MW01593026

Civil PE Professional Engineer Exam
Construction Module
Fifth Edition
By Ruwan Rajapakse, PE, CCM, CCE, AVS

Printed in the United States of America

ISBN 10:   1939493048

ISBN 13:   978-1-939493-04-0

Civil PE Construction Module, 5th Edition

Price $129.99

 www.geotechweb.com

Civil PE Construction Module, Fifth Edition

Civil PE exam has two sessions.

Morning session   (Breadth Exam)
(4 hours, 40 multiple choice questions)

Afternoon session (Depth exam)
(4 hours, 40 multiple choice questions)

Morning session is the breadth section. In this section, the candidate will be tested on all aspects of civil engineering.

During the afternoon session, the candidate has the choice of selecting a subject area he wishes. Following streams are available for the afternoon session.

1)   Structural
2)   Geotechnical
3)   Water Resources and Environmental
4)   Transportation
5)   Construction

The latest subject module is the construction module.

Good news about the construction module is that it is less mathematical compared to structural, geotechnical or transportation. The bad news is that construction module has more subject matter to study.

This book will provide theory and practice examples and various tips to successfully complete the construction module.
Increase your chances by buying the practice problems book also.

Errata for this book is provided in www.geotechweb.com

Four Sample Exams for the Civil PE Exam All Modules Covered

Four complete sample exams with illustrated solutions.

Many topics in all modules are covered...
Hydraulics, pumps, open channel flow, hydraulic jump, concrete beam design, column design, loadings, structural analysis, highway vertical curves, horizontal curves, signal lights, headway, velocity density relationships, shallow foundations, piles, earth retaining structures and many more problems and illustrated solutions...

PRACTICE, PRACTICE, PRACTICE.......KEY TO EXAM SUCCESS

Civil PE Geotechnical Module

Do you know that the sub module of construction depth is Geotechnical?

There are significant number of geotechnical problems in the afternoon construction exam. This book will help you understand core concepts and obtain necessary practice.

Civil PE Professional Engineer
Exam

Geotechnical Module

Illustrated Guide with Sample Questions and
Answers
Rapid Two Month Course!

Ruwan Rajapakse, PE, CCM, CCE, AVS

Civil PE Construction Module Practice Problems (Second Edition)

Nearly 1,000 practice problems with solutions!

Concrete, steel, rigging, earthwork, mass - haul diagrams, CPM, arrow diagrams, material quality, cranes, scaffolding, shoring/reshoring, estimating, construction operations, geotechnical topics and much more…..

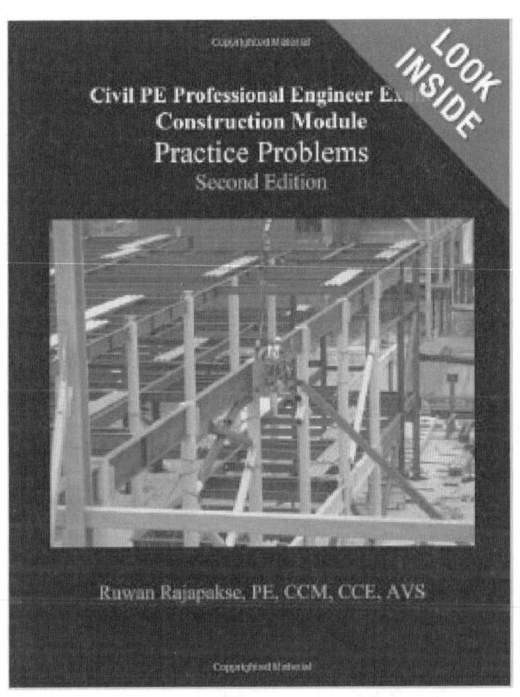

PRACTICE, PRACTICE, PRACTICE…….KEY TO EXAM SUCCESS

Three Sample Exams for the Civil PE Construction Module

Available in January 2014.
Please check Amazon.com

PRACTICE, PRACTICE, PRACTICE.......KEY TO EXAM SUCCESS

NCEES Principles and Practice of Engineering Examination
CONSTRUCTION Design Standards
Effective Beginning with the April 2012 Examinations
Revised January 6, 2012*
ABBREVIATION DESIGN STANDARD TITLE

ASCE 37-02 *Design Loads on Structures During Construction*, 2002, American Society of Civil Engineers, Reston, VA, www.asce.org.

NDS *National Design Specification for Wood Construction*, 2005, American Forest & Paper Association/American Wood Council, Washington, DC, www.awc.org.

CMWB *Standard Practice for Bracing Masonry Walls During Construction*, 2001, Council for Masonry Wall Bracing, Mason Contractors Association of America, Lombard, IL, www.masoncontractors.org.

AISC *Steel Construction Manual,* 13th ed., American Institute of Steel Construction, Inc., Chicago, IL, www.aisc.org.

ACI 318-08 *Building Code Requirements for Structural Concrete*, 2008, American Concrete Institute, Farmington Hills, MI, www.concrete.org.

ACI 347-04 *Guide to Formwork for Concrete,* 2004, American Concrete Institute, Farmington Hills, MI, www.concrete.org (in ACI SP-4, 7th edition appendix).

ACI SP-4 *Formwork for Concrete,* 7th ed., 2005, American Concrete Institute, Farmington Hills, MI, www.concrete.org.

OSHA *Occupational Safety and Health Standards for the Construction Industry,* 29 CFR Part 1926 (US federal version), US Department of Labor, Washington, DC.

MUTCD-Pt 6 *Manual on Uniform Traffic Control Devices—Part 6 Temporary Traffic Control,* 2009, US Federal Highway Administration, www.fhwa.dot.gov.

REFERENCE CATEGORIES FOR CONSTRUCTION DEPTH MODULE
• Construction surveying
• Construction estimating
• Construction planning and scheduling
• Construction equipment and methods
• Construction materials
• Construction design standards (see above)

Building Code Requirements for Structural Concrete (ACI 318) was updated to the 2008 edition on January 6, 2012.

1. The examination is developed with questions that will require a variety of approaches and methodologies including design, analysis, and application. Some questions may require knowledge of engineering economics.
2. The knowledge areas specified under 1, 2, 3, etc., are examples of kinds of knowledge, but they are not exclusive or exhaustive categories.

3. The breadth (AM) exam contains 40 multiple-choice questions. Examinee works all questions.

4. Score results are combined with depth exam results for final score.

8 hours (two 4-hour sessions)	80 multiple-choice (40 per session) Examinee takes a common breadth exam and chooses 1 depth exam (of 5 offered).	Both SI and USCS	Exam is open-book. Examinee must bring own copy of all relevant references in hard-copy format.

UNITS:

fps Units	SI Units
Length	
1 ft = 0.3048 m	1 m = 3.28084 ft
1 inch = 2.54 cm	
Pressure	
1 ksf = 1,000 psf	1 Pascal = 1 N/m^2
1 ksf = 0.04788 MPa	1 MPa = 20.88543 ksf
1 ksf = 47,880.26 Pascal	1 MPa = 145.0377 psi
1 ksf = 47.88 kPa	1 kPa = 0.020885 ksf
1 psi = 6,894.757 Pascal	1 kPa = 0.1450377 psi
1 psi = 6.894757 kPa	1 bar = 100 kPa
1 psi = 144 psf	
Area	
1 ft^2 = 0.092903 m^2	1 m^2 = 10.76387 ft^2
1 ft^2 = 144 in^2	1 Acre = 43,560 sq. ft
Volume	
1 ft^3 = 0.028317 m^3	1 m^3 = 35.314667 ft^3
1 gallon = 8.34 lbs	1 cu. ft = 7.48 gallons
Density	
1 lbs/ft^3 = 157.1081 N/m^3	1 kN/m^3 = 6.3658 lbs/ft^3
1 lbs/ft^3 = 0.1571081 kN/m^3	
Weight:	
1 kip = 1,000 lbs	1 kg = 9.80665 N
1 lb = 0.453592 kg	1 kg = 2.2046223 lbs
1 lb = 4.448222 N	1 N = 0.224809 lbs
1 ton (short) = 2,000 lbs	1 N = 0.101972 kg
1 ton = 2 kips	1 kN = 0.224809 kips

DENSITY OF WATER
1 g per cubic centimeter = 1,000 g per liter = 1,000 kg/m^3
           = 62.42 pounds per cu. feet

Table of Contents

A.0   Site Work: 20

A.1   Permanent and Temporary Site Work: 20

A.2   Site Clearing: 21

A.3   Demolition of Existing Structures and Utilities: 23

A.4   Mass Grading: 23

A.5   Fine Grading: 24

A.6   Temporary Drainage: 24

A.7   Erosion and Sediment Control: 25

A.8   Surveying: 26

A.9   Sheet piles: 27

A.10   Soil Stabilization: 28

A.11   Site Work - Permanent Construction; 28

A.12   Permanent Drainage: 28

A.13   Construction of Utilities (Water Pipes, Sewer Pipes, Electrical Conduits): ... 28

A.14   Landscaping: 29

B.0   Concrete Construction 30

B.1   Cement, fine aggregates and coarse aggregates: 30

Cement Types: 30

B.2.1   Fly Ash: 32

B.3   Concrete Admixtures: 33

Air Entraining Admixtures: 33

Water Reducing Admixtures: 33

Accelerating Admixtures 33

Superplasticizers (Commonly known as Super Ps): 33

Concrete Retarders: 33

B.4   Concrete Slump Test: 33

Slump Test Procedure: 33

B.5   Concrete Cylinders: 34

Procedure to obtain concrete cylinders; 34

B.6   Splitting Tensile Strength Test: 35

B.7   Mixing, Transportation and Placement of Concrete: (ACI 304R) 35

B.7.1   Concrete Plants: 35

B.7.2   Storage of Material: 37

B.7.3   Cement Silos: 37

B.7.4   Concrete Mixing: 37

B.7.5   Concrete Placement: 38

Pumping during Cold Weather: 41

Pumping of lightweight concrete: 41

Lightweight aggregates: 41

Tremie Pipes: 42

Free Fall of Concrete: 42

B.8   Concrete Vibration (Concrete Consolidation) ACI 309: 42

Adverse Conditions due to Inadequate Vibrating; 44

B.9   Concrete Finishing: 45

B.10   Concrete Grinding: 48

B.11   Concrete Scarifiers: 48

B.12   Tolerances: 49

B.13   Cold Weather and Hot Weather Concreting: 50

B.13.1   Cold Weather Concreting: 50

B.13.2   Hot Weather Concreting (ACI 305): 51

B.14   Concrete Elements: 53

B.15   Concrete Accessories: 53

B.15.1 Curing Compounds 53

B15.2   Bonding Admixture (Bonding Agent): 54

B15.3 Waterstops: 55

B.16   Concrete Formwork: 56

Prefabricated Formwork: 57

Formwork Material: 58

ACI (American Concrete Institute) Recommendations: 59

B.17   Shoring and Reshoring: 65

Reshoring: 65

B.18   Bracing Masonry Walls: 77

B18.1   Masonry Wall Construction Procedure: 78

B18.2   Reinforced Masonry Walls: 83

B.19   Typical Rebar Details: 85

B.20   Construction Joints in Slabs: 86

B.21   Concrete Practice Problems: 87

C.0   Steel Construction 90

C.1   Steel Construction Process: 91

C.1.1   Design Drawings and Shop Drawings: 91

C.1.2   Erection Drawings: 93

C.1.3   Steel Erection Process: 93

D.0   Construction Equipment 97

D.1	Mobile Cranes:	97
D.2	Tower Cranes:	101
D.3	Crane Selection, Erection and Stability:	102
D.4	Dozers:	106
D.5	Scrapers:	106
D.6	Loaders:	109
D.7	Excavators:	111
D.8	Draglines:	114
D.9	Graders:	115
D.10	Compaction Equipment:	117
D.11	Machine Power:	119
D.12	Grade:	121
1.0	Earthwork Construction and Layout	124
1.1	Excavation and Embankment (Cut and Fill):	124
1.2	Borrow Pit Volume Problems:	124
1.3	Soil Phase Relationships:	124
1.3.1	Borrow Pit Problems	130
1.3.2	Site Layout and Control:	133
1.3.3	Highway Curves (Horizontal and Vertical Curves):	139
1.3.4	Trench Excavations:	151
1.3.5	Construction Stakes and Markings:	152
1.4	Earthwork Mass Diagrams:	157
	Free Haul Distance (FHD):	168
	Limit of Profitable Haul (LPH):	170
1.5	Hauling:	171
2.0	Estimating	178
2.1	Quantity Takeoff:	178
2.2	Cost Estimating:	188
2.2.1	Equipment Depreciation:	191
2.2.2	Bank Volume, Loose Volume and Compacted Volume:	194
2.3	Engineering Analysis:	220
2.4	Earned Value Management:	229
3.0	Construction Operations and Methods	234
3.1	Introduction	234
3.2	Lifting and Rigging	234
3.2.1	Sheaves (Pulleys) and Blocks:	234
3.2.2	Block and Tackle:	236
3.2.3	Single Whip: Lifting with one sheave is known as single whip.	236
3.2.4	Pulleys with Friction:	241

3.2.5   Crane Mechanism: 243

3.2.6   Chain Hoists: 247

3.3 Dewatering and Pumping: 251

3.3.1 Pumps: 255

3.3.2   Pump Performance Curve, Pump Efficiency Curve and System Curve: 257

3.3.3   System Curve: 258

3.3.4   Net Positive Suction Head: 260

3.4   Equipment Production: 263

3.5   Productivity Analysis and Improvement: 265

3.6   Temporary Erosion Control: 265

3.7   Excavation Support: 267

4.0 Scheduling 270

4.1   Construction Sequencing: 270

4.2   Activity on Node Networks and CPM Network Analysis: 270

4.2.1   FLOATS: 286

4.3   Activity on Arrow Networks; 288

4.4   Resource Leveling: 290

4.5   Time - Cost Tradeoff: 293

4.6   Integration of CAD and Schedule: 293

5.0   Material Quality Control and Production 295

5.1   Material Testing: 298

Concrete Slump Test: 299

Laboratory Testing: 300

Sieve Analysis: 300

Soil Classification: 303

Soil Compaction: 304

Modified Proctor Test Procedure: 304

Liquid Limit: 306

Plastic limit: 306

Permeability Test: 307

Unconfined Un-Drained Compressive Strength Tests (UU Tests): 308

Asphalt: 309

5.2   Welding: 310

Butt Joints: 310

T – Joints: 311

Lap Joints: 312

Corner Joints: 313

Edge Joints: 313

Fillet Weld: 313

Welding Symbols: 314

Weld Testing: 316

Weld Material Weight: 316

5.3   Bolt Testing: 318

5.3.1 Washers: 319

5.3.2   Joint Types: 319

5.3.3   Slip Critical Joints: 319

5.3.4   Bearing Type Joints: 319

5.3.5   Bolt Tension: 320

5.3.6   Tension vs Torque Debate: 322

5.4   Quality Control Process: 323

5.4.1   Concrete Mix Design: 323

6.0 Temporary Structures 326

6.1   Construction Loads: 326

6.2   Formwork: 326

Timber Formwork: 326

Steel Formwork: 326

6.3   Falsework and Scaffolding: 327

6.4   Shoring: 335

6.4.1   Loads during Construction: 335

6.5 Concrete Maturity and Early Strength Evaluation: 338

Normal Distribution: 338

6.6 Bracing: 344

6.7 Anchorage: 345

6.8   Cofferdams: 347

Cofferdams in Bridge Pier Construction: 348

Forces acting on cofferdams: 350

Cofferdam Types: 352

7.0   Worker Health, Safety, and Environment: 356

7.1   OSHA Regulations (Introduction): 356

7.2   CFR 1926 Subpart A (Right of Entry): 356

7.3   CFR 1926 Subpart B (Health Standards): 356

7.4   CFR 1926 Subpart C: (General safety and health provisions): 356

7.5   CFR 1926 Subpart D: (Environmental Control): 357

7.6   Personal Protective Equipment: 1926 Subpart E: 357

7.7   Safety Nets 1926.105: 358

7.8   Fire Protection and Prevention: 1926 Subpart F: 359

7.9   Signs Signals and Barricade: 1926 Subpart G: 359

7.10   Materials Handling, Storage, Use, and Disposal: 1926 Subpart H: 359

7.11   Tools (Hand Tools and Power Tools) - Subpart I: 362

7.12   Welding and Cutting: OSHA 1926 Subpart J: 362

7.13   Electrical Safety: OSHA 1926 Subpart K: 364

7.14   Scaffolds: OSHA 1926 Subpart L: 367

7.15   Fall Protection: OSHA 1926 Subpart M: 368

7.16   Helicopters, Hoists, Elevators, and Conveyors: OSHA 1926 Subpart N: 371

7.17   Motor Vehicles, Mechanized Equipment, and Marine Operations: OSHA 1926 Subpart O: 374

7.18   Excavations: OSHA 1926 Subpart P: 374

         Sloping and Benching: 375

7.19   Concrete and Masonry Construction: OSHA 1926 Subpart Q: 380

7.20   Steel Erection Safety: OSHA 1926 Subpart R: 383

7.21   Safety Management: 387

7.22   Safety Statistics: 388

8.0   Other Topics: 389

8.1 Groundwater and well fields: 389

     Confined Aquifers: 389

8.2   Slurry Cutoff Wall Types: 390

8.3   Subsurface Exploration and Sampling: 390

8.4   Shallow Foundations: 394

8.5   Raft (Mat) Foundations: 396

8.6   Earth Retaining Structures: 397

     Gabion Walls: 405

     Mechanically Stabilized Earth Walls: 405

     Grouted Soil Anchors: 410

8.7   Rock Anchors: 411

     Mechanical rock anchors: 413

8.8   Pile Foundations: 417

8.9   Loadings: 422

     Load Paths: 423

8.10   Mechanics of Materials: Mechanics can be divided into two parts. 424

9.0   MUTCD: Manual of Uniform Traffic Control Devices 436

9.1   Brief Overview of MUTCD Part 6: 436

9.2   TTC: Temporary Traffic Control 437

     Traffic Control Devices: 437

Components of Temporary Traffic Control Zones: 439

Development of a TTC Plan: 440

Flaggers: 440

6D.01: Pedestrian safety around construction sites: 441

MUTCD Chapter 6D.03   Construction Worker Safety Near Traffic: 442

MUTCD Chapter 6E: Flagger Control: 443

9.3   Hand Signaling Devices: 443

General Introduction:

You will be doing plenty of addition, subtraction, multiplication and division. Fortunately that is the only mathematics you are required to do. We all know how to do these four fundamental processes but the question is how fast you are able to do them. In an exam setting when number of calculations has to be done quickly, it is possible that a mistake could occur.

Calculators make arithmetic easy. However, press one wrong button and you will get a wrong answer. If you have to multiply 543 x 657, then it makes sense to use the calculator. But if you have to multiply 25 x 23? Should you go for the calculator or do it by hand? Which is faster? It is advisable to figure these things prior to go to the exam.

Only arithmetic you would need is addition, subtraction, multiplication and division.

Concepts and Computations:

Civil PE construction module contains questions that require the knowledge of concepts and at the same time which require the ability to conduct simple computations. This book has provided worked examples that are similar in nature to the examination questions.

History of Construction:

Early Period: Probably around 5,000 years ago, cities started to appear in Mesopotamia, India Egypt and China. Egyptians took construction to a very high level by building large-scale pyramids. During later time periods construction activities became more and more diverse. Chinese great wall, Roman aqua ducts, large-scale temple structures etc were built.

Development of the Number System:

Early engineers used very little mathematics for construction work. Any mathematics that was used mainly limited to geometry. Simple computations such as addition, subtraction, multiplication and division were extremely cumbersome using Egyptian, Greek or Chinese numbers. They did not have the numbers we use today.

New era of construction industry started due to the discovery of modern number system by Indian/Sri Lankan mathematician Aryabhatta around 500 AD.

Four Fundamental Operations:

One hundred years later Brahmagupta (600 AD) gave arbitrary rules for the four fundamental operations. (Addition, subtraction, multiplication and division). Brahmagupta's system was transported to Europe through Arabia and to rest of the world. Today mathematics has become an integral part of construction. Interestingly even today, most construction work does not need any mathematics beyond the four fundamental operations.

Machinery:

Next major development to benefit construction was the use of machinery. Earlier construction workers used wedges, pulleys and other hand operated tools. Today construction is mostly an affair of labor and machinery. Backhoes, trucks, loaders, forklifts, cranes, derricks, conveyor belts, jackhammers, compactors, rollers, compressors are some of the few machines used in construction sites.

Internal Combustion Engine: Development of the internal combustion engine provided a new dimension to the construction industry. Nicklaus Otto, Gottlieb Daimler, Karl Benz and James Atkinson invented internal combustion engine around 1890. Internal combustion engine or its variations are needed for today's machinery.

Electricity:
Discovery of electricity by Michael Faraday, James Joule, Thomas Edison and Nicolai Tesla is another major development that affected the construction industry. It is unthinkable to do any construction activities without the use of electricity. Power drills, jackhammers, cutting machines, hoists, and conveyor belts are operated using electricity.

Computer: Computers have become an integral part of the construction industry. Scheduling, cost estimating, design and construction management highly dependent on computers. Development of the computer by US engineers such as Attanasof, Allen Turing and Von Neumann brought a new dimension to the construction industry.

Building Construction: All construction engineers will encounter building construction work eventually. Construction of a building starts with a need. A company may need more office space or new stores. Management of that company would meet an architect and explain their needs. Architect would come up with a set of architectural drawings. Owner would look at it and make comments. Owner may want the meeting hall to be larger or more bathrooms be added or change appearance of the building. Based on owner needs, architect would redraw the plans. After the architectural drawings are finalized, structural drawings and civil drawings will be prepared by structural engineers and civil engineers. Mechanical drawings and electrical drawings also would be prepared. Today network drawings are prepared for communication and computer networks.

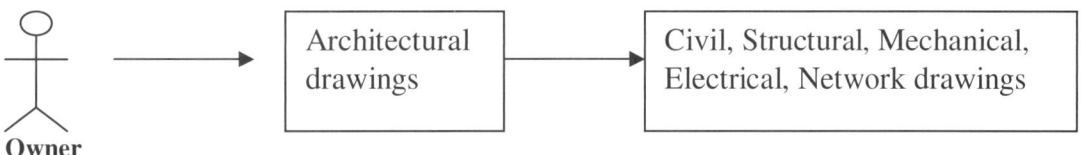

After all necessary drawings and specifications are prepared, bids would be called. Based on bids, a contractor would be selected.

Construction – Early Phase: Prior to any construction work, site has to be prepared. Site preparation work includes, cutting trees, constructing temporary roads for delivery trucks and concrete trucks, construct temporary parking lots for workers, dewatering to remove water from excavations, setup office trailers, security fences, erosion control mechanisms such as silt fences, setup temporary phone lines and power.

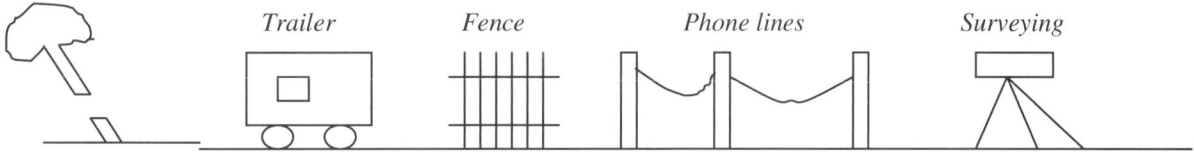

Cutting trees, setting up trailers, security fences, temporary power lines, surveying
Site Preparation Work

Soil Grading and Fill: After site preparation work, site has to be graded. High ground has to be cut and low ground has to be filled.

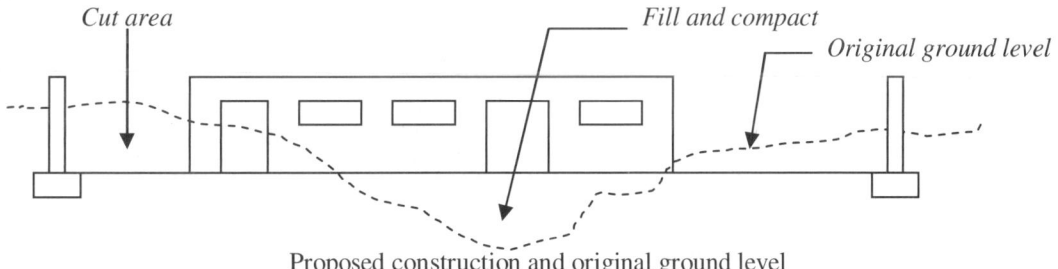

Proposed construction and original ground level

Soil grading is the process of cutting the original ground to the proposed level.

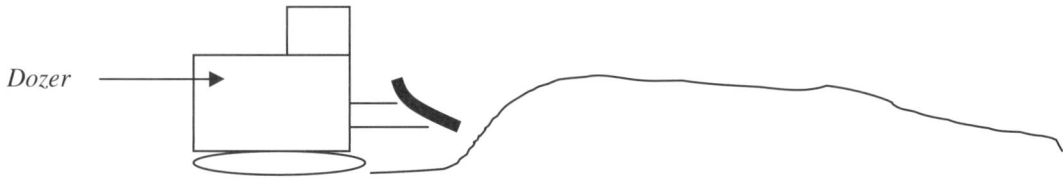

Fill and Compaction: As you could see from the above figure, some areas have to be filled and compacted. Prior to any fill activity, soils that will be used have to be approved by a geotechnical engineer. Usually poorly graded sandy soil or stones are used for fill work. Clay soils and silty soils are considered unsuitable for fill and compaction.

Removal of Rock: Rock removal is done using blasting and rock breakers. Generally, igneous rocks are hard and difficult to rip. Sedimentary rocks are relatively easier. Rippability of rock depends on rock type and degree of weathering,

Pile Driving: Some building requires piles when existing ground conditions are not suited for shallow foundations. Piles transfer loads to lower level.

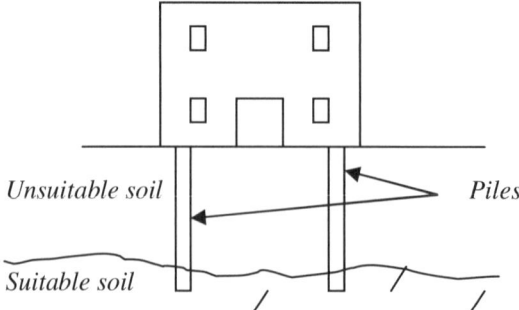

Pile diving is done using pile drivers.

Excavation: Excavation is needed for basements, shallow foundations, sewer pipes, drainage pipes, manholes and swimming pools.

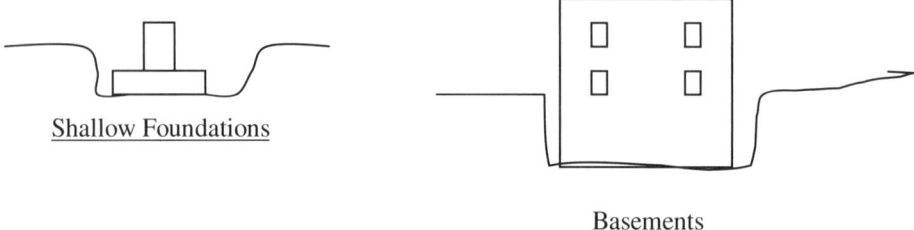

 Excavation work is usually done using backhoes.

Concreting: After completion of site preparation work, excavations, pile driving is completed, concreting work will start.
Concreting work can be divided into
  • Formwork preparation
  • Installation of reinforcement bars
  • Concreting and curing
Formwork is needed to hold the concrete in place. Concreting can be done by bringing pre mixed concrete from a concrete yard or concrete can be prepared on site using a mixer. Concrete can be pumped or lifted to high elevations.

Steel Erection: Some buildings are designed using steel beams and columns. Steel members are connected suing bolts or welding. Rivets were used in the past and not used anymore.

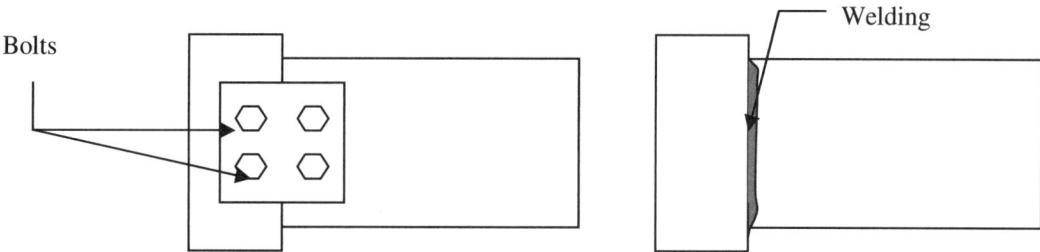

Moving and Lifting of Material (Rigging): Material such as concrete, timber, steel brought to the site using trucks. Then cranes are used to move them inside the site. There are many different types of cranes available.

- Tower cranes – Large tower crane can cover a large area. Material on one corner of a site can be moved to the other end in a second.
- Crawler Mounted Cranes – These are good for small sites.
- Gantry cranes – These cranes move on rail

A.0 Site Work:

A.1   Permanent and Temporary Site Work: In construction work, many things need to be done outside the main building or structure that is planned. Look at the photograph below. It shows an undeveloped plot of land.

Let us assume a developer is planning to build a shopping mall in this land.

Can you prepare a list of work items that need to be done other than construction of the building?
First the developer needs to cut the tress and clean the top soil. This is not a complicated activity. However, there are many state and federal permits have to be obtained prior to cutting trees. Above figure also shows a small water logged

area. This may be considered as a wetland. The developer needs to find out from relevant authorities whether he could fill that area.

Site work can be divided into permanent site work and temporary site work. A sheetpile wall may be erected to hold back the soil during construction. This could be considered as temporary retaining wall. Also some retaining walls can be a permanent structure that is part of the design. A contractor may decide to have a quick and dirty drainage lines during construction. Later he may build the permanent drainage lines to the site. Some areas may be temporarily paved for delivery trucks to come and go.

Some temporary site work;

- Site clearing or grubbing
- Demolition of abandoned structures
- Fill depressed areas
- Excavations
- Cut and fill
- Breaking rock
- Mass grading
- Fine grading
- Compaction of soil
- Removal of existing utilities
- Install temporary lighting, water or gas supply
- Provide temporary drainage to the site
- Provide temporary paving
- Temporary retaining walls, coffer dams, sheet pile walls
- Temporary sediment and erosion control structures (rip rap, silt fences etc)
- Soil stabilization (Vibroflotation, dynamic compaction, soil surcharging)

Some permanent site work;

- Retaining walls
- Roads
- Parking lots
- Construct permanent utilities (water supply, electricity, gas, cable, communication etc)
- Planting trees
- Ponds and canals
- Landscaping

A.2   Site Clearing:

Site clearing is also known as "grubbing". Site clearing involves cutting trees, removal of bushes, removal of top soil and roots etc. Typically backhoes, dozers and tree cutting machines are used for site clearing.

Some specialized equipment used for site clearing;

- Stump splitters
- Stump pullers
- Clearing rakes
- Grapples

Left: Backhoe clearing the site
Right: Stump splitter removing tree stumps

Left: Equipment removing grass and grading the soil
Right: Stump puller (This machine can remove deep rooted stumps)

Left: (Grapple):   Grapples are effective in removing boulders, roots and vegetation
Right: *Clearing Rake*:   Clearing rakes are used to remove small tress and vegetation. Some rough grading also   can be done with these machines

A.3   Demolition of Existing Structures and Utilities:

In many situations old abandoned structures need to be demolished. Typically, demolition involves demolition of concrete, steel structures, fences, masonry structures, roofs etc.

Left: Jack hammer: (Jack hammers are widely used for breaking concrete)
Right: Jack hammer mounted in a loader

Left: Wrecking balls are widely used for demolition of buildings
Right: Shear - These machines can cut thru pipes and metals

A.4   Mass Grading:

Grading is the process of attaining the required ground elevation. Depressed areas have to be filled and high areas have to be cut. After site clearing and demolition is completed, mass grading is done. Mass grading is done using dozers, excavators and loaders. Dozers are good to cut thru soil. But not a good machine to transport soil. Dozers are efficient when transportation of soil is kept to a minimum. Loader can transport soil in the bucket. Other widely used equipment is the scraper. Scarpers have an underbelly to transport soil and much more efficient in transporting soil than loaders. More details regarding these machines are provided under cut and fill chapter.

Scrapers have an underbelly to store and transport soil

A.5   Fine Grading:

Above figure shows a "grader" that is used for fine grading. The blade of a grader is not as robust as a blade of a dozer. Typically, blades of graders are at the center between wheels. On the other hand, dozer blade is much more robust and located in front.

A.6   Temporary Drainage: Once the trees and grass is removed, water tend make the site muddy.
Working becomes highly inefficient in a muddy site. Hence temporary drainage should be provided.
Temporary drainage is provided thru backfilling, gravel beds, perforated pipes and trenches. Typically one has to locate low areas where ponding could occur. These areas can be backfilled and bring it up. Also gravel could be placed and a perforated pipe can be installed.

Temporary drainage in a construction site

A.7   Erosion and Sediment Control:

Many states require an erosion and sediment control plan be submitted prior to start of any construction work. Silt fences are used to stop soil eroding away. Near river beds, rip rap is provided. Hay bales and geo-fabrics also can be used to stop erosion.

Left: Riprap to stop erosion near a stream
Silt Fence: Silt fence is a geo-fabric installed using posts. Silt fence should be buried few inches deep into
                   soil

Left: Protecting a manhole using hay bales
Right: Hay bales used to stop erosion of soil

A.8   Surveying:

Horizontal Control: Design documents would sepcify that the coordinates should be obtained using a monument nearby. Surveyors need to use the monuments provided and establish control points near the site. In many instances these control points get runover by machines and new control points need to be installed. It is important to make sure that the control points are protected. If not the building would be constructed at wrong cordinates.

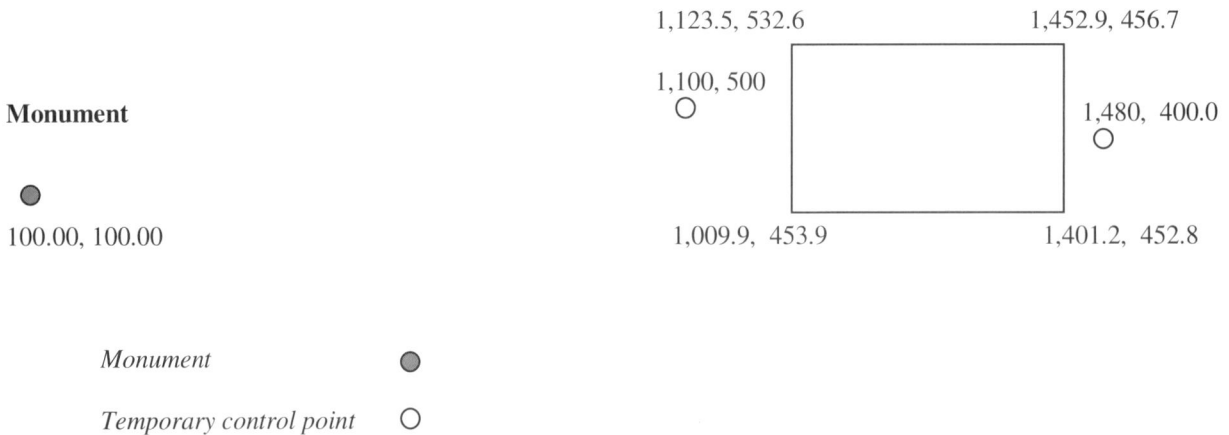

Above figure shows a prposed building, monument and two control points. Control points need to be closer to the site. However when too close they get damaged due to construction activities.

Vertical Control: Similar to horizontal control, design documenst would indicate the elevation and the datum used. Surveyors need to establish temporary bench marks near and around the site to be used for grading, establish footing and slab elevations and elevations of utility pipes.

Manhole Construction: Manholes are required to clean out pipes. Manholes can be temporary or permanent.

A.9   Sheet piles:

I have never seen a construction site without sheetpiles. Sheetpiles can be used as retaining walls, excavation support, trenching, cofferdams and temporary bearing platforms.

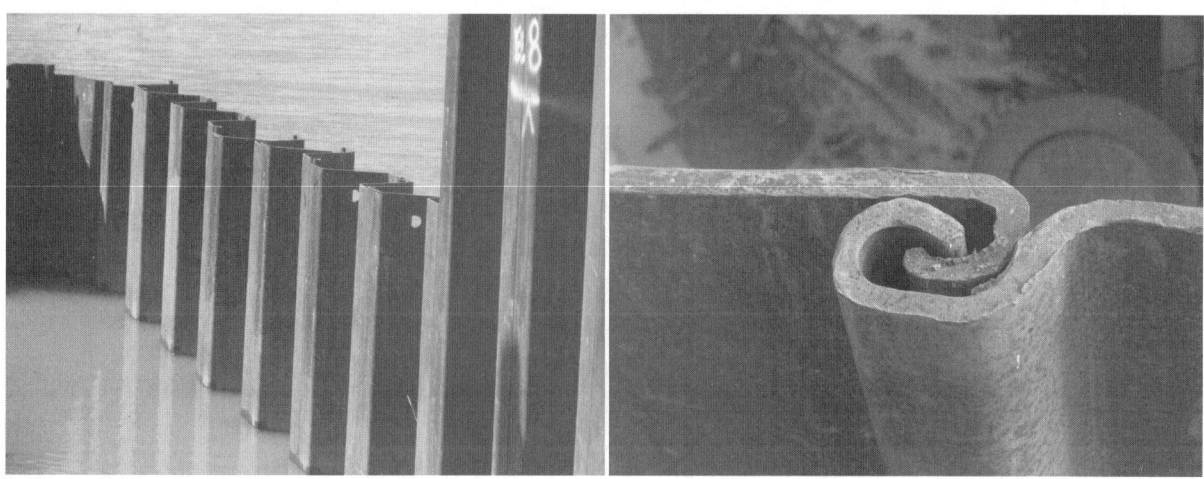

Left: Coffer dam built using sheetpiles
Right: Pipe to pile connection detail

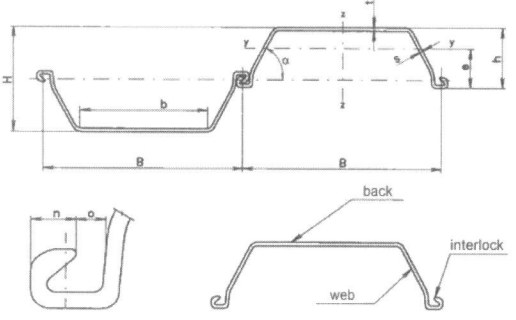

Left: Vibratory hammer is used to drive sheet piles
Right: Sheet pile configuration

A.10 Soil Stabilization:

Some sites are not suitable to have shallow foundations. In such cases, piles need to be driven. Piles are generally comes with a heavy price tag. Instead one can try to improve the soil bearing strength. This is known as soil stabilization. Many methods are used for soil stabilization. Vibroflotation, dynamic compaction, surcharging, Wick Drains and pressure grouting are some processes.

Note: Please see my geotechnical module for complete description on soil stabilization.

A.11 Site Work - Permanent Construction;

Any building needs roads and parking lots. Roads and parking lots are constructed by bringing the soil to the required grade and then providing a gravel base. This is known as subbase. After the gravel layer (sometimes crushed stone also used), asphalt base course is provided. On top of the asphalt base course, asphalt surface layer is provided. Surface course is designed to have better friction between tires and asphalt. Base course is designed to provide rigidity to the road.

Left: Layer of gravel or crushed stones is spread out prior to installation of asphalt
Right: Compaction of asphalt surface course. Gravel subbase and Asphalt base course is seen in the picture.

A.12 Permanent Drainage:

Drainage is provided thru installation of storm water pipes and manholes. Trenches need to be dug to install storm water pipes. Excavation support is provided with trench boxes or shoring.

A.13 Construction of Utilities (Water Pipes, Sewer Pipes, Electrical Conduits):

Any facility requires water, electricity, sanitary, cable and communication lines. These utilities are part of site work.

Other site work items include retaining walls, storm water detention systems, play grounds and landscaping.

Storm water detention pond -   During storms, all the storm water ends up in storm pipes. This could create overflow of manholes and flooding. Hence large sites are required to maintain storm water detention ponds. During a storm, water is drained to the storm water detention pond. Later when the storm is over, detention pond would discharge to the storm water pipes.

A.14 Landscaping:

Landscaping is the process of creating an aesthetic and natural environment around the facility. Generally trees, flowers, water ponds and plants are used to create a pleasant environment.

Well Designed Landscaping

B.0 Concrete Construction

Concrete is a product made of cement, sand, stones and water. Sand is known as fine aggregates and stone is known as coarse aggregates. Chemical compounds known as admixtures are also added to concrete to obtain special properties.

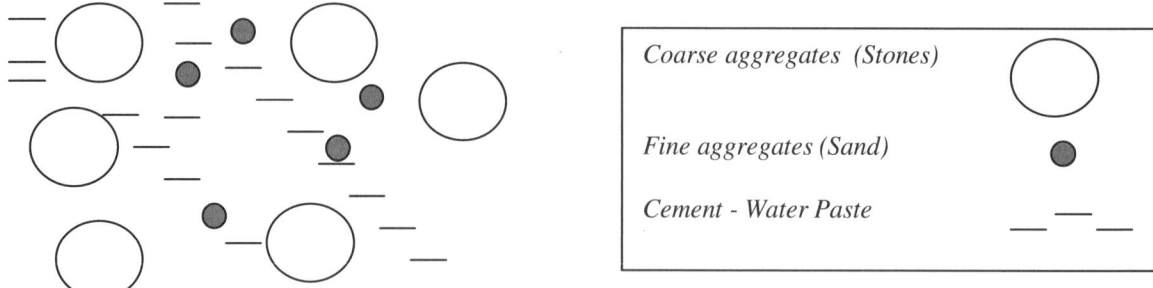

B.1   Cement, fine aggregates and coarse aggregates: Cement water mixture acts as the binder between coarse and fine aggregates. Generally higher the cement content, higher the strength. It has been found that high water content would lead to lesser strength. Hence, to achieve high strength, one should minimize the water content. If the water content is reduced, the concrete may not be workable. Also in most cases, concrete needs to be pumped. Certain amount of flowability is needed to pump concrete. When one needs to maintain high workability and also needs to have high strength then chemical admixtures can be added to increase the workability without reducing the strength.

High water content   ⟶   *Low strength + High workability*
Low water content   ⟶   *High strength + Low workability*
Low water content + Admixtures   ⟶   *High strength + High workability*

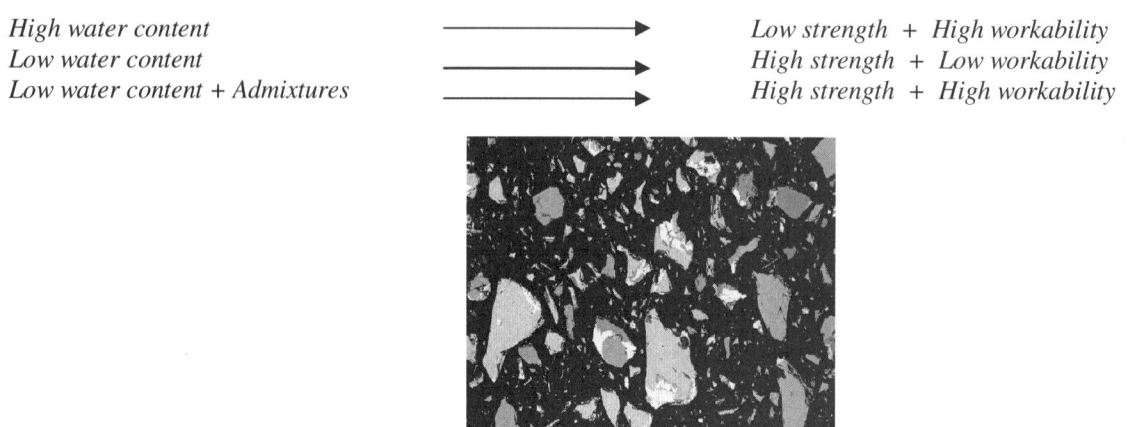

Cement particles seen with a high-resolution microscope

Cement Types: Five major types of cements are available in the US market.

Type I Cement -   Type I cement is known as general-purpose cement and widely used. This is the cheapest type of cement.

Type II Cement -   Type II cement generates less heat than type I cement. This property can be useful for mass concretes. When large mass of concrete is poured (ex. dams, large footings, retaining walls) heat generated inside the core may not be able to escape. High temperatures give rise to low strength. In such situations, type II cement can be used.

Another property of type II cement is its resistance to sulphate attack. Sulphates are present in some soils and groundwater.

Large mass of concrete is poured when building concrete dams. Heat inside the mass of concrete dissipate slowly and would give rise to high temperature in the core. Research has shown that development of high temperature leads to low strength.

Type III Cement: Type III cement is known as high early strength cement. High early strength is required to remove forms and move forward. Type III cement is expensive than type I cement. Hence, one may have to consider cost vs. schedule benefits when recommending type III cement. Typically, type III cement will achieve the 28-day strength of type I cement in 7 days. Eventually they both will have the same strength assuming other ingredients are the same.

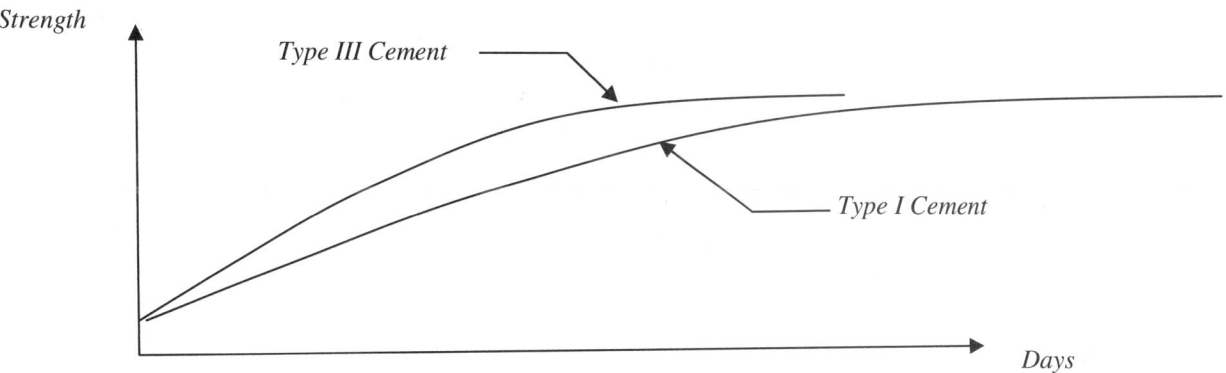

Type IV Cement:

Type IV cement generates much less heat during hydration. Hence, this cement is used for very large concrete structures. These cements have the lowest heat generation. Type IV cements are not readily available in the market.

Type V Cement: Type V cements are known as sulphate resistance cements. These cements are used when the groundwater or the soil contain large concentrations of sulphates.

B.2   Pozzalans: Pozzalans are known as supplementary cementitious material. Pozzalans can be mixed with cement to reduce cost without reducing the strength. Pozzalans react with byproducts of cement hydration. One of the main byproduct of cement hydration is Calcium Hydroxide. Pozzalans react with this byproduct to generate strength. Hence, Pozzalans do not contribute to initial strength. But later Pozzalans react with byproducts of cement hydration and generate additional strength.

Other than the cost benefit, there is another benefit of pozzalans. Since most pozzalans are materials that are wastes from other processes, owners can gain LEEDs environmental points by using them in the mixture.

Three widely used pozzolans are;

Fly Ash
Blast furnace slag
Micro silica or silica fume

B.2.1   Fly Ash:

Left: Coal Plant
Right: Fly Ash is a byproduct of coal burning

Coal is burnt to generate electricity. It has been reported that 50% of electricity generated in USA comes from coal plants. Fly ash is a byproduct of coal burning plants. In the past, fly ash was sent to landfills. Recently it has been found that fly ash could be used as a supplement to cement without affecting the strength. Fly ash is the most commonly used supplementary cementitios material.

Since fly ash particles are more spherical in shape than cement particles, workability and pumpability can be improved by adding fly ash. Some fly ashes cause low early strength. This can be a problem when strength needs to be attained sooner. Adding fly ash usually improve the resistance against sulphate attack. Another property of fly ash is to reduce the air content in concrete. In freezing and thawing conditions, air entrained concrete is preferred. In such situations, fly ash should be avoided.

B.2.2   Blast Furnace Slag:

Slag is produced in blast furnaces that produce iron and steel. Slag also can be used as a supplementary cementitious material. Slag tends to improve resistance for sulphate attack. In addition, it has been reported that slag develop higher long-term strength.

B.2.3   Silica Fume: Silica fume is a byproduct of silica alloy industry. Silica fume is also known as micro silica. Micro silica particles are 100 times smaller than cement particles. Main advantage of Silica fume is high durability. Since micro silica particles are extremely small, permeability of concrete is reduced. This is an important quality since rebars would be better protected from water permeation.

B.3   Concrete Admixtures:
Chemical admixtures are widely used to improve required properties of concrete.

Air Entraining Admixtures: Concrete that is subjected to repeated freezing and thawing would develop cracks. This can be avoided by increasing entrapped air. Wide array of chemicals are used for air entrainment. Vinsol resin is the most popular air entrainment admixture.

Water Reducing Admixtures: Less water in the concrete would generate higher strengths. On the other hand, there need to be enough water for workability. Water reducing agents can maintain a low water content while maintaining workability.

Accelerating Admixtures: Accelerating agents are used to accelerate the setting of concrete. Some accelerators are capable of increasing the early strength of concrete as well

Superplasticizers (Commonly known as Super Ps):   Superplastizers are used to maintain high workability at the same time maintaining strength. When concreting highly reinforced structures, concrete has to be able to flow freely. Superplastizers can be used in such situations to increase the flowability without compromising strength.

Concrete Retarders: Concrete retarders are added to delay the setting of concrete. Delaying of concrete setting is required in following situations.
Concrete has to be transported longer distances
   1)   Provide more time for the workers to carve grooves, curves and architectural features.
   2)   To avoid cold joints
   3)

B.4   Concrete Slump Test:
Concrete slump test should be done as described in ASTM C 143. Slump test is widely used to check the workability and consistency of concrete.

<u>Left</u>:   Above left photo shows the slump cone, rod and hand trowel.
<u>Middle</u>: After concrete is placed inside the slump cone, the slump cone is removed.
<u>Right</u>:   Next, the slump is measured. Higher the slump, higher the water content.

Slump Test Procedure:
STEP 1: Obtain fresh concrete from the truck.
STEP 2: Fill 1/3rd of the slump cone and tamp 25 times with a rod.   (This is commonly called rodding)
STEP 3: Fill another 1/3rd and tamp 25 times. Fill the last one third and tamp 25 times.
STEP 4: Lift the cone
STEP 5: Measure the slump.

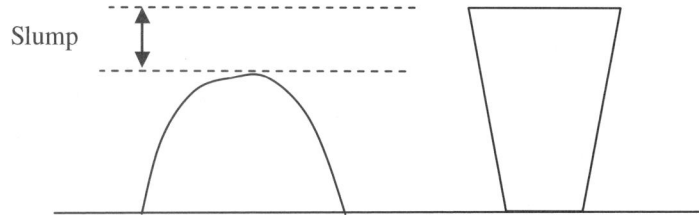

Kelly Ball Test: Kelly ball test also measures the consistency of concrete. Kelly ball is an apparatus consisting of a cylindrical weight 6 in. diameter, weighing 30 lb. Kelly ball is lowered to the concrete and penetration is

measured.   Higher the penetration, higher the flowability and water content.   One-inch penetration of Kelly ball is approximately equal to 2 inches of slump.

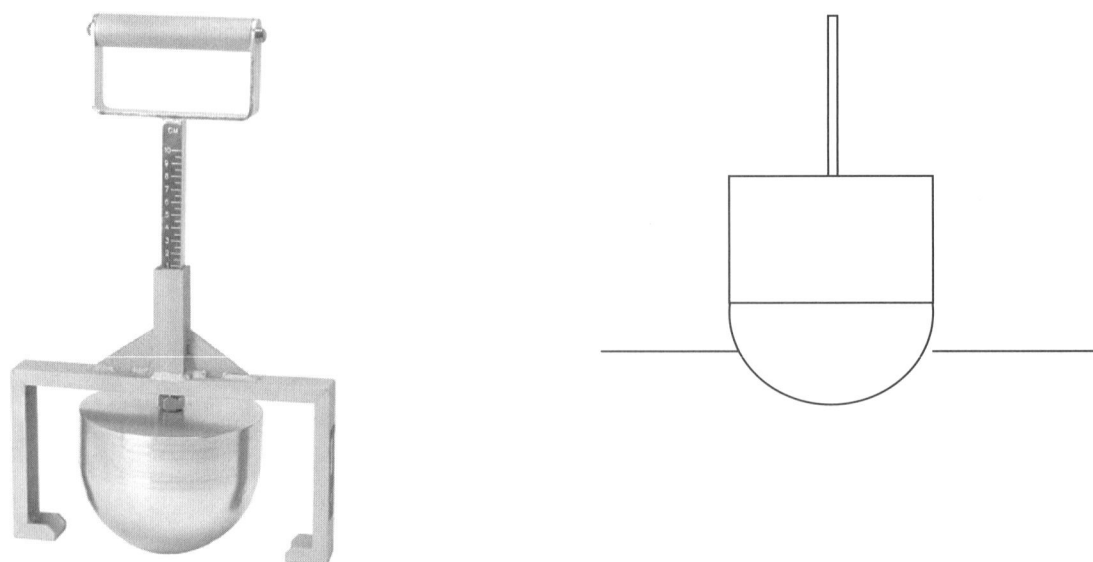

Kelly Ball Apparatus

B.5   Concrete Cylinders: Concrete cylinders are taken to conduct compressive strength tests. Concrete compressive strength tests need to be done as per ASTM C 31 and ASTM C 39. Concrete cylinders are 6 in diameter and 12 in. high. Small size cylinders (4 in. diameter and 8 in. tall) are also used.

Procedure to obtain concrete cylinders;

STEP 1: Fill 1/3rd of the cylinder and tamp 25 times with a rod.
STEP 2: Fill another 1/3rd of the cylinder and tamp 25 times. Finally, fill the last 1/3rd of the cylinder and tamp 25 times. Concrete cylinders should be placed in the job site in a controlled environment at temperature 60F to 80F. Cylinders should be transported to the lab within 48 hours.

Acceptance Criteria:
Typically, three cylinders are taken. One cylinder is broken after 7 days. The strength of the 7-day test should be approximately 65 to 70% of the 28-day strength. 7-day break is for informational purposes only.
Other two cylinders are broken after 28 days. Average of these two cylinders should be equal or more than the required strength. In addition, none of the 28 days tests should fall below required strength by more than 500 psi.
It is a good practice to obtain 4 cylinders. If the 28-day breaks do not reach the required strength, 4th cylinder can be tested at a later time.

Left picture shows concrete cylinders taken in the field. The cylinders are taken to the lab and covers are removed. Picture at the right shows compressive strength test.

Concrete cylinders should be placed in concrete curing boxes when on site. During wintertime, these boxes need to be powered and heat should be provided to attain proper temperatures.

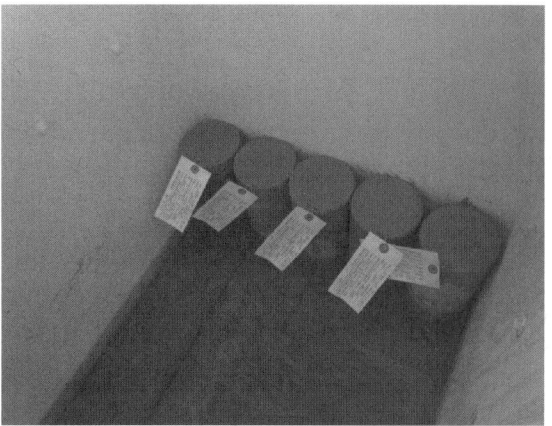

<u>Left</u>: Temperature controlled concrete curing box
<u>Right</u>: Concrete cylinders placed inside the box

B.6   Splitting Tensile Strength Test:

Tensile strength of concrete is not utilized for design. In rare cases, tensile strength of concrete is utilized. Tensile strength of concrete is found using splitting tensile strength test.

Splitting tensile strength test (This test is done to evaluate the tensile strength of concrete)

The cylinder is tested by placing horizontally. There are correlations between tensile strength and the compressive strength.

B.7   Mixing, Transportation and Placement of Concrete: (ACI 304R)

It is important to make sure that the design mix has not undergone major changes when the concrete truck arrives at the job site. One major problem that occurs during transportation is segregation. It is common sense that heavy particles such as aggregates tend to settle at the bottom if given the chance. Hence, it is important that drums of concrete trucks rotate during transportation.

Another major parameter that affects the strength is the water content. Higher water content would give rise to low strength and low durability. It is not possible to reduce the water content indefinitely, since workability will be reduced. It would be very difficult to get a smooth finish if the water content is too low.

B.7.1   Concrete Plants:

Concrete is a mixture of cement, sand, coarse aggregates, admixtures and water. In some cases as discussed before fly ash and various other pozzalans are also added. General functioning of a concrete plant is shown below.

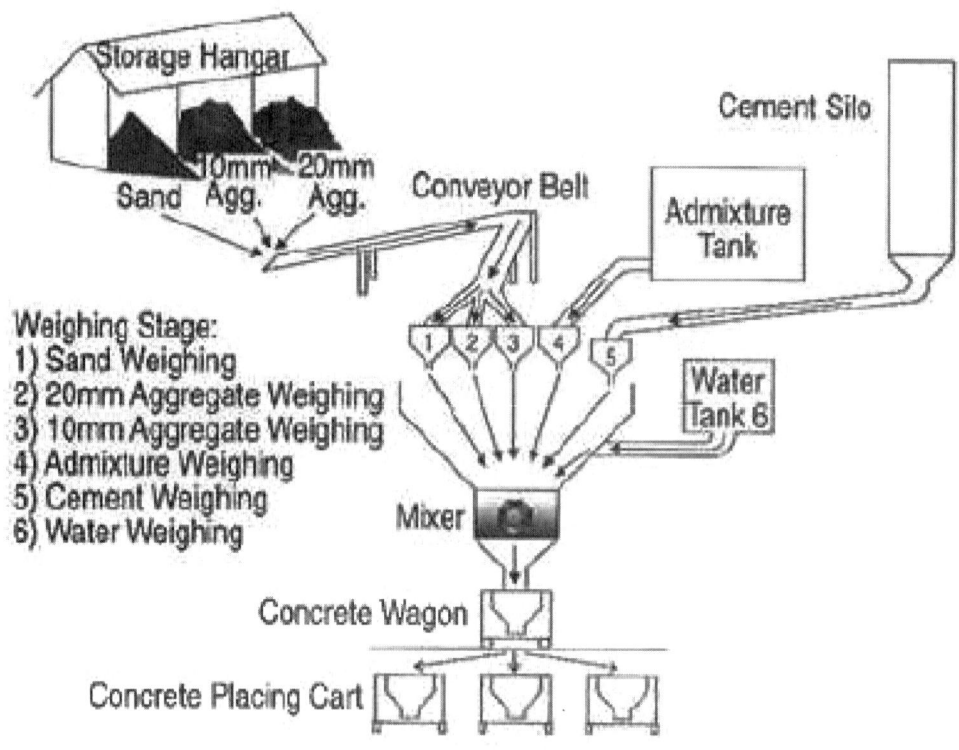

General outline of concrete batch plant

Concrete plant needs to have storage facilities for cement, fine aggregates, coarse aggregates, chemical admixtures and water. These ingredients need to be transported to the mixer. Typically, conveyor belts are used to transport materials in a concrete plant. Modern mixers are computer controlled. The operator input the proportions of material that need to be mixed. This data is used by a control system and correct amount of material is transported to the mixer. Concrete trucks are placed just under the mixer. In some plants, mixing is done inside the truck while travelling.

Concrete mixer is just above the concrete truck. Cone like figure on right is the cement silo. There is a conveyor belt from the cement silo to the mixer. Trapezoidal shaped container on left will be filled with sand and stones. Water usually comes from the street.

B.7.2   Storage of Material:

Some concrete plants tend to store sand and coarse aggregates outside exposed to elements. It is expensive to have indoor silos for sand and coarse aggregates. Storing sand and coarse aggregates in the open would allow dust and other contaminants getting into stones and sand. Also during winter times, stones and sand will freeze.

B.7.3   Cement Silos:

Storage of cement should be carefully planned. Cement tends to absorb moisture. Hence, it is important to make sure that cement silos are free of moisture. As per ACI 304R, cement silo should have a minimum bottom slope of 50 degrees from the horizontal for a circular silo and 55 to 60 degrees for a rectangular silo.

B.7.4   Concrete Mixing:

Concrete mixing can be done in the plant or in the truck. If the concrete has to travel far, then it is advantageous to mix in the truck. Well-proportioned mix is dropped into the truck and the mixer inside the truck would mix the concrete while going to the job site. This way time can be saved. On the other hand, mixing can be done in the plant. Still it is important for the concrete truck to have a rotating drum to make sure that no segregation would occur.

Concrete truck mixer

ACI 304R prefers all the water to be added at the plant so that water content can be properly controlled. Some water can be added at the job site to obtain the correct slump.

Concrete Mixing at the Job Site: For small projects, mixing of concrete can be done at the job site. Portable mixers of various sizes are available.

Mixing concrete at the job site

B.7.5   Concrete Placement:

Once the concrete arrives at jobsite, concrete placement can be done with many different equipment.

Concrete Buckets: Concrete trucks would dump concrete into buckets. Concrete buckets are lifted by a crane to the proper elevation for concreting.

Concrete bucket lifted by a crane

It is important to clean the concrete bucket end of each day so that the openings are not obstructed by hardened concrete. ACI 304R recommends side slopes of the bucket to be at least 60 digress from the horizontal.

Concrete Buggies: Concrete buggies are used for horizontal transportation of concrete. Concrete tends to segregate during transportation of concrete using buggies. Hence, it is not a very good way of transporting concrete. ACI limit the concrete transportation distance to 200 ft for manually operated buggies and 1,000 ft for power buggies. To minimize segregation, rails should be provided for the buggies. Hence, transportation can be made smooth. If rails cannot be provided, the surface should be made smooth as possible.

Left: Concrete manual buggy (maximum travel distance 200 ft)
Right: Concrete power buggy   (maximum travel distance 1,000 ft)

Concrete Chutes: Concrete chutes are typically used to transport concrete from a higher elevation to a lower elevation. ACI does not give a maximum allowed length that can be used to transport concrete using chutes.

Concrete chute

Concrete chutes should have rounded corners. Slope should be steep enough for the concrete to travel freely.

Concrete Pumping: Concrete pumping has become very popular in large projects. Concrete pumping requires less labor and easy to control.   Height of pumping is dependent on the size of the pump. Concrete pump design mixes typically have a higher slump compared to regular concrete mix. To obtain a high slump, one needs to increase the water content. Increasing the water content would affect the strength. Hence, water-reducing admixtures are used to obtain a higher slump without increasing the water content.

Concrete pump

Concrete pumping pipes can be rigid pipes or flexible pipes. Rigid pipes will have fewer problems during pumping. The major disadvantage of rigid piping is difficulty of handling. On the other hand, workers can take the flexible pipes to the location of placement without much difficulty. Concrete pumps have a maximum rate of flow and a maximum pressure. Both cannot be achieved at the same time. One ft of additional vertical height is equal to 3 to 4 ft of additional horizontal distance.

Pumping during Cold Weather:

Major problems are encountered when pumping concrete during winter months. Pipes freezing, concrete freezing, valves freezing and various other problems are common when pumping in cold weather conditions.

As per ACI, maximum size of angular aggregates should be less than 1/3rd of the internal diameter of pipe. Maximum size of round aggregates can be 2/5th of the internal diameter of pipe. If coarse aggregate sizes are larger than these recommended values, blocking of concrete can occur.

Fine aggregates also play a major role in concrete pumping. Fine aggregates, water and sand combines together to make a paste. If this paste consists of large particles, pumping would be difficult. Hence, it is important to control the size of fine aggregates (sand).

ACI recommendations on size of fine aggregates;

- At least 15 to 30% should pass the No. 50 sieve and
- 5 to 10% should pass the No. 100 sieve.

Pumping of lightweight concrete:

Lightweight concrete is needed to reduce the weight on metal decks, bridge decks and high-rise building slabs. Density of lightweight concrete is in the range of 115 pcf to 120 pcf while density of normal weight concrete is around 145 pcf. Lightweight is achieved by using light material. Density of cement and water cannot be changed. Lightweight concrete is achieved by using lightweight aggregates and lightweight sand.

Lightweight concrete is used in metal decks to reduce the load on beams and columns

Lightweight aggregates:

Lightweight aggregates typically manufactured by burning shale or clay and then fragmenting them into pieces. When clay or shale is burnt, these materials tend to expand. Hence, density of the material would decrease. Some naturally occurring sands may be less dense than normal sand. Lightweight sand may be costlier than normal sand. In many cases lightweight sand needs to be transported from far away quarries. Hence, transportation cost will be a factor when specifying lightweight sand.

Prior to pumping lightweight concrete, one needs to make sure that the aggregates are fully saturated. If the aggregates are not saturated, they tend to rise to the top of the pipe. This would create segregation

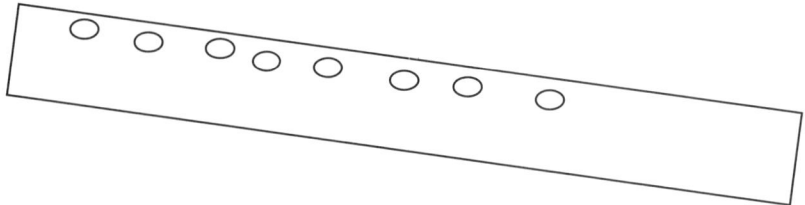

Lightweight aggregates tend to rise to top of the pipe. Hence, light weight aggregates need to be fully saturated prior to mixing.

Tremie Pipes:

Tremie pipes are used to concrete piers, caissons and bridge substructures. ACI recommends tremie pipes to be in the range of 8 to 12 inches diameter. Tremie should be embedded in fresh concrete 3 to 5 inches.

Tremie pipe

Free Fall of Concrete:
ACI does not limit the height of free fall of concrete. AS per ACI 304R. As long as the free fall path of concrete does not have rebars or any other obstructions, segregation is not an issue.

"The stream of concrete should not be separated by falling freely over rods, spacers, reinforcement, or other embedded materials. If forms are sufficiently open and clear so that the concrete is not disturbed in a vertical fall into place, direct discharge without the use of hoppers, trunks or chutes is favorable. Concrete should be deposited at or near its final position because it tends to segregate when it has to be flowed laterally into place".
ACI 304R

B.8   Concrete Vibration (Concrete Consolidation)   ACI 309:
ACI document 309 deals with concrete consolidation or vibration.
Following is a list of benefits one may obtain due to proper vibration of concrete.

- Higher compressive strength
- Higher bond between rebars and concrete
- Increase bond at cold joints
- Reduction of honeycombing and air pockets inside concrete
- Avoid segregation of cement paste and aggregates

External Vibrators:

In some cases, it is not possible to insert a regular vibrator into concrete. In such situations, external vibrators are used. External vibrators are attached to formwork and a motor inside creates vibration.

External vibrator is attached to formwork

Adverse Conditions due to Inadequate Vibrating;

Inadequate vibration would cause

- Honeycombing
- Voids due to high air entrapment - Proper vibration would allow air to escape.
- Sandstreaking - Sandstreaking is loss of cement water paste due to excessive bleeding. When cement water paste bleeds out between the form and mass of concrete sand lines would be exposed. Proper vibration can be useful in avoiding sandstreaking. Not enough fines in the concrete mix also could lead to sandstreaking.
- Placement lines - Concrete is not placed with one truck. There could be a time lag up to half hour in some cases between trucks. One may see placement lines if concrete is not properly vibrated.

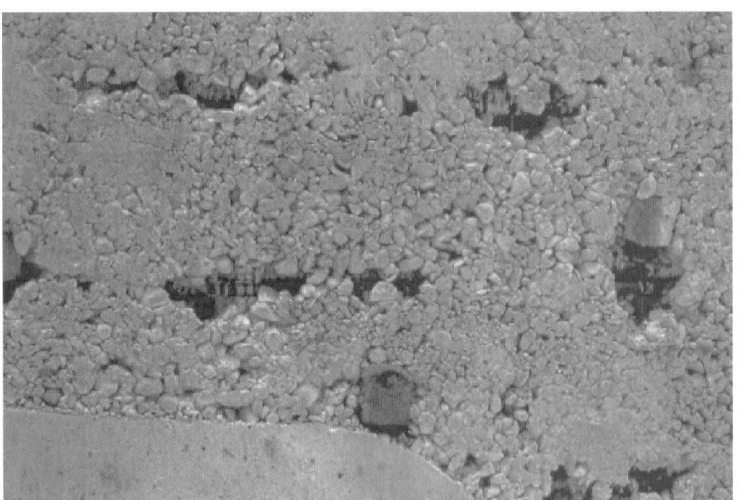

Honeycombing and large voids due to air entrapment in concrete

Sandstreaking

B.9   Concrete Finishing:

Concrete finishing is also known as concrete screeding is the process of achieving a smooth concrete surface. Most common screeding apparatus is the bull float. Bull float can be used for average size concrete slabs.

Bull Float

Concrete hand trowels are used for areas where bull float cannot reach. Curbs, inside edges of a slab, round surfaces etc. are finished with concrete hand trowels.

Concrete Hand Trowels

Bull float and hand trowels may be time consuming for larger slabs. In such situations, concrete trowel machines are used. Trowel machines come in various sizes. Small scale trowel machine is shown below.

Small trowel machine

Concrete Broom Finish:

Figure: Concrete Broom Finish

Some instances, concrete is finished with a broom to get a rough surface. This type of finish is required when epoxy or other layers were to be placed on concrete. The rough surface obtained will be useful to provide friction so that whatever the layer going on top could properly adhere to concrete.

Ride on Trowel Machines:

Large projects typically uses ride on trowel machines. A person can ride these machines and trowelling can be done faster.

Ride on Trowel Machine

Power screeds are also famous among concrete contractors.

Concrete power screed

B.10 Concrete Grinding:
Not all projects proceed smoothly. If a concrete slab is placed at a higher elevation than the specified elevation, one may have to grind the concrete to the correct elevation. In such situations, concrete grinding machines are used. Concrete grinding machines have a cutter that rotates. The cutter would grind the concrete to the correct elevation.

Concrete grinding machine

B.11 Concrete Scarifiers:
Scarifying of concrete is required to obtain a rough surface in the concrete. Rough surfaces are sometimes required for certain topping slabs, to avoid tripping, certain epoxies etc. In addition, clarifiers are used to remove concrete coatings.

Concrete scarifier

B.12 Tolerances: Concrete elements can never be constructed to exact dimensions. Column may be slightly off from the vertical. Slab may not be 100% flat. ACI 117 provides guidelines for tolerances for concrete construction.

Tolerance for Vertical Walls: As per ACI 117, wall height less than 83 ft 4 inches should have a tolerance of lesser of 1" or 0.3% of the height. For walls taller than 84 ft 4 inches, the tolerance is lesser of 0.1 times the height or 6 inches.

Example: Find the tolerance at the top for the vertical wall shown;

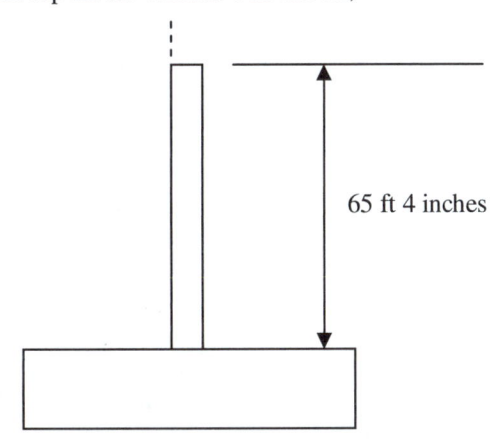

65 ft 4 inches

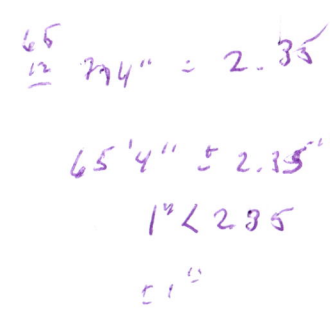

Solution:
This wall is less 83 ft 4 inches. Hence, the tolerance is lesser of 1" or 0.3% of the height.

0.3% of height = 0.3/100 x (65.33)
                = 0.196 ft = 2.35 inches

1 inch is less than 2.35 inches.
Tolerance at the top of wall = 1 inch.

Tolerance for Horizontal Distance between Concrete Elements:
In most cases, 1-inch tolerance is recommended for distance between concrete elements.

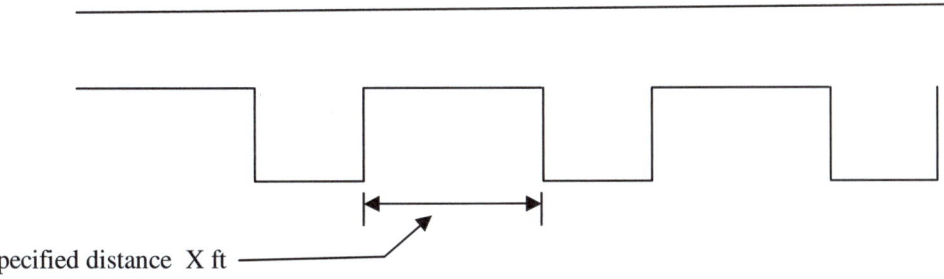

Specified distance X ft

Acceptable distance = X ft +/- 1 inch.

Tolerance for soil grading below slabs on grade:

Soil grading below slabs on grade is important. If the soil were at a higher elevation, then the slab thickness would reduce. ACI 117 recommends ¾ inches of tolerance for soil elevation below slab on grade.

Tolerance for slab thickness:

If one core is taken, the slab thickness should not be less than ¾ inches from the given value. ACI 117 does not mention of larger slab thicknesses. If more than one core sample is taken, the thickness should not be less than 3/8 inches from the given value. At least one sample should be taken for every 10,000 SF. Core samples should be taken after seven days of concrete placement.

Practice Problem:

Three core samples were taken for a 14-inch slab. Thicknesses of the three core samples are 13.25 in, 13.12 in and 13.32 inches. Is this slab within the tolerance limit?

Solution:

Average thickness = (13.25 + 13.12 + 13.32)/3 = 13.23

Deviation = 14 - 13.23 = 0.77 inches.   (Tolerance limit = 3/8 in. or 0.375 in)

The slab exceeds the tolerance limit and corrective measures should be taken.

B.13 Cold Weather and Hot Weather Concreting:

B.13.1 Cold Weather Concreting:

Hydration is the process of cement reacting with water and creating a binder. When the temperature is low, hydration process would slow down. Hence, cement water binder will not form or would take longer to form. Another problem of cold weather is freezing of water. When water freezes, intended chemical reactions would not take place.

ACI 306 defines cold weather as follows;

Cold weather is defined as a period when, for more than 3 consecutive days, the following conditions exist:
1) The average daily air temperature is less than 40 F (5 C) and
2) The air temperature is not greater than 50 F (10 C) for more than one-half of any 24-hr period.

The average daily air temperature is the average of the highest and the lowest temperatures occurring during the period from midnight to midnight.

Hence concrete inspectors need to keep an eye on the temperature to see cold weather conditions as defined by ACI 306 exists.

Laying blankets to protect concrete from cold weather

Solutions for cold weather:

- Heating aggregates
- Use hot water for mixing
- Lay blankets and sprinkle hot water
- Provide heat to formwork
- Provide heat to metal deck or other steel elements attached to wet concrete
- Provide heaters to heat the ambient air

B.13.2 Hot Weather Concreting (ACI 305): Concreting during hot weather can lead to many problems. ACI 305 deals with hot weather concreting.

As per ACI 305, following problems can be expected when concreting in hot weather.

•   Increased rate of slump loss and corresponding tendency to add water at the job site:
As per ACI, adding water at the job site is not a very good practice since one may not be able to control the water cement ratio properly.

•   Increased rate of setting:
Hydration reaction (or concrete setting) will take place at a faster rate during hot weather. This would create difficulty in handling, compacting and finishing. Another problem of fast setting is formation of cold joints.

•   Increased tendency for shrinkage cracking:
When the temperature in the surrounding goes down, concrete shrinks. Shrinkage of concrete would generate cracks. It has been reported that concrete poured during hot weather conditions are highly vulnerable for shrinkage cracking.

•   Increased difficulty in controlling entrained air content: High air content would give rise to low strength and low air content would give rise to cracking during freezing and thawing. Controlling air content is extremely difficult during hot weather conditions.

•   Decreased 28-day and later strengths resulting from high temperature:
Concreting during hot weather can result low strength concrete.

•   Cold Joint Formation: Since the concrete is setting fast due to high temperature, cold joints could form in between arrival of concrete trucks.

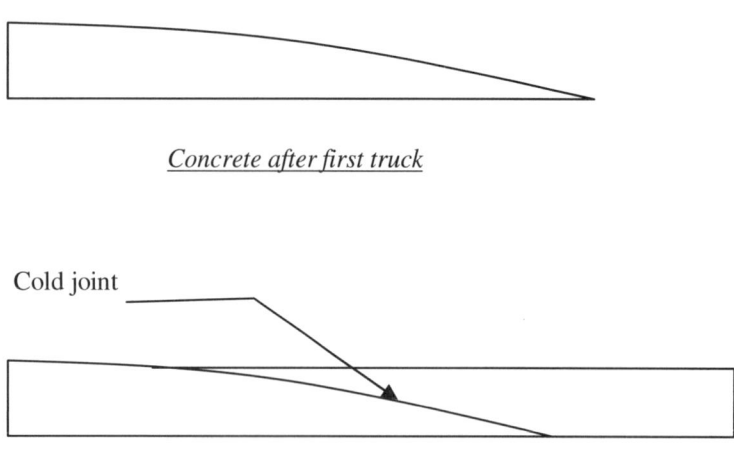

Concrete after first truck

Cold joint

Concrete after second truck

Formation of cold joints reduces the strength and durability of concrete.

Definition for Hot Weather Concreting;

Hot weather is defined as any combination of the following conditions;

• High ambient temperature;
• High concrete temperature;
• Low relative humidity;
• Wind speed and
• Solar radiation.

It is obvious that high ambient (air) temperature would give rise to high concrete temperature. In addition, it is possible that the temperature of concrete was high during mixing. Low relative humidity would cause water loss and have the same effect as high temperature in many cases.

Solutions for Hot Weather Concreting:

If concreting is planned during summer months, the contractor may need to submit a hot weather-concreting plan. In that plan, the contractor needs to address the issue of hot weather concreting.

Widely Used Solutions during Hot Weather:

• Use ice with mixing water: Ice absorbs large amount of heat during the melting phase. This would keep the concrete from reaching high temperatures. As per ACI 305, maximum of 20^0 F can be reduced by mixing ice with water.

• Use low hydrating cement: If the hydration rate of cement is lower, then heat generation would be lower at the initial stages,

• Use of flyash and other Porzalans.:
Porzallans react with byproducts of cement hydration. Hence, cement amount can be reduced and Porzallans can be introduced, This would decrease the heat generation during hydration.
• Use of retarding admixtures: Retarding admixtures increase the setting time. Hence, peak temperatures of the concrete is reduced.

Protecting the concrete from hot weather during curing:
Precautions should be taken to protect the concrete from high temperatures during the curing period. Concrete can be kept moist by continuously spraying water. One can also use wet blankets to keep the concrete at moderate temperatures.

B.14 Concrete Elements: Typically, there are many different types of concrete elements in a structure. Some of the concrete elements are beams, columns, slabs on grade, structural slabs, slabs on metal decks, concrete walls, retaining walls, concrete piles, pile caps, topping slabs, piers, footings, curbs, stairs, equipment pads, conduit encasements and concrete filled metal pan stairs.

B.15 Concrete Accessories:

Reinforcement Supports: Rebars need to be supported in slabs and beams to obtain proper concrete cover requirements. Concrete cover is needed to protect rebars from water and outside chemicals.

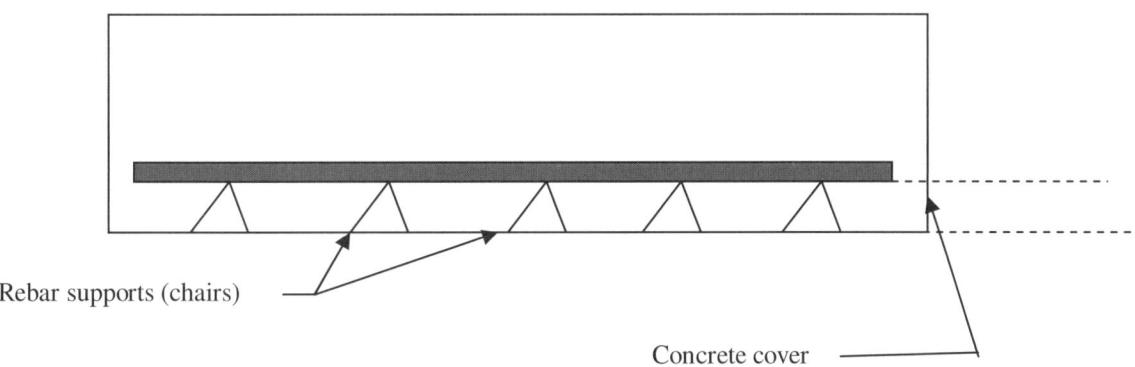

Rebar supports (chairs)

Concrete cover

Different types of rebar supports available in the market. In most cases, bricks are used as rebar supports.

Rebar chairs

B.15.1 Curing Compounds: Curing is the process of concrete hardening or hydration. The hardening process needs water. The concrete shall be kept in moist condition during curing. This can be achieved by flooding the concrete with water or sprinkling water during curing. Other methods include wet blankets and curing compounds.

Layer of water   Wet blankets

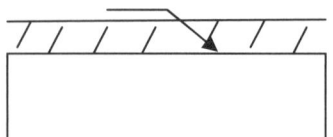   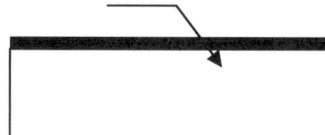

Left: Flooding the concrete with water
Right: Place a wet blanket and sprinkle water

Most contractors would prefer to apply a curing compound to the concrete. Curing compounds are a liquid that would seal the concrete surface and keep the water inside. After concrete is hardened, the curing compound would break down and sealing effect will disappear.

Application of a curing compound is shown in the photograph. Curing compounds come in 55-gallon barrels.

Curing compounds essentially act as a sealant during curing. It will not allow water to evaporate from the concrete.

B15.2   Bonding Admixture (Bonding Agent):   Fresh concrete do not bond well to old concrete. Bonding agents are used to bond new concrete to old concrete, metal to concrete, concrete to topping slabs etc.

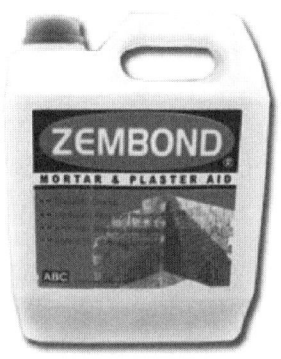

Left: Application of a bonding agent to old concrete
Right: Bonding agent container

B15.3   Waterstops:

Waterstop is an expanding material that is installed in footings and in walls to stop water from entering the concrete. Waterstops are made of PVC, stainless steel and swellable clays.

Swellable waterstop is shown above. When water is encountered, this waterstop will expand and stop water from getting inside. It is possible in some occasions to damage the concrete due to swelling of waterstop.

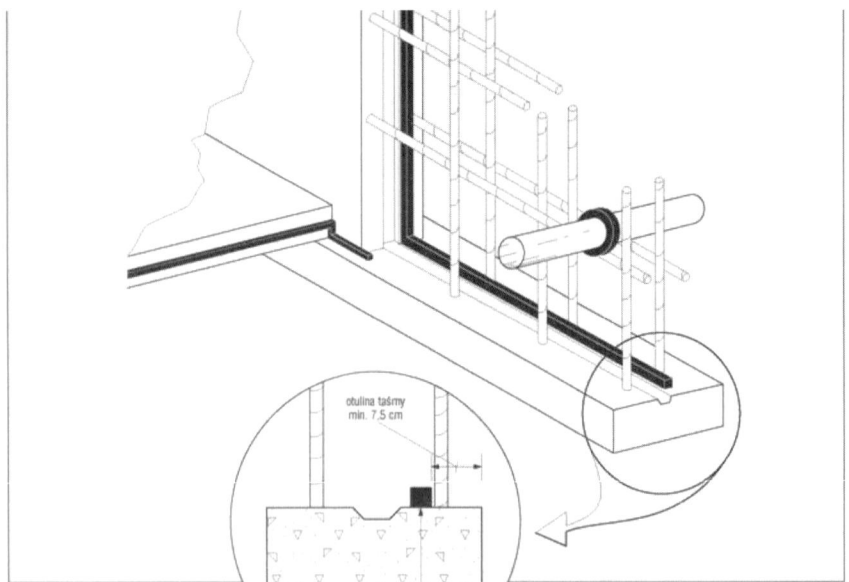

Waterstop installed in a shallow foundation is shown above. It is not advisable to install the waterstop inside the keyway since that would reduce the shear capacity of the keyway.

Most waterstop materials would expand when it encounter wet concrete. Due to the expansion, it would create a barrier for water.

B.16 Concrete Formwork:

In many projects, formwork cost exceeds the cost of concreting. Hence, one may need to pay proper attention to formwork. Formwork in the past was mostly constructed using timber. Still timber is widely used. Timber formwork though cheaper than metal or plastic formwork, cannot be reused several times due to damage. Hence, other products can be more economical than timber formwork.

Wall Formwork:

Wall formwork using timber is shown in the above figure.

Main items in a timber wall formwork system are;

1) Sheathing
2) Wales
3) Posts
4) Buttresses

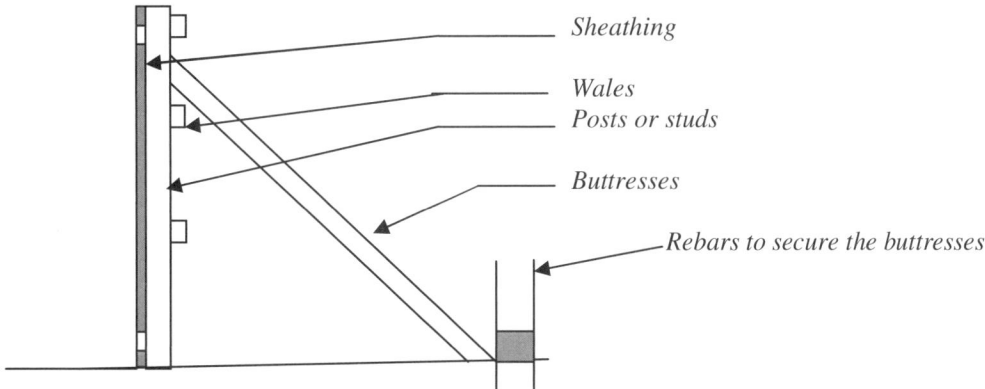

Timber formwork may be economical for small-scale projects.

Prefabricated Formwork:

For larger projects, it is more economical to rent or buy prefabricated formwork. In addition, it may be faster to install them than constructing timber formwork.

Prefabricated wall formwork

Formwork Material:

Plywood Forms: Plywood is the cheapest. They can be reused many times.

Steel Forms: Steel forms can be reused up to 300 times. Cost of steel forms are much higher than plywood forms. Steel forms come in different sizes and shapes hence work in the field can be reduced.

Aluminum Forms: Aluminum is lighter than steel. Hence, Aluminum forms can be erected with few men.

Lateral Concrete Pressure in Formwork: Exam questions are highly likely in computing pressure in formwork during concreting. When concrete is poured, pressure in concrete starts to build up. When the concrete starts to harden, lateral pressure starts to reduce and becomes zero after concrete is fully hardened.

Lateral Concrete Pressure assuming Concrete to be a Liquid (Hydrostatic Force):   Concrete flows freely and at the time of pouring, concrete can be considered to be a liquid. However, within hours, concrete starts to harden. When concrete is semi hardened, lateral force diminishes. When concrete is fully hardened, lateral force disappears completely and formwork is not needed.
Following formula can be used to find the hydrostatic pressure.

$$P = \gamma \cdot h$$

P = Lateral pressure
γ = Concrete density
h = Concrete height

Practice Problem: Find the hydrostatic concrete pressure at bottom of formwork. Assume concrete density to be 145 pcf.
a)   Draw the concrete pressure distribution diagram.
b)   Find the total force acting on the formwork per linear ft

10.7 ft

Solution: γ = 145 pcf   h = 10.7

$P = \gamma \cdot h = 145 \times 10.7 = 1,551.5$ psf

Concrete Pressure Distribution Diagram:

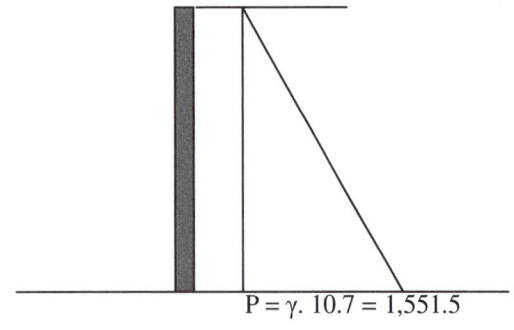

$P = \gamma \cdot 10.7 = 1,551.5$

b)   Total force per linear ft = Area of the pressure diagram

Total force per linear ft = 1,551.5 x 10.7/2 (Area of the pressure triangle) = 8,300.5 lbs per linear ft of formwork

Practice Problem: If a single form is 10.7 ft high and 3 ft wide, what is the total force on the form in the above example.

Solution: Total force per linear ft = 8,300.5 lbs

Total force per 3 ft wide formwork = 8,300.5 lbs x 3.0 = 24,901.6 lbs

ACI (American Concrete Institute) Recommendations:

It has been found that concrete does not stay a liquid during pouring. Concrete at lower depths starts to harden and lateral pressure would start to drop. Hence, ACI have following two equations.

Equations for Wall Forms:

For wall forms filled at a rate less than 7 ft per hour and total height less than 14 ft;

$$p_{max} = C_w \cdot C_c (150 + 9{,}000 \times R/T)$$

p_{max} = Maximum lateral pressure
R = Rate of pouring (ft/hr)
T = Temperature in degrees (F^0)
C_w = Unit Weight Coefficient (See below for ACI 347 table 2.1)
C_c = Chemistry coefficient (Lateral pressure on formwork depends on concrete type and concrete chemistry).
C_c is obtained from ACI 347 table 2.2

For wall forms filled at a rate larger than 7 ft per hour but less than 10 ft/hr, wall height less or higher than 14 ft.;

$$p_{max} = C_w \cdot C_c (150 + 43{,}400/T + 2800)R/T$$

Two Rules for the Above Equation:

- The maximum pressure value obtained from above equation should not be lower than 600 C_w. If it is less than 600C_w, use 600C_w as the maximum pressure. Use table 2.1 given below to find C_w.
- The maximum pressure value obtained from above equation should not exceed "wh". If it exceeds "wh", use "wh" as the maximum pressure. (w is the unit weight of concrete in pcf and h is the height of concrete in ft).

Unit Weight of Concrete (w)	C_w
Less than 140 pcf	$C_w = 0.5 [1 + (w/145)]$ w is the unit weight of concrete given in pcf or lbs/ft^3. C_w should not be less than 0.80
140 to 150 pcf	1.0
Greater than 150 pcf	$C_w = w/145$

ACI Table 2.1   (ACI 347-04) Unit Weight Coefficient C_w.

Cement Type	C_c (Chemistry Coefficient)
Cement Types I, II and III without retarding admixtures	1.0
Cement Types I, II and III with retarding admixtures	1.2
Other types of cements or blends containing less than 70% slag or 40% flyash without retarding admixtures	1.2
Other types of cements or blends containing less than 70% slag or 40% flyash with retarding admixtures	1.4
Blends containing more than 70% slag or 40% fly ash	1.4

ACI Table 2.2 (ACI 347-04)   Chemistry Coefficient C_c.

Practice Problem:

a)   Find the maximum concrete pressure acting on the formwork shown below using the ACI recommended equation. Rate of pouring is 6 ft/hr and temperature of concrete is 75 F. Density of concrete is 145 pcf. C_w and C_c coefficients are 1.0
b)   What is the highest point where maximum pressure occurs?
c)   Draw the pressure diagram
d)   What is the force acting on one linear ft of formwork?
e)   Find the total force acting on the form, if the form is 3 ft wide.

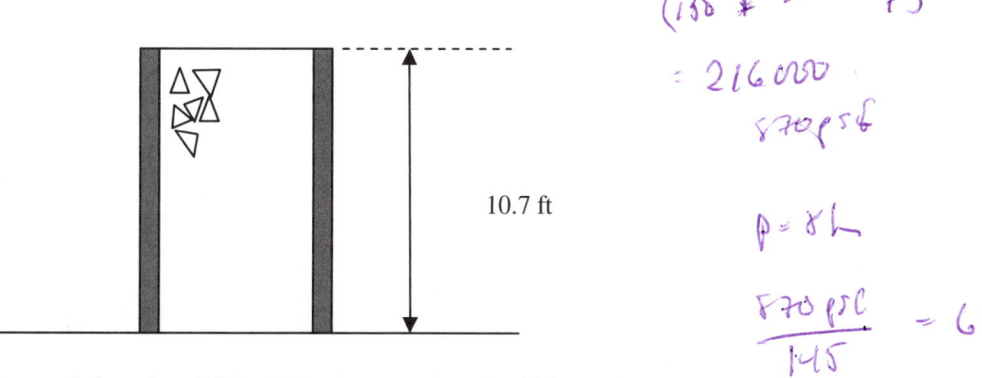

10.7 ft

Solution: a)   Since the rate is less than 7 ft/hr, following equation should be used.

$p_{max} = C_w \cdot C_c (150 + 9{,}000 \times R/T)$
C_w and C_c are given to be 1.0

$p_{max} = 150 + 9{,}000 \times 6/75$ psf $= 870$ psf.   (This is the maximum pressure as per ACI guidelines).

b)   Find the highest depth where maximum pressure occurs.

$870 = \gamma \cdot h = 145 \cdot h$
$h = 870/145 = 6.0$ ft

c)   Draw the pressure diagram:

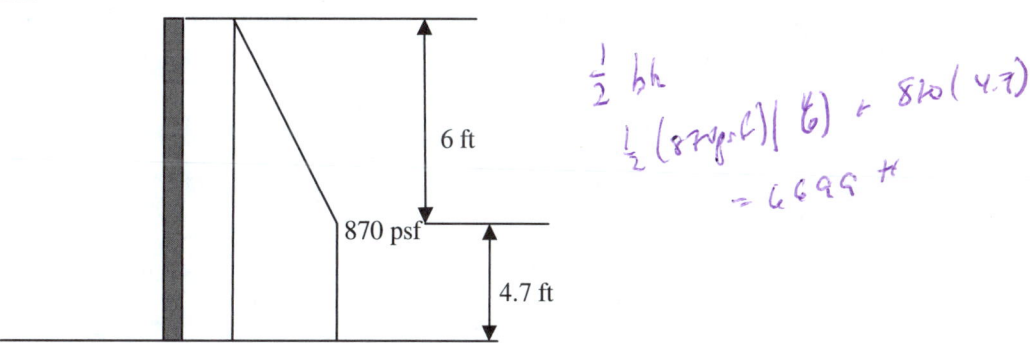

6 ft

870 psf

4.7 ft

d)   Find the force per one linear ft of formwork:

Total force is given by area of the pressure diagram.

Area of the pressure diagram = $(870 \times 6/2) + (870 \times 4.7) = 6{,}699$ lbs per 1 ft wide form

e)   Total force on a 3 ft wide form = $3 \times 6{,}699$ lbs $= 20{,}097$ lbs

Note that hydrostatic force for a 3 ft wide form was 24,901.6 lbs. (See the previous problem).

Wall Forms (General Configuration):

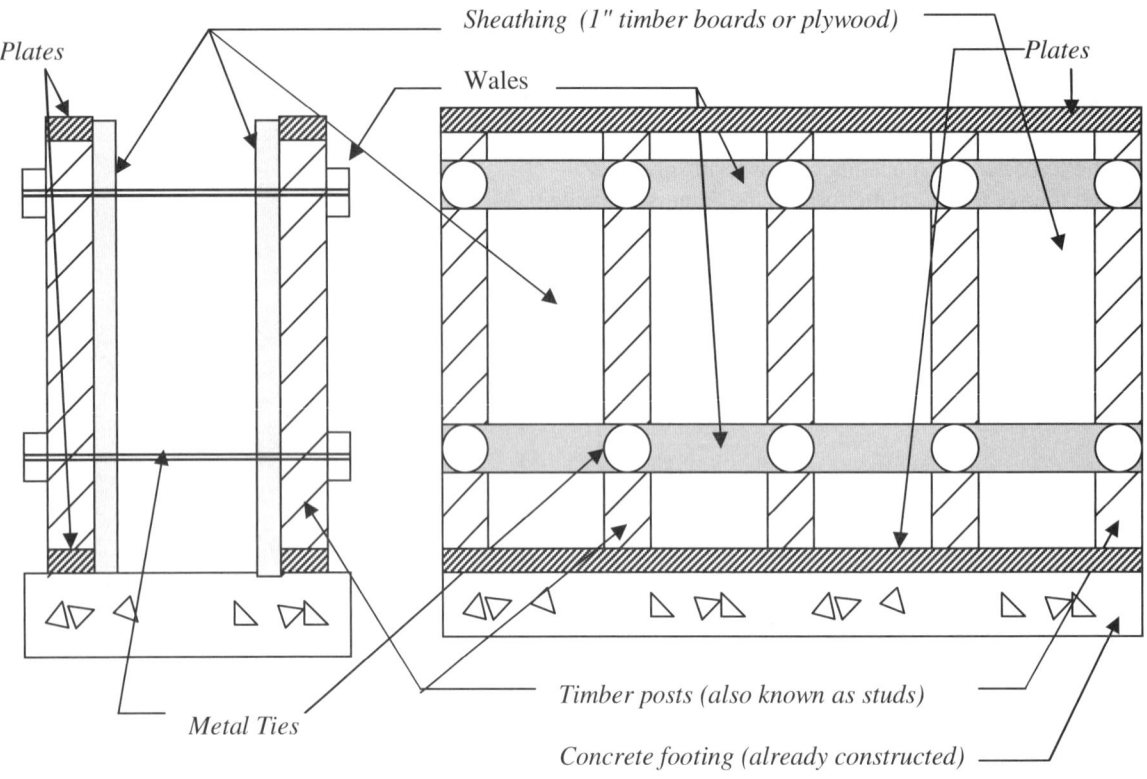

Elevation View   **Side View**

Sheathing: Sheathing keeps the concrete from falling. Sheathing could be 1" thick timber planks or ¾" plywood.

Studs (Vertical Timber Posts):   Vertical timber posts have to be erected to hold the sheeting. Function of studs is to hold the sheeting in place. Studs (timber posts) could be 2" x 4" timber. Studs are attached to the sheeting using nails.

Wales (Horizontal timber):   Horizontal timber is erected to hold the studs. These could be 2" x 4" or 2" x 2" timber depending upon the height. Nails are used to attach wales to studs.

Plates: Timber placed on top and bottom of studs are known as plates. Typically, 2 x 4 timber is used for plates. Studs are constructed on top of plates.

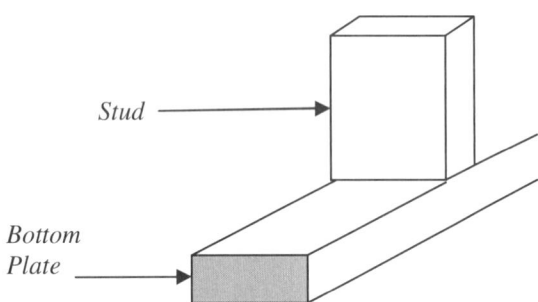

Metal Ties: Metal ties are used to hold the wales together. They usually break off when the concrete hardens.

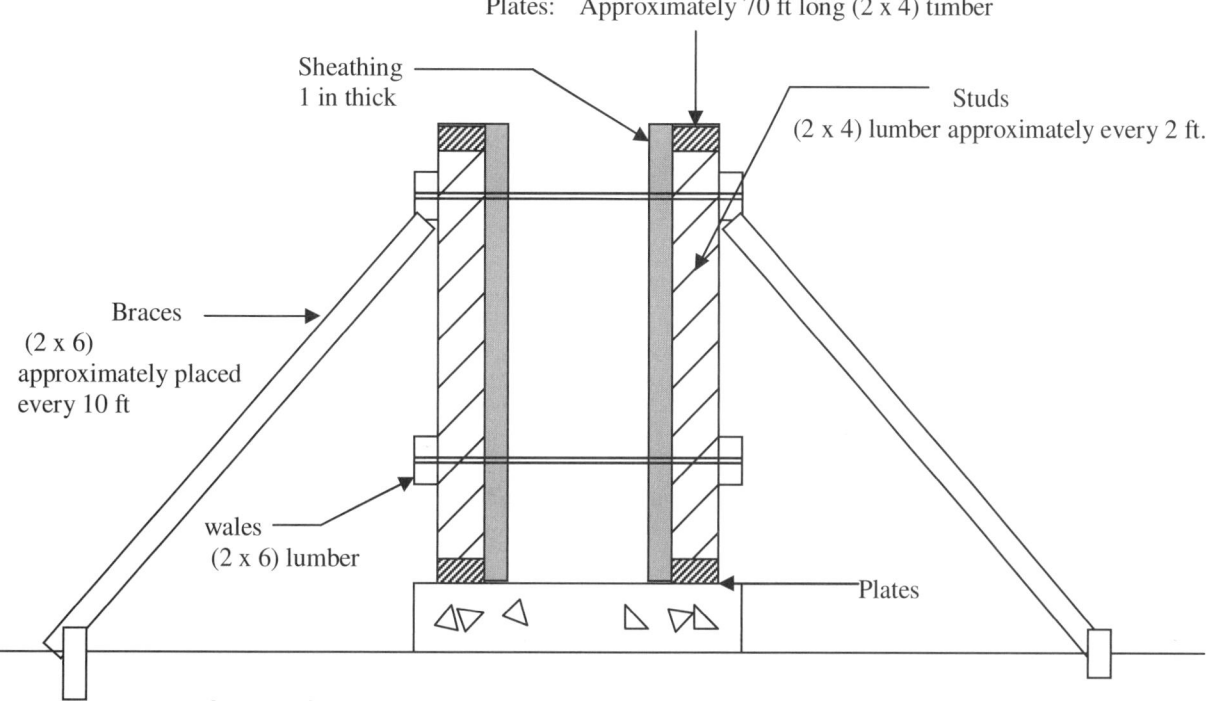

General Configuration of wall Forms (Dimensions would be different based on the situation)

<u>Load on Sheathing</u>:   Load on sheathing due to concrete is considered to be a uniformly distributed load for computation purposes.

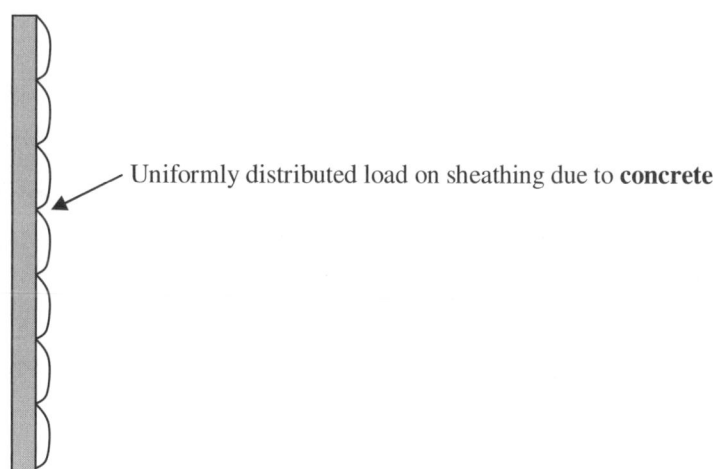

<u>Load on Studs:</u>   Load on studs due to sheathing is also can be approximated to a uniformly distributed load.

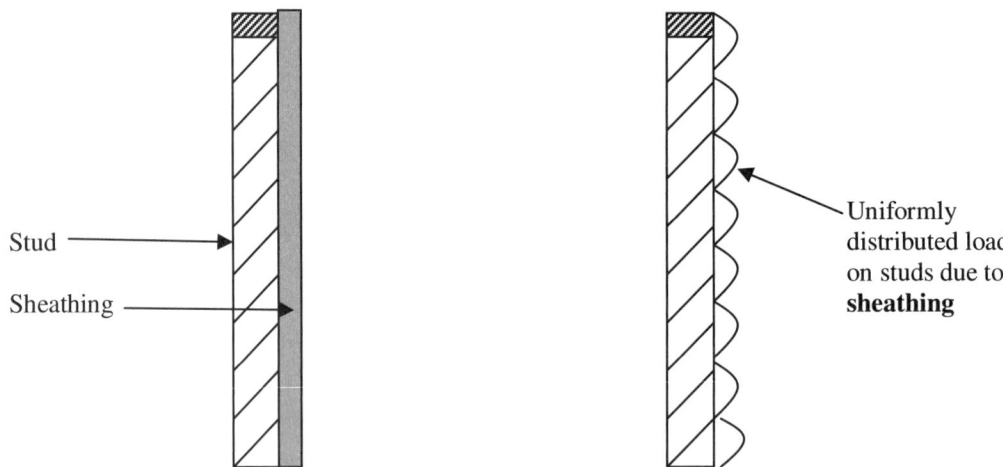

<u>Load on Wales due to Studs:</u>   Loads on wales due to studs are point loads. For practical purposes, load on wales also considered to be uniformly distributed.

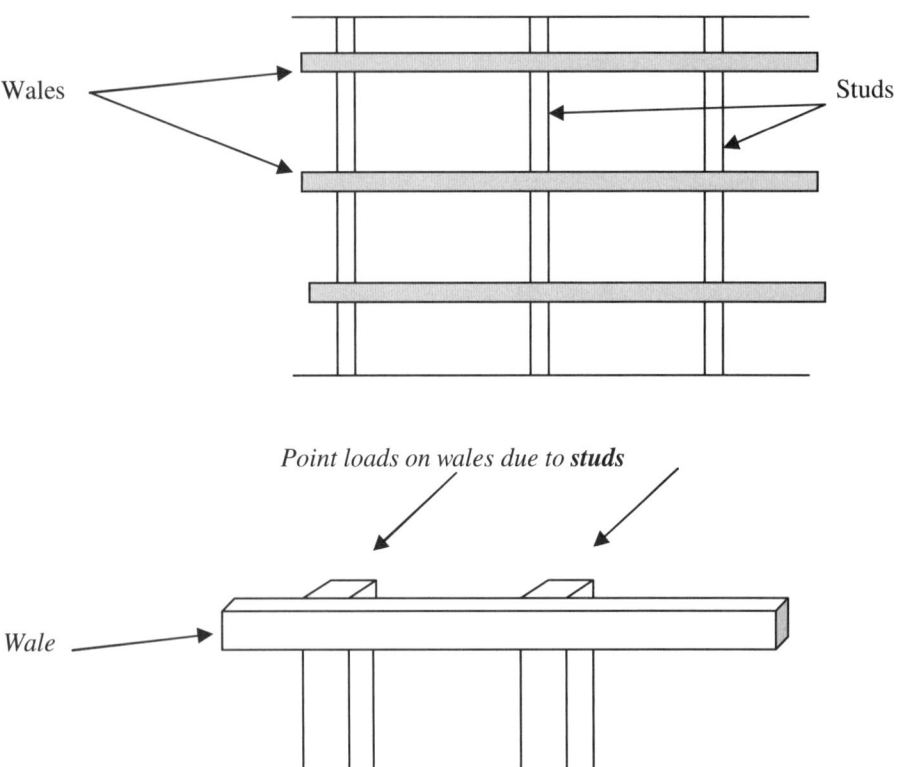

*Note: Refer to my **"practice problem book (second edition)"** and the **"Three sample Exams for the Construction Module"** for many problems and solutions.*

B.17 Shoring and Reshoring:

Shoring is the process of supporting wet concrete slabs or walls until they harden. Usually shores are placed below the formwork.

New slab

Shoring

Shoring

| Shoring is provided to support newly constructed slab |

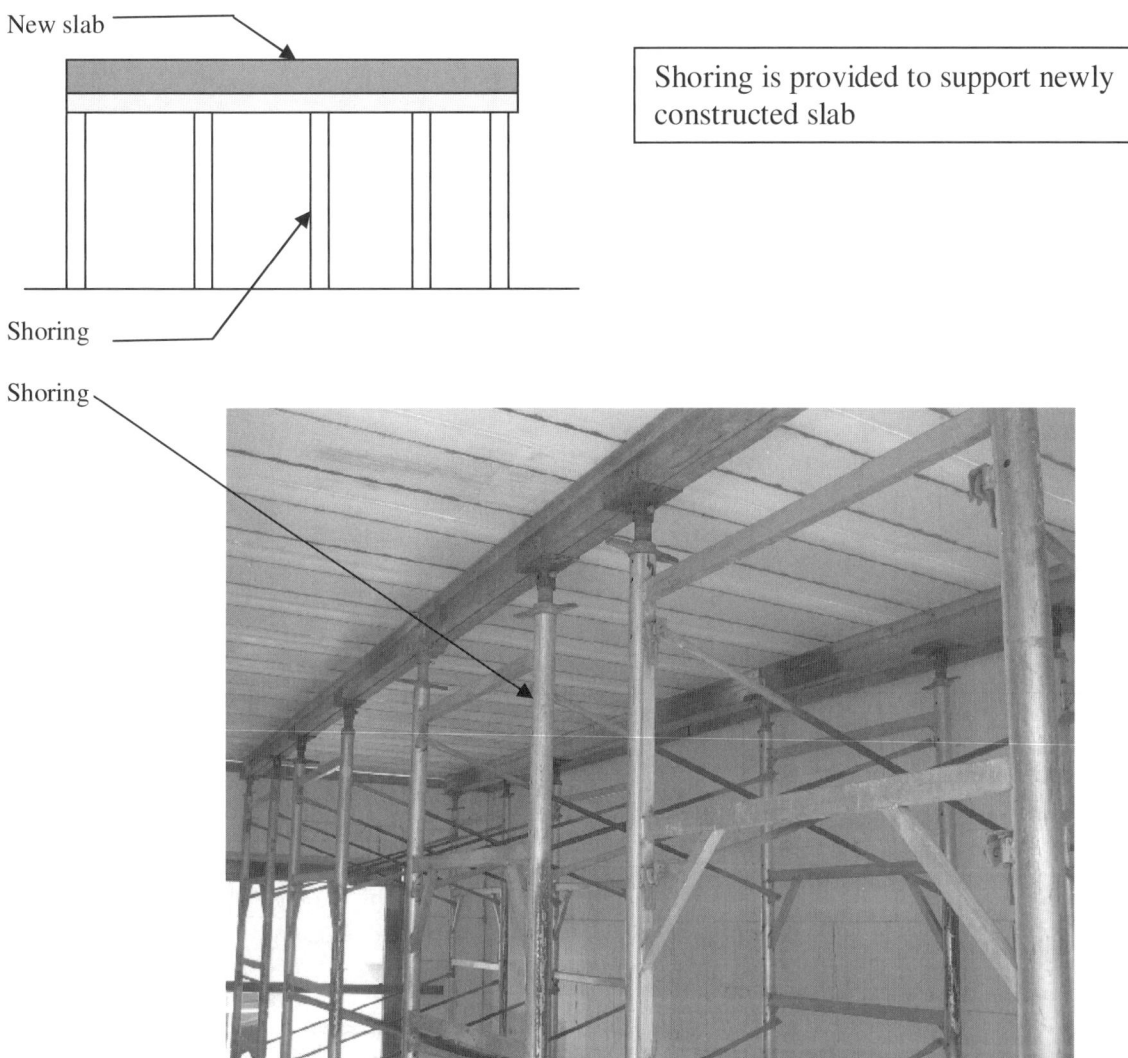

Shoring supporting a newly formed slab

It should be known that newly formed slabs are not capable of supporting themselves. With time, concrete would gain strength. In many cases, maximum strength is achieved in approximately 28 days. During this time, concrete slabs need to be supported.

Lateral Support: There are many situations where shoring has failed due to lack of lateral support. Lateral loads can be significant due to wind, motorized buggies on top of the slab and vibrations. It is important to consider adequacy of lateral support during design of shoring. Another major reason for failure is removal of shoring prior to slab gaining adequate strength.

Load Transfer during Shoring: Shoring should be designed to carry the total slab load + load due to form + any workers and equipment on top of the slab. It is no secret that concrete hardly has any strength during the time of pouring.

Reshoring: Reshoring is the process of supporting multiple floor slabs. During construction of high-rise buildings, multiple floor slabs will be supported by shores. Original shoring in lower floors needs to be removed and reshored to support higher-level slabs. If original shoring was not removed, the entire load coming from top floors would go to the original shoring at the lowest level. Hence, shoring at lower levels needs to be removed and let the hardened slab take its own weight. In addition, the slab should be allowed to deflect during the curing process. If the slab is not allowed to deflect, it would lead to cracks.

Following demonstration will show how load is transferred to shoring and reshores.

1st floor slab construction (Wet slab):

New wet floor slab (weight = W1)

Columns

Original shoring

Ground

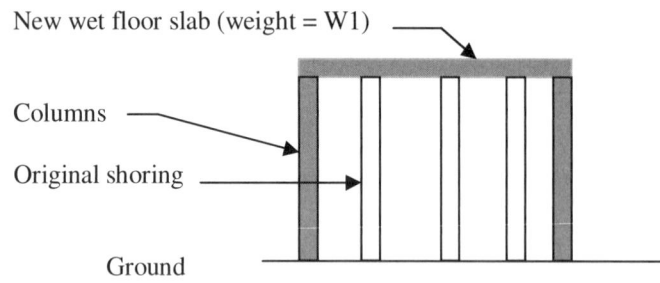

> Total slab load (W1) is taken by shoring. Note that slab is wet and cannot take any loads.

Load taken by slab = 0
Load taken by shoring = W1

Symbol for shoring

Symbol for reshores

Hardened slab:

Hardened floor slab (weight = W1)

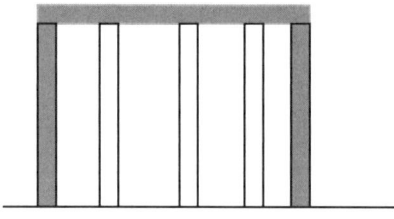

Ground

> Now the slab is hardened. Total slab load (W1) is still taken by shoring. Still no load is taken by the slab.

Load taken by slab = 0

Until shoring is removed, slab cannot take its own weight. Once the shoring is removed, slab will slightly deflect and take its own weight.

Load taken by shoring = W1

Shoring removed:

Hardened floor slab (weight = W1)

Ground

> Shoring is removed. Now slab is taking its own weight.

Load taken by slab = W1

Reshores installed:

Hardened floor slab (weight = W1)

Columns

Reshores

Ground

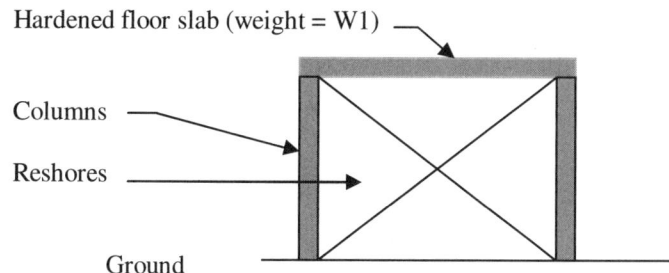

Next, reshores are installed. Reshores are snug fitted. Snug fitted means reshores are not loaded. They are just placed under the slab touching the slab.

Load taken by slab = Slab dead weight = W1
Load taken by reshores = 0 (Reshores are not loaded).

Construct second floor slab:

2nd floor slab (wet) W2

2nd floor shoring

Columns

Reshores

Ground

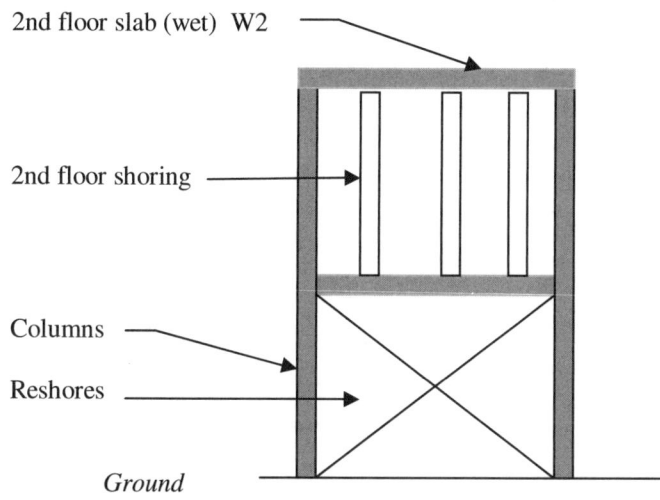

Next, second floor slab is constructed. 2nd floor slab is wet and will not take any load. It would pass the load to shoring below. Shoring will transfer the load to 1st floor slab. The 1st floor slab will try to deflect but it cannot. Reshores would immediately get loaded and absorb the load.

Load taken by 2nd floor slab = 0
Load taken by 2nd floor shoring = W2

Load taken by 1st floor slab = 1st floor slab dead weight = W1

Note that 1st floor slab is carrying its own weight (W1). W2 weight coming from top will be transferred to the reshores below.
Load taken by reshores = W2 (Reshores are now loaded).

<u>Second floor slab hardened. Remove second floor shoring:</u>

2nd floor slab (wet) W2

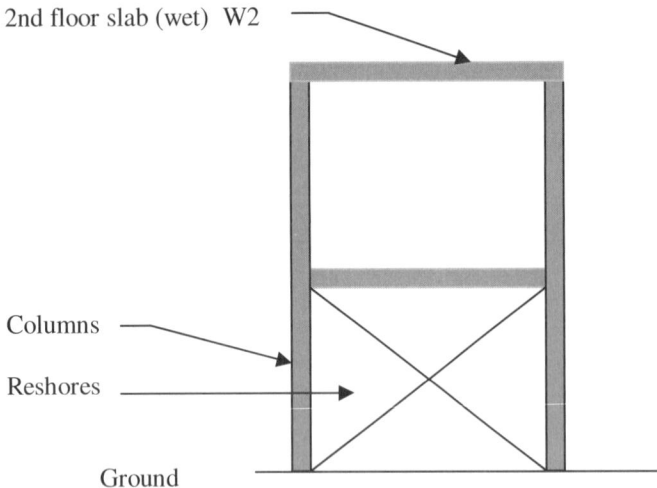

Columns

Reshores

Ground

Load taken by 2nd floor slab = W2
Load taken by 2nd floor shoring = 0   (shoring removed)

Load taken by 1st floor slab = Slab dead weight = W1
Load taken by reshores = 0 (W2 load is taken by the second floor slab).

<u>Second floor slab hardened. Install 2nd floor reshores:</u>

2nd floor slab (hardened) W2

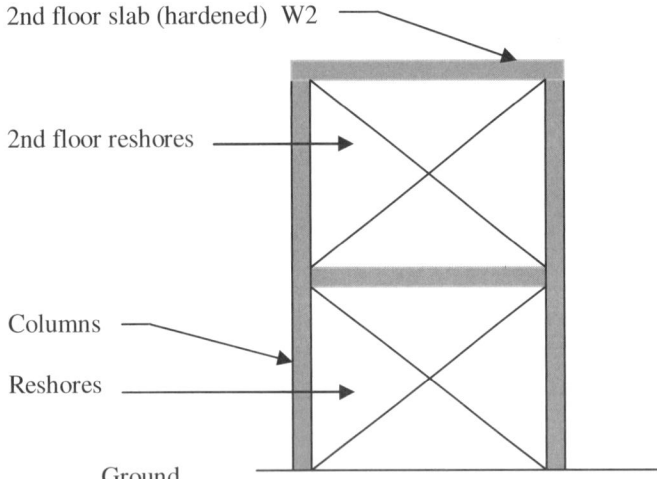

2nd floor reshores

Columns

Reshores

Ground

Load taken by 2nd floor slab = W2
Load taken by 2nd floor reshores = 0   (Reshores are snug fitted)

Load taken by 1st floor slab = Slab dead weight = W1
Load taken by 1st floor reshores = 0 (W2 load is taken by the second floor slab).

Construct the third floor slab (W3):

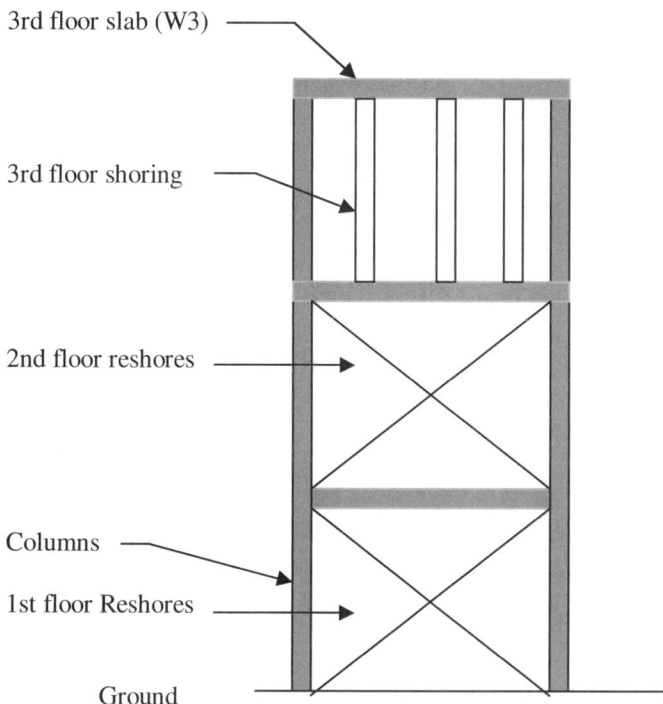

3rd floor slab (W3)

3rd floor shoring

2nd floor reshores

Columns

1st floor Reshores

Ground

Load taken by third floor wet slab = 0   (Slab is wet)
Load taken by 3rd floor shoring = W3

Load taken by 2nd floor slab = W2   (2nd floor slab takes only its own weight)
Load taken by 2nd floor reshores = W3   (W3 load coming from top will be transferred to the reshores)

Load taken by 1st floor slab = Slab dead weight = W1
Load taken by 1st floor reshores = W3

Basically new slab weight (W3) is transferred to 3rd floor shoring to 2nd floor reshores to 1st floor reshores and finally to the ground. Slabs will not take any of W3 load. Slabs will be taking only their own dead weight.

<u>Remove third floor shoring and install 3rd floor reshores. Also remove the first floor reshore:</u>

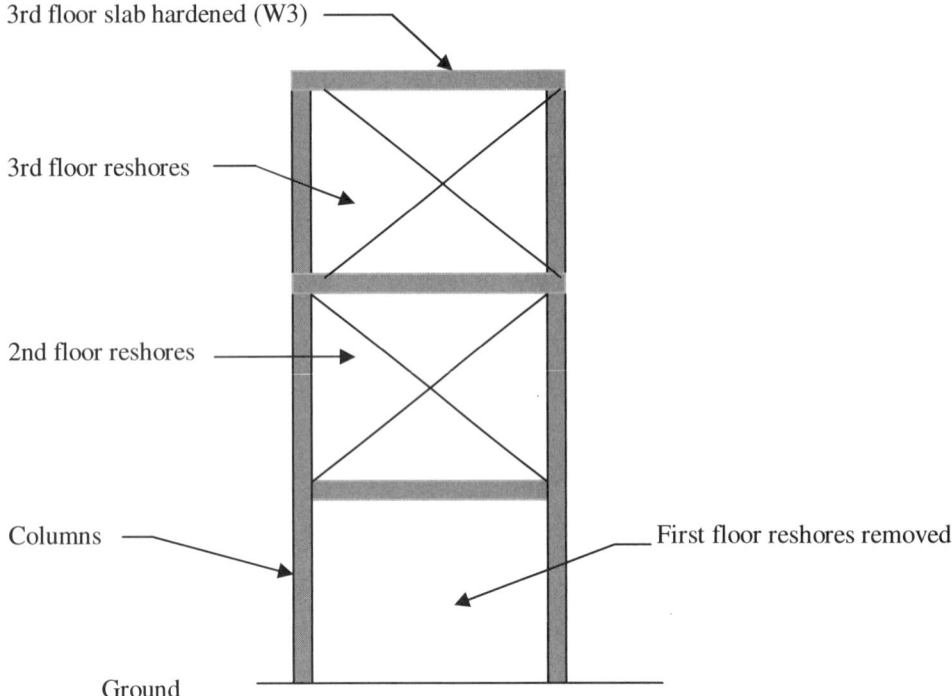

3rd floor slab hardened (W3)

3rd floor reshores

2nd floor reshores

Columns

First floor reshores removed

Ground

Load taken by third floor hardened slab = W3
Load taken by 3rd floor reshores = 0   (Reshores are snug fitted).

Load taken by 2nd floor slab = W2   (2nd floor slab takes only its own weight)
Load taken by 2nd floor reshores = 0   (W3 load is taken by the hardened third floor slab)

Load taken by 1st floor slab = Slab dead weight = W1
1st floor reshores are removed.

Construct the fourth floor slab: (VERY IMPORTANT STEP):

This step is very important and different than previous steps. Note that new load is NOT transferred to the ground.

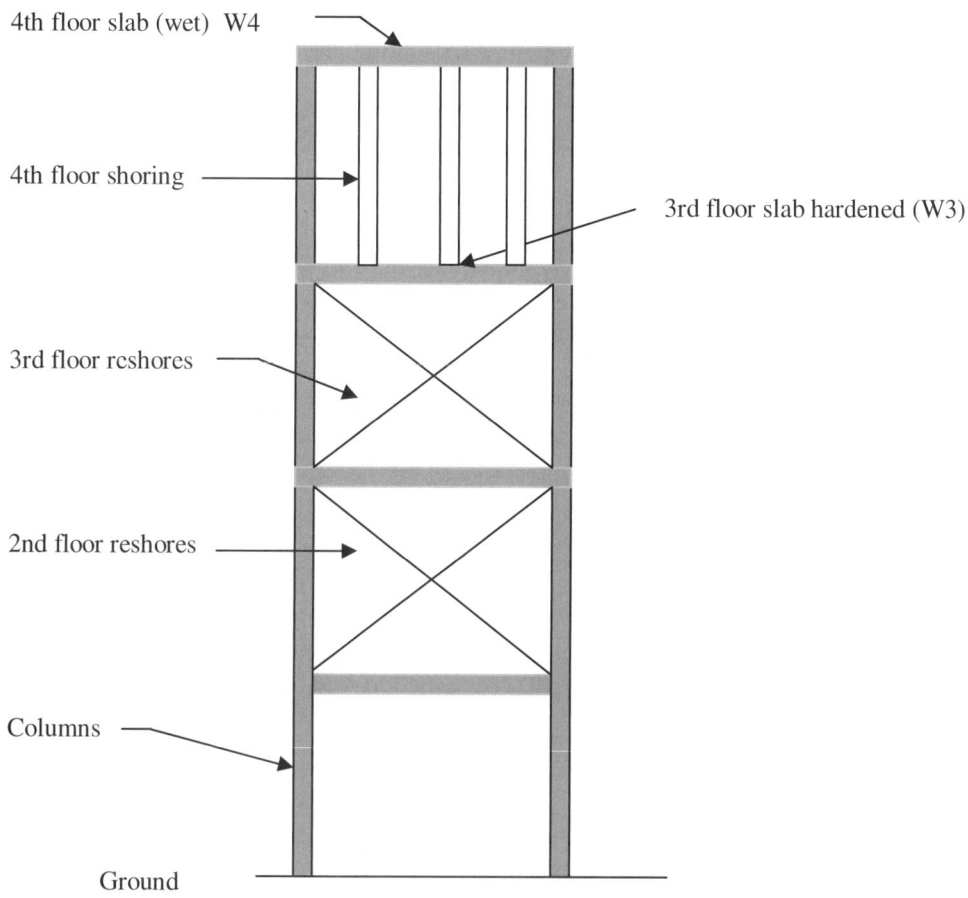

4th floor slab (wet) W4

4th floor shoring

3rd floor slab hardened (W3)

3rd floor reshores

2nd floor reshores

Columns

Ground

Load taken by 4th floor slab (wet) = 0
Load taken by 4th floor shoring = W4

4th floor slab is wet and will not take any load. It would transfer its weight to shoring below.

In the previous instances, load got transferred to the ground. Now the 1st floor reshores are removed, there is no way to transfer the W4 weight to ground.
W4 weight has to be shared by three slabs. (1st, 2nd and 3rd floor slabs).
Each of these slabs will take a load of W4/3.

Load taken by third floor hardened slab = W3 + W4/3

Now what is the load taken by 3rd floor reshores? W4 load is coming from top. W4/3 was taken by the third floor slab.
Hence remaining slab weight will be transferred to the 3rd floor reshores.
Load taken by 3rd floor reshores = 2W4/3

Load taken by 2nd floor slab = W2 + W4/3
We agreed to transfer the W4 load equally among three slabs. Hence second floor slab will take its own weight and W4/3.

Now what is the load transferred to 2nd floor reshores?
Load coming from third floor reshores is 2W4/3. Out of this load, W4/3 was taken by the second floor slab. Remaining load need to be taken by the second floor reshores.

71

Load taken by 2nd floor reshores = W4/3

Load taken by 1st floor slab = W1 + W4/3

W4 load is fully transferred among three slabs. After this, everything repeat the same way for upper floors.

This step is very important since slabs are taking its own weight plus a share of the fourth floor slab. If a slab were to fail, it would happen in this step. Previously, slabs were taking only their own weights.

Loads taken by slabs and reshores are shown below;

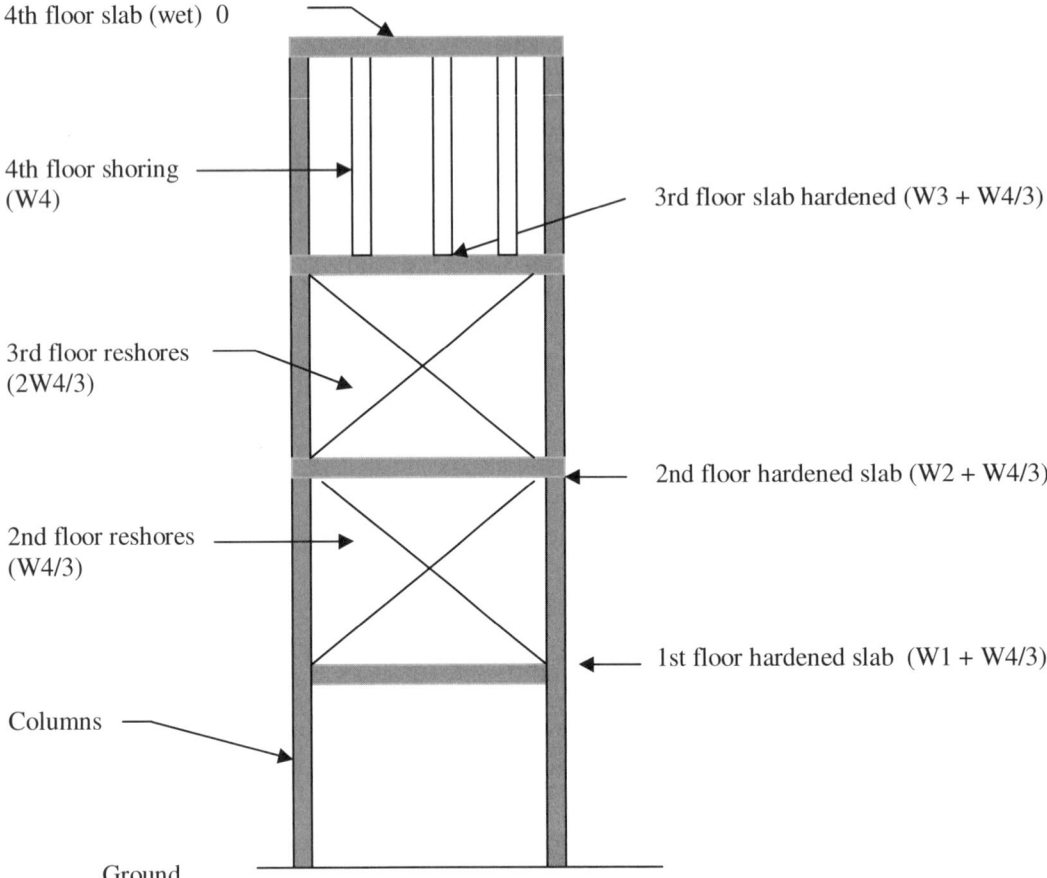

4th floor slab (wet) 0

4th floor shoring (W4)

3rd floor slab hardened (W3 + W4/3)

3rd floor reshores (2W4/3)

2nd floor hardened slab (W2 + W4/3)

2nd floor reshores (W4/3)

1st floor hardened slab (W1 + W4/3)

Columns

Ground

<u>ACI 347 Example</u>:

Now we are ready to discuss the method given in ACI 347. This is similar to method given above.

Building slabs are shored/reshored with one level of shoring and two levels of reshoring.
Following loads are given;
       Weight of each slab = D.
       Construction live load = 0.4D
       Shore and form weight = 0.1 D
       Reshore weight is ignored.

Construction live load is the load due to workers and their tools and buggies.

Symbol for shoring

Symbol for reshoring

Stage 1:   Slab is wet and will not carry any load. Total load will be taken by shoring.
Total load taken by shoring = 1.5D   (1D + 0.4D + 0.1D)
Load taken by wet slab = 0

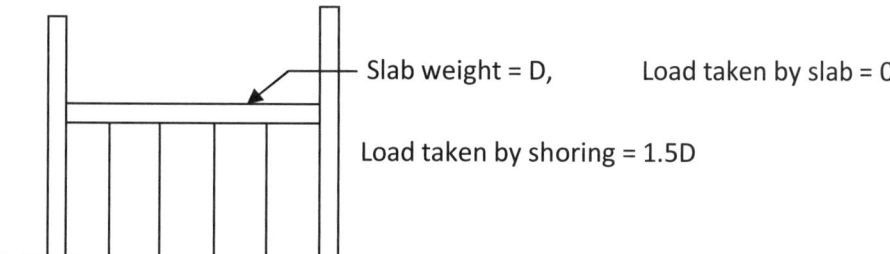

Slab weight = D,   Load taken by slab = 0

Load taken by shoring = 1.5D

Stage 2:   Once the slab is hardened, shoring is removed and reshores are installed. Reshores are lightly fitted or snug fitted. Hence reshores are not loaded. Once the slab is hardened there is no need of having any construction load on top of the slab. Hence construction live load = 0. Slab will take its own weight.
Load taken by slab = D
Load taken by reshores = 0

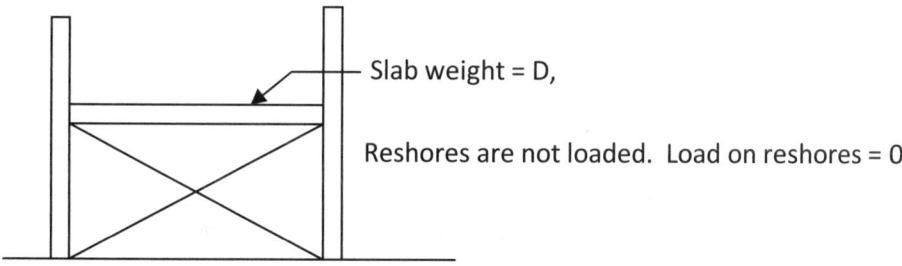

Slab weight = D,

Reshores are not loaded. Load on reshores = 0

Stage 3:   Shores are installed on top of hardened 1st floor slab and second floor slab is constructed.
Load taken by 2nd floor slab = 0   (This slab is still wet)
Load taken by shores between 1st and 2nd floor = 1.5D   (1D + 0.4D + 0.1D)
Load taken by 1st floor slab = D   (1st floor slab will carry its own weight. Any new load will be passed to the reshores below).
Load taken by 1st floor reshores = 1.5D

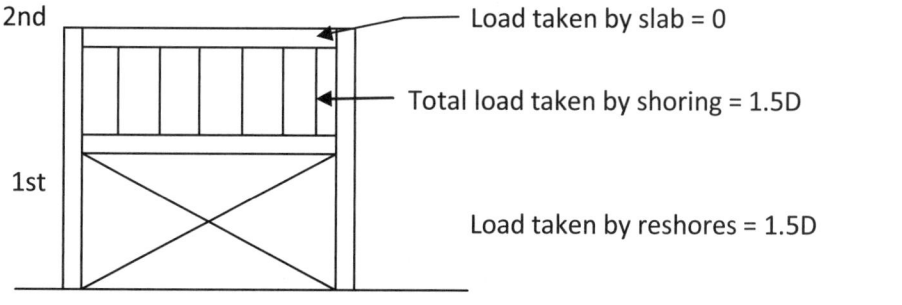

2nd   Load taken by slab = 0

Total load taken by shoring = 1.5D

1st

Load taken by reshores = 1.5D

Stage 4:   Once the second floor slab is hardened, shoring between 1st and 2nd floor is removed and reshores are installed. Construction live load and shoring is gone.

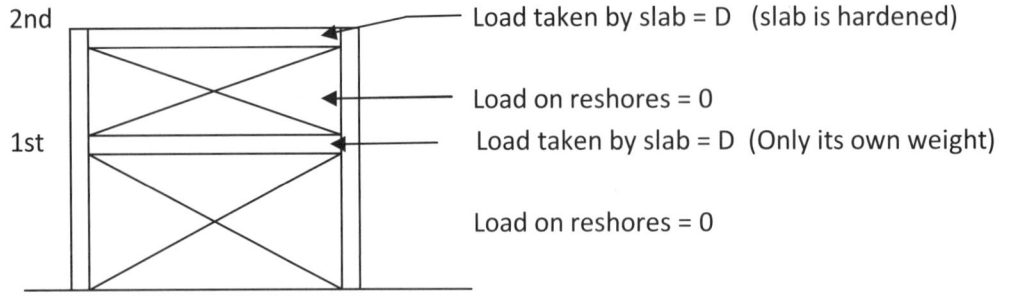

Stage 5:   Install shoring on second floor slab and build the third floor slab

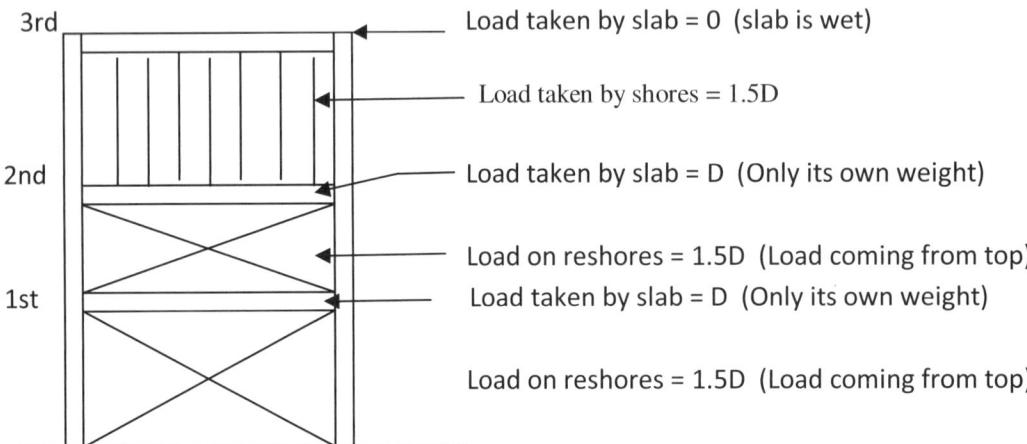

Load coming from 3rd floor will be taken by shores and then pass to reshores below. Finally the load is transferred to the ground. Slabs will not take any load other than its own weight since slabs are not allowed to deflect.

Stage 6:   Remove shoring below 3rd floor and install reshores. 3rd floor slab is now hardened. Construction live load is gone. Also remove reshores on ground floor.

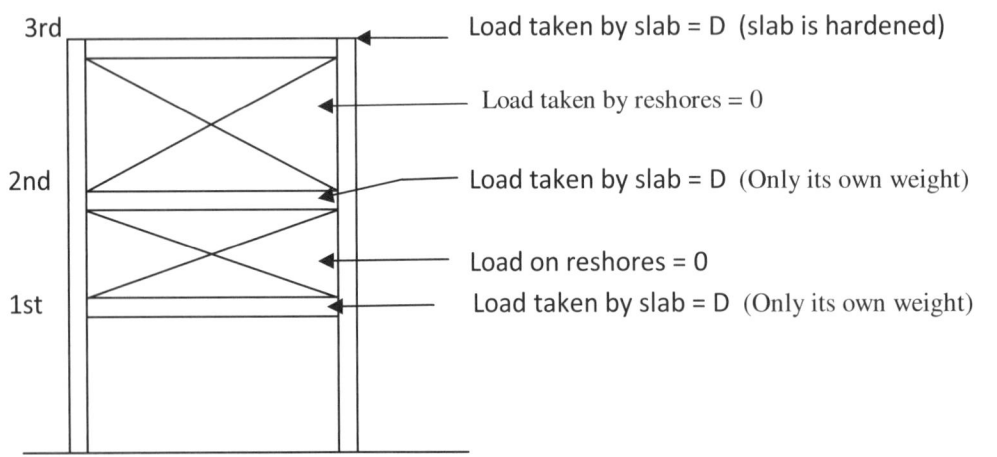

Stage 7: (Very important step):   Install shoring on third floor and build the 4th floor slab. Now this situation is slightly different than previous cases. If you notice reshoring on ground floor is removed. Hence load coming from top cannot be transferred to ground. Total load on 4th floor is 1.5 D. Where does this load end up? In previous cases, 1.5D got directly transferred to ground. Now this 1.5D cannot be transferred to ground. It has to be taken by three slabs. (3rd, 2nd and 1st floor slabs).
1.5D is equally distributed among three slabs.

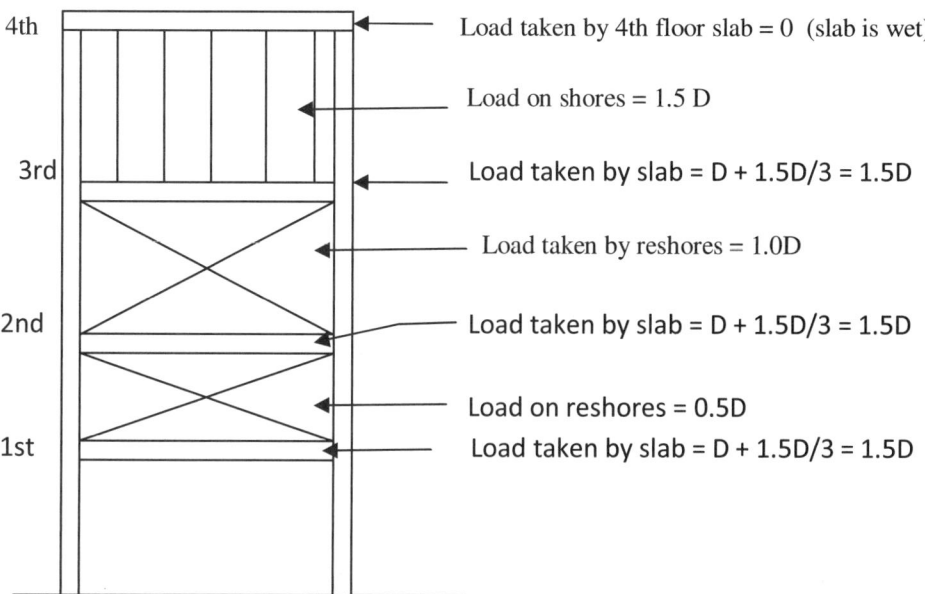

4th floor has a load of 1.5D including shoring weight and construction live load. This 1.5D will be taken by shoring below 4th floor.   3rd floor slab will take 1/3rd of the load that is coming from top. 1/3rd of 1.5D is 0.5D.

Hence 3rd floor slab will take 0.5D plus its own weight of 1.0D. 3rd floor slab will take a total of 1.5 D.

Now let us see how much loading will be taken by reshores below 3rd floor.
4th floor loading was 1.5D. 0.5D was already taken by 3rd floor slab. What is remaining is 1.0D.
Hence, reshores below 3rd floor will take 1.0D.

We agreed to distribute the 1.5D, equally among three slabs. Hence loading taken by 2nd floor slab will be 1.0D + 0.5D = 1.5D.

Now how much loading will be taken by reshores below 2nd floor?

Load coming from reshores above is 1.0 D. Out of that 0.5D was taken by the second floor slab. Hence loading below 2nd floor reshores would be 0.5D.
Load on first floor slab is 1.5 D, since we are equally distributing the 1.5D load among three slabs.

Stage 8:   Once the 4th floor slab is finished, workers will leave. Hence construction live load of 0.4D is removed. New load is 1.1D. This amount has to be distributed among three slabs equally.

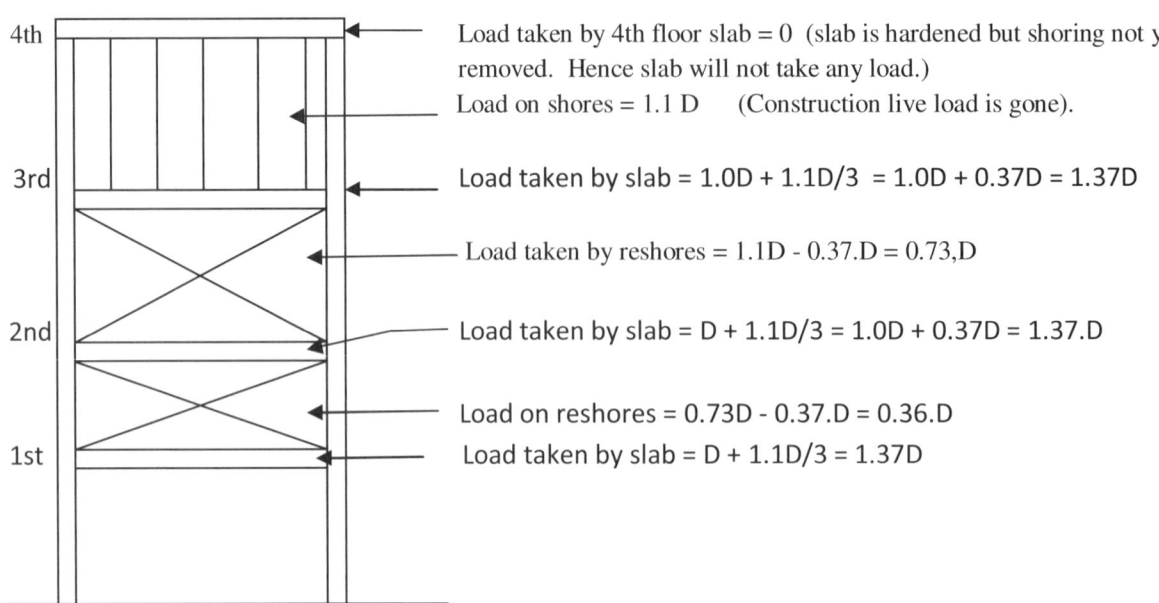

4th   Load taken by 4th floor slab = 0 (slab is hardened but shoring not yet removed. Hence slab will not take any load.)
Load on shores = 1.1 D   (Construction live load is gone).

3rd   Load taken by slab = 1.0D + 1.1D/3 = 1.0D + 0.37D = 1.37D

Load taken by reshores = 1.1D - 0.37.D = 0.73,D

2nd   Load taken by slab = D + 1.1D/3 = 1.0D + 0.37D = 1.37.D

Load on reshores = 0.73D - 0.37.D = 0.36.D

1st   Load taken by slab = D + 1.1D/3 = 1.37D

4th floor has a load of 1.1D including shoring weight. Construction live load is removed. This 1.1D will be taken by shoring below 4th floor.   3rd floor slab will take 1/3rd of the load that is coming from top. 1/3rd of 1.1D is 0.37D.

Hence, 3rd floor slab will take 0.37D plus its own weight of 1.0D. 3rd floor slab will take a total of 1.37 D.

Now let us see how much loading will be taken by reshores below 3rd floor.
4th floor loading was 1.1D. Out of that 0.37D was already taken by 3rd floor slab. What is remaining is 1.1D - 0.37D = 0.73D.
Hence reshores below 3rd floor will take 0.73D.

We agreed to distribute the 1.1D, equally among three slabs. Hence loading taken by 2nd floor slab will be 1.0D + 1.1D/3 = 1.37D.

Now how much loading will be taken by reshores below 2nd floor?

Load coming from reshores above is 0.73 D. Out of that 0.37D was taken by the second floor slab. Hence loading below 2nd floor reshores would be 0.73D- 0.37D = 0.36D
Load on first floor slab is 1.37 D, since we are equally distributing the 1.1D load among three slabs. (Note that there is rounding of decimals to second decimal).

See my other books "**Three Sample Exams for the Civil PE exam**" and "**Civil PE Construction Module Practice Problems**" books for more problems and solutions.

B.18 Bracing Masonry Walls:

Masonry walls need to be braced during and after construction. All masonry walls have to be supported laterally. In a building, masonry walls are tied to beams, columns and other walls. Until the masonry wall is laterally supported, it has to be braced.

In practice, bracing of masonry walls has to follow OSHA guidelines. For the exam purposes, NCEES recommends "Standard Practice for Bracing Masonry Walls Under Construction" by **Mason Contractors Association of America**. (MCAA). Hence you need to know both OSHA and MCAA guidelines.

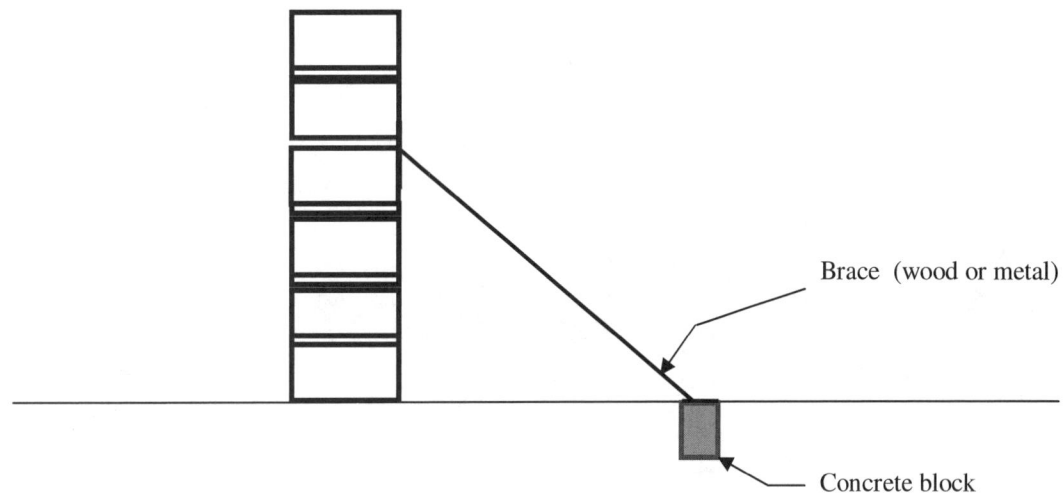

Schematic diagram of a masonry wall bracing is shown above. Bracing is required to maintain the lateral stability of a masonry wall.

Figure: Above system shows bracing, scaffolds, and worker platform. Worker platform is supported by scaffolding. Worker platform is needed for the workers to place bricks on the top.

Masonry walls are made of bricks and mortar. Until mortar brick joint is fully developed, masonry walls have little lateral stability. Even after mortar is hardened, standing masonry wall has little resistance against overturning. As per OSHA, any wall over 8 ft or taller need to be braced.

OSHA (1926.706 (b)) says the following;

"All masonry walls over eight feet in height shall be adequately braced to prevent overturning and to prevent collapse unless the wall is adequately supported so that it will not overturn or collapse. The bracing shall remain in place until permanent supporting elements of the structure are in place".

B18.1 Masonry Wall Construction Procedure:

Typically masonry walls are constructed using scaffolds and a worker platform. When the wall reaches 8 ft, the wall needs to be braced. Construction period is also known as "*Initial Period*". Initial period is the period that the wall is constructed or 24 hours whichever is shorter. Bracing has to be installed after initial period. In other words, if wall construction is ongoing after 24 hours, the bracing need to be installed after 24 hours. If the construction of the wall is finished after 8 hours, then bracing need to be installed after 8 hours.

Intermediate Period: After initial period, the workers will be attaching the wall to other elements of the building such as columns, beams and other walls. Bracing should be in place until the wall is properly attached to columns, beams and other walls. Bracing can be removed when lateral stability has achieved.

Restricted Zone: During the construction period (initial period) and the intermediate period, people who are not working on the wall should not go near the wall. Restricted zone is declared around the masonry wall. Restricted zone is equal to the height of the wall plus 4 ft on both sides of the wall.

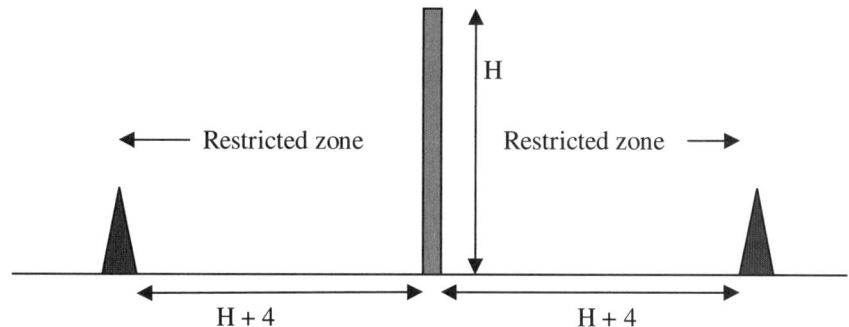

Note: There is some confusion between OSHA and MCAA standard practice. MCAA Standard practice says the restricted zone shall be established on both sides of the wall. OSHA says the following;
"The limited access zone shall be established on the side of the wall which will be unscaffolded" (**"1926.706(a)(3)**)

Limited access zone and restricted zone means the same thing. Only workers who are directly working on the wall can enter the restricted zone. For an instance, a worker who is concreting a side walk near the masonry wall is not allowed inside the restricted zone.

As per MCAA, work on masonry walls should stop when the wind speed exceeds 20 mph during the initial period. On the other hand, work is allowed till the wind speed is 35 mph during the intermediate period.

As per OSHA, limited access zone should be established whenever masonry walls are built. OSHA does not specify a height limitation for the limited access zone.

Tables are given in "Standard Practice for Bracing Masonry Walls Under Construction" indicating type of bracing required for a given wall height.

Factors that affect masonry bracing;

Not all masonry walls are the same. Some masonry walls are fully grouted. Some are reinforced. Some are not reinforced. Also some have higher density.

Some factors that affect the lateral stability;

- The wall is reinforced or not
- The wall is fully grouted or not
- Density of masonry
- Thickness of the wall
- Height of the wall
- Wind speed

Wind Force Calculation:

MCAA gives the following equation to calculate the force acting on a wall;

$$w = 0.00256 \ V^2$$

w = Wind pressure in psf
V = 5 second wind gust speed in mph

If the wind speed is 20 mph, $w = 0.00256 \times 20^2 = 1.042$ psf

Example: What is the wind force acting on a 12 ft tall wall when the wind is blowing at 20 mph. Assume the wind speed is the same on the wall from top to bottom.   Length of the wall is 100 ft.

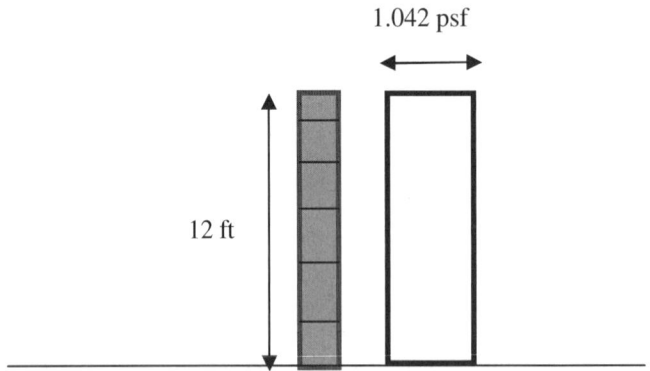

Total force acting on the wall = Wind pressure x Area of the wall
Total force acting on the wall = 1.042 x (12 x 100)
Total force acting on the wall = 1,250.4 lbs

Three different bracing types are considered by MCAA standard practice.
- Wood bracing
- Pipe bracing
- Cable bracing

Practice Problems:

Problem 1:   Wind speed of a site is measured to be 35 mph. The wall is 8 ft high and 60 ft long. Bracings are placed every 10 ft at a height of 8 ft as shown. What is the horizontal force acting on each concrete block?

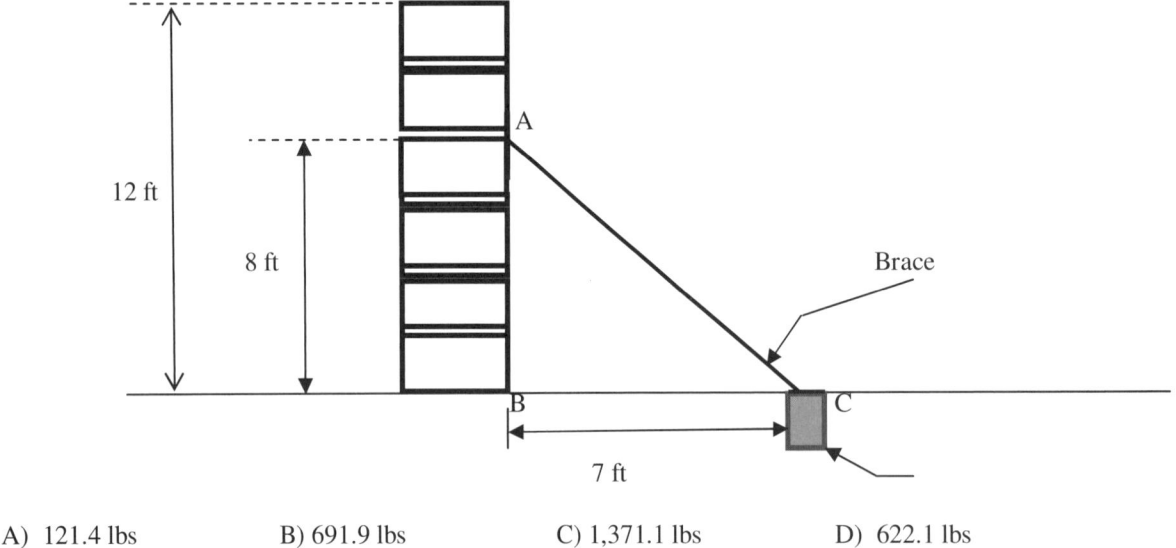

A) 121.4 lbs   B) 691.9 lbs   C) 1,371.1 lbs   D) 622.1 lbs

Problem 2):   Find the force in the bracing for the problem given above.

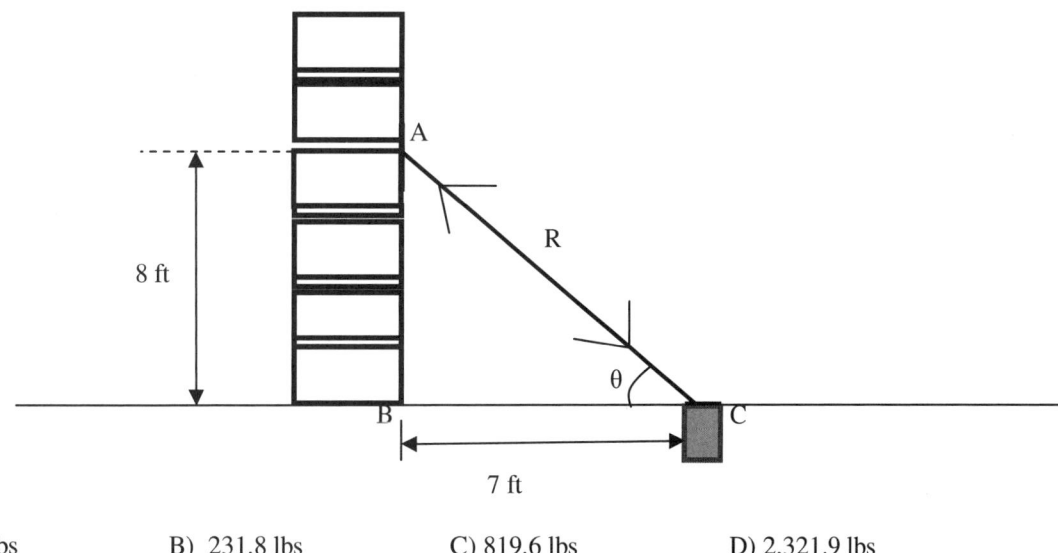

A) 944.5 lbs   B) 231.8 lbs   C) 819.6 lbs   D) 2,321.9 lbs

Problem 3)   18 ft high unreinforced masonry wall is braced as shown in the figure during the intermediate period. The wall is 10 inches thick and built using type N mortar. Is the bracing shown acceptable?

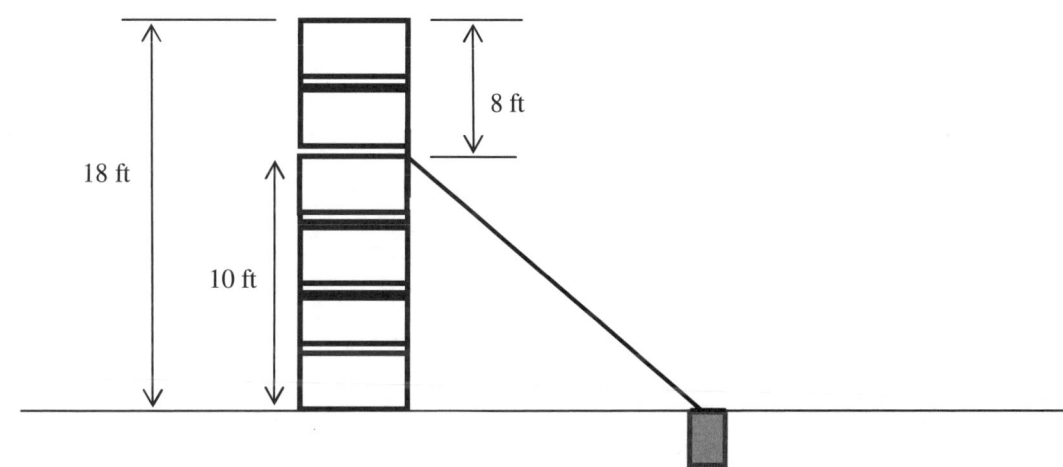

Problem 4):   8 inch thick 28 ft high unreinforced wall is braced as shown below during the intermediate period. Type N mortar is used. Is the configuration acceptable?

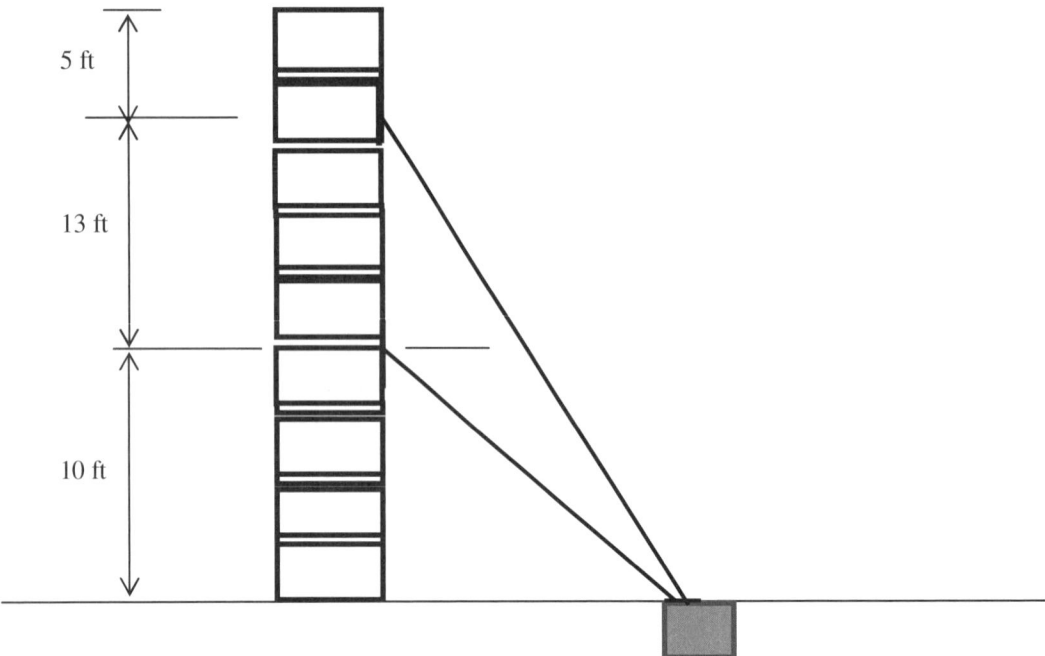

Problem 5):   Expansion joints are placed every 20 ft in an unreinforced masonry wall. The thickness of the wall is 10 inches and height is 35 ft. Type N mortar was used. Following configuration was used for bracing. Is this acceptable?

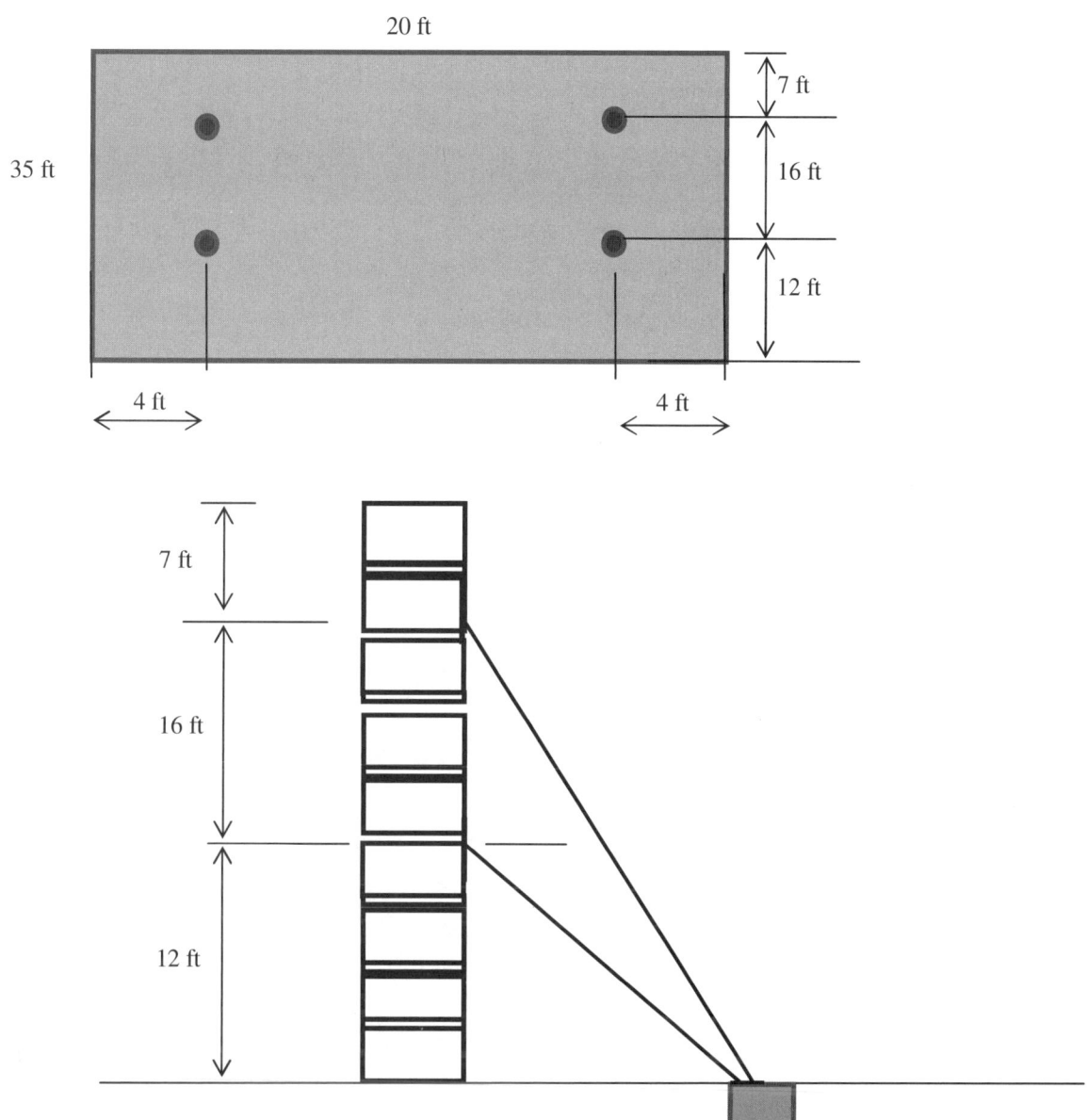

B18.2   Reinforced Masonry Walls:

Problem 6):   A contractor grouts reinforced masonry walls at 3.00 PM. At the end of the work day at 6 PM, he has to brace the wall. Should he consider the wall as a reinforced masonry wall or an unreinforced masonry wall?

Problem 7):   10 inch thick reinforced masonry wall was grouted 8 AM in the morning. The work for the day ended at 8 PM and wall was braced. Type M mortar was used for the wall. The wall was reinforced with #5 bars every 48 inches. Below shown bracing configuration was used. Is this configuration adequate?

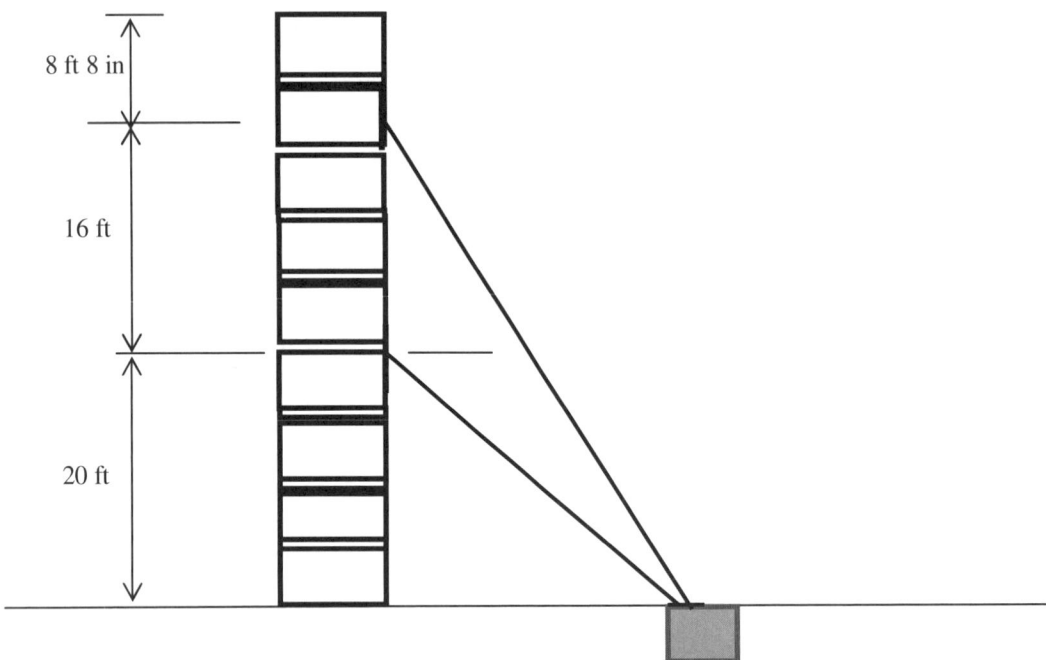

Solutions are given in "Civil PE Construction Module Practice Problems, Second Edition".

B.19 Typical Rebar Details:

Typical rebar details for various conditions are shown below.

Typical detail for corner of a wall:

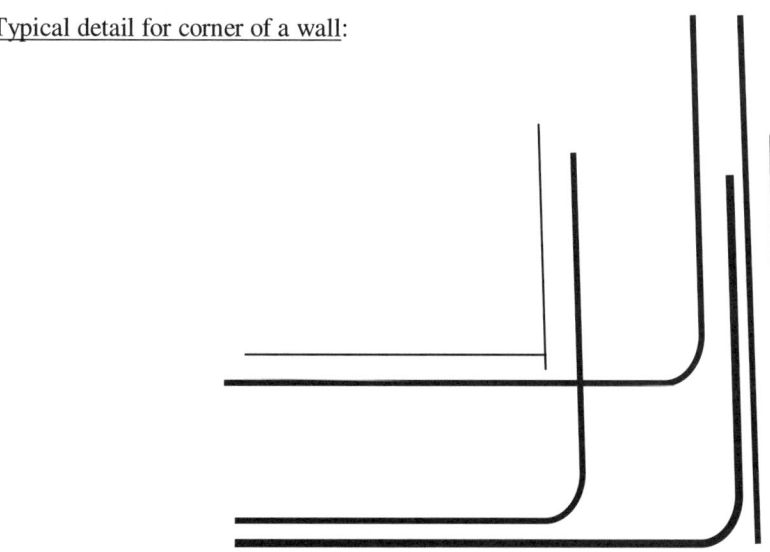

Typically, all external bars are hooked. As per ACI, standard hook is 12 x diameter.

Practice Problem: What is the length of a standard hook for a No. 9 bar?

Solution:

As per ACI 318, standard hook is 12d.

Diameter of a No. 9 bar = 9/8 inches.
Standard hook length = 12 x 9/8 inches = 13.5 inches

13.5 in

Dowels for Masonry Walls:

Typically, dowels are provided for masonry walls by the concrete contractor.

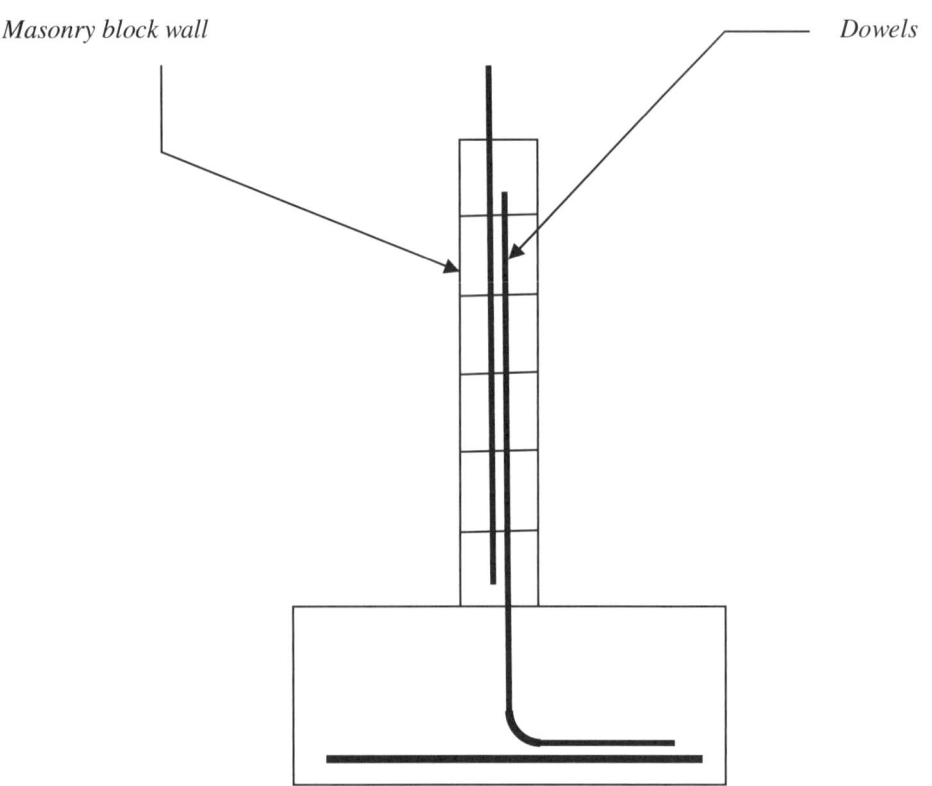

B.20 Construction Joints in Slabs: It is not possible to concrete a whole slab or a wall in one concrete pour. Hence, construction joints are needed. Typically, a keyway is provided to engage the old concrete with new concrete.

Construction Joints in Slabs

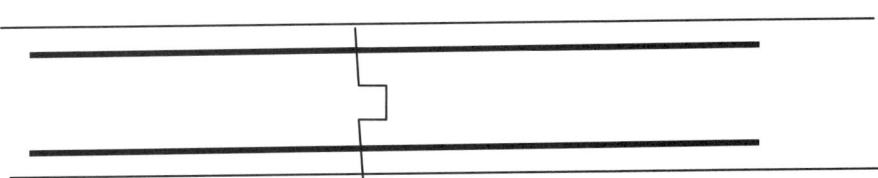

Typically, rebars are extended thru the joint.

B.21 Concrete Practice Problems:

Practice Problem 1:   Contractor is planning to pump concrete to a high rise building. The pump mix needs to have a higher water content. How could one design a pump mix without sacrificing the strength?
A) Add water reducing admixtures   B) Add fast setting admixtures   C) Increase the water content
D) Add mineral admixtures

Solution:
Increasing the water content would lead to lower strength. On the other hand, water reducing admixtures would increase the workability and pumpability without affecting the strength. Hence the correct answer is A.

Practice Problem 2:   What is the correct statement below;

A)   Type II cement can develop higher strength in a mass concrete than Type I cement.
B)   Development of high temperature in mass concrete would increase the strength
C)   Type I cement can develop higher strength in a mass concrete than Type II cement.
D)   None of the above

Solution: Ans (A)

In mass concretes, heat at the core is trapped. Hence the temperature at the core would rise. This would lead to low strength concrete. Type II cement generates less heat and the problem can be avoided.

Practice Problem 3:   Is the following statement correct?
Replacing cement with Pozzalans would reduce the strength of concrete

Solution: This may or may not be true. Pozzalans generally react with by products of cement hydration. Hence, it is not necessarily a bad thing to replace cement with porzallans.

Practice Problem 4:   Name three highly used Porzallans?

Solution:

- Fly Ash
- Blast furnace slag
- Micro silica or silica fume

Practice Problem 5:   Workability can be increased by introducing fly ash into a concrete mix. What is the reason for this?

Solution: Fly ash particles are more spherical in shape than cement particles. Hence, it is believed that fly ash particles can roll instead of slide. Hence, particles would move around easily increasing the workability.

Practice Problem 6:   What is the purpose of a bull float?

Solution: Bull floats are used for concrete finishing work. Bull float is not a good device to achieve strict flatness requirements. However, for many practical purposes, bull floats are suffice.

Practice Problem 7:   What is the length of a No. 6 standard hook?

Solution: Standard hook is 12d.

Length of standard hook = 12 x d = 12 x 6/8 = 9 inches.

Practice Problem 8:   Quality control inspector has been monitoring the ambient temperature. Following is his finding.

Sunday: Average air temperature 32F
Monday: Average air temperature 38F
Tuesday: Average air temperature 32F
Wednesday: Average air temperature 22F

Highest air temperature for one half the day from midnight to midnight = 55F
Should the contractor follow the cold weather plan.

Solution:

ACI 306 defines cold weather as follows;

Cold weather is defined as a period when, for more than 3 consecutive days, the following conditions exist:
1) The average daily air temperature is less than 40 F (5 C) and
2) The air temperature is not greater than 50 F (10 C) for more than one-half of any 24-hr period.

The average temperature is less than 40F for more than three consecutive days. Hence first condition implicates that cold weather protection should be used.

On the other hand, highest air temperature for one half the day was more than 50F. Cold weather plan should be followed if any of the conditions are met. Hence, the contractor needs to provide cold weather protection and any other required precautions specified.

Practice Problem 9:   Above what temperature should the contractor obligated to provide hot weather protection?

Solution:

ACI does not provide a temperature, in the case of hot weather condition.

Practice Problem 10:   What does a curing compound do?

A)   Curing compounds allow water to evaporate.
B)   Curing compounds do not allow water to evaporate.
C)   Curing compounds keep the concrete hot
D)   None of the above

Solution: Ans (B)

Practice Problem 11)   What is the maximum height that concrete can be dropped?

Solution: ACI does not provide a maximum height. However, ACI requires that there are no rebars or any other obstructions on the way when dropping concrete.

Practice Problem 12)   New concrete has to be poured next to old concrete. What shall contractor do prior to placing the new concrete?

Solution: Bond between new concrete to old concrete is very weak. Hence, the contractor should apply a bonding agent to the old concrete prior to concreting.

Practice Problem 13)   Concrete slab of a large warehouse need to be finished. What is the best equipment that can be used for this purpose?

A)   Hand trowel
B)   Bull Float
C)   Ride on trowel machine
D)   None of the above

Solution: Ans C

Practice Problem 14)   A concrete structure needs to be built in an area that has severe winters and very hot summers. The structural engineer has recommended flyash to be added to the concrete mix. Is this a good idea?

A)   Yes. Fly ash would generate less heat and that would be beneficial.
B)   Yes. Fly ash increases the air content and would resist cracking due to freezing and thawing.
C)   No.   Fly ash decreases the air content and would promote cracking due to freezing and thawing.
D)   None of the above

Solution: Ans C

Cracks could appear due to freezing and thawing of concrete. High air content is recommended when concrete is subjected to freezing and thawing conditions. Air in concrete would allow concrete to expand and contract without generating cracks. Fly ash particles are generally much smaller than cement particles. Hence, fly ash tends to decrease the air content. Adding fly ash would promote cracks.

Practice Problem 15)   Elevation of top of slab on grade is given to be 13.5 ft. The thickness of the slab is 8 inches. Soil grade is at elevation 12' 9". As per ACI 117, soil grade tolerance is 3/4 inches. Is the elevation of soil is within the tolerance limit?
A) Yes
B) No
C) Can't say

Solution:

Top of slab elevation = 13.5 ft
Slab thickness = 8 inches = 0.6666 ft
Top of soil elevation required = 13.5 - 0.6666 = 12.8333 ft
Measured top of soil elevation = 12 ft 9" = 12.75 ft

Difference = 12.83333 - 12.75 = 0.0833 ft = 0.996 inches

This is greater than ACI recommended tolerance of 3/4 inches. (0.75 inches).

Ans B

C.0 Steel Construction

Steel is still widely used in construction. Steel has many advantages over concrete. After 9/11, many proponents of concrete stated that if the world trade center towers were built using concrete, they would not have collapsed. Concrete is an extremely good fireproof material. Under high temperatures, steel connections tend to fail. Concrete beams and columns do not need additional fireproofing. On the other hand, steel beams and columns need to be fireproofed.

Left: *Steel beams and columns prior to fireproofing*
Right: *Steel columns after fireproofing*

On the other hand, performance of steel structures during earthquakes is much better. This is due to the fact that steel structures can be designed with more flexibility than concrete structures. But some argue with modern design techniques even concrete structures can be made very safe under earthquake loadings.

It is generally believed that cost of steel framed structures to be much higher than concrete structures. But some experts believe that with the advent of high strength steel combined with state of the art design techniques, one may able to design cheap steel structures. One of the main advantages of concrete is the availability. Concrete is available thru out the year in most parts of the country. On the other hand, availability of steel can be an issue if not ordered ahead of time.

Concrete structures can be built faster than steel frames. But if one can get design, detailing and fabrication done in time, steel erection can go faster. On the other hand, any errors during detailing or fabrication can delay the project.

Another advantage of concrete is that any shape an architect imagines can be easily achieved. Same cannot be said with steel. Though complex shapes are possible with steel, fabrication issues can delay the progress. However, one can argue that most aesthetic buildings are steel framed structures.

Left: Steel building
Right: Concrete building

C.1   Steel Construction Process:

C.1.1   Design Drawings and Shop Drawings:

Once the architect has completed the architectural drawings, structural engineers would design columns and beams. Structural engineers would size up the columns and beams and provide the type of sections needed at each location. In addition, they would provide the size of anchor bolts and various other structural information.

Design drawings and specifications would be part of the contract. Contractor who won the contract would provide the design drawings to a steel fabricator. Steel fabricator would use the design drawings and develop shop drawings. During the shop drawings stage many issues that were not considered during the design phase would be considered. What is the best method to attach a gusset plate to a beam? Should the plate be welded in the field or in the shop? Welding a steel member in a shop is always cheaper than welding in the field. On the other hand, if welded in the field, workers can make minor adjustments to the piece to fit into the structure. In many instances, design engineer would delegate design of connections to steel fabricating shop. This is known as design delegation. But as per law, this would not release the design engineer from the responsibility. Since two parties are involved, any issues arising due to bad connection design would be the responsibility of both the fabricator and the design engineer.

Steel Design Drawings: Design drawings would tell the erector what beams and columns need to be used. Beam elevations and column elevations are also given.

Building grid lines, beams and column schedule is shown below.

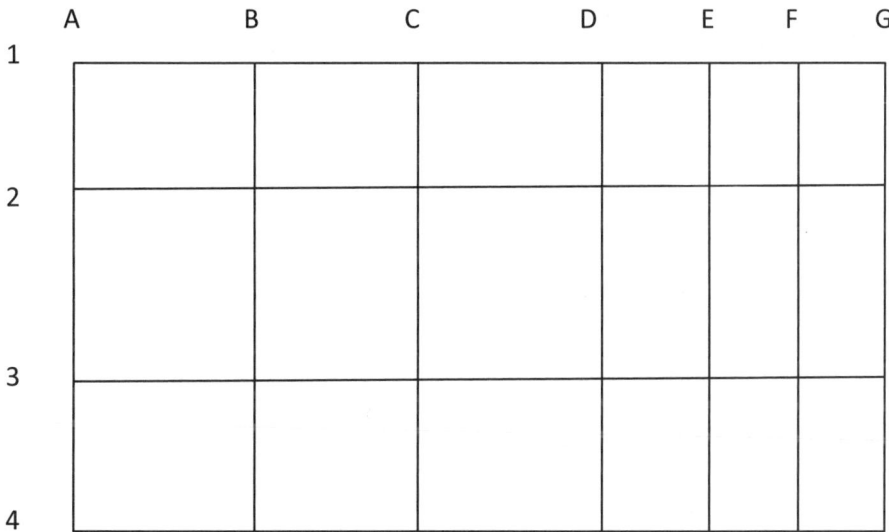

Building Grid

Civil PE Construction Module, Fifth Edition Ruwan Rajapakse, PE, CCM, CCE, AVS

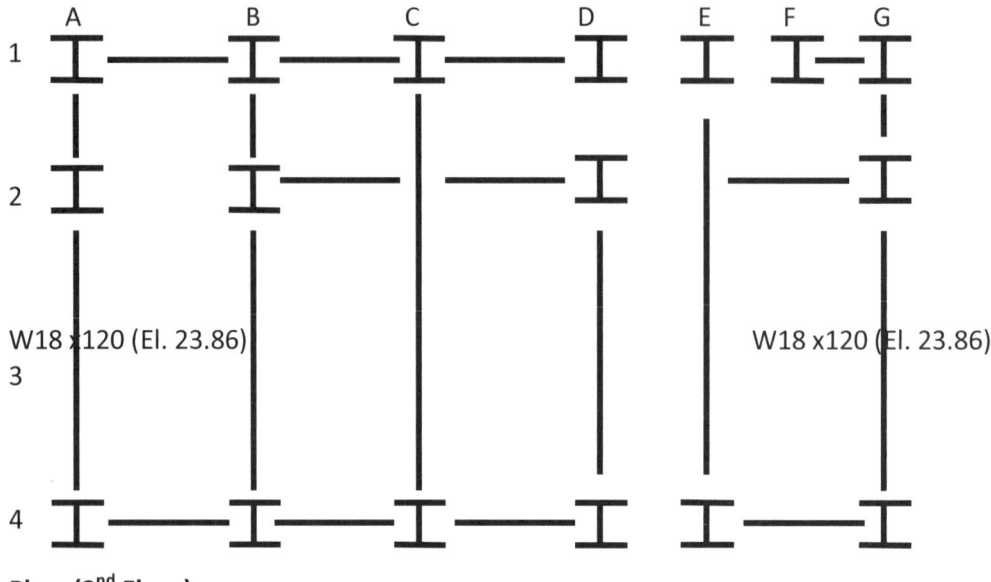

Plan (2nd Floor)

Above figure shows the plan view of second floor. Plan view of each floor should be provided. Size of each and every beam and top of the beam elevation should be given in the drawing. In the above figure, size of two beams shown. In addition, connection details also should be provided. Bolt pattern or weld information need to be provided.

Column schedule;

A1 A2 A3 A4	B1 B2 B3 B4	C1 C2 D1 D2	D3 D4 C3 C4	E1 E2 E3 E4 F1 F2	F3 F4 G1 G2 G3 G4	
W 24 x 40	W 24 x 40					EL. 114' 2"
		W18 x 40	W18x 56	W24x 60	W18x 60	EL. 104' 6"
						EL 94' 8"
W 24 x 56	W24x 56					EL. 81' 6"
						EL. 67' 4"

Column schedule should provide column location, column size, column start and end elevations. (ie. In the above figure at C1, install a column W18 x 40 at an elevation of 81' 6". Top of column elevation is 104' 6".

C.1.2   Erection Drawings:

Once the shop drawings are approved by the design engineer, the fabricator would develop erection drawings. Each steel member is given a piece number. Erection drawings would very specifically give where each steel member goes. The workers would pick the marked steel member and find out where it would be erected. Then they would erect the pieces as shown on erection drawings. When steel members come to the site, they would be sorted out as per location that they are supposed to be erected. This is known as shaking. Steel members would be transported to the location of erection using a crane.

C.1.3   Steel Erection Process:

Steel erection has different phases and different crews. Some of the steel working crews are;
- Connecting crew
- Bolting crew
- Detailing crew
- Welding crew
- Decking crew
- Rigging crew

93

Very first crew to go up is the connecting crew. These workers connect beams and columns with few bolts. Connecting is considered to be the hardest job in steel work. Connecting crew connect steel beams and columns while they are loose and dangling in air.

Following is a write up by a steel worker;
"As the steel pieces goes up, every time a beam is set onto a column, two pieces of steel meet in thin air. It's windy up there, and frames tend to sway without walls to stiffen them. A "connector" has to be at the top of that column, ready to pin the beam to it — and he may be 30 floors above the street. The work is simple to understand, but that doesn't make it easy. It is dirty, difficult and dangerous, and it takes a very determined man to do it. There are no gray areas. The reality of the work hits a man like a baseball bat each day. He can either do it or he can't".

Connecting Crew

Bolting Crew: Once the connecting crew had connected steel beams and columns with few bolts, bolting crew comes in. Bolting crew would bolt rest of the bolts and tighten them. Since the steel is already connected, steel pieces are not moving in air. Bolting crew need to know which bolt goes where. Also there is a way of fastening them. In addition, bolting men need to carry hefty amount of bolts with them in addition to various wrenches.

Left: Steel workers bolting a beam
Right: Bucket of bolts handed down to a worker

Detailing Crew: After the bolting crew had completed bolting, detailing crew would follow up. As the name implies they would go through all the details and make sure the connection is completed as per design specifications. Any changes that the design engineer had come up with will be done by the detailing crew.

<u>Welding Crew:</u>   Some connections also need welding. Welding crew will conduct any welding required.

<u>Decking Crew:</u>   After all the connections are completed, decking crew will install the deck.

<u>Metal deck installation</u>

<u>Rigging Crew:</u>   Riggers would tie up beams and columns and signal the crane operator to take steel pieces to steel workers. Riggers should know various knots and chokers.

<u>Iron worker putting a choker to steel pieces to be lifted</u>

<u>Steel Wire Ropes:</u>   Steel wire ropes are made of strands. Strands are made of wires. There is a fiber or steel core at the center.
6 x 24 - FC means there are 6 strands. Each strand has 24 wires and FC means fiber core.

 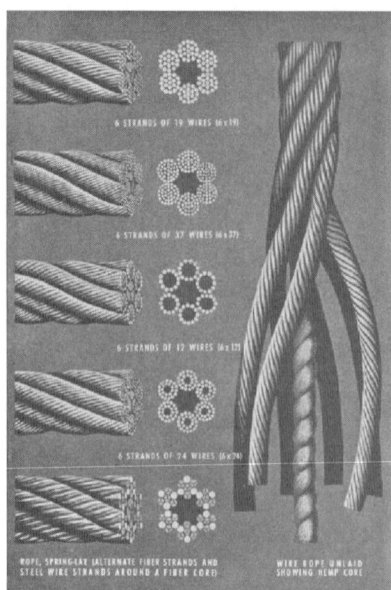

Left: Wire rope
Right: Different combinations of strands, wires and cores

See my "**Construction Module Practice problem Book**" and "**Three Sample Exams for the Civil PE Exam**" for more problems and solutions for steel construction and rigging.

D.0 Construction Equipment

Cranes:

D.1   Mobile Cranes:

Most common type of crane is a one, which is attached to a caterpillar type wheels.

These cranes can move to the location, rotate the arm and can lift objects. Height that can be lifted is limited to the height of the boom. Modern high-rise buildings could have 20 or more stories and in such situations, these cranes may not be suitable.

Things to consider during operation of cranes are:

Make sure that the weight is within the manufacturer's specified range of the crane. Never try to lift more than what is specified by the manufacturer of the crane.

Check all the cables and brake mechanisms prior to lifting.

If the crane is placed on unstable ground, it would sink. Make sure that the crane is placed on stable ground.

Make sure the object being lifted is not bolted, lagged or clamped to the floor or to other surface.

Make sure that the object is properly balanced.

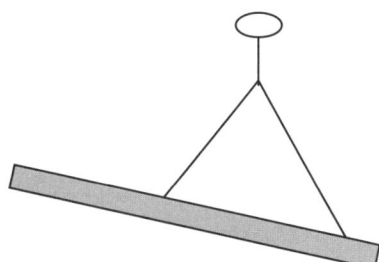

The object is not properly balanced

6)   Remove loose pieces from the load before lifting.

7)   Long loads such as beams tend to swing during lifting. Long loads can be controlled during lifting by attaching ropes to one or both ends of the load. Workers on the ground can work these ropes to help control load swinging.

8)   Workers should never ride on the load.

9)   Other workers should stand clear of the load.
10)   If the load is lifted over traffic, special permission should be obtained.
11)   Observe the chains and chain links for damages, nicks, bends or elongation prior to lifting.
12)   Never leave the load suspending for a long period of time.

Lattice Boom Cranes:
Lattice boom cranes have got that name due to the lattice structure. Below figure shows a crawler type lattice boom crane.

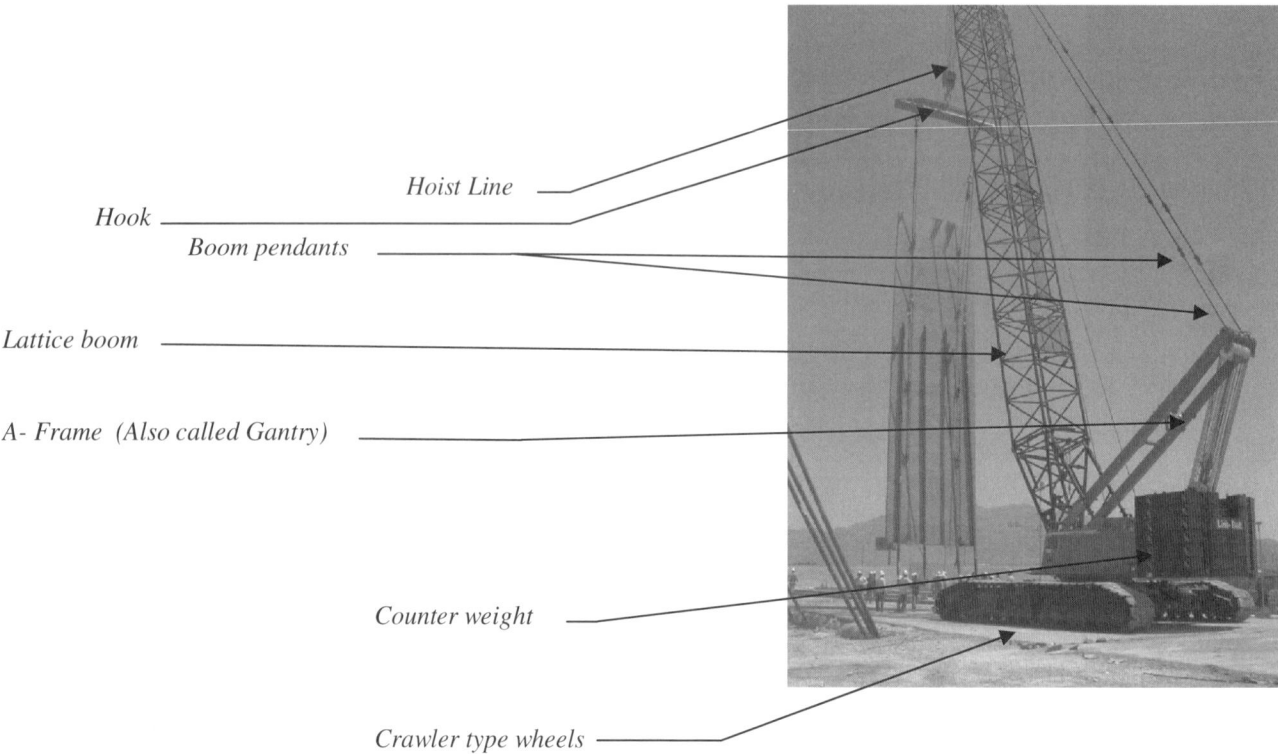

Hoist Line

Hook

Boom pendants

Lattice boom

A- Frame (Also called Gantry)

Counter weight

Crawler type wheels

The load is attached to a hook. The load is lifted using the hoist line. Two cables that are attached to the lattice boom are known as pendants. Counter weight is used to balance the load so that the crane would not tip over. The frame supporting the cables (pendants) is known as A-frame. Heavy lattice boom cranes are typically on crawler type wheels. These wheels are more stable than tires.

Lattice Boom Crane with a Luffing Jib:

Luffing jib

Lattice Boom

Luffing jib is a smaller lattice boom attached to extend the vertical and horizontal reach of the crane. Below figure shows a wheel mounted lattice boom crane.

Wheel mounted lattice boom crane

Some important parts of cranes:

Sheaves or pulleys:

Outriggers (Outriggers are used to improve the stability of cranes)

Boom Angle Detector:

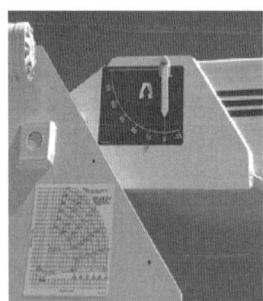

Boom angle detector

It is important to know the angle of the boom. The operator of the crane needs to closely monitor the boom angle.

Telescopic Cranes: Instead of a lattice boom, telescopic cranes have a boom similar to a telescope.

Telescopic Boom Crane

D.2   Tower Cranes:

Tower cranes are widely used for high-rise buildings since other cranes may not be able to lift to high elevations.

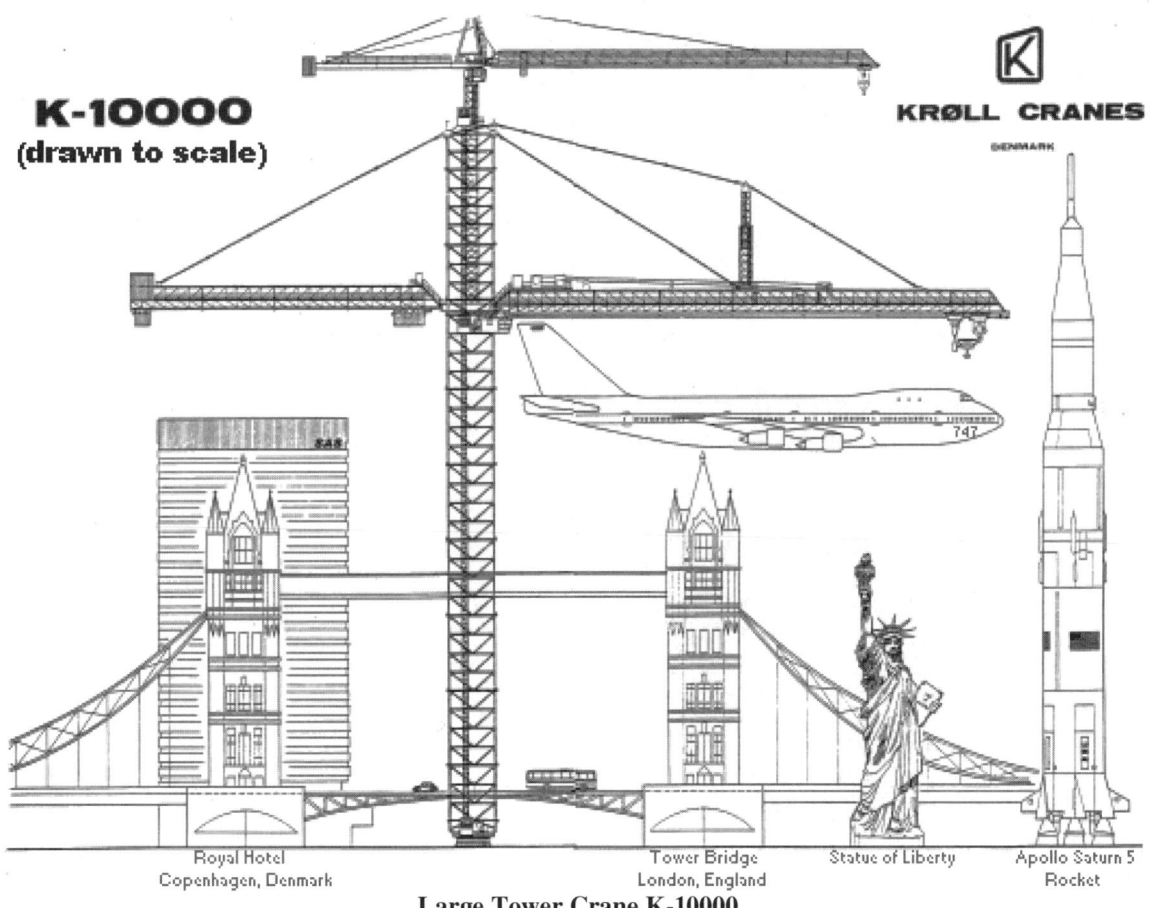

Large Tower Crane K-10000

Tower cranes cannot be moved. But thanks to long rotating arm, it can move loads effectively.

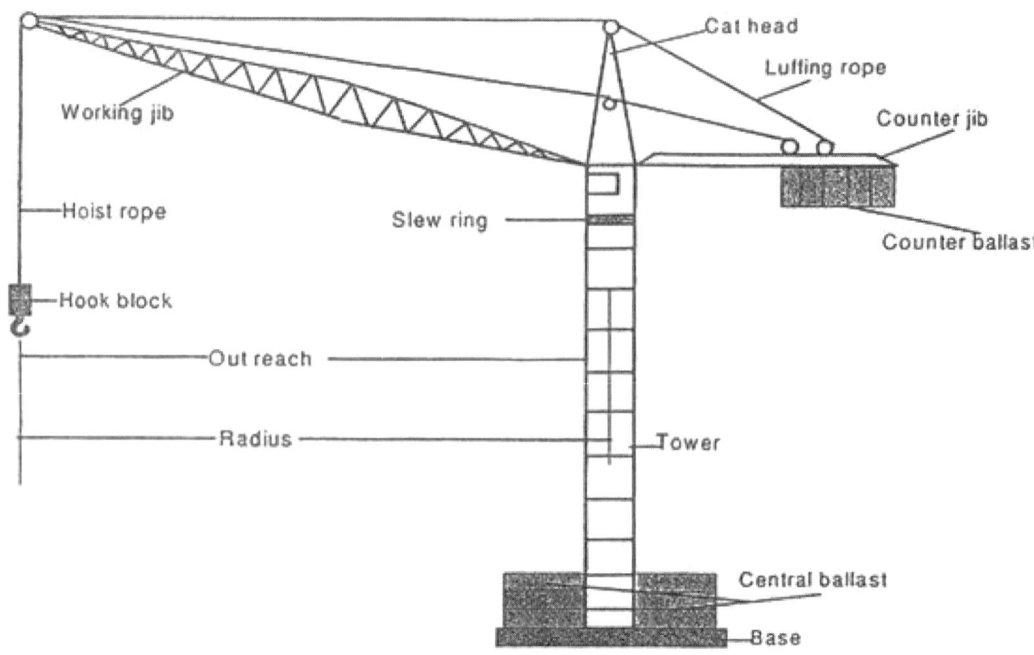

Different Parts of a Tower Crane

Gantry Cranes:　　　Gantry cranes are placed on trolleys so that they can move. They are not suitable for high-rise buildings.

Gantry Crane

D.3　Crane Selection, Erection and Stability:
Many factors have to be considered during selection of cranes to a particular construction site. Weight of typical loads, height needs to be lifted, stability of ground, cost implications, nearby traffic, safety of workers are some of the factors that need to be considered during the selection process of cranes. Tower cranes have become the most widely used crane type for high-rise buildings. Caterpillar cranes may be suitable for many construction projects as long as the height is not an issue. Gantry cranes are suitable for short buildings and warehouses.

The parts of cranes such as chains, chain links, hooks, moving parts constantly need to be inspected by qualified professionals. Crane failures can cause lives of workers and construction work to be delayed.

Practice Problem: Find the tension in two slings.

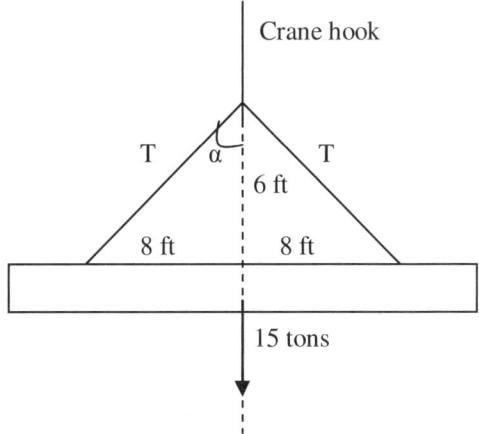

Solution:

From symmetry one can deduce that the tension in two slings to be equal.

From trigonometry

Tan α = 8/6 = 1.333

$\alpha = 53^0$.

Balance forces:

2 x T. Cos α = 15

T = 15/(2 x Cos α) = 15/(2 x 0.6) = 12.5 tons

Mobile Crane Stability: Mobile cranes have counter weights to balance the weights that need to be lifted and the weight of the boom.

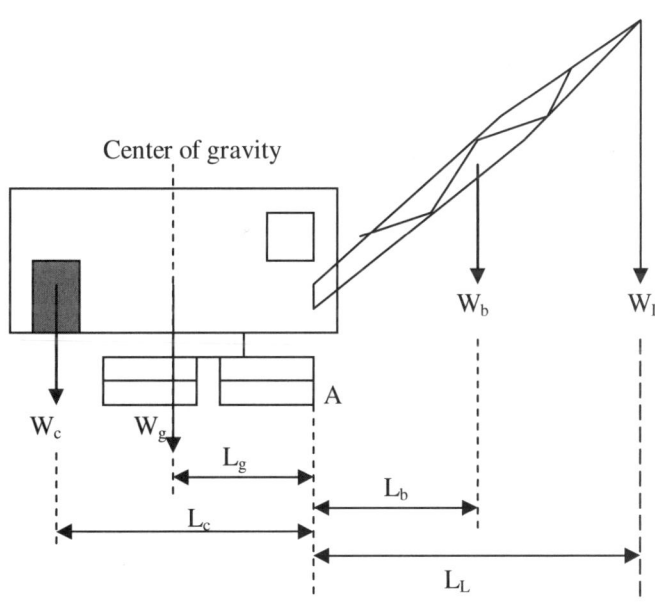

The crane will topple from the crawler track at point A.

W_L = Weight of the load; W_b = Weight of the boom; W_c = Weight of the counter weight

W_g = Weight of the crane body

Toppling moment = W_L x L_L + W_b x L_b

Resisting moment = W_c x L_c + W_g x L_g

Factor of safety against toppling = Resisting moment/Toppling moment

Practice Problem: A crane body weighs 20 tons and the boom weighs 2 tons. The crane is rated to lift a maximum load of 2 tons. Distances are as shown in the figure. Find the weight of the counter weight to have a factor of safety of 2.5.

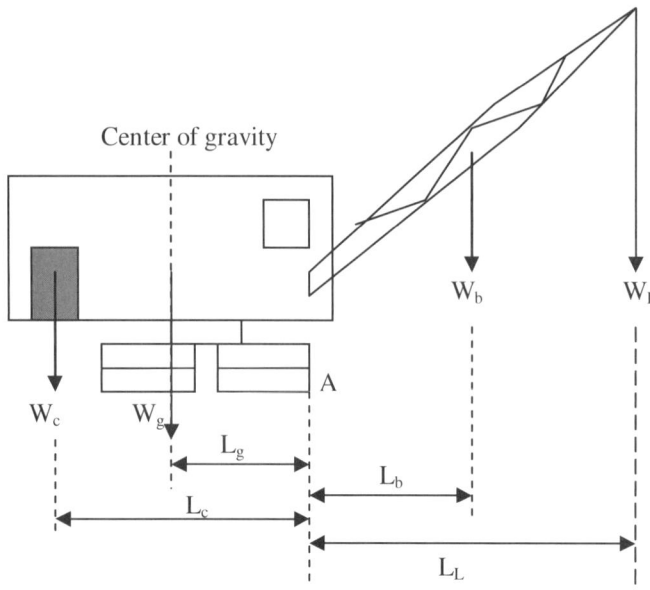

W_L = 2 tons; W_b = 2 tons W_c = Weight of the counter weight W_g = 20 tons

L_L = 20 ft L_b = 10 ft L_c = 10 ft L_g = 6 ft

Toppling moment = $W_L \times L_L + W_b \times L_b$ = 2 x 20 + 2 x 10 = 60 ton. ft

Resisting moment = $W_c \times L_c + W_g \times L_g$ = W_c x 10 + 20 x 6 = 10 W_c + 120

Factor of safety against toppling = 2.5 = Resisting moment/Toppling moment

2.5 = (10 W_c + 120)/60

150 = 10 W_c + 120

W_c = 3 tons

Practice Problem: 30 ft x 4 ft beam is shown. There are two openings in the beam with diameters 1 ft and 1.5 ft. One side of the wire rope is 25 ft. Find the length of the wire rope (y) required to properly balance the beam horizontally.

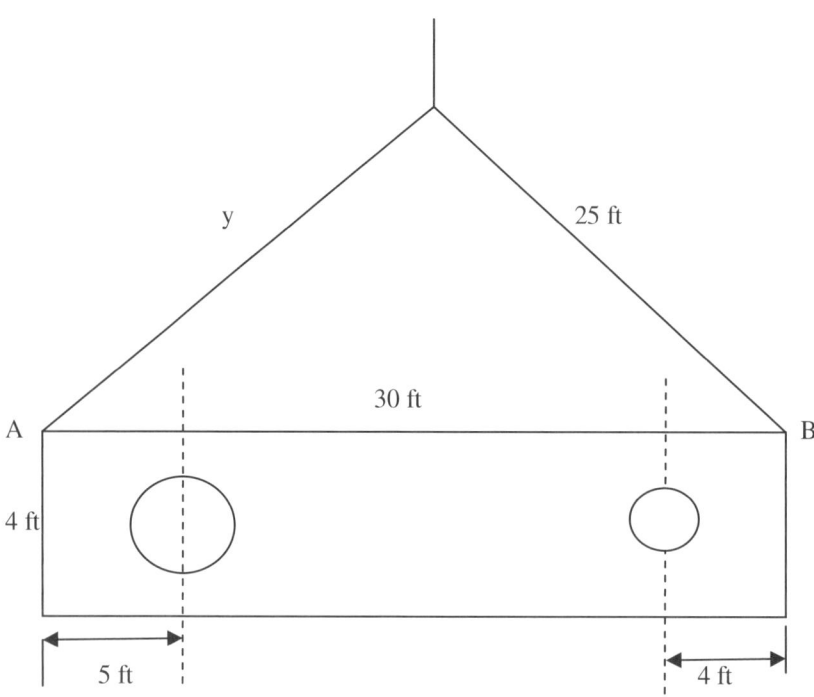

Solution:

To properly balance the beam, the vertical string should go thru the center of gravity of the beam.

STEP 1: Find the center of gravity (C.G) of the beam

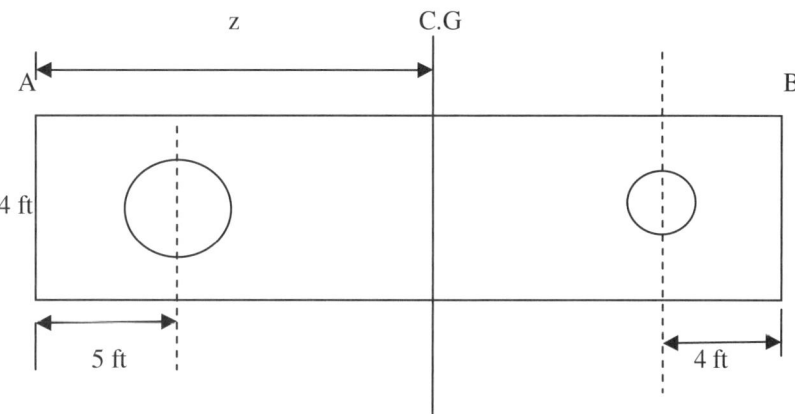

Equation for finding center of gravity;
Assume center of gravity of the beam with holes lies "z" distance from point A;
Total area x distance to center of gravity = Individual areas x distances to center of gravity of that area
Total area of the beam = (30 x 4) - Area of openings
Area of opening 1(1.5 diameter hole) = 1.767 sq. ft
Area of opening 2(1.0 diameter hole) = 0.785 sq. ft
Total area of openings = 2.553
Total area of the beam (minus openings) = $(30 \times 4) - \pi \times (1.5)^2/4 - \pi \times (1.0)^2/4 = 117.45$

$117.45 \cdot z = (30 \times 4) \times 15 - 1.767 \times 5 - 0.785 \times 26$

Area of original beam without openings = 120 sq. ft and its center of gravity is 15 ft away from point A.
Openings reduce the area. Hence, they need to be reduced from the original beam. First opening is 5 ft away from point A.
Second opening is 26 ft away from point A.
$z = 15.077$ ft

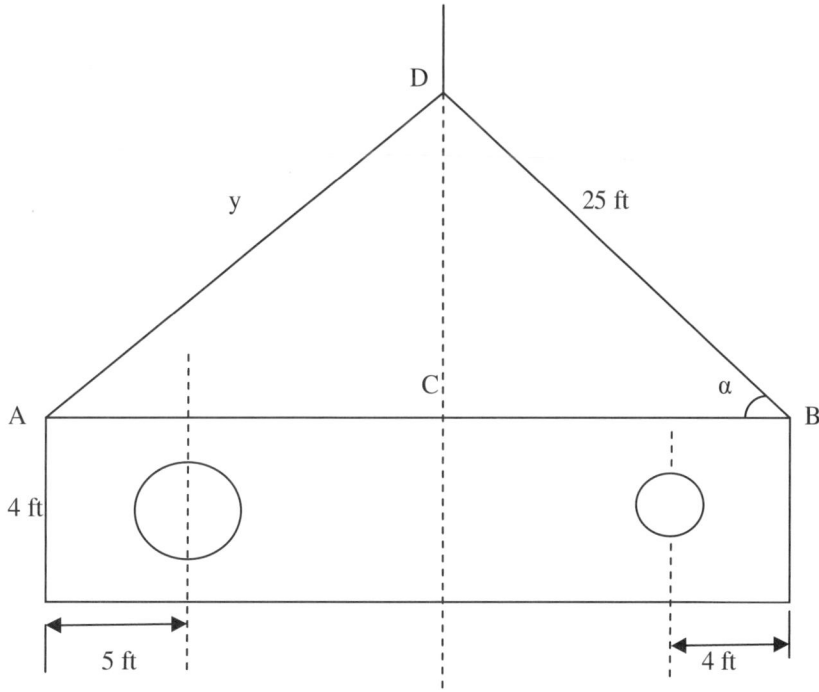

AC = 15.077
BC = 30 - 15.077 = 14.923
Assume angle DBC to be α.
BC/DB = Cos α = 14.923/25 = 0.59693
Hence α = 53.349^0.

DB. Sin α = DC
25 x Sin α = DC
Hence DC = 20.0573 ft

AD can be found using Pythagoras theorem.
$AD^2 = AC^2 + DC^2$
$AD^2 = 15.077^2 + 20.0573^2$
AD = y = 25.092 ft

D.4   Dozers:

Cutting of soil is most exclusively done using dozers. Dozers are exclusively used to cut soil. They also can transport soil for shorter distances by pushing the soil with the blade. When the distance of soil that needs to be moved exceeds 100 yards or so dozers become extremely inefficient in moving soil. For longer distances, scrapers can be used.

Dozer

D.5   Scrapers:

Unlike dozers, scrapers have an underbelly that can store soil. Scraper scrapes soil and stores inside the underbelly. Then it can transport soil to the final location, dump it, and level it.

Underbelly to store soil

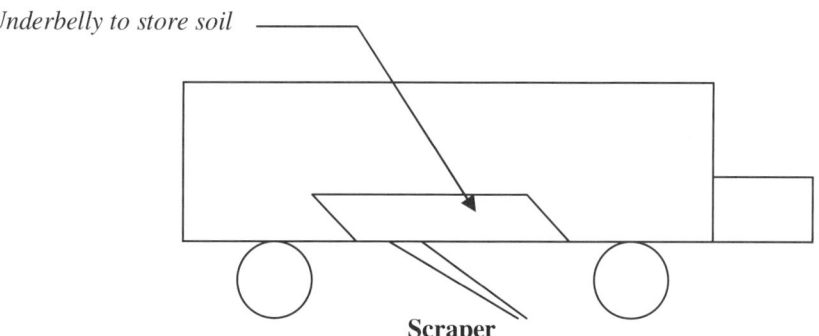

Scraper

There are different types of scrapers.

- <u>Elevating Scrapers</u>:   These scrapers can elevate the under belly after scraping the soil.
- <u>Towed Scrapers</u>:   This type of scrapers are been towed and the soil is moved up to the belly while in the move.

Elevating Scrapers

Dozer pushing a scraper (Dozer at left)

Scraper been pushed by a dozer

Above figure shows a scraper been pushed by a dozer. When the soil is hard, dozers are used to push the scrapers so that more soil can be scooped up quickly. If the scraper to work alone, it will take more time to scoop the soil. Using a dozer to push the scraper would accelerate the project. In addition, one should remember that dozer rental cost would add to the cost.

Bunch of scrapers can be towed by a dozer as shown (known as pull type scrapers)

T

D.6   Loaders:

Loaders have a bucket in front that can be used to load soil into trucks. The bucket can also be used for grading of soil.

Loaders are either wheel mounted or crawler mounted. Loaders dig out material, transport and dump to a truck. They are also capable of minor grading activities.

Loader capacity is measured using the size of the bucket. Size of the bucket can range from ¼ CY to 20 CY. Average loader would have a bucket capacity of 8 CY.

<u>Factor of Safety against Tipping</u>:   The tipping of the loader can happen due to heavy bucket loads. Typically, loaders are provided with a factor of safety of 2.5 to 3.5 against tipping when the bucket is loaded with material with density 3,000 lbs per cubic yard. (lbs/CY).

Loading a truck

Practice Problem: Heaped capacity of a bucket of a loader is 8 CY. The manufacturer claims a factor of safety of 3.0 against tipping when loaded with material of density 3,000 lbs/CY. What is the weight of the loader? Assume that moment arms are at equal distance from the tipping point.

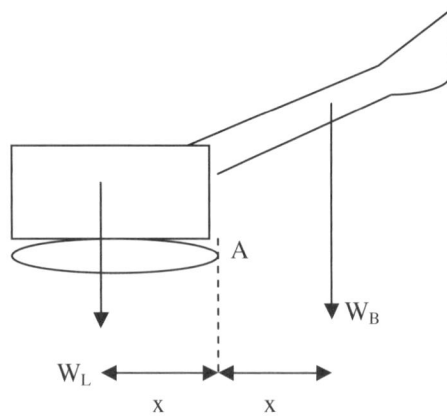

W_L is the weight of the loader and W_B is the weight of the bucket, arm and weight of soil.

Solution: Weight of the material in the bucket = 8 x 3,000 lbs = 24,000 lbs
                         Weight of the loader = 3.0 x 24,000 = 72,000 lbs

Practice Problem: A loader is loaded with 3,000 lbs/CY material. The capacity of the bucket is 6 CY. Loader has a safety factor of 3.5 against tipping. When the loader is fully loaded, its maximum speed is 15 mph. what is the horsepower of the loader?

Solution:

Weight of the bucket material when fully loaded = 6 x 3,000 = 18,000 lbs
Weight of the loader = 18,000 x 3.5 = 63,000 lbs
Total weight = 63,000 + 18,000 = 81,000 lbs

Speed = 15 mph = 22 ft/sec

Horsepower = weight x speed/550 = 81,000 x 22/550 = 3,240 HP

Bucket Fill Factor of Loaders: Some soil can be scooped by the bucket easily. Soils such as moist loam, has a bucket fill factor of 1.0 to 1.2. On the other hand, cemented material has a fill factor of 0.85.

Loader Cycle Time: Loader cycle time is the time taken for the loader to scoop up soil, transport it to the truck, dump and come back.

Breakdown of the Loader Cycle Time:

- Loading the bucket
- Spot the truck (In some cases loader may have to wait for the truck to arrive. This is due to poor planning)
- Transport the load to the truck
- Dump the load to the truck
- Return

Loading the bucket depends on type of material to be loaded. Hard soils may take more time to scoop than loose soils.
Spotting the Truck: Time required to spot the truck is dependent on the work location. In a large site, with many trucks doing many operations, it would take more time to spot the correct truck that is allocated for this operation. In a small operation, it would be easy to spot the truck sine there would be only one truck for the operation.

Transport the load to the truck depends on work conditions and distance to the truck. In a small area, that maneuvering is difficult, this time would be longer. Dumping the load is pretty much standard for a given loader and a truck combination. Return time after dumping also depends on terrain, distance and space available for loader movement.

Practice Problem: Following time, intervals have been computed for a loader operation.
Loading the bucket = 0.1 min,
Spot and transport to the truck = 0.15 min
Dump the load and return = 0.2 min
The loader has a bucket of 6 CY and bucket fill factor for the soil is 0.9.
Operator works 50 minutes per hour and 8 hours per day.
How many days would be needed to remove 20,000 CY of material?

Solution:
Total time required for one cycle = 0.1 + 0.15 + 0.2 = 0.45 min
Number of cycles per hour = 50/0.45 = 111.1
(Note that operator is only working 50 minutes per hour)

Number of CY soil removed in a cycle = 6 x bucket fill factor = 5.4 CY
Number of CY soil removed in a hour = 5.4 x 111.1 CY = 599.9 CY
Number of CY soil removed in a day = 599.9 x 8 CY = 4,799.2 CY
Number of days required to remove 20,000 CY of soil = 20,000/4,799.2 = 4.17 days

D.7   Excavators: Excavators are also known as backhoes. Excavators could be wheel type or crawler type. Normally small scale backhoes are wheel mounted while large backhoes are crawler mounted. When the weight of the bucket is large, arm length is made shorter. On the other hand, some backhoes have longer arms and small size buckets.

Heap Volume and Struck Volume: Backhoe bucket has two volumes. Heap volume and struck volume.

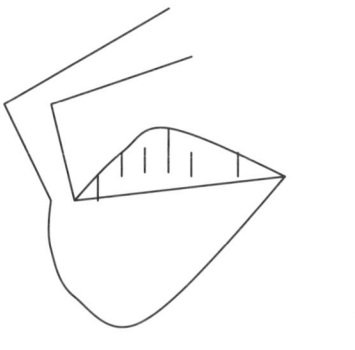   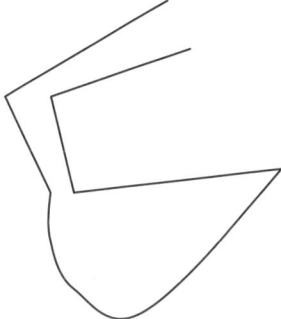

Heap volume   Struck volume

Soil Type: Hard cemented soil is difficult to excavate compared to loose sand or loam. Hence, soil type plays a major role in determining the efficiency of a backhoe operation. Bucket efficiency is high when the operator can obtain a full bucket in one scoop. It is possible to obtain a full bucket in one scoop for soils such as loam and loose sand. This is not possible for stiff clay and weathered rock.

Excavator

Soil Type	Bucket Fill Factor %
Loose sand	100
Medium dense sand	90
Dense sand	80
Soft clay	95
Medium stiff clay	90
Stiff clay	80
Clayey Gravel (stiff)	85
Shale and other rocks (weathered)	75
Shale and other rocks (medium hard)	50

Table A   Bucket Fill Factor vs. Soil Type

Efficiency of Backhoes: Backhoes have an optimum depth of excavation. Backhoe works at its highest efficiency at this depth. When the depth is too shallow, the efficiency goes down. Similarly, when the depth is too deep, efficiency decreases. Optimum depth of excavation of a given backhoe depends upon its arm lengths and bucket sizes. Backhoe manufacturers will provide optimum depth of the backhoe.

Angle of Operation: Backhoe bucket goes down into the excavation and digs soil. Then it would lift up and rotate to dump the soil. Angle that needs to be rotated to dump the soil to a truck is known as angle of operation.

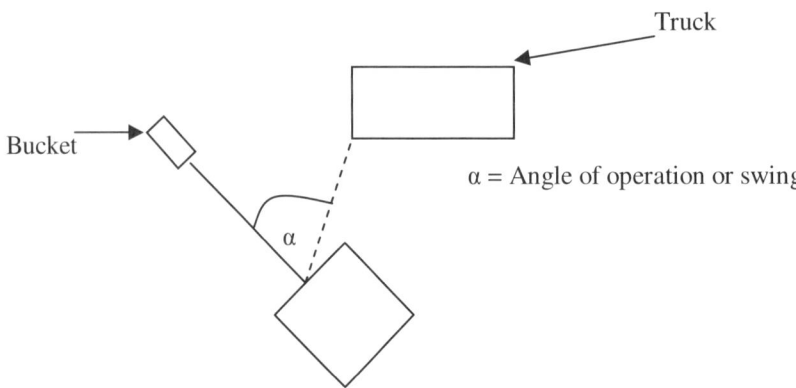

α = Angle of operation or swing

When the angle of operation is low, faster operation can be expected. When the angle of operation is high, excavation work slows down. Hence, it is important to make sure that truck to be placed so that the angle of operation is low. In some situations, it may not be possible to maintain a low angle of operation. There could be existing structures, trees or any other obstruction so that trucks have to be parked far away from the backhoe. Angle of operation is also known as angle of swing.

Angle of Operation and Depth of Operation: Following table gives the productivity factor for various depths of operation and various angles of swing. Productivity factor is also known as A:D factor.

Optimum Depth Ratio (D/D_o)	Angle of Swing (A) degrees					
	45	60	75	90	120	150
0.40	0.93	0.89	0.85	0.80	0.72	0.59
0.60	1.1	1.03	0.96	0.91	0.81	0.66
0.80	1.22	1.12	1.04	0.98	0.86	0.69
1.00	1.26	1.16	1.07	1.00	0.88	0.71
1.20	1.2	1.11	1.03	0.97	0.86	0.70
1.40	1.12	1.04	0.97	0.91	0.81	0.66
1.60	1.03	0.96	0.90	0.85	0.75	0.62

Table B: Productivity Factor (P) or A:D Factor

Source: Power crane and shovel association.

How to use the above table?   Let's assume a certain excavator has an 8 ft optimum depth of operation where it has the highest efficiency. Let's say it is excavating at a depth of 9.6 ft.

Optimum depth (D_o) = 8 ft
Depth of operation = 9.6 ft
$D/D_o = 9.6/8 = 1.2 = 120\%$

If you travel along row of 120% you would see productivity factor decreasing when the angle of operation increases. If possible, best productivity can be obtained when the angle of operation is closer to 45 degrees.

On the other hand, let's assume that this backhoe is operating at an angle of 75 degrees. If you come down along the 75^0 column line you would see productivity increasing until $D/D_o = 1.00$. Then the productivity starts to drop. Productivity is highest at optimum depth. When the operating depth is shallow, productivity decreases. Similarly, when the operating depth is more than the optimum depth, productivity decreases.

Look at $D/D_o = 1.00$ and angle of swing is 90 degrees. You would see productivity factor to be 1.00. This is the base. Productivity factor goes above 1.00 when the angle of swing is reduced.

Computation of Excavator Production:

Excavator production is given by the following equation;

$$q = \frac{3600 \, B \times E \times P}{C}$$

q = Volume of soil excavated and dumped in a truck by the excavator, (CY/hr)
B = Bucket struck capacity (CY)
E = Bucket efficiency factor from table A
P = Productivity factor from table B
C = Cycle time for 90 degree angle and optimum depth

Practice Problem: An excavator with a bucket that has a struck capacity of 1.2 cu. yds and an optimum depth of 8 ft was used to dig a pit that is 10 ft deep. The angle of operation is found to be 120 degrees. The soil is medium stiff clay. Manufacturer of the excavator lists cycle time for 90^0 angle and optimum depth to be 18 seconds. Find the productivity of the excavator in cu. yds per hr.

Solution:

$$q = \frac{3600 \, B \times E \times P}{C}$$

q = Volume of soil excavated and dumped in a truck by the excavator, (cu yds per hr)
B = Bucket struck capacity (cu. yds) = 1.2 cu. yds
E = Bucket efficiency factor from table A
E = 0.9 for medium stiff clay.

P = Productivity factor from table B

$D/D_o = 10/8 = 1.25$
Angle of operation = 120

$D/D_o = 1.2$ and angle of operation 120, gives a P value of 0.86.
Using interpolation P is found to be 0.85.

C = Cycle time for 90 degree angle and optimum depth = 18 seconds (Usually provided by the manufacturer).
If cycle time is not provided by the manufacturer, this value can be ascertained in the field by practice. Have an operator work at optimum depth with an angle of operation of 90 degrees and evaluate the cycle time.

$$q = \frac{3600 \text{ B x E x P}}{C} = \frac{3600 \times 1.2 \times 0.9 \times 0.85}{18} = 180 \text{ cu. yds/hr}$$

D.8   Draglines:

Dragline is a combination of a crane, bucket and two cables.

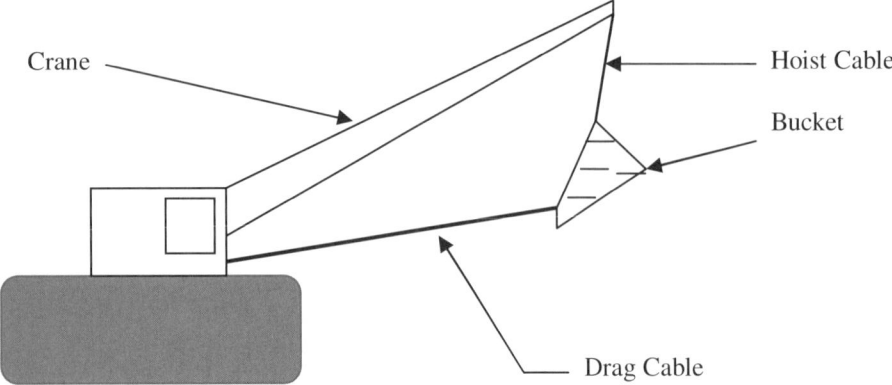

When the upper cable (hoist cable) is tightened, bucket moves up and to the right. When the lower cable (drag cable) is tightened, the bucket moves down and towards the crane. This way, the operator can manipulate the bucket to excavate and move soil.

Dragline is shown in the picture. Dragline has a much longer reach than an excavator does.

Draglines are used for dredging

Two large dragline buckets are shown above. Note the size of the cables.

Scrapers become too inefficient and expensive when soil has to be transported much longer distances. In such situations, trucks are used.

Backhoes and Trucks: Dozers would cut soil and make a small mound. Then backhoe would load the trucks. Trucks would take the soil to necessary location and dump there. Bunch of dozers at the destination would level and grade the soil.

D.9   Graders: Grading is a very important activity in any construction site. Graders are specialized equipment built for grading. Graders are equipped with a blade that is used for the grading purpose. Blade of a grader is designed to minor cutting and grading. First dozers should do the main cutting and rough grading. Graders cannot do the work of dozers since graders are not capable of cutting deep into the soil.

Grader

Grader Cycle: Graders would move forward with the blade. Then it would come back. Assume that the forward pass distance is d_f and return distance is d_r. In many cases $d_f = d_r$.

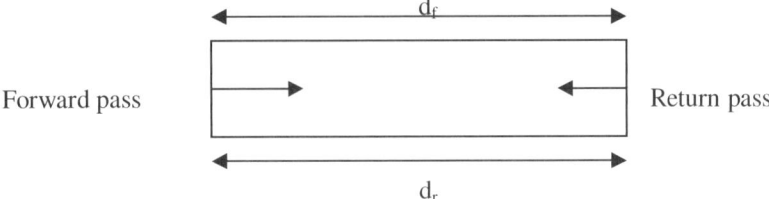

For most cases $d_f = d_r$

Time to go forward = $T_f = d_f/v_f$

d_f = Forward pass distance ; v_f = Velocity of the grader

Time to return = $T_r = d_r/v_r$

d_r = Return distance v_r = Return velocity of the grader   (probably in reverse gear)

Cycle Time = $T_c = T_f + T_r$ = Time to go forward and return

$T_c = T_f + T_r = d_f/v_f + d_r/v_r$

If the grader has a width of W ft, a grader can grade (W x d_f) sq. ft in going forward and it can grade (W x d_r) sq. ft during return.
Normally more than one pass may be necessary to grade a given area.
In many cases $d_f = d_r = d$ Then the above equation for cycle time can be simplified.
$T_c = T_f + T_r = d/v_f + d/v_r = d \left(1/v_f + 1/v_r\right)$

If we assume an average velocity (d_a) for the grader for forward movement and return movement, then this equation can be further simplified.

$$T_c = 2\ d/v_a$$

If each location has to be passed N times, then time to grade a distance of "d" = T_g

$$T_g = 2\ N\ d/v_a$$

Note that N passes are needed to grade one point. Each pass consists of one forward pass and one return pass. Sometimes efficiency term E is introduced to account for operator efficiency, other construction traffic, grading in slopes, movement by surveyors, masons and various other construction workers and dust control activities. Remember that no construction operation is done in complete isolation. Always other issues would delay a given operation. These other issues are dependent upon the specific site. To account for site-specific factors, efficiency term is introduced.

$$T_g = 2\ N\ d/(Ev_a) \qquad\qquad E = Efficiency$$

Practice Problems: 100 x 3,000 ft Area need to be graded. It has been noted that grader has to pass each location 2 passes. Each pass containing one forward pass and one backward pass. Grader has a width of 10 ft and has an average velocity (both forward and reverse) of 5 mph. The operator is new and do not have much experience in grading. Dust control activities and surveying work in the vicinity expect to delay the grading operation. Due to these reasons, efficiency of the grading operation was found to be 0.85. Operator works 50 minutes per hour. Find how many hours are required to grade the area.

Solution:

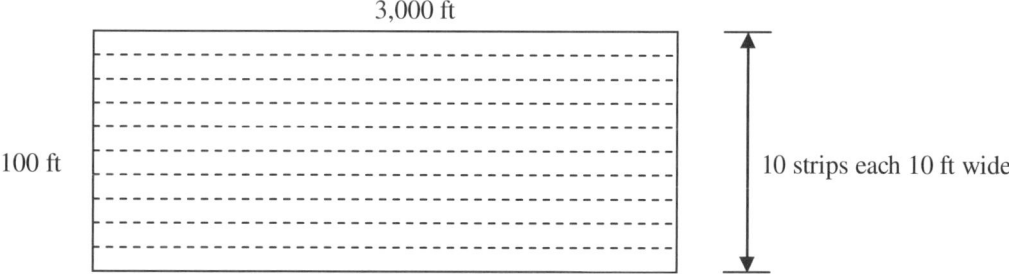

Grader is moving along the length. Grader width is 10 ft. There are 10 strips.
Average velocity of the grader = 5 mph = 7.33 ft/sec
Time for one pass (One forward pass and reverse to the initial position) = T_c = 6000 ft/7.33 = 818.5 sec
Number of passes needed for one strip = 2
Time to complete one strip with 100% efficiency = 2 x 818.5 seconds = 1637 seconds
Due to other activities, grading operation can be delayed. Hence, introduce the efficiency factor of 0.85.
Time to complete one strip with 85% efficiency = 1637/0.85 = 1926 seconds = 32.1 minutes
Time to complete 10 strips = 32.1 x 10 = 321 minutes
Operator works only 50 min per hour.
Number of hours required to complete the project = 321/50 = 6.42 hours

D.10 Compaction Equipment:
Compaction of fill material is required to make sure that no settlement will follow after construction. Typically, compaction is done 95% of modified proctor value. Modified proctor is a compaction test done in a laboratory. Typically, it is required to achieve at least 95% of that value. Compaction equipment has to be selected as per soil conditions.
- Sand and gravels - Static rollers, Vibratory rollers
- Clay soils – Sheep foot rollers (vibratory)
- Trenches – small size rollers, vibratory plates or jumping jacks

Static rollers could be steel drums or pneumatic tires. They could be made to vibrate increasing its compaction effort.

Productivity of Rollers: Heavy rollers will achieve the required compaction faster than a smaller roller. At the same time, smaller vibratory type roller can be more effective than a larger static roller. Suitable equipment need to be selected for the soil type that needs to be compacted.

Assume thickness "B" soil layer is compacted with a roller that has a width of "W" ft. Assume that each location needs to be rolled "N" times. The speed of the roller is "S".

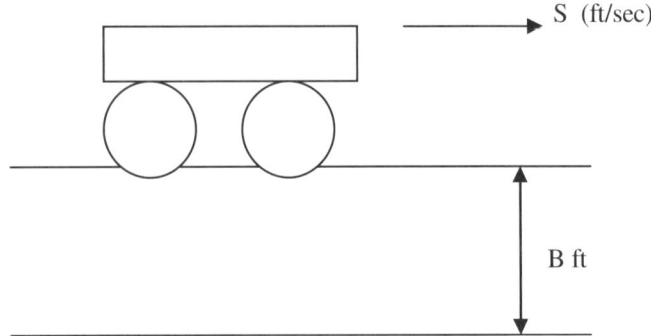

Width of the roller = W ft,   N = Number of passes required to compact one location
S = Speed (ft/sec)

Area of compaction sq. ft per second in one pass = (W x S)/N   Sq. ft/sec

"N' passes are required to compact one location. After N passes area (W x S) will be compacted. Only portion of area (W x S) will be compacted in one pass.

Assume 4 passes are required to compact one location. One pass will compact only 1/4th of the total compaction.

In other words, compaction of area (W x S) in one pass = (W x S)/4   Sq. ft/sec

Volume of compaction (cu ft per second) = (W x S x B)/N cu. ft/sec
Volume of compaction (cu ft per hour) = 3,600 x (W x S x B)/(N) cu. ft/hr
Volume of compaction (cu yards per hour) = 3,600 x (W x S x B)/(N x 27) CY/hr

---

Volume of compaction (cu yards per hour) = 3,600 x (W x S x B)/(N x 27) CY/hr

W (ft),   S (ft/sec)   B (ft)   N = Number of passes

Practice Problem: Soccer field (300 ft x 150 ft) has to be compacted with 18 inch lifts. Each lift has to be rolled three times to achieve the necessary compaction with a 10 ton static roller with a width of 6 ft. The speed of the roller is 5 mph. How many hours are required to compact one lift?

Solution:
Volume of compaction (cu yards per hour) = 3,600 x (W x S x B)/(N x 27) CY/hr

W in ft,   S in ft/sec and B in ft.

W = 6 ft   S = 7.33 ft/sec   B = 1.5 ft
Volume of compaction (cu yards per hour) = 3,600 x (6 x 7.33 x 1.5)/(3 x 27) CY/hr = 2932 CY/hr

Total cubic yards per lift = (300 x 150 x 1.5)/27 = 2500 CY
Hours required to compact 2,500 CY = 2,500/2932 = 0.85 hours

Jumping Jacks and Vibratory Plates: Jumping jacks have a plate that moves up and down. In the case of vibratory plates, as the name indicates compaction is done by a vibrating plate.

D.11 Machine Power:

Machine power is measured by horsepower and Watts (SI). When early engines were manufactured, it was important to compare the power of the engines with horses. It was known at that time, average horse could pull 550 lbs at a rate of 1 ft/sec. If a certain machine can pull or move a vehicle that would create a frictional force of 550 lbs at a rate of 1 ft/sec then we can say that particular machine has a horsepower of 1.0.

Average horse can pull 550 lbs at a rate of 1 ft/sec. (1 HP)

Note that pull force is not equal to the weight. Pull force of a vehicle is equal to the frictional resistance of wheels. This is also known as rolling resistance.

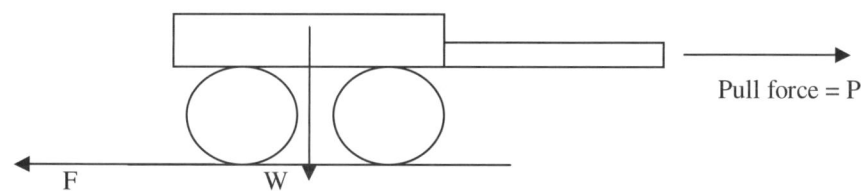

F = Friction or Rolling resistance   *W = Weight*   *P (Pull Force) =F.*
When P = 550 and speed = 1 ft/sec, the power of the engine is 1 horsepower (HP).
1 HP = 550 lb. ft/sec

Practice Problem: Steam engine can move a train that weighs 25 tons at a speed of 30 mph. The friction coefficient between rail and wheels is 0.13. Find the horsepower of the engine.

Solution: Pull force = Friction

Friction = 0.13 x 25 tons = 0.13 x 25 x 2000 = 6,500 lbs
Speed = 30 mph = 44 ft/sec
Work done per second = 6500 x 44 = 286,000 lbs. ft/sec
Work done per second in HP = 286,000/550 = 520 HP

Power in a Machine: Engines generate power. The power of the engine is then transferred to a flywheel. Energy loss occurs during this process. Power is then transferred to a gear mechanism and then to the axle.

Engine Power and Flywheel Power: Engine horsepower is much larger than the flywheel horsepower. Hence, it is important to know the flywheel HP of an engine rather than the engine HP.

Rim pull: Rim pull is the pull needed to overcome friction. Typically at lower gears of a vehicle (gears 1 and 2), the very high rim pulls can be generated. However, at low gears, one has to maintain a lower speed. At high gears of a vehicle, high speeds can be achieved but rim pull will be less.

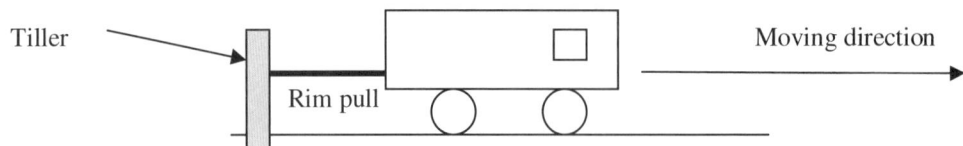

Practice Problem: A tractor needs to pull a tiller. The horsepower of the tractor is 70 HP. The tiller exerts a pull of 2,000 lbs. What is the maximum speed that the tractor can travel?

Solution:

70 HP = 70 x 550 lbs. ft/sec = 38,500 lbs. ft/sec.

Horsepower = Work done per second = Force x speed = 2,000 x speed

      70 HP = 38,500 = 2,000 x speed
      Maximum speed = 38,500/2,000 = 19.25 ft/sec.

Drawbar Pull: Drawbar pull is same as the rim pull except that this term is used for vehicles that do not have a rim but a crawler type tracks. It does not make a difference whether it is pull or push.

Crawler type tracks

Practice Problem: Dozer needs to cut through hard soil. The force exerted on the soil is computed to be 900 lbs. The dozer has to move at a speed of 10 mph to maintain the schedule. The contractor is planning to use a 30 HP dozer. Can this machine do the work required?

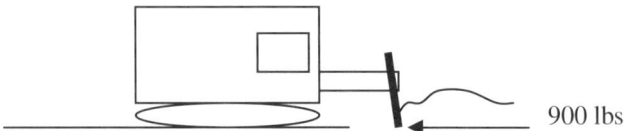

Solution:
10 mph = 14.67 ft/sec
Power needed = 900 x 14.67 lbs. ft/sec = 13,200 lbs. ft/sec = 24 HP
The machine is capable of performing the task as specified.

Rolling Resistance: There is a resistance to rolling of wheels. Rolling resistance depends on air pressure in tires, wear and tear of tires and road roughness.

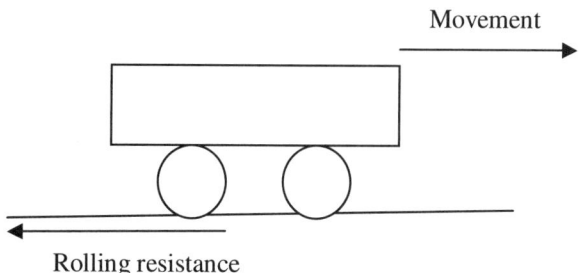

Rolling resistance typically given in lbs/ton.

Practice Problem: Rolling resistance of a truck is given to be 30 lbs/ton. What is the rolling resistance of a truck that weighs 12 tons?

Solution: Rolling resistance of the truck = 12 x 30 lbs = 360 lbs

D.12 Grade:

Grade of a road effect the work done by machines.

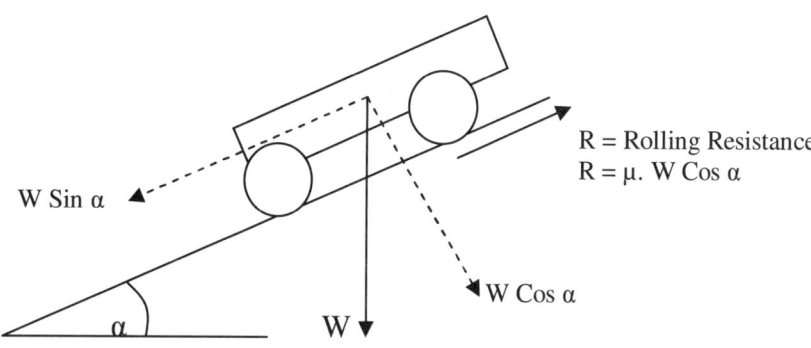

Component of weight W acts along the slope. (W Sin α)
Second component acts perpendicular to the slope (W Cos α)
Rolling resistance = μ. W Cos α   (μ = Rolling resistance coefficient)
For slope angles less than 10^0, Sin α is approximated with Tan α
tan α = V/H or the grade.

Practice Problem: A 5 ton loaded truck is moving uphill. The grade is 3.5%. What is the rim pull of the truck?
Solution: Force that needs to overcome is W sin α. For small angles Sin α is approximated to tan α.

Hence W Sin α = W Tan α
Tan α = Grade = 0.035
Rim Pull = W x 0.035 = (5 x 2000) x 0.035 lbs = 350 lbs

Traction: A truck may have super power engine but it may not be able to pull or haul anything if the road is slippery. Usable force of a truck, dozer, scraper or any other construction machine depends on the coefficient of traction.

```
Usable Force = Coefficient of Traction x Weight on Driving Wheels
```

If the truck tries to pull or haul any load greater than usable force, slippage of wheels would occur. High coefficient of traction would allow a truck to haul large loads. A truck can haul larger loads in a gravel road than in a smooth concrete road.

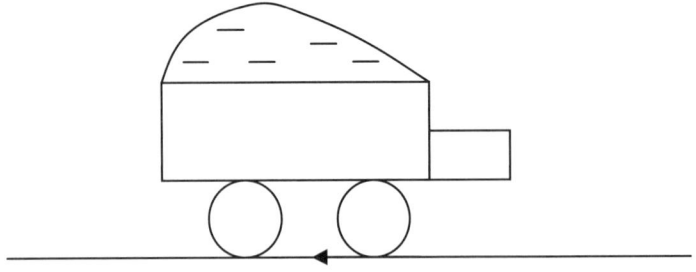

Traction at driving wheels

Practice Problem: Find the usable force of a truck if the fully loaded truck is 15,000 lbs and 55% of the weight is transferred to driving wheels. The coefficient of traction between wheels and road is 0.65. Find the usable force.

Solution: Weight transferred to driving wheels = 15,000 x 0.55 lbs = 8250 lbs

Usable Force = Coefficient of Traction x Weight on Driving Wheels
Usable Force = 0.65 x 8250 = 5362 lbs

Rim Pull and Usable Force: In some situations, maximum rim pull may not be usable due to slippage.
Practice Problem: An empty truck weighs 10,000 lbs. Rim pull of the truck is 9,000 lbs. 62% of the weight is transferred to driving wheels. The coefficient of traction between wheels and road is 0.65. What is the maximum volume of soil measured in CY, that can be hauled with the truck when using the maximum rim pull. (1 CY of soil weighs 3,000 lbs).

Solution:
Assume y lbs of soil are loaded.
Total Weight = y + 10,000
Weight on driving wheels = 0.62 x (y + 10,000)

      Usable Force = Coefficient of Traction x Weight on Driving Wheels
      Usable Force = 0.65 x 0.62 x (y + 10,000)
      At maximum rim pull,

      9,000 = 0.65 x 0.62 x (y + 10,000)
      y = 12,332 lbs
      y = 12,332/3,000 = 4.11 CY

Rim Pull or Drawbar Pull Vs Speed:

Horsepower of a vehicle depends on its engine power. Engine has a maximum capacity. When the vehicle is moving fast, its rim pull would be less. When the machine is moving at a lower speed, it has a higher rim pull capacity and could haul heavier loads.

Rim Pull or Drawbar Pull (lbs)

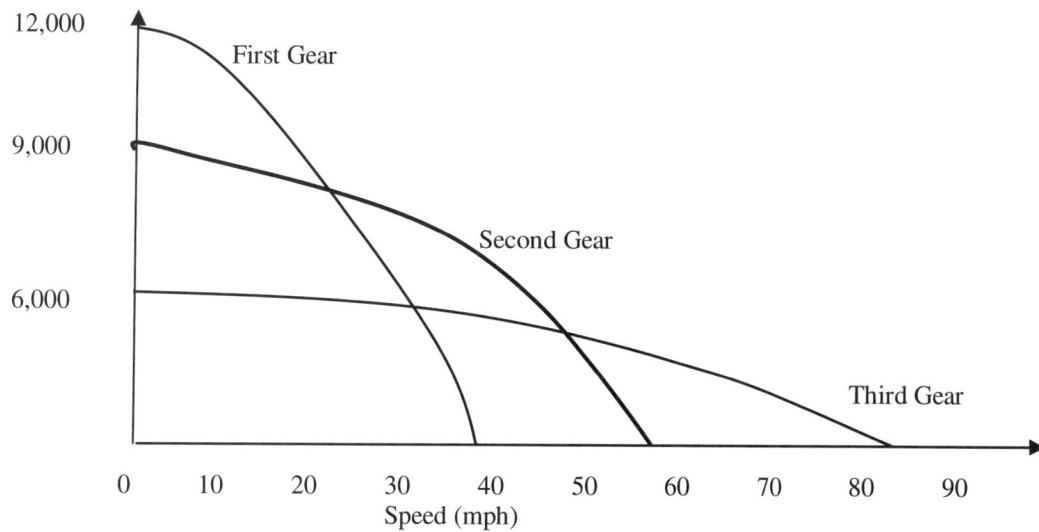

At first gear, rim pull can be as high as 12,000 lbs. The maximum speed that can be attained in first gear is 40 mph. If the gear is shifted to the second gear, higher speed can be achieved but the maximum rim pull or drawbar pull is 9000 lbs.

Practice Problem: A dozer has to cut soil and the push force is estimated to be 7,000 lbs. The contractor wants the machine to operate at 10 mph. What gear the operator should use? (Use the graph above).

Solution: At 10 mph, maximum drawbar pull for second gear is 8500 lbs approximately. Hence, it can spare 7,000 lbs at second gear. At 10 mph, maximum drawbar gear is 11,000 lbs at first gear.
Operator can use either the first gear or the second gear. On the other hand, at third gear with a speed of 10 mph, maximum drawbar pull is only 6,000 lbs. The dozer may not be able to exert 7,000 lbs drawbar pull at third gear.

Equipment Fuel Cost: Fuel consumption of a machine depends on horsepower of the machine and type of work it does. Excavator would burn more fuel when digging in hard soil than in soft soil. Dozer would burn more fuel when grading uphill. Older machines use more fuel than new machines.

Practice Problem: 350 HP dozer consumes fuel at a maximum rate (0.02 gal/HP per hr) when grading 4% grade uphill. Dozer uses 50% of the maximum rate when grading downhill. Dozer uses 30% of the maximum rate when moving from one location to another location. It has been noted that 40% of the time dozer is grading uphill, 35% of the time grading downhill and 25% of the time moving from location to location. What is the fuel consumption per hour if the operator works only 50 min per hour?

Solution:
Maximum fuel consumption = 0.02 x 350 = 7 gal/hr = 0.117 gal/min

Operator works only 50 min/hour.

Number of minutes grading uphill = 0.4 x 50 min = 20 min
Fuel consumption grading uphill = 20 x 0.117 = 2.34 gal
Number of minutes grading downhill = 0.35 x 50 min = 17.5 min
Fuel consumption grading uphill = 17.5 x (0.117 x 0.5) = 1.02 gal
Note that dozer uses only 50% of the maximum rate when grading downhill.
Number of minutes moving from one location to another = 0.25 x 50 min = 12.5 min
Fuel consumption during moving = 12.5 x (0.117 x 0.3) = 0.44 gal

Total fuel consumption per hour = 2.34 + 1.02 + 0.44 = 3.8 gal/hr

1.0 Earthwork Construction and Layout

1.1   Excavation and Embankment (Cut and Fill):

Roads are constructed over uneven ground. During construction of a road, some locations required to be cut and other locations have to be filled. Consider the terrain shown below. Point A to B has to be **cut** and point B to C has to be **filled**.

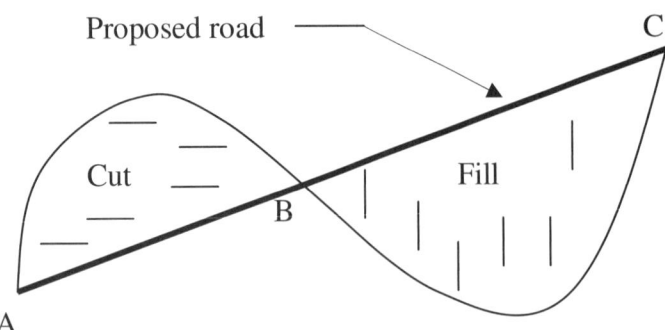

Cut and Fill: In some situations, the soil removed due to cut can be used for fill. If the soil removed is not suitable, then suitable soil has to be imported to the site for fill purposes.

1.2   Borrow Pit Volume Problems: To solve borrow pit problems, the student needs a good knowledge of phase relationships in soil.

1.3   Soil Phase Relationships: Soil consists of solids, air and water. Solids are soil particles. Soil matrix can be schematically represented as shown below.

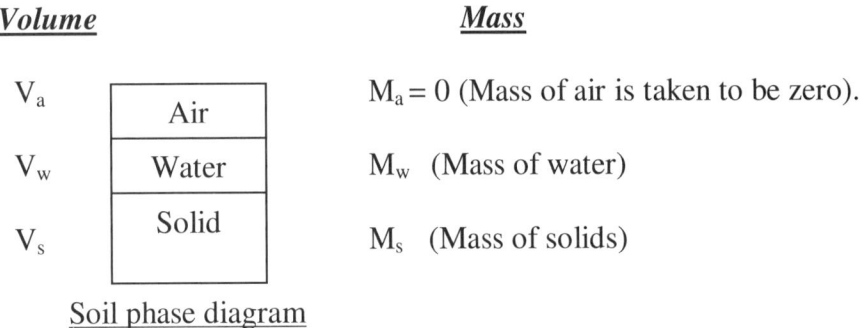

Volume   *Mass*

V_a — Air — $M_a = 0$ (Mass of air is taken to be zero).

V_w — Water — M_w (Mass of water)

V_s — Solid — M_s (Mass of solids)

Soil phase diagram

M_a = Mass of air = 0 (Usually taken to be zero)
V_a = Volume of air (Volume of air is **not** zero)

M_w = Mass of water
V_w = Volume of water

M_s = Mass of solids
V_s = Volume of solids

M = Total mass of soil $= M_s + M_w$ (mass of air ignored).
V = Total volume of soil $= V_s + V_w + V_a$
V_v = Volume of voids $= V_a + V_w$

Density of Water (γ_w) = Density of water can be expressed in many units.

$\gamma_w = M_w/V_w$
SI Units: $\gamma_w = 1 \text{ g/cm}^3 = 1{,}000$ g per liter $= 1{,}000 \text{ kg/m}^3 = 9.81 \text{ kN/m}^3$.
fps Units: $\gamma_w = 62.42$ pounds per cu. feet (pcf)

Total Density of Soil γ_t, γ_{wet} or γ: Some books use γ_{wet} and some other books uses γ_t or simply γ to denote total density of soil. Total density (also known as wet density) is simply mass of soil (including water) divided by the volume of soil.

$\gamma_{wet} = M/V$
$M = M_w + M_s$ and $V = V_w + V_a + V_s$
{M = Total mass of soil including water. Mass of air ignored}
{V = Total volume of soil including soil, water and air. Volume of air is **not** ignored.}

Dry Density of Soil (γ_d): $\gamma_d = M_s/V$
M_s = Mass of solid only.
V = Total volume of soil including soil, water and air
$V = V_w + V_a + V_s$

Density of Solids = M_s/V_s

Specific Gravity (G_s):   Specific gravity is defined as density of solids divided by the density of water. Density of solids represented by G_s or by simply G.
Specific Gravity (G_s) = $M_s/(V_s. \gamma_w)$

Void Ratio (e):   Void ratio (e) is defined as the ratio of volume of voids to volume of solids.
                    $e = V_v/V_s$
V_v = Volume of voids (Volume of water + Volume of air) = $V_a + V_w$
V_s = Volume of solids

Moisture Content (w):   Moisture content (w) = M_w/M_s
M_w = Mass of water; M_s = Mass of solids

Porosity (n):
                    $n = V_v/V$
V_v = Volume of voids   V = Total volume = $V_s + V_w + V_a$

What does porosity means? If you look at the top term V_v, basically tells us how much voids are there in the soil. The ratio between voids and total volume is given by porosity. In other words, porosity gives us an indication of pores in a soil. Soil with high porosity would have more pores than soil with low porosity. It is reasonable to assume that soils with high porosity would have a higher permeability.

Degree of saturation (S): $S = V_w/V_v$

                    V_w = Volume of water
                    V_v = Total of volume of voids

When total volume of voids is filled with water S = 100%.
Degree of saturation tells us how much water is in the voids.

Some Relationships to Remember:

Relationship 1:

$$\gamma_d = \gamma_{wet}/(1 + w)$$

This relationship appears in soil compaction section as well.
It can be proven as follows.

$\gamma_{wet} = M/V$, hence $V = M/\gamma_{wet}$

$\gamma_d = M_s/V;$
Replace V with M/γ_{wet}

$\gamma_d = M_s/(M/\gamma_{wet}) = M_s \times \gamma_{wet}/M$
$M = M_s + M_w$ (mass of air is ignored)
$\gamma_d = M_s \times \gamma_{wet}/(M_s + M_w)$

Divide both top and bottom by M_s.
$$\gamma_d = \gamma_{wet}/(1 + w)$$

Relationship 2:

$$S.e = G_s.w$$

This relationship can be shown to be true as below.
$S = V_w/V_v \qquad ; \qquad e = V_v/V_s$

$S.e = V_w/V_s$ -- (1)
$G_s = M_s/(V_s . \gamma_w); \qquad\qquad \gamma_w = M_w/V_w; \qquad$ Replace γ_w in the equation.
$G_s = M_s/(V_s) \times (V_w/M_w)$

Hence $G_s = (M_s \times V_w)/(V_s . M_w);$
$w = M_w/M_s$

$G_s.w = [(M_s \times V_w)/(V_s . M_w)] \times (M_w/M_s)$
By simplification;
$G_s.w = V_w/V_s$ ---------------------------------- (2)
Equations (1) and (2) are equal. Hence $S.e = G_s.w$.

Relationship 3:

$$n = e/(1 + e)$$

Proof:
     Replace "e" with V_v/V_s in the above equation.
     $n = e/(1 + e) = (V_v/V_s)/[1 + V_v/V_s]$

Multiply top and bottom by V_s.
     $e/(1 + e) = (V_v)/[V_s + V_v]$
     $V_s + V_v = V$
     $e/(1 + e) = V_v/V = n \qquad$ (V_v/V is porosity)

Relationship 4:

$$e = n/(1 - n)$$

Proof: From relationship 3;
     $n = e/(1 + e)$
     $n + ne = e$
     $n = e - ne$
     $n = e (1 - n)$
     $e = n/(1 - n)$

Relationship 5:

$$\gamma_d = \gamma_w . G_s/[1 + (w/S)G_s]$$

Proof:

$$\gamma_d = \frac{\gamma_w \cdot G_s}{[1 + (w/S)G_s]}$$

$$\gamma_d = \frac{\gamma_w \cdot M_s/(V_s \cdot \gamma_w)}{[1 + (M_w/M_s/(V_w/V_v) \times M_s/(V_s \cdot \gamma_w)]}$$

$$\gamma_d = \frac{\cancel{\gamma_w} \cdot M_s/(V_s \cdot \cancel{\gamma_w})}{[1 + (M_w/\cancel{M_s}/(V_w/V_v) \times \cancel{M_s}/(V_s \cdot \gamma_w)]}$$

$$\gamma_d = \frac{M_s/V_s}{[1 + (M_w/(V_w/V_v) \times 1/(V_s \cdot \gamma_w)]}$$

$$\gamma_d = \frac{M_s/V_s}{[1 + (\cancel{\gamma_w} \cdot V_v) \times 1/(V_s \cdot \cancel{\gamma_w})]}$$

$$\gamma_d = \frac{M_s/V_s}{[1 + (V_v) \times 1/(V_s)]}$$

Multiply top and bottom by V_s

$$\gamma_d = \frac{M_s}{[V_s + V_v]}$$

$$V_s + V_v = V$$

$$\gamma_d = \frac{M_s}{V}$$

Relationship 6:

$$\gamma_{wet} = \frac{\gamma_w \cdot G_s \times (1 + w)}{[1 + e]}$$

Proof:

Write down relationship 5.

$$\gamma_d = \frac{\gamma_w \cdot G_s}{[1 + (w/S)G_s]}$$

Substitute for γ_d and S.
$\gamma_d = \gamma_{wet}/(1 + w)$ and $S.e = G_s.w$
Hence $S = G_s.w/e$

$$\gamma_{wet}/(1 + w) = \frac{\gamma_w \cdot G_s}{[1 + (w.e/G_s.w)G_s]}$$

$$\gamma_{wet} = \frac{\gamma_w \cdot G_s \times (1 + w)}{[1 + e]}$$

Relationship 7:

$$\gamma_d = \frac{\gamma_w \cdot G_s}{[1 + e]}$$

Proof:

$$\gamma_d = M_s/V; \qquad G_s = M_s/V_s / \gamma_w \qquad e = V_v/V_s$$

Apply the values in the equation;

$$M_s/V = \gamma_w. (M_s/V_s / \gamma_w)/(1 + V_v/V_s)$$

γ_w cancels out.

$$M_s/V = (M_s/V_s)/(1 + V_v/V_s)$$

M_s cancels out.

$$1/V = (1/V_s)/(1 + V_v/V_s)$$

$$V_s/V = 1/(1 + V_v/V_s)$$
$$= 1/[(V_s + V_v)/V_s] = V_s/[(V_s + V_v)] = V_s/V$$

Left hand side and right hand side are equal.

Practice Problem 1.1:   Specific gravity of a soil sample is given to be 2.65. Moisture content and degree of saturation are 0.6 and 0.7 respectively. Find the void ratio.

Solution: S.e = G.w
0.7 x e = 2.65 x 0.6
e = 2.27

Practice Problem 1.2:   Total density of a soil sample was found to be 110 pcf and moisture content to be 60%. What is the dry density of the soil sample.

Solution: $\gamma_d = \gamma_{wet}/(1 + w) = 110/(1 + 0.6) = 68.75$ pcf

Practice Problem 1.3:   Soil sample obtained from the ground and measured the weight to be 1 lb and total soil volume to be 0.01 cu. ft. The soil sample is then put in the oven and dried. Dried soil sample was weighed to be 0.7 lbs. Specific gravity of the soil was known to be 2.6.
Find the following;
   a) Total density or wet density
   b) Dry density
   c) Porosity
   d) Void ratio
   e) degree of saturation

Solution:
   a) Total Density = M/V = 1/0.01 = 100 lbs/ft^3.
   b) Dry density = $\gamma_d = \gamma/(1 + w)$
Weight of dry soil (M_s) = 0.7 lbs
Weight of water in the soil sample (M_w) = 1 – 0.7 = 0.3 lbs

Water content (w) = M_w/M_s = 0.3/0.7 = 0.428
Dry density = $\gamma_d = \gamma/(1 + w) = 100/(1 + 0.428) = 69.9$ lbs/ft^3.

   c) Porosity (n) = V_v/V
V = 0.01 cu. ft. This is the total volume of the soil sample
Specific gravity (G) of the soil is given to be 2.6.

Find V_s:
          G = 2.6 = $M_s/(V_s. \gamma_w) = 0.7/(V_s \times 62.4)$
          Since $\gamma_w = 62.4$ lbs/ft^3.
          Hence $V_s = 0.0043$ ft^3.
          V = $V_v + V_s$ (Total volume = Volume of voids + Volume of solids)
          0.01 = $V_v + 0.0043$

$V_v = 0.01 - 0.0043 = 0.0057$
Porosity (n) = $V_v/V = 0.0057/0.01 = 0.57$

d) Void ratio (e) can be found using the following equation
$$e = n/(1 - n)$$
$$e = 0.57/(1 - 0.57) = 1.326$$

e) S.e = G.w
$$S = 2.6 \times 0.428/(1.326) = 0.839$$

Practice Problem 1.4:   Soil sample obtained from the ground was measured and weighed. The soil sample has a diameter of 4 in and a height 6 in. The weight of the soil sample was measured to be 4.8 lbs. The soil sample was oven dried and weighed again. Dry weight of the soil sample was found to be 3.9 lbs. Specific gravity of the soil sample is known to be 2.65.
Find the following;
   a) Total density
   b) Water content
   c) Dry density
   d) Porosity
   e) Void ratio
   f) Degree of saturation

Solution:
Total Density:
   Volume of the soil sample (V) = $\pi \times d^2/4 \times h = \pi \times (4/12)^2/4 \times (6/12) = 0.044$ cu. ft
   Wet weight of the soil sample = 4.8 lbs
   Total density (or wet density) = M/V = 4.8/0.044 = 109.1 lbs/cu. ft

Moisture Content (w) = M_w/M_s
$M_s = 3.9$ lbs; $M_w = 4.8 - 3.9$ lbs = 0.9 lbs
w = 0.9/3.9 = 0.23
$\gamma_d = \gamma/(1 + w) = 109.1/(1 + 0.23) = 88.7$ lbs/cu. ft

Find V_s:
G = 2.65 = $M_s/(V_s \cdot \gamma_w) = 3.9/(V_s \times 62.4)$,   Since $\gamma_w = 62.4$ lbs/ft^3.
Hence $V_s = 0.024$ ft^3.
$V = V_v + V_s$ (Total volume = Volume of voids + Volume of solids)
$0.044 = V_v + 0.024$

$V_v = 0.02$

Porosity (n) = $V_v/V = 0.02/0.044 = 0.45$
Void Ratio (e) = n/(1 - n) = 0.45/(1 - 0.45) = 0.82

Degree of saturation (S): S.e = G.w
                 S = 2.65 × 0.23/0.82 = 0.74

Practice Problem 1.5:   Degree of saturation, water content and specific gravity are respectively 75%, 42% and 2.68.
Find
   1) Total density (γ_{wet}) 2) Void ratio (e)   3) Porosity (n)

Solution:
STEP 1: Use relationship 5;
$$\gamma_d = \frac{\gamma_w \cdot G_s}{[1 + (w/S)G_s]}$$

$$\gamma_d = \frac{62.4 \times 2.68}{[1 + (0.42/0.75) \times 2.68]} = 66.9 \text{ pcf}$$

From relationship 1, $\gamma_d = \gamma_t/(1 + w)$

                          $\gamma_{wet} = \gamma_d \times (1 + w) = 66.9 \times (1 + 0.42) = 95$ pcf

From relationship 2, $S.e = G.w$

                   $e = 2.68 \times 0.42/0.75 = 1.5$

From relationship 3, $n = e/(1 + e) = 1.5/(1.5 + 1) = 0.6$

1.3.1 Borrow Pit Problems

Note: The student should master the previous chapter on soil relationships thoroughly in order to understand borrow pit problem.

Fill material for civil engineering work is obtained from borrow pits. The question is how much soil should be removed from the borrow pit for a given project?

Usually, final product is the controlled fill or the compacted soil. Total density, optimum moisture content and dry density of the compacted soil will be available. This information can be used to obtain the mass of solids required from the borrow pit. If the soil in borrow pit is too dry, water can always be added in the site. If the water content is too high, then soil can be dried prior to use. This could take some time in the field since one has to wait for few sunny days to get rid of water.

Water can be added or removed from soil.

What cannot be changed is the mass of **solids**. Mass of solids is the link between borrow pit soil and soil that has been transported.

Procedure:

Find the mass of solids required for the compacted fill

Excavate and transport the same mass of solids from the borrow pit.

Practice Problem 1.6:   Road construction project needs compacted soil to construct a road 10 ft wide, 500 ft long. The project needs 2 ft layer of soil. Soil density after compaction was found to be 112.1 pcf at optimum moisture content at 10.5%.

500 ft

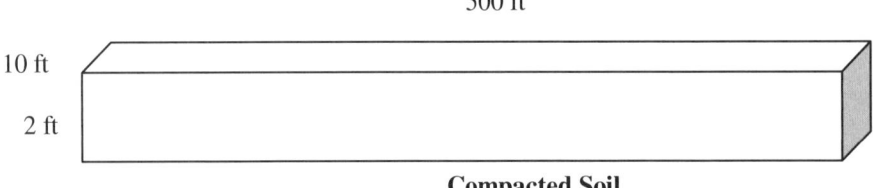

10 ft

2 ft

Compacted Soil

The soil in the borrow pit has following properties:

Total density of the borrow pit soil = 105 pcf

Moisture content of borrow pit soil = 8.5%.

Find the total volume of soil that need to be hauled from the borrow pit.

Total Density = $(M_w + M_s)/V$

Dry density = M_s/V

(See below for definitions of all terms).

Solution:

STEP 1:   Find the mass of solids (M_s) required for the controlled fill:

Volume of compacted soil required = 500 x 10 x 2 = 10,000 cu. ft

Soil density after compaction (dry density) = 112.1 pcf

Moisture content required = 10.5%

Draw the phase diagram for the controlled fill:

Volume   **Mass**

V_a

Air
Water
Solid

$M_a = 0$ (Usually mass of air is taken to be zero).

V_w M_w (Mass of water)

V_s M_s (Mass of solids)

Soil phase diagram

V = Total Volume = $V_s + V_w + V_a$
M = Total mass = $M_w + M_s$ (Note that mass of air is taken to be zero)
V_a = Volume of air (Volume of air is not zero)

M_w = Mass of water
V_w = Volume of water

M_s = Mass of solids
V_s = Volume of solids

M = Total mass of soil   = $M_s + M_w$
V = Total volume of soil   = $V_s + V_w + V_a$
Total Density = $(M_w + M_s)/V$
Dry density = M_s/V

Soil in the site after compaction has a dry density of 112.1 pcf and moisture content of 10.5%.

Dry density = M_s/V = 112.1 pcf
Note that total density is $(M_w + M_s)/V$
Moisture content = M_w/M_s = 10.5% = 0.105
The road needed 2 ft layer of soil at a width of 10 ft and length of 500 ft.
Hence the total volume of soil = 2 x 10 x 500 = 10,000 cu. ft.
V = Total volume = 10,000 cu. ft
Since M_s/V = Dry density
$M_s/10,000$ = 112.1
M_s = 1,121,000 lbs.
M_s is the mass of solids. This mass of solids should be hauled in from the borrow pit.

STEP 3:   Find the mass of water in compacted soil:
Moisture content in the compacted soil = M_w/M_s = 10.5% = 0.105
M_w = 0.105 x 1,121,000 lbs = 117,705 lbs

STEP 4:   Find the total volume of soil that needs to be hauled from the borrow pit:
The contractor needs to obtain 1,121,000 lbs of solids from the borrow pit.
Contractor can add water to the soil in the field if needed.
Mass of solids needed (M_s) = 1,121,000 lbs.
Density and moisture content of borrow pit soil is known.
Total density of borrow pit soil = M/V = 105 pcf
Moisture content of borrow pit soil = M_w/M_s = 8.5% = 0.085
Since M_s = 1,121,000 lbs,   (M_s is the mass of solids required).
M_w/M_s = 0.085
M_w = 0.085 x 1,121,000 lbs = 95,285 lbs.

Solid mass of 1,121,000 lbs of soil in the borrow pit contains 95,285 lbs of water.
Total mass of borrow pit soil = 1,121,000 + 95,285 = 1,216,285 lbs
Total density of borrow pit soil is known to be 105 pcf.
Total density of borrow pit soil = M/V = $(M_w + M_s)/V$ = 105 pcf

Insert known values for M_s and M_w.

$M/V = (M_w + M_s)/V = (95,285 + 1,121,000)/V = 105$ pcf
Hence $V = 11,583.7$ cu. ft

The contractor needs to extract 11,583.7 cu. ft of soil from the borrow pit.
The borrow pit soil comes with 95,285 lbs of water.
Compacted soil should have 117,705 lbs of water. (see above step 3).
Hence water needs to be added to the borrow pit soil
Amount of water needs to be added to the borrow pit soil =   117,705 – 95,285 = 22,420 lbs.
Weight of water is usually converted to gallons. One gallon is equal to 8.34 lbs.
Amount of water needs to be added = 2,688 gallons.

Summary:

STEP 1: Obtain all the requirements for compacted soil.
STEP 2: Find M_s or the mass of solids in the compacted soil.
         This is the mass of solids that needs to be obtained from the borrow pit.
STEP 3: Find the information about the borrow pit. Usually the moisture content in the borrow pit and total density of the borrow pit can be easily obtained.
STEP 4: The contractor needs to obtain M_s of soil from the borrow pit.
STEP 5: Find total volume of soil that needs to be removed in order to obtain M_s mass of solids.
STEP 6: Find M_w of the borrow pit. (mass of water that comes along with soil).
STEP 7: Find M_w (mass of water in compacted soil).
STEP 8: The difference in above two masses is the amount of water needs to be added.

Soil Borrow Pit

*Note: Refer to my "**practice problem book (second edition)**" and the "**Three sample Exams for the Construction Module**" for many problems and solutions.*

1.3.2   Site Layout and Control:

Surveying: Knowledge of surveying is important for construction work. Hence, you will be tested in the exam on surveying topics.

Magnetic North and Geographic North:

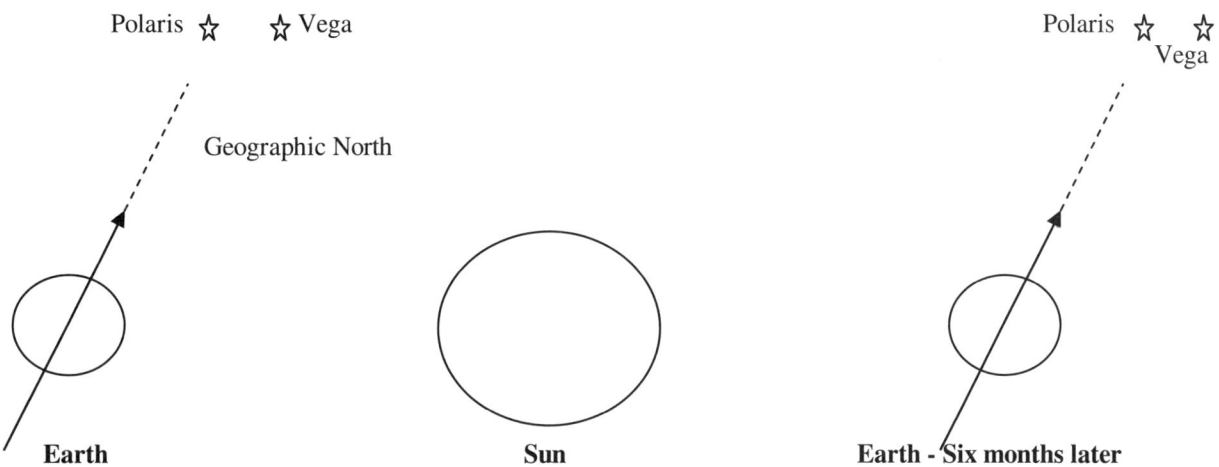

Geographic north is the direction of the axis of rotation and pointed to polar star. However, axis of rotation is not a constant. The axis of rotation of the earth is changing every year by a very small amount. It has been calculated that 25,000 years from now axis of rotation would point to a different star known as Vega.

Magnetic North: Geographic north depends on the rotation of the earth. Magnetic north depends on the magnetic field of the earth. It is a coincidence that earth's magnetic north is very close to the earth rotational axis. For an instance, the difference between Neptune's rotational axis and its magnetic north is 40^0.

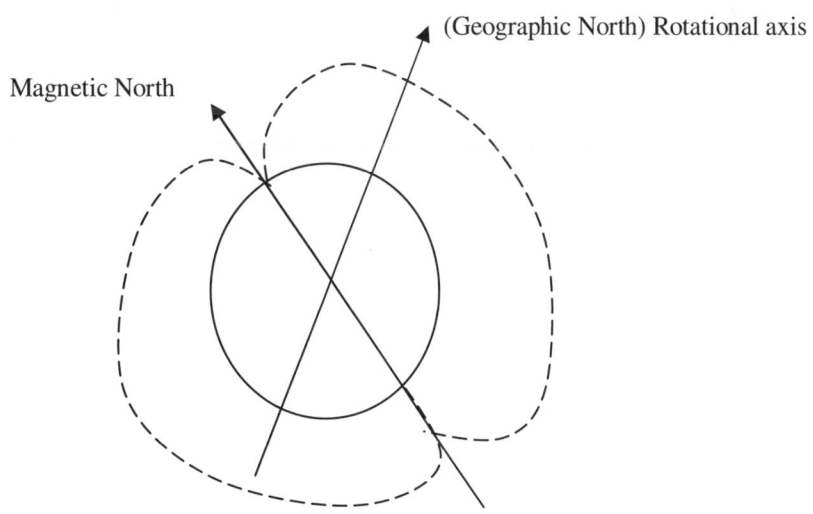

Neptune's rotational axis and magnetic north are 40^0 apart

In the case of earth, the difference between geographic north and magnetic north is very small.

Meridian: Meridian is any longitude. Meridian at a location is the longitude of that location.

Azimuth: Azimuth is the horizontal angle made with respect to the **geographic north**.

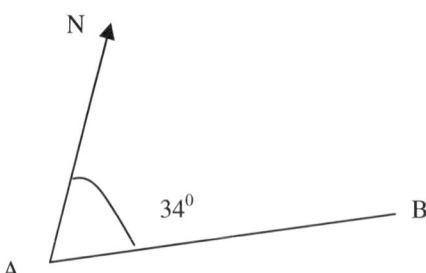

Azimuth of line AB is 34^0 in this case.

Zenith and Nadir: Line drawn vertically to the sky is known as zenith. Line drawn directly to the center of the earth is known as Nadir.

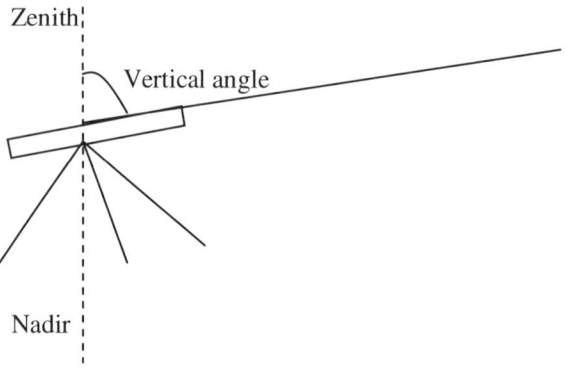

Surveying Instruments:

Level: levels are used to measure the vertical lengths. Some levels are equipped with a cross hair so that they can be used to measure horizontal distances. Cross hairs are located in such a manner, the length is computed by multiplying the distance between cross hairs by 100.

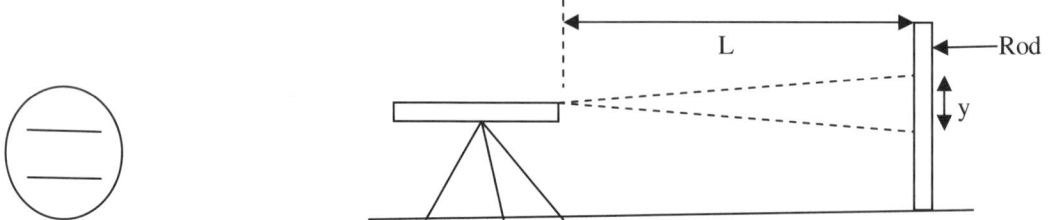

The instruments are designed in a such a manner so that L = 100 x y
If the reading y is 1.2 ft, then the distance (L) would be 120 ft.
Levels cannot be used for measurement of angles.

Theodolites: Theodolites are designed to measure horizontal and vertical angles.

EDM: Electronic distance measurement or EDM can be used to measure horizontal and vertical distances.

Total Stations: Total stations are electronic instruments equipped with computers that can be used to measure angles and distances.

Bearing: Bearing is the angle measured from North or South.

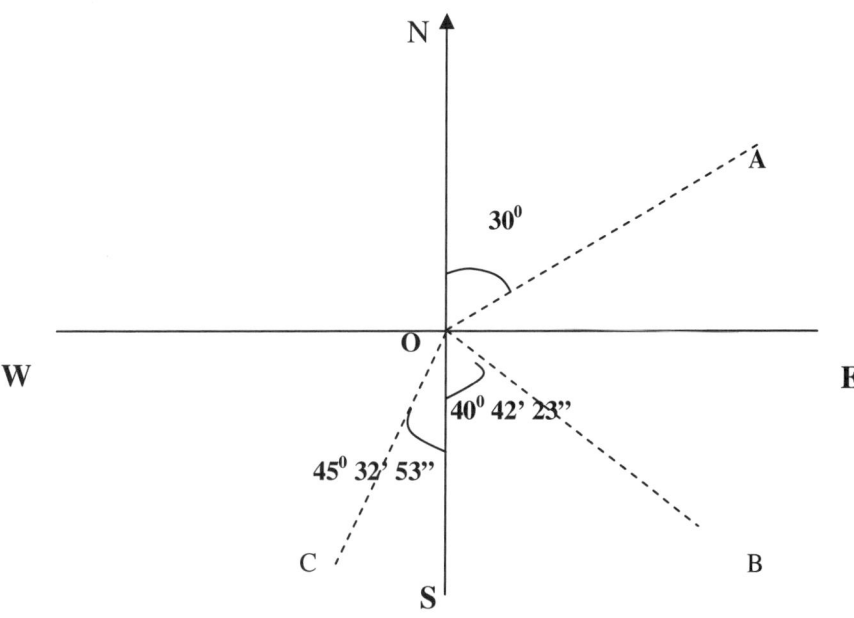

Bearing of OA = N 30^0 E
This means OA line is 30 degrees measured from N towards east.
Similarly, bearings of other lines are given below.
        OB = S 40^0 42' 23" E
        OC = S 45^0 32' 53" W

Practice Problem: Provide the bearing for above line OC from North.

Angle between OC and North is 180 + 45^0 32' 53" = 225^0 32' 53"

Traverse: Traverse is conducted by starting from a known point. Angles and distance measurements are taken to new points from the initial point.

Practice Problem: Bunch of new houses were built in a remote area. Surveyors were called upon to locate the new houses with better accuracy relative to a known benchmark in the vicinity.

Solution:

STEP 1:   Select a point B, which is closer to existing houses. Find the angle of AB relative to geographic north.

STEP 2:   Measure the distance AB. Now point B can be located in a map.

STEP 3:   Measure distance Ap.

STEP 4:   Measure pp' perpendicular to AB. Now point p' can be located in a map. If the house has to be exactly located in a map, more than one measurement is needed to its edges.

STEP 5:   Select another convenient point C, closer to houses that need to be measured. Find the interior angle ABC and the distance BC. Now point C can be established in a map.

STEP 6:   Measure Br and rr' distances.
This way all houses can be located in a map.

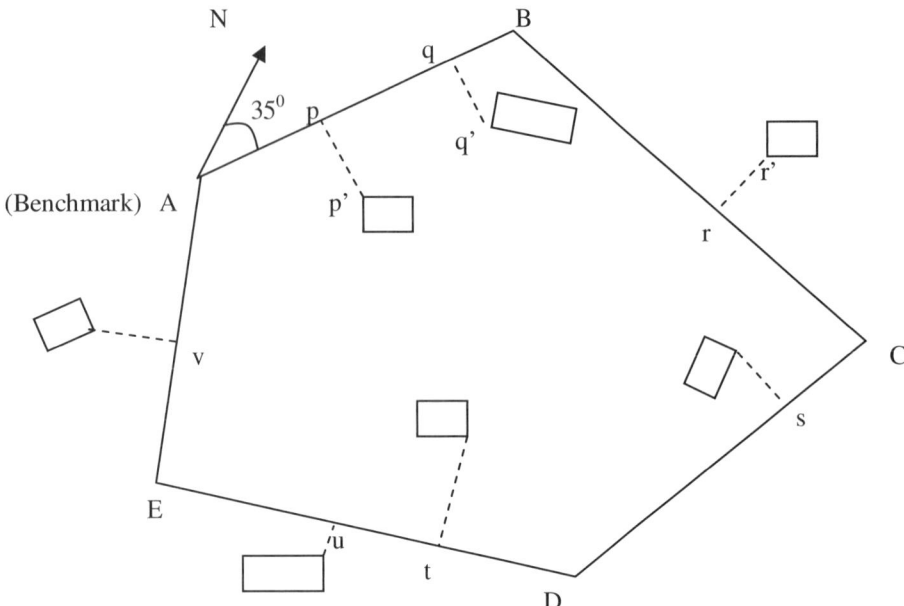

Accuracy of such a procedure heavily depends upon the interior angle measurements at points A, B, C, D and E.

Construction workers need to know the building footprint, column locations and wall lines. Locations of these structural elements are provided by surveyors. Nevertheless, construction engineers need to have a good understanding of the process.

Building Line: Surveyors usually provide a string line to indicate the building footprint. The string line may indicate the edge of the footing.

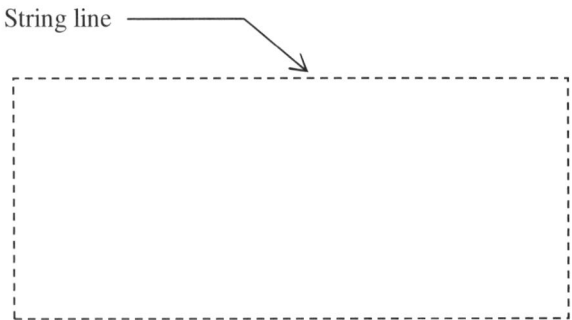

Using the string line, the contractor can excavate for footings.

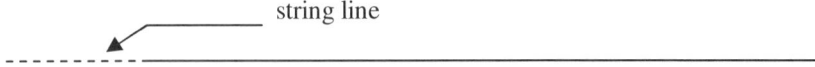

Elevations: It is important to obtain elevations for construction. Elevations are obtained with reference to a given benchmark.

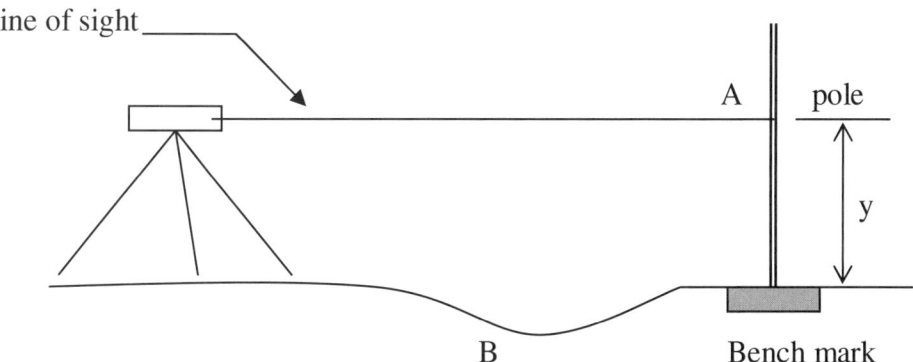

Assume the benchmark elevation is 100 ft.
Assume pole reading is 5.5 ft.
Elevation of line of sight = 100 + 5.5 = 105.5
Now place the pole in point B.

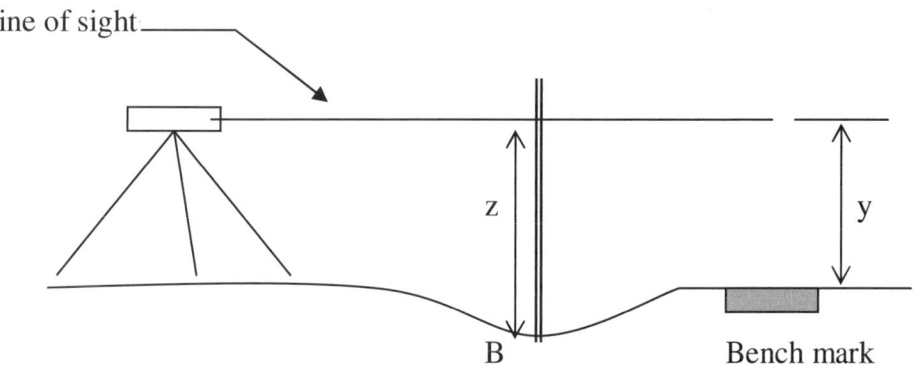

Obtain the new reading "z'.
Assume that new reading "z" is 7 ft.
Elevation of point B = Line of sight elevation - z   = 105.5 - 7 = 98.5 ft

Practice Problem 1.7:   Surveyor finds a US geological benchmark in the site. The benchmark elevation was found to be 98.7 ft above mean sea level. (MSL). The surveyor places the pole on top of the benchmark and obtained a reading of 5.7 ft. Then surveyor obtained a reading of 3.2 for point A, 6.7 for point B and 5.0 for point C. Find elevations of point A, B and C.

Solution:
Benchmark elevation = 98.7
Pole reading on top of the benchmark = 5.7 ft
Elevation of line of sight = 98.7 + 5.7 = 104.4 ft
Reading of point A = 3.2
Elevation of point A = 104.4 - 3.2 = 101.2 ft
Reading of point B = 6.7
Elevation of point B = 104.4 - 6.7 = 97.7 ft
Reading of point C = 5.0
Elevation of point C = 104.4 - 5.0 = 99.4 ft

Practice Problem 1.8:   Portion of surveyor's logbook is shown below. Elevation of known benchmark is given to be 101.23 ft. Find the elevation of point C.

Location	Back sight	Fore sight	Elevation of line of sight	Elevation
BM	5.23			101.23
Point A		6.12		
Point B		7.23		
Point C		2.45		

Solution:

It is advisable to draw a level and line of sights until you are familiar with back sight and fore sight readings.

Elevation of line of sight = 101.23 + 5.23 = 106.46 ft

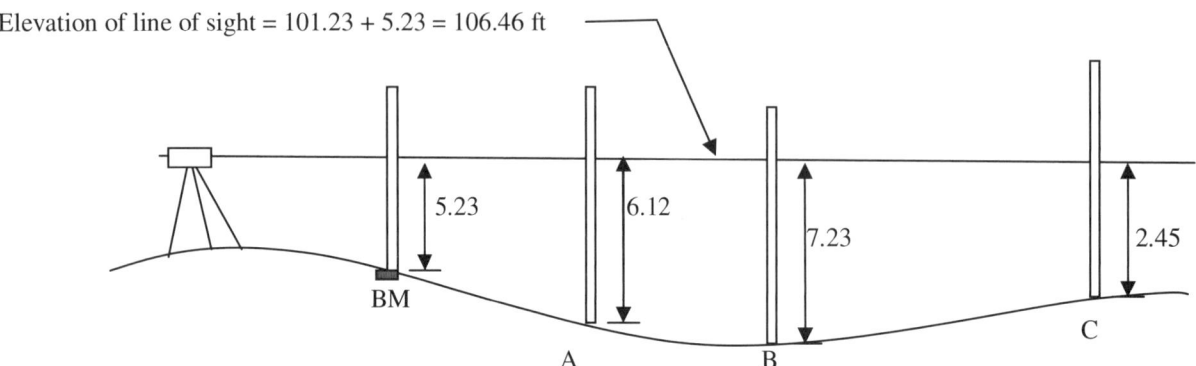

Elevation of line of sight can be computed by adding the reading at benchmark to the elevation of benchmark.

Elevation of line of sight = 101.23 + 5.23 = 106.46 ft

Elevation of point A   = Elevation of line of sight - Reading at point A
                        = 106.46 - 6.12 = 100.34

Elevation of point B   = Elevation of line of sight - Reading at point B
                        = 106.46 - 7.23 = 99.23

Elevation of point C   = Elevation of line of sight - Reading at point C
                        = 106.46 - 2.45 = 104.01

Hence, elevation of point C is 104.01.

You do not need to find elevations of points A and B to find the elevation of point C.

Though it is not necessary to fill the table in the exam, it may be useful to learn how to fill the table.

Location	Back sight	Fore sight	Elevation of line of sight	Elevation
BM	5.23		106.46	101.23
Point A		6.12		100.34
Point B		7.23		99.23
Point C		2.45		104.01

<u>Distance Measurement</u>:   Distances are measured with tapes, Theodalites and EDM (Electronic distance measurement).

Practice Problem: Surveyor had to measure the distance between points A and B. Surveyor locates a third point C and obtains angle measurements as shown. Find the distance AB.

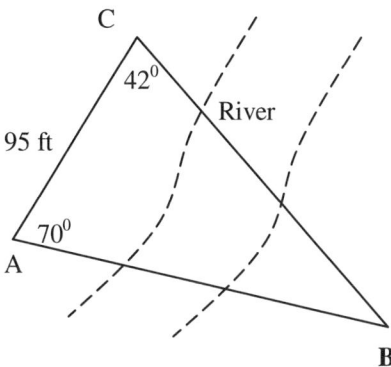

<u>**Solution:**</u>   This problem can be easily solved using the Sine law.

Sine Law: AC/Sin B = AB/Sin C = BC/Sin A

Angle B = 180 – (42 + 70) = 68

     AC/Sin B = AB/Sin C

     95/Sin 68 = AB/Sin 42

     AB = 68.6 ft

1.3.3   Highway Curves (Horizontal and Vertical Curves):
Surveyors are required to layout highway curves. There are two types of highway curves.
     1)   Horizontal curves
     2)   Vertical curves
Horizontal Curves: Prior to venture into horizontal curves it is important to spend little time in trigonometry.

<u>Trigonometry Refresher</u>:   Knowledge of trigonometry is essential for the civil PE exam.
It is highly unlikely that you would require any more trigonometry than sin, cos and tan functions.

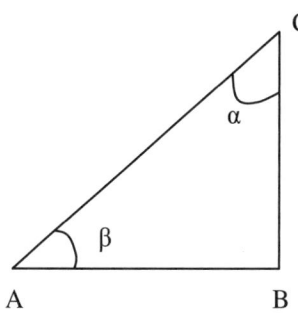

Sin β = BC/AC
Sin α = AB/AC
Cos β = AB/AC
Cos α = BC/AC

β = 90 - α
Sin β = Sin (90 – α) = Cos α
Cos β = Cos (90 – α) = Sin α

Tan α = AB/BC
Tan β = BC/AB
α = 90 – β

BC = AC Sin β

BC = AB Tan β
AB = AC Sin α
AB = BC Tan α

AC = BC/Cos α
AC = AB/Cos β
AC = BC/Sin β
AC = AB/Sin α
BC = AB/Tan α
AB = BC/Tan β

Practice problem: Find α, β, γ, AD, DC and BC

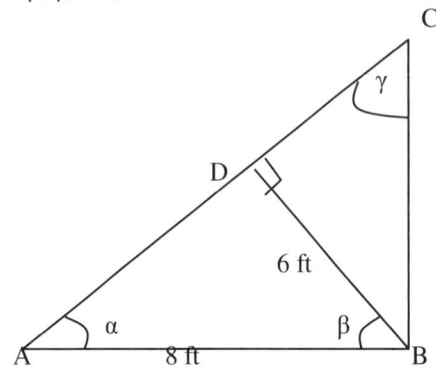

Solution:

Sin α = 6/8;   α = 48.6⁰
Hence β = 90 – α = 41.4⁰.
γ = 90 – α = 41.4
Note that β = γ in this case.
AD = 8 Cos α = 8 Cos (48.6) = 5.29
DC = AC – AD
AC = 8/Cos α = 8/ Cos (48.6) = 12.1 ft
Hence DC = 12.1 – 5.29 = 6.81
BC = 8 Tan α = 8 Tan (48.6) = 9.1

Radians: Angles can be measured with radians as well.
$360^0 = 2\pi$ radians

$2\pi \cdot r$ = Circumference of a circle
The length of an arc is given by multiplication of the angle measured in radians by the radius.

Length of an arc = Angle measured in radians x radius

Practice Problem: Find the length of an arc that projects an angle of 45^0 at the center of the circle. The radius of the circle is 2.5 m.

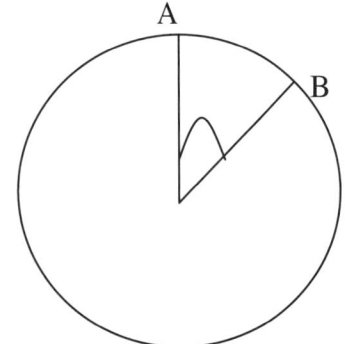

Solution: $360^0 = 2\pi$ radians
          $1^0 = (2\pi/360^0)$ radians
          $45^0 = (2\pi/360 \times 45)$ radians $= 0.785$ radians

Length of an arc = Angle measured in radians x radius
Length of arc AB = 0.785 x 2.5 = 1.96 m

Practice Problem: Find the length AB of the figure shown. O is the center of the circle and radius of the circle is 50 m.

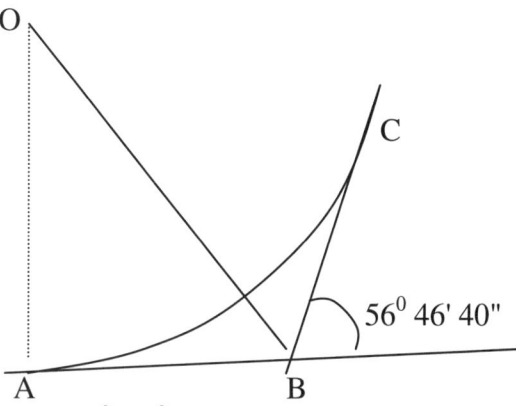

Solution: Angle ABC = 180^0 - 56^0 46' 40"

It is easy to work with decimals rather than minutes and seconds.

56^0 46' 40" = $56 + 46/60 + 40/3600$ = 56.78^0
Angle ABC = 180 - 56.78 = 123.22^0

Angle OBA = =123.22/2 = 61.61^0

Tan (angle OBA) = OA/AB
Tan (61.61^0) = radius/AB
Since radius is given to be 50 m,

AB = 50/Tan (61.61^0) = 50/1.85 = 27.03 m

Horizontal Curves:

Straight road would start to curve at the point known as *"Point of curvature"* or PC. The curve ends and straight road starts again at a point known as PT or point of tangent. Tangents drawn at each point intersects at PI or point of intersection.

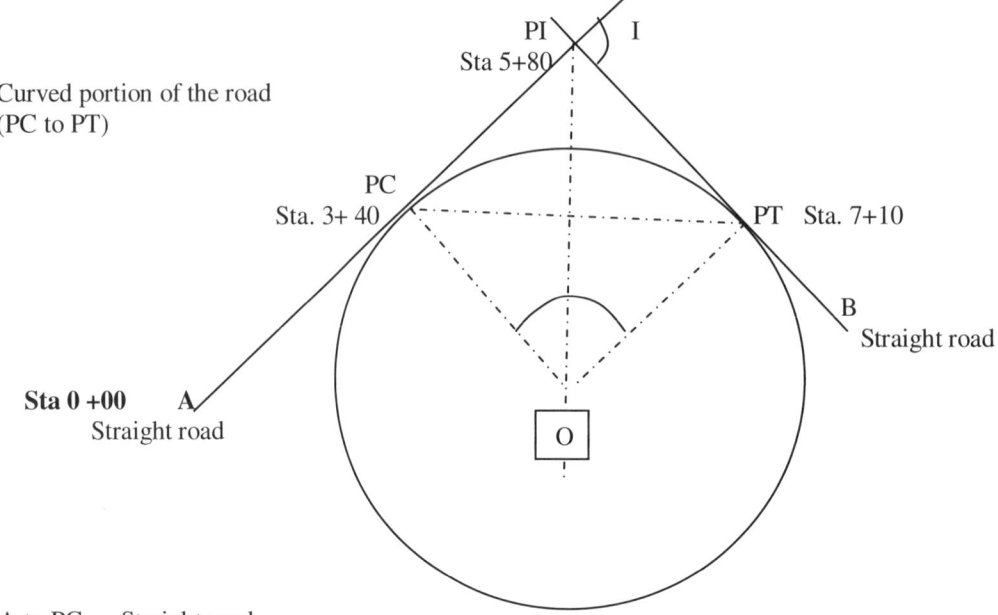

Curved portion of the road (PC to PT)

A to PC – Straight road
PC to PT – Curved portion of the road
PT to B – Straight road again

Station Markings: Station at PC is 3+40 (or 340 ft from the origin of stations). Station at PI is 5+80. The length between PC and PI = 580 – 340 = 240 ft

Station at PT = 7+10.
This station is measured along the curved portion of the road from PC to PT.
Length of the curved portion of the road from PC to PT = 710 – 340 = 370 ft

Angle at the Center of the Circle: Curved length of the road from PC to PT is 370 ft. If the radius is known, angle at the center of the circle can be calculated.

Assume the radius is 850 ft.
Whole circle is 360^0. Whole circle generates the perimeter of the circle.

360 degrees ------------------> $2 . \pi . R = 2 \times 3.14 \times 850 = 5,338$ ft
Or
5,338 ft generates an angle of 360 degrees at the center.
One (1) ft generates an angle of 360/5,338 degrees at the center.
370 ft arc will generate an angle of 360/5,338 x 370 = 24.9 degrees.

Practice problem: What is the length of an arc generated by an angle of 23.5 degrees. The radius of the circle is 575 ft.

Solution:

360 degrees -----------------> $2 . \pi . R = 2 \times 3.14 \times 575 = 3,613$ ft
1 degree----------------------> 3,613/360 = 10.03 ft
1-degree arc generates a curve of 10.03 ft.
23.5 degrees generates a curve of 10.03 x 23.5 ft = 235.7 ft

Angle Computation:

Curved portion of the road
(PC to PT)

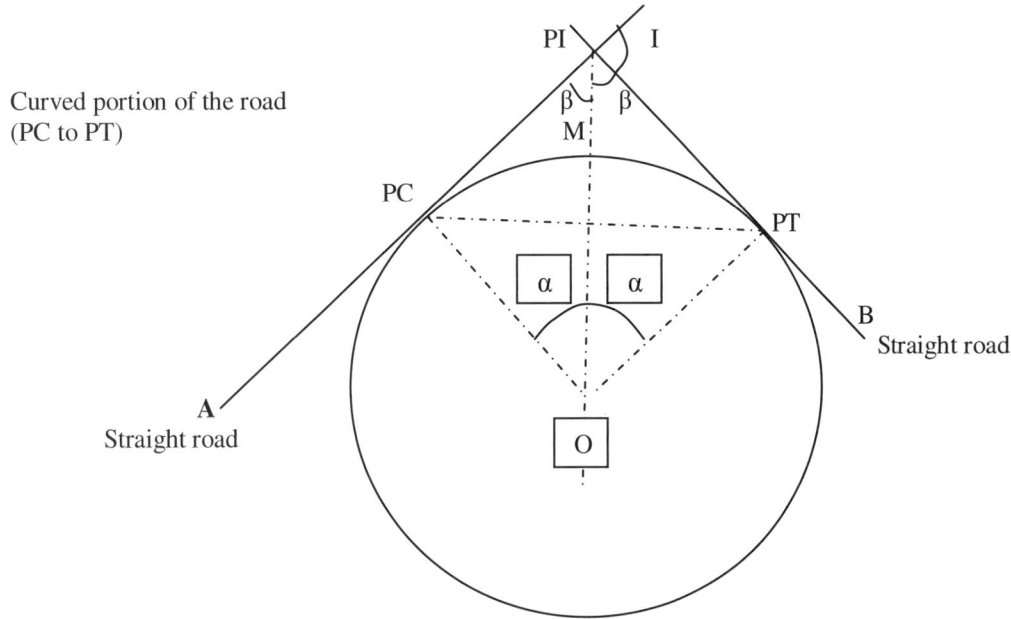

Straight road

A to PC – Straight road
PC to PT – Curved portion of the road
PT to B – Straight road again

Following properties are easily determined.

Intersection angle at point PI is known as I.
Consider two legs, PCPI and PTPI.

Angle PC PI PT = 180^0 - I   (Angle at point PI, between two legs PCPI and PIPT)

From symmetry, angle PC PI O = β = (180 – I)/2 = 90 – I/2
Hence α = 90 – β = I/2

If the radius of the circle is R and I are known, lengths PIPC, PCO and PIO can be deduced.

1) PIPC = PCO tan α = R Tan α = R Tan I/2

2) PCO = PIO Cos α
    PCO = R
    Hence PIO = PCO/Cos α = R/Cos α = R/Cos (I/2)

3) PIM = PIO – R = R/Cos α – R = R/Cos (I/2) - R

4) Length of the curved portion PC to PI can be found as follows.

Total perimeter of the circle = 2π R
Total perimeter of the circle is due to 360^0.
Hence, 360^0 extends a curve of 2πR
Hence 1^0 extends a curve of 2πR/360
$α^0$ extends a curve of 2πR/360 x α
$2α^0$ extends a curve of 2πR/360 x 2α
Length of the curved portion of the road from PC to PT = 2πR/360 x 2α

Practice Problem: Station of a road at PC is 5 + 30. Station at PI is 8 + 20. The angle of intersection (I) is 40^0.
   a)   Find the radius. (Refer to above figure)
   b)   Find the station at PT (measured along the curved portion of the road).

Solution: a) Length between PC and PI is 820 – 530 = 290 ft

   PCPI = 290 = R tan α

   α = I/2 = 20^0
   290 = R tan 20^0.
   R = 290/Tan 20^0 = 796.8 ft

   b.)   Length of the curved portion of the road from PC to PT = 2πR/360 x 2α
   = 2π x 796/360 x 2 x 20 = 555.7 ft

   Station at PC = 5 + 30 = 530
   Station at PT = 530 + 555.7 = 1,085.7
   Station at PT = 10 + 85.7

Note: Stations can be marked along a curved road or a straight line.
**   See the Practice Problem Book for more Practice Problems and solutions***

Vertical Curves:

Elevations and Grades: Prior to dealing with vertical curves, it is important to understand elevations and grades.

Practice Problem: Find the elevation of point B, if the grade is 5%. Grade = Vertical/Horizontal

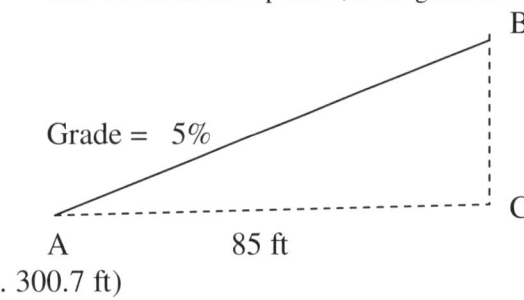

$$\text{Grade} = \frac{\text{Vertical}}{\text{Horizontal}} \times 100$$

Elevation at point A = 300.7 ft;   Grade = 5% = BC/AC
BC = 5% x 85 = 0.05 x 85 = 4.25 ft
Elevation at B = 300.7 + 4.25 = 304.95 ft

Grade Change: Grade changes are common in vertical curves.

Practice Problem: Find the average grade between point A and point B.
Find the change of grade per foot between points A and B

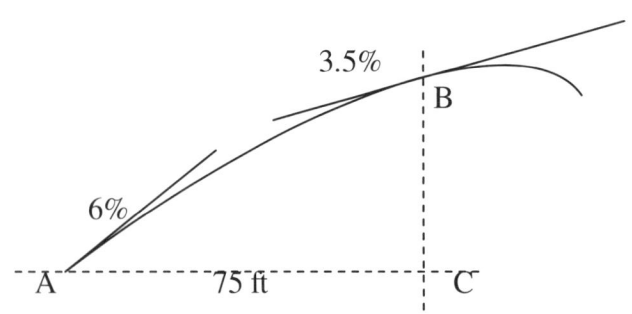

Solution:
Grade at point A = 6%
Grade at point B = 3.5%
Average grade between two points = (6 + 3.5)/2 = 4.75%

Change of grade between points A and B:
Grade at point A is 6%. The grade has gone down to 3.5% at point B.
Change of grade = 6 – 3.5 = 2.5%
Change of grade per foot = 2.5/75 = 0.0333% per foot

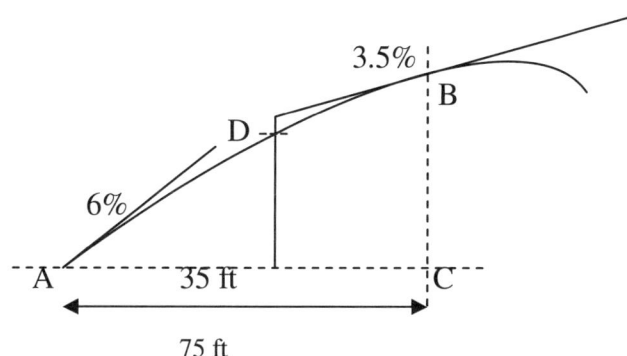

What is the grade at point D if the horizontal distance between points A and D is 35 ft.

Change of grade = 0.0333 per foot.
Change of grade for 30 ft = 0,0333 x 35 = 1.167%
Grade at point D = 6% – 1.167% = 4.833%

PVC, PVT and PVI:

PVC (Point of Vertical Curvature):	In a vertical curve where straight road starts to curve is known as PVC.
PVT (point of Vertical Tangent):	Point where curved road becomes a straight road again is known as PVT.
PVI (Point of Vertical Intersection):	Intersection of two tangents crossing PVC and PVT is known as PVI.

Practice Problem:
a)   Find the change of grade between PVC and point A. Grade at point A is 3%.
b)   Find the change of grade between PVC and PVT
b)   Find the change of grade between PVC and highest point in the curve.

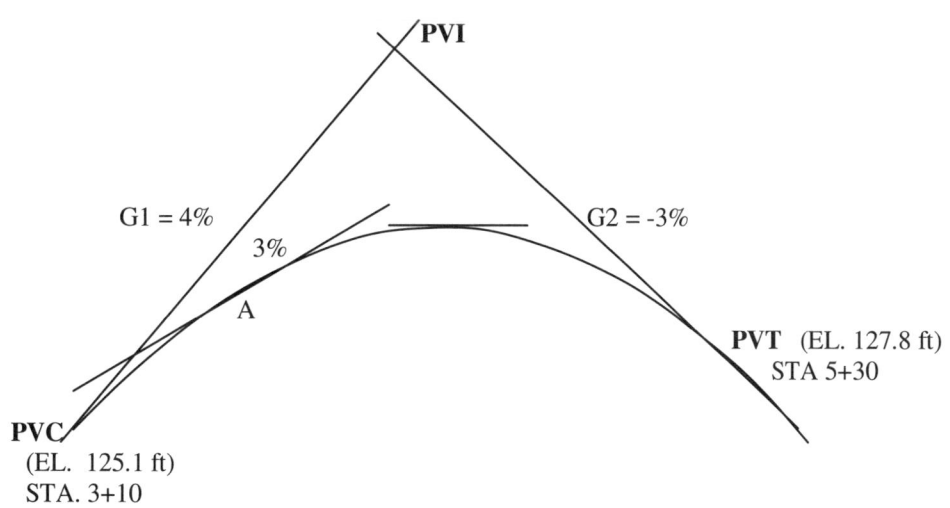

Solution:

PVC = Point of vertical curvature. Straight road start to curve at PVC. In this case, PVC is at an elevation of 125.1 and at station 3+10.
G1 = Grade of the tangent drawn at PVC. = 4%
G2 = Grade of the tangent drawn at PVT. = -3%

PVT = point of vertical tangent. Curved portion of the road becomes straight. In this case, PVT is at elevation 127.8 and station 5+30.
Point A = Point A is an arbitrary point in the curve. Grade at point A is 3%.
a)   Change of grade between PVC and point A = 4 – 3   = 1%
Since the change is a reduction from 4 to 3, change of grade is -1%. Minus sign indicates that the change is a reduction. In other words going from PVC to A, grade reduces by 1%.
b)   Change of grade between PVC and PVT   = 4 – (-3)   = 7%
Again, the change is a reduction. Hence change of grade is -7%.
c)   Find the change of grade between PVC and highest point in the curve = 4 – 0 = 4%
Change of grade is -4%
Note that in a crest curve, highest point has a zero grade. Similarly, in a sag curve, lowest point has zero grade.

Practice Problem: a)   Find the change of grade between PVC and point A
b)   Find the change of grade between PVC and PVT
c)   Find the change of grade between PVC and lowest point in the curve.
d)   Find the rate of grade change from PVC to PVT

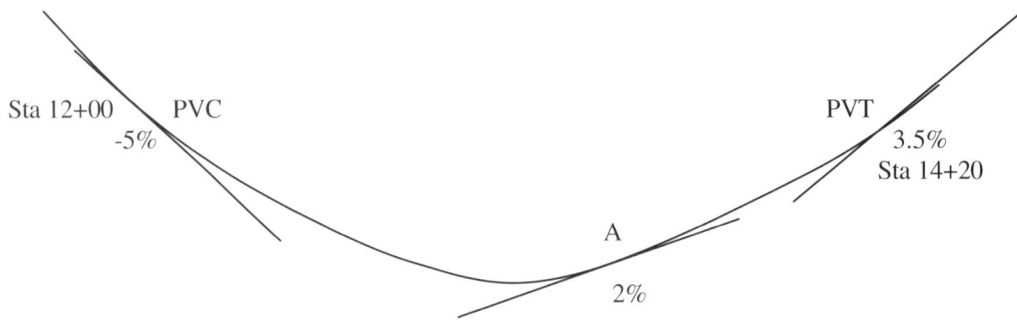

Solution:

a)   The change of grade between PVC and point A:

Grade at PVC is -5%. This goes up to 2% when reaching point A. The grade change is from -5% to +2%. Grade change is a positive one. Total grade change is +7%.

b)   The change of grade between PVC and PVT:

Grade at PVC is -5%. Grade at PVT is +3.5%. The grade is going up from PVC to PVT.
Grade change from PVC to PVT is positive. It is +8.5%.

c)   The change of grade between PVC and lowest point in the curve:

Grade at the lowest point of curve is zero. Grade at PVC is -5%. Hence, grade change from PVC to lowest point of the curve is positive. It is +5%.

d)   The rate of grade change from PVC to PVT:

Grade change from PVC to PVT = +8.5%.
Horizontal distance between PVC and PVT = 1,420 – 1,200 = 220 ft
Note that stations are measured horizontally.

Rate of grade change per foot = 8.5/220 = 0.038% per foot.

In other words, the grade **increases** by 0.038% per every foot.

Practice Problem: Find the horizontal distance required to have a grade change of 1% in the curve shown.

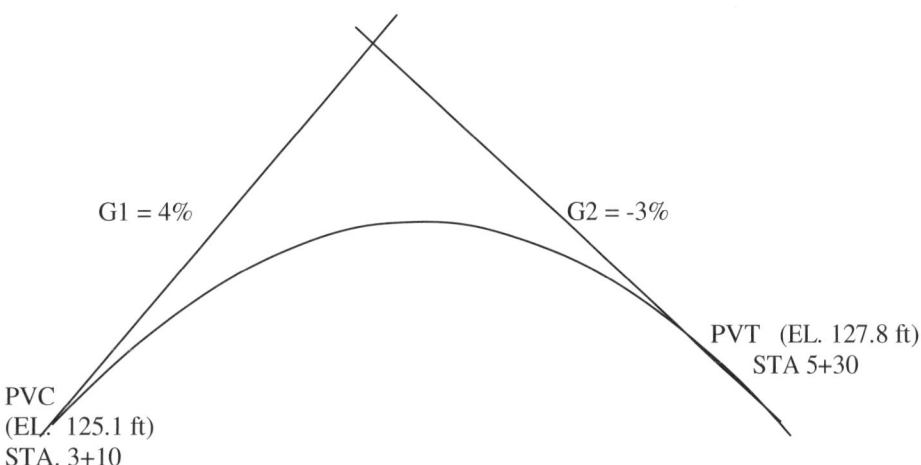

Solution: Horizontal distance required to have a grade change of 1% is required.

Grade change from PVC to PVT is negative. +4% at PVC becomes -3% at PVT.
Hence grade change from PVC to PVT is -7%.

Horizontal distance from PVC to PVT = 530 – 310 = 220 ft   (Station 3 + 10 to 5 + 30)
Horizontal distance for 7% grade change is 220 ft.
Horizontal distance for 1% grade change is 220/7= 31.4 ft.

Crest Curves and Sag Curves: Vertical curves could be crest curves or sag curves.

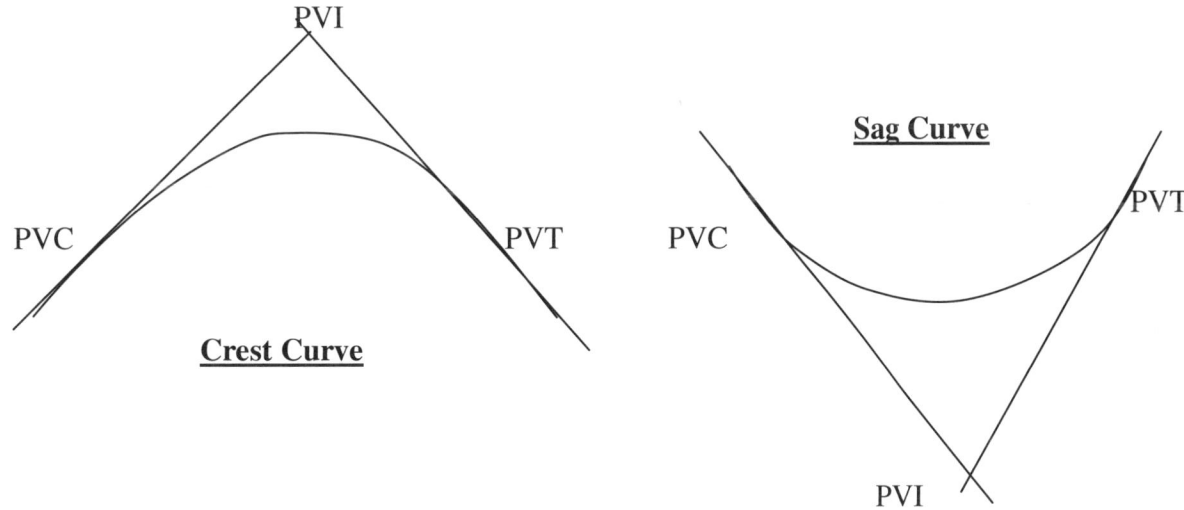

PVC = Point of vertical curvature (starting point of the vertical curve)
PVT = Point of vertical tangent (End point of the vertical curve)
PVI = Point of vertical intersection

Practice Problem:
a)   Find the grade change from PVC to PVT for the crest curve shown.
b)   Find the change of grade per foot from PVC to PVT

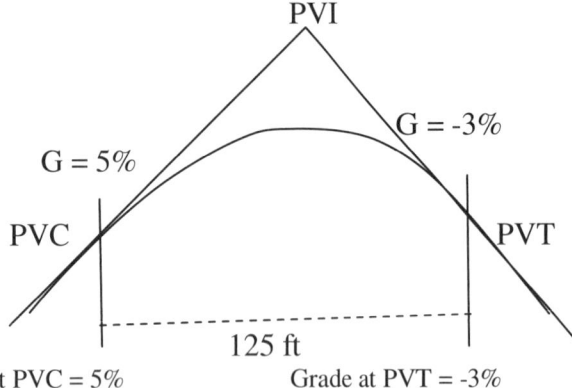

Grade at PVC = 5%   Grade at PVT = -3%
Total grade change = -3 - 5 = -8%
5% at PVC goes down to -3 at PVT. Hence, the change of grade is negative.

Grade change per foot = -8/125 = -0.064% per foot. The grade **goes down** by 0.064% per every foot.

General Equation for Vertical Curves:

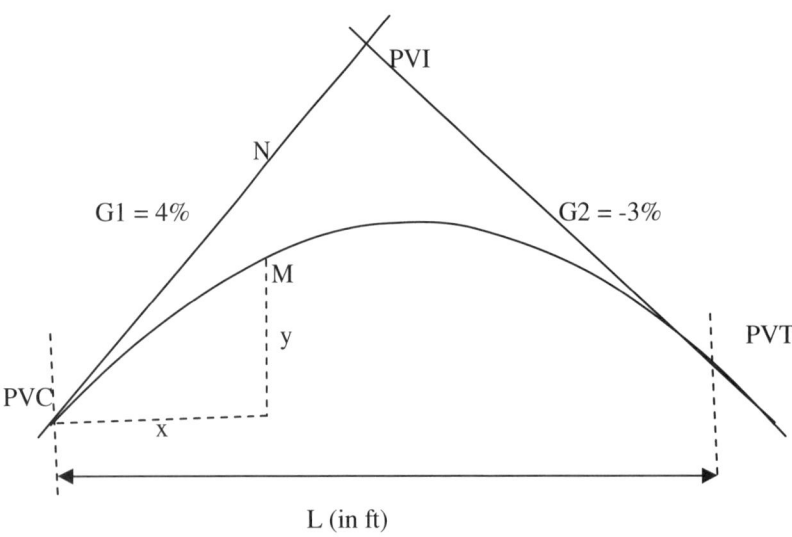

The elevation to point M from PVC is "y".
Horizontal distance to point M from PVC is "x". Both "x" and "y" are measured in ft.
General equation for vertical curves shown below.

$$y = \frac{(G2 - G1)}{200\ L}.\ x^2 + \frac{G1.\ x}{100}$$

y = Vertical height to point in the curve from BVC in ft
x = Horizontal distance between two points in ft.
G1 and G2 are gradients in percent.
Upward gradient is taken to be positive (+) ve.

Downward gradient is taken to be (-) ve.
L = Horizontal distance between BVC and EVC in ft.

Practice Problem):   Sag vertical curve of a roadway is shown in the figure. The roadway goes under an overpass.
Station of BVC = 115+45,
Elevation of BVC = 134.56 ft
Station of PVI = 120 + 34
Station of overpass = 123 + 13
Elevation of overpass = 143.25 ft

What is the maximum height of trucks that can be allowed in the roadway assuming 1 ft clearance between roof of trucks and the overpass.
Note that vertical curves are constructed in a manner so that PVI station is at the center of BVC and EVC.

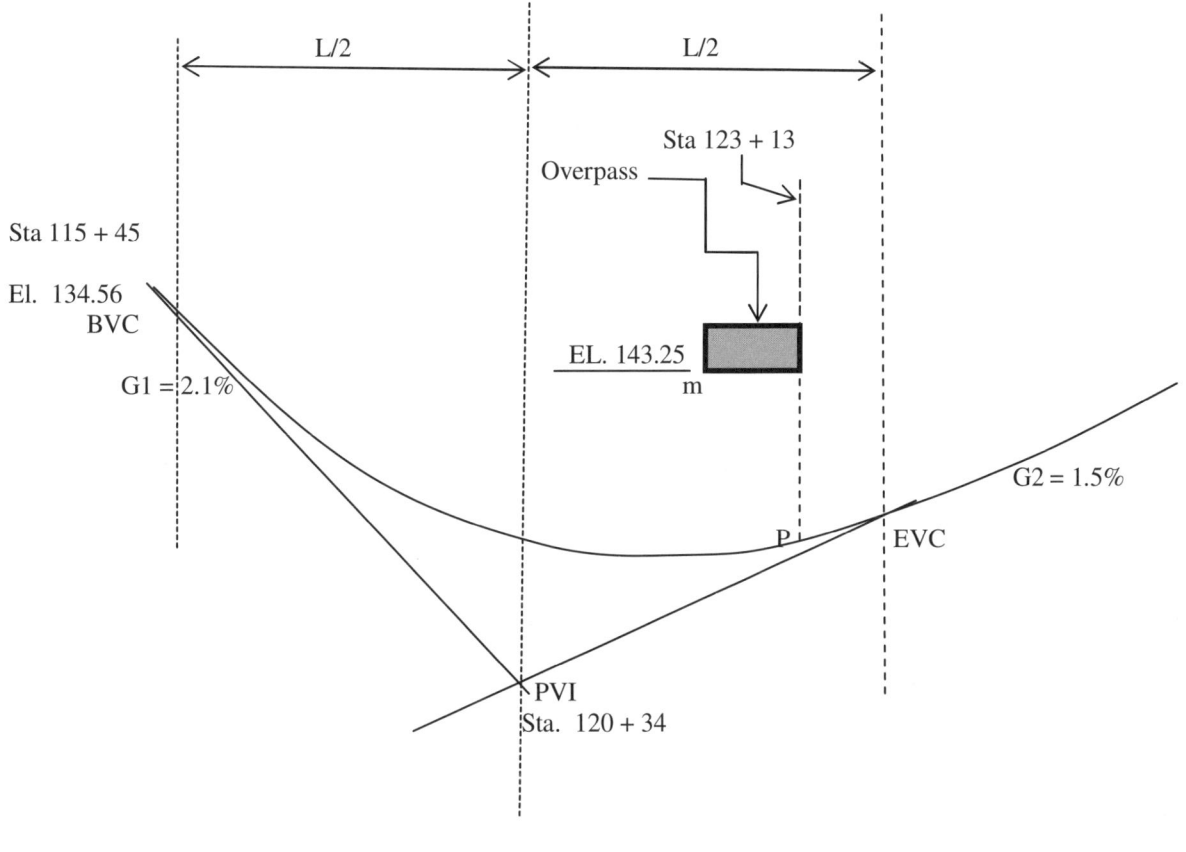

A) 13.45 ft   B) 12.97 ft   C) 14.56 ft   D) 10.89 ft

Solution 4.23):

Vertical Curve Equation;

$$y = \frac{(G2 - G1)}{200.\,L}\,x^2 + \frac{G1.\,x}{100}$$

y = Vertical height to point in the curve from BVC in ft
x = Horizontal distance between two points in ft.
G1 and G2 are gradients in percent.

Upward gradient is taken to be positive (+) ve.
Downward gradient is taken to be (-) ve.
L = Horizontal distance between BVC and EVC in ft.

Let's write down the given parameters.
BVC station = 115 + 45
PVI station = 120 + 34
The horizontal distance between BVC and PVI = 12,034 – 11,545 = 489 ft

Note that PVI station is located midway between BVC and EVC.

Hence L = 2 x 489 = 978 ft

$G1 = -2.1$ (Downward gradient is considered to be negative)
$G2 = 1.5$ (Upward gradient is considered to be positive)
We need to find the horizontal distance between the overpass (point P) and BVC.
Horizontal distance to the overpass measured from BVC (x) = 12313 – 11545 = 768 ft

STEP 1:   Find the elevation at point P:

$$y = \frac{(G2 - G1)}{200\,L}\,x^2 + \frac{G1\,x}{100}$$

$$y = \frac{(1.5 - -2.1)}{200 \times 978}\,768^2 + \frac{(-2.1 \times 768)}{100}$$

$y = 10.855 – 16.128 = -5.273$

Note that "y" is measured from BVC.

Elevation at point P = 134.56 – 5.273 = 129.28

Elevation of the overpass = 143.25

The total clearance between the roadway and overpass = 143.25 – 129.28 = 13.97 ft

Clearance of 1 ft is needed between overpass and roof of trucks.
Hence maximum height of trucks = 12.97 ft   (Ans B)

1.3.4   Trench Excavations:

Trench excavations are mostly done by using a string line. The procedure is easily explained with an example.

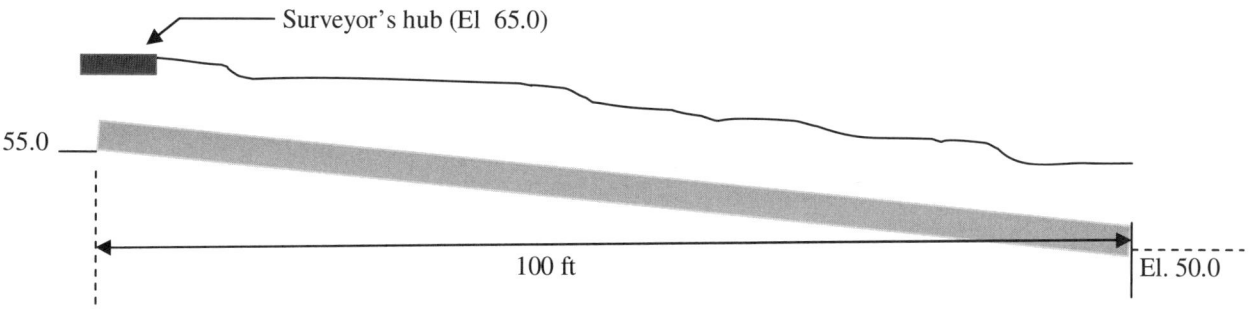

In the above example, elevation of the surveyor's hub is known. Contractor will establish a string line, probably 3 ft above the surveyor's hub as shown below. Elevation of the string line would be 68.0. Machine operator will excavate 13 ft measured from the string line. (68 – 55 = 13). Depth to bottom of trench measured from ground level would vary depending upon the ground elevation.

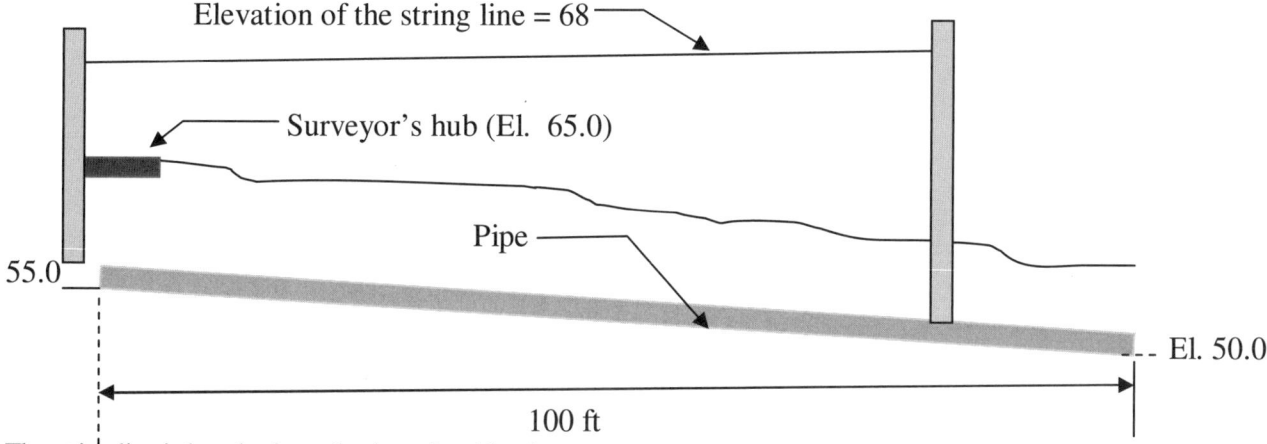

The string line is kept horizontal using a hand level.

Elevation at bottom of pipe at 50 ft is 52.5.

Elevation of the string line is 68. The contractor has to excavate 15.5 ft measured from the string line, at 50 ft distance.

(68 – 52.5 = 15.5 ft). Depth to bottom of trench measured from ground level would vary depending upon the ground elevation.

1.3.5   Construction Stakes and Markings:

We all have seen stakes planted in the ground for various construction work. In this chapter, we will look what information these stakes have and how to read them.

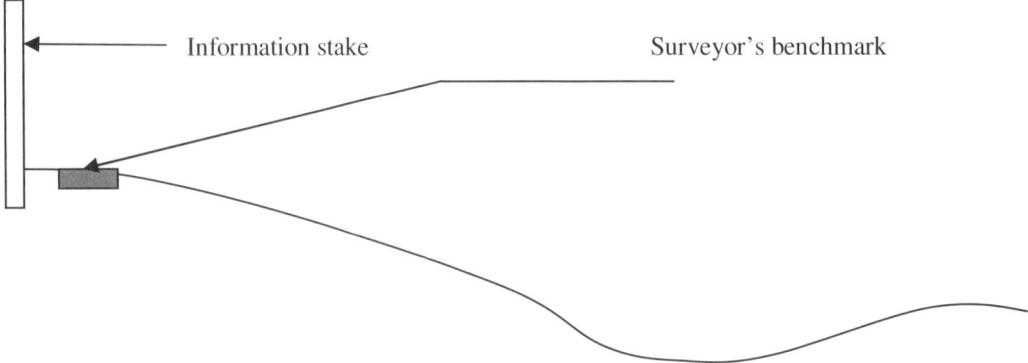

Surveyor's Benchmark (Surveyor's Hub):   All measurements are taken from the surveyor's benchmark also known as surveyor's hub. It is a solid plate strongly embedded in the ground.

Information Stake: Next to the surveyor's benchmark, there is an information stake. This stake would give what action need to be taken at a given point. You should remember that all measurements are taken from the surveyor's benchmark or the hub.

Practice Problem: Draw the cut section as for the marking in the following stake.

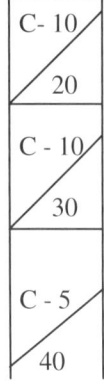

Solution: STEP 1:   Very top item in the above stake shows C – 10/20   This means a cut of 10 feet at a distance of 20 feet. (C-10/20).   This is shown below.

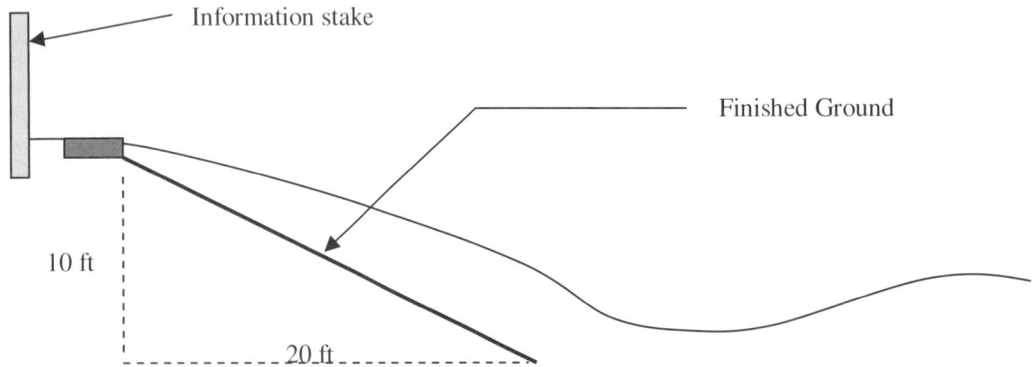

First point is 20 feet away and 10 ft below the surveyor's hub.

<u>STEP 2</u>:   Next item is C-10/30. This means, next point is 30 feet away (horizontal distance) and 10 ft below the surveyor's hub.

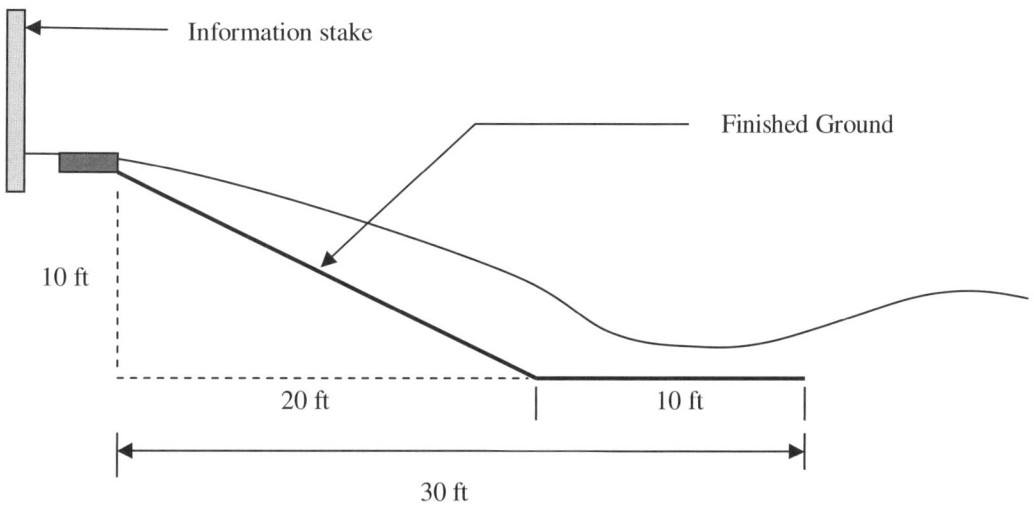

At 30 ft, the finished ground is 10 ft below the surveyor's hub.

<u>STEP 3</u>:   Last item is C-5/40. This means the next point is 40 ft away and 5 ft below the surveyor's hub.

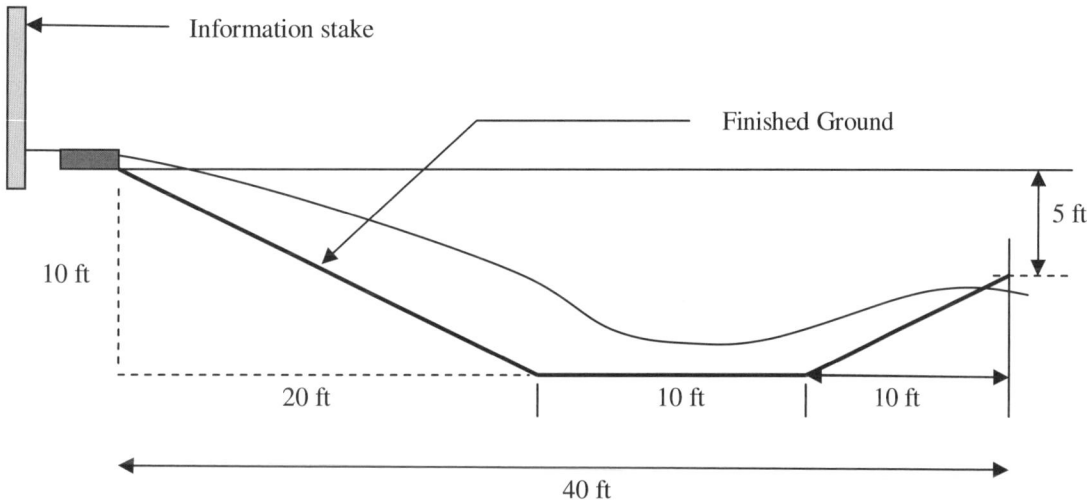

<u>Establishing a Reference Stake</u>: If you look at the above profile, there is a small problem. Cutting of the ground from the surveyor's hub is not a good idea since that could move the surveyor's hub. If the surveyor's hub is moved or lost then the surveyor needs to come back to the site again. Due to this reason, surveyors provide a reference stake.
Typically, surveyor would make a note as shown below.

   RS

   2.0/ 10.0

This indicates to establish a stake 10 feet away and 2 feet below the surveyor's hub. Let's assume information stake indicates the following.

   RS
   2.0/10.0

Below figure shows the reference stake. The measurement for the reference stake is taken from the surveyor's hub.

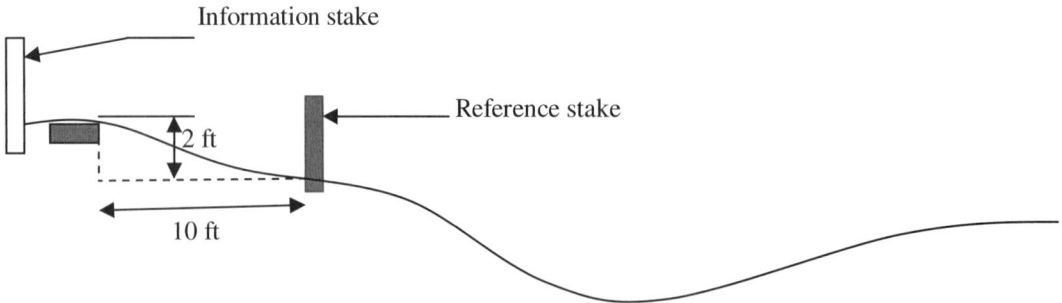

Practice Problem: Draw the cut section as for the marking in the information stake given below.

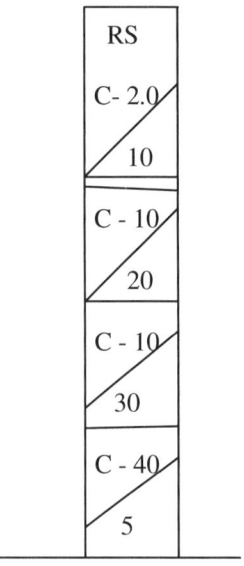

Solution: STEP 1: Establish the reference stake.

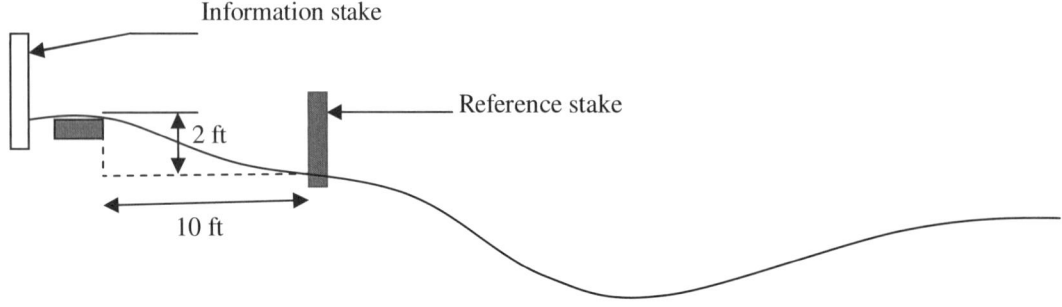

STEP 2:   Look at the information stake. Double line after the RS means that all the measurements to be taken from the reference stake. It is also known as reference point or RP.

C-10/20

After establishment of the reference stake, a cut of 10 feet need to be done at a point 20 ft away from the **reference stake**. Make sure that all measurements are taken from the reference stake.

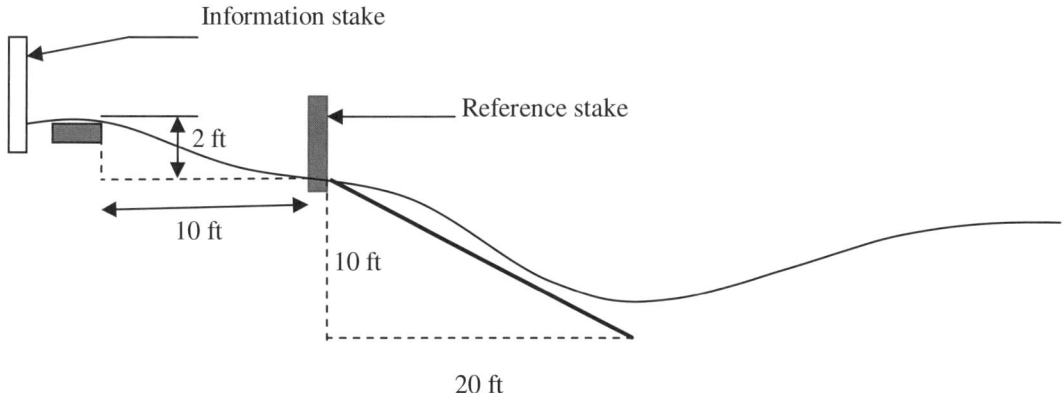

STEP 3:   Next item indicates a cut of 10 feet, 30 feet away from the reference stake. (C – 10/30)

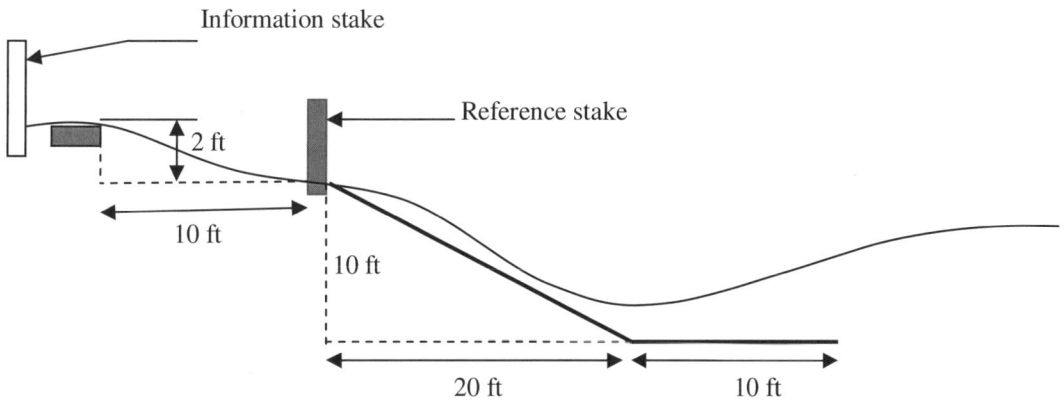

STEP 4:   Next item indicates a cut of 5 ft, 40 ft away from the reference stake. (C – 5/40)

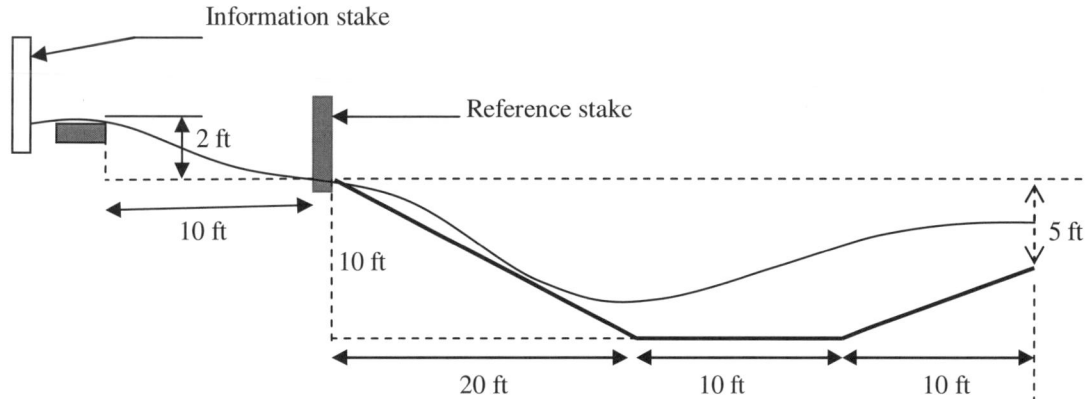

Grading: Grading is leveling the ground to the desired elevation. Surveyor would provide stakes for the dozer
operators.

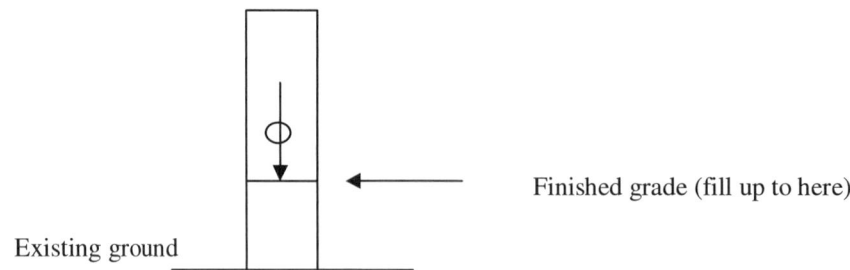

Circle and an arrow indicate that finished grade should be at the end of the arrow. In this case, soil has to be filled

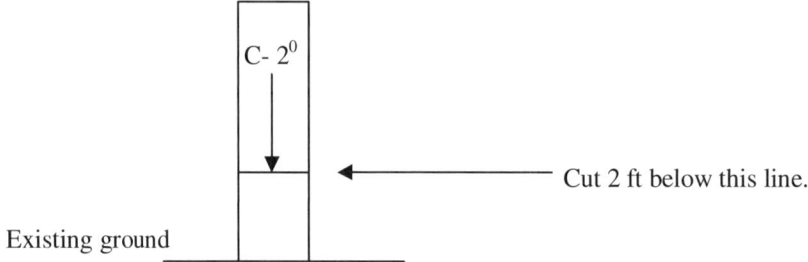

1.4   Earthwork Mass Diagrams:

Earthwork and mass diagrams are used to compute the cut and fill quantity required for road construction projects.

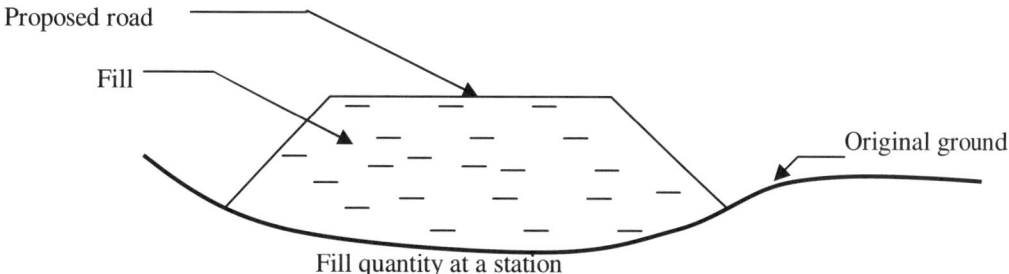

Fill quantity at a station

During road projects, the road is divided into stations. Typically, stations are given as 0+00, 1+00, 2+00 etc. 1+00 means 100 ft from the reference point and 2+00 means 200 ft from the reference point. Similarly, 2+30 means 230 ft from the reference point. Fill quantity required at each station varies since the ground surface tends to vary.

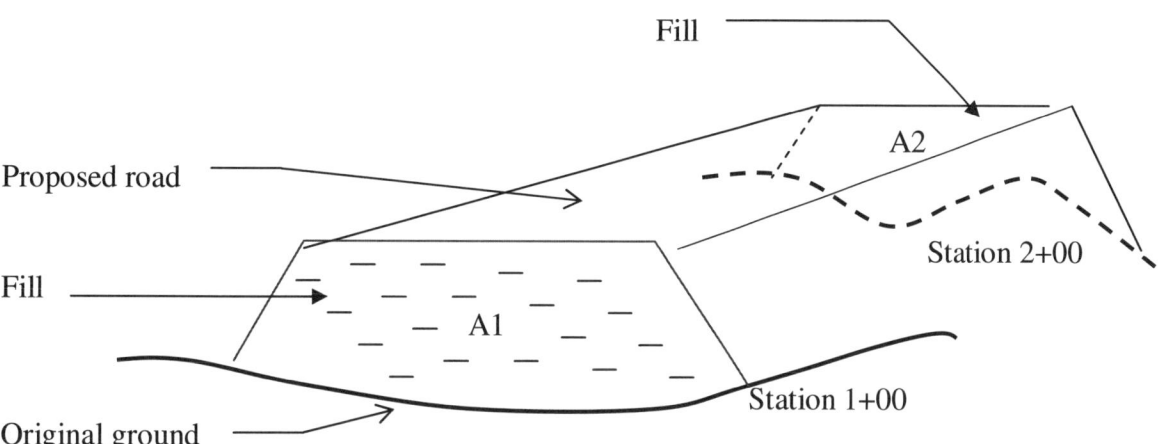

Placement of fill in road construction

Fill quantity required at station 1+00 is different from the quantity required at station 2+00.
Volume of fill required is obtained by multiplying the average area of two stations by the distance between stations.

Volume of fill required = (A1 + A2)/2 x d
d = distance between stations

How to obtain the areas A1 and A2?
In the real world, computer programs and planimeters are used to obtain A1 and A2 areas since they cannot be computed due to their irregular shapes. In the exam, these areas will be provided.

Above figure shows a highway been constructed thru a mountain range. Such projects involve huge quantity of soil been cut, transported and filled.

Practice Problem 1.8:   Find the volume of fill required from station 1+00 to 1+50. Fill area at station 1+00 is found to be 60 ft^2 and station 1+50 found to be 80 ft^2.

Solution: Volume of fill required = (A1 + A2)/2 x distance between stations
          = (60 + 80)/2 x 50 ft^3.
          = 3,500 ft^3 = 129.6 yd^3.

Cut: During road construction, some locations may have to be cut. This happens when the proposed road is at a lower elevation than the existing ground.

Original ground

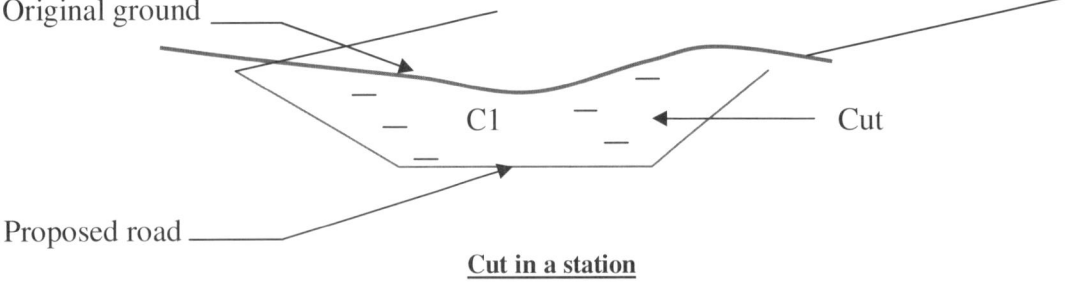

C1   Cut

Proposed road

Cut in a station

In some stations both cut and fill can occur.

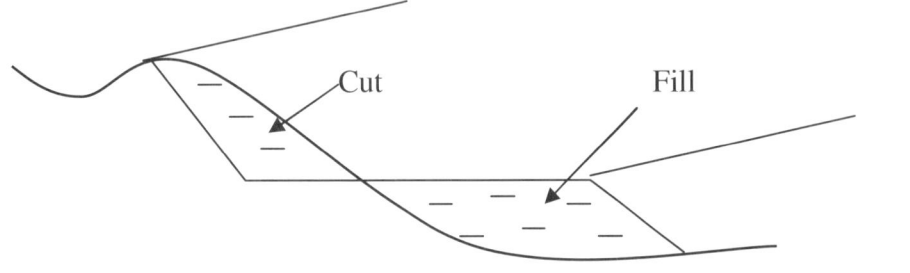

Cut   Fill

Cut and fill at the same station

When both cut and fill occurs at the same station, net value is obtained. The process is easily explained using an example.

Practice Problem 1.9:   Find the net cut or fill between station 1+50 and 2+00.

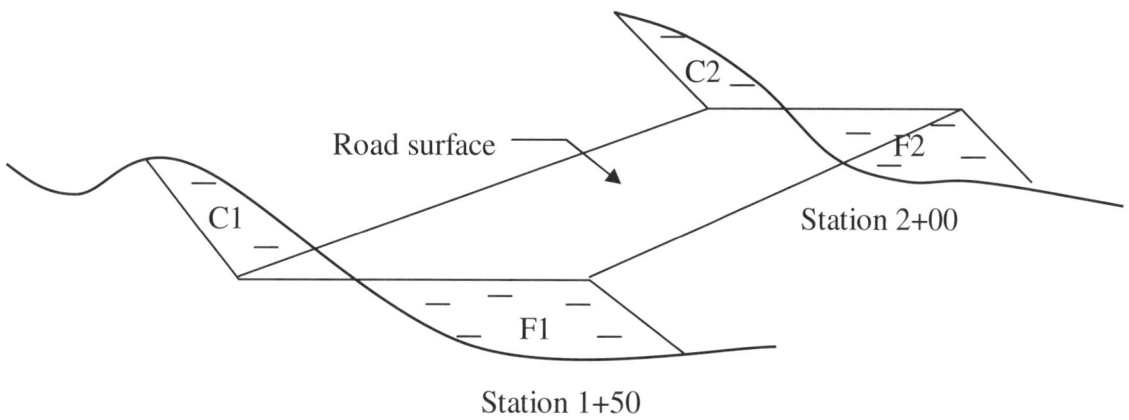

Station 1+50
Cut and fill diagram

Following information provided.

Station 1+50 $C1 = 120 \text{ ft}^2$ $F1 = 170 \text{ ft}^2$
Station 2+00 $C2 = 200 \text{ ft}^2$ $F2 = 60 \text{ ft}^2$

Usually this information is tabulated.

Station No.	Cut Area	Fill Area	Cut Vol	Fill Vol	Net Cut (yd^3)
1+50	120	170			
2+00	200	60			

Solution:

Total cut between two stations = (C1 + C2)/2 x 50
$$= (120 + 200)/2 \text{ x } 50 = 8{,}000 \text{ ft}^3 = 296.3 \text{ yd}^3.$$

Total fill between two stations = (F1 + F2)/2 x 50
$$= (170 + 60)/2 \text{ x } 50 = 5{,}750 \text{ ft}^3 = 213 \text{ yd}^3.$$

Net amount = 296.3 – 213 = 83.3 yd^3. (cut)

Cut is represented with positive while fill is represented with negative.

Station No.	Cut Area	Fill Area	Cut Vol (ft^3)	Fill Vol (ft^3)	Net Cut (ft^3)
1+50	120	170			
2+00	200	60	296.3	213	83.3

Mass Diagrams: Mass diagram is drawn using the net cut values. Mass diagrams are easily explained using an example.

Practice Problem 1.10:   Mass diagram example:

Cut areas and fill areas are tabulated as shown. Complete the blank columns and draw a mass diagram.

Station No.	Cut Area	Fill Area	Cut Vol (ft^3)	Fill Vol (ft^3)	Net Cut (ft^3)	Cumulative Cut (ft^3)
0+00	175	125				
0+50	117	123				
1+00	238	250				
1+50	211	240				
2+00	198	180				
2+50	140	141				
3+00	258	200				

Solution:
STEP 1: Complete the "Cut Vol" column.

Cut volume (1st entry) = (175+117)/2 x 50   = 7,300
Cut volume (2nd entry) = (117+238)/2 x 50   = 8,875
Cut volume (3rd entry) = (238+211)/2 x 50   = 11,225
Cut volume (4th entry) = (211+198)/2 x 50   = 10,225
Cut volume (5th entry) = (198+140)/2 x 50   = 8,450
Cut volume (6th entry) = (140+258)/2 x 50   = 9,950

Station No.	Cut Area	Fill Area	Cut Vol (ft^3)	Fill Vol (ft^3)	Net Cut (ft^3)	Cumulative Cut (ft^3)
0+00	175	125	0	0	0	
0+50	117	123	7,300			
1+00	238	250	8,875			
1+50	211	240	11,225			
2+00	198	180	10,225			
2+50	140	141	8,450			
3+00	258	200	9,950			

STEP 2: Complete the "Fill Vol" column.

Fill volume (1st entry) = (125+123)/2 x 50   = 6,200
Fill volume (2nd entry) = (123+250)/2 x 50   = 9,325
Fill volume (3rd entry) = (250+240)/2 x 50   = 12,250
Fill volume (4th entry) = (240+180)/2 x 50   = 10,500
Fill volume (5th entry) = (180+141)/2 x 50   = 8,025
Fill volume (6th entry) = (141+200)/2 x 50   = 8,525

Station No.	Cut Area	Fill Area	Cut Vol	Fill Vol	Net Cut (ft^3)	Cumulative Cut
0+00	175	125	0	0	0	
0+50	117	123	7,300	6,200		
1+00	238	250	8,875	9,325		
1+50	211	240	11,225	12,250		
2+00	198	180	10,225	10,500		
2+50	140	141	8,450	8,025		
3+00	258	200	9,950	8,525		

STEP 3: Complete the "Net Cut" column

Net cut (1st entry) = 7,300 – 6,200 = 1,100
Net cut (2nd entry) = 8,875 – 9,25 = -450
Net cut (3rd entry) = 11,225– 6,200 = -1,025
Net cut (4th entry) = 7,300 – 6,200 = -275
Net cut (5th entry) = 7,300 – 6,200 = 425
Net cut (6th entry) = 7,300 – 6,200 = 1,425

Station No.	Cut Area	Fill Area	Cut Vol	Fill Vol	Net Cut (ft^3)	Cumulative Cut
0+00	175	125	0	0	0	0
0+50	117	123	7,300	6,200	1,100	
1+00	238	250	8,875	9,325	-450	
1+50	211	240	11,225	12,250	-1,025	
2+00	198	180	10,225	10,500	-275	
2+50	140	141	8,450	8,025	425	
3+00	258	200	9,950	8,525	1,425	

STEP 4: Complete the "Cumulative Cut" column:
Cumulative cut is obtained by adding the present net cut to the previous net total.

Cumulative cut (1st entry) = 1,100 + 0   = 1,100
Cumulative cut (2nd entry) = 1,100 + (-450) = 650
Cumulative cut (3rd entry) = 650 + (-1,025) = -375
Cumulative cut (4th entry) = -375 + (-275)   = -650
Cumulative cut (5th entry) = -650 + 425   = -225
Cumulative cut (6th entry) = -225 + 1,425   = 1,200

Station No.	Cut Area	Fill Area	Cut Vol	Fill Vol	Net Cut (ft^3)	Cumulative Cut
0+00	175	125	0	0	0	0
0+50	117	123	7,300	6,200	1,100	1,100
1+00	238	250	8,875	9,325	-450	650
1+50	211	240	11,225	12,250	-1,025	-375
2+00	198	180	10,225	10,500	-275	-650
2+50	140	141	8,450	8,025	425	-225
3+00	258	200	9,950	8,525	1,425	1,200

STEP 5: Draw the mass diagram:
Mass diagram is drawn between the "cumulative cut and the stations.

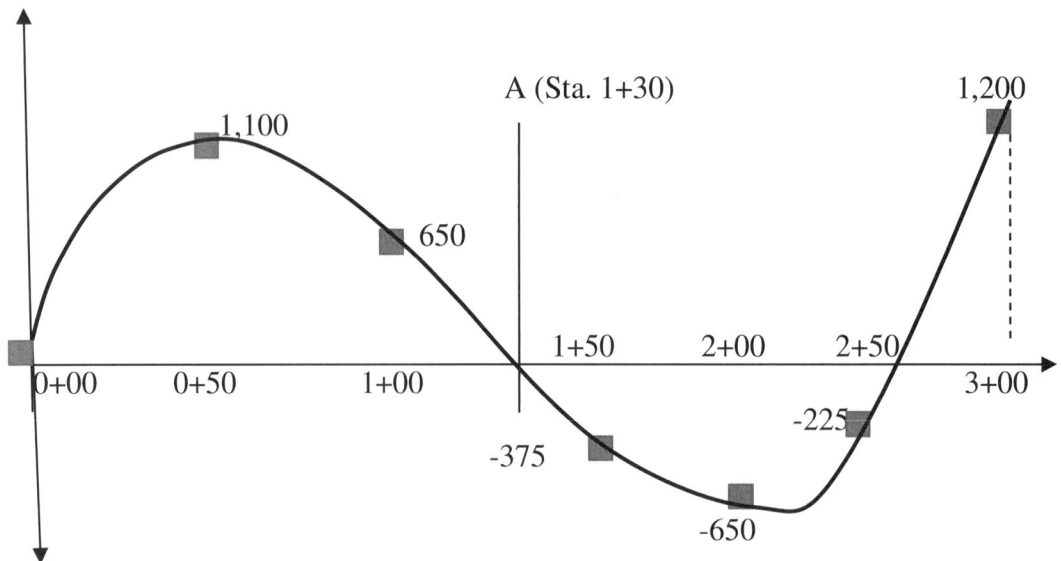

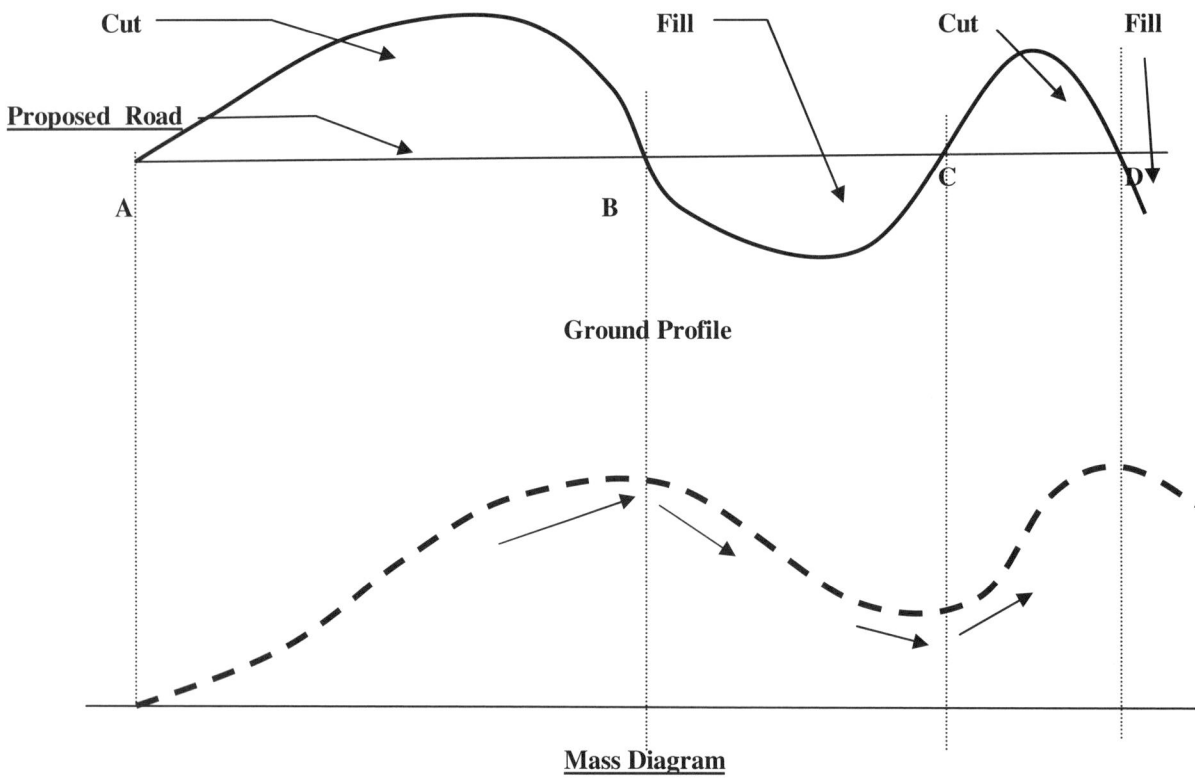

Point A to B: This section is all cut. Hence, mass diagram keeps going up.
Point B to C: This section is fill. Mass diagram changes direction at point B and start going down.
Point C to D: Point C to D is all cut. Mass diagram changes direction and start going up.
Beyond Point D: Beyond point D is fill. Mass diagram changes direction and start pointing down.

Mass Diagram Implications: Consider point "A" shown with a vertical line. At point "A", the curve crosses the "X" axis. Point "A" lies between station 1+00 and 1+50. Let's assume point "A" to be at station 1+30.
At station 1+30, the curve crosses the "X" axis.
What does this mean?

It means that between station 0+00 and station 1+30, total required fill is zero. In other words, all the cut material has been used for fill purposes.

Balanced points: Net cut between balanced points is zero. Sta. 0+00 to 1+30, net cut is zero. Hence, station 0+00 and 1+30 are balanced points. In other words, all the cut material in this region is utilized for fill. Similarly, station 1+30 to 2+60 also are two balanced points.

Volume Reduction due to Compaction: When soil is compacted, the volume reduces. Let's assume that a contractor has found out that portion of the road needs 200 cu. yds of fill after compaction. It is common sense for him to bring more than 200 cu. yds of fill since the volume decreases after compaction.

Volume reduction factor = (Additional volume of soil required)/Volume of soil after compaction

Practice Problem 1.11: The contractor has to fill and compact a portion of the road. The volume of the fill needed (after compaction) is calculated to be 200 cu. yds. Calculate the volume of soil need to be brought to the site if the volume reduction factor is 10%.

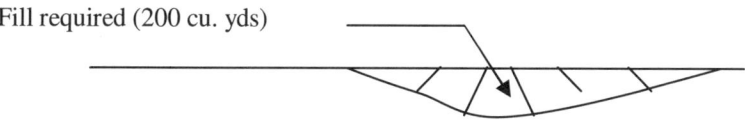

Fill required (200 cu. yds)

Fill required after compaction

Solution:
Volume reduction factor = (Additional volume of soil required)/Volume of soil after compaction
Volume reduction factor = 10%
Volume of soil after compaction = 200 cu. yds

Volume reduction factor = 0.10 = (Additional volume of soil required)/200

Additional volume of soil required = 0.10 x 200 = 20 cu. yds
Total volume of soil required = 200 + 20 = 220 cu. yds

Expansion: Expansion occurs when soil is cut and removed from ground. Expansion is defined as follows.

Expansion = Additional volume after cut and removal from ground/Volume in ground
Soil volume increases after cut and removed from ground.

Practice Problem 1.12:   During a road project, 150 cu. yds has to be cut and removed from site. Expansion factor of soil is 7%. Each truckload can carry 10 cu. yds. Find how many truckloads are required to remove the soil from site.

Solution:

Expansion = Additional volume after cut and removal from ground/Volume in ground

Expansion = 7%
Volume of soil in ground = 150 cu. yds

        0.07 = Additional volume after cut and removal from ground/150

Additional volume after cut and removal from ground = 0.07 x 150 = 10.5 cu. yds

Total volume of soil after cut and removed from ground = 150 + 10.5 = 160.5
Sixteen truck loads will be needed to carry 160 cu. yds, since each truck can carry 10 cu. yds. One final truck is required to carry last remaining 0.5 cu. yds. Hence total of 17 truckloads are required.

Practice Problem 1.13:   Mass diagram example (considering expansion and volume reduction):
Cut areas and fill areas are tabulated as shown. Complete the blank columns and draw a mass diagram. Volume reduction factor is given to be 9% and expansion factor is given to be 8%.

Solution:

A	B	C	D	E	F	G	H	I
							H = E-G	
Station No.	Cut Area	Fill Area	Cut Vol. (in ground)	Cut Vol. after expansion	Fill Vol. required	Fill Volume required considering volume reduction	Net Cut (ft³)	Cumulative Cut (ft³)
0+00	175	125						
0+50	117	123						
1+00	238	250						
1+50	211	240						
2+00	198	180						
2+50	140	141						
3+00	258	200						

STEP 1: Complete the "Cut Vol (in ground) column.

Cut volume (1ˢᵗ entry) = (175+117)/2 x 50   = 7,300
Cut volume (2ⁿᵈ entry) = (117+238)/2 x 50   = 8,875
Cut volume (3ʳᵈ entry) = (238+211)/2 x 50   = 11,225
Cut volume (4ᵗʰ entry) = (211+198)/2 x 50   = 10,225
Cut volume (5ᵗʰ entry) = (198+140)/2 x 50   = 8,450
Cut volume (6ᵗʰ entry) = (140+258)/2 x 50   = 9,950

A	B	C	D	E	F	G	H	I
							H = E-G	
Station No.	Cut Area	Fill Area	Cut Vol. (in ground)	Cut Vol. after expansion	Fill Vol. required	Fill Volume required considering volume reduction	Net Cut (ft³)	Cumulative Cut (ft³)
0+00	175	125	0					
0+50	117	123	7,300					
1+00	238	250	8,875					
1+50	211	240	11,225					
2+00	198	180	10,225					
2+50	140	141	8,450					
3+00	258	200	9,950					

STEP 2: Complete the "Cut Vol. after expansion" column:
As we discussed earlier, when the soil is cut and removed from ground it expands. Expansion factor is given to be 8%.
Cut volume in ground = 7,300
Expansion = 7,300 x 0.08 = 584
Volume of soil after expansion = 7,300 + 584 = 7,884 cu. ft

Simply this can be done by multiplying 7,300 x (1 + 0.08) = 7,884 cu. ft
Similarly 8,875 x (1.08) = 9,585
11,225 x 1.08 = 12,123 cu. ft
10,225 x 1.08 = 11,043 cu. ft
8,450 x 1.08 = 9,126 cu. ft

9,950 x 1.08 = 10,746 cu. ft

Input these values in column "E".

A	B	C	D	E	F	G	H	I
							H = E-G	
Station No.	Cut Area	Fill Area	Cut Vol. (in ground)	Cut Vol. after expansion	Fill Vol. required	Fill Volume. required considering volume reduction	Net Cut (ft^3)	Cumulative Cut (ft^3)
0+00	175	125	0	0				
0+50	117	123	7,300	7,884				
1+00	238	250	8,875	9,585				
1+50	211	240	11,225	12,123				
2+00	198	180	10,225	11,043				
2+50	140	141	8,450	9,126				
3+00	258	200	9,950	10,746				

STEP 3: Complete the "Fill Vol" column.

Fill volume (1st entry) = (125+123)/2 x 50   = 6,200
Fill volume (2nd entry) = (123+250)/2 x 50   = 9,325
Fill volume (3rd entry) = (250+240)/2 x 50   = 12,250
Fill volume (4th entry) = (240+180)/2 x 50   = 10,500
Fill volume (5th entry) = (180+141)/2 x 50   = 8,025
Fill volume (6th entry) = (141+200)/2 x 50   = 8,525

A	B	C	D	E	F	G	H	I
							H = E-G	
Station No.	Cut Area	Fill Area	Cut Vol. (in ground)	Cut Vol. after expansion	Fill Vol. required	Fill Volume. required considering volume reduction	Net Cut (ft^3)	Cumulative Cut (ft^3)
0+00	175	125	0	0	0			
0+50	117	123	7,300	7,884	6,200			
1+00	238	250	8,875	9,585	9,325			
1+50	211	240	11,225	12,123	12,250			
2+00	198	180	10,225	11,043	10,500			
2+50	140	141	8,450	9,126	8,025			
3+00	258	200	9,950	10,746	8,525			

STEP 4: When fill material is compacted, volume is reduced. Complete the "Fill volume required considering volume reduction":
Volume reduction factor is given to be 9%.

If fill volume required is 6,200 cu. ft, the contractor has to bring 6,200 x 1.09 cu. ft
= 6,758 cu. ft
Similarly

9,325 x 1.09 = 10,164 cu. ft
12,250 x 1.09 = 13,352 cu. ft
10,500 x 1.09 = 11,445 cu. ft
8,025 x 1.09 = 8,747 cu. ft
8,525 x 1.09 = 9,292 cu. ft

Input these values in column "G".

A	B	C	D	E	F	G	H	I
							H = E - G	
Station No.	Cut Area	Fill Area	Cut Vol. (in ground)	Cut Vol. after expansion	Fill Vol. required	Fill Volume. required considering volume reduction	Net Cut (ft^3)	Cumulative Cut (ft^3)
0+00	175	125	0	0	0			
0+50	117	123	7,300	7,884	6,200	6,758		
1+00	238	250	8,875	9,585	9,325	10,164		
1+50	211	240	11,225	12,123	12,250	13,352		
2+00	198	180	10,225	11,043	10,500	11,445		
2+50	140	141	8,450	9,126	8,025	8,747		
3+00	258	200	9,950	10,746	8,525	9,292		

STEP 5:   Complete column "H".
Net cut (1st entry) = 7,884 – 6,758   = 1,126 cu. ft
Net cut (2nd entry) = 9,585 – 10,164   = -579 cu. ft
Net cut (3rd entry) = 12,123 – 13,352 = -1,229 cu. ft
Net cut (4th entry) = 11,043 – 11,445 = -402 cu. ft
Net cut (5th entry) = 9,126 – 8,747   = 379 cu. ft
Net cut (6th entry) = 10,746 – 9,292   = 1,454 cu. ft
Input these values in column "H".

A	B	C	D	E	F	G	H	I
							H = E-G	
Station No.	Cut Area	Fill Area	Cut Vol. (in ground)	Cut Vol. after expansion	Fill Vol. required	Fill Volumes. required considering volume reduction	Net Cut (ft^3)	Cumulative Cut (ft^3)
0+00	175	125	0	0	0	0	0	
0+50	117	123	7,300	7,884	6,200	6,758	1,126	
1+00	238	250	8,875	9,585	9,325	10,164	-579	
1+50	211	240	11,225	12,123	12,250	13,352	-1,229	
2+00	198	180	10,225	11,043	10,500	11,445	-402	
2+50	140	141	8,450	9,126	8,025	8,747	379	
3+00	258	200	9,950	10,746	8,525	9,292	1,454	

STEP 6:   Complete the "Cumulative Cut" column:

Cumulative cut is obtained by adding the present net cut to the previous net total.

Cumulative cut (1st entry) = 1,126 + 0   = 1,126
Cumulative cut (2nd entry) = 1,126 + (-579) = 547
Cumulative cut (3rd entry) = 547 + (-1,229) = -682
Cumulative cut (4th entry) = -682 + (-402)   = -1,084
Cumulative cut (5th entry) = -1,084 + 379   = -705
Cumulative cut (6th entry) = -705 + 1,454   = 749

Input these values in column "I".

A	B	C	D	E	F	G	H	I
							H = E-G	
Station No.	Cut Area	Fill Area	Cut Vol. (in ground)	Cut Vol. after expansion	Fill Vol. required	Fill Volume required considering Volume reduction	Net Cut (ft³)	Cumulative Cut (ft³)
0+00	175	125	0	0	0	0	0	0
0+50	117	123	7,300	7,884	6,200	6,758	1,126	1,126
1+00	238	250	8,875	9,585	9,325	10,164	-579	547
1+50	211	240	11,225	12,123	12,250	13,352	-1,229	-682
2+00	198	180	10,225	11,043	10,500	11,445	-402	-1,084
2+50	140	141	8,450	9,126	8,025	8,747	379	-705
3+00	258	200	9,950	10,746	8,525	9,292	1,454	749

STEP 7:   Draw the mass diagram:

Mass diagram is drawn between the "cumulative cut" and the "stations".

Cumulative Cut (ft³)

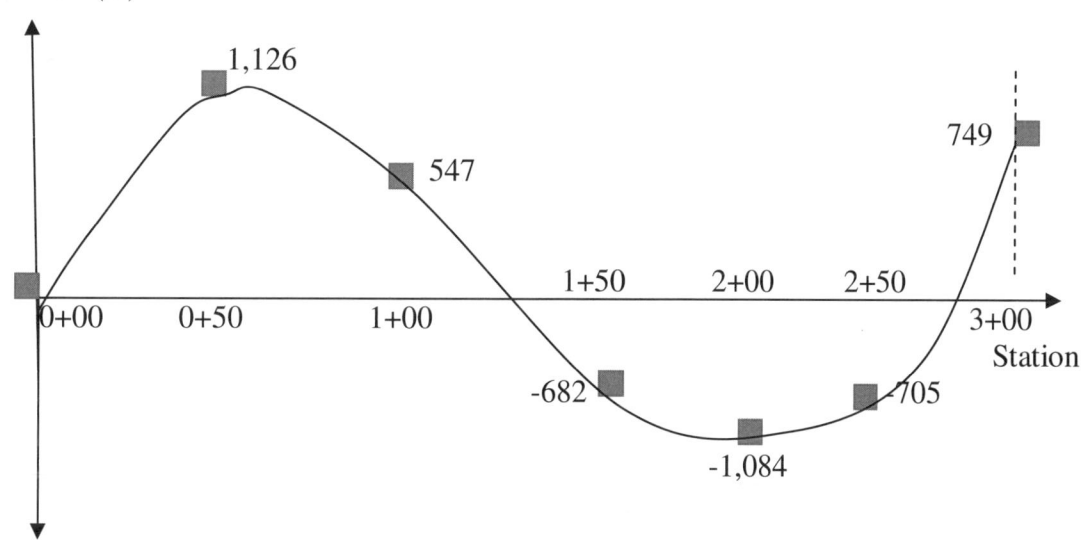

Practice Problem 1.14: Draw the mass diagram for the road construction project shown. The volume of soil cut or filled shown in the drawing.

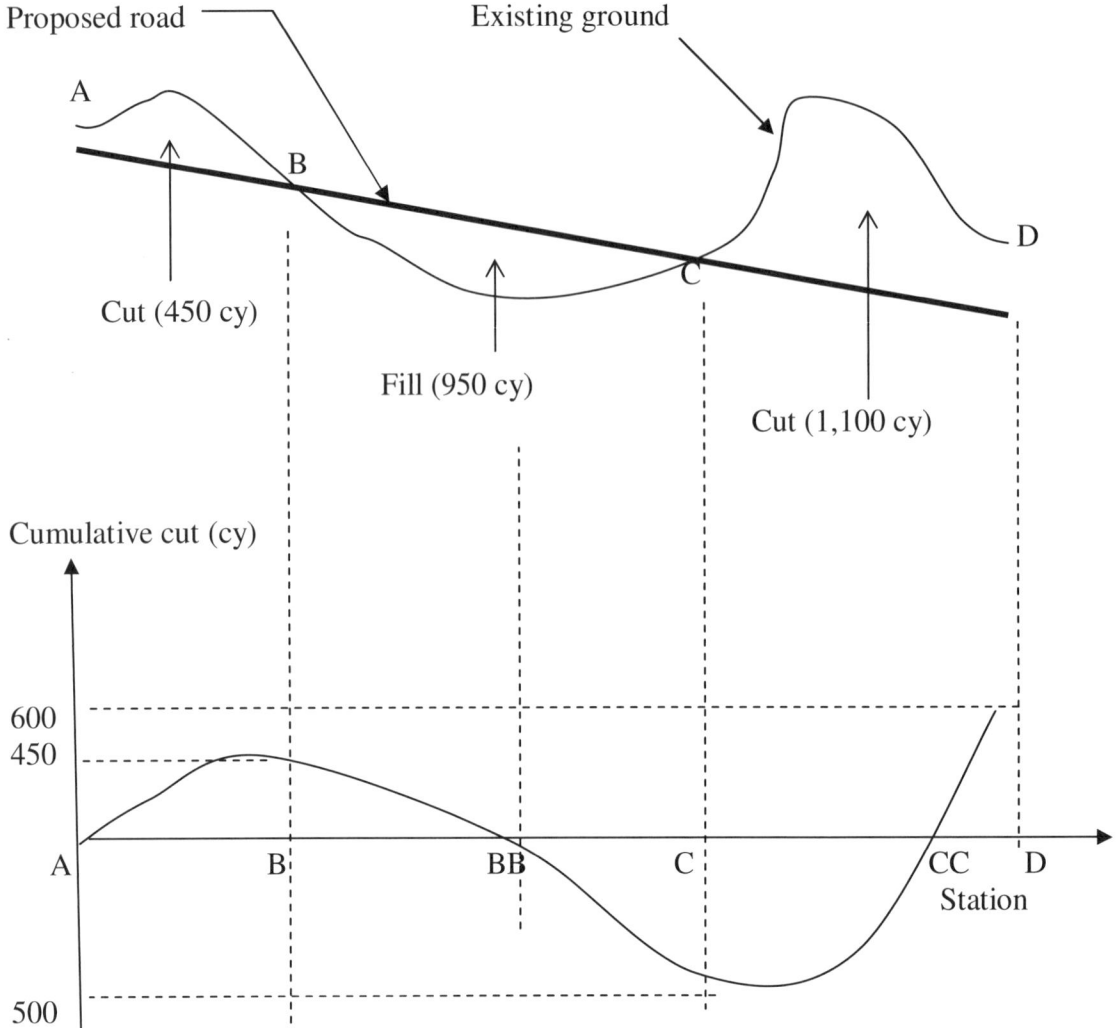

Solution:

Point A to B - The ground has to be cut. 450 CY of soil will be cut from point A to B.
Point B to C - The ground has to be filled. 950 CY of soil needed.
Point C to D – The ground has to be cut. 1,100 CY of soil will be cut from point C to D.
Total cut = 450 + 1,100 = 1,550 cy
Total fill = 950 cy
Waste = 1,550 – 950 = 600 cy

Cumulative cut volume increases from point A to B. Cumulative cut volume start to decrease after point B, since filling has started. At point BB, cut volume will be equal to fill volume. There is not enough information given in this example to find point BB.
Point BB to C, the fill volume increases. Cutting starts again at point C. Hence cumulative cut volume start to increase.
At point CC, cut and fill becomes equal again. There is not enough information given in this example to obtain point CC.
Point CC to D, cut volume increases. There is excess of 600 cy of soil that would be left at the end of the project.

Free Haul Distance (FHD):   Free haul distance is known as the "distance soil is moved" without additional compensation. This distance is agreed upon prior to construction.
Free haul distance can be explained using an example.

Practice Problem 1.15:   Free haul distance for a cut and fill project is given to be 100 yds. Find the free haul areas of the mass diagram shown.
Point A to B = Cut volume = 600 cy
Point B to C = Fill volume = 600 cy
Point C to D = Fill volume = 350 cy
Point D to E = Cut volume = 500 cy

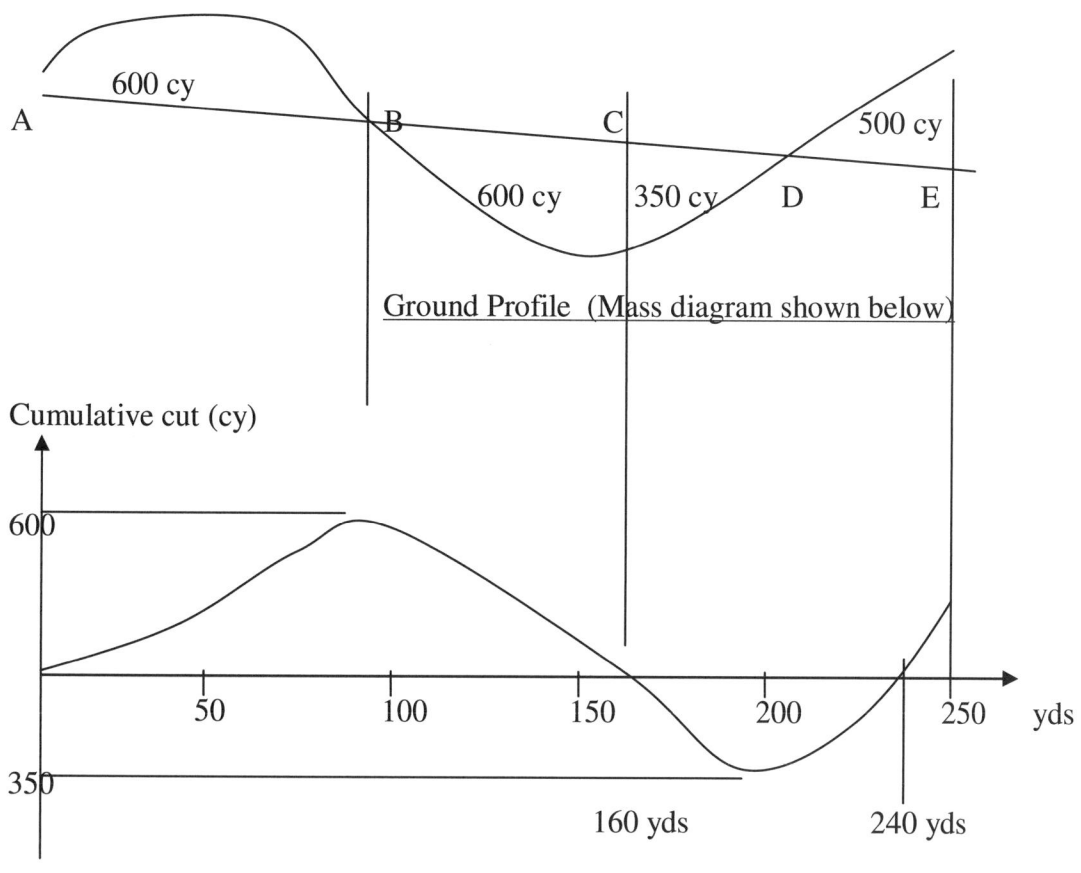

Solution:
Free haul distance is given to be 100 yds. Point A to C all cut material can be used for the fill. The distance between points A to C is 160 yds. This is greater than the free haul distance.
Draw a horizontal line (GH) to a distance of 100 yds as shown below.

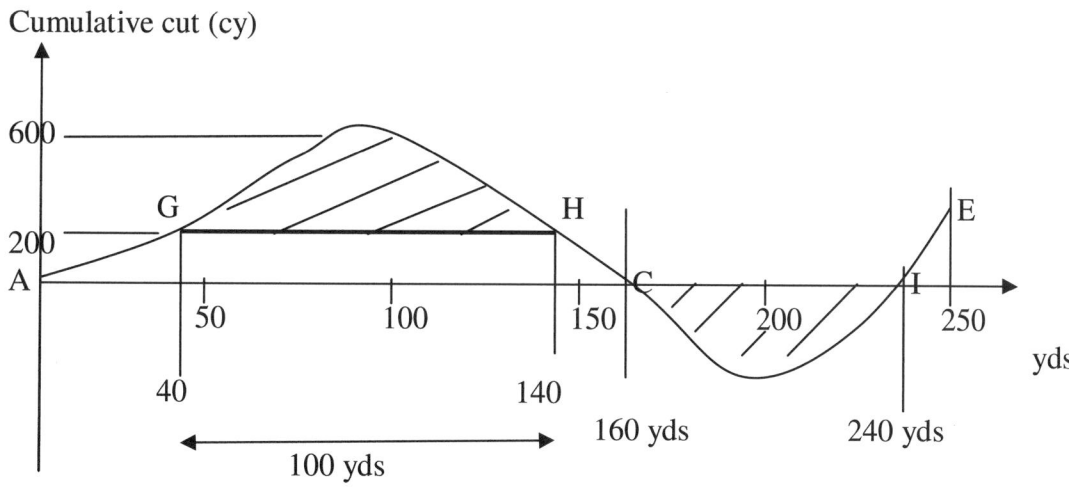

169

Find the coordinates of point G and H.
Point G = Cumulative cut = 200 cy, station = 40
Point H = Cumulative cut = 200 cy, station = 140
Between points G and H, all the cut material has been used for fill purposes. Hence, the contractor cannot charge additional funds for hauling of material in this section of the road. (Point G to H is the free haul distance).

Point A to G = Not within the free haul distance. Additional cost will incur for hauling material.
Point H to C = Not within the free haul distance. Additional cost will incur for hauling material.
Point C to I = Distance is 80 yds   (240 – 160).
This is less than the free haul distance. Hence, no additional cost will incur for points C to I.
Cut material from I to E is waste.

Overhaul: When soil is moved beyond the free haul distance, it is known as overhaul. The contractor required to be compensated for overhaul.

Limit of Profitable Haul (LPH):   Soil can be profitable moved from point A to point B. If the distance between two points is larger than the LPH, then it is more profitable to obtain soil from an outside source.

Borrow: Volume of soil obtained from an outside source.

Waste: Volume of soil that has to be discarded.

1.5   Hauling:

Soil that is cut has to be hauled to fill areas. Small distances can be hauled using dozers. Typically, distances closer to mile is hauled using scrapers. Scrapers may not be economical for anything beyond one mile. In such situations, trucks are used. It is the judgment of the site super to decide what machines to be used for a given project.

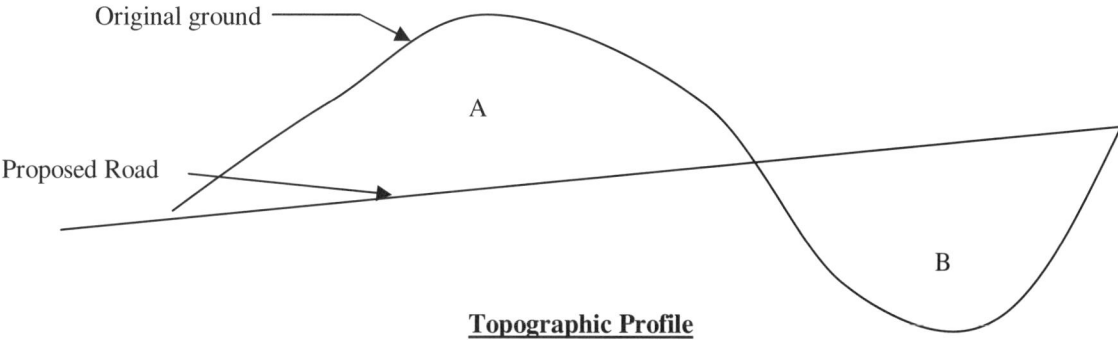

Topographic Profile

Volume A has to be cut and volume B has to be filled. Small haul distances can be one using dozers.

STEP 1:   Cut the volume of soil A1 and fill volume B1. Hauling can be done using dozers since the distance is short.

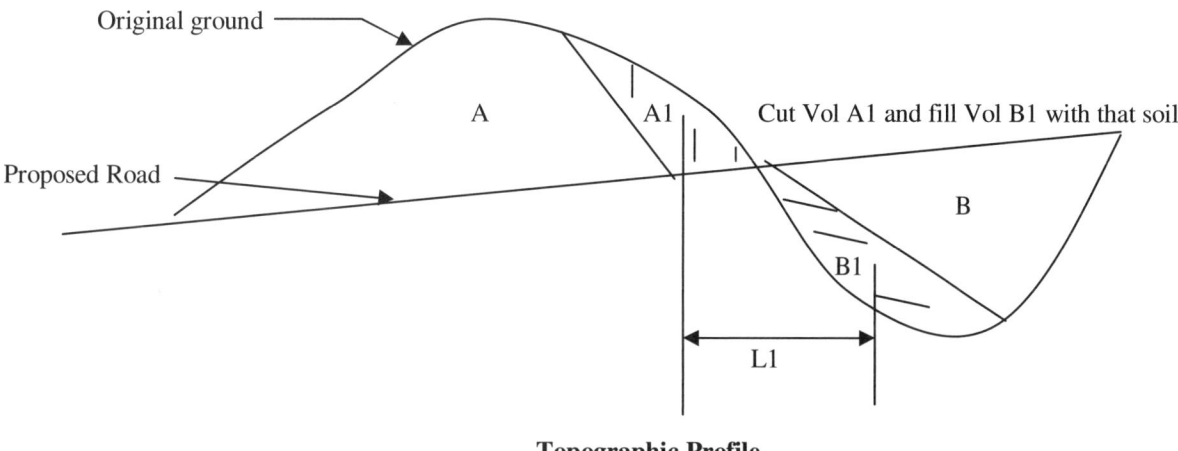

Topographic Profile

L1 is the average transportation distance.
Cut Vol A1 and fill Vol B1 with that soil

L1 = Average transportation distance = Distance from center of gravity of A1 to center of gravity of B1.
At the beginning of a cut and fill operation soil can be moved with dozers. The distance from cut site to fill site would be small.

STEP 2:   Cut a volume of soil A2 and fill volume B2 with the same soil. (Soil at A2 goes to B2).

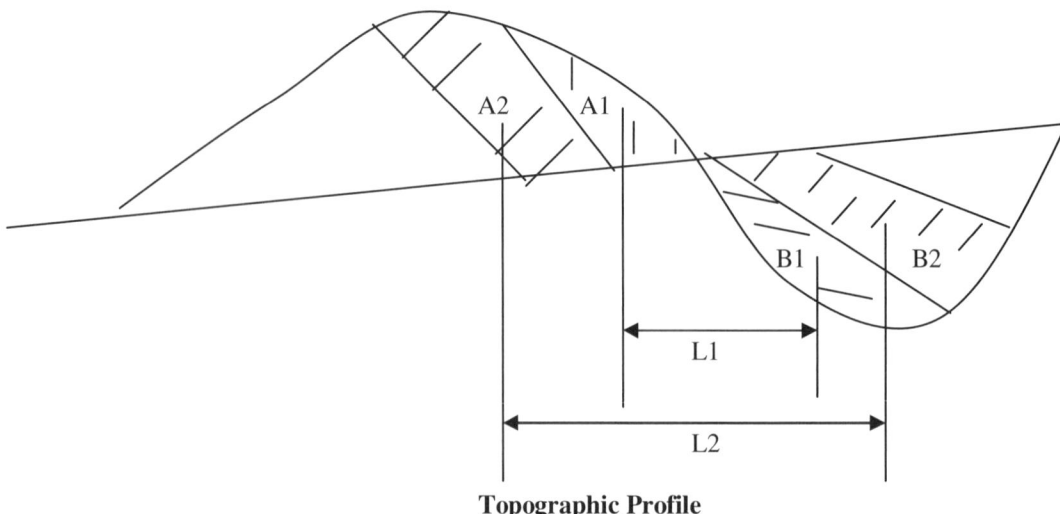

Topographic Profile

Cut volume A2 and fill B2 with that soil.
L2 is the average transportation distance from A2 to B2.
One can see soil has to be transported longer distances. $L2 > L1$
Depending upon the site conditions it may not be efficient to use dozers to move soil. Hence, scrapers can be utilized.

STEP 3:   Cut a volume of soil at A3 and fill volume B3.

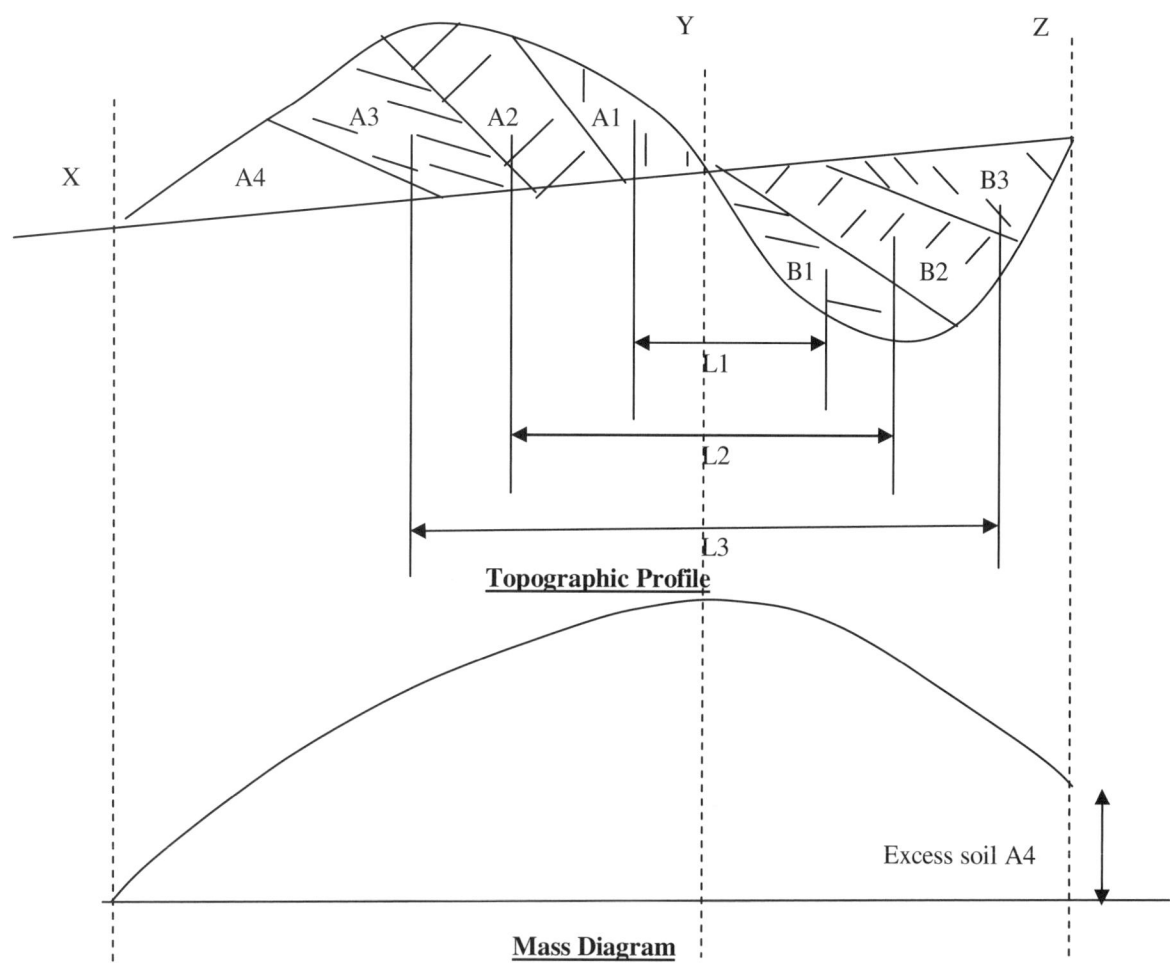

Cutting occurs from X to Y. Hence cutting cumulative volume increases until Y. After Y, fill begins.
Cumulative cut volume increases from point X to Y. Fill starts at point Y. Hence, mass diagram will start to bend down. Since there is more cut in this section, there is excess soil at the end that needs to be trucked away.

Moving soil volume A3 to B3 involves transportation of soil for much longer distances. In such situations, trucks may be the most efficient method.

Volume of soil A4 is the surplus. This soil may be cut and transported out of the site.

Most Efficient Method to Conduct a Cut and Fill Operation: Cutting of soil is mostly done using dozers. Some time backhoes may be needed for cutting of soil due to steep slopes or loose soil situations where dozers are unable to access the location. Moving of soil at shorter distances can be done using dozers efficiently. Dozers become increasingly inefficient when the distance increase. In such situations, scrapers are used to scrape and move soil. One has to understand rental cost of a scraper may be twice as much as a dozer. Trucks are needed for much longer distances. In many situations, trucks may have to use local roads that could have significant traffic. Hence it is advisable to move the soil early in the morning before the rush hour and then after the rush hour. The foreman of the site has to plan his work in a most efficient manner.

Contour Lines: Contour lines represent elevations.

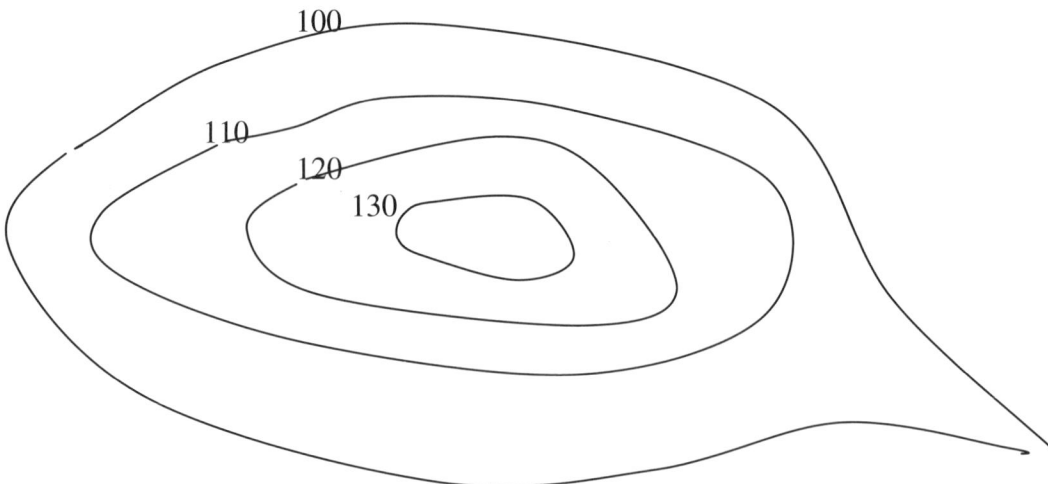

If you look at the above figure, contour elevation increases from 100 to 130. This represents a hill. On the other hand, below figure represents a lake or a crater.

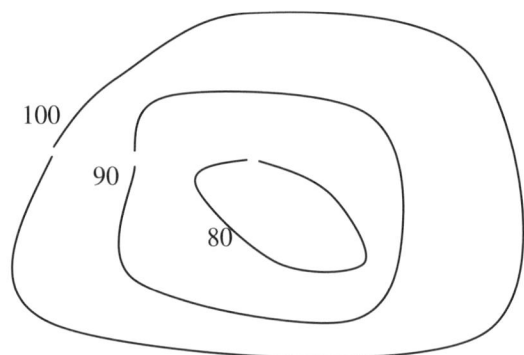

Cut and Fill Computations Using Contour Lines: Cut and fill can be computed using contour lines. Example below shows how to compute cut and fill volumes using contour lines.

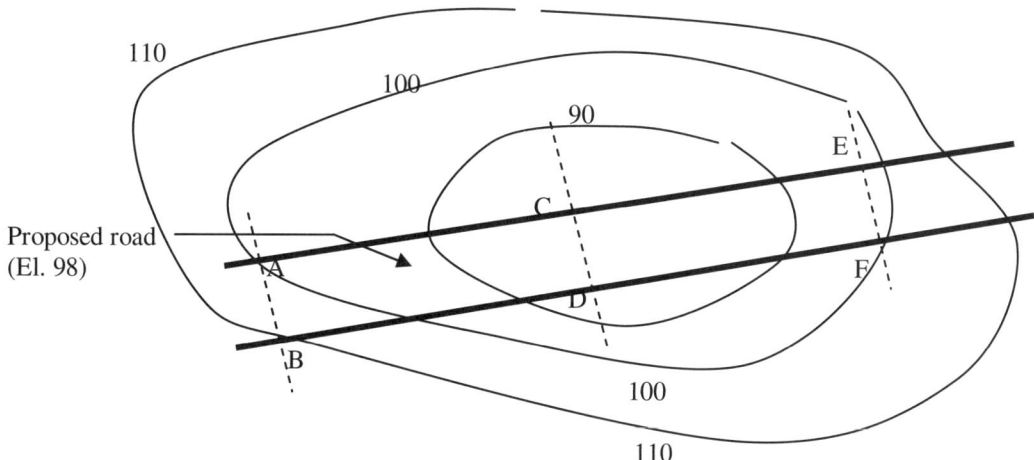

The width of the road is 30 ft and BD = 500 ft and DF = 500 ft. Elevation of the proposed road is 98 ft.
Find the following;
    A)   Cross sectional areas at sections AB, CD and EF.
    B)   Find the cut and fill volumes from B to F.

Solution:

STEP 1: Find the cross sectional area at section AB.
Elevation at point A = 100   (See the contour 100)
Elevation at point B = 110
Proposed road elevation = 98 ft

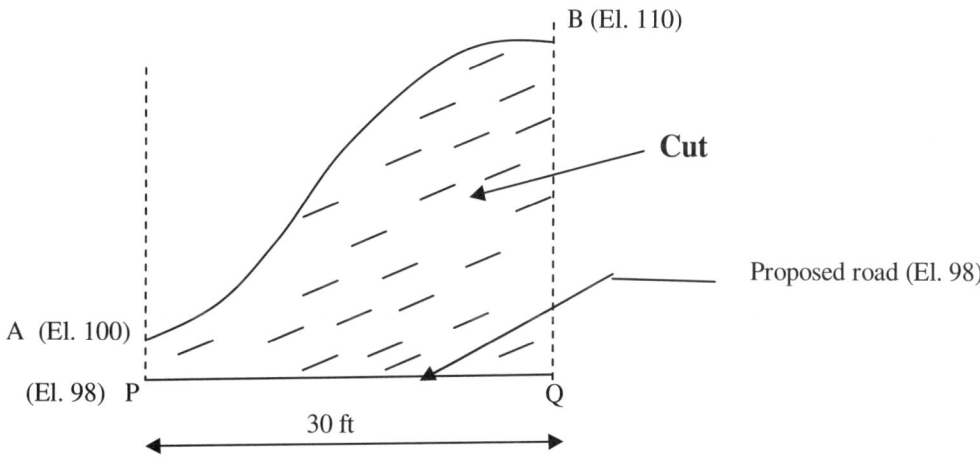

Points P and Q are on the proposed road. Hence elevation of both P and Q is 98.0
AP = 2;   BQ = 12
              Area of the trapezoid (APQB) = (2 + 12)/2 x 30 = 210 sq. ft

STEP 2:   Find the cross sectional area at section CD.
Elevation at point C = 85   (Elevation at C can be <u>approximated</u> to 85 ft. Both points C and D are inside the contour 90).
Elevation at point D = 87   (Point D is closer to 90 ft contour. Hence, it should be around 87).
Proposed road elevation = 98 ft

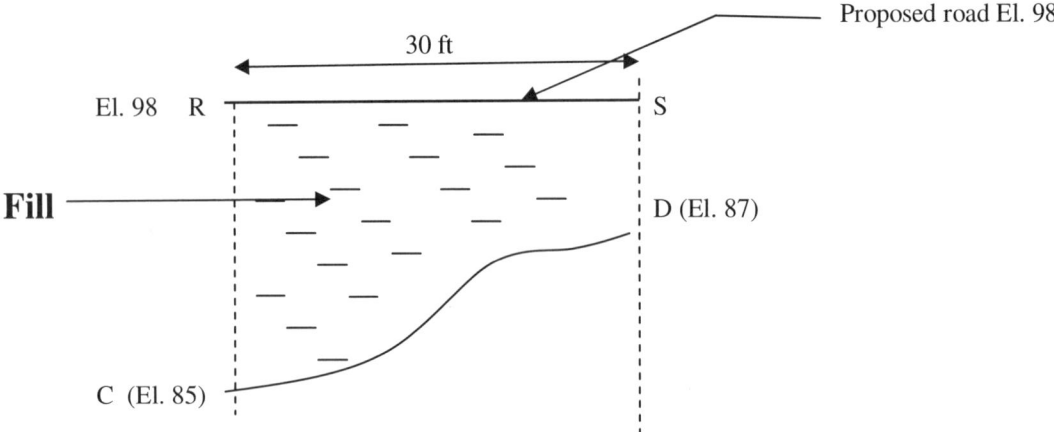

Assume points R and S to be on proposed road.
RC = 13 ft,   SD = 11 ft
Area of trapezoid (RCDS) = (13 + 11)/2 x 30 = 360 sq. ft

Cut at station AB = 210 sq. ft   (Found in step 1)
Fill at station AB = 0 sq. ft

Cut at station CD = 0 sq. ft
Fill at station CD = 360 sq. ft

Average cut between two stations = (210 + 0)/2 x 500 cu. Ft = 1,944 CY
Average fill between two stations = (0 + 360)/2 x 500 cu. Ft = 3,333 CY

STEP 3: Find the cross sectional area at section EF.
Elevation at point E = 98 (approximately)
Elevation at point F = 100
Proposed road elevation = 98 ft

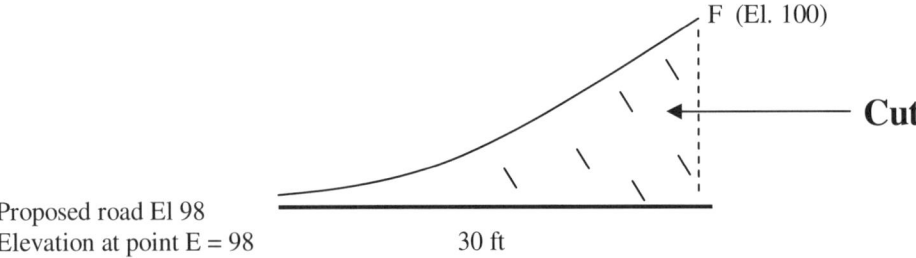

There is no fill at this station.
Cut area can be calculated by considering an approximate triangle.

Cut area = 2 x 30/2 = 30 sq. ft
Fill area = 0

Average fill volume between stations CD and EF = (360 + 0)/2 x 500 cu. Ft = 3,333 CY
Average cut volume between stations CD and EF = (0 + 30)/2 x 500 cu. Ft = 278 CY

Practice problems:

1)   Three proposed roads are shown. What's the best route to build a road at elevation 90,
      a) Considering cut and fill costs only?
      b) Considering drainage infrastructure build up costs only
      c) Considering retaining wall construction costs only

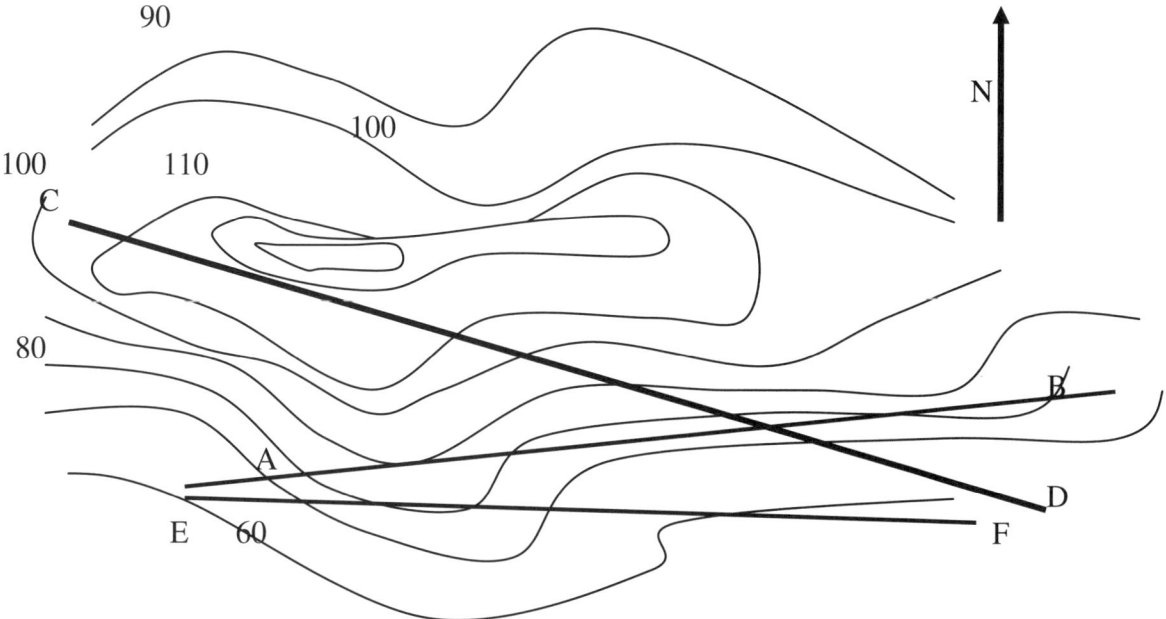

Cut and Fill Costs:
AB-   Proposed road elevation is at 90 ft. AB passes mostly thru contours 80 and 70. When the proposed road passes thru 80 and 70 contours, fill is needed to bring it to 90 ft. Proposed route requires large amount of fill that need to be brought in from outside.
EF – Proposed road EF goes mostly thru 60 and 70.   EF route needs more fill than AB route.
CD – CD route has plenty of cut (North Western end) while southeast requires fill. It can be argued that cut from North Western end to be utilized for the fill in southeast end of the road. Since on site cut material could be used, cost could be cheaper.

Drainage Costs:
As per contours given, hills to the north would drain to the proposed routes AB and EF. Drainage to route EF would be higher than route AB, hence drainage costs for the route EF would be higher than AB. On the other hand, CD is at high grounds. Hence, less drainage can be expected. Drainage infrastructure build up costs would be less for CD.

Retaining Wall Costs:
Northwestern end of route CD goes thru contour 110. Just north of the road CD, contours 120 and 130 are located. Large retaining wall is needed in this section. Contours for the most part are tightly packed along CD. This indicates steep slopes and costly and high retaining walls. Retaining wall heights for proposed routes AB and EF would be moderate compared to CD.

2.0 Estimating

Introduction: In USA, cost estimating is done as per Master format created by Construction Specifications Institute (CSI). Due to this reason, Master format is also known as CSI format. Master format is a list of titles that has specific numbers. First two numbers describe the division. There are 16 major divisions. These divisions are shown below. Complete list of items can be obtained by visiting the CSI website.

For example,   03 indicates concrete.
              03 20 indicates concrete reinforcing

03 20 to 03 29 is allocated for concrete reinforcing.

03 21 16 indicates Epoxy coated reinforced steel.

Division 00 – Procurement and Contracting Requirements: This division deals with activities related to procurement of contracts. Pre bid meetings, site surveys, environmental impact studies, geophysical data and various other activities that need to be conducted prior to selecting a contractor is provided in this division.

Division 01 – General Requirements: This section deals with quality control, regulatory requirements, temporary facilities, product delivery requirements, closeout procedures, etc.

Division 02 – Existing Conditions: This division deals with maintenance of existing facilities during construction, site assessments, subsurface investigations, site remediation etc.

Division 03 – Concrete: Some of the sub items are Concrete forms, reinforcements, heavyweight concreting, pre-cast concrete and architectural concrete.

Division 04 – Masonry: Some of the sub items are grouting, mortar, maintenance of masonry and masonry cleaning.

Division 05 – Metals: Some of the sub items are structural steel, joist framing, steel stairs and roof decking.

Division 06 – Wood, Plastics, and Composites: Carpentry items, wood treatment, finished carpentry.

Division 07 – Thermal and Moisture Protection: Roofs, waterproofing, dampproofing, siding, membranes etc.

Division 08 – Openings: Doors and windows.

Divisions 09 – Finishes: Plastering, tiling, ceiling, flooring, wall finishes, painting and coating

Division 10 – Specialties: Fireplaces, stoves, telephones, partitions, toilet accessories, emergency exits

Division 11 – Equipment: Vehicle washing equipment, Parking meters, valves, dock lifts etc.

Division 12 – Furnishings: Arts, paintings, statues, window blinds, office accessories, bedroom furnishings, furniture

Division 13 – Special Construction: Swimming pools, ice rinks, basketball courts

Division 14 – Conveying Equipment: Elevators, scaffolding, lifts, sidewalk lifts, chutes

Division 15 – Mechanical:

Division 16 – Electrical

2.1   Quantity Takeoff: The first step in cost estimating is to conduct a quantity take off using design drawings. Quantity takeoff can be explained easily using examples. You are required to obtain quantities using design drawings.

Practice Problem 2.1:   Find the following quantities using the design drawing given.
a)   Volume of soil to be excavated
b)   Concrete volume for footings
c)   Area of formwork required for footings

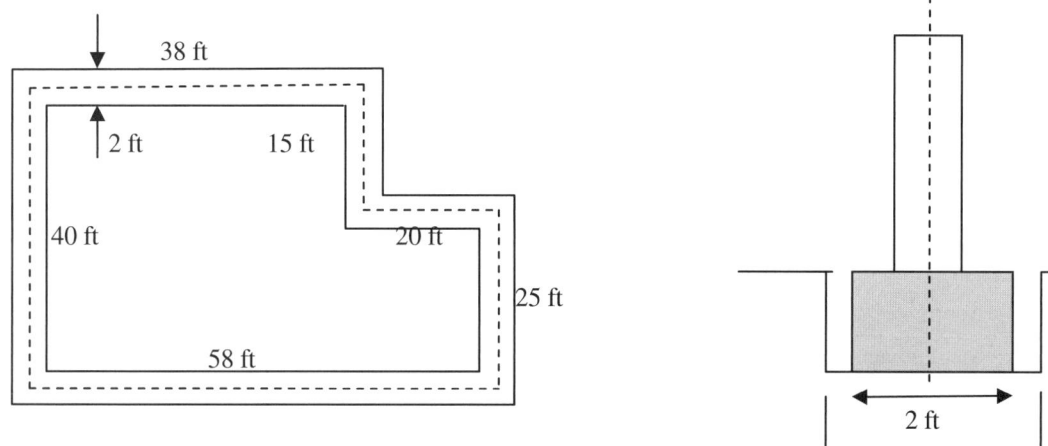

Footing Plan (Lengths are given along the centerline of the footing)
Thickness of the footing is 2 ft.

Solution: Note: When you are measuring the distances you need to measure along the centerline. Other method is In to In and Out to Out method. In this method, one side is measured In to In while perpendicular side is measured out to Out.

STEP 1)   Volume of soil to be excavated = (3 x 3) x length of the footing
Length of the footing = 38 + 15 + 20 + 25 + 58 + 40 = 196 ft
Note: If distances are not given along the centerline of the footing, you have to compute the lengths. In some cases, lengths are given along the outer perimeter.
Volume of soil to be excavated = (3 x 3) x 196 = 1,764 cu. ft = 65.3 cu. yds   (1 cu. yd = 27 cu. ft)

STEP 2)   Concrete volume of footings = 2 x 3 x 196 = 1,176 cu. ft = 43.6 cu. yds

STEP 3)   Area of formwork required for footings:

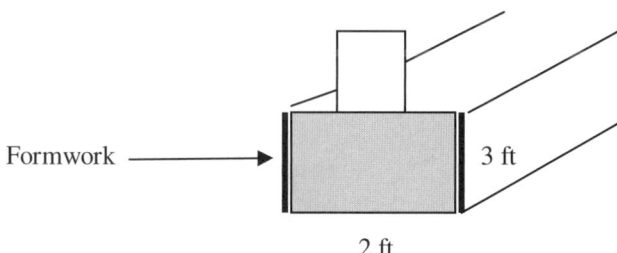

Formwork has to be erected on either side of the footing.
Formwork area for one side of the footing = (3 x 196) sq. ft = 588 sq. ft
Formwork area for both sides of the footing = 2 x 588 sq. ft = 1,176 sq. ft

Practice Problem 2.2:   Find the area of formwork required for the footing shown.

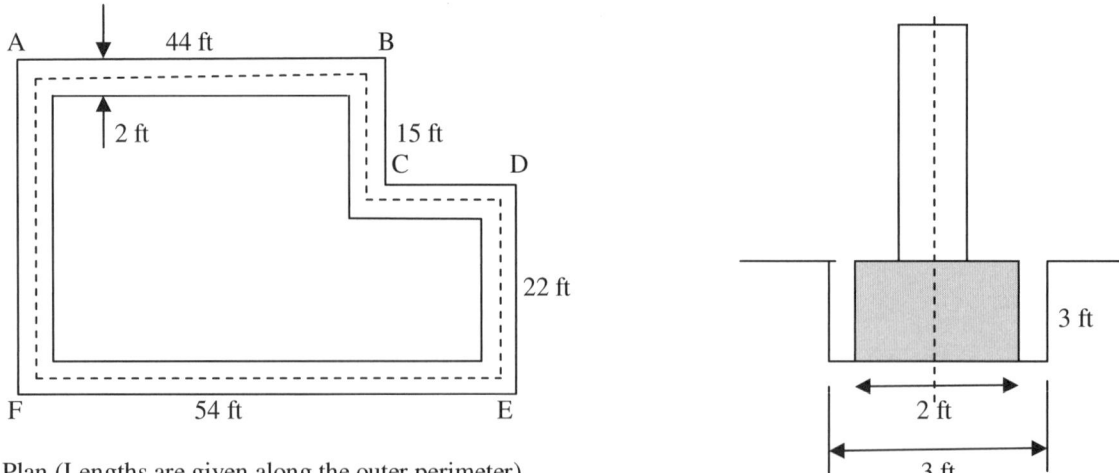

Footing Plan (Lengths are given along the outer perimeter)

Solution: Find the length of footing along the centerline:

In to In and Out to Out method:

Horizontal sides are measured In to In. Vertical distances are measured out to out.

Distance along AB = 40 ft   (44 - 4) (In to In) (measured wall to wall from inside the house)
Distance along BC = 15   (Out to out) (measured wall to wall from outside the house)
Distance along CD = 10 ft   (In to In) (measured wall to wall from inside the house)
Distance along DE = 22 ft   (Out to out) (measured wall to wall from outside the house)
Distance along EF = 50 ft   (In to In) (measured wall to wall from inside the house)
Distance along AF = 37 ft   (Out to out) (measured wall to wall from outside the house)
Total = 174 ft
This can be double-checked using centerline method.
Total lengths of footings along the centerline = 42 + 15 + 10 + 20 + 52 + 35 = 174 ft
(Note: lengths in this example has no connection to the lengths in the previous example)
Area of formwork per side = 3 x 174 = 522 sq. ft
Area of formwork for both sides = 1,044 sq. ft

Practice Problem 2.3:   Find the quantities for following items for the 200 ft long retaining wall shown.
1)   Excavation volume
2)   Concrete volume
3)   Gravel volume
4)   Backfill volume

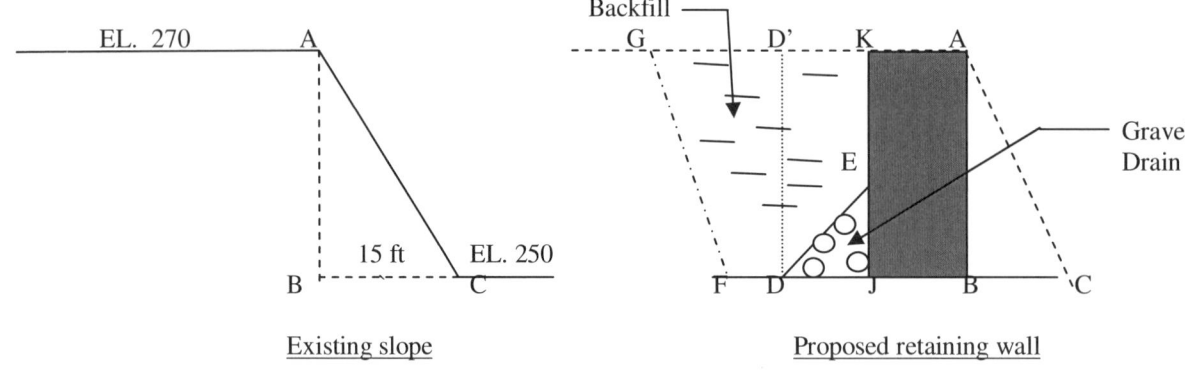

Existing slope   Proposed retaining wall

Following distances are given:
BC = 15 ft,   JB = 10 ft;   DJ = 3 ft;   EJ = 2.5 ft   FD = 3 ft;   GA = 20 ft

Construction Procedure:
STEP 1)   Excavate and remove soil volume GFCA
STEP 2)   Construct the retaining wall KAJB
STEP 3)   Construct the gravel drain EDJ
STEP 4)   Backfill   GKEDF

Quantity Takeoff:
STEP 1)   Excavation volume = Area GFCA x 200   (200 ft is the length)
Area of GFCA = (GA + FC)/2 x Height KJ
GA is given to be 20 ft.
FC = BC + FB = 15 + (10 + 3 + 3) = 31 ft
Area of GFCA = (GA + FC)/2 x Height KJ = (20 + 31)/2 x (EL 270 - El 250)
= (20 + 31)/2 x 20 = 510
Excavation volume = 510 x 200 cu. ft = 102,000 cu. ft = 3,778 cu. yds

STEP 2)   Concrete volume for the retaining wall = Area KAJB x 200 = (20 x 10) x 200
                 = 40,000 cu. ft = 1,481 cu.yds

STEP 3)   Volume of gravel required = Area EDJ x 200 = (3 x 2.5)/2 x 200 = 750 cu. ft = 28 cu. yds

STEP 4)   Backfill Volume = Area GKEDF x 200
Area GKEDF can be broken down to GD'DF and D'KED.
Area GD'DF = (FD + GD')/2 x D'D = (7 + 3)/2 x 20 = 100
Area D'KED = (D'D + EK)/2 x D'K = (20 + 17.5)/2 x 3 = 56.3
Area GKEDF = 100 + 56.3 = 156.3
Backfill volume = 156.3 x 200 = 31,260 cu. ft = 1,158 cu. yds

Masonry: Quantity takeoff for masonry work is considered.

Practice Problem 2.4:   Find the mortar volume required per brick in the wall shown. Bricks are 15" x 4" x 4". Mortar thickness is 1 inches.

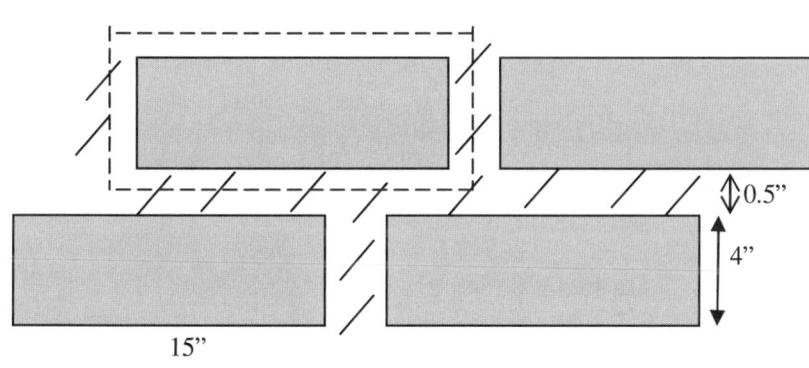
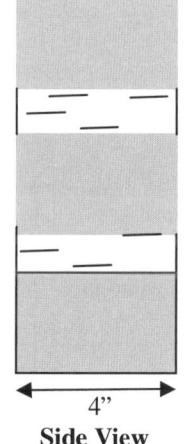

Elevation

Side View

Solution: Length of a brick with the mortar = 15 + 1/2 + 1/2 = 16 in
Height of a brick with the mortar =   4 + 1/2 + 1/2 = 5 in
Total volume of a brick with mortar = 16 x 5 x 4 = 320 cu. inches
Volume of the brick without mortar = 15 x 4 x 4 = 240 cu. inches
Volume of mortar per brick = 80 cu. inches

Practice Problem 2.5:   100 ft long, 4 in wide and 11 ft high wall is constructed using above shown brick (15" x 4" x 4")
and 0.5" mortar. Find the following:
a)   Number of bricks required
b)   Volume of mortar required
Solution:
Total volume of the wall = (100 x 12) x (11 x 12) x 4 in = 633,600 cu. inches

Total volume of a brick with mortar = 16 x 5 x 4 = 320 cu. inches   (see the previous example)
Number of bricks required = 633,600/320 = 1,980 bricks
Note: To obtain the number of bricks required for a wall, use the volume of a brick with the mortar. If you use bare volume of the brick (in this case 240 cu. in), you would get a wrong answer.

Volume of brick alone = 15 x 4 x 4 = 240 cu. in
Mortar volume in each brick = 320 - 240 = 80 cu. inches
Mortar volume = Number of bricks x Mortar vol. per brick = 1980 x 80 = 158,400 cu. in
Your answers can be checked.
Total volume of the wall = Volume of bricks + volume of mortar
Volume of bricks only = 1980 x 240 = 475,200 cu. in
Volume of bricks + Volume of mortar = 475,200 + 158,400 = 633,600 cu. in
This is equal to the volume of the wall.

Standard Bricks: Bricks come in various sizes. Bricks known as standard bricks are 2 ¼ x 3 ¾ x 8 inches.

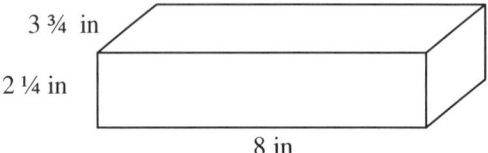

3 ¾ in

2 ¼ in

8 in

Practice Problem 2.6:   A wall is built using standard bricks. The wall is one brick thick. How many bricks are required for 100 sq. ft of the wall. Assume mortar is ¼ in thick.
Solution:
Length of one brick with the mortar = 8 +1/8 + 1/8 = 8 ¼ in
Height of one brick with mortar = 2 ¼ + 1/8 + 1/8 = 2 ½ in
Area of one brick with mortar = (8 ¼) x (2 ½) = 8.25 x 2.5 = 20.625 sq. in
Bricks in 100 sq. ft of wall = (100 x144)/20.625 = 698
Practice Problem 2.6:   Rectangular building has a length of 120 ft and width 80 ft. Building walls are 9 ft high. There are total of 180 sq. ft of openings for windows and doors. Walls are built of standard bricks and are of one brick thick. Find the number of bricks and volume of mortar. Standard bricks are 8 in x 2 ¼ in x 3 ¾ in. Assume mortar thickness to be 0.5 in.

Solution:

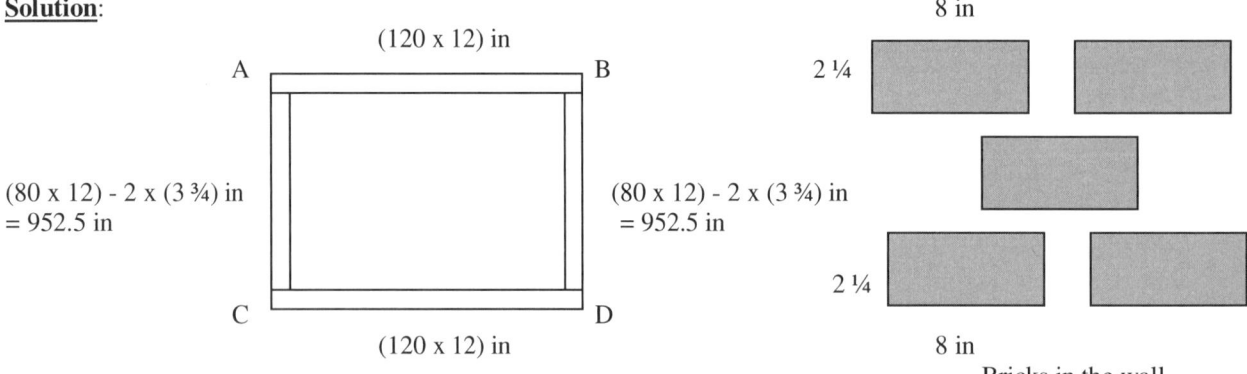

(120 x 12) in

A   B

(80 x 12) - 2 x (3 ¾) in
= 952.5 in

(80 x 12) - 2 x (3 ¾) in
= 952.5 in

C   D

(120 x 12) in

8 in

2 ¼

2 ¼

8 in
Bricks in the wall

Note: The brick at the edge need to be deducted to avoid double counting.

STEP 1: Find the area of brick walls:
Area of side AB = (120 x 12) x height = (120 x12) x (9 x 12) = 155,520 sq. in
Area of side AC = width x height = 952.5 x (9 x 12) = 102,870 sq. in
Total area of four sides = 2 x (155,520 + 102,870) = 516,780 sq. in
Area of doors and windows = 180 sq. ft = 180 x 144 = 25,920 sq. in
Area of walls after reducing for openings = 516,780 - 25,920 = 490,860 sq. in
Effective brick area including the mortar thickness = (8 + 0.5) x (2.25 + 0.5) = 23.375 sq. in

STEP 2:   Number of bricks = 490,860/23.375 = 20,999 bricks

STEP 3:   Find the mortar volume:

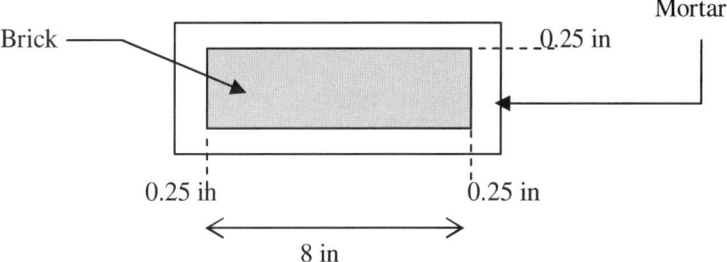

Area of mortar per brick = Total area with mortar - brick area = (8.5 x 2.75) - (8 x 2.25) = 5.375 sq. in
Wall is one brick thick. The thickness of the brick is 3.75 in.
Volume of mortar per brick = 5.375 x 3.75 = 20.156 cu. in
Number of bricks = 20,999   (See step 2)
Volume of mortar required = 20,999 x 20.156 cu. in = 423,255 cu. in = 245 cu. ft = 9.07 cu. yds

Note to candidates: Each question would have four answers. Depending upon the answers given in the exam one may opt to use a quick and dirty analysis. For an instance, area of the wall can be obtained as follows quickly, without paying attention to edges.

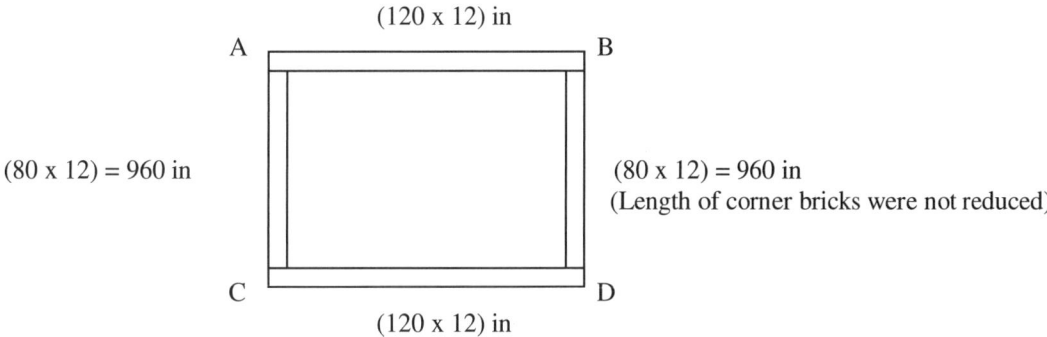

STEP 1:   Find the area of brick walls:
Area of side AB = (120 x 12) x height = (120 x12) x (9 x 12) = 155,520 sq. in
Area of side AC = 960 x (9 x 12) = 103,680 sq. in
Total area of four sides = 2 x (155,520 + 103,680)   = 518,400 sq. in
Area of doors and windows = 180 sq. ft = 25,920 sq. in
Area of walls after reducing for openings = 518,400 - 25,920 = 492,480 sq. in
Effective brick area including the mortar thickness = (8 + 0.5) x (2.25 + 0.5) = 23.375 sq. in

STEP 2:   Number of bricks = 492,480/23.375 = 21,069 bricks
As you could see, analysis that is more precise gave 20,999 bricks while quick and dirty analysis gave 21,069 bricks.

Quantity Takeoff (Steel):   Steel structures contain W - sections, S - sections, L - shapes, Channels, Angles, Hollow tubular sections and hollow rectangular sections.

W Shapes: **(Wide Flange)**

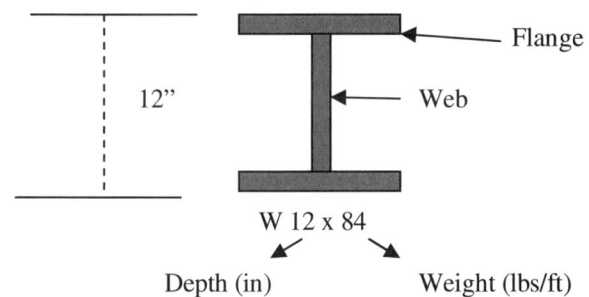

Above 12 indicates the approximate depth. Above 84 indicates weight of the section in lbs per foot.

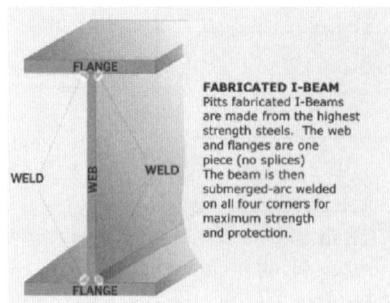

Channels: **(American Standard Channel)**

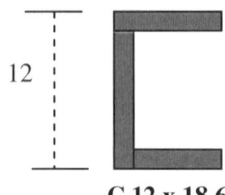

C 12 x 18.6

Above 12 indicates the approximate depth. Above 18.6 indicates weight of the channel section in lbs per foot.

S - Sections: S sections are similar to W - sections. They are known as American Standard Steel. W sections have a wider flange than S sections.

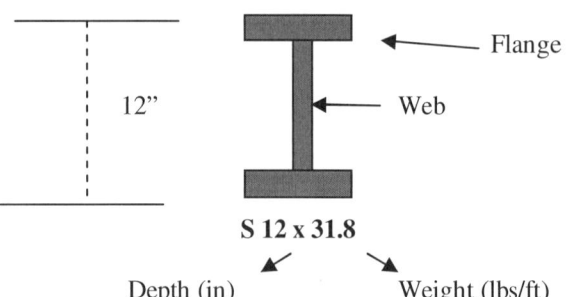

S 12 x 31.8

Depth (in)   Weight (lbs/ft)

M - Sections: M - Sections are known as "Miscellaneous Beam". These beams are manufactured by various steel manufacturers with varying thicknesses and depths.

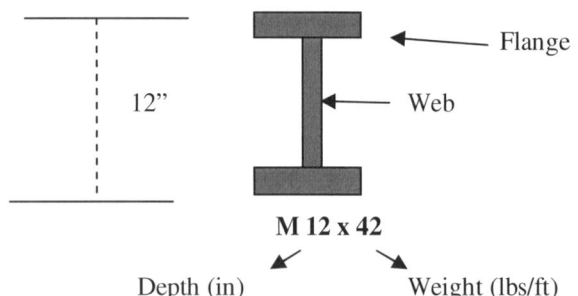

M 12 x 42

Depth (in)   Weight (lbs/ft)

MC Sections: MC stands for "Miscellaneous Channel". These channels are produced by various manufacturers with varying thicknesses and depths.

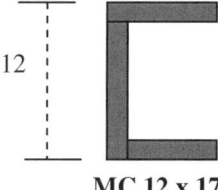

MC 12 x 17

Above 12 indicates the approximate depth. Above 17 indicates weight of the channel section in lbs per foot.

L - Angles: Angles are represented with "L". Angles may have equal or unequal legs.

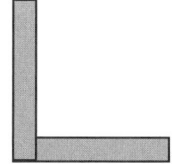

L 9 x 4 x 5/8

Above 9 indicates the length of one leg in inches and 4 indicates the length of the other leg in inches and 5/8 represents the thickness of the section. Weight of the L section has to be obtained from steel tables. Steel angles are shown below.

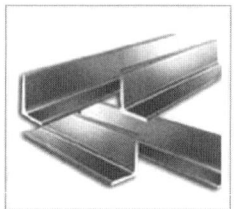

HP - Piles (Or simply H - Piles):   HP sections are used for piles.

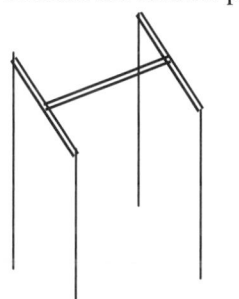

HP 12 x 72

(12 is the depth and 72 is the weight of the pile per linear foot given in lbs.

WT Sections: MT sections are cut from W (Wide flange) sections. Typically, a W section is obtained and one flange is cut off to obtain a T shape.

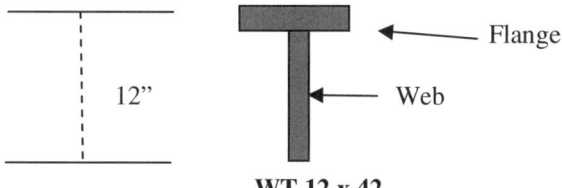

WT 12 x 42

(Above 12 is the depth and 42 is the weight per foot in lbs)

MT Sections: M section is obtained and one flange is removed to obtain a MT section. Similar to WT sections.

ST Sections: S section is obtained and one flange is removed to obtain a ST section. Similar to WT sections.

Practice Problem 2.7:   Find the weight of steel in the building shown.

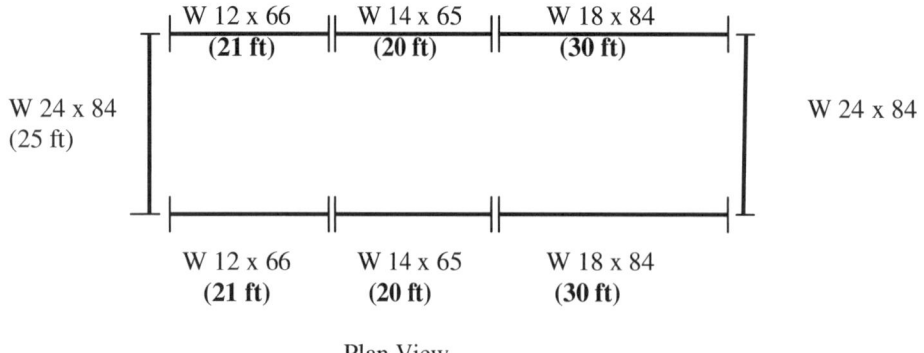

Plan View

STEP 1:   Find the weight of each beam:
W 12 x 66 (21 ft):   Weight = 21 x 66 lbs = 1,386 lbs
W 14 x 65 (20 ft)   Weight = 20 x 65 lbs = 1,300 lbs
W 18 x 84 (30 ft)   Weight = 30 x 84 lbs = 2,520 lbs
Subtotal = 5,206 lbs
Multiply by 2 to get the weight of other side. (This is possible since the structure is symmetrical).
Subtotal = 10,412 lbs

Two side beams:
W 24 x 84 (25 ft)   Weight = 25 x 84 lbs = 2,100 lbs
Subtotal = 4,200 lbs
Total weight of beams = 10,412 + 4,200 = 14,612 lbs = 7.306 tons

Quantity Takeoff - Reinforcement Bars (Rebars):   Concrete itself do not have tensile strength. Tensile strength for concrete is provided by reinforcing bars or simply known as rebars. Below table provide rebar sizes and weight per foot.

Bar No:	Nominal diameter (in)	Nominal diameter (mm)	Nominal Weight (lb/ft)
3	0.375 (3/8)	9.5	0.376
4	0.500 (4/8)	12.7	0.668
5	0.625 (5/8)	15.9	1.043
6	0.750 (6/8)	19.1	1.502
7	0.875 (7/8)	22.2	2.044
8	1.000	25.4	2.670
9	1.128	28.7	3.400
10	1.270	32.3	4.303
11	1.410	35.8	5.313
14	1.693	43	7.650

Practice Problem 2.8:   Construction site needs 2,000 ft of #3 rebars and 150 ft of #7 rebars. Find the total weight of rebars.

Solution: #3 rebars (0.376 lbs per foot) -   2000 x 0.376 = 752 lbs
                       #7 rebars (**2.044** lbs per foot) -   150 x 2.044 = **306.6**
                       Total weight = 1,058.6 lbs

Practice problem 2.9:   60 ft long 7.5 ft high wall needs rebars as shown. Find the total rebars needed in tons.

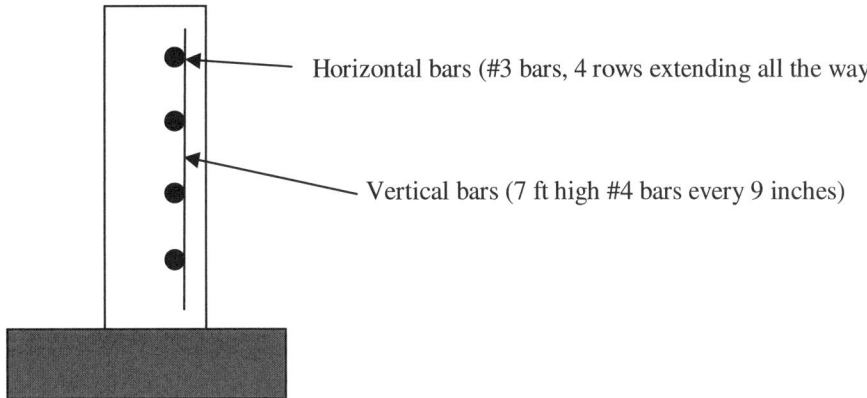

Solution:

Horizontal bars: The wall is 60 ft long. Four rows of horizontal bars needed as shown in the drawing. Weight of #3 bars is 0.376 lbs per foot.
        4 x 60 x 0.376 = 90.24 lbs

Vertical bars: The wall is 60 ft long. That is 720 inches. Vertical bars are placed every 9 inches.
Number of vertical bars = 720/9 + 1= 81
Each vertical bar is 7 ft long.
Total length of vertical bars = 7 x 81 = 567 ft
Weight of 567 ft of #4 bars = 567 x 0.668 = 378.8 lbs
Total weight of rebars = 90.24 + 378.8 = 469 lbs = 0.234 tons

Practice Problem 2.10:   Find the weight of steel rebars in the drilled shaft shown. Drilled shaft is 35 ft long and ties are attached every 5 ft. There are 8 ties. Diameter of the shaft is 2 ft.

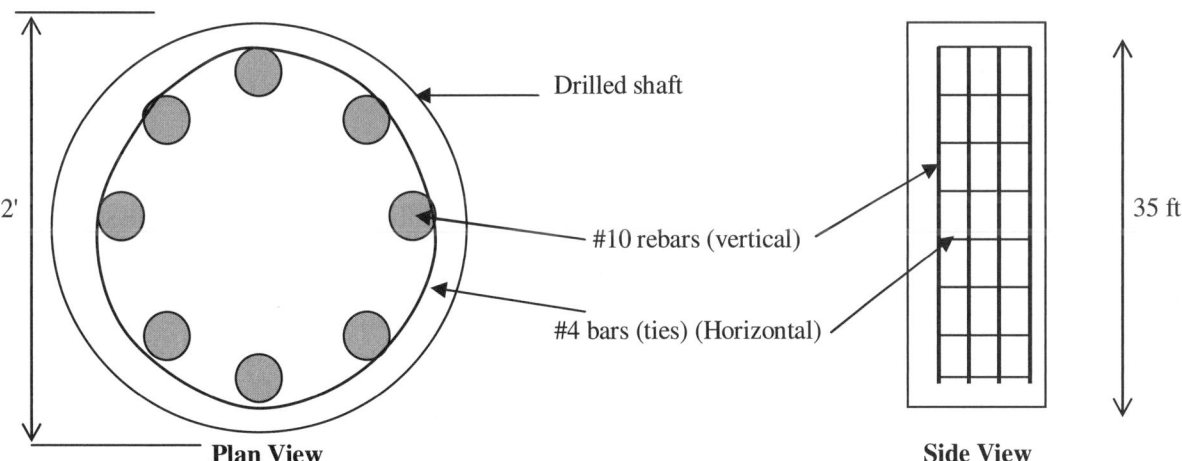

Solution:

STEP 1:   Length of #10 vertical bars = 35 ft
                Number of vertical bars = 8
                Total length of vertical bars = 35 x 8 = 280 ft
                Weight of #10 vertical bars = 4.303 lbs/ft
                Weight of vertical bars = 4.303 x 280 = 1,205 lbs

STEP 2:   Length of ties = Circumference of the drilled shaft (approximately)
Length of ties = π x Diameter = π x 2 = 6.283 ft
Number of ties = 8
Total length of ties = 8 x 6.283 = 50.3 ft
Weight of ties (#4 bars) = 0.668 lbs/ft
Total weight of ties = 0.668 x 50.3 = 33.6 lbs
Total weight of rebars = 1,205 + 33.6 = 1,238.6 lbs

2.2 Cost Estimating:

Cost estimating is a very important function in any project.
Basic steps involved in cost estimating are;

- Quantity takeoff (Which was covered in the previous chapter)
- Assess the cost of labor, equipment and material
- Assess overhead and profits

The estimator should take into account of the location, time of the year and any other factors that could impact the cost. Cost of a project during winter could be higher than the summer. Construction project on top of a hill or middle of a major city could also be high due to efficiency, traffic and various other factors.

The estimator needs to pay attention to complexity of a project. For example, construction of a car dealership may be straight forward compared to a waste water plant. Each company has their own specialty. A company that is specialized in building construction may not be able to construct a highway in a cost effective manner. In such situations, it may be profitable to have a subcontractor on board.

Average construction project always start with site clearing. Then the contractor may decide to build temporary roads for truck traffic and construction vehicles. Almost all construction projects will have some concreting. In today's world concrete is the most common construction material followed by steel. Following major subject areas can be seen in an average building project.

1) Site clearing (Includes cutting down trees, removal of debris)
2) Earthwork (Grading)
3) Excavation for footings
4) Pile driving (In some building projects, piles may not be necessary)
5) Construction of footings
6) Construction of walls and columns
7) Construction of slabs
8) Construction of upper floors
9) Plumbing (sewer, water, drainage, fire standpipes)
10) Mechanical and electrical work

Labor:
Crew hour rate is defined as cost per crew hour. Let's assume formwork crew consists of 3 carpenters plus 2 laborers. Let's say carpenters earn $50 per hour while laborers earn $30 per hour.
The crew rate would be (3 x 50 + 3 x 30) = $240 per hour. In other words if the crew cannot work for some delay, the contractor will lose $240 per hour.
Crew production rate is the output per hour by the crew. Output can be increased by increasing the crew. If the contractor adds more carpenters, he may be able to get more formwork done. On the other hand, cost of the crew will also increase.

Practice Problem 2.11: what crew is better?
Crew A: 3 carpenters + 3 laborers (Production 100 sq. ft of formwork per hour)
Crew B: 5 carpenters + 3 laborers (Production 125 sq. ft of formwork per hour)

Carpenter = $60 per hour   Laborer = $30 per hour

Solution:
Crew A - Cost per crew hour = (3 x 60) + (3 x 30) = $270
Crew A - Production = 100 sq. ft per crew hour
Cost per sq. ft = 270/100 = $2.7 per sq. ft of formwork
Crew B - Cost per crew hour = (5 x 60) + (3 x 30) = $390

Crew B - Production = 125 sq. ft per crew hour
Cost per sq. ft = 390/125 = $3.12 per sq. ft of formwork
The contractor has to pay $3.12 for each sq. ft of formwork if he uses crew B. Obviously, crew A is cheaper than crew B. On the other hand, crew B produces 125 sq. ft per hour compared to crew A, who produce only 100 sq. ft per hour. If the project has to be completed sooner, then crew B should be used even though that crew costs more.

Labor Hour (LH):   Examples given by NCEES guidebook uses labor hours (LH). Hence, it is important that you should be familiar with LH. Labor hour is obtained by dividing the crew hour by number of workers.
Practice Problem 2.12:   Concreting crew consists of 3 masons and 2 laborers.
Mason = $70 per hour   Laborer = $30 per hour
Crew production = 10 cu. yds per hour
Find crew hour and labor hour. (LH)

Solution:
Crew hour = (3 x 70) + (2 x 30) = $270
Labor hour is obtained by dividing the cost of crew hour by total number of workers in the crew. In this case, there are total of 5 workers.

Hence cost of labor hour = $270/5 = $54
Crew production is given to be 10 cu. yds per hour.
Production per labor hour is obtained by dividing the production per crew hour by number of workers in that crew.
Production per labor hour = 10/5 = 2 cu. yds per labor hour (LH)

Labor Rates: Workers need to be paid various insurances beyond the base wages. It is important to understand benefits and fringes involved in payment to workers.

Base Pay: Base pay is the starting pay rate for a worker. Base wages are negotiated or agreed upon with the union.

Social Security Tax: All employers and employees have to pay social security tax by national law. Social security tax goes to a collective fund maintained by the federal government.

Unemployment Insurance: When workers are unemployed, they are eligible for unemployment benefits. Unemployment insurance will be maintained by the state.

Workers Compensation Insurance: Workers are entitled for payment in the case of an injury while at work. Workers compensation insurance covers injury to workers.

General Liability Insurance;   General liability insurance covers any harm or injury to third party due to the action of the worker. This insurance may cover property damage to public or any other entity.

Fringe Benefits: Fringe benefits covers workers health, vacation and pension plans.

Overtime Pay: Normal workday in USA is 8 hours a day. Typically any hours worked beyond 8 hours is paid at 50% extra known as time and a half. Usually workers get paid double time on Sundays and holidays. Some workers get double time on Saturdays while some others get time and a half. These rates are dependent upon union agreements in the locality.

Practice Problem 2.13:   Mason works 11 hours per day from Monday to Friday. He works 7 hours on Saturday and 7 hours on Sunday. As per union agreement, worker is entitled to time and a half on any hours beyond 8 hours during weekdays. Worker is entitled to time and half on Saturdays and double time on Sundays.
a)   Worker is entitled to how many hours of pay?

Solution:
Monday to Friday (Hours per day) = (8 Standard time + 3 Overtime) = 8 + (3 x 1.5) = 12.5 hours
Total hours for Monday to Friday = 5 x 12.5 = 62.5 hours
Saturday = 7 x 1.5 = 10.5 hours
Sunday = 7 x 2 = 14 hours
Total hours = 62.5 + 10.5 + 14 = 87 hours

Practice Problem 2.14:   Carpenter's base wage is $45 per hour. Unemployment insurance is 3% of his actual wages. Social security tax is 6% of actual wages. Worker's compensation insurance is 7% of base wages. General liability insurance is 4.5% of base wages. Fringe benefits are $5.30 per hour. Carpenter works 40 hours a week. (all standard hours).

a)   What is the weekly cost of the carpenter?
b)   What is the hourly rate of the carpenter?

Solution:
STEP 1:   Find the base wages per week;
Base wages per week = $45 x 40 = $1,800
STEP 2:   Add insurance and benefits;
Unemployment insurance 3% of actual wages = 3/100 x 1,800   = $54
Social security tax 6% of actual wages = 6/100 x 1,800   = $108
Worker's compensation insurance 7% of base wages   = 7/100 x 1,800   = $126
General liability insurance 4.5% of base wages = 4.5/100 x 1,800   = $81
Fringe benefits are $5.30 per hour. Carpenter works 40 hours a week. Hence fringe benefits are 40 x 5.30 = $212

a)   Total cost per week to hire a carpenter = 1,800 + 54 + 108 + 126 + 81 + 212 = $2,381
b)   Hourly cost of the carpenter = $2,381/40 = $59.525

Practice Problem 2.15:   To meet schedule obligations, contractor is planning to have the carpenter in the above problem work additional 8 hours on Saturday. As per union agreement, contractor is required to pay time and a half for Saturdays.

Data Given: Carpenter's base wage is $45 per hour. Unemployment insurance is 3% of his actual wages. Social security tax is 6% of actual wages. Worker's compensation insurance is 7% of base wages. General liability insurance is 4.5% of base wages. Fringe benefits are $5.30 per hour. Carpenter works 40 hours a week from Monday to Friday and 8 hours on Saturday.

a)   What is the new weekly cost of the carpenter?
b)   What is the new hourly rate of the carpenter?

Solution:
STEP 1:   Find the base wages per week;
Carpenter works total 48 hours including the 8 hours on Saturday.
Base wages per week = $45 x 48 = $2,160
STEP 2:   Find the actual wages per week without insurance and benefits;
Carpenter works 40 hours during the week and 8 hours on Saturday. Saturday 8 hours has to be paid at time and half.
Hours carpenter should get paid = 40 + 1.5 x (8) = 52 hours
Actual wages without insurance and benefits = $45 x 52 = $2,340
STEP 3:   Add insurance and benefits;
Unemployment insurance 3% of actual wages = 3/100 x 2,340   = $ 70.2
Social security tax 6% of actual wages = 6/100 x 2,340   = $ 140.4
Worker's compensation insurance 7% of base wages = 7/100 x 2,160   = $151.2
General liability insurance 4.5% of base wages = 4.5/100 x 2,160   = $97.2

Fringe benefits are $5.30 per hour. Carpenter works 48 hours a week. Hence fringe benefits are 48 x 5.30 = $254.4

a)   Total cost per week to hire a carpenter = 2,340 + 70.2 + 140.4 + 151.2 + 97.2 + 254.4 = $ 3,053.4
b)   New hourly rate of the carpenter = $ 3,053.4/48 = $ 63.6
(Note: Carpenter is paid for 52 hours but he works only 48 hours.)

Alternative Solution: Above problem can be solved using base rate and actual rate. Following is the solution using rates.

STEP 1:   Base rate = $45/hour

STEP 2:   Find the actual rate:
Carpenter works 48 hours but gets paid for 52 hours, since he get paid time and half for Saturday.

Actual rate = Base rate x hours paid/hours worked
Actual rate = 45 x 52/48 = $48.75

STEP 3:   Add insurance and benefits to the actual rate;

Hourly rate (Actual)	= $ 48.75
Unemployment insurance 3% of actual rate = 3/100 x 48.75	= $ 1.4625
Social security tax 6% of actual rate = 6/100 x 48.75	= $ 2.925
Worker's compensation insurance 7% of base rate = 7/100 x 45	= $3.15
General liability insurance 4.5% of base rate = 4.5/100 x 45	= $2.025
Fringe benefits	= $5.30 per hour

Total hourly rate = 48.75 + 1.4625 + 2.925 + 3.15 + 2.025 + 5.30 = 63.61
Total weekly wages = 48 x 63.61 = 3,053

2.2.1 Equipment Depreciation:

Depreciation is the loss of value due to use. Most of us have bought cars. Imagine you bought a car for 20,000 dollars. One year later, you would like to sell the car. You would advertise in newspapers and the best price you can get is $15,000. You have lost $5,000 in one year. Depreciation of your car is $5,000. If you decide to sell the car in two years instead of one year, you will find that the value of the car has depreciated further. Let's say two years later, the maximum you can get for your car is $12,000. Total depreciation for two years is $8,000. If you wait for three years, let's say value of the car has further dropped to $10,000. Now total depreciation for three years is $10,000.

	Value	Total Depreciation	Depreciation per Year
Purchase price	20,000		
Value after one year	15,000	5,000	5,000
Value after two years	12,000	8,000	4,000
Value after three years	10,000	10,000	3,333

You could see that value drops rapidly during initial years.

Straight Line Depreciation:

There are many methods to compute depreciation. Easiest method is the straight-line depreciation. Straight-line depreciation assumes that depreciation to be same every year. This method can be explained using an example.

Practice Problem 2.16: (Straight Line Distribution):   Contractor has bought a dozer for 100,000. He estimates that the salvage value of the equipment after four years is 20,000. Find the depreciation of the equipment after each year.

Solution: STEP 1:   Find the total depreciation:
Purchase price = 100,000
Salvage value after four years = 20,000
Total depreciation after four years = 80,000

STEP 2:   Find the depreciation per year:
Depreciation per year = 80,000/4 = 20,000

STEP 3:   Find depreciation end of each year:
Purchase price = 100,000
Depreciation after one year = 20,000
Hence value after one year = 100,000 - 20,000 = 80,000

Depreciation after 2 years = 2 x 20,000 = 40,000
Value after two years = 100,000 - 40,000 = 60,000

Depreciation after 3 years = 3 x 20,000 = 60,000
Value after three years = 100,000 - 60,000 = 40,000

Depreciation after 4 years = 4 x 20,000 = 80,000
Value after three years = 100,000 - 80,000 = 20,000

Note: Straight-line distribution is not realistic. In the real world, equipment depreciates faster at the initial years as you saw with the example of the car. To alleviate this problem, other methods such as Sum of the years digit method and declining balance method have been introduced.

Sum of the Years Digits Method: This method is devised to have a higher rate of depreciation during initial years. As the name indicates, add the sum of each year. If we are planning to depreciate the equipment for 2 years, sum of the digits is $(1 + 2 = 3)$.

If we are planning to depreciate for three years, sum of the digits; $1 + 2 + 3 = 6$
If we are planning to depreciate for four years, sum of the digits; $1 + 2 + 3 + 4 = 10$
If we are planning to depreciate for five years, sum of the digits; $1 + 2 + 3 + 4 + 5 = 15$
If we are planning to depreciate for six years, sum of the digits; $1 + 2 + 3 + 4 + 5 + 6 = 21$

This method can be better explained using an example:

Practice Problem 2.17:   (Sum of the years digit method):   Find the depreciation of the equipment in the previous problem using sum of years digit method. Contractor has bought a dozer for 100,000. He estimates that the salvage value of the equipment after four years is 20,000. Find the depreciation of the equipment after each year using sum of the years digit method.

Solution:

STEP 1:   Find the total depreciation:
Purchase price = 100,000
Salvage value after four years = 20,000
Total depreciation after four years = 80,000

STEP 2:   Find sum of the digits
Depreciation is done for four years; $1 + 2 + 3 + 4 = 10$

STEP 3:   Find the depreciation after each year:
Depreciation first year = 4/10 x (Total depreciation) = 4/10 x 80,000 = 32,000
(4 is the last number in the series and 10 is the sum of the series)
Value after one year = Purchase price - Depreciation = 100,000 - 32,000 = 68,000

Depreciation second year = 3/10 x (Total depreciation) = 3/10 x 80,000 = 24,000
Value after two years = Remaining value - Depreciation = 68,000 - 24,000 = 44,000

Depreciation third year = 2/10 x (Total depreciation) = 2/10 x 80,000 = 16,000
Value after three years = Remaining value - Depreciation = 44,000 - 16,000 = 28,000
Depreciation fourth year = 1/10 x (Total depreciation) = 1/10 x 80,000 = 8,000
Value after four years = Remaining value - Depreciation = 28,000 - 8,000 = 20,000

Practice Problem 2.18:   (Sum of the years digit method): Contractor has bought a backhoe for $200,000.   He estimates that the salvage value of the equipment after six years is $10,000. Find the depreciation of the equipment after each year using sum of the years digit method.

Solution:
STEP 1:   Find the total depreciation:
Purchase price = 200,000
Salvage value after six years = 10,000
Total depreciation after six years = 190,000
STEP 2:   Find sum of the digits
Depreciation is done for six years; $1 + 2 + 3 + 4 + 5 + 6 = 21$
STEP 3:   Find the depreciation after each year:

Depreciation first year = 6/21 x (Total depreciation) = 6/21 x 190,000 = 54,286
Value after one year = Purchase price - Depreciation = 200,000 - 54,286 = 145,714

Depreciation second year = 5/21 x (Total depreciation) = 5/21 x 190,000 = 45,238
Value after second year = Remaining Value - Depreciation = 145,714 - 45,238 = 100,476

Depreciation third year = 4/21 x (Total depreciation) = 4/21 x 190,000 = 36,190
Value after third year = Remaining Value - Depreciation = 100,476 - 36,190 = 64,286

Depreciation fourth year = 3/21 x (Total depreciation) = 3/21 x 190,000 = 27,143
Value after fourth year = Remaining Value - Depreciation =   64,286 - 27,143 = 37,143

Depreciation fifth year = 2/21 x (Total depreciation) = 2/21 x 190,000 = 18,095
Value after fifth year = Remaining Value - Depreciation =   37,143 - 18,095 = 19,048

Depreciation sixth year = 1/21 x (Total depreciation) = 1/21 x 190,000 = 9,048
Value after sixth year = Remaining Value - Depreciation =   19,048 - 9,048 = 10,000

Declining Balance Depreciation:

In this method, average depreciation rate is obtained per year. Same rate is used each year to compute the depreciation. This method is better explained using an example.

Practice Problem 2.19:   Contractor buys a loader for $100,000. He is planning to use the equipment for 5 (five) years. Find the depreciation of the equipment after each year using the declining balance method.

Solution:

$$\boxed{\text{Average Depreciation Rate} = 100/\text{number of years}}$$

STEP 1:   Find the average depreciation rate
Average depreciation rate = 100/number of years = 100/5 = 20% = 0.2

It is assumed that 100% depreciation would occur in five years. End of 5 years, there would be a book value for the equipment. In this method, salvage value does not come into equations.

STEP 2:   Find the depreciation after each year;
Depreciation first year = 0.2 x (Value of the equipment) = 0.2 x 100,000 = 20,000
Value after one year = Value of the equipment - Depreciation = 100,000 - 20,000 = 80,000

Depreciation second year = 0.2 x (Value of the equipment) = 0.2 x 80,000 = 16,000
Value after second year = Value of the equipment - Depreciation = 80,000 - 16,000 = 64,000

Depreciation third year = 0.2 x (Value of the equipment) = 0.2 x 64,000 = 12,800
Value after third year = Value of the equipment - Depreciation = 64,000 - 12,800 = 51,200

Depreciation fourth year = 0.2 x (Value of the equipment) = 0.2 x 51,200 = 10,240
Value after fourth year = Value of the equipment - Depreciation = 51,200 - 10,240 = 40,960
Depreciation fifth year = 0.2 x (Value of the equipment) = 0.2 x 40,960 = 8,192
Value after fifth year = Value of the equipment - Depreciation = 40,960 - 8,192 = 32,768

Book value of the equipment after five years 32,768

200% Declining Balance Depreciation:

This method is a variation of the previous method. In this method, average depreciation is obtained per year and then doubled and applied to the remaining value of the equipment.

$$\boxed{\text{Double Average Depreciation Rate} = 2 \text{ x } (100/\text{number of years})}$$

Practice problem 2.20:   Contractor buys a loader for 100,000. He is planning to use the equipment for five years. Find the depreciation of the equipment after each year using the declining balance method.

Solution:
STEP 1:   Find the average depreciation rate
Average depreciation rate = 100/number of years = 100/5 = 20% = 0.2
It is assumed that 100% depreciation would occur in five years. Then the rate is doubled. Value at the end of five years is known as book value.

STEP 2:   Double the average depreciation rate = 2 x 20% = 40% = 0.4

STEP 3:   Find the depreciation after each year;
Depreciation first year = 0.4 x (Value of the equipment) = 0.4 x 100,000 = 40,000
Value after one year = Value of the equipment - Depreciation = 100,000 - 40,000 = 60,000

Depreciation second year = 0.4 x (Value of the equipment) = 0.4 x 60,000 = 24,000
Value after second year = Value of the equipment - Depreciation = 60,000 - 24,000 = 36,000

Depreciation third year = 0.4 x (Value of the equipment) = 0.4 x 36,000 = 14,400
Value after third year = Value of the equipment - Depreciation = 36,000 - 14,400 = 21,600

Depreciation fourth year = 0.4 x (Value of the equipment) = 0.4 x 21,600 = 8,640
Value after fourth year = Value of the equipment - Depreciation = 21,600 - 8,640 = 12,960

Depreciation fifth year = 0.4 x (Value of the equipment) = 0.4 x 12,960 = 5,184
Value after fifth year = Value of the equipment - Depreciation = 12,960 - 5,184 = 7,776
Book value of the equipment after five years = 7,776

Soil Excavation: Soil is a very important construction material. Soil is used for roads, buildings and retaining walls. Some of the terminology in soil excavation is need to be understood.

2.2.2   Bank Volume, Loose Volume and Compacted Volume:

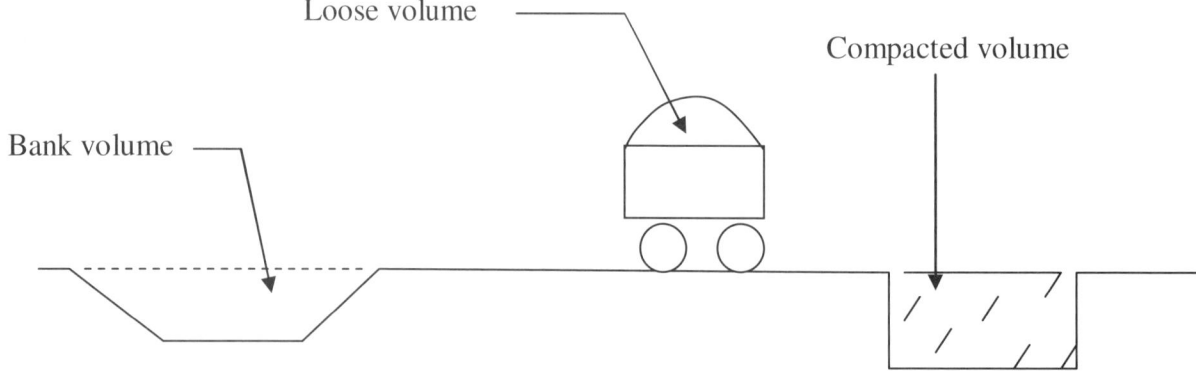

Bank Volume: Volume of naturally existing soil
Loose volume: When natural soil is excavated and loaded into trucks, new volume is known as loose volume.

It is easy to see that loose volume is greater than bank volume.

$$\text{Loose Volume} = (1 + S_w) \times \text{Bank Volume}$$

S_w = Swell factor

When the soil is compacted, volume is reduced.

$$\text{Compact Volume} = (1 - S_H) \times \text{Bank Volume}$$

S_H = Shrinkage factor

$$\text{Compact Volume} = \text{Loose Volume} \times (1 - S_H)/(1 + S_w)$$

Practice Problem 2.21:   a)   Derive an equation for compact volume using loose volume.
b) 10 trucks each carrying 10 cu. yds of soil was compacted. Find the bank volume and compact volume. Swell factor is 20% and shrinkage factor is 15%.

Solution:
Loose Volume = $(1 + S_w)$ x Bank Volume----------------------------- (1)
Compact Volume = $(1 - S_H)$ x Bank Volume------------------------- (2)

From (1)   Bank Volume = Loose Volume/$(1 + S_w)$

Replace Bank Volume in equation 2.
Compact Volume = $(1 - S_H)$ x Loose Volume/$(1 + S_w)$ = Loose Volume x $(1 - S_H)/(1 + S_w)$

b)   Loose volume = 10 x 10 = 100 cu. yds
        Loose Volume = $(1 + S_w)$ x Bank Volume
        100 = (1 + 0.2) x Bank Volume
        Bank Volume = 83.33 cu. yds
        Compact Volume = $(1 - S_H)$ x Bank Volume = (1 - 0.15) x 83.33 = 71 cu. yds

Installation of Underground Pipes:
Installation of underground sewer pipes, water pipes, electrical duct banks, drain pipes, cables are a very common construction activity.

Installation of an underground pipe

Activities involved in installation of an underground pipe:

- Excavation for the trench
- Stockpiling of excavated material (Usually usable soil and un-usable soil are separated).
- Shoring of trench sides
- Installation of the pipe
- Backfill and compaction

Practice Problem 2.22:   Contractor is excavating a 5 ft deep 3 ft wide and 100 ft long trench to install a 6" pipe. Contractor is planning to re-use the excavated soil for backfill. If swell factor is 15% and shrinkage factor is 12% will he be able to backfill the trench with excavated soil? If not how many truckloads of soil does he need? Assume each truck carries 3 cu. yds of soil.

Solution:
STEP 1)   Find the volume of the soil in the trench (Bank volume) = 5 x 3 x 100 = 1,500 cu. ft

STEP 2)   What is the volume of this soil after compacted?

Compact Volume = (1 - S_H) x Bank Volume = (1 - 0.12) x 1,500 = 1,320 cu. ft

STEP 3)   Find the volume of soil needed (after compacted).

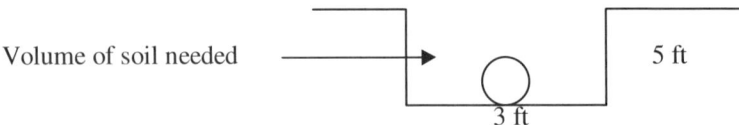

Volume of soil needed   5 ft

3 ft

Volume of compacted soil needed = Volume of the trench - Volume of the pipe
= 5 x 3 x 100 - (π x d^2/4) x 100 = 1,500 - π x 0.5^2 x 100 = 1,480 cu. ft

From step 2, we know we could get only 1,320 cu. ft from the excavated soil.

Volume of soil contractor needs = 1,480 - 1,320 = 160 cu. ft (after compacted).
Convert this compacted volume to bank volume.

Compact Volume = (1 - S_H) x Bank Volume
160 = (1 - 0.12) x Bank Volume
Bank Volume = 182 cu. ft

Convert bank volume to loose volume;

Loose Volume = (1 + S_w) x Bank Volume = (1 + 0.15) x 182 = 209.3 cu. ft = 7.75 cu. yds
Since each truck carries 3 cu. yds, contractor needs 2.58 trucks.

Concrete Work: Concrete is the most used building construction material in the world today. Prior to concreting, formwork is erected and rebars are placed. Next concreting is conducted. After the concrete is set, the formwork is removed. Reinforcing bars are placed by ironworkers. Formwork is erected by carpenters and concreting is conducted by concrete masons. Stripping of formwork is typically done by laborers. In most cases, formwork is re-used. During re-use, certain percentage of formwork could be damaged and has to be discarded. It is fair to assume 10% of formwork to be damaged during each use.

<u>Concreting Steps for a Footing</u>:
Excavation for the footing:

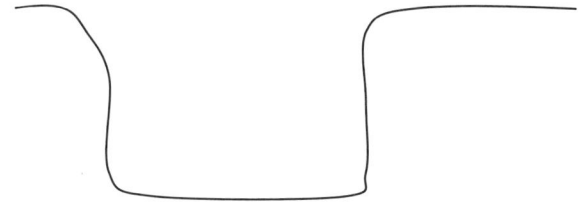

Erect Formwork:

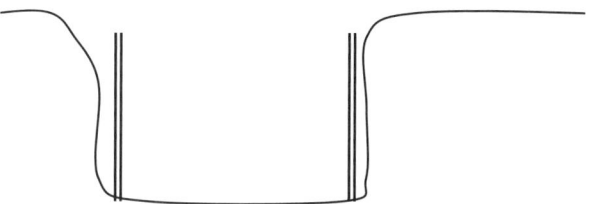

Place rebars and concrete:

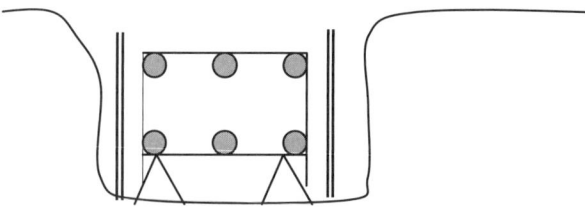

In the case of footings, the sides have to be backfilled.

Practice Problem 2.23:   (Cost estimating for concreting)
Find the cost involved in concreting the walls and footings of the building shown.

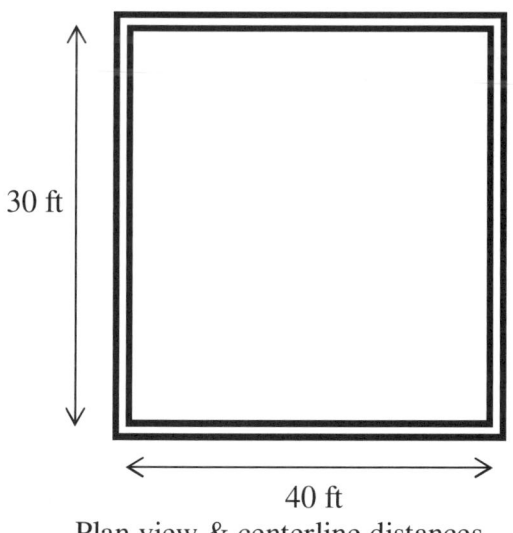

Plan view & centerline distances	Side view

Following information is given:

Concreting crew: 1 – Foreman,   3 – Laborers

Foreman wages = $60/hr,   Laborer = $ 30/hr
The crew can concrete 30 cu. yds per day (8 hr shift)
Find the total cost involved in concreting.

Solution:
STEP 1: Find the total quantity of concrete involved.
Quantity of concrete in footings = Perimeter length x footing cross sectional area
Length along center lines = 2 x (40 + 30) = 140 ft
Footing cross sectional area = 3 x 4 = 12 sq. ft
Concrete volume in footings = 140 x 12 = 1,680 cu. ft
= 1,680/27 cu. yds = 62 cu. yds
Quantity of concrete in walls = Perimeter length x wall cross sectional area
Concrete volume in walls = 2 x (40 + 30) x 10 x 1 = 1,400 cu. ft
= 1,400/27 cu. yds = 52 cu. yds
Total concrete volume = 52 + 62 = 114 cu. yds
STEP 2: Find the crew rate
The cost for crew hour = (1 x 60) + (3 x 30) = $ 150
(The crew consists of 1 foreman and 3 laborers.)
STEP 3: Number of days required = Concrete volume/Concrete production per day
                = 114/30 = 3.8 days
Concrete production is given to be 30 cu. yds per day.
Number of hours = 3.8 x 8 = 30.4 hours
Each hour costs $150 for the crew. (see step 2).
Total cost = 30.4 x 150 = $4,560
Please note that in this example, material cost, cost of forming, overhead and equipment costs were neglected to keep the example simple.

Practice Problem 2.24:   Cost estimating for formwork:
Find the cost for formwork required for walls and footings.

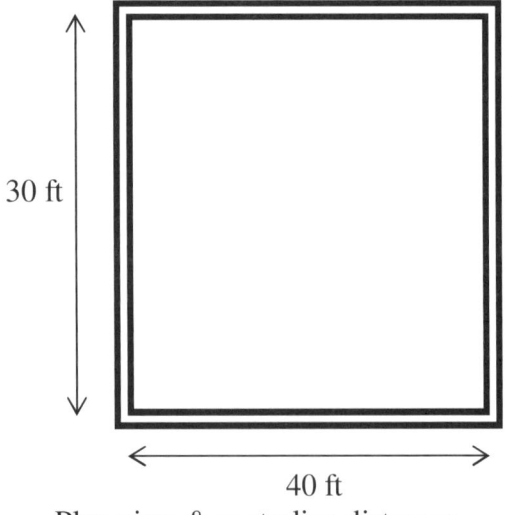

30 ft

40 ft

Plan view & centerline distances

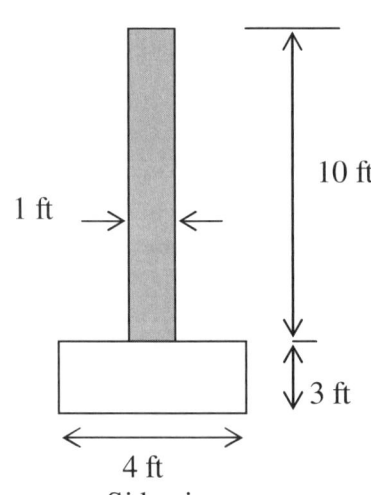

10 ft

1 ft

3 ft

4 ft

Side view

Following information is provided.
Crew required for formwork: 2 Carpenters,   3 laborers
Carpenter wages = $50/hr,   Laborer = $ 30/hr
The crew can form 60 sq. ft per hour.
Find the total cost involved in formwork.

Solution: STEP 1: Find the total quantity of formwork involved.
Quantity of formwork in footings = Perimeter length x footing side area

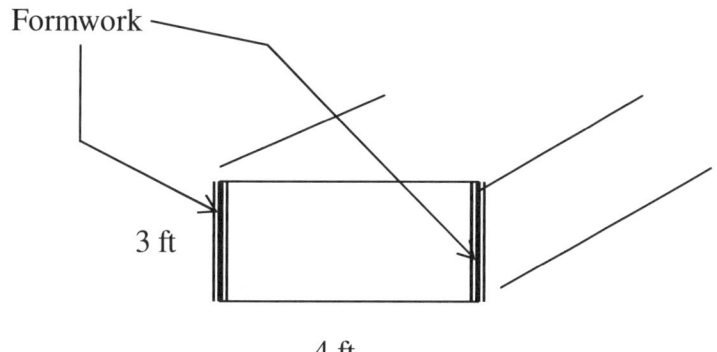

Formwork

3 ft

4 ft

Centerline length = 2 x (40 + 30) = 140 ft
Depth = 3 ft
Formwork required (one side) = 140 x 3 =   420 sq. ft
Formwork required (both sides) = 840 sq. ft
Quantity of formwork in walls = Perimeter length x wall side area
Quantity of formwork in walls (one side) = 2 x (40 + 30) x 10 = 1,400 sq. ft
Quantity of formwork in walls (both sides) = 2 x 1,400 = 2,800 sq. ft
Total formwork for walls and footings = 840 + 2,800 = 3,640 sq. ft

STEP 2:   Find the crew rate
The cost for the crew per hour (2 carpenters + 3 laborers)
= (2 x 50) + (3 x 30) = $ 190

Production rate of the crew is given to be 60 sq. ft per hour.
Number of hours required = Formwork area/Formwork production per hour
                    = 3,640/60 = 61 hours
Total cost = 61 x 190 = $11,590

Practice Problem 2.25:   Concreting:

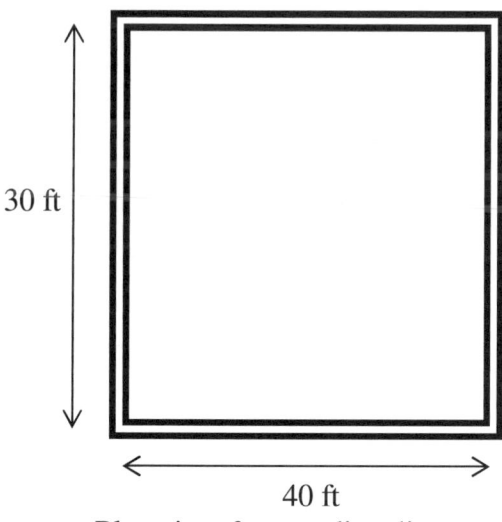

30 ft

40 ft
Plan view & centerline distances

1 ft

10 ft

3 ft

4 ft
Side view

Following information is provided.
Crew required for concreting: 2 Masons,   3 laborers
Mason wages = $55/hr,   Laborer = $ 30/hr
The crew can concrete 9 cu. yds per 8 hr shift.
Concrete material cost = $110 per cu. yd. (Assume 10% waste)
Find the total cost involved in concreting.

Solution:
Volume of concrete for footings:
= Centerline length of the footing x footing cross section
= 2 x (40 + 30) x (4 x 3) = 1,680 cu. ft
= 1,680/27 cu. yds = 62.2 cu. yds

Volume of concrete for walls:
Perimeter length of the wall x Wall cross section
= 2 x (40 + 30) x (1 x 10) = 1,400 cu. ft
= 1,400/27 cu. yds = 51.9 cu. yds
Total concrete volume = 62.2 + 51.9 = 114.1 cu. yds

STEP 2: Find the crew rate
The cost for the crew per hour (2 masons + 3 laborers)
= (2 x 55) + (3 x 30) = $ 200
Crew production rate per 8 hours = 9 cu. yds
Crew production per hour = 9/8 = 1.125 cu. yds per hour
Number of hours required = Concrete volume/Concrete production rate per hour
$$= 114.1/1.125 = 101.4 \text{ hours}$$
Total cost = 101.4 x 200 = $20,280
(200 is the crew rate per hour).

STEP 3: Material cost:
Concrete volume required = 114.1
Add 10% for waste = 114.1 + (10% x 114.1) = 125.5 cu. yds
Material cost = 125.5 x 110 = $13,805
Total cost = Labor + Material = 20,280 + 13,805 = $34,085

Labor Hour Method: Above examples were done using crew hour method. Some estimators perform calculations using labor hours. It is prudent to know both methods since it is possible that exam question could be in labor hours.
Labor hour rate = Crew hour rate/Number of workers in the crew.

Practice Problem 2.26:   Steel erection crew consists of 1 – foreman, 4 steel workers and 1 laborer.
Find the crew hour rate and labor hour rate.
Following hourly rates are available.
Foreman - $60,   Steel worker - $50,   Laborer - $35

Solution:
Crew hour rate = (1 x 60) + (4 x 50) + (1 x 35) = $295
Labor hour rate = Crew hour rate/Number of workers in the crew
Labor hour rate = 295/6 = $49.2

Practice Problem 2.27:   Formwork erection is done by 1 – foreman and 3 – carpenters.
Foreman - $60,   Carpenter - $45
Productivity of formwork erection is 7.2 sq. ft/LH   (LH = Labor hour)
Find the cost of erection of formwork if the project consists of 1,000 sq. ft of formwork.

Solution:
Crew hour rate = (1 x 60) + (3 x 45) = $195
Labor hour rate = Crew hour rate/Number of workers in the crew
Labor hour rate = 195/4 = $48.75
Total sq. ft of the project = 1,000 sq. ft
Productivity of formwork erection is 7.2 sq. ft/LH
Labor hours required = 1,000/7.2 = 138.9
Total cost = 138.9 x 48.75 = $6,770

Formwork Re-Use: In most cases, the contractor will not buy formwork for the whole project. He would buy only certain percentage of formwork and re-use them. If the project requires 10,000 sq. ft of formwork, the contractor may decide to purchase 3,000 sq. ft of formwork and re-use them. Typically, 10% of the formwork may not be re-usable due to damage.

Practice Problem 2.28: A project requires to complete 5,000 sq. ft of formwork. The contractor purchases 2,500 sq. ft of formwork at a price of $3 per sq. ft and plans to re-use them. The contractor believes he may have to replace 10% of formwork due to damage. Find the cost of formwork for the project.

Solution:
Cost for purchasing 2,500 sq. ft of formwork = 3 x 2,500 = $7,500
Loss of formwork due to damage = 10% x 2,500 = 250 sq. ft
Cost of replacement of damaged formwork = 3 x 250 = $750
Total cost of formwork = 7,500 + 750 = $8,250

Practice Problem 2.29: 12 ft high, 200 ft long wall will be concreted in three pours. Contractor plans to reuse the formwork. Initial cost of formwork is $5.10 per sq. ft. After that contractor would purchase formwork only to replace the damaged formwork. Contractor believes 10% of formwork will be damaged during every use.
Estimate the cost of formwork.

Solution:

STEP 1: Cost of formwork for pour 1:
Since the 12 ft high wall is concreted in three pours, each pour is 4 ft high.

Formwork for the first pour:

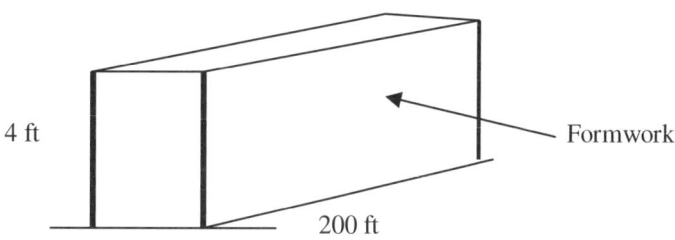

Formwork for the first pour (per side) = 4 x 200 = 800 sq. ft
Formwork for the first pour (both sides) = 1,600 sq. ft
Cost of formwork for the first pour = 5.10 x 1,600 = $ 8,160
Formwork for the second pour:

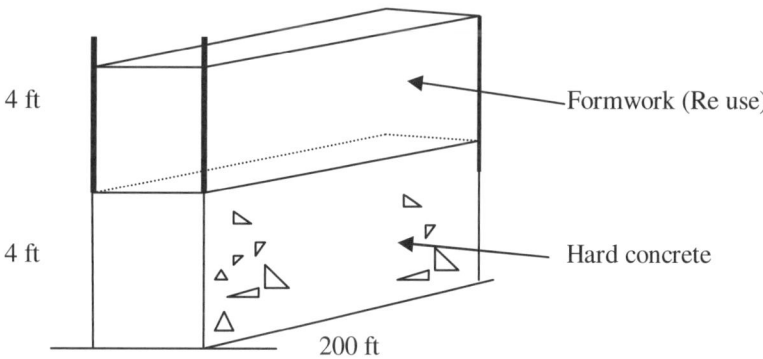

Formwork for the second pour (both sides) = 2 x 4 x 200 = 1,600 sq. ft
Formwork from the first pour will be re-used. However, 10% of the formwork will be damaged. Hence, contractor has to buy 160 sq. ft of formwork.
Formwork for the second pour (both sides) = 160 sq. ft
Additional cost of formwork for the second pour = 5.10 x 160 = $ 816

Formwork for the third pour:

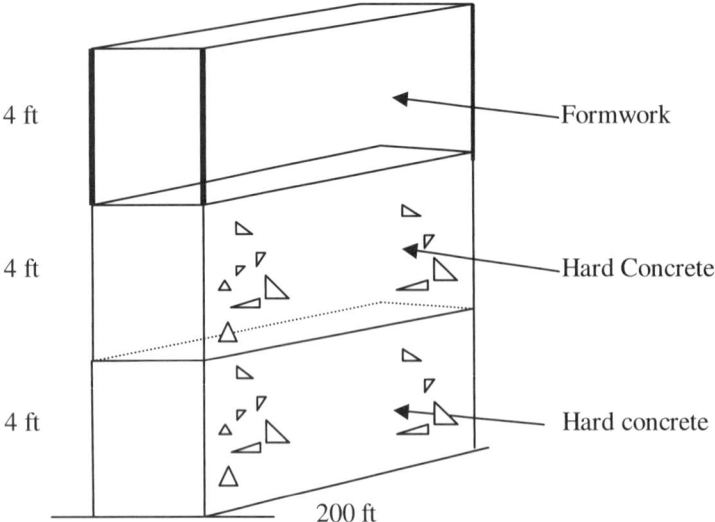

Formwork for the third pour (both sides) = 2 x 4 x 200 = 1,600 sq. ft
Formwork from the second pour will be re-used. However, 10% of the formwork will be damaged. Hence, contractor has to buy another 160 sq. ft of formwork.
Formwork for the third pour (both sides) = 160 sq. ft
Additional cost of formwork for the third pour = 5.10 x 160 = $ 816
Total cost of formwork   = Cost for the first pour + Cost for the second pour + cost for the third pour
                          = 8,160 + 816 + 816 = $ 9,792

Alternative Method of Formwork Re-Use Cost Computation (Unit Cost Method):
Contractor may compute the formwork cost using unit costs. Unit cost for formwork for the first pour is purchasing cost of formwork. Unit cost for the second pour is much smaller since he is planning to re-use formwork from first pour. Hence based on experience he may assign a unit cost for formwork for the second pour and third pour etc. This can be demonstrated using an example.

Practice Problem 2.30:   Contractor is planning to concrete a 12 ft high 200 ft long wall in three pours.
Purchasing cost of formwork is $5.10 per sq. ft. Contractor is planning to re-use the formwork.
Unit cost of formwork for the second and third pours is 10% of the initial cost.

Solution: STEP 1:   Cost of formwork for the first pour = 2 x 4 x 200 x 5.10 = $8,160
Note that formwork unit cost for the first pour is 5.10 per sq. ft and unit cost for the second and third pours are 0.51 per sq. ft.
STEP 2:   Cost of formwork for the second pour = 2 x 4 x 200 x 0.51 = $816
STEP 3:   Cost of formwork for the third pour = 2 x 4 x 200 x 0.51 = $816
Total cost of formwork = 8160 + 816 + 816 = $9,792

Formwork Construction: Forms are needed to hold the wet concrete in place until it hardens. Formwork cost in concrete work is significant. Some of the different timber sizes used in practice to build forms:

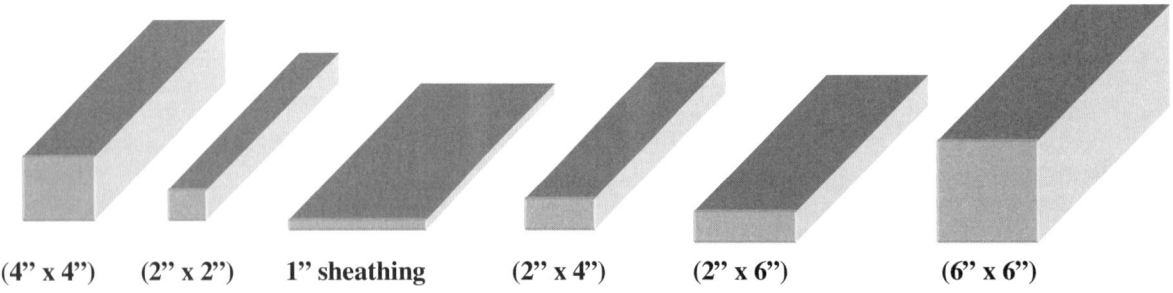

(4" x 4")   (2" x 2")   1" sheathing   (2" x 4")   (2" x 6")   (6" x 6")

It is important that you understand all the elements involved in formwork and the function of each element.

<u>Measure of Timber (fbm)</u>: Timber quantities are measured using fbm (footboard measure). Footboard measure is also known as board feet (BF). Some abbreviate it as fbm and some other authors abbreviate it as BF.

1 fbm (or BF) = 144 cu. inches

To find the fbm of a timber multiply length, width and depth using inches and then divide by 144.

Practice Problem 2.31:   Find the fbm of a 10 ft long 2" x 4" timber.

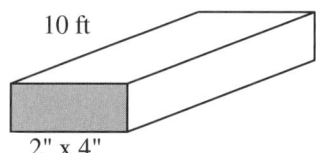

Solution: To obtain fbm multiply length, width and depth using inches and divide by 144.
(10 x 12) x 2 x 4/144 = 6.67 fbm

Practice Problem 2.32:   Find the fbm of 9 pieces of 10 ft long 2" x 4" timber and 13 pieces of 20 ft long 2 x 2 timber.

Solution: Multiply length, width and depth using inches and divide by 144.

9 x (10 x 12) x (2 x 4)/144 = 60 fbm
13 x (20 x 12) x (2 x 2)/144 = 86.7 fbm
<u>   Total   = 146.7 fbm</u>

Formwork for Columns:

Formwork for columns are built using 1" sheathing or ¾" in plywood. Typical arrangement is shown below.

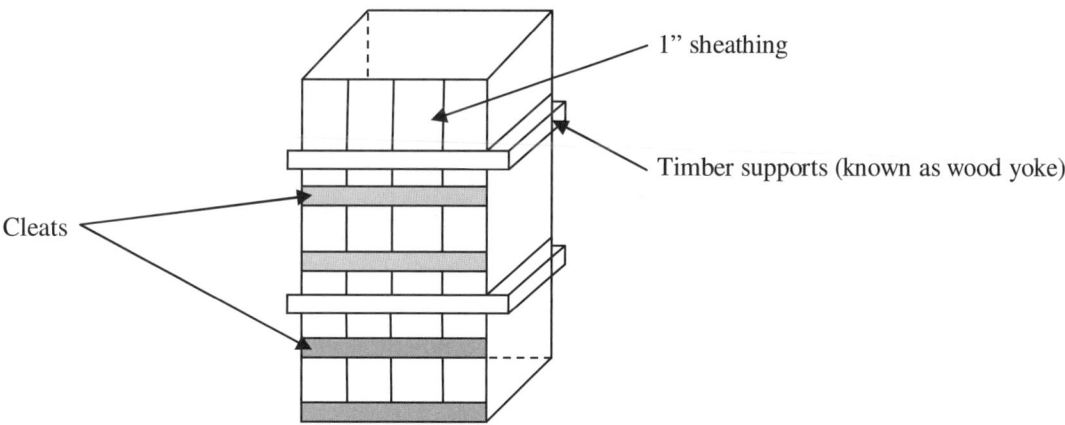

Elements in a column formwork:
1" sheathing: 1" sheathing comes in vertical strips as shown.
Cleats: Cleats are nailed to the sheathing. Typically 1" thick and 4" wide timber is used for cleats.
Timber supports (yoke):   Yoke holds the structure together. Yoke is built using 4" x 4" timber. Typically, timber supports are held together with bolts as shown below.

Column Configuration (Plan view):

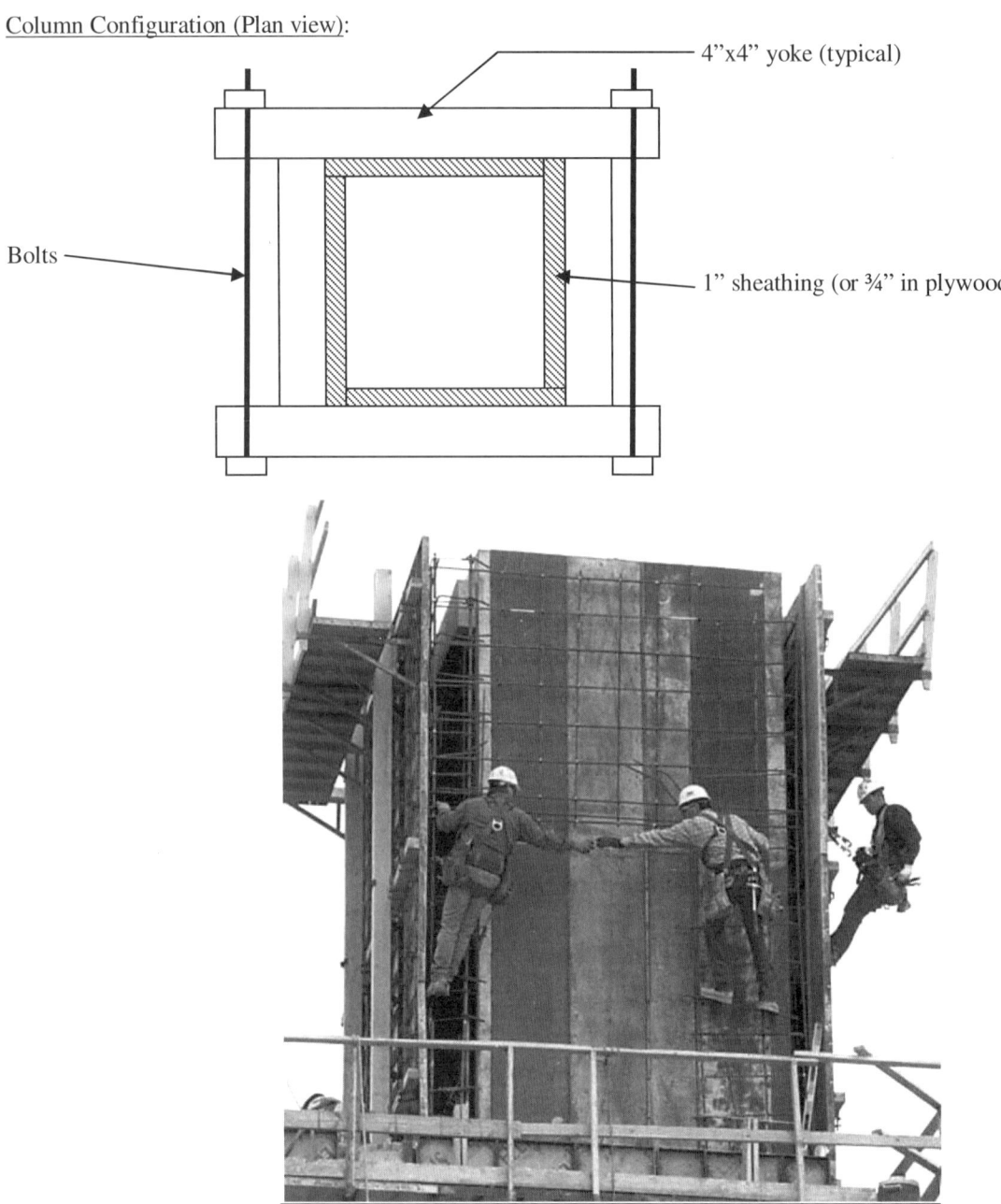

Computation of Material for a Column Formwork: You need to compute the square footage of 1" sheathing. Quantity of timber required for cleats and wood yokes. Labor required for construction has to be computed based on labor wage rates and production rate.

Practice Problem 2.33:   Compute the quantity of timber required for formwork for a 2ft x 2ft column with a height of 10 ft. Following information is given.
Formwork is prepared using 1" sheathing.
1" x 6" wood cleats are provided every 18 inches.
4" x 4" wood yokes are provided every 2 ft. (six)

Wood yokes are held together with ½" diameter bolts.

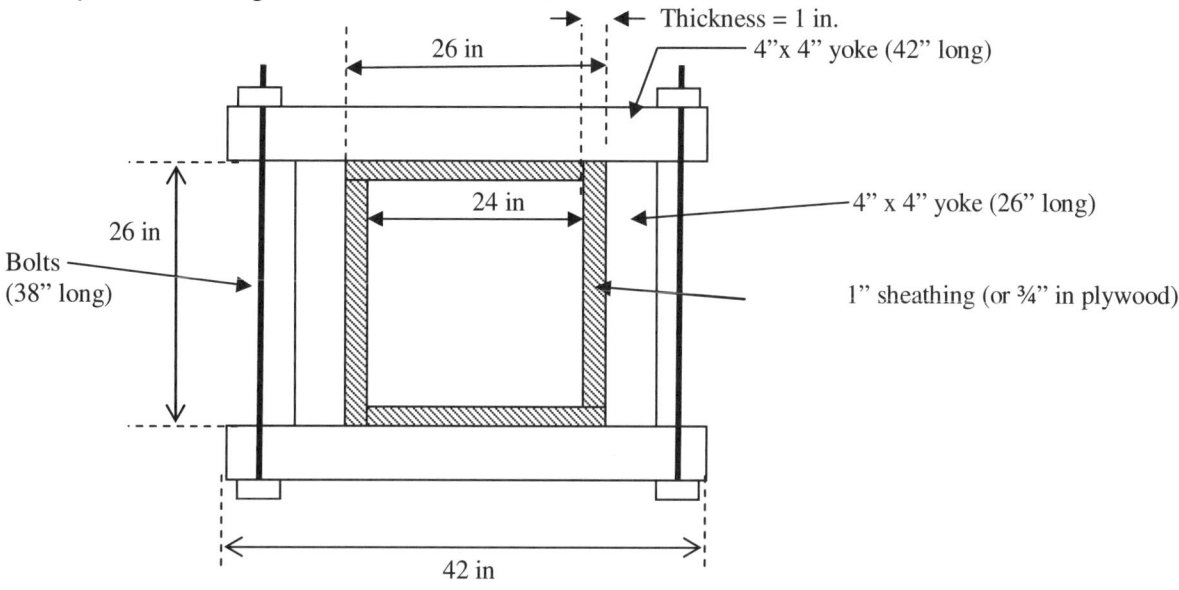

Solution: STEP 1:   Compute the 1" sheathing required:
1" sheathings have to be 25" wide. (not 24").
Required 1" sheathing per side = 25" x 10 ft = 25 x 120 x 1/144 fbm = 20.83 fbm
Required 1" sheathing for four sides = 4 x 20.83 = 83.3 fbm

STEP 2:   Compute the quantity of wood cleats:
Height of the column = 10 ft = 120 inches.
Cleats are provided every 18 inches.
Number of wood cleats = 120/18 = 6.67 = 7 wood cleats per side.
Total column requires 28 wood cleats. Each cleat is 1" thick, 6" wide and 26 in long. (Outside width of the formwork considering the thickness of the 1" sheathing)

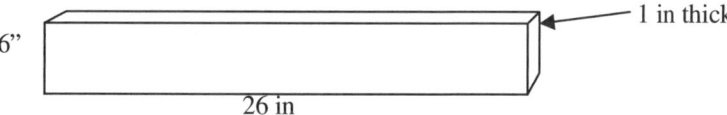

Quantity of required wood cleats = 28 x (1 x 6 x 26)/144 fbm = 30.3 fbm

STEP 3:   Compute the quantity of wood yokes:
Six wood yokes are provided for the column.
Each wood yoke needs two 42" long pieces and two 26" long pieces. (see the figure)
Required 42" long pieces for six wood yokes = 12
Timber quantity of 42" long pieces = 12 x 42 x (4 x 4)/144 = 56 fbm
Timber quantity of 26" long pieces = 12 x 26 x (4 x 4)/144 = 34.7 fbm
Total timber required = 83.3 + 30.3 + 56 + 34.7 = 204.3 fbm
STEP 3:   Compute the quantity of bolts required:
Two bolts are required per one wood yoke.
Total bolts required are 12, since there are six wood yokes.
Each bolt is 38" long.
Total length of bolts = 12 x 38 in = 38 ft

Practice Problem 2.34:   Compute the cost of labor required for the above problem. Following information is given.
Carpenter wages: $70 per hour,   Helper wages: $40 per hour
Saw cutting cleats and wood yokes per 100 sq. ft of contact area =   (0.5 carpenter hours + 2.0 helper hours)
Nailing wood cleats per 100 sq. ft of contact area =   (0.5 carpenter hours + 0.5 helper hours)
Erecting of wood york per 100 sq. ft of contact area =   (1.0 carpenter hours + 1.0 helper hours)

Solution:

STEP 1:   Contact area means the contact area between column forms and concrete.

In this case, it is 2 ft x 10 ft per side. There are four sides.

Hence contact area = 20 x 4 = 80 sq. ft

STEP 2:   Saw cutting of cleats and wood yokes:

Labor cost for 100 sq. ft of contact area = (0.5 x 70 + 2.0 x 40) = $115   (0.5 carpenter hrs + 2 helper hrs)

Labor cost for 80 sq. ft of contact area = $115/100 x 80 = $92

STEP 3:   Nailing wood cleats:

Labor cost for 100 sq. ft of contact area = (0.5 x 70 + 0.5 x 40) = $55   (0.5 carpenter hrs + 2 helper hrs)

Labor cost for 80 sq. ft of contact area = $55/100 x 80 = $ 44

STEP 4:   Erecting wood yokes:

Labor cost for 100 sq. ft of contact area = (1.0 x 70 + 1.0 x 40) = $110   (1.0 carpenter hours + 1.0 helper hours)

Labor cost for 80 sq. ft of contact area = $110/100 x 80 = $ 88

Total cost of labor for the column form = 92 + 44 + 88 = $ 224

Formwork for columns

Elements in a Wall Formwork:

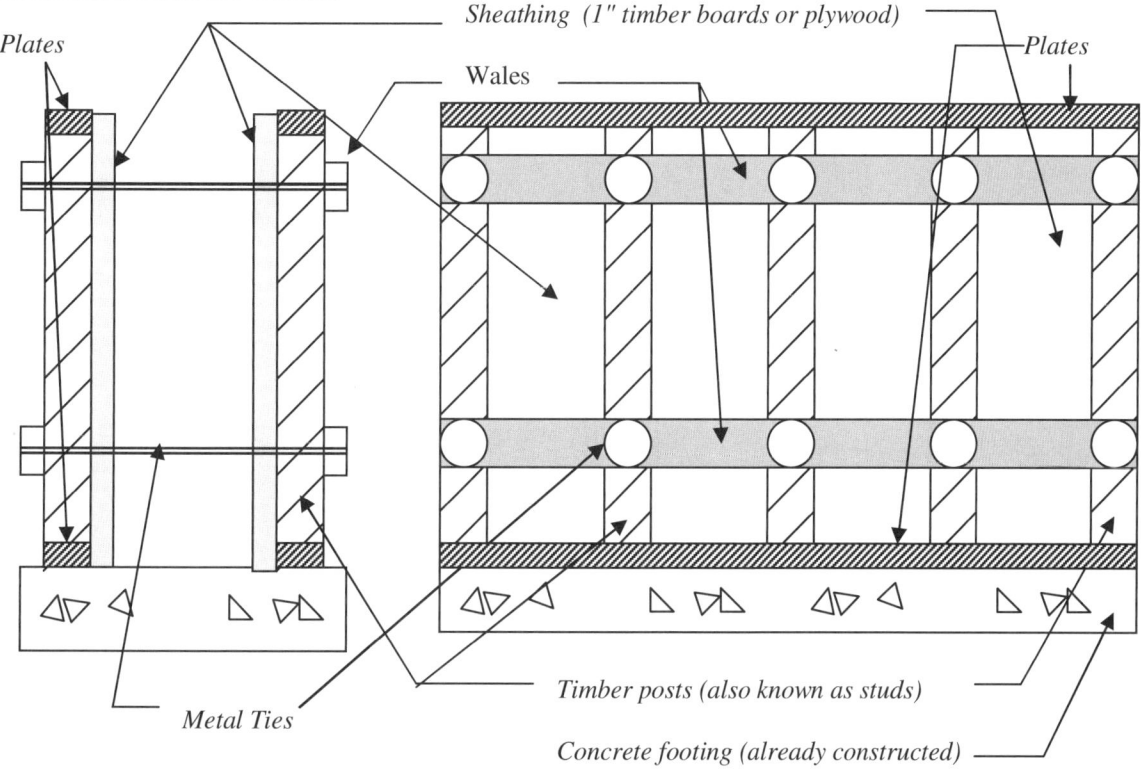

Elevation View   **Side View**

Practice Problem 2.35:   Find the quantity of timber required to construct formwork for a 70 ft long and 8 ft high wall. Assume the following. (See the section under "Wall Form General Configuration" for in length description).

Sheathing: 1 inch thick
Studs: Use 8 ft high studs. Ignore the thickness of timber plates. (2 x 4) timber posts placed every 2 ft.
Wales: (2 x 6) timber is used. Two wales per side are used.
Plates: (2 x 4) plates are used top and bottom of studs
Braces;   11 ft long 2 x 6 braces are provide every 10 ft on either side as shown below.

Wastage: 10%

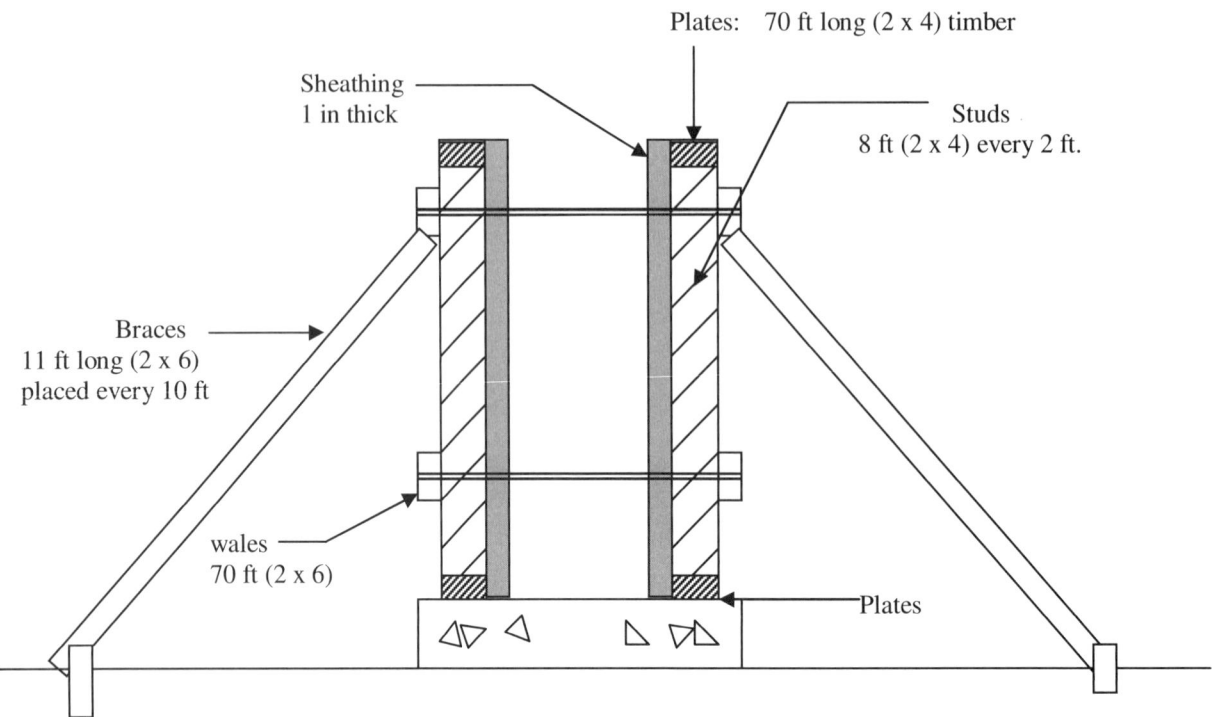

Solution: STEP 1:   Sheathing: Length = 70 ft, Height = 8 ft, thickness = 1in.
(70 x 12) x (8 x 12) x 1/144 = 560 fbm for one side
STEP 2:   Studs: Studs are used every 2 ft. Hence, (35 + 1) studs are needed for one side.
36 x (8 x 12) x (2 x 4)/144 = 192 fbm per one side.
STEP 3:   Wales;   Length of wales = 70 ft. Two wales are needed for one side.
2 x (70 x 12) x (2 x 6)/144 = 140 fbm per one side.
STEP 4:   Plates: Length of plates = 70 ft. Two plates are needed per side. (top and bottom)
2 x (70 x 12) x (2 x 4)/144 = 93.3 fbm per side
STEP 5:   Braces: Braces are provide every 10 ft. Hence, (7 + 1) braces are needed per side.
8 x (11 x 12) x (2 x 6)/144 = 88 fbm per one side.
Total timber quantity per side = 560 + 192 + 140 + 93.33 + 88 = 1.073.3 fbm
Total timber quantity needed for both sides = 2,146.6 fbm
10% waste of material anticipated. Hence total timber required = 1.1 x 2,146.6 = 2,361.6 fbm

<u>Labor Costs for Formwork</u>:   Formwork is done by carpenters and helpers. Typically, helpers will be moving wood, hoisting and saw cutting pieces. Carpenters will be measuring timber and erecting the formwork.

Practice Problem 2.36:   Compute the cost of labor for the erection of the formwork in the previous example. Following information is given.
Carpenter wages: $70 per hour,   Helper wages: $40 per hour
Saw cutting timber (for 100 fbm):   (1.0 carpenter hours + 0.5 helper hours)
Measurement and erection (for 100 fbm):   (2.0 carpenter hours + 1.0 helper hours)

Solution:

STEP 1:   <u>Cost for saw cutting:</u>
Cost for 100 fbm of saw cutting = (1 x 70) + (0.5 x 40) = $90
Total fbm in the formwork = 2,146.6 fbm (Not including wastage)
Cost for 2,361 fbm = 90/100 x 2,146.6 = $1,932

STEP 2:   Cost for measurement and erection:
Cost for 100 fbm of measurement and erection = (2 x 70) + (1.0 x 40) = $ 180
Total fbm in the formwork = 2,146.6 fbm
Cost for 2,361 fbm = 180/100 x 2,146.6 = $ 3,864
Total cost = 1,932 + 3,864 = $ 5,796

Roofing Estimates:

Roofing is a very important aspect of construction. Some of the concepts involved in roofing are discussed here in this chapter. Most roofing frames are built using lumber. Roof material could be shingles or tiles.

Nomenclature:

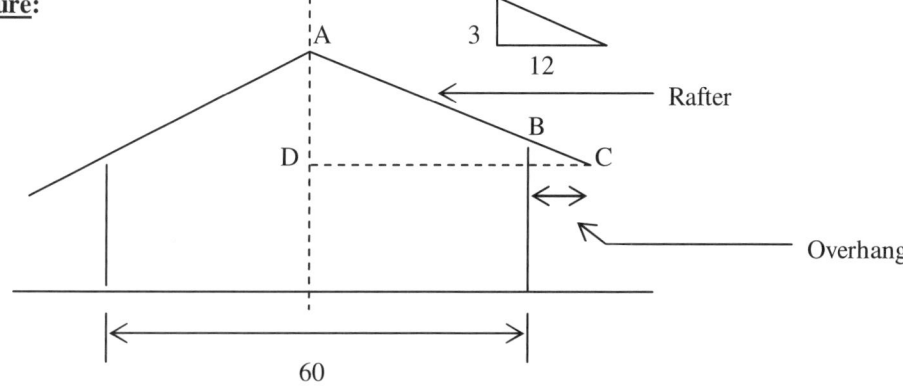

If the overhang is 2 ft what is the length of the rafter if the slope is 3 to 12. This is a simple trigonometric problem.
Length of the rafter is AC.
DC = 30 + Overhang = 32 ft
Tan (angle ACD) = 3/12 = 0.25
Angle ACD = 14^0.
AC Cos (14^0) = DC = 32
AC = Length of the rafter = 32/ Cos (14^0) = 32/0.970 = 32.98 ft
Roofing area = 2 x (Length of the rafter x Length of the building)

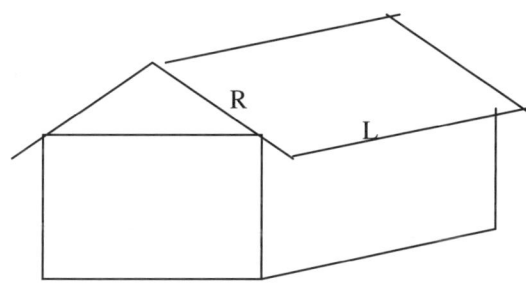

Practice problem 2.37:   Find the roofing cost of the building shown below. Overhang of the roof is 2 ft. Roofing material cost $6.90 per sq. ft.
Roofing installation crew: 2 roofers + 4 laborers
Wages: Roofer = $60/hr,   Laborer = $40/hr.
Productivity = 2.5 sq. ft/LH   (LH = Labor hour)

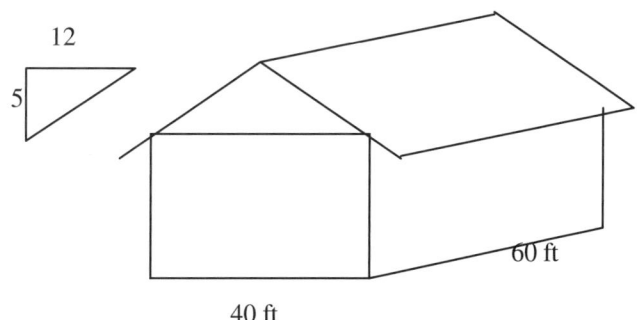

Solution: STEP 1:   Find the length of the rafter

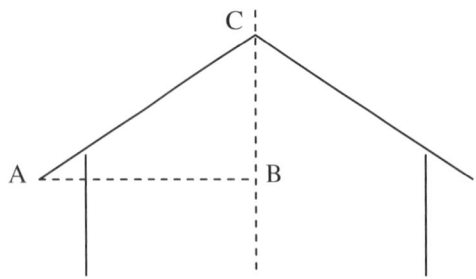

AB = 20 + Overhang = 22

Tan (Angle CAB) = 5/12

Angle CAB = 22.5^0

AC Cos (22.5^0) = AB = 22

AC = Length of the rafter = 22/ Cos (22.5^0) = 23.8 ft

STEP 2:   Find the area of the roof:

Roof area = 2 x (Length of the rafter x Length of the building) = 2 x 23.8 x 60 = 2,856 sq. ft

STEP 3:   Find the cost of roofing material:

Cost of roofing material = 6.90 x 2,856 = $19,706.4

STEP 4:   Find the cost of labor hour:

Crew = 2 roofers + 4 laborers

Cost of crew hour = (2 x 60) + (4 x 40) = $280

Cost of labor hour = Cost of crew hour/Number of workers in the crew = 280/6 = $46.7

STEP 4:   Find the labor hours required:

Labor hours required = 2,856/2.5 = 1,142

Note: 2.5 is the productivity. 2.5 sq. ft of roof is installed per labor hour (LH)

STEP 5:   Find the total cost of labor:

Cost of labor = Labor hours required x Cost of labor hour

Cost of labor = 1,142 x 46.7 = $53,350

STEP 6:   Find the total cost of the project:

Total cost of the project = Cost of material + Cost of labor = 19,706.4 + 53,350 = $73,056

Roof Trusses: Roof trusses are needed to support roofs. Most roof trusses are built of lumber or metal.

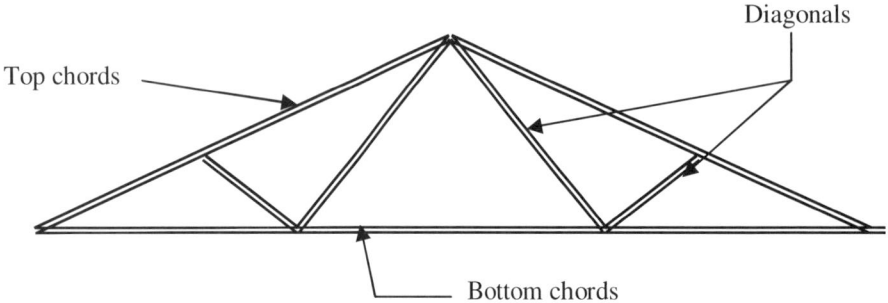

**   Refer to my Practice Problem Book and Three sample exam book for more Problems***

Miscellaneous Practice Problems: Exam questions can come from any segment of construction. Following practice problems are designed to cover major activities in construction. Following problems are little longer than typical exam questions. This is due to the fact that I have tried to cover all different aspects of activities involved in each problem. It is important for the student to have a good knowledge of the construction process to develop an estimate.

Practice Problem 2.38 (Borings):   Boring program is planned by a consulting company. Local building code requires a boring to be conducted every 400 sq. ft of the building footprint. Borings need to 15 ft below the bottom of footings. Building is 80 ft x 100 ft and bottom of footing is 3 ft below the ground. Following information available:
Mobilization = 2 hrs.   Demobilization = 2 hrs
Material:
Drilling mud mix: 20 bags (Cost $10 per bag)
Sampling spoons: 5   (Cost $100 per spoon)
Equipment:
Drill rig rental = $ 1,000 per day
Crew:
Drilling crew = 1 - Drill rig operator + 1 Helper
Wages: Drill rig operator = $75/hr   Helper = $55/hr

Productivity: 80 ft/day
Find the cost of the project.

Solution: STEP 1:   Total length of drilling required:
Building area = 80 x 100 = 8,000 sq. ft
Boring is required for every 400 sq. ft
Number of borings required = 8,000/400 = 20
Depth of borings = 15 ft below the depth of footings = 3 + 15 = 18
Total length of borings = 18 x 20 = 360 ft

STEP 2:   Number of days required:
Number of days of drilling = 360/Productivity = 360/80 = 4.5 days
Mobilization and demobilization = 4 hrs = 1/2 day
Total project duration = 5 days

STEP 3:   Equipment Rental:
Drill rig rental = 5 x 1,000 = $ 5,000

STEP 4:   Material:
Drilling mud   = 20 x 10 = $ 200
Sampling spoons = 5 x 100 = $ 500
Total material cost = $ 700

STEP 5:   Labor:
Drilling crew = 1 - Drill rig operator + 1 Helper
Crew hourly rate = 75 + 55 = $130

Number of hours = 5 x 8 = 40
Labor = 130 x 40 = $5,200
Total Direct Cost (Without Overhead and Profit) = 5,000 + 700 + 5,200 = $10,900

Practice Problem 2.39 (Excavation):   Photograph shows an excavation for a basement.   The excavation is 150 ft long, 80 ft wide and 40 ft deep. Following activities are identified.

      a)   Excavation
      b)   Hauling material out of site
      c)   Driving of sheet piles
      d)   Construction of wales and struts

Overhead is agreed at 15% and profits at 10%.   Find the cost of above items.

Wales ⎯⎯⎯   ⎯⎯ Struts

Following information is provided.

a)   Excavation: $10 per CY
b)   Hauling material out of site: $120 per truck   (truck capacity = 10 CY)
c)   Driving of sheet piles: Sheet piles are driven 2 feet below the bottom of excavation and 2 ft section above the ground level will be left alone.
            Sheetpile material cost = $15/sq.ft
            Rental cost of sheetpile driver = $1,200/day
            Pile driving crew;   1 - Operator,   3 - Laborers
            Wage rates: Operator = $70/hr,   Laborer = $45/hr
            Productivity of sheetpile installation: 60 sq. ft/hr
d)   Construction of wales and struts: W26 x 82 sections would be used for wales and struts.
            Material cost of W26 x 82 section = $2 per lb.
            Wales and struts are installed by a crew of 7 ironworkers and 5 Laborers.
            Wage rates: Iron worker = $60/hr,   Laborer = $45/hr
            Productivity = 1.2 ft/LH   (LH = Labor Hour)
            Total length of wales and struts = 800 ft

Solution: STEP 1:   Find the cost of excavation:

Excavation volume = 150 x 80 x 40 = 480,000 cu. ft = 17,778 CY
Cost of excavation = 17,778 x 10 = $177,780

STEP 2:   Cost of hauling material:
Cost of hauling material = 17,778/10 x 120 = $ 213,333

STEP 3:   Material cost of sheetpiles:
Length of sheet piles = 40 +2 + 2 = 44 ft
Perimeter length of the excavation = (2 x 150) + (2 x 80) = 460 ft
Total square feet of sheetpiles = 460 x 44 = 20,240 sq. ft
Sheetpile material cost = 15 x 20,240 = $303,600

STEP 4:   Rental cost of sheetpile driver:
Duration of driving sheetpiles = square footage of sheetpiles/productivity = 20,240/60 = 338 hrs = 42.25 days (8 hrs per day)
Rental cost of sheetpile driver = 42.25 x $1,200 = $50,700

STEP 5:   Labor cost of driving sheetpiles:
Sheetpile driving crew;   1 - Operator,   3 - Laborers
Cost of crew hour = (1 x 70) + (3 x 45) = $205/hr
Number of hours required = 338 (see step 4)
Cost of labor = 338 x 205 = $ 69,290

STEP 6:   Material cost of wales and struts:
Total length of wales and struts = 800 ft
W26 x 82 sections weighs 82 lbs per linear foot.
Total weight of wales and struts = 800 x 82 = 65,600 lbs
Material cost of wales and struts = $2 x 65,600 = $ 131,200

STEP 7:   Labor cost of installation of wales and struts:
Cost of crew hour = (7 x 60) = (5 x 45) = $645/hr
Cost of labor hour (LH) = 645/number of workers in the crew = 645/12 = $ 53.75
Productivity = 1.2 ft/LH
Labor hours required = 800/1.2 = 667
Cost of labor for installation of wales and struts = 667 x 53.75 = $ 35,851
STEP 8:   Total direct cost = $177,780 + $213,333 + $303,600 + $50,700 + $69,290 + $131,200 + $35,851
     = $981,754
Overhead = 0.15 x $981,754 = $147,263
Cost including overhead = $1,129,017
Profit = 0.1 x $1,129,017 = $112,901.7
Total cost including overhead and profit = $1,241,919

Wooden Floors:

Wooden floors are common in many parts of the world. Wooden floors are built above the ground using timber.

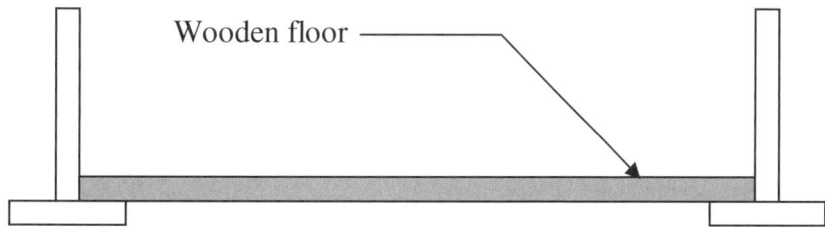

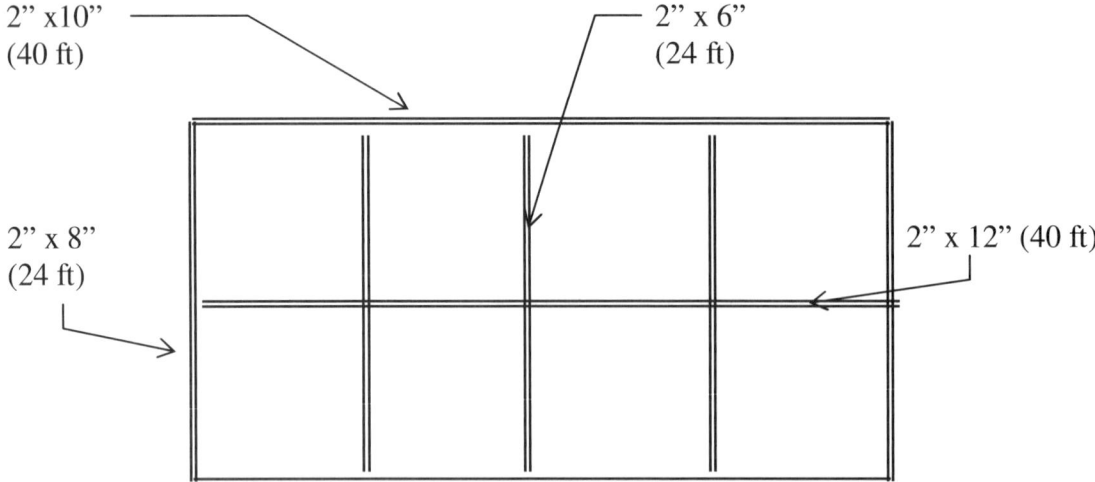

2" x10"
(40 ft)

2" x 6"
(24 ft)

2" x 8"
(24 ft)

2" x 12" (40 ft)

Practice Problem 2.40:   Find the costs associated with construction of the wooden floor shown above. Following information is available.

Cost of lumber = $4.2 per fbm

Framing crew consists of 2 carpenters and 3 laborers.

Wages: Carpenter = $75/hr   Laborer = $55/hr

Productivity = 2.1 fbm/LH   (LH = Labor Hour)

Fork lift rental rate = $200/day

(Assume 8 hr workday and full crew is working all the time)

Solution:

STEP 1:   Find the cost of lumber:

2 pieces of 2" x 10" (length 40 ft) =   2 x (2 x 10) x (40 x 12)/144 = 133.3 fbm

2 pieces of 2" x 8" (length 24 ft) =   2 x (2 x 8) x (24 x 12)/144 = 64 fbm

3 pieces of 2" x 6' (length 24 ft) =   3 x (2 x 6) x (24 x 12)/144 = 72 fbm

1 piece of 2" x 12" (length 40 ft) =   1 x (2 x 12) x (40 x 12)/144 = 80 fbm

Total = 349 fbm

Cost of lumber = 4.2 x 349 = $1,467

STEP 2:   Find the cost of labor:

Cost of crew hour = (2 x 75) + (3 x 55) = $315

Cost of labor hour (LH) = Cost of crew hour/number of workers in the crew = 315/5 = $63

Productivity is given to be 2.1 fbm per labor hour (LH)

Number of labor hours needed = 349/2.1 = 166.2

Cost of labor = Number of labor hours x cost of labor hour = 166.2 x 63 = $ 10,470

STEP 3:   Find the time required for construction:

At any given time 2 carpenters and 3 laborers are working. That is a total of 5 workers.

Productivity of crew hour = number of workers in the crew x productivity of labor hour

Productivity of crew hour = 5 x 2.1 = 10.5 fbm/crew hour

Number of crew hours needed = 349/10.5 = 33.2

Since the workers are working 8 hrs per day

Number of days needed = 33.2/8 = 4.15

Fork lift is needed for 5 days.

Equipment rental cost = 5 x 200 = $ 1,000

Total cost = 1,467 + 10,470 + 1,000 = $ 12,937

Steel Structures: Steel structures are common in the world. Main activities involved in erection of steel structures are;

1)   Fabrication of Steel Members -   Contractor has to buy columns, beams, connections, angles, channels and plates. These steel members come in standard sizes. Contractor has to cut the beams, angles, channels to the correct length, drill holes for bolts, taper steel members for installation. These activities are known as fabrication.

Gusset plate

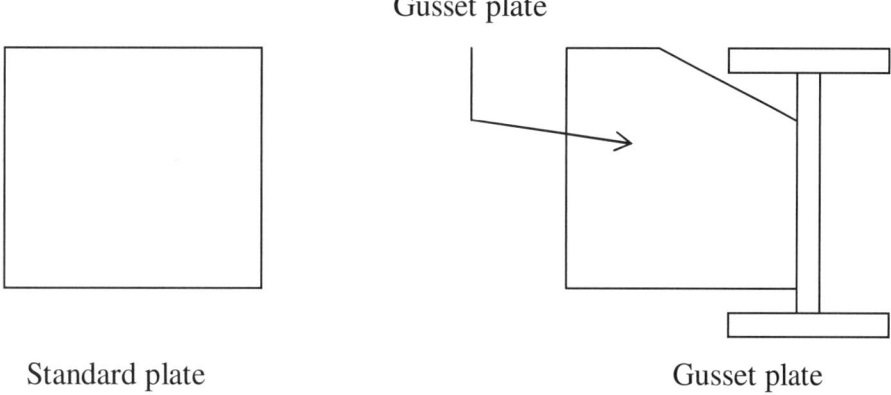

Standard plate   Gusset plate

Above figure shows fabrication of a gusset plate using factory manufactured standard plate.   Sometimes beams are fabricated using angles or channels.

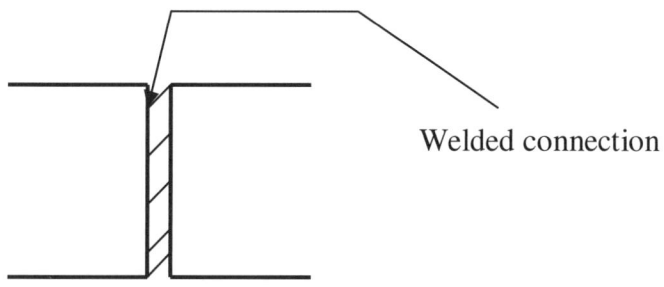

Welded connection

Fabrication of a beam using two channel sections using welding

2)   Transportation to the Site and Storage: After fabrication of steel members, they are transported and stored in the site.
3)   Steel Erection: Erection of steel requires lifting to the correct location using a crane and making connections. Erection of steel is a highly specialized profession. Bolts are done by drilling holes. Some holes are factory drilled and some other holes are field drilled.
4)   Member Connections: Steel members are connected using bolts or welding. In the past, rivets were used for steel connections. Today most riveted connections are converted to bolts.

Practice Problem 2.41:   12 columns each with height 11 ft has to be constructed.

Following labor rates are known:
Carpenter = $70/hr;   Iron Worker = $60/hr   Concrete Mason = $70/hr
Laborer = $40/hr
Formwork Crew = 2 Carpenter + 3 laborers
Rebar crew = 2 iron workers + 1 laborer
Concreting crew = 2 concrete masons + 5 laborers
Productivity:
Formwork = 6 ft^2/LH
Rebar placement = 100 lbs/LH
Concreting = 0.5 cu. yds/LH
Note: LH = Labor hour
Material Cost: Formwork for 4 columns (initial erection) = $2.1/sq. ft

Formwork reuse cost = $0.3/sq. ft
Concrete = $120/Cu. yd
Rebar cost = 0.50/lb

Find the cost of the project.

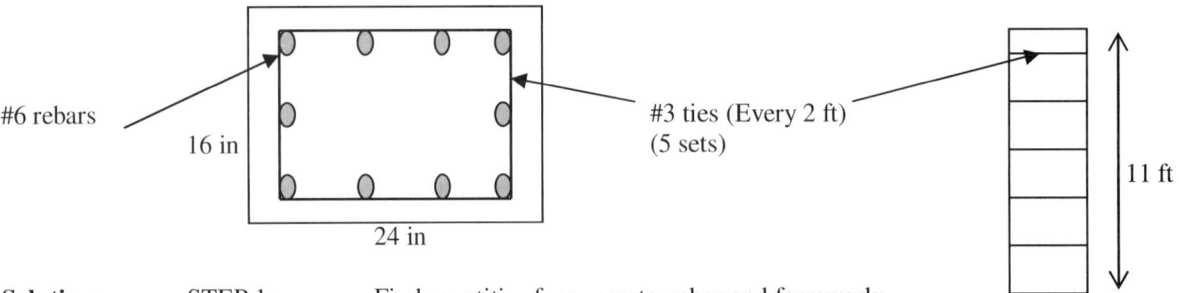

Solution: STEP 1:   Find quantities for concrete, rebar and formwork:
Find the quantity of #6 bars:
Number of #6 bars per column = 10
Length of each bar = 11 ft
Total length of #6 bars per column = 110 ft
Total length of #6 bars for 12 columns = 110 x 12 = 1,320 ft
Total weight of #6 bars = 1,320 x 1.502 lbs = 1,983 lbs

STEP 2:   Find the quantity of #3 Ties:
Length of one #3 tie bar = 24 + 24 + 16 + 16 = 80 in (Approximately)
Number of tie bars per column = 5
Length of #3 bars per column = 5 x 80/12 = 33.33 ft
Total length of #3 bars for 12 columns = 33.33 x 12 = 400 ft
Total weight of #3 bars = 400 x 0.376 lbs = 150 lbs
Total weight of rebars = 1,983 + 150 = 2,133 lbs

STEP 3:   Material cost of rebars = 2133 x 0.5 = $1,067
STEP 4:   Formwork (Material Cost):
Formwork per column = Perimeter x Height = (24 + 24 + 16 + 16)/12 x 11 = 73.33 sq. ft
Formwork quantity for 12 columns = 12 x 73.33 = 880 sq. ft
Formwork for first four columns bought at $2.1/sq. ft = 4 x 73.33 x 2.1 = $616
Formwork reuse cost = 0.3/sq. ft
Area of formwork for remaining 8 columns = 8 x 73.33 = 586.6 sq. ft
Cost of formwork for remaining 8 columns = 0.3 x 586.6 = $176
Total material cost of formwork = 616 + 176 = $792
STEP 5:   Concrete (Material Cost):
Volume of concrete per column = (16 x 24)/144 x 11 = 29.33 cu. ft = 1.09 cu. yds
Concrete volume for 12 columns = 12 x 1.09 = 13.1 cu. yds
Cost of concrete for 12 columns = 12 x 1.09 x 120 = $1,570
STEP 6:   Total Material Cost = 1,067 + 616 + 176 + 1,570 = $3,429

STEP 7:   Labor (Formwork):
Formwork Crew = 2 Carpenter + 3 laborers
Cost of crew hour = (2 x 70) + (3 x 40) = 260
Labor Hour = 260/Number of workers = 260/ 5 = $52
Productivity for Formwork = 6 ft^2/LH
Total formwork quantity = 880 sq. ft (See step 4)
Required labor hours = 880/6 = 147
Cost of labor for formwork = 147 x 52 = $ 7,644
STEP 8:   Labor (Rebars)
Rebar crew = 2 iron workers + 1 laborer
Cost of crew hour = (2 x 60) + (1 x 40) = 160
Labor Hour = 160/Number of workers = 160/ 3 = $53.3

Productivity for rebars = 100 lbs/LH
Total rebar quantity = 2,133 lbs (See step 2)
Required labor hours = 2,133/100 = 21.3

Cost of labor for formwork = 21.3 x 53.3 = $ 1,135

STEP 9:   Labor (Concreting)
Concreting crew = 2 concrete masons + 5 laborers
Cost of crew hour = (2 x 70) + (5 x 40) = 340
Labor Hour = 340/Number of workers = 340/7 = $48.6

Productivity for concreting = 0.5 cu. yds/LH
Total concrete quantity 13.1 cu. yds (See step 5)
Required labor hours = 13.1/0.5 = 26.2
Cost of labor for concreting = 26.2 x 48.6 = $ 1,273

Total Labor Cost = 7,644 + 1,135 + 1,273 = $10,052
Total Material Cost = $3,429 (see step 6)
Total project cost = $13,481

Concreting of an Upper Slab:

Formwork and shoring for concreting of an upper slab (see schematic below)

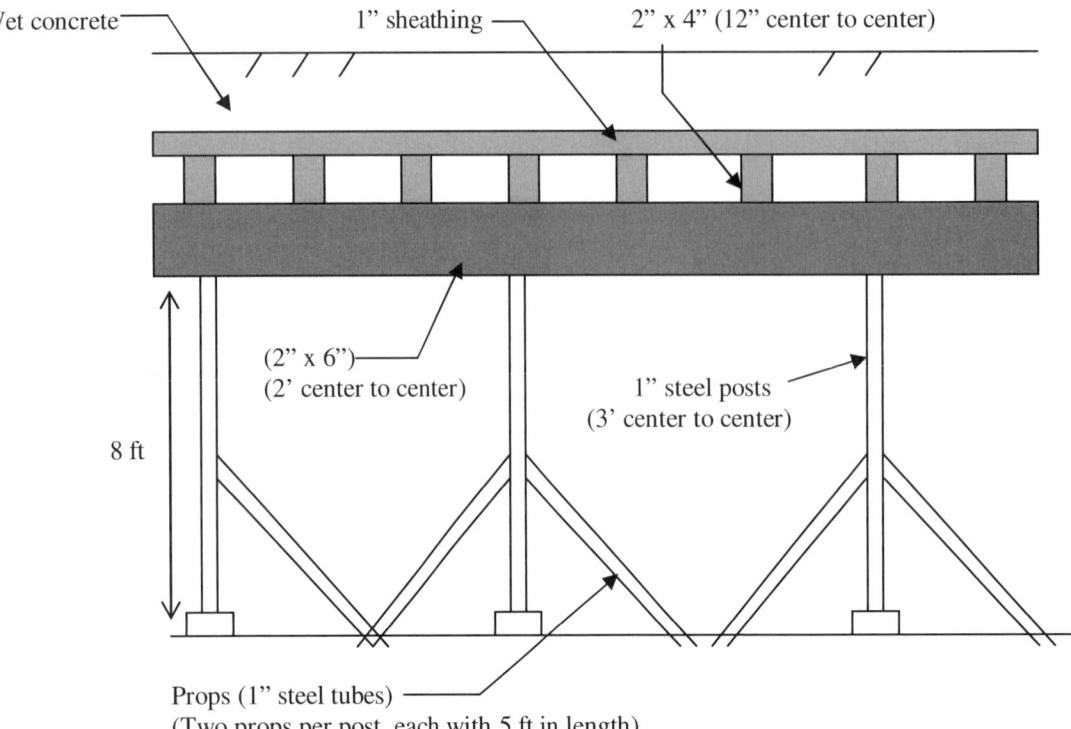

Wet concrete   1" sheathing   2" x 4" (12" center to center)

(2" x 6")
(2' center to center)

1" steel posts
(3' center to center)

8 ft

Props (1" steel tubes)
(Two props per post, each with 5 ft in length)

Practice Problem 2.42:   50 ft by 50 ft slab has to be concreted. Formwork and shoring is as shown above. (Please see the sketch and the photograph above).
a)   Compute the total fbm of timber
b)   Find the total length of steel posts
c)   Find the total length of steel props

Labor costs: Mason = $65/hr   Laborer = $40/hr
Crew: 2 masons + 4 laborers

Productivity:
1" sheathing = 10 sq. ft/LH
2" x 4" beams = 9 ft/LH
2" x 6" beams = 8 ft/LH
Posts and Props = 1 post and 2 props/LH   (2 Props per post)
Find the total cost.

Solution: STEP 1: Find the fbm of timber:

Calculate the fbm of 1" sheathing;

1" sheathing = (50 x 12) x (50 x 12) x 1/144 fbm = 2,500 fbm
Explanation: fbm is calculated by calculating the total volume of timber by 144.
Total volume of timber sheathing is area x thickness.

Calculate the fbm of (2" x 4") lumber:
Length is 50 ft. (Length = 50 x 12 inches)
They are placed 1 ft center to center. Hence, there are 51 pieces.
51 x (50 x 12) x (2 x 4)/144 fbm = 1,700 fbm

Calculate the fbm of (2" x 6") lumber:
Length is 50 ft. (Length = 50 x 12 inches)

They are placed 2 ft center to center. Hence, there are 26 pieces.
26 x (50 x 12) x (2 x 6)/144 fbm = 1,300 fbm

Total fbm = 2,500 + 1,700 + 1,300 = 5,500 fbm

STEP 2:   Find the number of steel posts and props:
Steel Posts: Steel posts are placed along 2 x 6 lumber.
There are 26 pieces of (2 x 6) lumber.
Each (2 x 6) lumber is 50 ft long and posts are located every 3 ft.
Number of posts per one length of (2 x 6) lumber = (50/3) = 16.667
Number of posts per one length of (2 x 6) lumber cannot be a fraction hence number of posts = 17
Total number of posts = (17) x 26 = 442
Number of props = 2 x 442 = 884

STEP 3:   Find the cost of labor hour (LH):
Crew = 2 masons + 4 laborers
Cost of crew hour = (2 x 65) + (4 x 40) = $290
Cost of labor hour (LH) = 290/6 = $48.3

STEP 4:   Find the total cost:

1" sheathing = 10 sq. ft/LH
LH required = 2500/10 = 250
Labor cost of 1" sheathing = 250 x $48.3 = **$12,075**

2" x 4" beams = 9 ft/LH
Total length = 51 x 50 = 2,550
LH required = 2550/9 = 283.3
Cost of 2 x 4 beams = 283.3 x $48.3 = **$13,685**

2" x 6" beams = 8 ft/LH
Total length = 26 x 50 = 1,300
LH required = 1,300/8 = 162.5
Cost of 2 x 6 beams = 162.5 x $48.3 = **$7,848.8**

Posts and props = 1 post and 2 props/LH
Total number of posts = 442
Number of props = 884
(See step 2)
One post has two props. Let's call it a post-prop unit.
One labor hour is required to install one unit. (One unit = One post and 2 props).
Number of posts and prop units = 442
Labor hours required to install 442 units = 442 LH
Cost = 442 x 48.3 = **$21,348.6**

Total Cost = $12,075 + $13,685 + $7,848 + $21,348.6= **$54,956.6**

2.3   Engineering Analysis:

Important Note on Economic Problems: Economic problems can be solved using either interest tables or equations. It is easier to use interest tables to solve economic problems. However, interest tables can be used only for very simple problems. Difficult problems **cannot** be solved with interest table. In such situations, equations need to be used.   Due to this reason, problems in this book are solved using both interest tables and equations.

Present Worth and Future Worth: It is not a secret that value of money goes down with time. One thousand dollars today has more value than one thousand dollars one year from now.
If the interest rate is " i ", present worth is "P" number of years is "n" and future worth is "F", following equation can be used.

Representation:

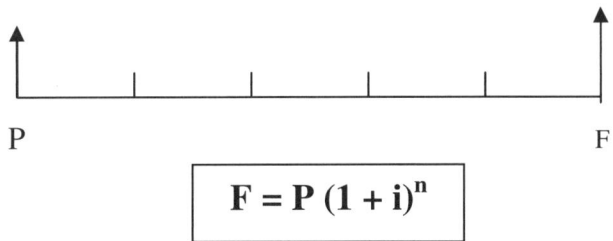

$$F = P (1 + i)^n$$

Practice Problem 2.43:   Find the value of \$1,200 in a savings account that generates 9% interest per year after 5 years.

Solution Using Interest Tables:

P = Present value = 1,200
i = 9%   n = 5
F needs to be found.

Go to interest tables and locate n = 5 and i = 9%.
Then look for the **F/P** column. This means value of **F** when **P** is given.
From the tables F/P = 1.5386
Hence F = 1.5386 x P = 1.5386 x 1,200 = \$1,846.32

Please note that interest tables are not provided in this book but available in any economic book.

Solution using equations:

    P = \$1,200
i = 9%   n = 5

    $F = P (1 + i)^n$

F = 1,200 $(1 + 0.09)^5$
F = 1,846.4

Finding Interest Rate (i) when F and P are Given:
When interest arte i need to be found using given F and P values, using interest tables may be little difficult.. In such situations, following equation can be used.

    $F = P (1 + i)^n$
    $F/P = (1 + i)^n$

    $(F/P)^{1/n} = (1 + i)$

    $i = (F/P)^{1/n} - 1$

$$i = (F/P)^{1/n} - 1$$

Practice Problem 2.44: An investor invests $7,000 dollars and receives $11,000 after 7 years. What is the interest rate?
Answers A) 5% B) 4.3% C) 6.6% D) 7.2%

Solution Using Interest Tables:
F = Future value = 11,000
n = 7
i = Interest rate need to be found.

F/P = 11,000/7,000 = 1.571
Locate n = 7 and F/P = 1.571.

Now you could see this is not easy to do since i (interest rate) is not given.
If you look at n = 7 and i = 6%, F/P = 1.5036
However, we are looking for F/P = 1.571. Hence, we have to look for a higher interest rate.
Now look at n = 7 and i = 7%, and F/P = 1.6057.
Now you can extrapolate.

n = 7 and i = 6% ---------- F/P = 1.5036
n = 7 and i = 7% ---------- F/P = 1.6057

Find i for F/P = 1.571
Use the following extrapolation equation:

$$(i - 6)/(1.571 - 1.5036) = (7 - 6)/(1.6057 - 1.5036)$$

If you look at the above equation, i matches with 1.571, 6% matches with 1.5036 and 7% matches with 1.6057.
Solve the above equation to find i.
i = 6.660

Solution using equations:

$F = P (1 + i)^n$
F = 11,000
P = 7000   n = 7

$i = (F/P)^{1/n} - 1$
$i = (11,000/7,000)^{1/7} - 1$
$i = 0.067 = 6.7\%$

Series Payments (A): Business loans are paid using series payments. Assume a contractor obtained a loan and agreed to pay the loan in a yearly basis. This could be represented in an arrow diagram. Money coming into the contractor is represented with an upward arrow and money paid is represented with a downward arrow.

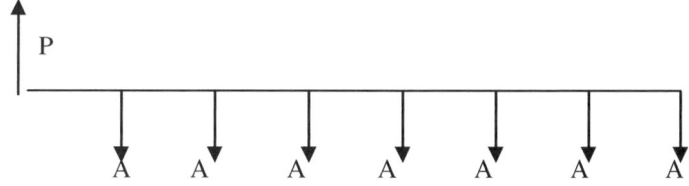

P = Present worth (shown with an upward arrow to indicate money coming in)
A = Series payments (shown with a downward arrow to indicate money going out)

$$P = A \, [(1 + i)^n - 1]/[i \, (1 + i)^n]$$

Practice Problem 2.45: A contractor obtained a 3 million dollar loan from a bank at an interest rate of 4% and agreed to make yearly payments for 5 years. What is his yearly payment?

Solution:

$P = 3{,}000{,}000 \quad i = 4\% \quad n = 5$

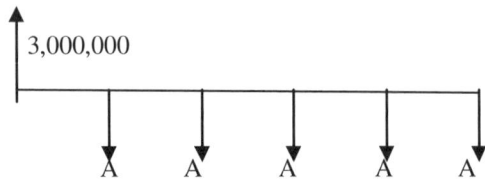

$P = A \, [(1 + i)^n - 1]/[i \, (1 + i)^n]$

$3{,}000{,}000 = A \, [(1 + 0.04)^5 - 1]/[0.04 \, (1 + 0.04)^5]$
$3{,}000{,}000 = A \, [(1.04)^5 - 1]/[0.04 \, (1.04)^5]$
$3{,}000{,}000 = A \times 4.45$
$\quad\quad A = 3{,}000{,}000/4.45 \; = \; 674{,}157$

Series Payments and Future Value: An employee can make series payments to a pension fund and expect to obtain a lump sum in the future.

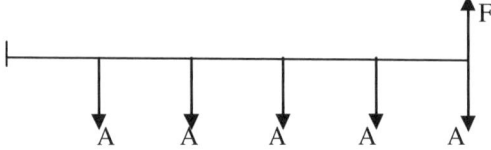

$F = A \, [(1 + i)^n - 1]/[i]$

Practice Problem 2.46 An employee makes yearly payments for 20 years for a pension fund. His yearly payment is $10,000 and interest rate is 7%. How much money he would be able to collect at the end of the 20-year period.

Solution:

$F = A \, [(1 + i)^n - 1]/[i]$
$A = 10{,}000$
$i = 0.07 \quad\quad n = 20$

$F = 10{,}000 \, [(1 + 0.07)^{20} - 1]/[0.07]$
$F = 10{,}000 \, [(1.07)^{20} - 1]/[0.07]$
$F = 409{,}954$

Future Value and Arithmetic Gradient: (F and G)   Payments can increase after every payment. Such schemes are known as arithmetic gradients (G).

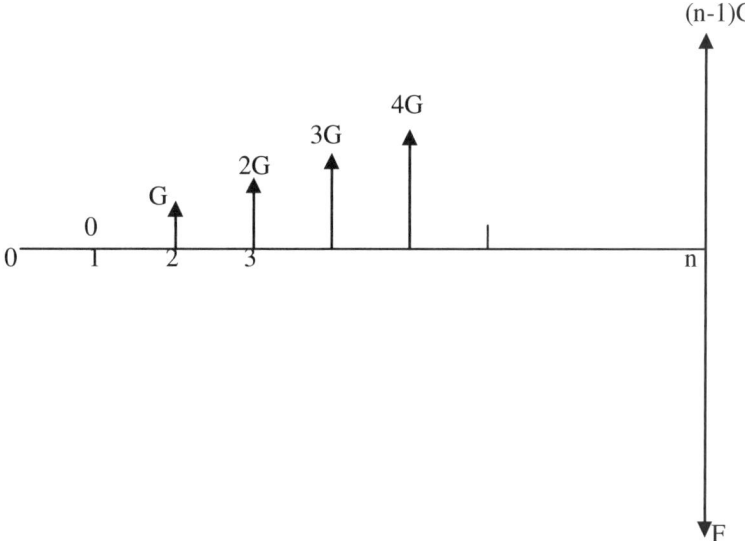

Note that first year increment is 0. Second year it is G and 3rd year it is 2G and so forth. In the above figure, an individual is making constantly increasing payments to a bank and eventually obtain a future one-time sum of F.

Above series is equal to one final payment of F. F is given as

$$F = \frac{G}{i} \left[\frac{(1 + i)^n - 1}{i} - n \right]$$

If F is known P or A can be calculated from equations given before.

Uniform Series (A) and Arithmetic Gradient (G): (A and G):

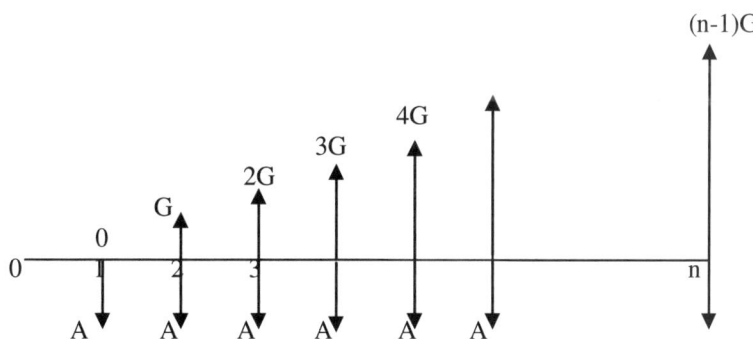

In the above series, a man is making constantly increasing sum of money and in return obtain uniform series payments (A). Please note the figure is not drawn to a scale.

$$A = G \left[\frac{1}{i} - \frac{n}{(1 + i)^n - 1} \right]$$

Practice Problem 2.47:   A man is making monthly payments of 0, 500, 1000, 1500 etc for 11 years. After 11 years he wishes to obtain a lump sum payment. What is his lump sum payment if the interest rate is 5%?

Solution:

G = 500,   i = 5%   n = 11   F = ?

Use the interest tables.   Since F needs to be found, look for F/G.
From interest tables F/G = 64.135
Hence F = 64.135 x G = 64.135 x 500 = $ 32,067

Finding the Interest Rate when G, n and F are Given:

Practice Problem 2.48:   A man is making monthly payments of 0, 500, 1000, 1500 etc for 11 years. After 11 years, he wishes to obtain a lump sum payment of $40,000. What is the interest rate?
It is easier to use equations to solve such problems than using interest table.

Solution:
G = 500,   i = ?   n = 11   F = 40,000

$$ F = \frac{G}{i} \left[\frac{(1+i)^n - 1}{i} - n \right] $$

$$ 40,000 = \frac{500}{i} \left[\frac{(1+i)^{11} - 1}{i} - 11 \right] $$

In the exam, four answers will be given. The student can insert the values and see which one works. In the real world, the problem has to be solved thru iteration.
Use an interest rate of 5% and check the value in the right hand side of the equation.
For interest rate of 5%, the value on the right hand side is 32,067.
Use a higher interest rate and check the value again.
For interest rate of 6%, the value on the right hand side is 33,097.
For interest rate of 12%, the value on the right hand side is 40,227.
This value may be close enough for many situations.

Uniform Series (A) and Arithmetic Gradient (G): (A and G):

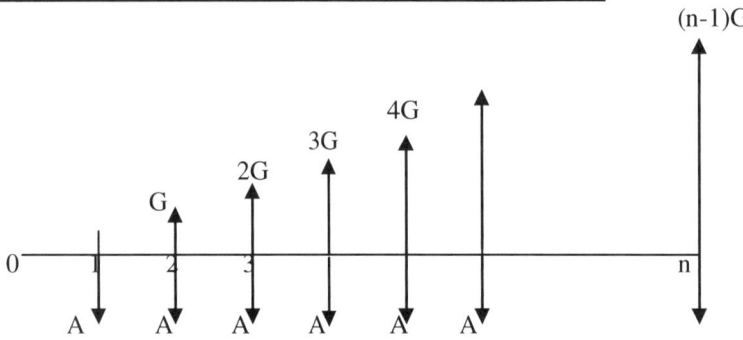

In the above series, a man is making constantly increasing sum of money and in return obtain uniform series payments (A).
Please note the figure is not drawn to a scale.

$$ A = G \left[\frac{1}{i} - \frac{n}{(1+i)^n - 1} \right] $$

Practice Problem 2.49:   A man is making monthly payments of 0, 600, 1200, 1800 etc for 7 years. During this time period, he likes to obtain a uniform payment every year. If the interest rate is 8% what is the uniform payment.

Solution:

        G = 600,   i = 8%   n = 7   A = ?
Since A needs to be found, from the interest tables find A/G.
A/G = 2.6936   (From interest tables)
A = 2.6936 x 600 = $1,616.2

Cost - Benefit Analysis: All projects have costs and benefits. It is important to investigate the costs and benefits involved in a project.

Practice Problem 2.47   Developer is considering two development projects. First project is a housing complex and the other one is a shopping mall. Following information is available.
Initial construction cost for the housing complex = 12 million dollars
Initial construction cost for the shopping mall = 17 million dollars
Yearly income from rental payments from the housing complex = 1.5 million dollars
Yearly income from rental payments from the shopping mall = 2.2 million dollars
Interest rate is at 6% and both projects have a lifetime of 20 years.
What is the better investment?

Solution:

Arrow diagram for the housing complex:

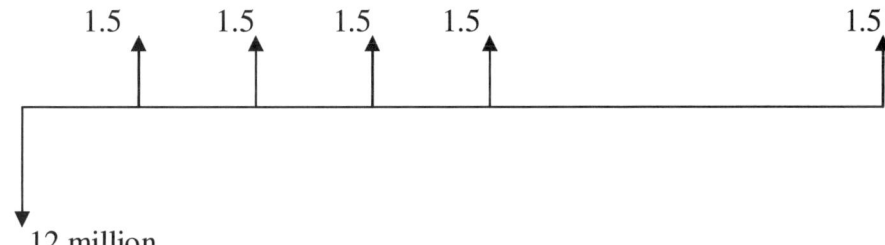

Housing complex has an initial cost of 12 million dollars. However, the developer will get yearly payments of 1.5 million dollars for next 20 years.

It is important to convert yearly payments to present worth.
What is the present worth of the yearly payments?
$P = A [(1 + i)^n - 1]/[i (1 + i)^n]$
A = 1.5   n = 20   i = 6%

$P = 1.5 [(1 + 0.06)^{20} - 1]/[0.06 (1 + 0.06)^{20}]$
$P = 1.5 [(1.06)^{20} - 1]/[0.06 (1.06)^{20}]$
P = 17.2 million dollars
Above arrow diagram can be represented as follows:

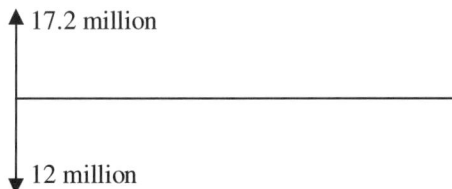

Initial investment = 12 million
Present value of return = 17.2 million

Benefit = 5.2 million

Shopping Mall: Shopping mall has an initial cost of 17 million dollars. However, the developer will get yearly payments of 2.2 million dollars for next 20 years.

$P = A [(1 + i)^n - 1]/[i (1 + i)^n]$

A = 2.2   n = 20   i = 6%

$P = 2.2 [(1 + 0.06)^{20} - 1]/[0.06 (1 + 0.06)^{20}]$
$P = 2.2 [(1.06)^{20} - 1]/[0.06 (1.06)^{20}]$
P = 25.2 million dollars

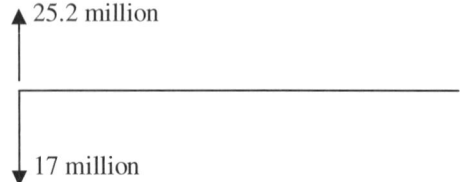

Initial investment = 17 million
Present value of return = 25.2 million
Benefit = 8.2 million
Shopping mall will bring a profit of 8.2 million.

Practice Problem 2.48:   A city is considering building a new power plant or to upgrade the existing power plant. The new power plant costs 2.5 million dollars. It has a maintenance cost of 50,000 dollars per year for the first year and expected to increase by $5,000 per year. Existing plant can be upgraded by spending $300,000 per year for the next 5 years. Existing plant has a maintenance cost of 60,000 per year and expected to increase by 6,000 per year. Which alternative cost is smaller if you consider the costs for next 10 years? Assume an interest rate of 5%.

Solution:

All costs and benefits need to be transformed to present value.

Alternative A: Initial cost = 2,500,000
                 Annual maintenance cost (A) for next 10 years = 50,000
                 Gradient (G) = 5,000

Alternative B: Initial cost = 0
                 Annual cost for upgrading (A1) for next 5 years = 300,000
                 Annual maintenance cost (A2) for next 10 years = 60,000
                 Gradient (G) = 6,000

Alternative A: Arrow diagram;

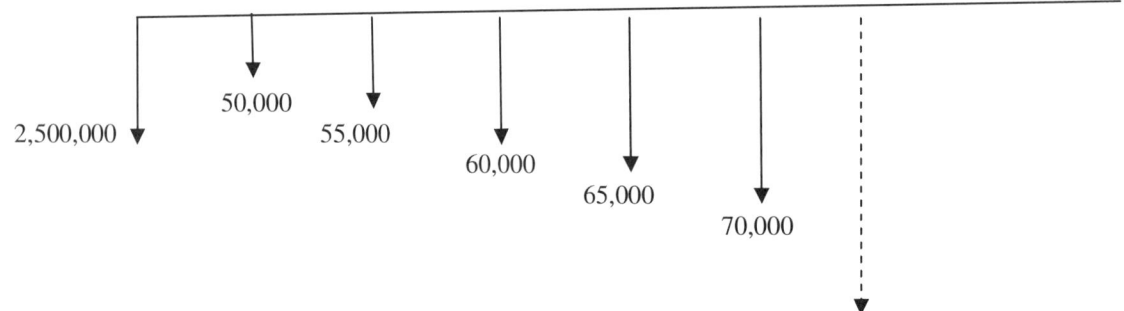

Convert all costs and benefits to present value.

Maintenance cost is divided into a uniform series and a gradient.

Maintenance cost = Uniform series (A) + Gradient (G)
        A = 50,000   G = 5,000

Uniform series (A) of $50,000 and a Gradient (G) of 5,000.

Present value of uniform series of 50,000.

Use the interest table to find P/A value for n = 10 and i = 5%.
P/A = 7.722
Hence P = 7.722 x 50,000 = -$386,100

(Negative value is used since it is a cost).

Convert the Gradient (G = 5,000) to present value.
Find using interest tables P/G for i = 5% and n = 10
P/G = 31.652
Hence   P = 31.652 x 5,000 = - 158,260

Total maintenance cost = -$386,100 - $158,260 = -$544,360
Total cost   = Cost to build the new power plant + Total maintenance cost
                  = $-2,500,000 - $544,360 = -$3,044,360

Alternative 2:   Alternative cost is divided into two arrow diagrams. First arrow diagram shows the plant upgrade cost. Second arrow diagram shows the

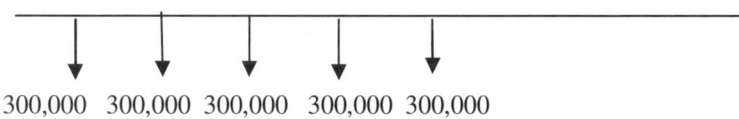

300,000   300,000 300,000   300,000 300,000

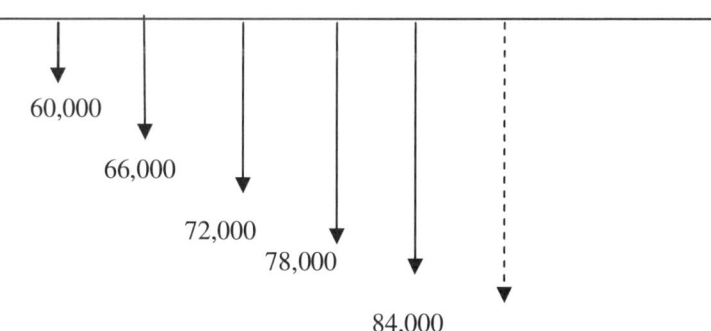

60,000

66,000

72,000

78,000

84,000

Upgrade Cost:

Upgrade cost is 300,000 per year for 5 years.

(P/A, i = 5, n = 5) = 4.329   (From interest tables)

Present cost of the upgrade cost = 4.329 x 300,000 = -$1,298,700

<u>Maintenance Cost:</u>

Maintenance cost is divided into a uniform series and a gradient.

Maintenance cost = Uniform series (A) + Gradient (G)
         A = 60,000   G = 5,000

Uniform series (A) of $60,000 and a Gradient (G) of 6,000.

Present value of uniform series of 60,000.

Use the interest table to find P/A value for n = 10 and i = 5%.
P/A = 7.722
Hence P = 7.722 x 60,000 = -$463,320

(Negative value is used since it's a cost).

Convert the Gradient (G = 6,000) to present value.
Find using interest tables P/G for i = 5% and n = 10
P/G = 31.652
Hence   P = 31.652 x 6,000 = - 189,912

Total maintenance cost = -$463,320 - $189,912 = -$653,232
Total cost   = Cost to upgrade the power plant + Total maintenance cost
            = -$1,298,700 - $653,232 = -$ 1,951,932

Alternative 2 is better.

2.4   Earned Value Management:

Earned value management section is one of the easiest sections in the examination. Questions from this section are highly likely.

Consider the following scenario. Contractor receives a lump sum contract to construct a 1,000 ft long pipeline for $500 per linear foot. Contractor is required to complete the project in 10 months. Contractor would be paid monthly based on work completed.

Budgeted cost = 1,000 x 500 = $500,000

Assume that the contractor has completed 80 ft of pipe after one month and he has expended $55,000. This is contractor's actual cost (AC).

Cost Implications: Since contractor has completed only 80 ft, he is entitled to $40,000. (80 ft x 500). Contractor's entitlement is known as earned value (EV).

Contractor's actual cost after one month (AC) = $55,000

Contractor's earnings (EV) = $40,000

Contractor's loss after one month = $15,000

It is clear that contractor has to cut costs, otherwise he would end up with a loss at the end of the project.

Schedule Implications: Contractor is supposed to complete 1,000 ft of pipe in 10 months. Hence, he is scheduled to complete 100 ft every month. Hence, his planned value after one month is $50,000 (100 x 500).

However, he has completed only 80 ft of pipes after one month. It is clear that the contractor is behind schedule.

Scheduled cost or planned value (PV) = 100 x 50 = 50,000.

Hence, for this project, following information can be formulated after one month.

	month 1	month 2	month 3	month 4	month 5	month 6	month 7	month 8	month 9	month 10
PV	50,000	100,000	150,000	200,000	250,000	300,000	350,000	400,000	450,000	500,000
EV	40,000									
AC	55,000									

Assume after the second month he has completed a total of 190 ft of pipes (including the 80 ft he did on the first month) and his total expenses (including the first month) is $102,000.

Find EV, PV and AC.

Actual cost (AC) = $102,000.
Planned value (PV) = 100,000 (as per schedule)
Earned value (EV) = 190 ft x 500 = $95,000

	month 1	month 2	month 3	month 4	month 5	month 6	month 7	month 8	month 9	month 10
PV	50,000	100,000	150,000	200,000	250,000	300,000	350,000	400,000	450,000	500,000
EV	40,000	95,000								
AC	55,000	102,000								

Practice Problem 2.48:   Mr. Sanath of ABC contracting has obtained a project to drive 600 ft of piles in 4 months. Contractor would be paid $200 per each foot of piling. After 2 months, contractor has completed 350 ft of piling and his actual cost happened to be $82,000.

As a construction engineer what is your advice to the contractor?

Solution:

Total budget = 600 ft x 200 = $ 120,000

After 2 months as per schedule, 50% of the project should be completed.

Planned value (PV) = 50% x 120,000 = $60,000

After two months contractor has completed 350 ft of piles.

Earned value (EV) = 350ft x 200 = $70,000

Actual cost for the contractor (AC) = $82,000

Analysis: Contractor has earned 70,000 but expended 82,000. Hence, contractor has lost 12,000 dollars after two months.

As per schedule contractor should have earned $60,000 (PV).

However, contractor has earned 70,000. Hence, contractor is ahead of schedule.

Contractor is moving faster than the original schedule.

Your advice to the contractor: Mr. Sanath, you are spending more than you earn. Hence, you are losing money. If you want to be profitable, you have to cut costs.

As per progress, you are moving faster than the schedule. You can slow down little bit if that helps in cutting costs.

Fancy Terms for Earned Value, Planned Value and Actual Value:

Some prefer to use terms such as BCWP, ACWP, BCWS for earned value, actual cost and planned value.

Earned value (EV) = BCWP (Budgeted cost for work performed)
Actual cost (AC) = ACWP (Actual cost for work performed)
Planned value (PV) = BCWS (Budgeted cost for work scheduled)

Unfortunately, you have to remember these terms as well.

Cost Performance Index (CPI):   CPI is defined as follows;

$$\text{CPI} = \text{EV/AC} = \text{BCWP/ACWP}$$

CPI = 1.0:   If CPI is equal to 1.0, earned value is equal to actual cost. In other words, contractor is spending exactly what he is earning. Contractors are in business to make money. If he is spending exactly what he is earning, that is not productive.

CPI < 1.0:   In this case, earned value is less than the actual cost.   In other words, he is earning less than what he is spending. Contractor is losing money.

CPI > 1.0:   In this case, earned value is greater than the actual cost.   In other words, he is earning more than what he is spending. Contractor is making a profit.

Schedule Performance Index (SPI):

SPI is defined as follows;

$$\text{SPI} = \text{EV/PV} = \text{BCWP/BCWS}$$

SPI = 1.0:   If SPI is equal to 1.0, earned value is equal to planned value. In other words, contractor is earning exactly what he planned as per schedule. Contractor is moving along as per schedule.

SPI < 1.0:   In this case, earned value is less than the planned value.   In other words, he is earning less than what he planned as per schedule. Contractor is falling behind the schedule.

SPI > 1.0:   In this case, earned value is greater than the planned value.   In other words, he is earning more than what he planned as per schedule. Contractor is ahead of schedule.

Some Questions and Answers:

Question: SPI of a project is 1.5. Is the contractor making a profit?
Answer: It is not possible to tell whether the contractor is making a profit by looking at SPI.

Question: If SPI is 1.5, is the contractor ahead of the schedule?
Answer: If SPI is 1.5, then contractor is earning more than what he planned. Hence, he is ahead of schedule.

Question: If CPI is 0.8, is the contractor ahead of the schedule?
Answer: CPI cannot be used to answer questions about the schedule.

Question: If CPI is 0.8, is the contractor making a profit.

Answer: If CPI is 0.8, EV is less than AC. He is earning less than what he is spending. Contractor is losing money.

Cost Variance: (CV):   Cost variance (CV) is defined as follows;

$$CV \text{ (Cost Variance)} = EV - AC = BCWP - ACWP$$

If CV is a positive value, then contractor is earning more than what he is spending. That is a positive development. If CV is negative then the contractor is losing money.

Schedule Variance: (SV):   Schedule variance (SV) is defined as follows;

$$SV \text{ (Schedule Variance)} = EV - PV = BCWP - BCWS$$

If SV is a positive value, then contractor is earning more than what he planned at the start of the project. That means contractor is ahead of schedule. If SV is negative, then the contractor is earning less than what he planned at the beginning. Contractor is behind schedule.

Summary:

CPI = EV/AC= BCWP/ACWP

CPI > 1   Contractor is making a profit
CPI < 1   Contractor is losing money
CPI cannot be used to tell whether contractor is ahead of schedule or behind schedule.
SPI = EV/PV = BCWP/BCWS

SPI > 1   Contractor is ahead of schedule
SPI < 1   Contractor is behind schedule

SPI cannot be used to tell whether contractor is making a profit or not.

CV (Cost Variance) = EV - AC = BCWP - ACWP

If CV is positive, contractor is making a profit
If CV is negative, contractor is losing money

SV (Schedule Variance) = EV - PV = BCWP - BCWS

If SV is positive, contractor is ahead of schedule.
If SV is negative, contractor is behind schedule.

Earned Value Graphs:

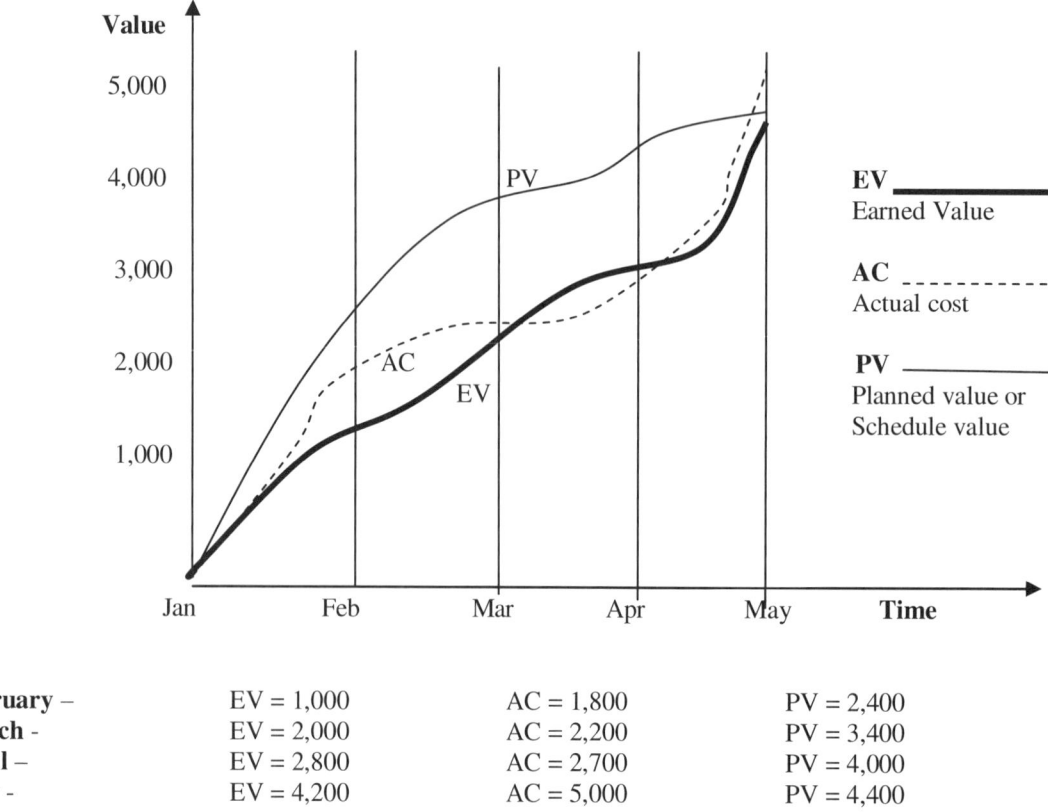

February –	EV = 1,000	AC = 1,800	PV = 2,400
March -	EV = 2,000	AC = 2,200	PV = 3,400
April –	EV = 2,800	AC = 2,700	PV = 4,000
May -	EV = 4,200	AC = 5,000	PV = 4,400

In the above graph contractor agreed with the client to get paid $1 per each square foot of painting.

February:

- **Earned Value (EV):**   By February, contractor has completed 1000 sq. ft of painting and client would pay him $1,000 (EV) as per contract.

- **Actual Cost (AC):**   But contractor found out that he has spent $1,800 by February. The owner was furious and after investigating, he was able to find the reason.   He found out that some workers were inefficient and highly paid. To cut costs, he decides to replace highly paid workers with low paid workers. Further, he takes steps to increase the productivity.
  CPI = EV/AC = 1,000/1,800 = 0.56
  In other words, to earn 1 dollar, he has to spend approximately 1.8 dollars. This is not a healthy situation.

  CV (Cost Variance) = EV – AC = 1,000 – 1,800 = -800 (Cash flow is negative)

- **Planned Value: (PV):**   If contractor had completed everything as per schedule, he would be paid the planned value. Very rarely any project goes as exactly as the schedule. As per schedule, contractor is supposed to finish 2400 sq. ft of painting by February. If he was able to stick to the schedule, he would have earned $2,400 by February. However, the contractor had painted only 1000 sq. ft, hence the contractor is behind schedule.

  SPI = EV/PV = 1,000/2,400 = 0.41
  SV (Schedule Variance) = EV - PV = 1,000 – 2,400 = -1,400

  The contractor is way behind the schedule. He should have completed approximately $2,400 worth of work. But he has completed only 1000 sq. ft.

March:

- **Earned Value (EV):**   By March, contractor has completed 2,000 sq. ft of painting and client would pay him $2,000 (EV) as per contract.
- **Actual Cost (AC):**   Due to hiring low salary workers, actual cost of the contractor has reduced. Now the actual cost is $2,200.
- $CPI = EV/AC = 2,000/2,200 = 0.91$
  Still his actual costs are higher than his earnings. But the situation has significantly improved.
  CV (Cost Variance) = $EV - AC = 2,000 - 2,200 = -200$ (Cash flow is still negative. Things have vastly improved)

- **Planned Value: (PV):**   As per schedule, contractor is supposed to finish 3400 sq. ft of painting by March. If he was able to stick to the schedule, he would have earned $3,400 by March. However, the contractor had painted only 2000 sq. ft, hence the contractor is behind schedule.
- $SPI = EV/PV = 2,000/3,400 = 0.59$
  SV (Schedule Variance) = $EV - PV = 2,000 - 3,400 = -1,400$

April:

- **Earned Value (EV):**   By April, contractor has completed 2800 sq. ft of painting and client would pay him $2,800 (EV) as per contract.
- **Actual Cost (AC):**   Due to hiring low salary workers, actual cost of the contractor has reduced. Now the actual cost is $2,700.
- $CPI = EV/AC = 2,800/2,700 = 1.03$
  His CPI has gone above 1.0. His actual costs are lower than his earnings.

  CV (Cost Variance) = $EV - AC = 2,800 - 2,700 = 100$ (Cash flow is now positive. Things are looking good for the contractor).

- **Planned Value: (PV):**   As per schedule, contractor is supposed to finish 4,000 sq. ft of painting by April. If he was able to stick to the schedule, he would have earned $4,000 by April. But the contractor had painted only 2800 sq. ft, hence the contractor is still behind schedule.
- $SPI = EV/PV = 2,800/4000 = 0.70$
  SV (Schedule Variance) = $EV - PV = 2,800 - 4000 = -1,200$

May:

- **Earned Value (EV):**   By May, contractor has completed 4200 sq. ft of painting and client would pay him $4,200 (EV) as per contract.
- **Actual Cost (AC):**   Now the actual cost is $5000.
- $CPI = EV/AC = 4200/5000 = 0.84$
  Contractor is losing money.
  CV (Cost Variance) = $EV - AC = 4200 - 5000 = -800$

- **Planned Value: (PV):**   As per schedule, contractor is supposed to finish 4400 sq. ft of painting by May. If he was able to stick to the schedule, he would have earned $4,400 by May. However, the contractor had painted only 4200 sq. ft, hence the contractor is still behind schedule.
- $SPI = EV/PV = 4200/4400 = 0.95$
  SV (Schedule Variance) = $EV - PV = 4200 - 4400 = -200$

  Contractor is behind schedule. Contractor will exceed the contract duration.

**   See my Practice Problem Book and three sample exams for more Practice Problems***

3.0 Construction Operations and Methods

3.1 Introduction: Construction work requires many operations. Lifting and rigging, dewatering, concreting, bracing of temporary structures, underpinning, jacking, grouting and pumping are some common construction operations.

3.2 Lifting and Rigging: No construction can be done without lifting and rigging of material and equipment to the proper location. Rigging is a word that comes from the early sailing days. Rigging meant moving a ship which involved many operations. In the construction industry, the word "rigging" is used to indicate moving and lifting of material and equipment.

You cannot build if you do not move it to the correct location. Moving involves lifting, rolling, pulling and pushing. Ancient Egyptians used wooden cylinders to move large stones. Today many other forms of equipment are used. As a construction engineer, you need to be familiar with equipment and methods used to lift and move material and equipment.

Typically, in the construction industry, steel beams, steel columns have to be lifted. In high-rise building construction, concrete has to be lifted. Construction equipment such as jacks, tools, concrete mixers, testing equipment also have to be moved and lifted to the place where they are needed.

Note: I have covered cranes, derricks, rigging equipment such as thimbles, spreader beams, hooks, shackles, also rigging methods and rigging computations in "**Civil PE Construction Module Practice Problems – Second Edition**". Hence I will not cover that subject matter in this book.

3.2.1 Sheaves (Pulleys) and Blocks:

Sheaves (Pulleys):

In construction, sheaves and blocks are widely used. Sheave and pulley means the same thing.

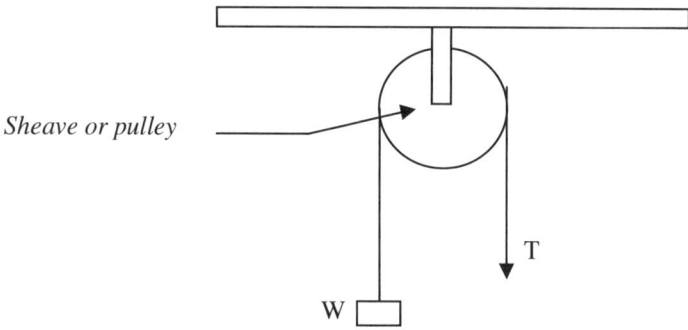

In a sheave, mechanical advantage is 1. In other words, $T = W$.
This is assuming that pulley and rope has no friction. We would later discuss how to calculate the force when friction is present,

Blocks:
When more than one sheave is connected together it is known as a *block*.

Look at the above figure. It shows a pulley or a sheave on upper left. Lower left shows a block. It has two sheaves. Upper right shows another block which has three sheaves.

Figure: A block with sixteen sheaves

3.2.2   Block and Tackle:

When two or more blocks are combined together it is known as a block and tackle.

Figure: Block and Tackle

Above figure shows two blocks. Both blocks have two sheaves each. When more than one block is used, it is known as block and tackle.

3.2.3   Single Whip: Lifting with one sheave is known as single whip.

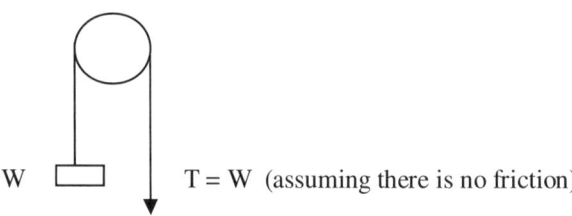

W   T = W (assuming there is no friction)

Single whip

Mechanical advantage of a single whip is 1.0. In other words, there is no advantage. Force required to lift weight W is W.

Parts of Line: Parts of line is defined as number of ropes attached to the weight. In this case, only one rope is attached to the weight. Hence parts of lines is 1.0.

Movement of Single Whip: When weight move one ft upwards, the effort moves 1 ft downward.

Gun Tackle:

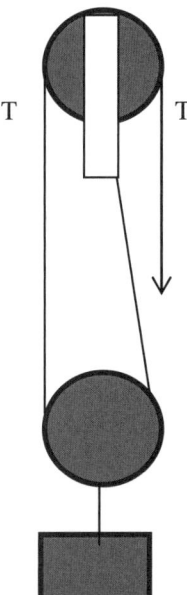

Weight = 2. T
Gun Tackle

Two sheaves assembled one below the other is known as gun tackle.

Let us assume applied force is "T". Then this tension travels thru the ropes as shown if there is no friction. Now if you look at the lower block, it has two ropes pulling up. Hence the block is been pulled by a force of 2.T.
The force applied = 100 lbs
The weight that can be lifted = 200 lbs
Mechanical advantage = 2.0

Parts of Line: In this case, two ropes are attached to the weight. Hence parts of lines for a gun tackle is 2.0. Note that mechanical advantage and parts of line are the same.
Movement of Gun Tackle: Let us see how much weight moves when the effort moves by 1 ft.

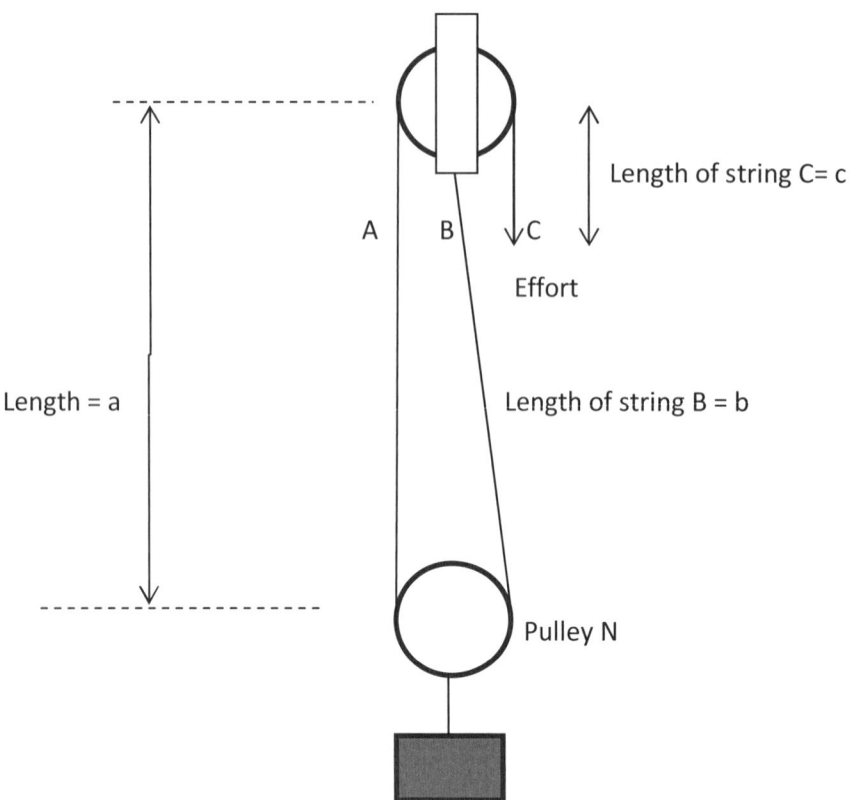

Length of string C= c

A   B   ↓C

Effort

Length = a

Length of string B = b

Pulley N

Strings are named A, B and C.
Length of string A = "a"
Length of string B = "b"
Length of string C = "c"
Total length of strings = a + b + c
Now let us assume that effort moves by X ft downward.

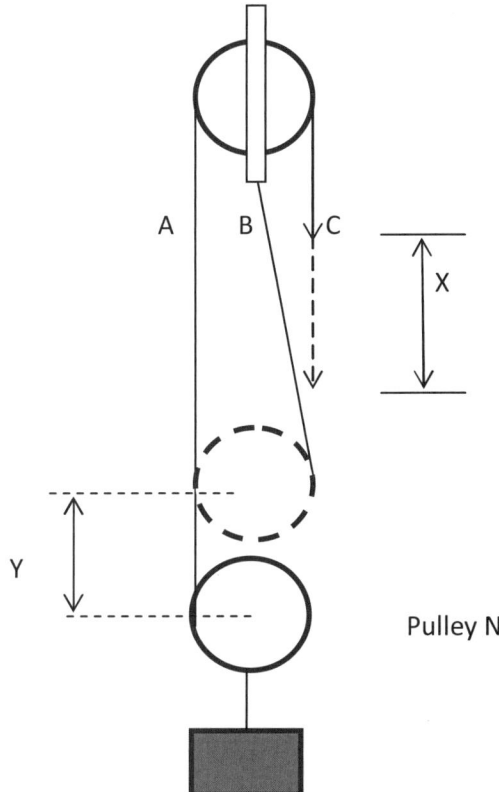

Let us say string C is pulled by distance X downwards.

Then let us assume pulley N would go up by distance Y

New lengths of strings;

Length of string A = a - Y
Length of string B = b - Y
Length of string C = c + X
Total length of strings = (a – Y) + (b – Y) + c + X
Total lengths of strings do not change;
Hence
  a + b + c = (a – Y) + (b – Y) + c + X

  0 = -2Y + X
  Y = X/2

Hence we can see that when the string is pulled by a distance of X, the pulley would go up by a distance of X/2.
When effort moves by a distance of 1 ft, the weight moves up by a distance of 1/2 ft.
Also we can say that when weight moves 1 ft, effort has to move 2 ft.

Luff Tackle:

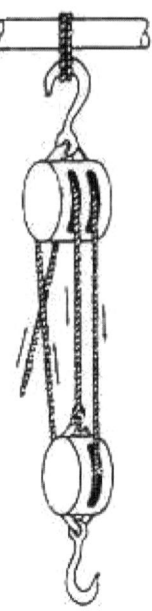

Luff Tackle

Luff tackle has a top block with two sheaves and a bottom block with one sheave. The weight is lifted by three ropes. Parts of line for Luff tackle is 3.0. Mechanical advantage is 3.0.

Luff tackle can be used to lift a 300 lb weight using a force of 100 lbs. When the weight move 1 ft upwards, pulling rope will move 3 ft.

Work done by the weight = 300 x 1.0 = 300 lbs. ft
Work done by the puller = 100 x 3.0 = 300 lbs. ft

Twofold Purchase:

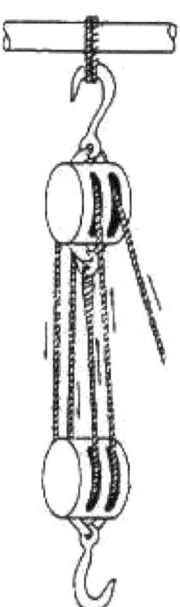

Twofold Purchase

Twofold purchase has an upper block with two sheaves and a lower block with two sheaves.

Parts of line for twofold purchase is 4.0. Note that the weight is attached to 4.0 lines. Mechanical advantage of a twofold purchase is 4.0. In other words, with a force of 100lbs, one can lift 400 lbs.

Luff Upon Luff:

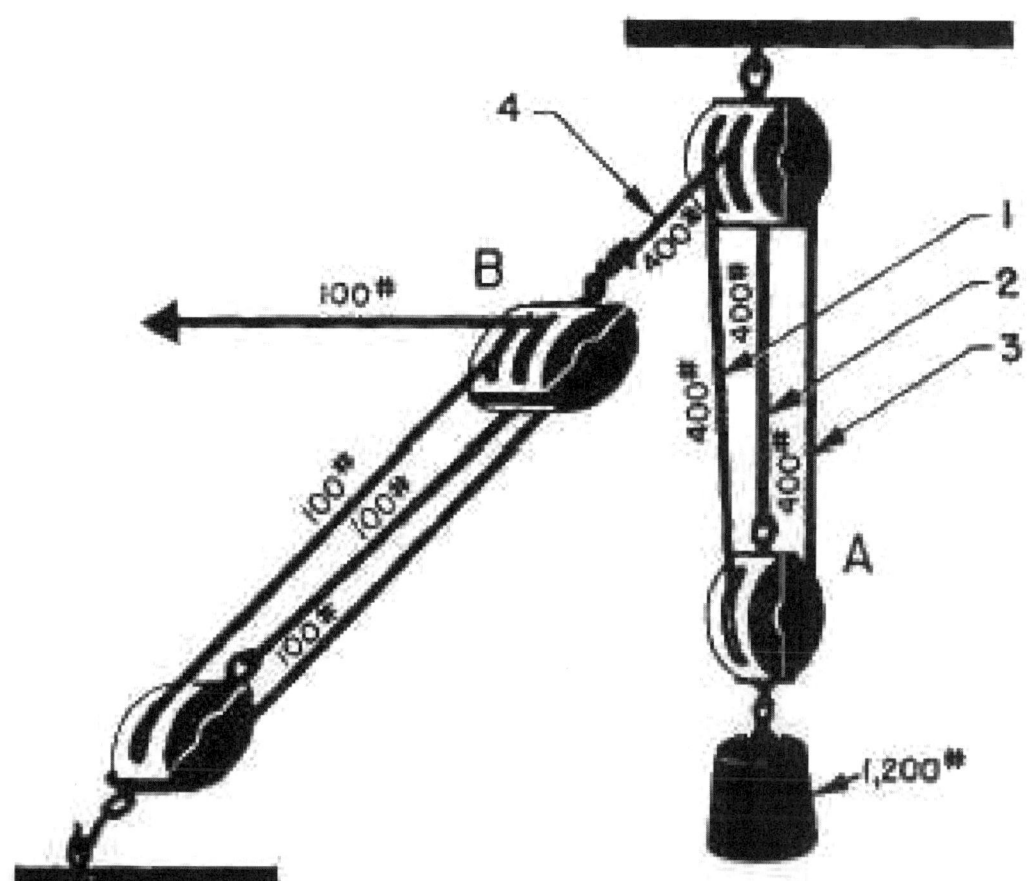

Figure: Luff Upon Luff

Above figure shows a Luff upon luff arrangement. Let us assume an effort of 100 lbs is provided.
Then rope marked 4, will have a force of 400 lbs. Similarly ropes marked 1, 2 and 3 also have 400 lbs each. Hence a weight of 1,200 lbs can be lifted with an effort of 100 lbs.
Mechanical advantage = 12.
In this case parts of lines is not equal to mechanical advantage.

3.2.4 Pulleys with Friction:

So far we considered only pulleys without friction. In real world, friction can be significant. Let us look at the simple pulley. Assume the weight is W and the force required to pull the weight is T. Note that T is NOT equal to W when friction is present. Also assume that the friction coefficient is μ.

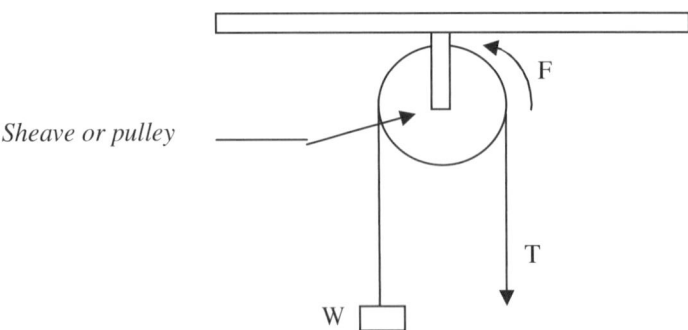

Sheave or pulley

When the rope is pulled down, friction (F) is acting against the movement of the rope.
Hence we can write;
T = W + F ----------------------------(1)

W and F are acting in the same direction.
Now F = µ. T ------------------------(2)

One may think why F is not equal to µ. W.
In reality, portion of the rope has a tension of T and other portion has a tension of W. F = µ. T is larger than F = µ. W.
Hence it is conservative.
T = W + µ. T
W = T - µ.T = T (1- µ)
T = W/(1- µ)

Example: Assume the friction factor of a rope and pulley is 0.24. Load of 150 lbs needs to be lifted with a simple pulley. What is the force required?
T = W/(1- µ)
T = 150/(1 - 0.24) = 197.37 lbs

Gun Tackle with Friction:

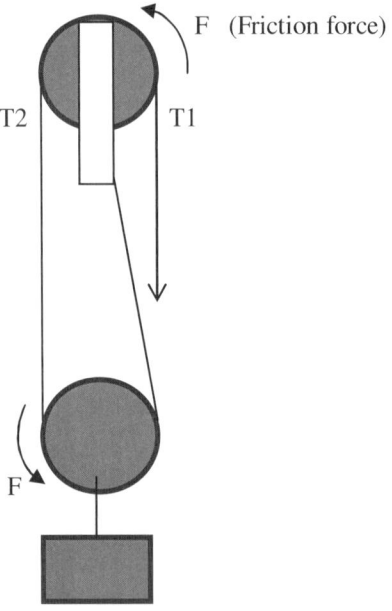

Weight = W
Gun Tackle

$T1 = T2 + F$
T2 and F acts on the same direction.

$T1 = T2 + \mu . T1$
$T2 = T1x (1- \mu)$ -----------------------(1)

Similarly;
$T3 + F = T2$
T3 and F acts in the same direction.
$T3 + \mu . T2 = T2$
$T3 = T2 \times (1- \mu)$ ----------------------(2)

From (1); $T2 = T1x (1- \mu)$

Hence $T3 = T1x (1- \mu) \times (1 - \mu) = T1 \times (1 - \mu)^2$

$W = T3 + T2$
$W = T1 \times (1 - \mu)^2 + T1x (1- \mu) = T1 \times [(1 - \mu)^2 + (1- \mu)]$

Example: Gun tackle is used to lift a weight of 230 lbs. Friction coefficient of two pulleys is 0.13. Find the force required to lift the weight.

$W = 230$ lbs and $\mu = 0.13$

$W = T1x [(1 - \mu)^2 + (1- \mu)]$
$230 = T1 [(1 - 0.13)^2 + (1 - 0.13)]$
$230 = T1 \times 1.6269$
$T1 = 141.37$ lbs

230 lbs load can be lifted with an effort of 141.37 lbs. If there was no friction, the same load could have lifted with 115 lbs.

3.2.5   Crane Mechanism:

Now we have acquired enough knowledge to tackle the crane mechanism. Simple crane consists of a winch, upper pulley and a moving block. Winch provides power to the rope through an internal combustion engine. Let us look at the figure below. You can see the upper pulley and moving block. The winch is not seen.

Upper pulley ————

Moving Block ————

Winch (Not seen) ————

Figure: Typical crane

Figure: Winch of a crane

Winch provides power to the ropes.

Example: Typical hoisting mechanism for a crane is shown in the figure. Load lifted is 900 lbs. Friction coefficient of ropes and pulleys is 0.15. What is the effort required to lift the weight?

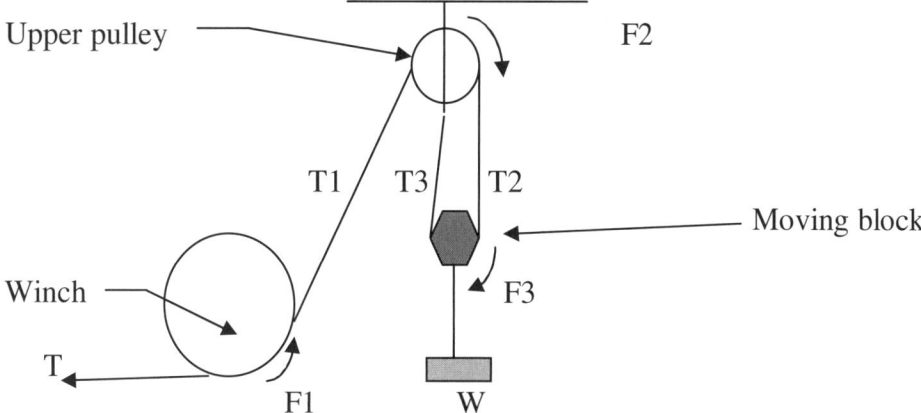

F1, F2 and F3 are frictional forces.   Assume the effort to be T and rope tensions as shown. Friction always acts against the movement of the rope.

$T = T1 + F1 = T1 + \mu. T$
Friction force and T1 act in the same direction.

$T1 = T \times (1 - \mu)$ ----------------------------(1)

Similarly at upper pulley;

$T1 = T2 + F2 = T2 + \mu. T1$
$T2 = T1 \times (1 - \mu)$ -------------------------(2)

From (1)
$T2 = T \times (1 - \mu)^2$---------------------------(3)

Also;
$T2 = T3 + F3 = T3 + \mu. T2$
$T3 = T2 \times (1 - \mu)$

From above (3)
$T3 = T \times (1 - \mu)^2 \times (1- \mu) = T \times (1 - \mu)^3$

$W = T3 + T2$
$W = T \times (1 - \mu)^3 + T \times (1 - \mu)^2$
$W = T \times [1 - \mu)^3 + (1 - \mu)^2]$

$T = W/[1 - \mu)^3 + (1 - \mu)^2]$
$T = 900/[1 - 0.15)^3 + (1 - 0.15)^2] = 673.33$ lbs

In this case, 900 lb load is lifted with an effort of 673.33 lbs.
If there is no friction, load could have lifted with an effort of 450 lbs since the mechanical advantage is 2.0.

When the hook has to be lowered, the moving block should move down. It should have enough weight to overcome the friction.

Example: In the above figure, the load has to be lowered. The friction coefficient between ropes and pulleys is 0.15. Assume the weight of pulleys and ropes to be negligible. The tension of the rope at the winch should not be zero. The rope in the winch should have some tension so that the rope will not get entangled. What is the minimum weight of the moving block?

Solution: When the hook has to be lowered, the moving block needs to overcome friction of cables and come down by itself. Hence the moving block should be heavy enough to overcome the friction in ropes. The weight of the moving block allows the hook to be brought down when there is no weight attached.

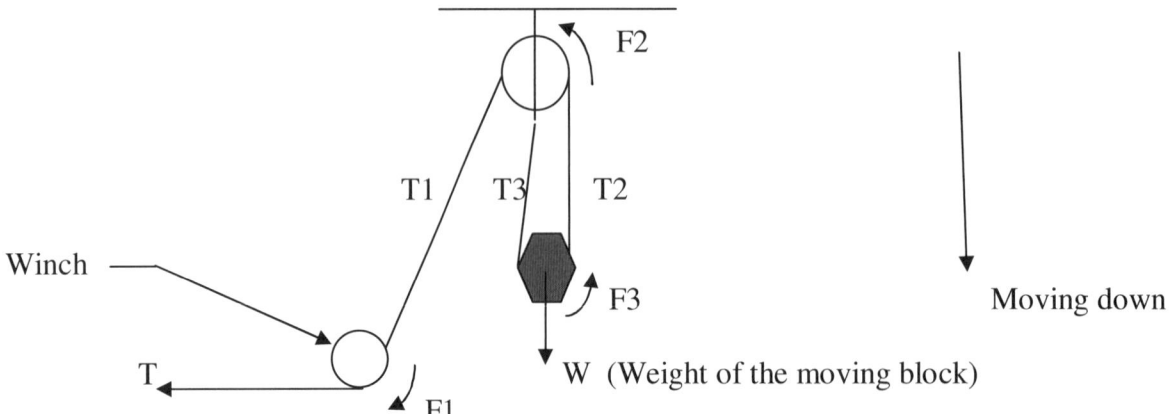

When the moving block comes down, friction is acting against the movement of ropes.

$T1 = F1 + T$
$F1 = \mu . T1$
$T1 = \mu . T1 + T$
$T = T1. (1- \mu)$
$T1 = T/(1- \mu)$ ----------------------------(1)

Also;
$T1 + F2 = T2$
$T1 + \mu.T2 = T2$
$T1 = T2 . (1 - \mu)$ -----------------------(2)

From (1)
$T1 = T/(1- \mu)$
$T/(1- \mu) = T2 . (1 - \mu)$
$T2 = T/(1 - \mu)^2$ ------------------------ (3)

At moving block;
$T3 = T2 + F3$
$F3 = \mu . T3$
$T3 = T2 + \mu . T3$
$T3 = T2/(1 - \mu)$

From (3) $T2 = T/(1 - \mu)^2$
$T3 = T/(1 - \mu)^3$ --------------------------(4)

$W = T2 + T3$
Hence;
$W = T/(1 - \mu)^2 + T/(1 - \mu)^3$

$W = T. [1/(1 - \mu)^2 + 1/(1 - \mu)^3]$

$\mu = 0.15$ and $T = 100$

$W = 100 \times 3.012 = 301.2$ lbs

Headache Ball:
In some instances a headache ball is used instead of a moving block to keep the ropes tight when a load is not attached.

Left: Headache ball.
Right: Headache ball attached as an additional weight to moving block. In this case, weight of moving block is not enough to bring the hook down. Hence a headache ball also attached to the moving block.

3.2.6   Chain Hoists:
Chain hoists are different than block and tackles. In the case of block and tackles, the radius of sheaves did not come into the equations. On the other hand, radius of sheaves are important for the mechanism of chain hoists. Chain hoists are largely used to lift heavy weights. The main advantage of chain hoists is that a large load can be lifted with little force. The mechanism of chain hoist is different than the mechanism of block and tackles.

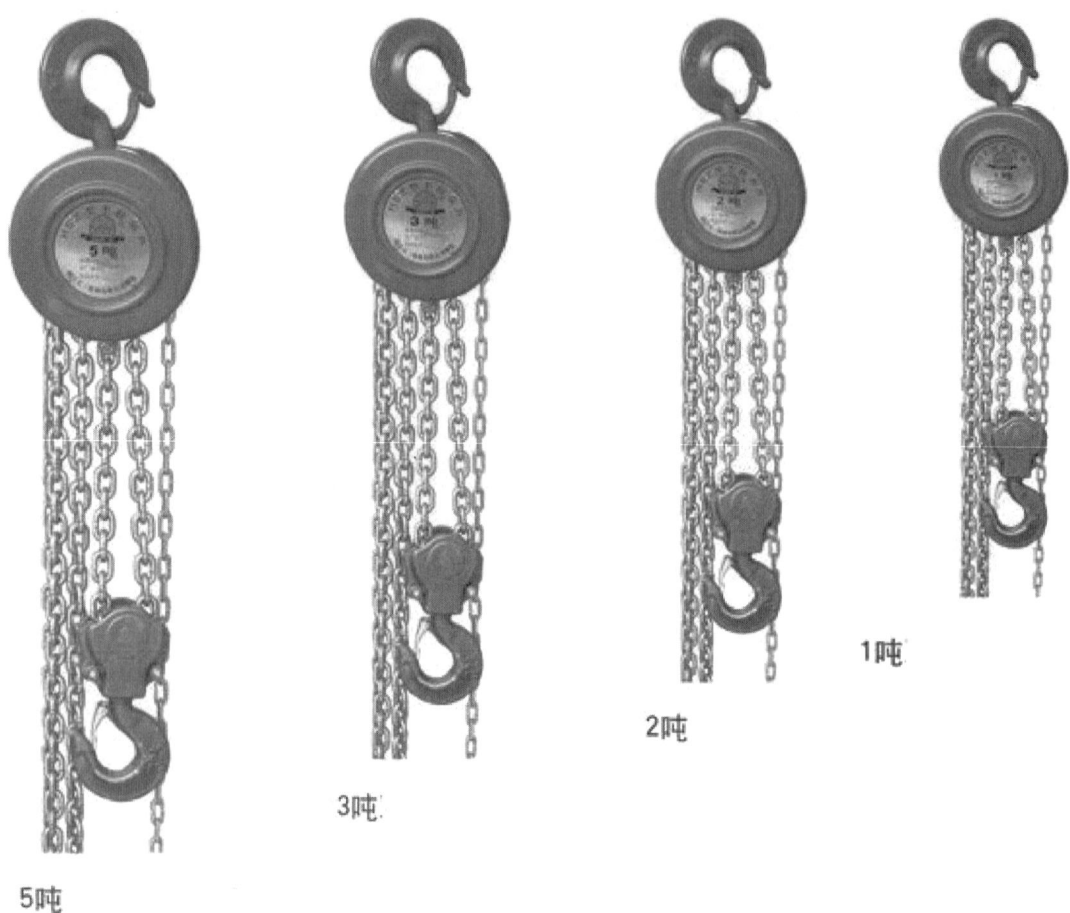

5吨

3吨

2吨

1吨

Chain hoists

<u>Chain Hoist Mechanism:</u>   Let us look at an example to understand the mechanism of chain hoists.

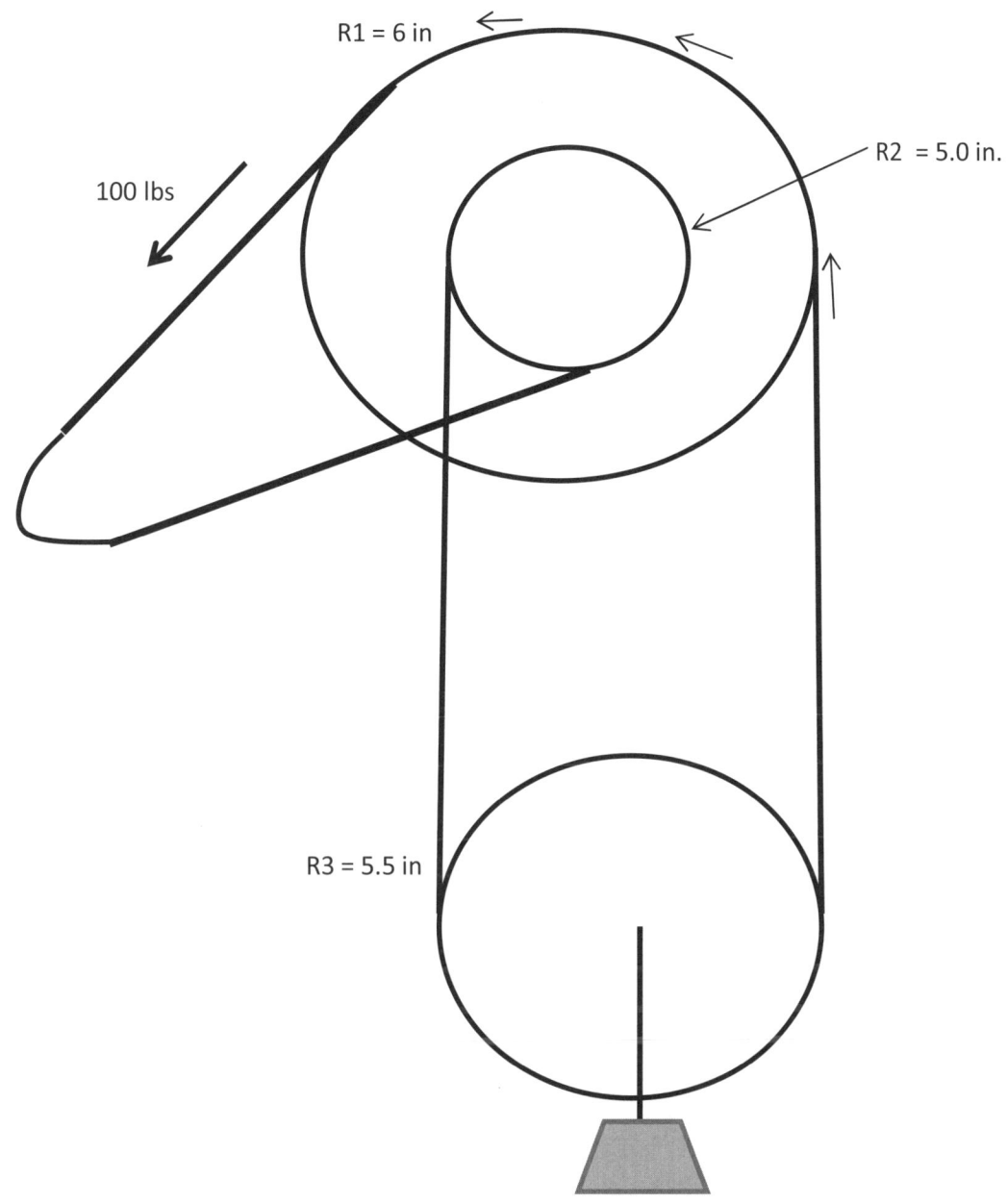

A chain hoist is shown in the above figure. Let us assume radii of pulleys are 6.0 in, 5.0 in and 5.5 in as shown. Assume a force of 130 lbs is applied.

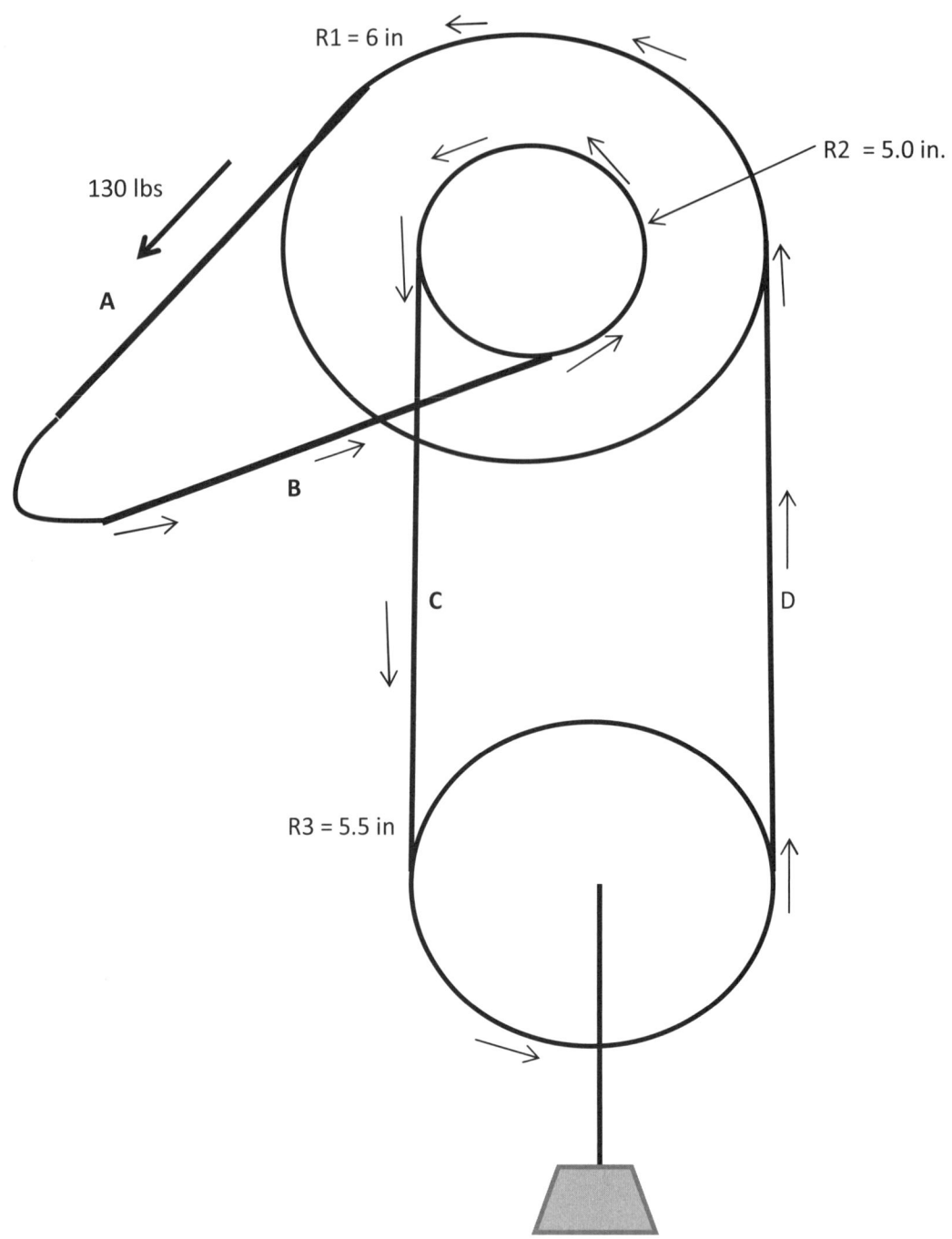

Wheels R1 and R2 are rigidly attached. When the wheel R1 makes one revolution, wheel R2 also makes one revolution. Though it is the same chain that goes around, the chain segments are named A, B, C and D.
Now let us look at the mechanism.

STEP 1:   Find the movement of the weight;
A worker pulls the chain and the wheel R1 makes one revolution. When wheel R1 makes one revolution, wheel R2 also makes one revolution since two wheels are rigidly attached.
The chain is pulled by a distance of $2.\pi. R1$
The chain segment D would go **up** by $2.\pi. R1$.
When chain segment D goes up by $2.\pi. R1$, the weight "W" will go up by $(2.\pi. R1)/2$.

When wheel R2 makes one revolution, chain segment C goes **down** by $2.\pi.$ R2
Net movement of the weight is $(2.\pi.$ R1 $- 2.\pi.$ R2$)/2 = \pi.$ (R1 – R2)

STEP 2:   Work done by weight and effort is the same if there is no friction.
The effort is given to be 130 lbs. The weight that can be lifted is to be found.

Work done by effort = Effort x Distance travelled by effort
Work done by weight = Weight x Distance travelled by the weight

Work done by effort = 130 x $2.\pi.$ R1
Work done by weight = W x $\pi.$ (R1 – R2)
130 x $2.\pi.$ R1 = W x $\pi.$ (R1 – R2)
130 x 2 x 6 = W (6 – 5)   lbs. in

Weight is in lbs and distance is in inches on both sides of the equation.
W = 1,560 lbs

3.3 Dewatering and Pumping:

<u>Dewatering</u>:   Construction work is difficult or sometimes impossible when water is present. Dewatering is conducted to facilitate construction work in excavations. Excavations are needed for shallow foundations, retaining walls and basements.
Construction engineers need to investigate the elevation of groundwater prior to a dewatering plan. Stability of the bottom may be affected by the presence of groundwater. In such situations, dewatering method needs to be planned. Maintaining side wall stability is another problem that needs to be addressed.

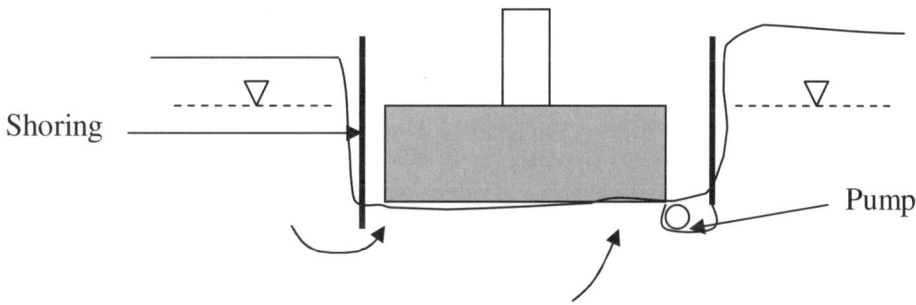

Shoring

Pump

<u>Dewatering for a shallow foundation</u>

Concreting work for shallow foundations are conducted by installing a pump Continuous pumping can be used to maintain a dry bottom. Stable side slopes can be maintained by providing shoring supports.

<u>Well Points</u>:   In some cases, it is not possible to pump enough water to maintain a dry bottom for concrete shallow foundations. In such situations, well points are constructed to lower the groundwater table.

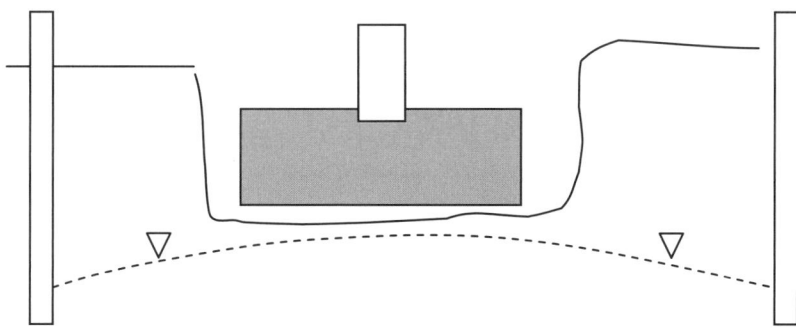

Use of well points to lower the groundwater table
Small Scale Dewatering for Column Footings: (Pump water from the excavation)

Groundwater level is lowered by constructing a small hole or a trench inside the excavation (as shown in the figure) and placing a pump (or several pumps) inside the excavation. For most column footing construction work, this method will be sufficient.

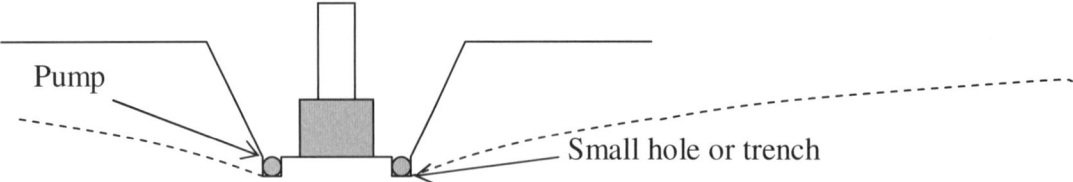

Dewatering of a column footing: Medium Scale Dewatering for Basements or Deep Excavations: (Pump water from trenches or wells). For medium scale dewatering projects, trenches or well points can be used.

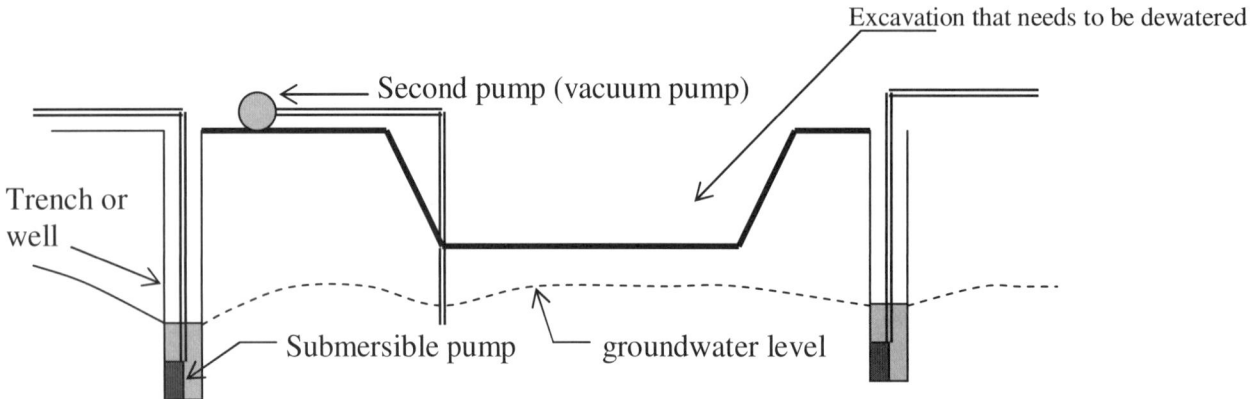

Groundwater lowering using well points

Add more pumps as necessary to keep the excavation dry. Combination of submersible pumps and vacuum pumps can be used. Large Scale Dewatering for Basements or Deep Excavations:

Alternative 1: Well points or trenches are constructed. Main artery pipe is connected to each pump as shown. A strong high capacity pump would suck water out of all the wells as shown.

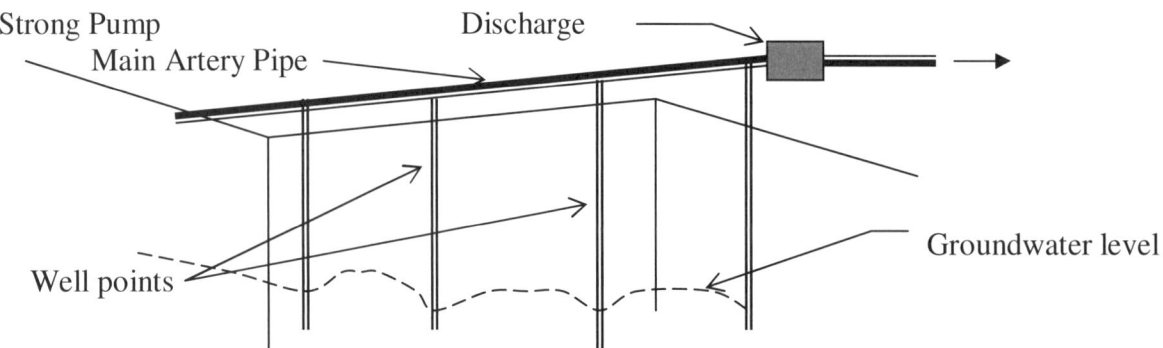

Well points in series with one large pump

Alternative 2: Similar dewatering system can be designed using submersible pumps. In this case, instead of one pump, each well would get a submersible pump as shown below.

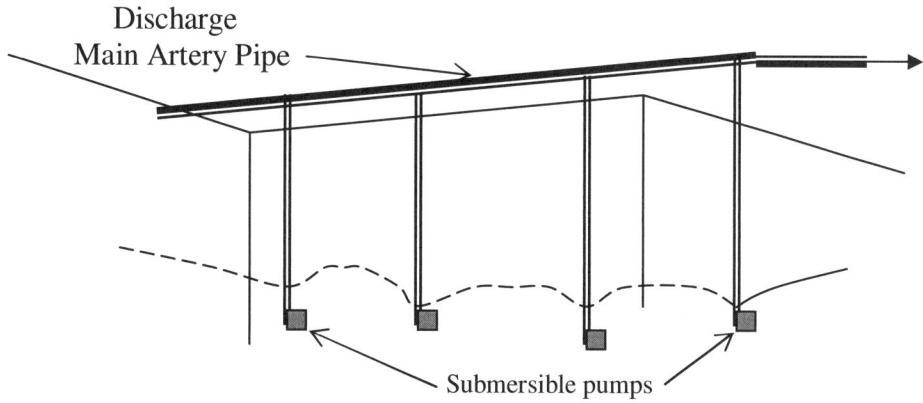

Discharge
Main Artery Pipe

Submersible pumps

Well points in series with submersible pumps

This method is more effective than alternative one. The main disadvantage is high maintenance. Since there is more than one pump, more maintenance work will occur compared to alternative one. On the other hand alternative two can be modified to include less well points since pumping effort can be increased significantly.

For most construction work, groundwater should be lowered at least 2 ft below the excavation.

If water needs to be treated prior to discharge, dewatering may become extremely expensive. In that case, "cutoff walls" or "ground freezing" options may be cheaper.

Design of Dewatering Systems:

Initial study: Study the surrounding area and locate nearby rivers, lakes and other water bodies. Groundwater normally flows towards surface water bodies such as rivers and lakes. If the site is adjacent to a major water body (such as a river or lake), the groundwater elevation will be same as the water level in the river.

Construct Borings and Piezometers: Soil conditions – Create soil profiles based on borings. Assess the permeability of the existing soil stratums. (Sandy soils will transmit more water than clayey soils).

Seasonal Variations - Groundwater elevation readings should be taken at regular intervals. In some sites, groundwater elevation could be very sensitive to seasonal changes. The groundwater elevation during the summer could be drastically different than the winter.

Tidal Effects - Groundwater elevation changes with respect to tidal flow. In some sites, groundwater elevation may show a very high sensitivity to high and low tides.

Artesian Conditions - Check for artesian conditions. Groundwater could be under pressure and well pumping or any other dewatering scheme could be a costly procedure.

Groundwater contamination: If contaminated groundwater is found, then groundwater cutoff methods should be studied.

Monitoring Wells: Monitoring wells are installed to obtain the groundwater elevation. Monitoring wells are typically constructed using PVC pipes.

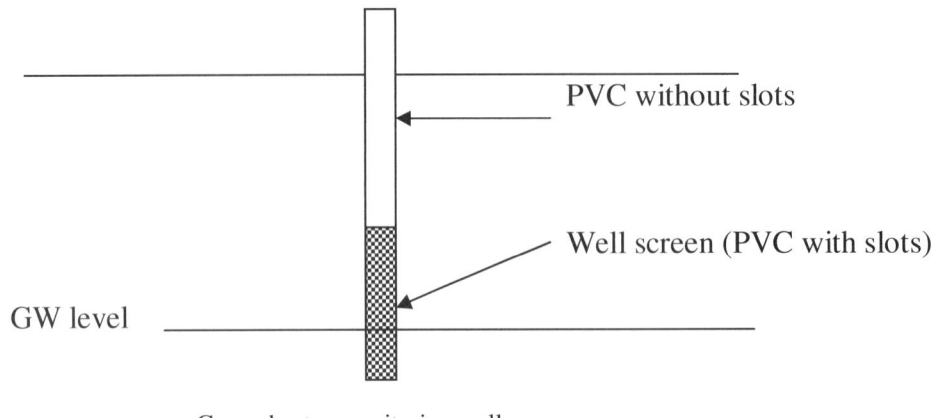

Groundwater monitoring well

Slotted section of the PVC is known as the well screen and allows water to flow into the well. If there is no pressure, water level in the well indicates the groundwater level.

Aquifers with Artesian Pressure: Groundwater in some aquifers can be under pressure. The monitoring wells will register a higher water level than the groundwater level. In some cases, water would spill out from the well due to artesian pressure.

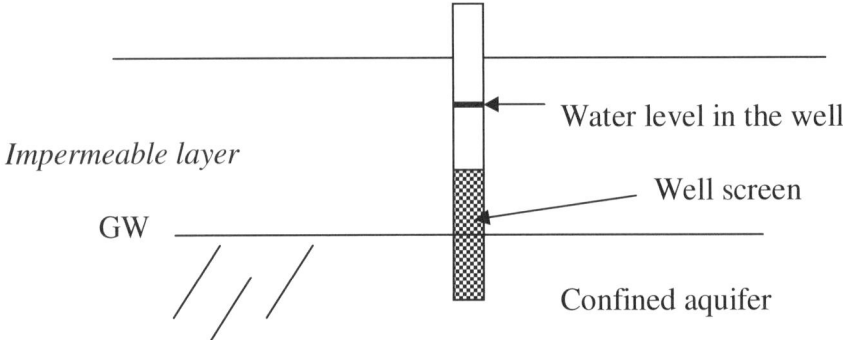

Monitoring well in a confined aquifer: Water level in the well is higher than the actual water level in the aquifer since the aquifer is under pressure.

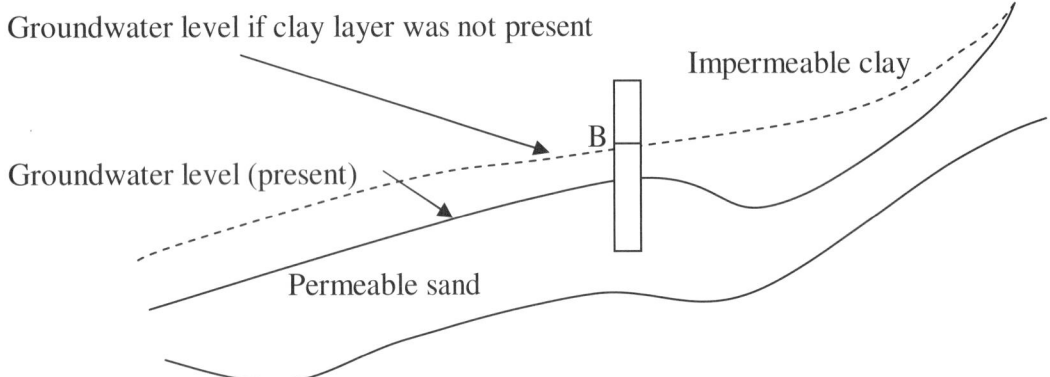

Artesian conditions: In the above figure, impermeable clay layer is shown lying above the permeable sand layer. The dotted line shows the groundwater level if the clay layer is absent. Due to impermeable clay layer, groundwater cannot reach the level shown by the dotted line. When a well is installed, the water level will rise to point B, higher than the initial water level due to artesian pressure.

3.3.1 Pumps: Pumps are required in construction to pump water from excavations and trenches. Also in larger scale, pumps are required to dewater cofferdams.

Head Added by a Pump: Let us look at the pump shown. Assume the head loss due to friction is *f*.

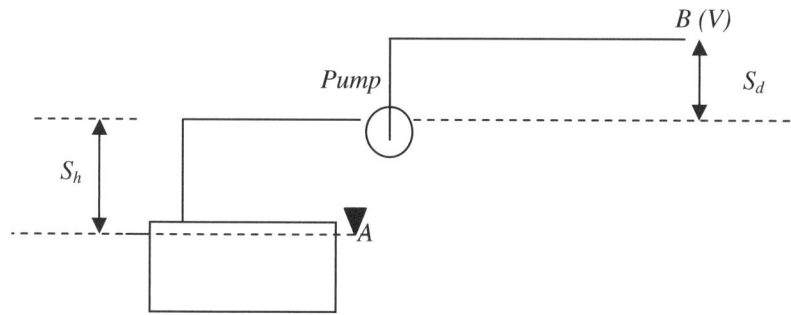

Water level in the excavation is at A. Water needs to be sucked into the pump. S_h is known as the suction head. Once the water is sucked into the pump, it has to discharge it. S_d is known as the discharge head. Also the pump has to overcome the friction in pipes.

Head added by the pump $(h_A) = S_h + S_d + f + V^2/2g + P_b/\gamma$

P_b = Pressure at point B
V = Velocity at point B
f = Head loss due to friction.

Above equation can be obtained using the energy equation.

Energy equation:

Energy of water in the excavation + Head added by the pump = Energy at point B + Head loss due to friction ---(1)

There is energy in water in the excavation. Energy has to be added to the water in the excavation to pump out.

Energy of water has three terms. They are;
Energy due to pressure = Pressure/Density = P/γ
Energy due to velocity = $V^2/2g$
Energy due to datum = h
Energy of water in the excavation = 0

In the excavation, water is exposed to atmosphere. Hence pressure energy is zero.
Water in the excavation is not moving. Hence kinetic energy is zero.
If we assume the datum to be the water level in the excavation, then datum head is also zero.
Hence from energy equation;
Energy at point A + Head added by the pump = Energy at point B + Friction head loss
$0 + h_A = S_h + S_d + f + V^2/2g + P_b/\gamma$

Horse Power of Pumps:

Pump horse power is given by the following equation.

$$\text{Pump horse power (HP)} = h \times m'/550$$

h = Head added by the pump.

m' = Flow in lbs/sec.
Note that in pump horsepower calculations unit of flow is NOT cu.ft/sec but lbs/sec.

Problem 4.7):   Suction head of a pump is 6 ft and the discharge head is 7 ft. The flow is 300 gal/min. Find the horse power of the pump. Head loss due to friction is 3 ft. Ignore the velocity head and pressure head in pipes.

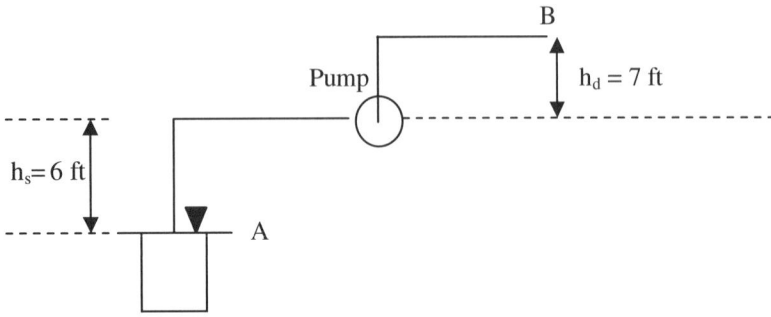

Solution 4.7):

Pump horse power is given by the following equation.

$$\text{Pump horse power (HP)} = h \times m'/550$$

h = Head added by the pump.
m' = Flow in lbs/sec.
Note that in pump horsepower calculations unit of flow is NOT cu.ft/sec but lbs/sec.

Typically flow is given in cu.ft per sec or gallons/minute. This has to be converted to lbs/sec.

STEP 1:   Find the head added by the pum

Head added by the pump = $S_h + S_d + f + V^2/2g + P_b/\gamma$
Ignore the velocity head and pressure head.
Hence;

Head added by the pump = $S_h + S_d + f$ = 6 + 7 + 3 = 16 ft

STEP 2:   Find the flow in lbs/sec.

Flow is given in gallons/minute. This has to be converted to lbs/sec.
Flow = 300 gal/min = 300/60 gal/sec = 5 gal/sec

1 gallon = 8.342 lbs;   Hence 5 gal/sec = 5 x 8.342 lbs/sec.= 41.71 lbs/sec

STEP 3:   Find the pump horse power;

Pump horse power (HP) = h x m'/550

h = 16 ft;   m' = 41.71 lbs/sec

Pump horse power = h x m'/550 = 16 x 41.71/550 = 1.21 HP

3.3.2   Pump Performance Curve, Pump Efficiency Curve and System Curve:

As a construction engineer, you may have to pick the correct pump for the job. Let us say in one project you have to pump water to an elevation of 25 ft at a rate of 100 gallons per minute. In another project you need to pump water to an elevation of 15 ft at a rate of 200 gallons per minute. Same pump may not be the best choice for both cases.

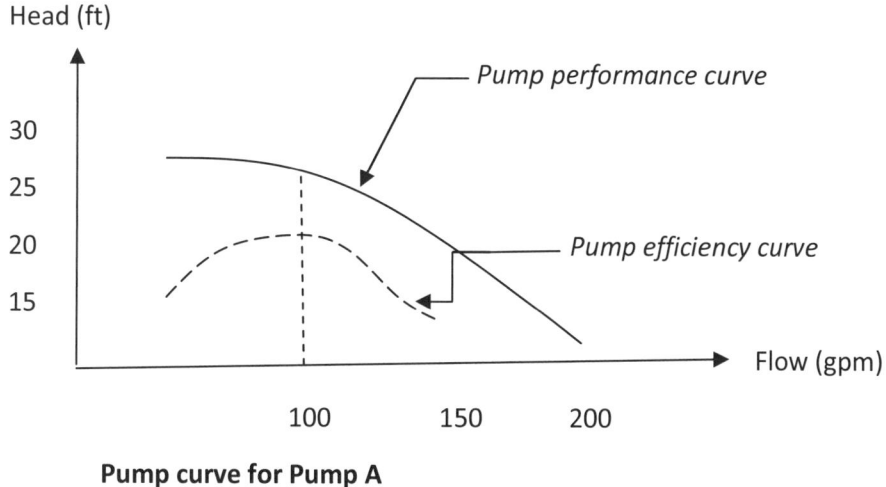

Pump curve for Pump A

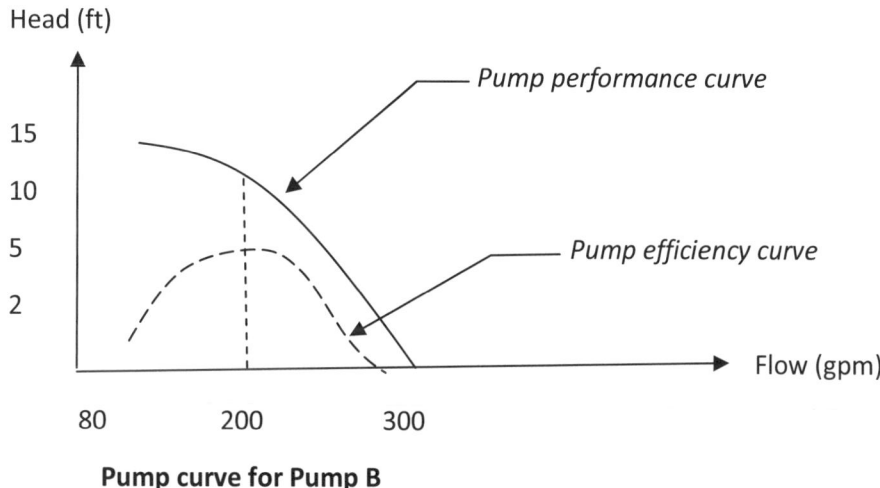

Pump curve for Pump B

When a pump is operating at its highest efficiency, energy bill would be lowest. Hence you need to find a pump that would operate at its highest efficiency. Highest efficiency of pump A is attained when pumping at 100 gpm. The highest effieciency of pump B is attained when pumping at 200 gpm.

Let us say you need to pump at a rate of 100 gpm to an elevation of 25 ft, then pump A should be your best choice. But if you want to pump at a rate of 150 gpm to an elevation of 20 ft, pump A is not very efficient. Yet pump A can do the job.

Now if you want to pump at a rate of 150 gpm to an elevation of 50 ft, pump A may not be able to do the job. (See the pump performance curve).

If you look at pumps A and B, pump A can pump to higher elevations but a a slower rate. On the other hand, pump B can pump at a faster rate, but it cannot lift the water to higher elevations.

3.3.3   System Curve:

System curve has nothing to do with pump curve. System curve depends on the friction head loss in pipes in the system. Let us assme a pipe line. The pipe line has certain characteristics. When water is flowing at a certain velocity, it would have a certain friction. Friction head loss is given by;

Friction head loss = H_f = f.L. $V^2/(2g.d)$

f = Friction coefficient
L = Length of pipe
V = Velocity of water
d = Diameter of the pipe

Length of pipes, friction coefficient and diameter of pipe are dependant on the specific system you have.
Also you would notice that higher the flow, higher the friction head loss.
Let us look at a typical dewatering scheme.

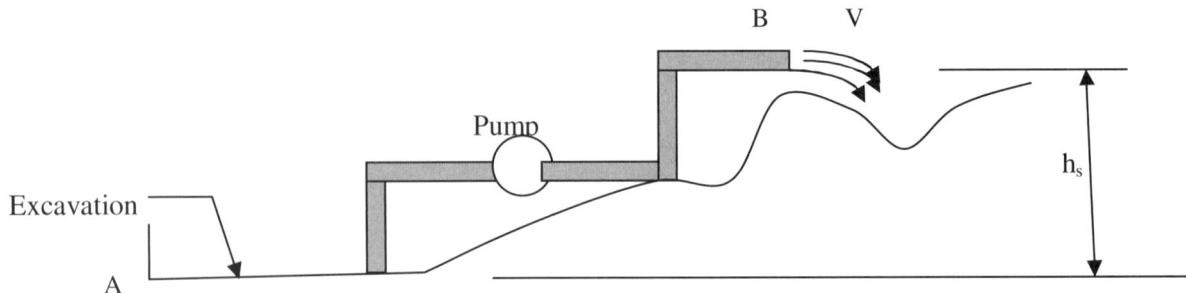

Water in the excavation is exposed to atmosphere. Hence the pressure head is zero. Also water does not move. Hence kinetic head is zero. We are required to pump water at velocity V.

Energy at point A = 0
Energy at point B = $h_s + V^2/2g + P_B/\gamma$
h_s = Static head;   V= Velocity; P_B = Pressure at point B
In this case, water at point B is exposed to atmosphere. Hence P_B is zero.

H_R = Head added by the pump = $H_f + h_s + V^2/2g$
H_f is the friction head loss.
Above H_f and $V^2/2g$, depends on velocity of water. Higher the velocity, higher the head loss due to friction.

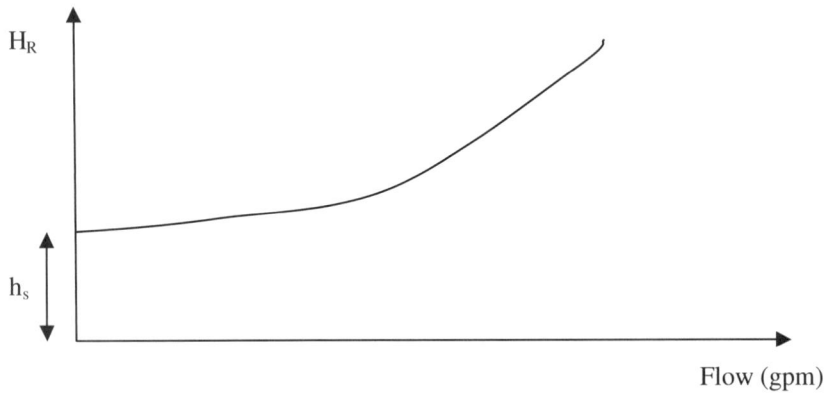

Figure: System Curve

Higher the flow, higher the head required. Above curve depends on length of pipes, friction coefficient and static head. All these parameters are dependant on the system.

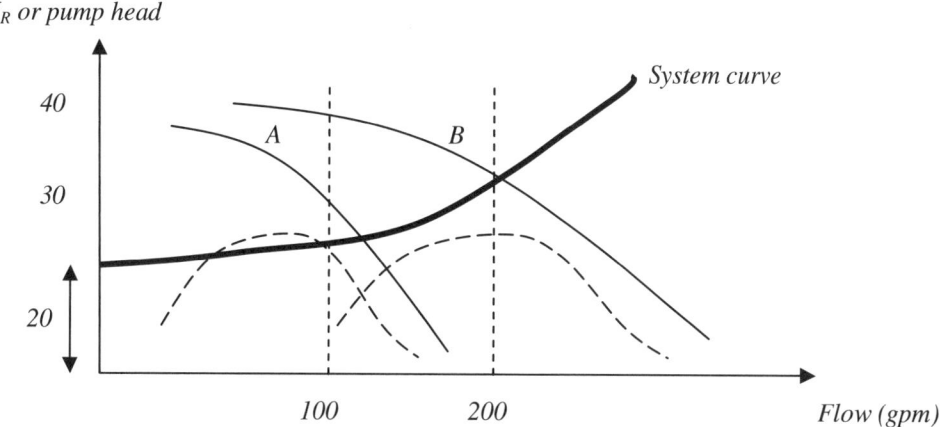

Now let us look at some pump curves drawn along side with the system curve.

Two pump performance curves (A and B) and their efficincy curves are shown.
Let us assume that we need to pump at 100 gpm. To pump at 100 gpm, we need a pump that can deliver a head of around 22 ft as per the system curve given. The system requires at least 22 ft of head to pump at 100 gpm to provide the static head required and to overcome the friction. Both pumps A and B are capable of doing so. But pump A is better suited for the job since it has a higher efficiency than pump B at 100 gpm. Now if we want to pump at 200 gpm, pump A is not suitable. Pump A is not capable of providing a flow of 200 gpm. Then we find pump B to be a better candidate.

<u>System curve when pumping horizontally;</u>

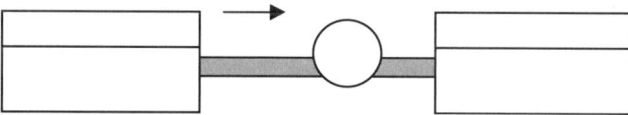

Water is pumped from one reservoir to the other. Both are at same elevation. System curve for this situation is shown below.

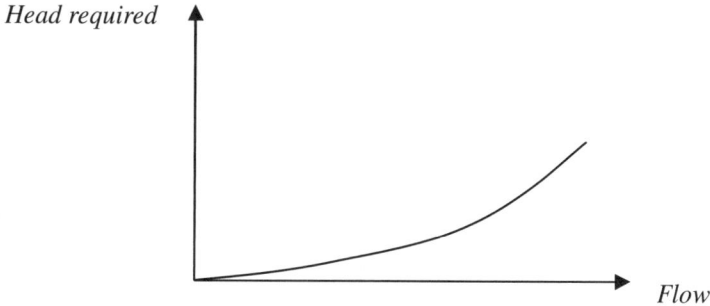

When the flow is increased head required goes up since friction head loss and velocity head depends on flow.

3.3.4   Net Positive Suction Head:

When selecting pumps, one has to look for the net positive suction head of the pump as well. Now let us look what this means.

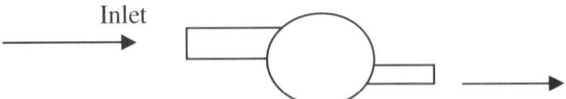

In the above pump, water comes in from the inlet. For the impellers to work properly, certain amount of head is required. If the head available at the inlet is very low, there would be air pockets inside the pump. This is known as cavitation. Cavitation means cavities of air has developed. In such situations, pump will not operate as designed. Hence every pump would indicate the net positive suction head (NPSH) required for the pump to operate properly. Some pumps may require a larger NPSH while some other pumps may require a smaller NPSH.

On the other hand, head available in the system has nothing to do with the pump. Available NPSH at the inlet of the pump depends on the suction head, friction head loss and vapor pressure.

If water is pumped from an open reservoir, available NPSH is given by the following equation.

$NPSH_{Available}$ = Atmospheric head - Suction head - Friction loss - Vapor pressure.

Let us look at an example;

Example: Water is pumped from an excavation 12 ft deep. Friction head loss in suction pipes is 10 ft. Vapor pressure of water is 0.6 ft. Atmospheric pressure is 35 ft. What is the available NPSH at the inlet of the pump?

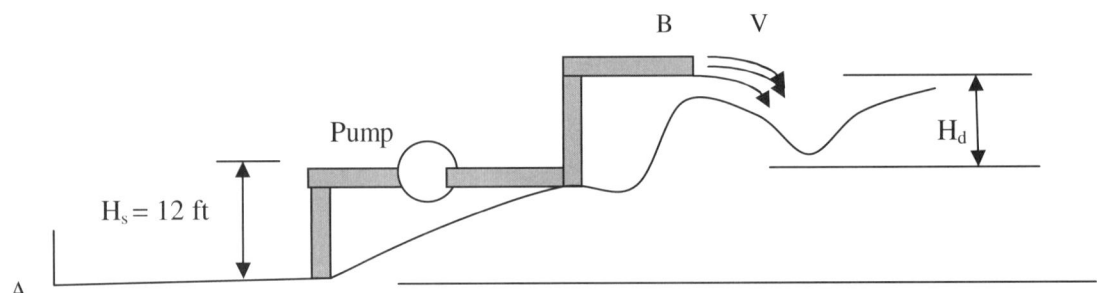

H_s = Suction head

$NPSH_{Available}$ = Atmospheric head - Suction head - Friction loss - Vapor pressure.
$NPSH_{Available}$ = 35 - 12 - 10 - 0.6 = 12.4

$NPSH_{Available}$ is dependent on the friction head loss and the suction head. These two parameters have nothing to do with the pump.

Once you have calculated the $NPSH_{Available}$, you need to find a pump that requires a NPSH less than what is available. If $NPSH_{required}$ of the pump is greater than the $NPSH_{Available}$, then the pump will not work.

For the pump to work;

$NPSH_{Available} > NPSH_{required}$

Example: Two pumps are available at a job site.
Pump A ----> $NPSH_{required}$ = 15 ft
Pump B ----> $NPSH_{required}$ = 8 ft

Which pump is best suited for the previous example?

$NPSH_{Available} = 12.4$ (Computed earlier)

Pump A requires a NPSH of 15 ft. What is available is 12.4. This pump will not perform properly. When the available NPSH is less than required NPSH, water vapor and air pockets will form inside the pump. This is known as cavitation. This is not a desirable situation.

On the other hand, NPSH required for pump B is only 8 ft of water. For this application, pump B should be selected.

Example: Dewatering from an excavation is shown below.

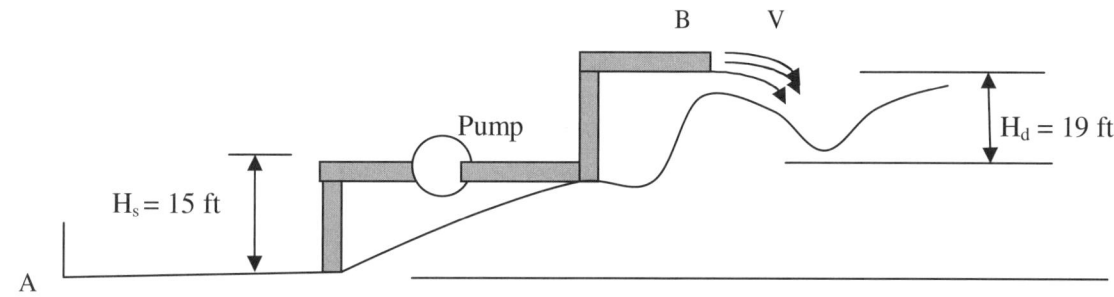

Vapor pressure = 0.6 ft.   Atmospheric head = 35 ft
Pump rate required = 400 gpm.
Ignore the velocity head.

System curve is shown below;

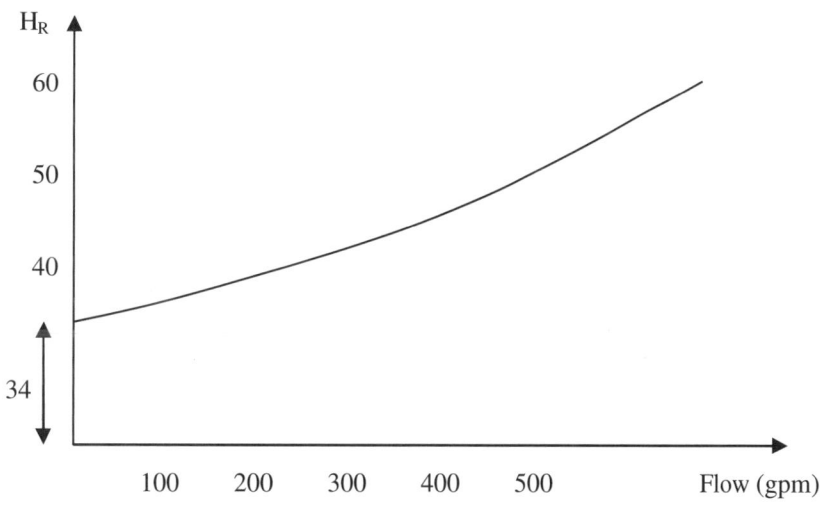

Performance curves for two pumps are given below.

Pump A: (NPSH = 7 ft)

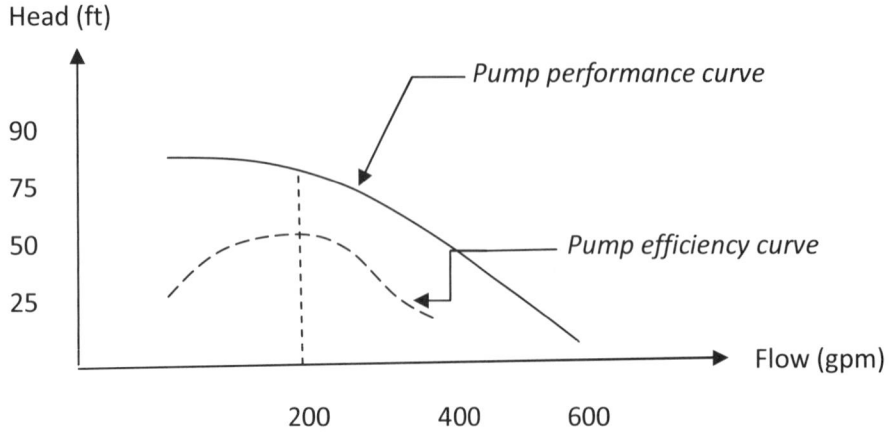

Pump curve for Pump A

Pump B: (NPSH = 15 ft)

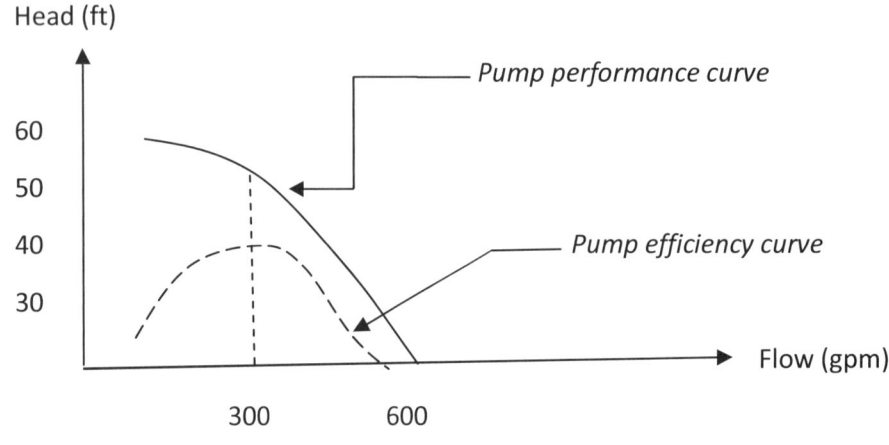

Pump curve for Pump B

Friction head loss in suction pipes is given by the following table;

Flow (gpm)	Friction head loss in suction pipes
100	8
150	10
200	11
400	12
500	19

Which pump is best suited for the project?

Solution:

If you look at the system curve, to pump at a rate of 400 gpm, you need a head of 45 ft.
Now let us look at the pump curve of pump A.

Can pump A, pump at a rate of 400 gpm and at the same time provide a head of 45 ft?
The answer is yes. But there is a problem. The efficiency of the pump at 400 gpm is very low.

Now let us look at pump B. We will ask the same question.
Can pump B, pump at a rate of 400 gpm and at the same time provide a head of 45 ft?
The answer is yes. The efficiency of the pump B at 400 gpm seems to be reasonable.

Now let us look whether the pumps would operate properly.

Find available NPSH;

$NPSH_{Available}$ = Atmospheric head - suction head - friction head in suction pipes - vapor pressure

$NPSH_{Available}$ = 35 - 15 - 12 - 0.6 = 7.4 ft

A table has been provided to find the friction head loss in suction pipes. For a rate of 400 gpm, friction head loss in suction pipes is 12 ft.

NPSH required by pump A is 7 ft. Available NPSH is larger than required NPSH.

On the other hand, NPSH required for pump B is 15 ft. Required NPSH is much larger than what is available. Hence pump B cannot be used.

Pump A has to be selected. This pump has a low efficiency level and high energy bill to be expected. But there is no choice. Pump B cannot be used since available NPSH is not enough for this pump to operate.

Example: What can be done to increase the $NPSH_{avialable}$?

$NPSH_{Available}$ = Atmospheric head - suction head - friction head in suction pipes - vapor pressure

One can replace the old piping with new piping. This would decrease the friction head. Also suction head can be reduced. This can be done by placing the pump at a lower elevation. This option may not be feasible depending on the conditions of the site.

Note: Read my other books **"Four Sample Exams for Civil PE exam All Modules"** and **"Civil PE Construction Module Practice Problems"** and **"Three Sample Exams for the Construction Module"** for worked examples.

3.4   Equipment Production:
Productivity or the effectiveness of labor and equipment are of paramount importance to project success. There are situations where contractor would decide to utilize cheaper equipment compared to high capacity equipment that cost more. The contractor needs to study the productivity of the equipment and assess which equipment are the most cost effective.
Factors that affect the effectiveness of equipment for a given project:
- Suitability of the equipment for the specific project
- Production rate
- Safety
- Repair cost
- Fuel consumption
- Cost of operators
- Need for specialized operators (difficulty of replacement in the event one leaves)
- Cost of parts if any parts are broken
- Lead time to obtain parts
- Cost of transportation
- Security of equipment from vandalism

Practice Problem 3.2:   Excavation contractor has the choice to use one large backhoe or two small size backhoes for a specific project. The backhoes are used to excavate and load soil into trucks for transportation. The contractor needs to excavate and remove 1,500 cu yds of soil. The project duration is 30 workdays.

Which is the cheaper alternative?
Following information is known of the backhoes.

Large backhoe:
Rental cost = $700 per day
Production rate = Can excavate and load one truck in 45 minutes. One truck has a capacity of 10 cu. yds.
Labor required = 1 operator + 1 laborer
Operator cost = $70 per hour with benefits
Laborer cost = $50 per hour with benefits
Company overhead allocated to this project = $ 15 per hour
Average maintenance cost per day (oiling, repairs, parts) = $30
Fuel consumption = 1 gallon of diesel per hour (Diesel cost $3 per gallon)

Small Backhoe:
Rental cost = $300 per day
Production rate = Can excavate and load one truck (10 cu. yds) in 1 hr and 15 minutes
Labor required = 1 operator + 1 laborer
Operator cost = $60 per hour with benefits
Laborer cost = $50 per hour with benefits
Company overhead allocated to this project = $ 15 per hour
Average maintenance cost per day for one small backhoe (oiling, repairs, parts) = $20
Fuel consumption = 0.6 gallons of diesel per hour (Diesel cost $3 per gallon)

Solution:
Find the cost of the project if the large backhoe is used.
To complete the project, the contractor has to load and remove 150 trucks. (1,500/10)
If the large backhoe is used, the project can be completed in 150 x 0.75 = 112.5 hours
(45 minutes = 0.75 hours)
Assuming 8-hour workday, the project can be completed in 14.1 days. (112.5/8)

Hence, the project can be successfully completed within the schedule if the large backhoe is used since the project contract duration is 30 working days.

Cost of the large backhoe: (Convert all costs to dollars per hour)
Rental cost = $700 per day = $87.5 per hour
Operator cost = $70 per hour with benefits
Laborer cost = $50 per hour with benefits
Company overhead allocated to this project = $ 15 per hour
Average maintenance cost per day (oiling, repairs, parts) = $30 per day
= $3.75 per hour
Fuel cost = $3 per hour
Total cost per hour = 87.5 + 70 + 50 + 15 + 3.75 + 3 = 229.25 per hour
Total number of hours needed = 112.5
Total cost = 112.5 x 229.25 = $25,790

Option of using two small backhoes:
First, check whether the project can be completed with two small backhoes.
To complete the project, the contractor has to load and remove 150 trucks. (1,500/10)
Production rate per one small backhoe = 1.25 hours to load one truck
Production rate for two small backhoes = 0.625 hours to load one truck
If two small backhoes are used, the project can be completed in 150 x 0.625 = 93.8 hours = 11.7 working days
Available days = 30
The project can be successfully completed with two small backhoes.
Cost of two small backhoes: (Convert all costs to dollars per hour)
Rental cost = $600 per day = $75 per hour
Operator cost = $120 per hour with benefits for two operators
Laborer cost = $100 per hour with benefits for two laborers
Company overhead allocated to this project = $ 15 per hour

Average maintenance cost per day for two backhoes (oiling, repairs, parts) = $40 per day = $5 per hour
Fuel consumption = 1.2 gallons per hour
Fuel cost = $3.6 per hour

Total cost per hour = 75 + 120 + 100 + 15 + 5 + 3.6 = 318.6 per hour
Total number of hours needed = 93.8 hours
Total cost = 93.8 x 318.6 = $29,884

Using the large backhoe is cost effective in this case.
There are other factors that cannot be quantified.

Safety factor: If the workspace is too tight, using two backhoes may be relatively unsafe compared to using one large backhoe.

Cost of parts if any parts are broken: Equipment can break down. If new parts are needed it is important to know the possible cost for parts and lead time to obtain them.

Specialized Operators: Unlike small backhoes, large backhoes may require operators with high skill. If the present operator leaves the company, it is important to know the availability of large backhoe operators in the market.

3.5   Productivity Analysis and Improvement: The contractor needs to analyze the equipment usage with respect to suitability, productivity, safety, reliability and cost. For example, contractor may find concreting a high-rise building is easier using a concrete lift mechanism compared to pumping. Good contractors constantly in the process of investigating new methods and equipment. Productivity analysis of a construction operation needs to be considered with respect to other alternatives. One method may be faster but costly. On the other hand, another method may require specialized equipment where spare parts are not easy to find.
In many cases, it is not easy to quantify advantages and disadvantages of different alternatives.

3.6   Temporary Erosion Control: During construction, trees will be cut down and natural plants will be removed. This would inevitably cause erosion of soil. Prior to start of site clearing work, erosion control measures have to be taken. Temporary erosion control methods are used to control erosion during the construction phase of the project. Permanent erosion control methods are used to protect the site after construction is completed.
Temporary Erosion Control Methods:
During construction, existing vegetation will be removed hence opening the site for erosion. The design engineer should identify downstream and provide an erosion control measure.
Silt Fences:
Silt fences are made of black plastic curtains and often seen in construction sites.

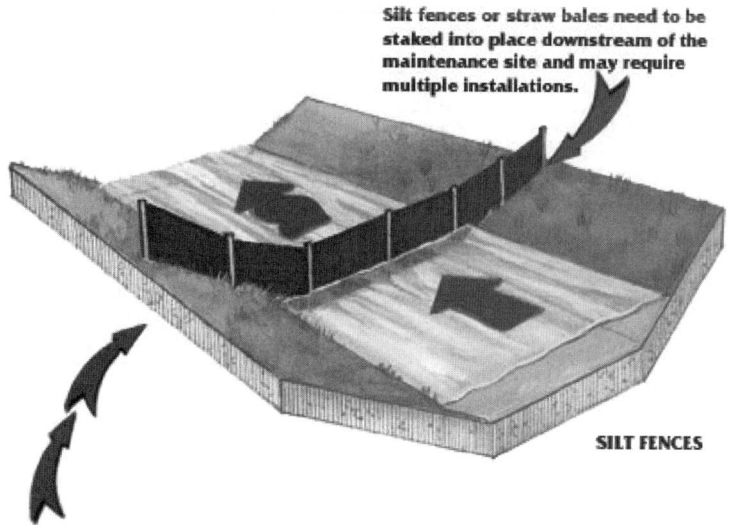

Silt fence

Silt fences stops sediments but let water go. Silt fences are an effective and inexpensive way of controlling erosion. Geotextile in the silt fence allows water to flow through it. Silt and sediments are trapped. Silt fences are easy to install, cheap and widely accepted. On the other hand, silt fences have to be properly maintained. Frequently silt fences need to be observed for damage and proper repairs need to be made.

Straw Bales: Straw bales are used to stop silt and sediments moving down a stream at the same time allow water to pass above them.

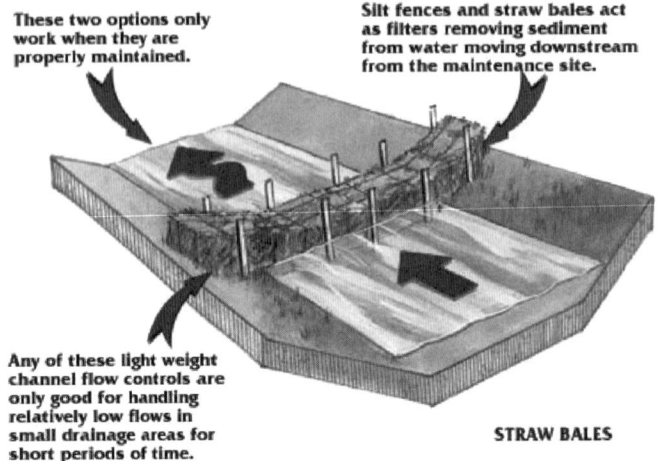

These two options only work when they are properly maintained.

Silt fences and straw bales act as filters removing sediment from water moving downstream from the maintenance site.

Any of these light weight channel flow controls are only good for handling relatively low flows in small drainage areas for short periods of time.

STRAW BALES

Straw Bales

Straw bales are typically staked into place downstream of the maintenance site. They act as filters removing sediment from water.

Sand Bags: Sand Bags are also used instead of straw bales and silt fences.

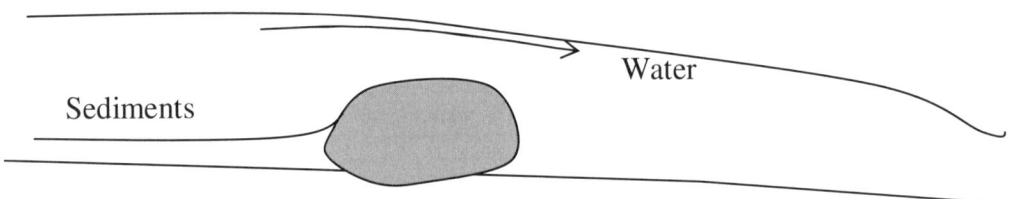

Sand bags stops sediments and let water go over

Erosion Control in Slopes: Slopes are subjected to erosion due to running water. Methods adopted to fight erosion in slopes are:
- Rip Rap
- Vegetation (Green method)
- Geowebs and plants

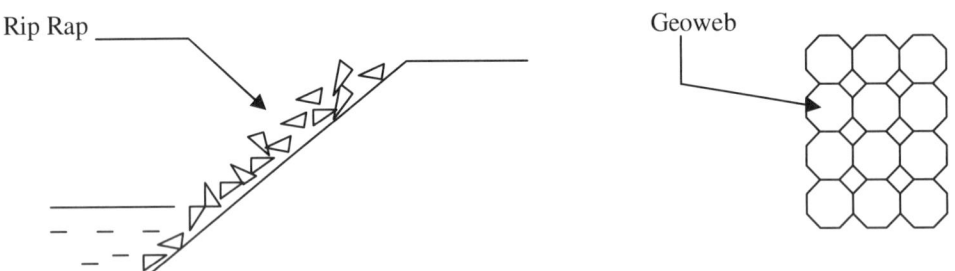

<u>Rip Rap</u>:   Rip Rap is basically stones of different sizes. If heavy water flow is expected along the slope, large stones are used. Rip Rap is also used to guard slopes against waves. Rip Rap does not facilitate animals and plants to prosper. On the other hand, using Rip Rap is fast, easy and cheap.

<u>Vegetation</u>:   Roots of trees and plants hold soil together. Main problem of using vegetation is the difficulty of growing required plants and trees in the slope. This could be a time consuming affair compared to Rip Rap. On the other hand, there is no method to stop erosion while the plants and trees are grown.

<u>Geoweb</u>:   Geoweb is made of plastic or biodegradable material. Geoweb is laid on the slope and trees are planted at the center of webs.

<u>Erosion Controlling Mats</u>:   Biodegradable mats are laid on the slope and trees are planted.   Erosion controlling mat hold the soil until trees and plants are grown.

3.7   Excavation Support: Excavations are needed for building basements and underground facilities. Excavations have to be kept stable during work.

I beams and large pipes are used to keep the excavation supported.

Sheetpiles are driven and supported by horizontal I beams. Pipes are anchored to the ground and attached to I beams

Timber lagging are supported by H sections known as soldier piles.

Timber lagging and soldier piles

4.0 Scheduling

4.1   Construction Sequencing: It is important to sequence construction activities. Walls cannot be built without constructing the footings. Footings cannot be built before the earthwork is finished. The contractor needs to identify activities that need to be completed and sequence them.

Site clearing → Excavation for footings → Formwork for footings → Footing construction

4.2   Activity on Node Networks and CPM Network Analysis: There are two types of networks. They are;

- Activity on node networks
- Activity on arrow networks

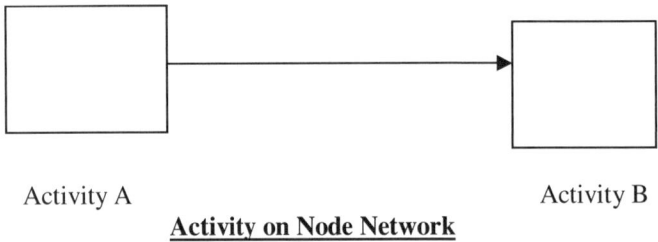

Activity A   Activity B
Activity on Node Network

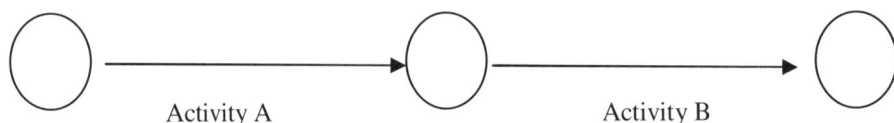

        Activity A   Activity B

Activity on Arrow Network

Activity on Node Networks: Let us first look at activity on node networks. It is fair to say that activity on node networks are widely used than activity on arrow networks.

Critical path method is the most popular technique adopted for scheduling using both networks.
In critical path method, all activities have following attributes.
Start time
Finish time
Duration

Let us look at the following example.

Practice Problem 4.1:   The contractor has forecasted that he would be able to complete site clearing in 10 days and construct footings in 9 days.

Site clearing (10 days)   Construction of footings (9 days)

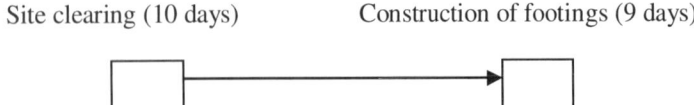

Site clearing is the first activity. It can be started on day 1. Some authors start the activity in day 0. However, NCEES examples book uses day 1 as the first day.

Site Clearing: Early Start (ES) = 1
Site Clearing: Early Finish (EF) = 1 + 10 = 11

Construction of footings: Early Start (ES) = 11
Construction of footings: Early Finish (EF) = 11 + 9 = 20

Activity name		
ES	Duration	LS
EF		LF

Site Clearing (A)		
1	10	?
11		?

Footings (B)		
11	9	?
20		?

Late start (LS) and late finish (LF) has to be completed.
What is the late finish of activity B?
Early finish time of activity B is 20. Since there is no any other information available, late finish also would be 20.

Late finish of footing construction (LF) = 20
Late start of activity B = LF - duration = 20 - 9 = 11

Now late finish of activity A can be found.
Late finish of activity A = 11
Late start of activity A = LF - duration = 11 - 10 = 1

These values can be included in the schedule.

Site Clearing (A)		
1	10	1
11		11

Footings (B)		
11	9	11
20		20

Practice Problem 4.2:   The contractor can complete construction of building walls in 20 days. He is planning to start construction of the roof immediately after construction of building walls. Contractor has estimated that he needs 12 days to construct the roof.

Activity (A) = Construction of walls
Activity (B) = Construction of roof

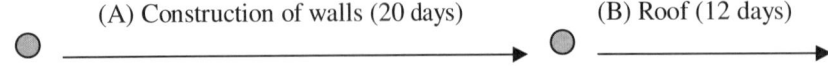

(A) Construction of walls (20 days)   (B) Roof (12 days)

Forward Pass: Forward pass is going forward starting from first activity. During forward pass early start time (ES) and early finish time (EF) of activities will be completed.

Late start time (LS) and late finish time (LF) of activities will NOT be completed during forward pass.

LS and LF are completed during backward pass.

Construction of walls (A):   ES = 1,   EF = 1 + 20 = 21

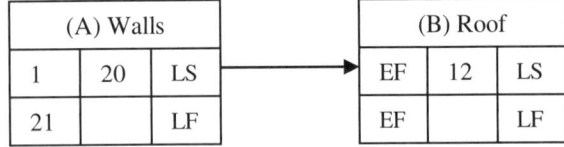

The contractor can start the roof construction immediately. Hence, early start (ES) of roof construction is 21.

Construction of the roof "B" :   ES = 21,   EF (Early Finish) = 21 + 12 = 33

Early finish time (EF) of roof construction is 21 + 12 = 33

Now these numbers can be inputted into the CPM diagram.

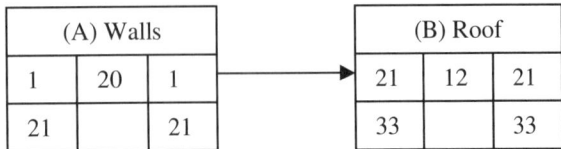

Now the forward pass is completed.

Backward Pass:

Late finish time of activity B = 33

Now you will be able to compute the late finish time of activity "A".

Late finish time of activity A = Late start time of activity B = 21

Late start time of activity A = Late finish time of activity A – duration of A = 21 – 20 = 1

Predecessor and Successor:

Activity A is the predecessor and activity B is the successor.

Dependence:

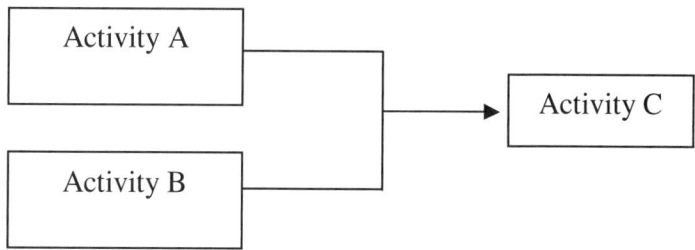

Activity C is dependent upon activity A and activity B.
Activity B does NOT depend on activity A.

Practice Problem 4.3:   The contractor has to complete construction of walls and fabrication of the roof truss before constructing the roof. The roof truss is constructed outside and brought in and installed.

Activity A = Wall construction (Duration = 20 days)
Activity B = Fabrication of the roof truss (Duration = 25 days)
Activity C = Installation of the roof (Duration = 15 days)

Activity A – No predecessors
Activity B – No predecessors
Activity C - Predecessors (A and B)
Conduct the forward and backward passes.

Solution:

STEP 1: Draw the activity diagram. (Input the durations)

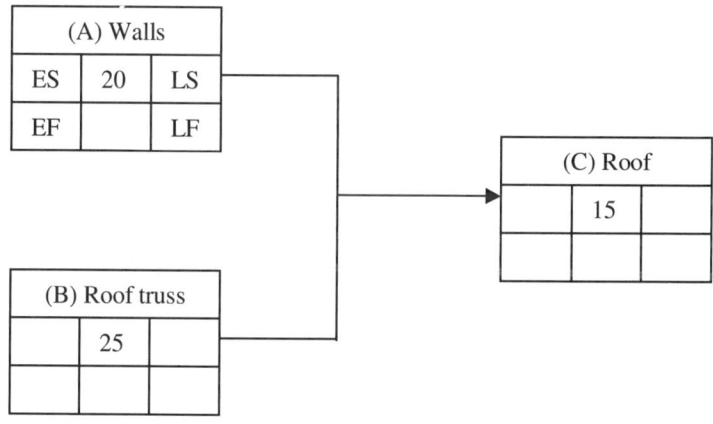

STEP 2:   Forward pass: (Find early start time and early finish time of each activity)
Activity A:
Early start time (ES) = 1
Early finish time (EF) = 21

Activity B:
Early start time (ES) = 1
Early finish time (EF) = 26

Activity C:
Activity C cannot be started until both activities A and B are completed. Activity A is completed on 21 and B is completed on 26.

Early start time of activity C (ES) = 26
Early finish time of activity C (EF) = 26 + 15 = 41
Forward pass is completed. Input the above values in CPM diagram.

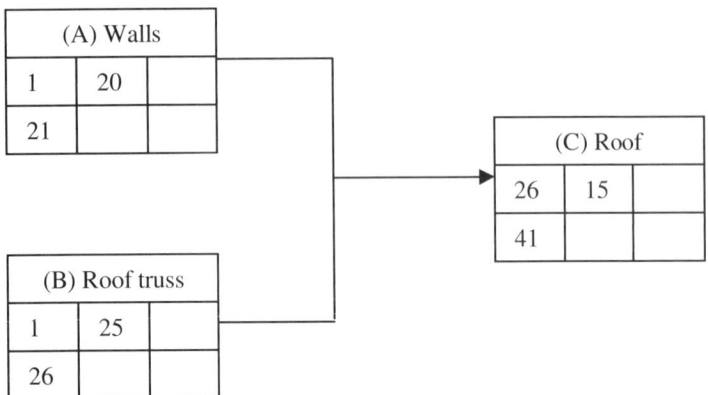

STEP 3:   Backward pass: (Late start time and late finish time of each activity)
Start to compute the late start time and late finish time of each activity starting from activity C.

Activity C: Since there is no any other information available, late finish time of activity C is 41.
Late start time of activity C = 41 – 15 = 26.

Activity B: Activity C cannot be started until B is finished. Late start time of activity C is 26. Hence, activity B has to be finished by 26.

Late finish time of activity B (LF) = 26
Late start time of activity B (LS) = 26 – 25 = 1
Activity A: Activity C cannot be started until A is finished as well. Late start time of activity C is 26. Hence, activity A has to be finished by 26.
Late finish time of activity A (LF) = 26
Late start time of activity A = 26 – 20 = 6
Look at the late start time of activity A.
Activity A **can** be started on day 6, without affecting the schedule.

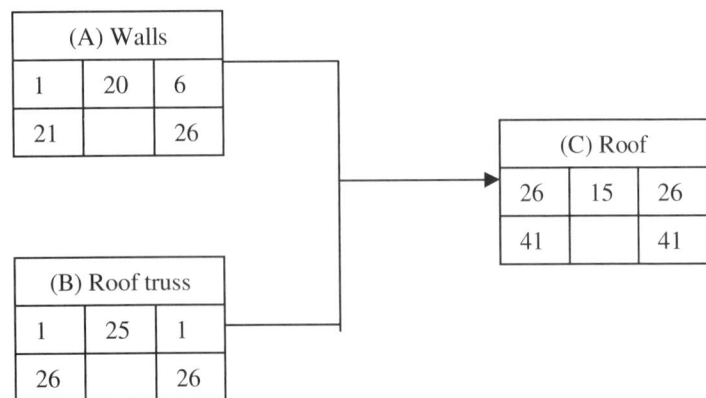

Practice Problem 4.4:   Following information is given. Draw the CPM diagram.

Activity A = No Predecessors (Duration = 12 days)
Activity B = No Predecessors (Duration = 15 days)
Activity C = Predecessors (A and B), (Duration = 16 days)
Activity D = Predecessors (A and B), (Duration = 18 days)
a)   Draw the CPM diagram.
b)   Conduct the forward and backward passes.

Solution: STEP 1: Draw the activity diagram. (Input the durations)

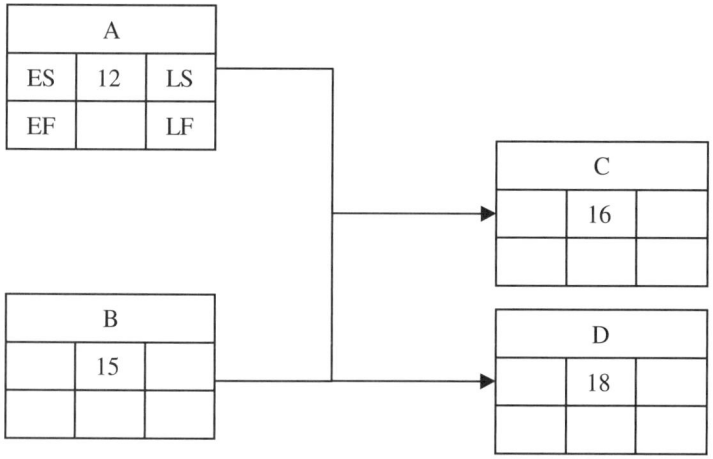

STEP 2: Forward pass: (Early start time and early finish time of each activity)
Activity A:
Early start time (ES) = 1
Early finish time (EF) = 1+ 12 = 13

Activity B:
Early start time (ES) = 1
Early finish time (EF) = 1 + 15 = 16

Activity C:
Activity C cannot be started until both activities A and B are completed. Activity A is completed on 13 and B is completed on 16.
Early start time of activity C (ES) = 16
Early finish time of activity C (EF) = 16 + 16 = 32

Activity D:
Activity D cannot be started until A and B are completed. Activity B is completed on 16 and activity A is completed on 13.
Early start time of activity D (ES) = 16
Early finish time of activity D (EF) = 16 + 18 = 34
Forward pass is completed. Input the above values in CPM diagram.

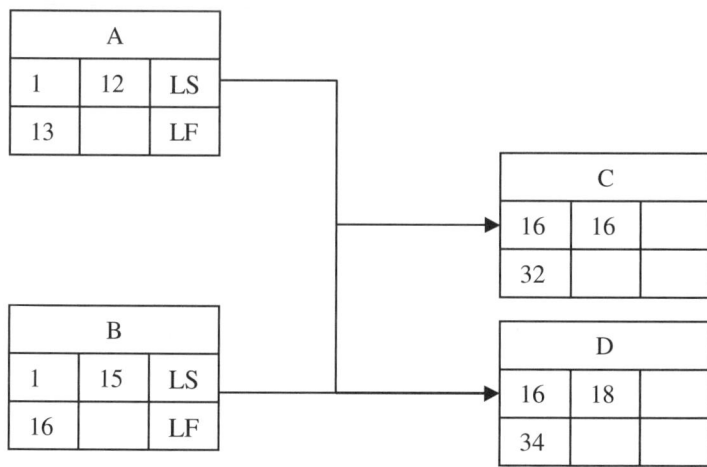

STEP 3: Backward pass: (Late start time and late finish time of each activity)
Start to compute the late start time and late finish time of each activity from activity D.

<u>Activity D</u>:   Late finish time of activity D is 34.
Late start time of activity D = 34 – 18 = 16

<u>Activity C</u>:   Activity C can be completed by 32. But it can be delayed till day 34 without affecting the project schedule.
Why?
Activity D will be completed by day 34 for the project to be completed. Hence, if required, activity C can be delayed till day 34.
Late finish time of activity C (LF) = 34
Late start time of activity C (LS) = 34 – 16 = 18
Let us input the numbers we acquired so far in the CPM diagram.

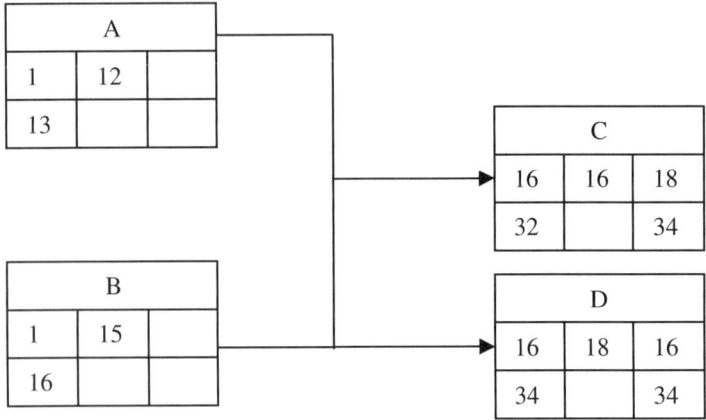

<u>Activity B</u>:   Activity C and D cannot be started until B is finished. Late start time of activity C is 18 and late start time of activity D is 16. Hence, activity B has to be finished by 16.
If activity B is finished after 16, activity D cannot be started by 16.
Late finish time of activity B (LF) = 16
Late start time of activity B = 16 – 15 = 1

<u>Activity A</u>:   Activity A has to be completed to start activities C and D.
Late start time of activity C is 18 and late start time of activity D is 16.   Hence activity A has to be finished by day 16.
Late finish time of activity A (LF) = 16
Late start time of activity A (LS) = 16 – 12 = 4
Now you can input the numbers in the CPM diagram.

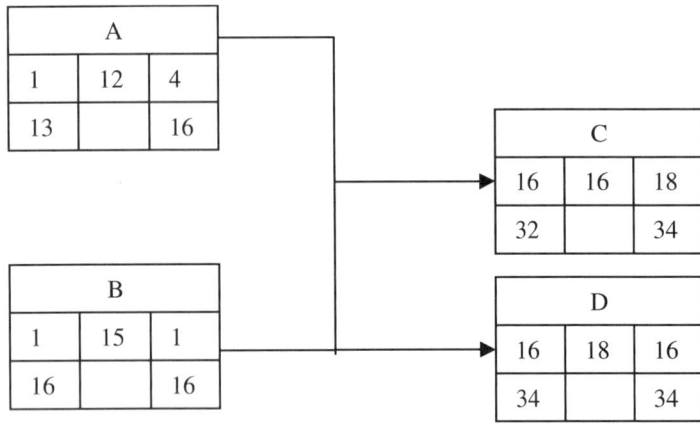

What is the critical path of the above project?
Activities A and C can be delayed without delaying the project. Activities B and D cannot be delayed.
Hence the critical path of the project is

B ——————→ D

Practice Problem 4.5:   Complete the network shown. Durations are as shown.

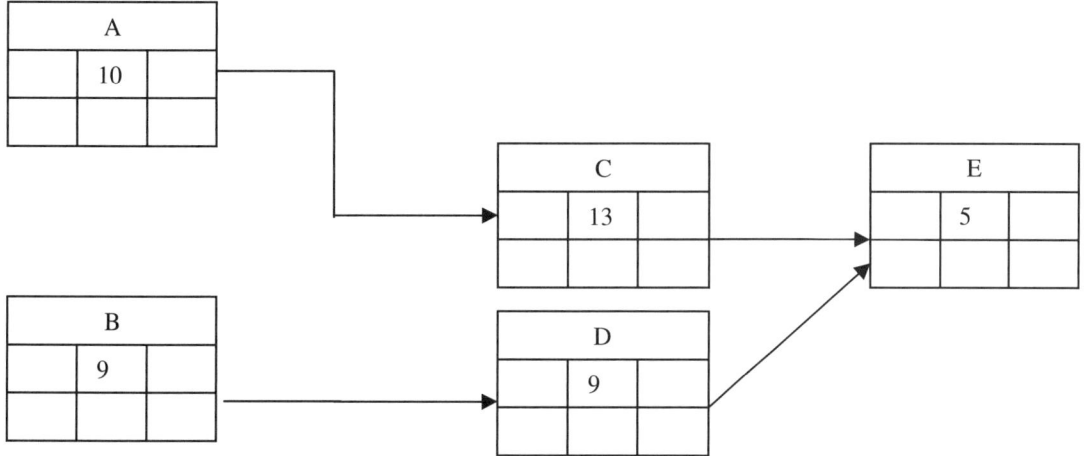

Solution: Complete the forward pass: During the forward pass early start times and early finish times are found.

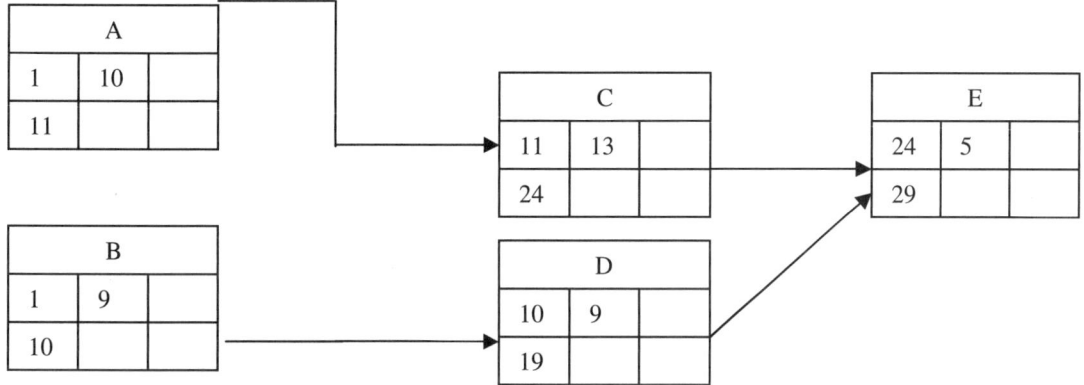

Complete the backward pass:

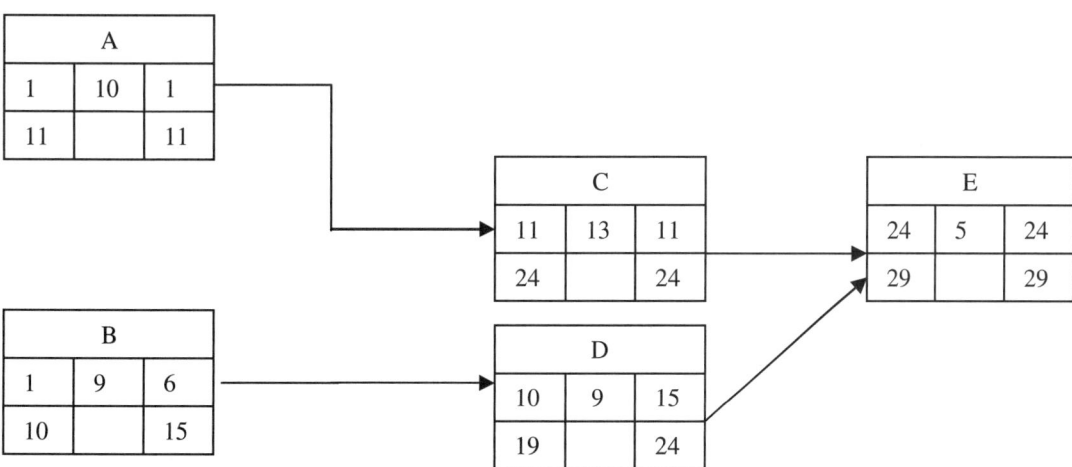

Critical path is the path with zero float.

Critical Path: A ----> C ------> E

Finish to Start Lag Time: So far, we considered that next activity would start just after the previous activity is finished. There are some situations where this is not possible. Concrete footing has to be constructed and a steel column has to be placed on the footing. After construction of the footing, there is a lag of 10 days for the concrete to cure.

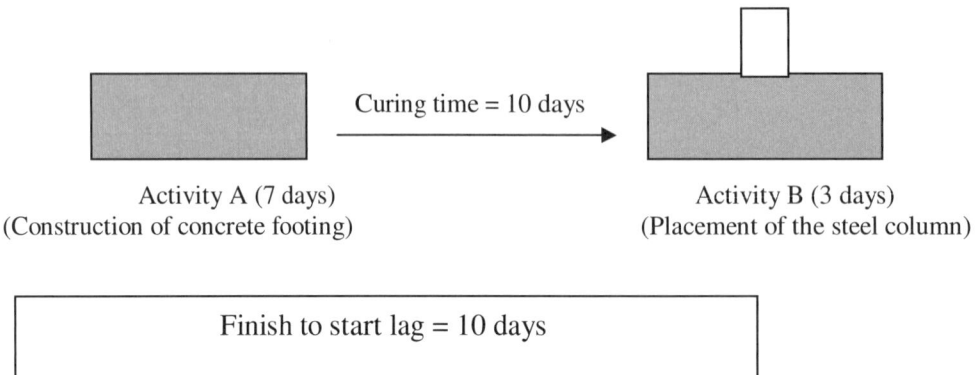

Activity A (7 days)   Activity B (3 days)
(Construction of concrete footing)   (Placement of the steel column)

Finish to start lag = 10 days

In the above example, steel column cannot be placed on the concrete footing until 10 days after the construction of the footing. This can be shown symbolically as below.

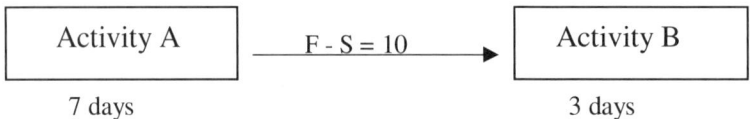

7 days   3 days

F - S = 10 indicates that finish to start there is a delay of 10 days. In this case, it is for the curing of concrete. It is important to note that this equation is valid for both early and late times.

$F - S = 10$
$EF - ES = 10$
(Early finish of activity A to Early start of activity B, there is a delay of 10 days).
And also
$LF - LS = 10$
(Late finish of activity A to Late start of activity B, there is a delay of 10 days).

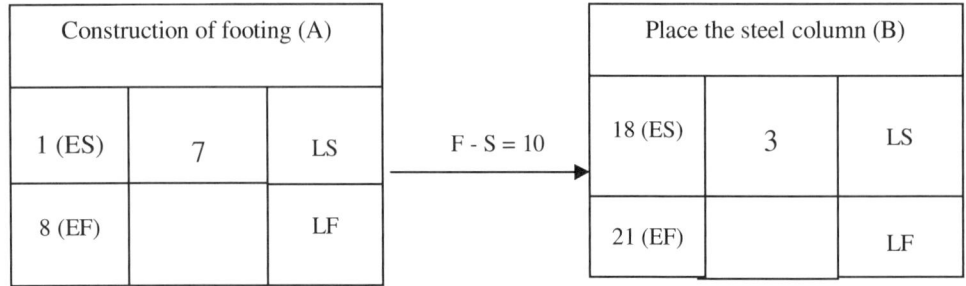

Early start of activity A = 1
Early finish of activity A = 1 + 7 = 8

Early start of activity B = 8 + 10 = 18   (10 is the finish to start delay)
Early finish of activity B = 18 + 3 = 21

Now let us find LS and LF of two activities. Note that finish to start lag exists for both forward pass and backward pass.

LF of activity B is 21.
LS of activity B = 21 - 3 = 18

LF of activity A = 18 - 10 = 8   (remember there is a 10 day delay between activity A and B).
LS of activity A = 8 - 7 = 1

Construction of footing (A)				Place steel column (B)		
1	7	1	F - S = 10 →	18	3	18
8		8		21		21

Start-to-Start Relationships: Contractor is erecting steel columns. He is supposed to erect 100 steel columns. He could deliver all 100 steel columns and start erecting steel columns.

But contractor is planning to deliver portion of steel columns and start erecting prior to completion of delivery of all steel. He is planning to deliver portion of steel columns in first two days and start erecting right away. While erecting, he will keep delivering steel to the site. Hence, two activities, delivering steel and erecting steel would happen simultaneously.

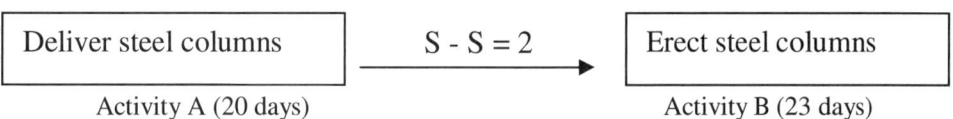

Deliver steel columns   S - S = 2   Erect steel columns
Activity A (20 days)   Activity B (23 days)

S - S = 2 means two days after start of activity A, activity B would start. After that, activity A and activity B would happen simultaneously.

S - S = 2 can be represented as follows.
Early start of activity B = Early start of activity A + 2
It will be true for late start as well.
Late start of activity B = Late start of activity A + 2

Now let us fill the boxes.
Early start of activity A = 1
Early finish of activity A = 1 + 20 = 21

Early start of activity B = 1 + 2 = 3
(Contractor is planning to start activity B, just two days after starting activity A).
Early finish of activity B = 3 + 23 = 26

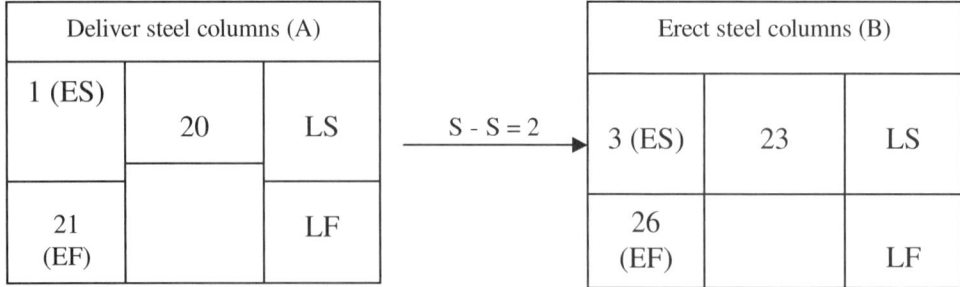

Now let us find LS and LF of two activities.
LF of activity B is 26.
LS of activity B = 26 - 23 = 3

LS of activity B = LS of activity A + 2
(Remember two activities are connected by S - S relationship.)
Hence   LS of activity A = LS of activity B - 2 = 3 - 2 = 1
LF of activity A = 1 + 20 = 21

Deliver steel columns (A)				Erect steel columns (B)		
1 (ES)	20	1	S - S = 2 →	3 (ES)	23	3
21 (EF)		21		26 (EF)		26

<u>Finish-to-Finish Relationships</u>:   Let us consider the same example above. Contractor is planning to start delivering steel columns and start erecting steel columns while steel been delivered. Contractor is planning to complete erecting all steel columns 12 days after completion of delivery of all steel. This can be represented as follows.

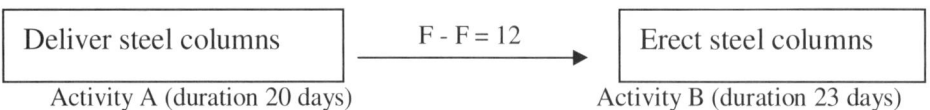

Deliver steel columns   F - F = 12 →   Erect steel columns
Activity A (duration 20 days)   Activity B (duration 23 days)

F - F = 12 means 12 days after activity A is **finished**, activity B would be **finished**.
Early finish (EF) of activity B = EF of activity A + 12
Similarly,
Late finish (LF) of activity B = LF of activity A + 12
Let us fill the boxes.
Early start of activity A = 1
Early finish of activity A = 1 + 20 = 21

Early finish (EF) of activity B = EF of activity A + 12
Early finish (EF) of activity B = 21 + 12 = 33
ES of activity B = 33 - duration = 33 - 23 = 10

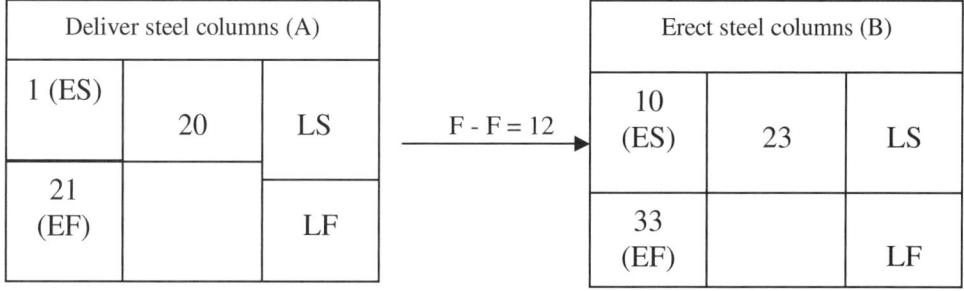

Deliver steel columns (A)		
1 (ES)	20	LS
21 (EF)		LF

F - F = 12 →

Erect steel columns (B)		
10 (ES)	23	LS
33 (EF)		LF

Backward pass:
LF of activity B = 33
Now we can find the LF of activity A.
Since,
Late finish (LF) of activity B = LF of activity A + 12
LF of activity A = LF of activity B - 12 = 33 - 12 = 21
LS of activity A = 21 - 20 = 1
LS of activity B = LF of activity B - duration = 33 - 23 = 10
Now all boxes can be filled.

Deliver steel columns (A)		
1 (ES)	20	1
21 (EF)		21

F - F = 12 →

Erect steel columns (B)		
10 (ES)	23	10
33 (EF)		33

S - S and F - F Relationships Together:

S - S and F - F relationships can be used together. Let us look at the same steel column example.

Contractor is planning to start delivering steel columns and start erecting steel columns while steel been delivered. Contractor is planning to start erecting steel columns 5 days after start delivering steel columns. At the same time contractor is planning to finish erection of steel columns 15 days after completion of delivery of all steel. This can be represented as follows.

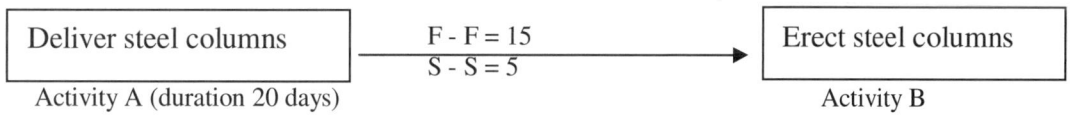

| Deliver steel columns | F - F = 15 / S - S = 5 → | Erect steel columns |
| Activity A (duration 20 days) | | Activity B |

Note that duration of activity B is not given. If duration of activity B is given, there would be a conflict. Duration of activity B is not needed if two relationships are given.
We can write the following;
ES of activity B = ES of activity A + 5
LS of activity B = LS of activity A + 5

EF of activity B = EF of activity A + 15
LF of activity B = LF of activity A + 15

Forward pass:
ES of activity A = 1
EF of activity A = 1 + 20 = 21

ES of activity B = ES of activity A + 5 = 1 + 5 = 6

EF of activity B = EF of activity A + 15
EF of activity B = 21 + 15 = 36
Now these numbers can be represented in the boxes.

Deliver steel columns (A)		
1 (ES)	20	LS
21 (EF)		LF

F - F = 15
S - S = 5

Erect steel columns (B)		
6 (ES)		LS
36 (EF)		LF

Backward Pass:
LF of activity B = 36
Now we can use the F - F relationship.
LF of activity B = LF of activity A + 15
LF of activity A = LF of activity B - 15
LF of activity A = 36 - 15 = 21
LS of activity A = 21 - 20 = 1

Now we can use the S - S relationship.
LS of activity B = LS of activity A + 5
LS of activity B = 1 + 5 = 6
Now all boxes can be filled.

Deliver steel columns (A)		
1 (ES)	20	1 (LS)
21 (EF)		21 (LF)

F - F = 15
S - S = 5

Erect steel columns (B)		
6 (ES)		6 (LS)
36 (EF)		36 (LF)

S - F Relationships:　Start to finish relationships rarely occur in the construction industry. Hence many textbooks ignore start to finish relationships. Many software programs do not allow start to finish relationships. Start to finish relationship can be represented as follows.
ES of activity A + 5 = EF of activity B
Can you think of a practical application of such a situation?

Negative Lags:　Above paragraph, we discussed positive lag between activities. Positive lag occurs due to curing of concrete or lead time of an item tc. Next, we consider **negative lag**.

Finish to Start (Negative Lag):　It is possible to have a negative lag between two activities. Let us assume that a contractor has to complete two activities, erection of steel and painting. Contractor can start painting prior to finish of steel erection. Contractor can erect 50% of steel and then start painting while steel erection is going on.

F - S = -5
Above equation means contractor is planning to erect steel. At the same time, he is planning to start painting 5 days prior to completion of steel erection.
Finish to start difference is -5 days. It does not matter whether it is early or late start and finish times. Nevertheless, one has to be consistent. If it is early start time, then finish should be early finish time. Similarly, if F is late finish time then S should be late start time. Hence, two equations can be developed for early and late times.

EF - ES = -5
And
LF - LS = -5
Above equation means, that contractor is planning to start painting 5 days before the finish of steel erection.

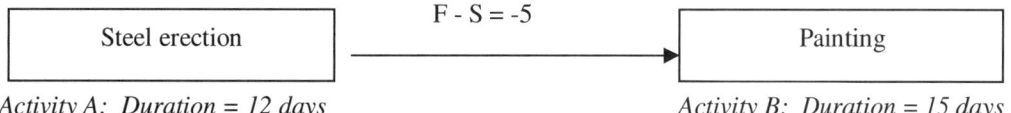

Steel erection

F - S = -5

Painting

Activity A: Duration = 12 days   *Activity B: Duration = 15 days*

ES of Activity B = EF of activity A – 5
(Activity B would start 5 days before activity A is finished).
And
LS of Activity B = LF of activity A – 5
Lets' do the forward pass:

ES = 1	D = 12	LS =
EF = 13		LF =

F – S = -5

ES = 8	D = 15	LS =
EF = 23		LF =

F - S = -5
Early finish of activity A is 13.
ES of Activity B = EF of activity A – 5
ES of Activity B = 13 – 5 = 8

Next, we can do the backward pass:

ES = 1	D = 12	LS = 1
EF = 13		LF = 13

F – S = -5

ES = 8	D = 15	LS = 8
EF = 23		LF = 23

LS of Activity B = LF of activity A – 5
LS of activity B = 8
Hence
8 = LF of activity A – 5
LF of activity A = 13

<u>Finish-to-Finish (Negative Lag):</u>   It is possible to have a negative lag between two activities with finish-to-finish relationship. Let us assume that a contractor has to build a retaining wall and paint it. The client does not want to paint the whole wall. The client wants only 75% of the wall to be painted. He believes that 25% of the wall is out of public view and need not be painted.

In this scenario, wall painting cannot be started until wall is built.
Wall painting **can be** completed prior to completion of the wall. (This is possible since only 75% of the wall need to be painted).

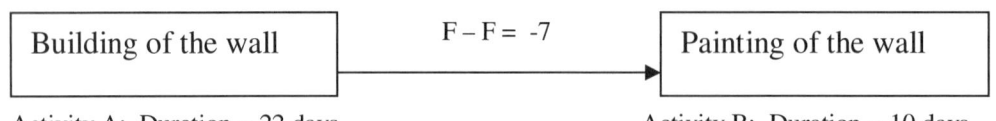

Building of the wall	F – F = -7	Painting of the wall

Activity A: Duration = 22 days   Activity B: Duration = 10 days

EF of Activity B = EF of activity A – 7
(Activity B finishes 7 days before activity A).
And
LF of Activity B = LF of activity A – 7

Lets' do the forward pass:
Activity A: ES = 1 and EF = 23
EF of Activity B = EF of activity A – 7 = 23 – 7 = 16
ES of activity B = EF of activity B – duration = 16 – 10 = 6

ES = 1	D = 22	LS =		ES = 6	D = 10	LS =
EF = 23		LF =	F – F = -7	EF = 16		LF =

Backward Pass:
LF of Activity B = 16
LF of Activity B = LF of activity A – 7
LF of activity A = LF of Activity B + 7 = 16 + 7 = 23
LS of activity A = 23 – duration = 23 – 22 = 1

ES = 1	D = 22	LS = 1		ES = 6	D = 10	LS = 6
EF = 23		LF = 23	F – F = -7	EF = 16		LF = 16

Practice Problem 4.6:   Complete the network below. Relationship between activity C to E is F – F = -4. Durations are as shown.

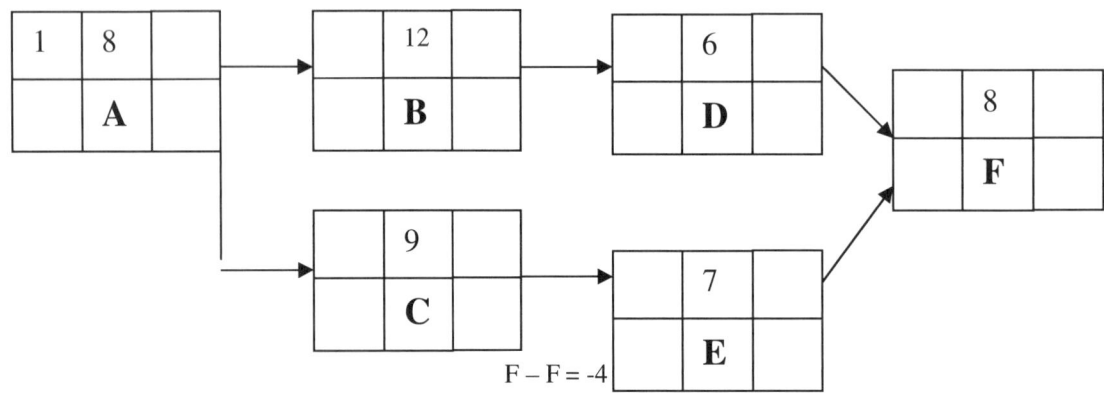

Solution: STEP 1:   Complete the forward pass.

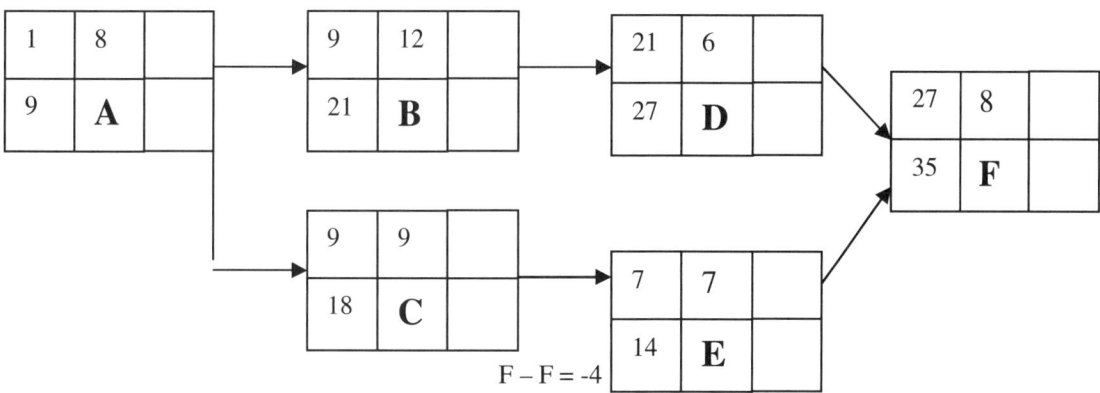

Forward pass of activities A, B, C and D are straightforward.

Activity C to E: Activity C to E, one has to worry about the relationship given.
EF of activity C is 18.
Hence, EF of activity E should be 18 – 4 = 14. Note that the relationship is finish to finish and it is negative.
If EF of activity E is 14, then ES of activity E = 14 – duration = 14 – 7 = 7.

Activity F cannot be started until activity D and E are completed. Activity E is completed by 14 and activity D is completed by 27. Hence ES of activity F is 27.

STEP 2:   Backward Pass:

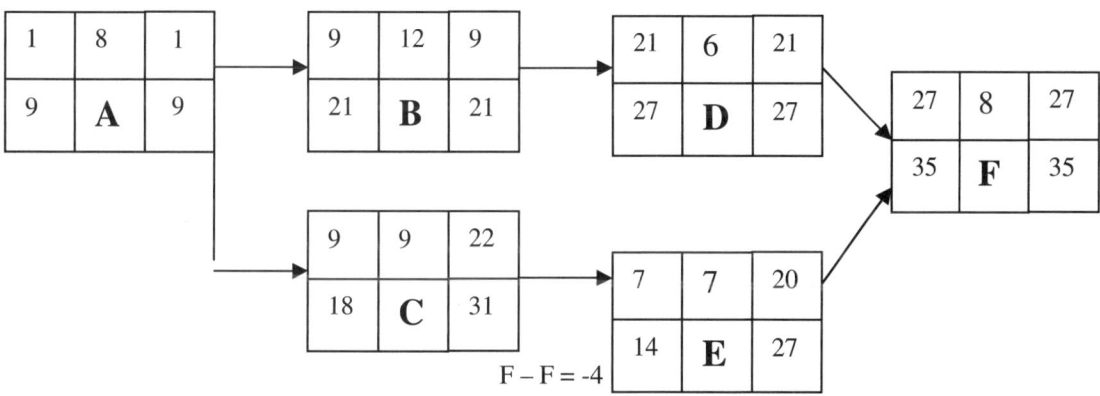

Backward Passes from F to D and F to E are standard.

Backward Pass from E to C: LF of activity E is 27. Hence, LF of activity C is 31. This may be little confusing.
Look at EF of activities C and E.
F – F = -4
LF of activity E = LF of activity C – 4
27 = LF of activity C – 4
LF of activity C = 27 + 4 = 31

4.2.1   FLOATS: **(Total Float, Free Float and Independent Float):**

ES = Early Start , LS = Late Start   EF = Early Finish,   LF = Late Finish,
D = Duration

Activity No:		
ES	D	LS
EF		LF

Floats: Three types of floats are identified.

Total Float:

$$\text{Total Float} = \text{LF} - \text{EF}$$

LF – EF is same as LS – ES.

This can be shown as follows.   LF = LS + D   (D = Duration)
EF = ES + D
LF – EF = (LS + D) – (ES + D) = LS – ES

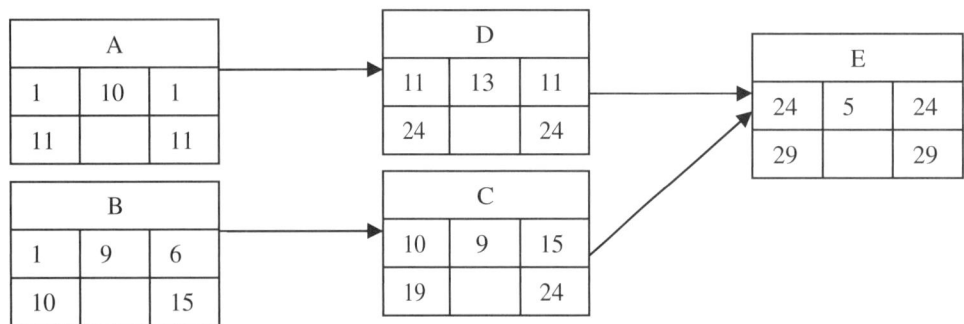

Total float of activity A = LF – EF = 11 – 11 = 0
Total float of activity B = LF – EF = 15 – 10 = 5
Total float of activity C = LF – EF = 24 – 19 = 5
Total float of activity D = LF – EF = 24 - 24 = 0
Total float of activity E = LF – EF = 29 -29 = 0
Note: All floats are zero for critical path activities.

Free Float:

$$\text{Free Float of Activity A} = \text{ES}_{\text{successor}} - \text{EF of activity A}$$

Free Float of A = $\text{ES}_{\text{successor}}$ – EF of Activity A
Successor of A is D. Hence $\text{ES}_{\text{successor}}$ = 11
EF of Activity A = 11
Free Float = 0

Free Float of B = $\text{ES}_{\text{successor}}$ – EF of Activity B
Successor of B is C. Hence $\text{ES}_{\text{successor}}$ = 10
EF of Activity B = 10
Free Float = 0

Free Float of C = ES $_{successor}$ – EF of Activity C
Successor of C is E. Hence ES $_{successor}$ = 24
EF of Activity C = 19
Free Float **= 24 – 19 = 5**

Free Float of D = ES $_{successor}$ – EF of Activity D
Successor of D is E. Hence ES $_{successor}$ = 24
EF of Activity D = 24
Free Float = 24 – 24 = 0

Free float and total float are zero along critical path.

Note that total float of B is 5 but free float is zero.
Total float and free float of C is 5.

Discussion of Total Float and Free Float: Let's assume that a certain project is of interest to the senator of the state and the governor of the state. Governor tells the project manager that he does not want to move any of the early start times of major activities. On the other hand, senator tells the project manager that he don't give a damn about early start times of activities but cares only of the final completion date.

If the project manager was to work without changing early start times of activities then he has to work with free floats.
If the project manger is interested only of the completion date then he can work with total floats.

For an example, if the project manager were to delay activity B by 5 days, he will delay the early start time of activity C, but will not delay the final completion date. The governor of the state would be a very angry man since activity C cannot be started at the early start time as scheduled. But on the other hand, senator may not have a problem with delaying activity B by 5 days. Senator would ask the governor why you care about early start time of activity C. The governor would say what if there is an unseen situation in activity C and has to be delayed? Then the whole project would be delayed.

Why some do not want to change early start times of activities?
There is a fear that if all the available slack (Total float) is utilized at the start of a project, there would not be any slack at the end. If any contingency were to occur at the end, the project would be delayed. Hence, some executives do not want to change early start times of activities.

Independent Float:

Independent Float of activity A = ES $_{successor}$ – LF $_{Predecessor}$ – Duration of A

If you need to find the independent float of activity A, obtain the early start time of successor. Then obtain the LF time of predecessor. Use the above given equation to find the independent float.

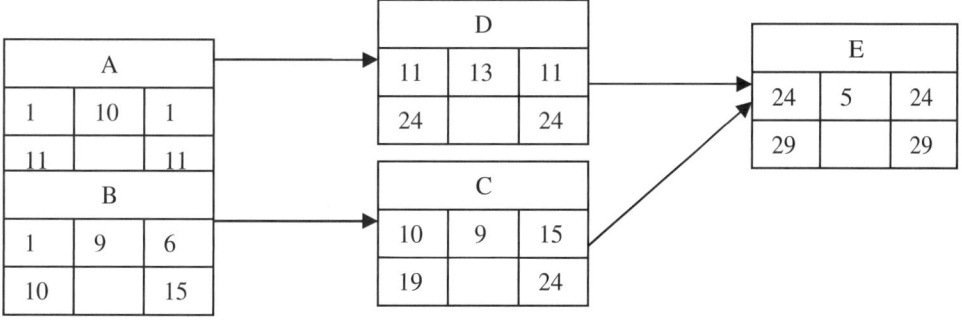

Independent float of activity A = There is no predecessor. Hence, no independent float

Independent float of activity B = There is no predecessor. Hence, no independent float.
Independent float of activity C = ES of activity E – LF of activity B – Duration of C = 24 – 15 – 9 = 0
Independent float of activity D = ES of activity E – LF of activity A –Duration of D = 24 – 11–13 = 0
Independent float of activity E = There is no successor. Hence, no independent float.

Discussion: Independent float indicates the slack that each activity has so that it will have absolutely no impact on preceding and successive activities. In other words, preceding activity can be finished at late finish time and succeeding activity can start at early start time. In most cases, independent float is zero.

4.3   Activity on Arrow Networks;

In activity on arrow diagrams, activities are represented in arrows. Nodes are considered to be events. The very first event is the "Start" event. Very last event is the "End" event. Activity cannot stat until the event prior to that activity is accomplished. An event to be completed, all activities coming to that event (node) should be completed.

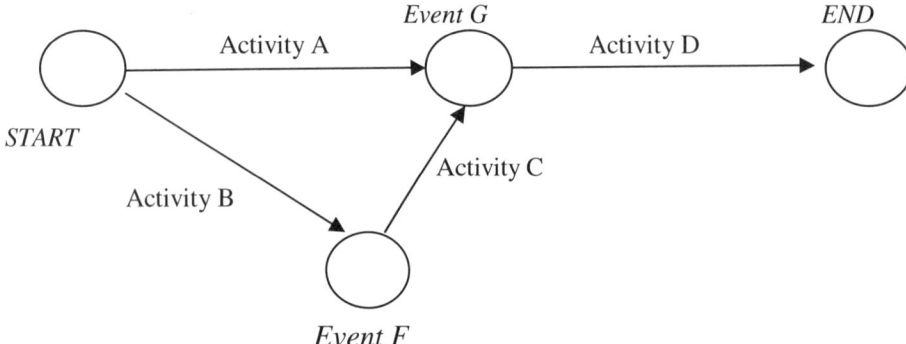

Above is an activity on arrow network. It has three activities. (activity A, B and C). It also has three events. (START event, Event F, Event G and END event).
Activity D cannot start until event G is accomplished. Event G is accomplished when both activities A and A have been completed.

Practice Problem)   Activity on arrow diagram is shown below. Find the duration of the project.

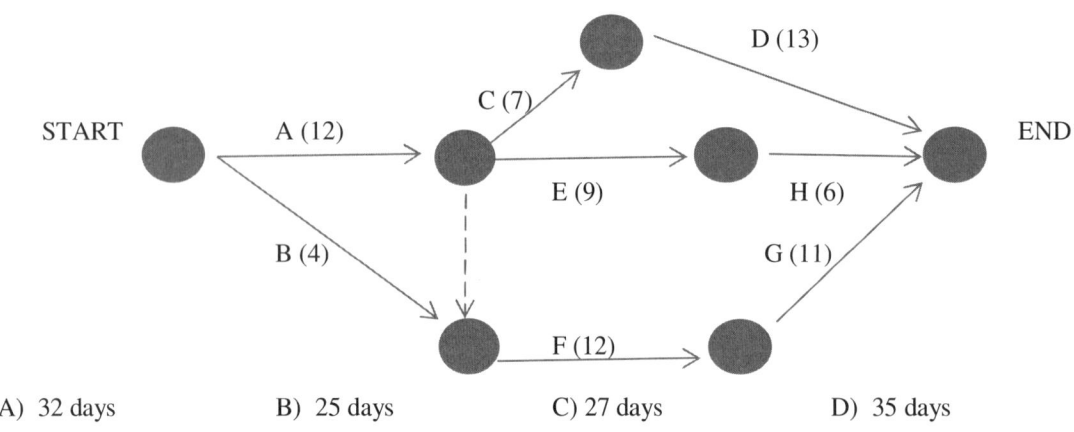

A) 32 days   B) 25 days   C) 27 days   D) 35 days

Solution):   Activities are shown on arrows in activity on arrow diagrams

In activity on arrow diagrams, arrows are used to show activities.
In activity on arrow diagrams, nodes are called events.
First node is always the "START" event and last node is the "END" event.
On the other hand, in activity on node diagrams, activities are shown on the node.

Dummy Activities: Broken arrows are used to indicate dummy activities. Activity F cannot be started until activities A and B are completed. If the dummy activity is not shown, activity F can be started as soon as activity B is completed.

There are number of paths exist from start to end.

Duration of path A, C, D = 12 + 7 + 13 = 32
Duration of path A, E, H = 12 + 9 + 6 = 27
Duration of path A, F, G = 12 + 12 + 11 = 35
Duration of path B, F, G = 4 + 12 + 11 = 27

To complete the project, longest path needs to be completed.

Duration of the project = 35   (Ans D)

Practice Problem: Find the early start and late start of activity D for the project given in the previous problem.

A) ES = 12,   LS = 15   B) ES = 13,   LS = 22   C) ES = 19,   LS = 22
D) ES = 22,   LS = 24

Solution:

Activity D, cannot be started until activity C is completed.

Early start of activity D = 12 + 7 = 19   (ES = 19)

Find the late start (LS) of activity D

Finding late start of an activity can be tricky.

We found that project duration to be 35 days.
Now we need to find what is the latest day that activity D can be started without delaying the project?

Latest day that activity D can be started without delaying the project = 35 – 13 = 22
35 is the duration of the project and 13 is the time need to complete activity D.
If activity D is started on day 22, there would not be any delay to the project. LS = 22
(Ans C)

Practice Problem: Find the total float of activity D.

A) 1   B) 3   C) 9   D) 2

Solution:

Total float of an activity is given by the following equation;

$$\boxed{\text{Total Float of an activity} = LS - ES}$$

LS = Late start;   ES = Early start

LS of activity D = 22
ES of activity D = 19
Float = LS – ES = 3

Activity Time Analysis: Activity times can be changed in order to change the critical path. Activity time of an activity can be either increased or decreased. Activity time can be decreased by increasing manpower. Similarly, activity time can be increased by reducing resources to that particular activity.

4.4   Resource Leveling:

Resource Leveling:

We may develop a fast schedule that completes the project on time. But what about the resources? Does the contractor have resources (Equipment and manpower) to do two or three activities at the same time? If the contractor does not have enough equipment and manpower to do two or three simultaneous activities, then resources should be increased. This can be done by renting new machines and hiring new personnel. Renting more machines will be an expensive thing to do. Hiring new people can also be a problem. It is not easy to find people who have suitable expertise.
Hence, the next option is to manipulate the activities

Construction resources are labor, material and equipment. In construction scheduling, conflicts can arise when activities compete for common resources that are available in limited quantities. After development of the critical path schedule, resource utilization chart is developed.

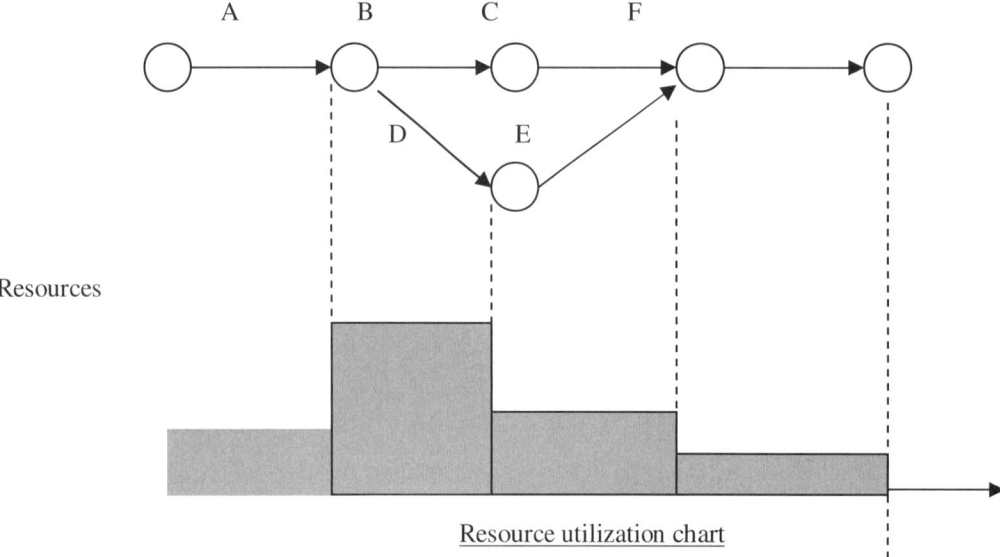

Resource utilization chart

Resources need to be allocated evenly, during the lifetime of the project. In the above figure, when activities B and D are conducted, demand for resources increases. It is important to level the resources during the project duration. In many cases, it is not an easy task. In the above figure, it is possible to stretch activities B and D and shorten the duration of activities A and F.
Increase the duration of activities B and D. This can be done by reducing the daily quantity of resources.
Decrease the duration of activities A and F. This can be done by increasing the daily quantity of resources.
It is possible to level resources by manipulating duration of activities. In some cases, it is possible to move activities around for the purpose of resource leveling.
Various computer algorithms are developed to level resources without affecting the schedule.
Competition for resources among activities:

Resource Leveling Procedure: Following procedure is normally adopted.
Construct the critical path schedule
Develop the resource schedule
Move around the activities to level the resources

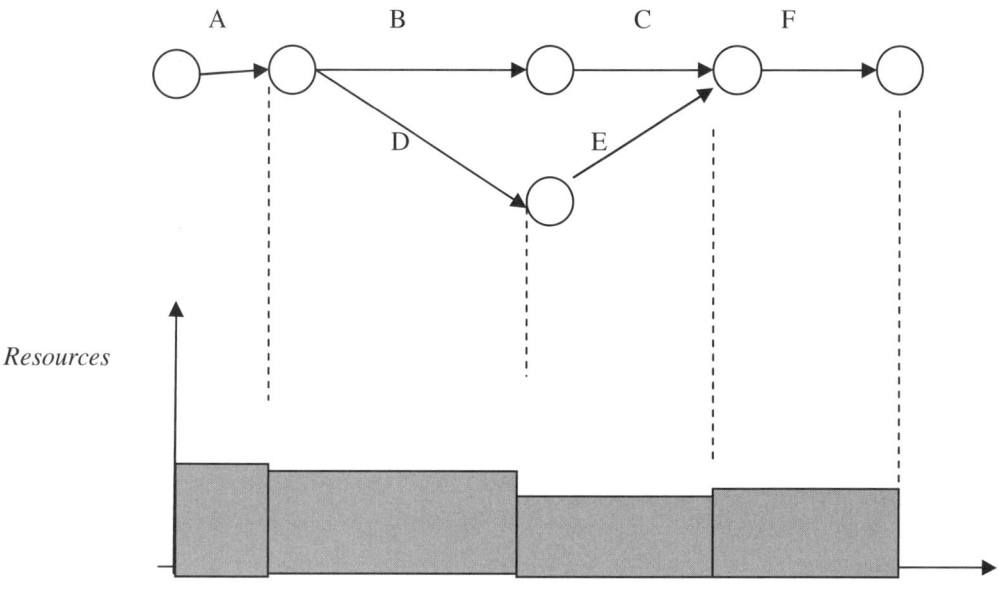

Resources

Resource utilization chart (after resource leveling)

Practice Problem: Contractor has developed durations and resources required for construction of two slabs.

Resources required for each activity is given below;

Activity 1:	Formwork slab in building A:	1 foreman, 8 carpenters, 6 laborers
Activity 2:	Rebar installation of slab in building A:	1 foreman, 5 iron workers, 3 laborers
Activity 3:	Concreting of slab in building A:	1 foreman, 8 concrete masons, 6 laborers

Activity 4:	Formwork of slab in building B:	1 foreman, 8 carpenters, 6 laborers
Activity 5:	Rebar installation of slab in building B:	1 foreman, 5 iron workers, 3 laborers
Activity 6:	Concreting of slab in building B:	1 foreman, 8 concrete masons, 6 laborers
Activity 7:	Opening ceremony	

Activity 1:	Duration	7 days
Activity 2:	Duration	10 days
Activity 3:	Duration	7 days

Activity 4:	Duration	12 days
Activity 5:	Duration	11 days
Activity 6:	Duration	7 days
Activity 7:	Duration	1 day

Logic of activities:

Activities 1 and 4 can start at any time.
Predecessor of activity 2 is activity 1.
Predecessor of activity 3 is activity 2.

Predecessor of activity 5 is activity 4.
Predecessor of activity 6 is activity 5

Predecessors of activity 7 are 3 and 6.

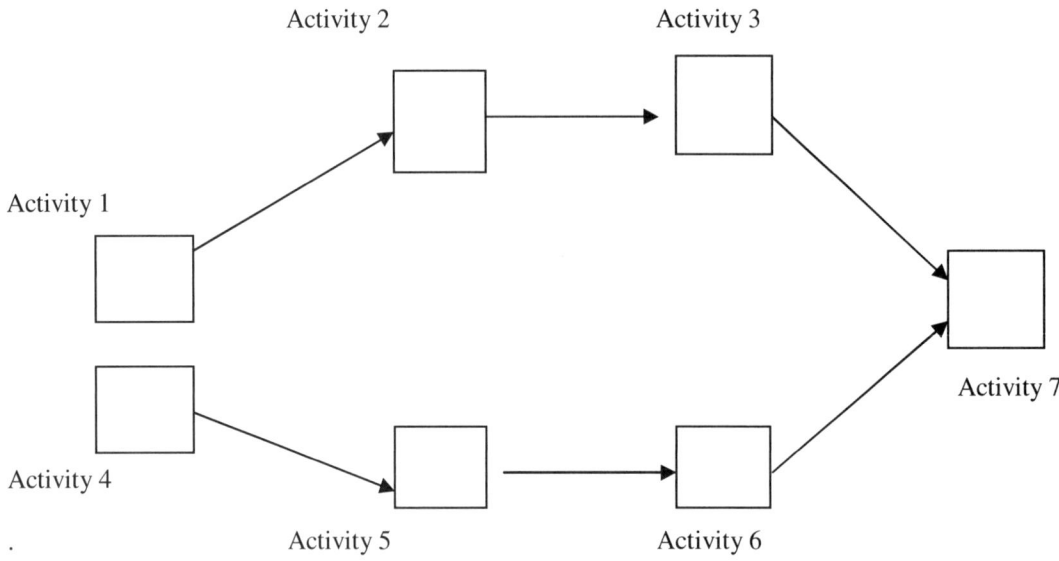

Maximum resources available at a given time;

2 Foremans
8 carpenters
10 iron workers
16 concrete masons
12 laborers

What is the project duration?

Solution:

There are only 8 carpenters available. Hence, activities 1 and 4 cannot go parallel.

There are 10 ironworkers available. Hence, there are enough ironworkers to conduct activities 2 and 5 in parallel.

There are 16 concrete masons available. Hence, activities 3 and 6 can be done parallel.

Hence, new network can be drawn as shown.

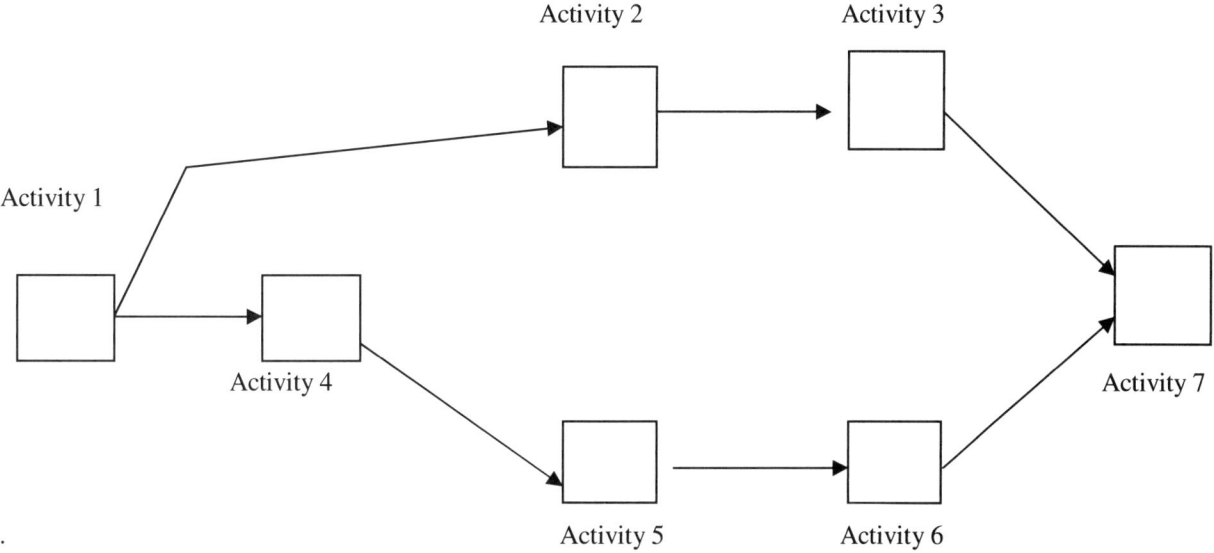

There are two paths.

Path 1, 2,3, 7
Path 1, 4, 5, 6, 7

Duration of path 1, 2, 3, 7 = 7 + 10 + 7 + 1 = 25 days
Duration of path 1, 4, 5, 6, 7 = 7 + 12 + 11 + 7 + 1 = 38 days

Project duration = 38 days

4. 5   Time - Cost Tradeoff:

Acceleration of a project can be done by increasing the labor. Unfortunately, in some situations increasing manpower may bring diminishing returns. This could be due to number of reasons.

More management staff is needed to manage a bigger crew. The crew may not have enough space to work.
There may not be enough machinery to support a bigger crew. Delays would have a bigger cost impact due to the larger crew size.

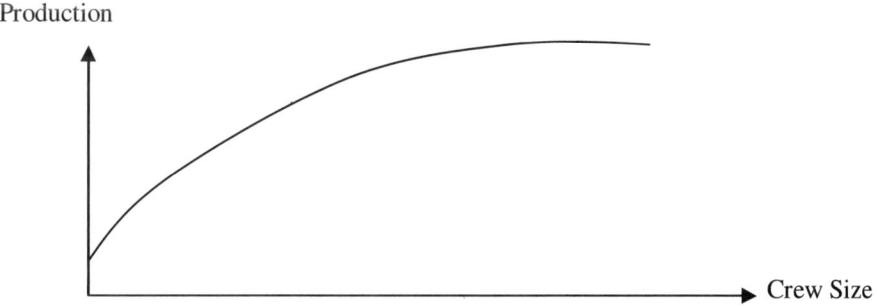

4.6   Integration of CAD and Schedule:

Three decades ago, CAD software or scheduling software were not available. All drawings were done by draughtsman. Scheduling of the project also conducted using manual methods. Following sets of drawings are needed for any construction project.

- Architectural Drawings - These drawings show the final view of the project after completion. In the past, these drawings were done manually. Today all drawings are done by using CAD.
- Civil Drawings - Civil drawings would show concrete rebar details, structural details, masonry details and many other information required to construct the project.

- •   <u>Mechanical Drawings</u> -   Mechanical drawings would show plumbing details, ducts, underground piping, piping inside walls, boilers, air conditioning units and all other mechanical devices.
- •   <u>Electrical Drawings</u> -   Electrical drawings would show electrical wiring, electrical panels, transformers and switches.
- •   <u>Communication Drawings</u> -   Communication network details such as communication cables, wiring, routers, telephone lines and computers are shown in these drawings.

As far as scheduling is concerned, CPM technique is widely used for scheduling.   Computer software such as Primevera is used for scheduling. Let us look at a simplified example of constructing small building.

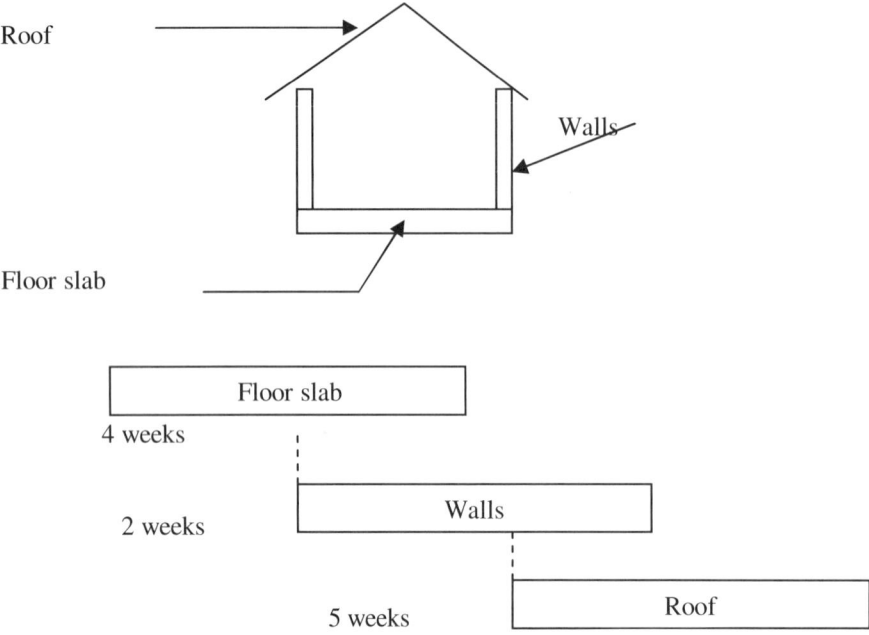

According to the schedule, 2 weeks after starting the project, wall construction would start. Floor slab will be completed in 4 weeks. Roof will be started in 5 weeks and completed in 8 weeks.

As mentioned earlier CAD drawings would show how the building would look at the end of the project. Integrated software such as *Rivet* can show how the site would look during construction. For an instance, it is possible for such software to show how the site would look after 3 weeks. After 3 weeks, most of the floor slab is completed and some of the walls also have been completed.

<u>Advantages of Integrated Software</u>:   Integrated software can show conflicts that could occur during construction. For an instance it is possible to visualize an underground piping been done while a footing is been constructed. The resident engineer may decide to slow down the piping construction to facilitate the footing construction. Another main advantage is that owners (mostly laymen) can better visualize the construction process.   Integrated software provides a better understanding between subcontractors.

5.0 Material Quality Control and Production

Construction Material: It is important to have a sound understanding on construction material. Some of the widely used construction materials are:
Concrete
Steel
Timber
Masonry

Concrete: Concrete is the most common building construction material in the world. Concrete is a mixture of cement, sand, aggregates (gravel) and water. Cement and water is known as binder. Sand and aggregate act as filler material. Cement and water is known as binder since it glues all ingredients together.

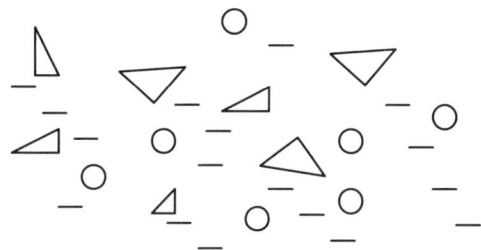

Concrete Ingredients

Legend:

Aggregates (gravel)

Sand:

Cement and water mixture

Cement: Limestone ($CaCO_3$) has a property of solidifying when water is added. This property of limestone is utilized to create cement. Cement is manufactured by burning limestone and clay together at very high temperatures. Portland cement due to its superior qualities has become most widely used cement type.
Limestone is crushed into small pieces. The crushed limestone is then mixed with clay, sand and iron ore and ground together to form a homogeneous powder.
This mixture is heated to a very high temperature and the powder is collected and packaged in bags and known as cement.
Water: Water when mixed with cement, forms a paste that binds the aggregates together. The water causes the hardening of concrete through a process called hydration. Hydration is a chemical reaction in which the major compounds in cement form chemical bonds with water molecules.
The water needs to be free of impurities. Impurities may cause side reactions that would reduce the strength of concrete.

Water Cement Ratio: The strength of concrete directly depends on the water cement ratio. Higher the water content, lesser the strength. Lesser the water content, higher the strength.
When the water content is too low, one may not be able to pump it. At the same time, concrete should flow and occupy the entire structure.

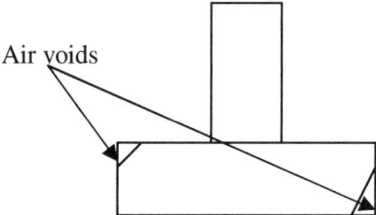

Air voids may form if water content is too low

Hence, the water content should be high enough to make sure it would flow freely to all corners of the structure. Too much water reduces concrete strength, while too little will make the concrete unworkable.

Aggregates: Gravel is known as coarse aggregates and sand is known as fine aggregates. Aggregates (both gravel and sand) are chemically inert, meaning that they do not participate in the chemical reactions. Aggregates are known as filler material that would bring weight and volume to the structure. Aggregates come in various shapes, sizes, and materials ranging from fine gravel to large coarse rocks. Because cement is the most expensive ingredient in making concrete, it is desirable to minimize the amount of cement used. The type of aggregates to be used depends on the final concrete required. For example, high-density concrete requires high-density aggregates. If lightweight concrete is needed, then it is desirable to use low-density aggregates.

Sand (Fine Aggregates):   Sand also does not participate in chemical reactions. The main function of sand is to provide weight and density to concrete and to act as a filler material.

Reinforcing Bars: Concrete is very weak in tension. Hence, rebars are added to provide tensile strength. Structural engineers compute tension members and add rebars to provide much-needed tensile strength.

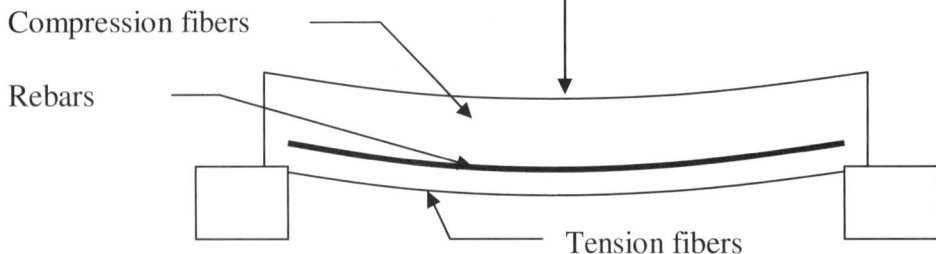

Compression fibers

Rebars

Tension fibers

Rebars provide tensile strength in concrete

Properties of Concrete: Concrete has many advantages compared to other construction materials. Construction work can be easily done using concrete. Good-quality concrete has many advantages that add to its popularity. Properly designed concrete has a long life span. In many instances concrete is cheaper than steel. Low maintenance of concrete structures is another advantage that designers consider. Concrete has the ability to be molded into almost any desired shape. Concrete is a non-combustible material, which makes it fire safe, and has the capacity to withstand high temperatures.
Concrete also has some disadvantages. Concrete can deteriorate if acidic water is encountered. Concrete has low strength to weight ratio compared to steel. In other words, to obtain the same strength as steel, one needs a larger concrete structure.

Steel: Steel is one of the most important construction materials. For some construction, work steel surpasses concrete. Steel bridges, buildings, domes, roofs are still commonly built using steel.

Steel structural shapes:
W Shapes (Wide Flange):
W sections are widely used for beams and columns.

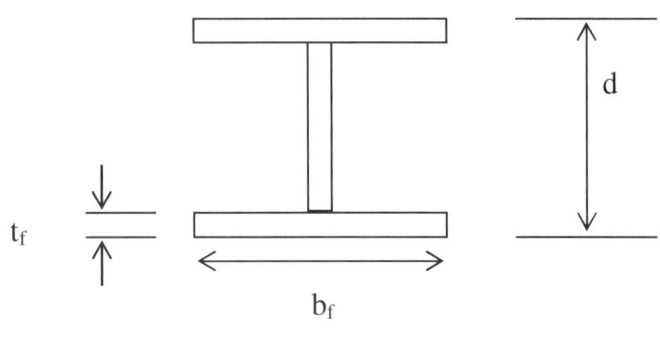

d = Depth   b_f = Width   t_f = Thickness

Description:

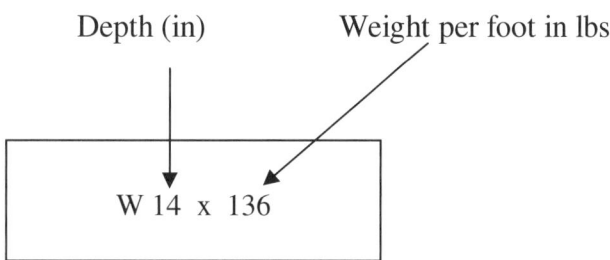

W shapes are available in many different sizes and widely used in USA.

S – Shapes:

S – Shapes have a slightly shorter flange. Description of S shapes are as same as W – shapes.

C – Shapes (Channels):

Channels are widely used for beams and columns depending on the situation.

C 15 x 50

Above 15 is the depth and 50 is the weight given in lbs per linear foot.

L – Shapes: (Angles)

Angles are also used for beams and columns.

Angles could be of equal length legs or un-equal legs.

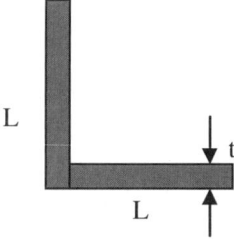

Description:

L 8 x 8 x 1 ½

Above 8 is the lengths of two legs and 1 ½ is the thickness (t).

HP – Shapes: HP shapes are widely used for piling work. Description of HP shapes is similar to W – shapes.

Structural Steel Pipes: Structural steel pipes are used mostly for columns. Structural steel pipes are also known as HSS (Hollow structural shape).

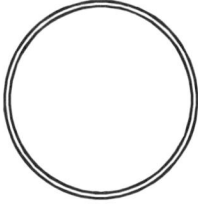

Nominal diameter, thickness and weight per linear foot are provided.

Square Structural Tubing:

Square structural tubing is used for columns and beams.

Masonry: Masonry is an important construction material.   Masonry structures could be bricks, cement blocks, stones or concrete blocks. Typically, mortar is used to bond the units together.

Mortar

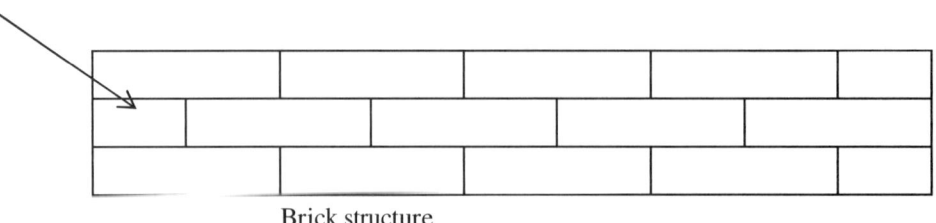

Brick structure

Hollow Cement Blocks: Hollow cement blocks filled with grout also widely used.

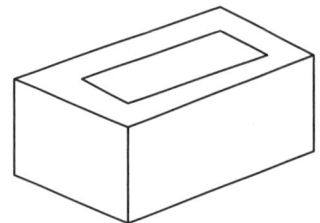

Hollow cement blocks

5.1   Material Testing: Material-testing section is one of the easiest sections and the student should take full advantage of it. Be thoroughly prepared to answer all questions in this section. This book will cover most of the common material testing procedures in this chapter. The student is encouraged to conduct his own research and obtain a good knowledge of various testing methods and procedures.

Construction materials such as concrete, soil, asphalt and steel need to be tested to assure the quality. This chapter is devoted to testing of construction materials.

Testing of Concrete: It is necessary to make sure that concrete has achieved the specified strength requirements. Typically, concrete cylinders are obtained during construction and sent to a laboratory for testing.

Concrete testing procedure (Concrete Cylinders):

STEP 1: Obtain concrete test cylinders. Concrete is poured into the test cylinder in five layers and compact them with a steel rod. Obtain a minimum of three cylinders.

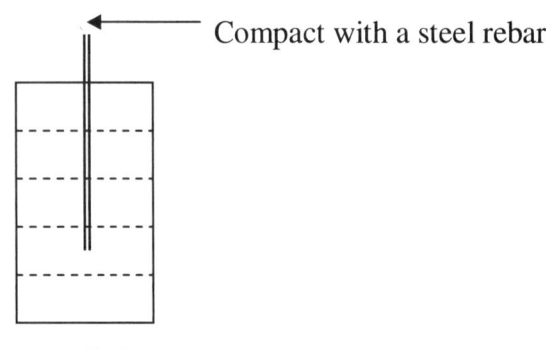

Compact with a steel rebar

Concrete cylinders

STEP 2: Leave concrete cylinders close to the construction site for few days to emulate the curing conditions in the site. Then send the cylinders to a testing laboratory. The cylinders are typically broken after 7 days, 14 days and 28 days.

Practice Problem 5.1:   Assume 3,000 psi concrete (which means that the strength expected after 28 days is 3,000 psi) cylinders were taken and sent to the laboratory. Following test values were received. Is the concrete acceptable?

Seven-day strength -   1,000 psi
Fourteen-day strength -   2,200 psi
Twenty-eight day strength – 3,100 psi
Required 28 day strength is 3,000 psi. Achieved strength is 3,100 psi. The concrete is acceptable.

Practice Problem 5.2:   Assume 5,000 psi concrete cylinders were taken and sent to the laboratory. Following test values were received. Is the concrete acceptable?
Seven-day strength -   2,200 psi
Fourteen-day strength -   3,700 psi
Twenty-eight day strength – 4,700 psi
Required 28-day strength is 5,000 psi.

Solution: Achieved strength is 4,700 psi. The concrete is not acceptable. In such situations, following options are available.

In such situations, inform the design engineer immediately. Ask him whether the concrete is used for a structural member. If the concrete is used for a structural member, can this low strength concrete support the loading?

If the low strength concrete is not adequate and does not comply with the design intent, the concrete has to be demolished and new concrete has to be placed.

If the concrete is used for non-structural members (such as steps, slab on grade, handicap ramp) then low strength concrete may be acceptable. This type of situation, structural engineer who designed the structure needs to be involved.

Concrete Slump Test: Slump test is conducted by packing concrete to a standard cone. After compaction of concrete in three layers, the cone is removed. When the cone is removed, the concrete is left unsupported and will slump. Bigger the slump, higher the water content.
Concrete with high water content is low in strength. To increase the strength, one has to decrease the water content. On the other hand, concrete with low water content has low workability.

Concrete Slump Test

Slump test procedure:

STEP 1: Compact concrete to a standard cone. The standard cone is 12 in (300 mm) in height. The concrete is placed in three layers and tamped with a steel rebar 25 times per layer.
STEP 2: The cone is removed and left the concrete un-supported.
STEP 3: The slump is measured. Compare the slump obtained in the field to the slump specified by the engineer.
High slump means high water content. High water content means low strength.
Low slump means low water content. Low water content means high strength.
Hence, to achieve high strength, the water content needs to be kept low. However, when the water content is too low, it is difficult to pour concrete. Hence, the engineer needs to specify the range of slump that is acceptable.

Standard Cone Size for the Slump Test:
300 mm (12 in.) high cone, 200 mm (8 in.) wide at the bottom and 100 mm (4 in.) wide at the top.

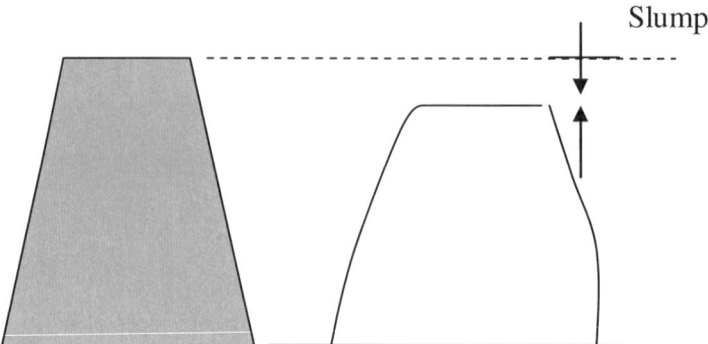

Soil Tests:

Laboratory Testing: After completion of the boring program, laboratory tests are conducted on the soil samples. Laboratory test program is dependent on the project requirements. Some of the laboratory tests done on soil samples are given below.
- Sieve analysis
- Water content
- Atterberg limit tests (Liquid limit and plastic limit)
- Permeability test
- UU tests (Undrained unconfined tests)
- Density of soil
- Consolidation test
- Tri-axial tests
- Direct shear test

Sieve Analysis: Sieve analysis is conducted to classify soil into sands, silts and clays. Sieves are used to separate soil particles and group them based on their size. This test is used for the purpose of classification of soil.
Standard sieve sizes are shown below.

Sieve No:	Mesh size (mm)
No. 4	4.75
No. 6	3.35
No. 8	2.36
No. 10	2.00
No. 12	1.68
No. 16	1.18
No. 20	0.85
No. 30	0.60
No. 40	0.425
No. 50	0.30
No. 60	0.25
No. 80	0.18
No. 100	0.15
No. 200	0.075
No. 270	0.053

US sieve No. and mesh size

Gravel: Particles greater than #4 sieve is considered to be gravel.
Sands: Particles in the range #4 to #200 are considered to be sands.

Silts and Clays: Particles smaller than #200 is considered to be silts and clays.

Differentiation of silts and clays cannot be done using sieve analysis. Clays are bound together due to chemical and electromagnetic forces. Silt particles are not bound together due to chemical forces.

Hypothetical sieve analysis test based on selected group of sieves are given below as an example.

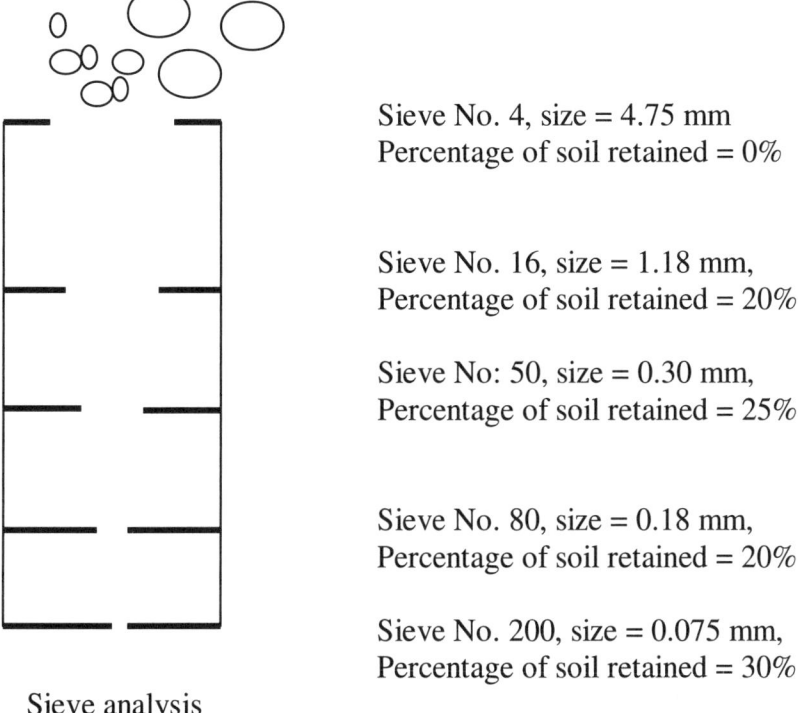

Sieve No. 4, size = 4.75 mm
Percentage of soil retained = 0%

Sieve No. 16, size = 1.18 mm,
Percentage of soil retained = 20%

Sieve No: 50, size = 0.30 mm,
Percentage of soil retained = 25%

Sieve No. 80, size = 0.18 mm,
Percentage of soil retained = 20%

Sieve No. 200, size = 0.075 mm,
Percentage of soil retained = 30%

<u>Sieve analysis</u>

If we know the percentage of soil passed from a given sieve, we can find the percentage of soil retained in that sieve.

Sieve No 4 (size 4.75 mm):   All soil went passed sieve No. 4.
 Percent retained at this sieve is 0%.
Percent passed = 100%.

Sieve No 16 (1.18 mm):   20% of soil was retained in sieve No. 16.
 Percent retained at sieve No. 16 = 20%
Percent passed = 100 – 20 = 80%.

Sieve No 50 (0.30 mm):   25% of soil was retained in sieve No. 50.
Total retained so far = 20 + 25 = 45%
Percent passed = 100 – 45 = 55%

Sieve No 80 (0.18 mm):   20% retained in sieve No. 80.
 Total retained so far = 20 + 25 + 20 = 65%
Percent passed = 100 – 65 = 35%.

Sieve No 200 (0.075 mm):   30% retained in sieve No. 200.
Total retained so far = 20 + 25 + 20 + 30 = 95%
Percent passed through sieve No. 200 = 100 – 95 = 5%.

Now it is possible to draw a graph indicating % passing at each sieve.

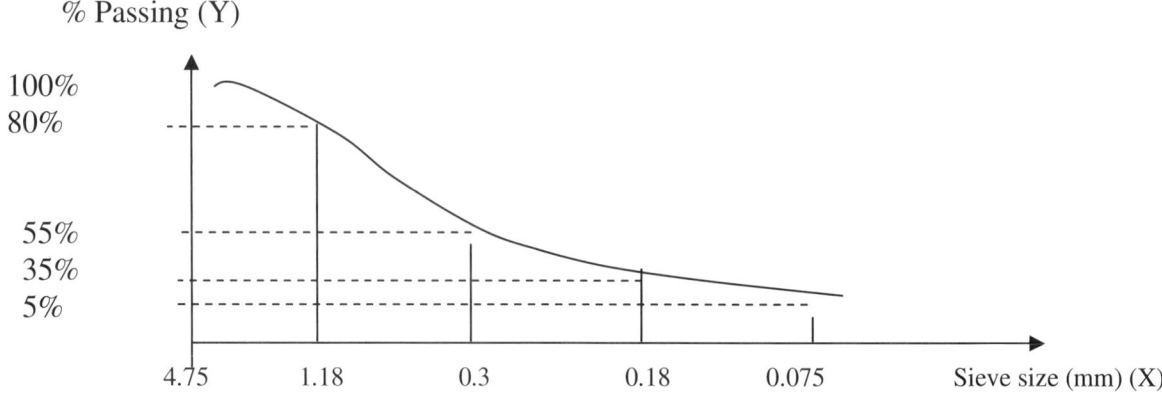

X – axis - Sieve size.   Y - axis - Percent passing.

Percent passing vs particle size

D_{60}: D_{60} is defined as the size of the sieve that allows 60% of the soil to pass. This value is used for soil classification purposes and frequently appears in geotechnical engineering correlations.

To find the D_{60} value, draw a line at 60% passing point. Then drop it down to obtain the D_{60} value.

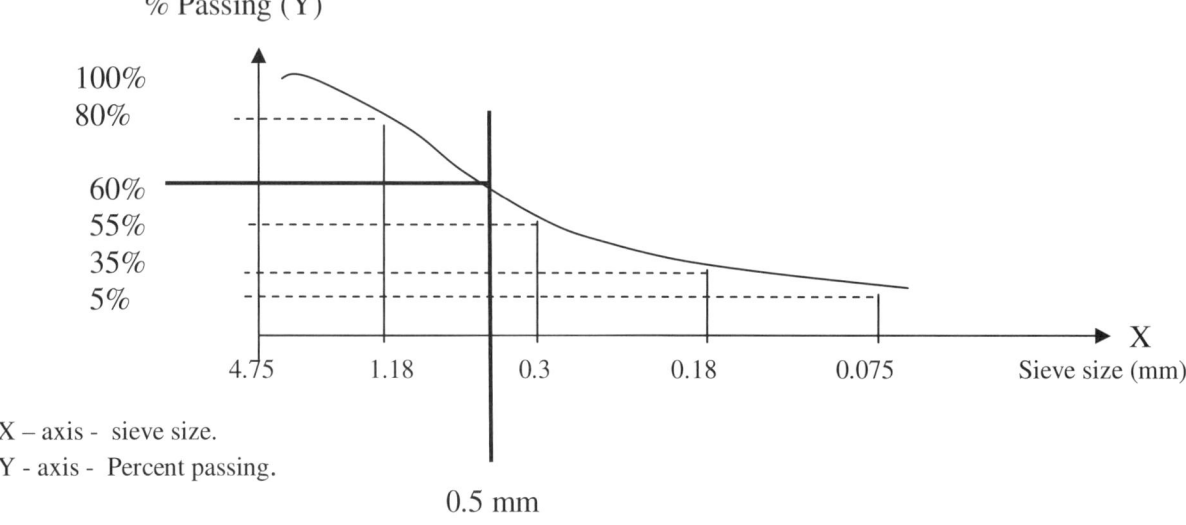

X – axis - sieve size.

Y - axis - Percent passing.

0.5 mm

Finding D_{60}:   In this case D_{60} is closer to 0.5 mm.

Find D_{30}:   As before, draw a line at 30% passing line. In this case, D_{30} happened to be approximately 0.1 mm.

Gradation: When a sand sample contains sand particles of all sizes, it is called a well graded sand. When sand particles are of more or less similar in size, the sand is considered to be poorly graded.

Well graded sands can be compacted better than poorly graded sands.

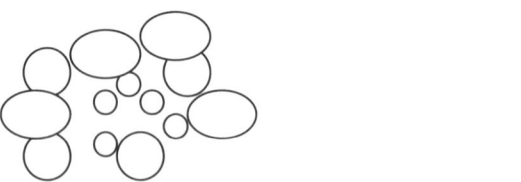

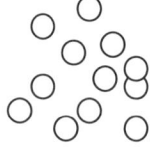

Well Graded Sands (various sizes)   *Poorly Graded Sands (similar sizes)*

Soil Classification:

Soils are classified into different categories.
Major categories of soils are:

Gravels
Sands
Silts
Organic Clays
Inorganic clays
Peat

Silts and Sands: Sand particles can be seen with naked eye. Silt and clay particles cannot be seen with the naked eye. The difference between silts and clays is that clay particles bind together. Silt particles do not have cohesive properties.

In many cases, silt particles and clay particles are mixed together. Such soils are known as silty clay or clayey silt. When the predominant constituent is clay and silt is the secondary component, such soils are known as silty clay. If the predominant constituent is silt, such soils are known as clayey silt.

Symbols:

> SP - Poorly graded sand
> SW - Well graded sand

Since symbol "S" was used for sands, another symbol was needed to represent silts. Symbol "M" is used to represent silts.

> ML - Low plastic silts
> MH - High plastic silts

Clays: Some clays contain plenty of organic matter. Organic matter is mainly decomposed tress and roots. Clays with large quantity of organic matter is known as organic clays.

Clays could be high plastic to low plastic. Highly cohesive clays are known as high plastic clays and vice versa. High plastic clays are known as fat clays also.

> CL - Low plastic inorganic clays
> CH - High plastic inorganic clays
> OL - Low plastic organic clays or silts
> OH - High plastic organic clays or silts
> PT - Predominantly organic soils, peat, muck, marsh soils.

Soil Classification Procedure:

Coarse Grained Soils and Fine Grained Soils:
Sands and silts are known as coarse grained soils and silts and clays are known as fine grained soils.

Particles larger than 0.075 mm (No. 200 sieve size) are classified as coarse grained soils or coarse fraction. (sands and gravel)
Particles smaller than 0.075 mm (No. 200 sieve size) are classified as fine grained soils or fine fraction. (silts and clays)

Classification of Gravels:

If 50% or more of the coarse fraction is larger than 4.75 mm (No. 4 sieve) such soils are classified as gravels.
If 50% or more of the coarse fraction is smaller than 4.75 mm (No. 4 sieve) such soils are classified as sands.
How to differentiate between poorly graded gravel and well graded gravel?

Conditions for well graded gravels (GW):   Two conditions have to be satisfied for well graded gravel.

Condition 1: $D_{60}/D_{10} > 4$
Condition 2: $1 < D_{30}^2/(D_{10} \times D_{60}) < 3$

If any of these conditions are violated such soils are classified as GP.

If gravel contains silts, then it would be classified as GM.
Similarly, if the gravel contains clays, it would be classified as GC.

Classification of Sands:

If more than 50% of the soil sample is larger than 0.075 mm (No. 200 sieve) such soils are classified as gravels and sands.

If 50% or more of the coarse fraction is smaller than 4.75 mm (No. 4 sieve) such soils are classified as sands.
Conditions for well graded sands (SW):

Condition 1: $D_{60}/D_{10} > 6$
Condition 2: $1 < D_{30}^2/(D_{10} \times D_{60}) < 3$

If any of these conditions are violated such soils are classified as poorly graded sands (SP).

If sand contains silts, then it would be classified as SM.
Similarly, if the sand contains clays, it would be classified as SC.

Plasticity Index

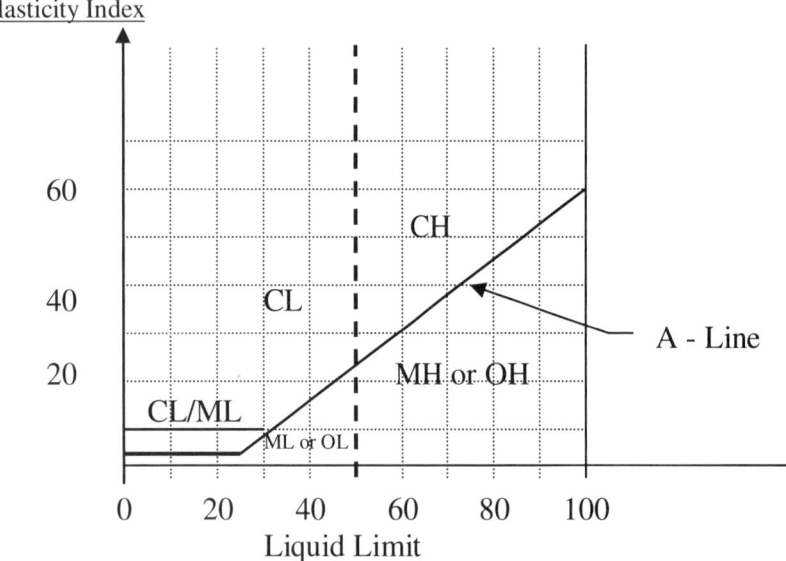

Soil Compaction: Shallow foundations can be rested on controlled fill, also known as engineered fill or structural fill. Typically such fill material are carefully selected and compacted to 95% of the modified Proctor density.

Modified Proctor test is conducted by placing soil in a standard mould and compacted with a standard ram.

Modified Proctor Test Procedure:

STEP 1:

Soil that needs to be compacted is placed in a standard mould and compacted.

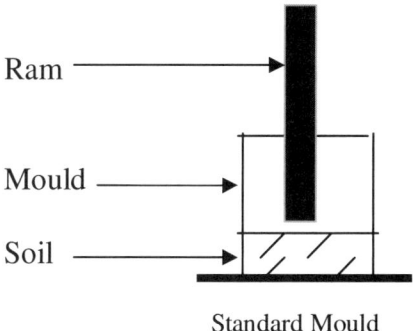

Standard Mould

STEP 2: Compaction of soil is done by dropping a standard ram 25 times for each layer of soil from a standard distance. Typically, soil is placed in five layers and compacted.

STEP 3: After compaction of all five layers, the weight of the soil is obtained. The soil contains solids and water. Solids are basically soil particles.

$$M = M_s + M_w$$

M = Total mass of soil including water
M_s = Mass of solid portion of soil
M_w = Mass of water

STEP 4: Find the moisture content of the soil.
Moisture content is defined as M_w/M_s
Small sample of soil is taken and placed in the oven and measured.

STEP 5:
Find the dry density of soil.
Dry density of soil is given by M_s/V
M_s is the dry weight of soil and "V" is the total volume.

STEP 6: Repeat the test few times with different moisture content and plot a graph between dry density and moisture content.

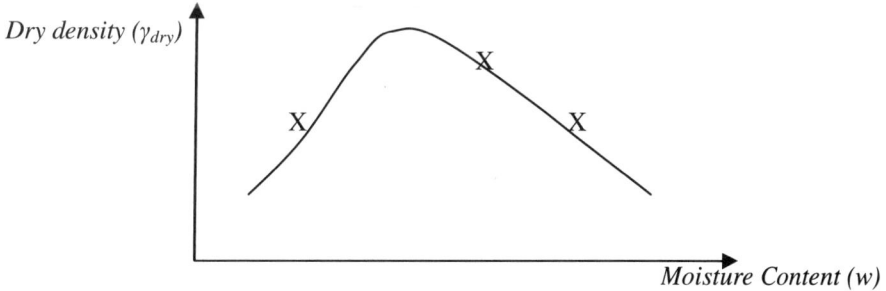

Dry density and moisture content

STEP 7: Obtain the maximum dry density and the optimum moisture content.

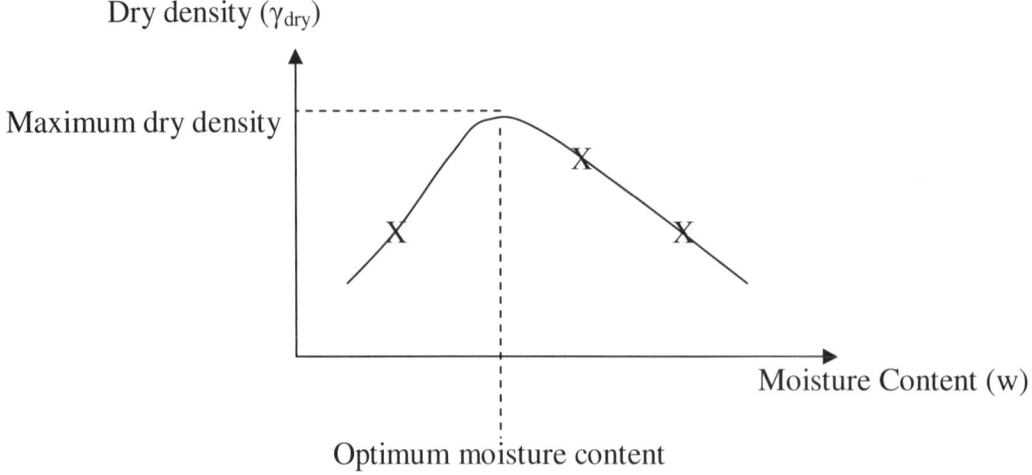

For a given soil, there is an optimum moisture content that would provide the maximum dry density.
It is not easy to attain the optimum moisture content in the field. Usually soil that is too wet is not compacted. If the soil is too dry, water is added to increase the moisture content.

Liquid Limit:

Liquid limit is the water content where soil start to behave as a liquid.
Liquid limit is measured by placing a clay sample in a standard cup and making a separation (groove) using a spatula. The cup is dropped till the separation vanishes. Water content of the soil is obtained at this sample. The test is performed again by increasing the water content. Soil with low water content would yield more blows and soil with high water content would yield less blows.
A graph is drawn between number of blows and the water content.

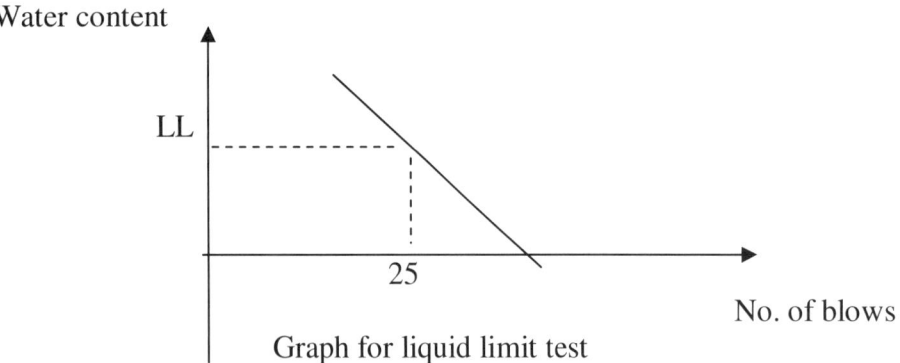

Graph for liquid limit test

Plastic limit:

Plastic limit is measured by rolling a clay sample to a 3 mm diameter cylindrical shape. During continuous rolling at this size, the clay sample tends to lose moisture and cracks start to appear. Water content where cracks start to appear is defined as the plastic limit.

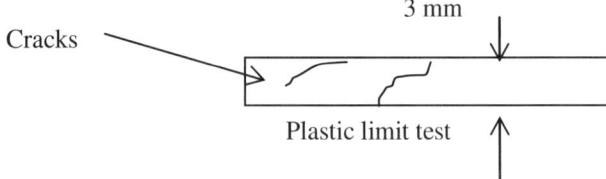

Plastic limit test

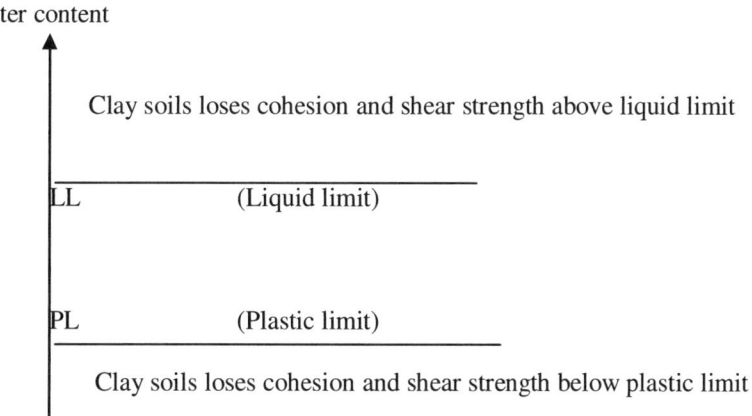

Water content

Clay soils loses cohesion and shear strength above liquid limit

LL   (Liquid limit)

PL   (Plastic limit)

Clay soils loses cohesion and shear strength below plastic limit

Permeability Test: Transport of water through soil media depends on the pressure head, velocity head and the potential head due to elevation. In most cases, most important parameter is the potential head due to elevation.

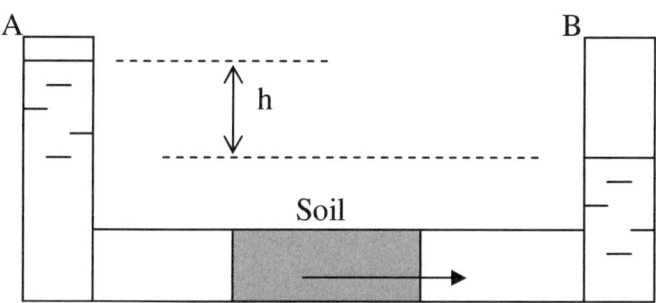

A   B

h

Soil

Water flowing through soil

Water travels from "A" to "B" due to high potential head. Velocity of traveling water is given by the Darcy equation.

$$v = k \cdot i \qquad \text{(Darcy's Equation)}$$

v = Velocity;

k = Coefficient of Permeability (cm/sec or in/sec)

i = Hydraulic gradient = h/L

L = Length of soil

Volume of water flow = $Q = A \times v$

A = Area; v = Velocity

Practice Problem 5.3:   Find the volume of water flowing in the pipe shown. Soil permeability is 10^{-5} cm/sec. Area of the pipe is 5 cm². Length of soil plug is 50 cm.

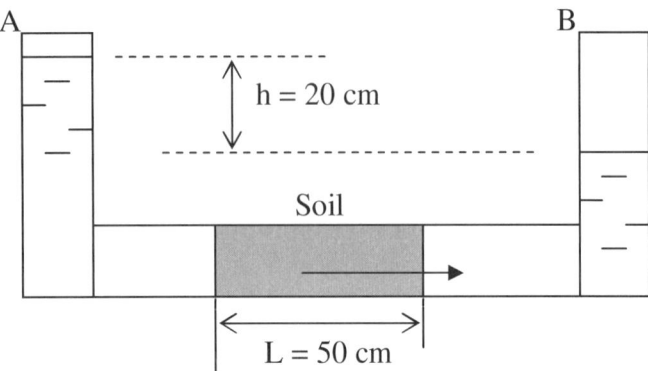

Water flow due to 20 cm gravity head

Solution: Apply the Darcy equation;

$v = k \cdot i$ (Darcy's Equation)

v = Velocity;
k = Coefficient of permeability (cm/sec or in/sec)
i = Hydraulic gradient = h/L
L = Length of soil
A = Area of the pipe = 5 cm².
     $v = k \times (h/L)$
     $v = 10^{-5} \times 20/5 = 4 \times 10^{-6}$ cm/sec
Volume of water flow = $A \times v = 5 \times 4 \times 10^{-6}$ cm³/sec = 2×10^{-5} cm³/sec

Unconfined Un-Drained Compressive Strength Tests (UU Tests):

Unconfined compressive strength test is designed to measure the shear strength of clay soils. This is the easiest and most common test done to measure the shear strength.
Since the test is done with the sample in an unconfined state and the load is applied fast so that there is no possibility of draining, The test is known as unconfined – undrained test. (UU test).
UU Test Procedure:
Soil sample is placed in a compression machine and compressed until failure. Stresses are recorded during the test and plotted.

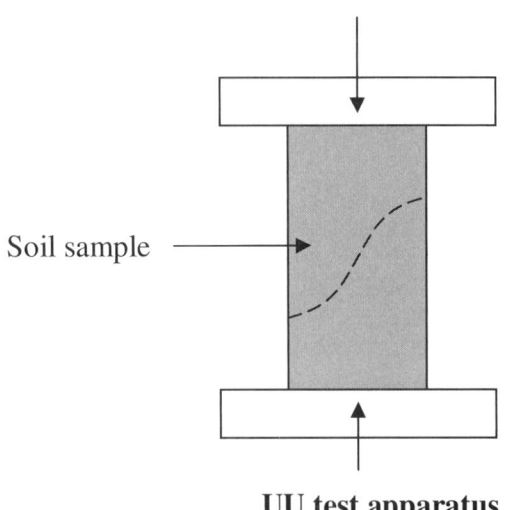

UU test apparatus

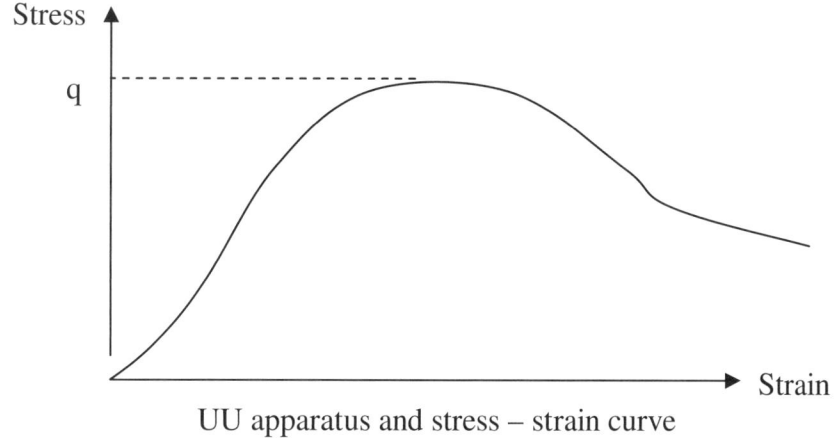

UU apparatus and stress – strain curve

<u>Tensile Failure</u>:   When a material is subjected to a tensile stress, it would undergo tensile failure.

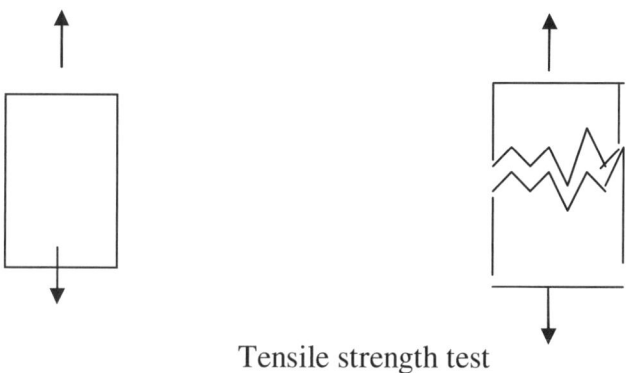

Tensile strength test

Two figures above show material failure under tension. Tensile failure of soil is not as common as shear failure and tensile tests rarely conducted. On the other hand, tensile failure is common in tunnels.

Asphalt: Asphalt is a bituminous material manufactured using petroleum bi-products. Asphalt is mixed with aggregates and base course is manufactured. The base course is laid on top of compacted soil and rolled. Another layer of asphalt known as top is laid on top of the base course.

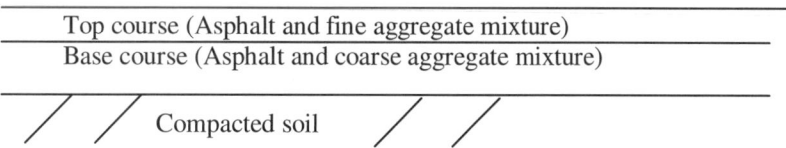

Both base course and top course are manufactured by mixing asphalt with aggregates. The main difference is that base course is mixed with coarse aggregates while top course is mixed with fine aggregates.

Asphalt density in the field can be tested with a nuclear gauge. Most famous manufacturer of these nuclear gauges is Troxler Inc. The gauge indicates the density of asphalt. If the density of asphalt is less than the specified density, the asphalt needs to be rolled with a heavy roller.

5.2   Welding:

Welding is done for aircrafts, ships, bridges and pipelines. Following five joint types are commonly used. Word joint and weld are in many cases interchanged in textbooks. One textbook may call a lap joint while another book may call it a lap weld. Similarly, one book may call **butt joint** and another one may call it **butt weld**.

    1)   Butt joints
    2)   T joints
    3)   Lap joints
    4)   Corner joints
    5)   Edge joints

Butt Joints: Two members need to be welded are **butted** together, hence, the joint is known as butt joints. In most cases, members to be welded are provided with grooves.

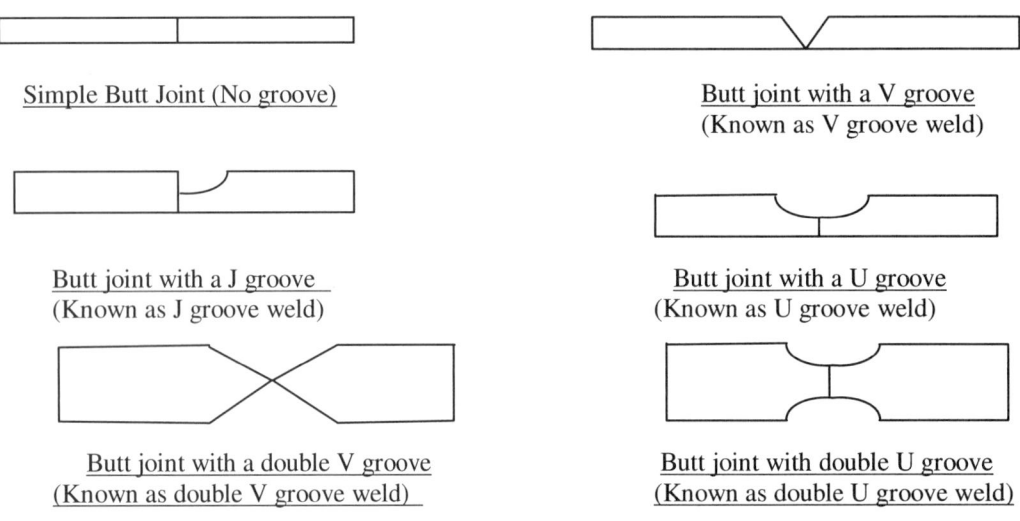

Simple Butt Joint (No groove)

Butt joint with a V groove
(Known as V groove weld)

Butt joint with a J groove
(Known as J groove weld)

Butt joint with a U groove
(Known as U groove weld)

Butt joint with a double V groove
(Known as double V groove weld)

Butt joint with double U groove
(Known as double U groove weld)

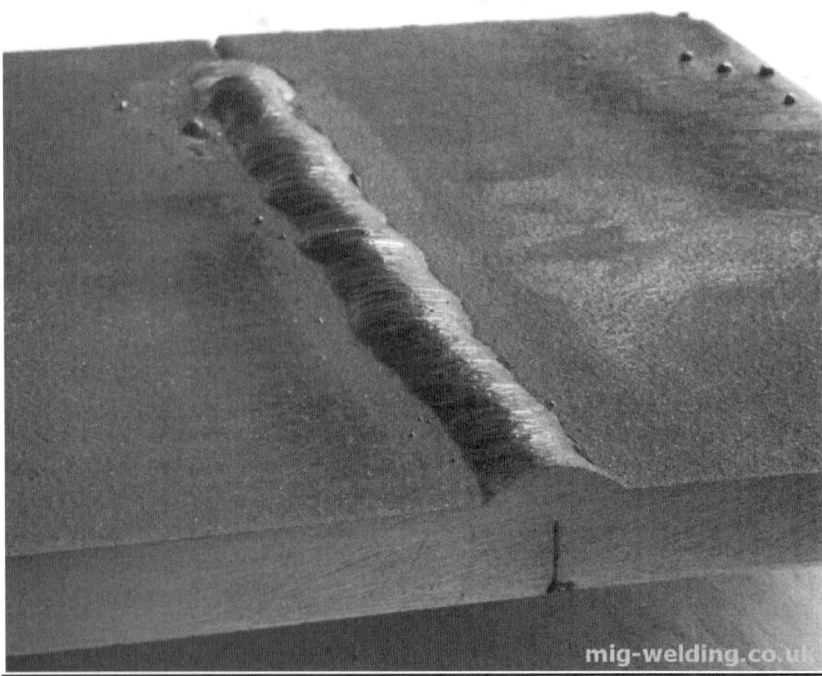

Photo of a simple butt weld   (Two plates are butted together. No groove in plates)

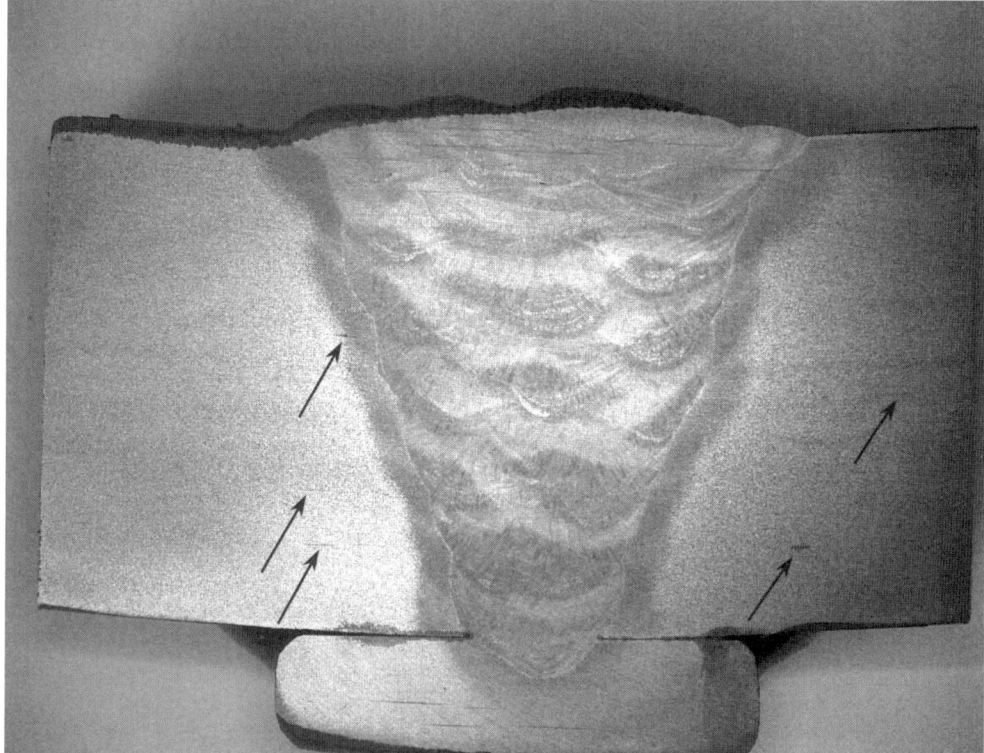

Figure: V-groove butt weld   (Also a backer rod is used under the plates for a better weld)

Above figure show a V groove weld.

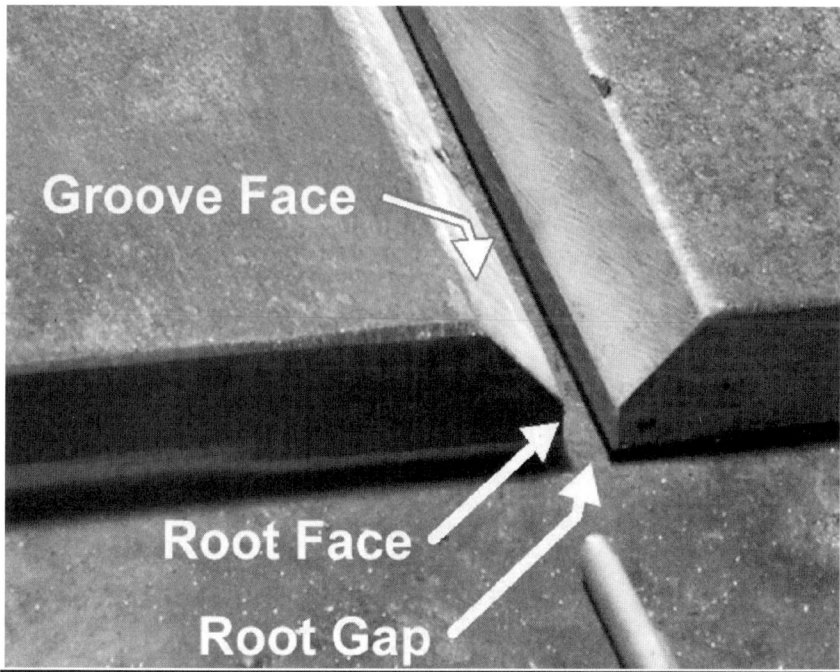

Figure: V-Groove butt weld with a root gap

In the above figure shows the root gap. Root gap is provided to insert more weld material to get a better weld between plates.

T – Joints:

T joints are used when members are perpendicular to each other.

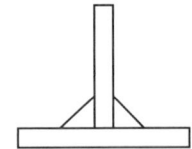

T joint without a groove
(Known as fillet weld)

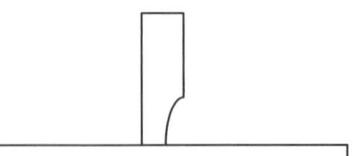

T joint with a J groove
(Known as J groove weld)

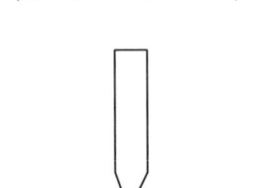

T joint with double bevel
(Known as double bevel weld)

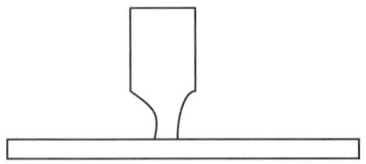

T joint with double J groove
(Known as J groove weld)

T- joint (Fillet weld)

Lap Joints: When steel members are overlapped, lap joints are used.

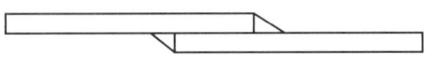

Lap joints
(Also known as lap weld)

Lap weld

Corner Joints: Corner joints as the name implied applied at corners.

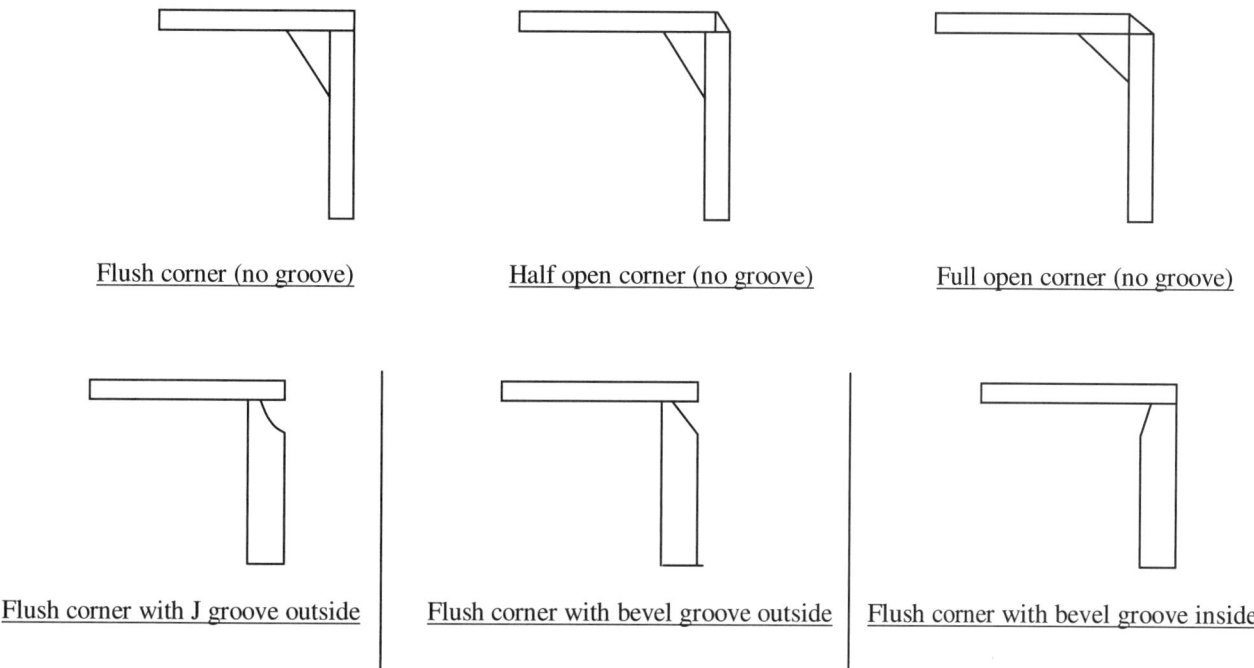

Flush corner (no groove)   Half open corner (no groove)   Full open corner (no groove)

Flush corner with J groove outside   Flush corner with bevel groove outside   Flush corner with bevel groove inside

Grooves can be J grooves, bevel grooves, U grooves or V grooves. These grooves could be inside or outside as necessary.

Edge Joints: As the name implies edge joints are applied at the edges.

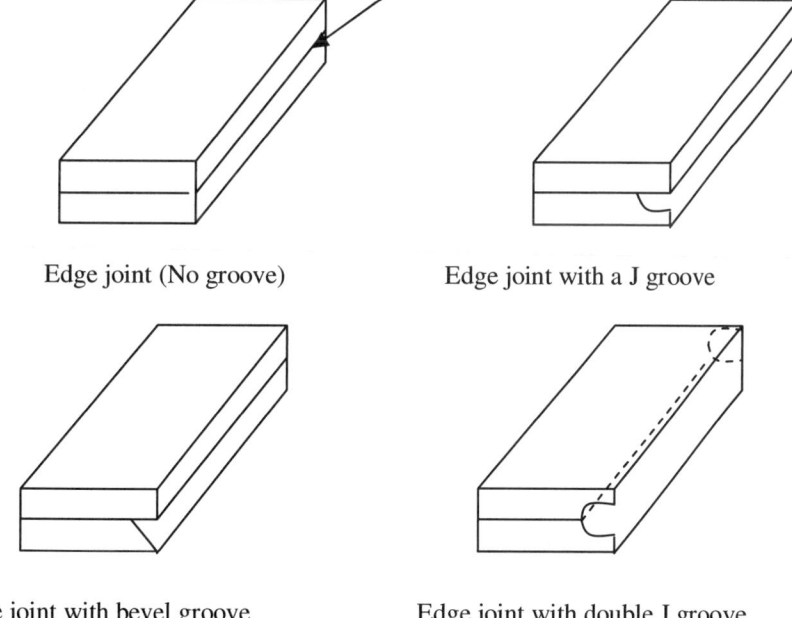

Edge joint (No groove)   Edge joint with a J groove

Edge joint with bevel groove   Edge joint with double J groove

Some Commonly used Terms:

Fillet Weld: Whenever there is no groove, such welds are called fillet welds. When there is a groove present, it is called by its groove shape. (Ex: J groove weld, U groove weld, double U groove weld etc).

Fillet Weld Examples:

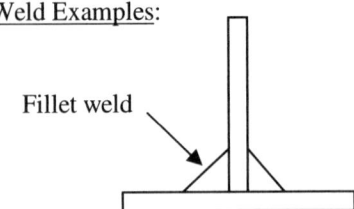

Fillet weld

Simple T joint with fillet welds

Fillet weld (Also a T-joint)

Seam Weld: When the seam of a pipe or any other object is welded, it is called seam weld.

Welding Symbols: Following welding symbols are as per AWS (American Welding Society). All the symbols are available in their website.
Fillet welds (No groove):

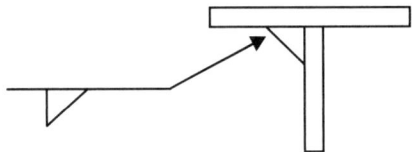

The triangle represents the fillet weld. If the triangle is at the bottom of the line, it means weld is required only on the arrow side.

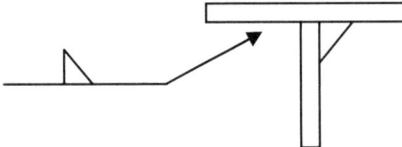

If the triangle is on top of the line, it means the weld is on the opposite side of the arrow as shown above.

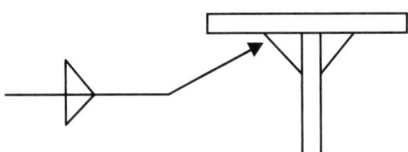

If two triangles are present, above and below the arrow line, both sides have to be welded.

Size of the Weld: It is necessary to indicate the size and length of welds as well.

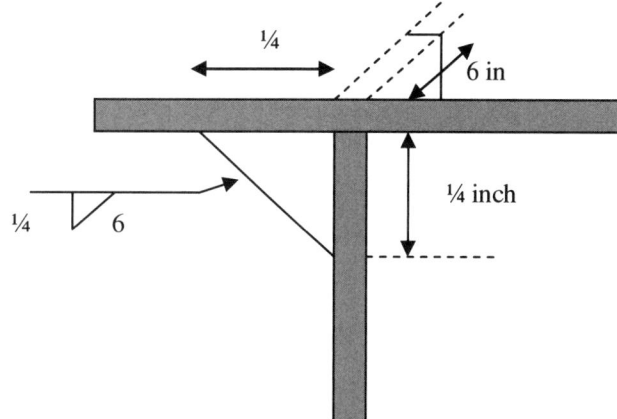

Since the triangle is at the bottom, the weld is on arrow side. The number before the triangle (1/4) indicates the size of the weld. The number after the triangle (6) indicates the length of the weld. Above symbol indicates to provide a fillet weld on the arrow side with ¼ inch size extending to a length of 6 inches.

Size of the weld uneven:

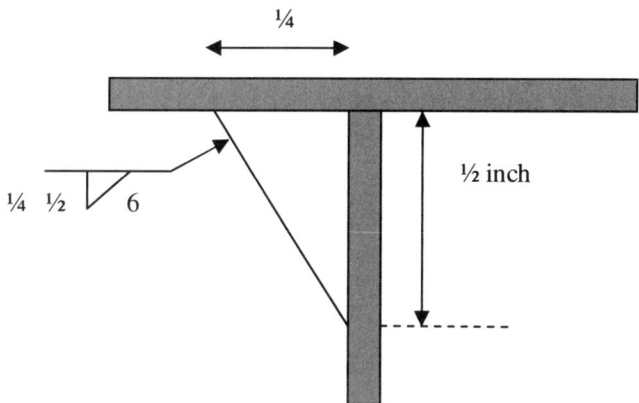

Side of the arrow: Above symbol indicates to provide a weld that is ½ inch and ¼ inch on the side of the arrow to a length of 6 inches. The question is how would the welder know which side is ½ inch and which side is ¼ inch? Typically, the drawing would be prepared with the longer side drawn longer as shown above. Vertical length of the triangle is drawn longer, so that the welder would know ½ inch weld is on the vertical side.

Size of the weld uneven (Weld on both sides):

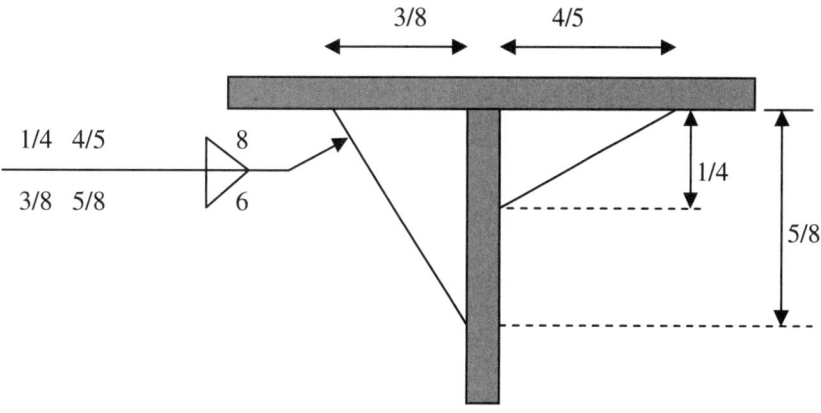

Arrow Side: Triangles on top and bottom indicate welds on both sides. Bottom triangle indicates arrow side. Size of the weld on arrow side is 3/8 and 5/8. Since the vertical edge of the triangle is drawn longer 5/8 weld should be provided on the vertical leg. Length of the weld in arrow side is 6 inches.

Other Side: The weld on other side of the arrow is ¼ and 4/5 inches. The horizontal leg of the triangle is drawn longer. Hence, horizontal leg is 4/5 inches and vertical leg is ¼ inches. Length of the weld is 8 inches.

V - Groove Weld Symbol:

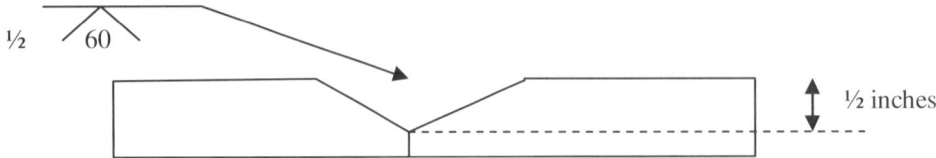

V groove symbol is placed below the arrow. This indicates weld is on the side of the arrow. The depth of the groove is ½ inch and the angle of the groove is 60 degrees.

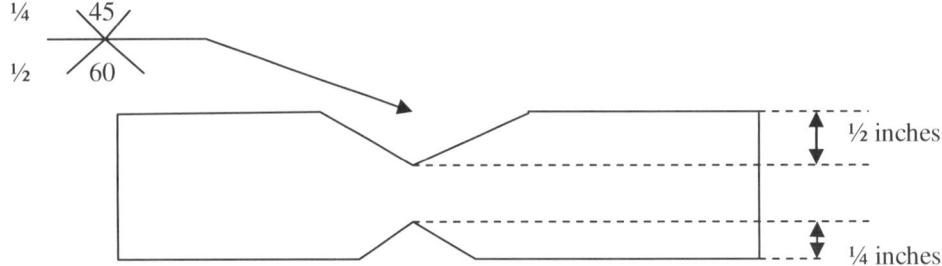

Arrow side: The V groove is ½ inch deep and has an angle of 60 degrees on arrow side.

Opposite of the Arrow: The V groove is ¼ inch thick and has an angle of 45 degrees.

Square Weld:

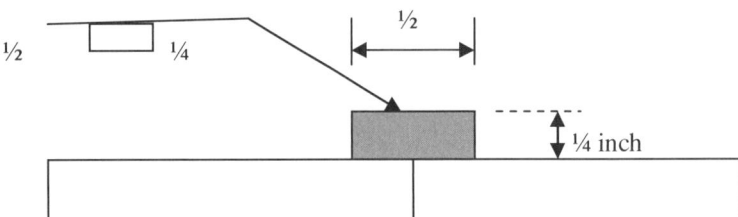

Above first number is the base dimension of the square. Second number is the thickness or the height of the weld.

Note: Complete coverage of the subject of welding is beyond this book. This book would provide you with background information to further improve your knowledge. AWS website is a very good reference source for welding.

Weld Testing: Welding defects are observed by obtaining X-ray photographs. Typical welding defects are
*   incomplete penetration
*   Incomplete fusion
*   Porosity and longitudinal cracking.

Weld Material Weight:

Cost of welding dependant on amount of weld material deposited. Weld material alone is not the best way to assess the cost of welding. Welding in a 10th story is not the same as welding in ground floor. Also welding above head is more difficult than welding at hand level. Other factors such as type of weld, complexity of weld also affects the cost of welding.

Computation of weld material quantity is still important.

Example: Find the weight of weld material deposited in the weld shown. The weld is 15 ft long. Weight of weld material is 0.283 lbs/cu. in.

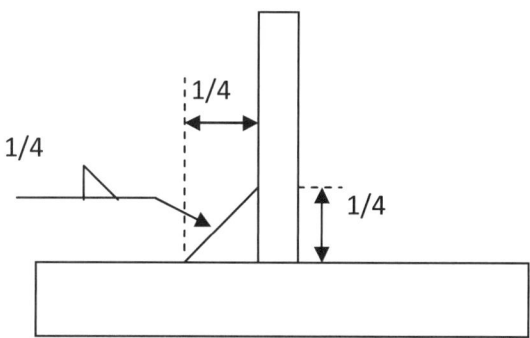

Volume of deposited material in cu. in = 1/2 x 1/4 x 1/4 x (15 x 12) = 5.625 cu. in
Weight of deposited material = 0.283 x 5.625 = 1.59 lbs

Note: See my "**Three Sample Exams for the Civil PE construction Module**" and "**Civil PE Construction Module Practice Problems, Second Edition**" for more problems involving estimating and welding take off.

5.3   Bolt Testing:

Parts of a bolt:

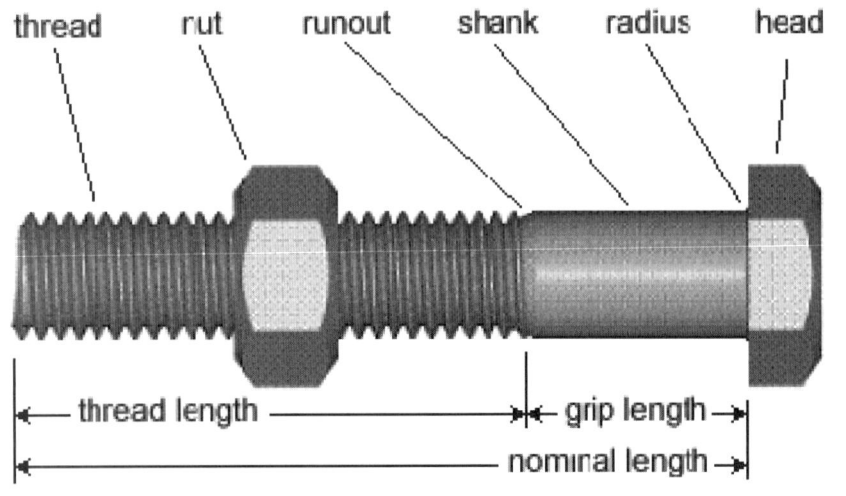

Washers are not shown in the above figure

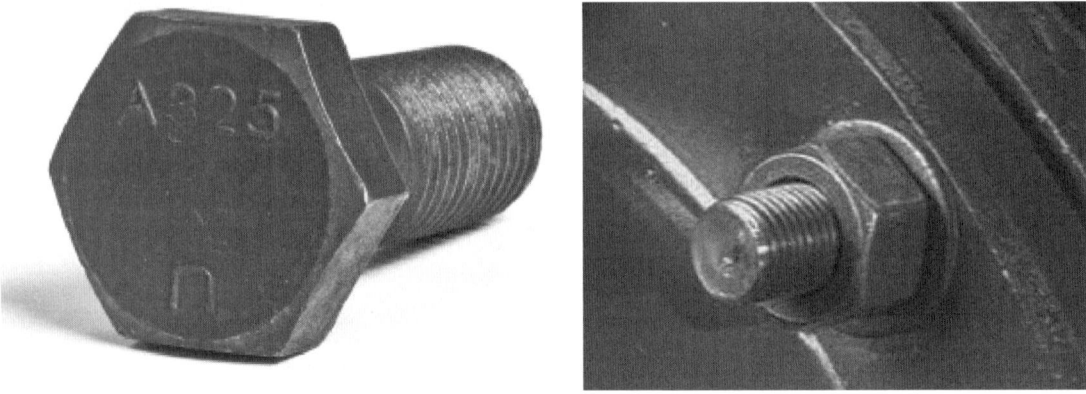

Left: Bolt head
Right: Bolt nut.

Assume two plates need to be connected using a bolt. Insert the bolt and tighten with the nut. Rotation occurs on nut side.

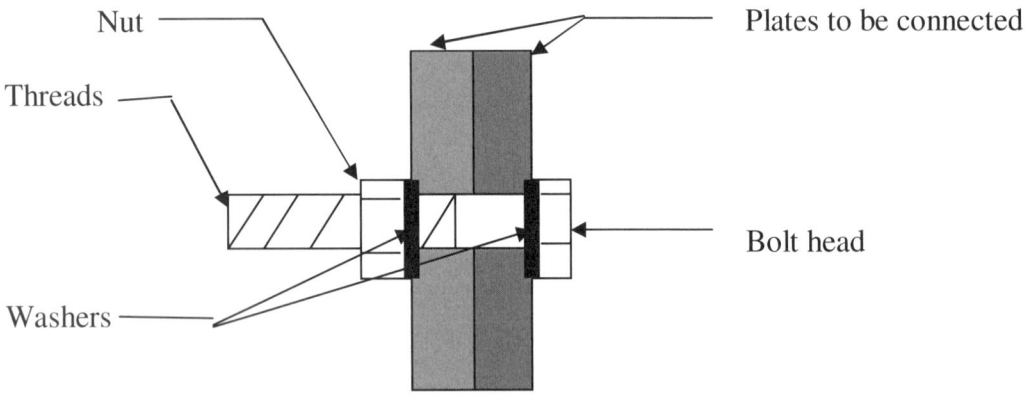

5.3.1   Washers:

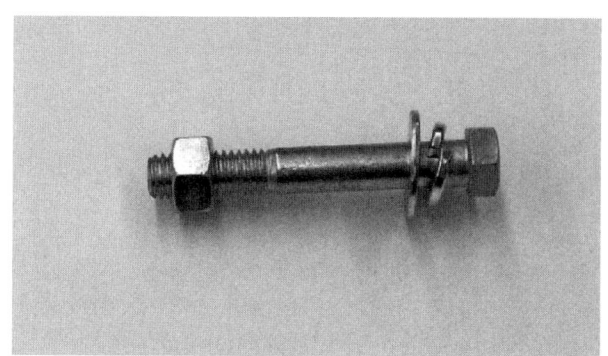

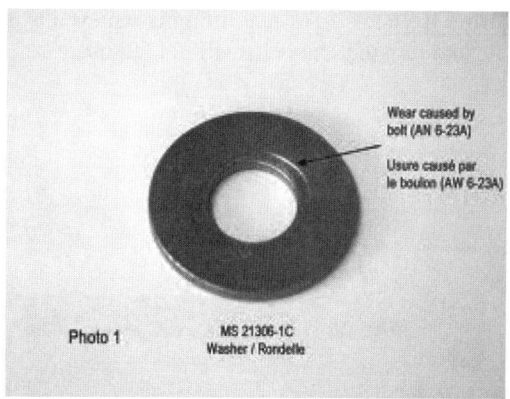

What is the purpose of washers?
- Washers spread the load evenly on the plate.
- When the nut is tightened, the plate surface could get damaged. The washer will protect the surface of the plate.
- It is a good practice to use washers on both sides. (Nut side and head side). But many use the washer only on the nut side. The argument to use the washer only on the nut side is that the nut is what is rotating. Since the head is not rotating, there is no need to have a washer on head side. Also some may argue that occasionally head also can rotate. Since washer helps spreading the load, it is good practice to use washers on both sides. In large jobs, one may be able to save some money by providing washers only on one side.

5.3.2   Joint Types:

Bolts are used for attaching two elements together. There are basically two types of bolted connections to resist shear.
- a)   Slip critical joints or friction type joints
- b)   Bearing type joints

5.3.3   Slip Critical Joints:

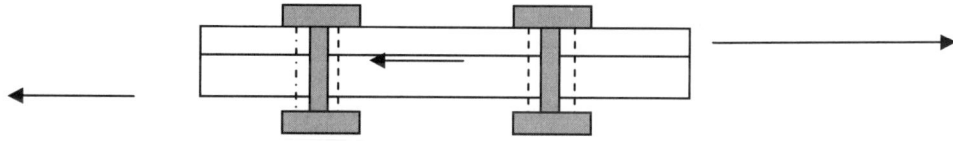

When the two plates try to move due to shear, friction develops between the two surfaces. Friction would resist the shear force. Such joints are known as slip critical joints. Holes are oversized since the bolt shaft need not butt against the metal plates. Shear resistance is achieved thru friction between plates. In this type of connection, proper tightening of bolts are important. Design engineer will provide the tension required in the bolt. Tension in bolts are proportional to the frictional resistance.

5.3.4   Bearing Type Joints:

Shear resistance is attained by bolt shaft butting against the metal plates. Holes should not be oversized for bearing type bolts.

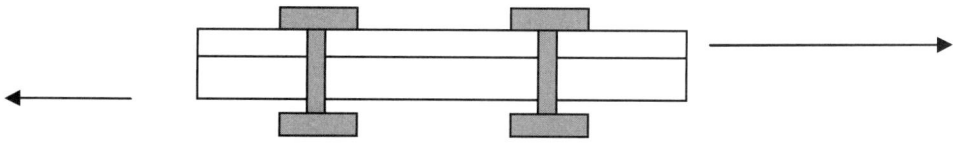

Bolts need not tightened to a pre-specified tension. Bolts are typically snug fitted.

Snug Fitted Bolts: Snug fitting is achieved by the force of an average worker using a spud wrench. Snug fitting is done to make sure that the bolts will not fall off.

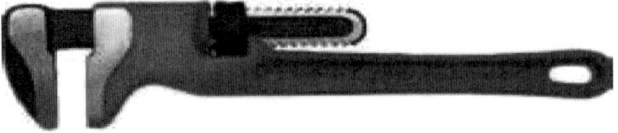

Figure: Spud Wrench

5.3.5   Bolt Tension: When the bolt is turned, bolt body would be under tension.

Torque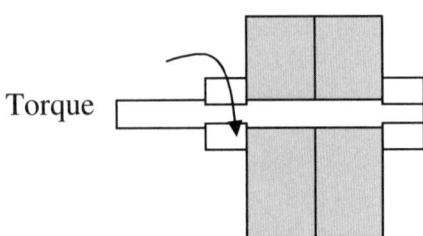

When a torque is applied to the nut, the two plates would compress together. The plates will be under compression and the bolt shaft will be under tension. But there are some reservations in obtaining the tension in bolts by measuring the torque. I will discuss that issue later in the chapter.

Bolt Tightening Methods:

As mentioned earlier, tightening of bolts to the specified tension is extremely important for friction type bolts.

Turn of the Nut Method: In this method, the bolt is snug fitted first. This is done by an average worker tightening the bolt with a spud wrench. After that the bolt is tightened with the rotation specified. For an instance bolts with length less than 8 inches, should be rotated 1/2 turn after snug fitting. Bolts with lengths exceeding 8 inches should be rotated 2/3 turns. In this method, the worker should mark the initial position of the nut and then rotate to the correct rotation specified.

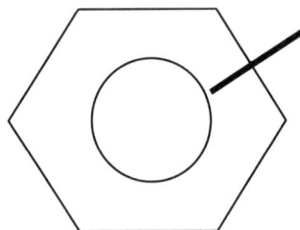

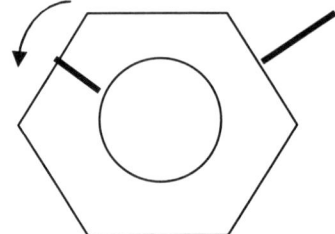

Mark the bolt and the steel plate prior to turning   Bolt after turning 1/3 rotation

Calibrate d Wrench Tightening:

Calibrated wrenches are used to obtain the proper tension in bolts.

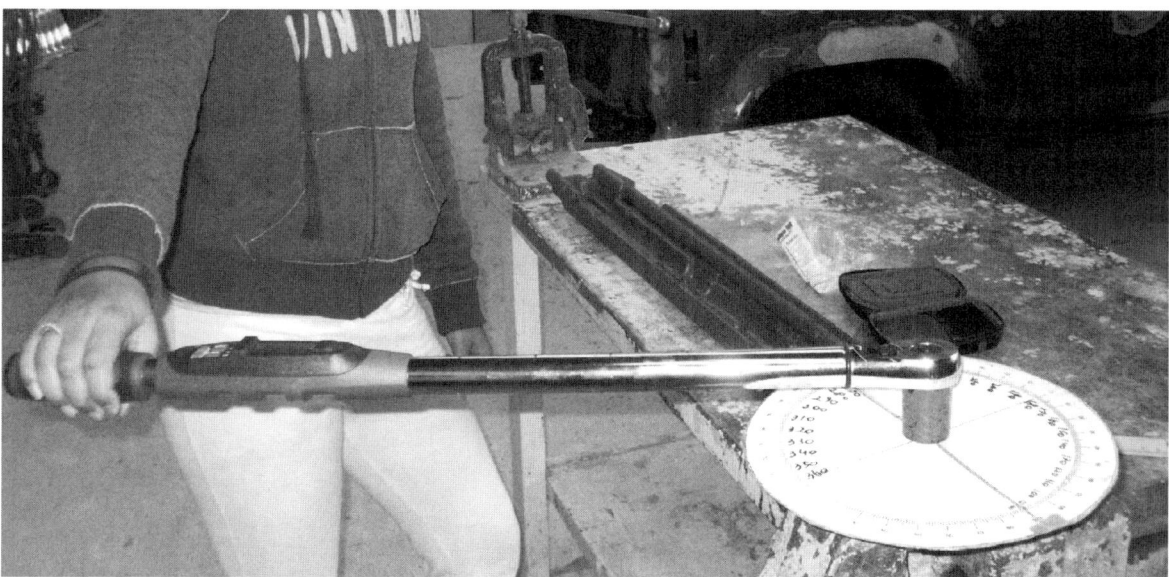

Torque wrench

Direct Tension Indicator: Instead of a torque wrench, direct tension indicator can be used. These machines show the tension in bolts. The bolt is tightened until the bolt has achieved the required tension. This method cannot be used for all the bolts.

Figure: Bolt tension indicator

Direct Tension Indicating Washers (DTI washers):
The whole idea is to find the tension in the bolt. The tension in bolts would create compression in plates. Design compression between plates needs to be attained to get the required friction.

Left: DTI: Pouches break when the specified compression is applied by the nut.
Right: Pouches are flattened due to the pressure from the nut. Pouches are designed to break at the correct compression of the nut.

DTI washer is shown in the figure. The DTI washers have pouches containing ink. Seven pouches are shown in the figure. When these pouches are subjected to compression they break and flatten. Then the ink would flow out. Pouches are designed to the required compression. If the compression required is 12,000 psi, one may need to buy a 12,000 psi DTI. The bolt is tightened until the pouches are broken and the washer is flattened.

5.3.6   Tension vs Torque Debate:

What is required is the friction between plates. Achieving the correct compression is required to obtain the required friction between plates. Compression between plates are achieved by tensioning the bolt shaft. Nut is rotated to create tension in the bolt shaft. The question is can we predict the tension in the bolt shaft by measuring the torque?

It is easy to measure the torque. Torque wrench can easily be used to measure the torque. It is not easy to measure the tension in bolts. DTI washers or Direct tension indicators are required to measure the tension in bolt shaft. Hence many measure the torque and extend the torque results to calculate the tension in the bolt shaft.

If the bolt is slightly rusted, large portion of the torque would go to get the bolt rotated. Also if a bolt is slightly out of tolerance then that would also create additional torque. Other factors that would affect the torque is the washer type and rust in washers. Friction between parts are not the same for each and every bolt. Hence torque is not a good indicator of tension in bolts.

5.4   Quality Control Process:

It is important to control quality during a project. Typically, the project should have a quality control manual at the beginning of the project. The contractor should follow the quality control plan during construction of the project.

Items of a typical quality control program are:
Inspection checklist
Documentation and filing procedure
Testing program
Closeout procedure

Inspection Program: Inspection checklist is developed to help the inspectors. The contractor is supposed to complete the project as per contract drawings and specifications. It is the responsibility of inspectors to make sure that the project is completed as per contract documents. The inspection checklist should contain items to be inspected and the frequency. If the contractor is not following the contract documents, the inspector should generate a non-compliance report and distributed to the engineer and the owner of the project.

Documentation and Filing Procedure:
Project documents include:
Non-compliance reports
RFIs (Request for information)
Change order requests
Safety violations
Daily field reports, weekly reports and monthly reports
Test results
Permits
Closeout documents
Quality control plan should include a methodology to file project documents.
Testing Program:
Testing program is developed to facilitate the inspectors and project managers. The testing program should include what items to be tested, testing methodology and testing frequency.

Closeout Procedure: Closeout is the process of terminating any activity that started. For an example, if there was a change order request by the contractor, the change order has to be either granted or rejected. If the change order was negotiated, the amount and the scope of the change order have to be properly documented.

5.4.1   Concrete Mix Design:

Concrete contains cement, sand, aggregates (gravel) and water. Fine aggregates is another name for sand.

Mix Ratios:
Concrete mix ratios are provided in weights.

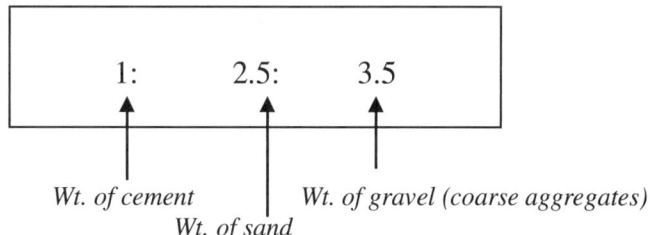

Wt. of cement   Wt. of gravel (coarse aggregates)
Wt. of sand

Practice Problem 5.4:
Find the cement, sand, aggregate ratio if 6 sacks of cement were mixed for 1 cu. yd of concrete. The contractor mixed 1,700 lbs of sand and 2,200 lbs of aggregates. Find the cement, sand, aggregate ratio. Assume one sack of cement is 94 lbs.

Solution:
     Wt. of cement = 6 x 94 = 564 lbs
     Wt. of sand = 1,700 lbs
     Wt. of aggregates (gravel) = 2,200 lbs
     Total = 564 + 1,700 + 2,200 = 4,464 lbs

Cement Ratio = 564/4464 = 0.126
Sand ratio = 1,700/4,464 = 0.381
Aggregate ratio = 2,200/4,464 = 0.493

Make cement ratio to be 1.0.

This can be done by dividing the cement ratio by 0.126.

Cement ratio = 0.126/0.126 = 1.0
Divide sand ratio and aggregate ratio by 0.126 also.

Sand ratio = 0.381/0.126 = 3.02
Aggregate ratio = 0.493/0.126 = 3.91

Cement: Sand: Aggregates   (by weight)
 1.0:   3.02:   3.91

Practice Problem 5.5:   Cement, sand, aggregate ratio of a concrete mixture is 1: 2.5: 3.0. Specifications require 7.2 bags of cement to be mixed for 1 cu. yd of concrete.
Following *specific gravities* are provided:
Cement: 3.1
Sand: 2.6
Aggregates: 2.65
Find the water cement ratio of the concrete. (One bag of cement weighs 94 lbs).

Solution:
Cement, sand, aggregate ratio = 1:   2.5:   3.0
Weight of cement per cu. yd = 7.2 x 94 = 676.8 lbs
Weight of sand = 2.5 x 676.8 = 1,692 lbs
Weight of aggregates = 3.0 x 676.8 = 2,030 lbs

Density = Weight/Volume
Specific Gravity = Density/Density of water

Cement:
Specific gravity of cement = Density of cement/ Density of water ------------(1)
Density of cement = Weight of cement/Volume of cement
Density of cement = 676.8/Volume of cement
From equation (1)
Specific gravity of cement = 676.8/(Volume of cement x Density of water)

3.1 = 676.8/(Vol. of cement x 62.4)
Vol. of cement = 676.8/(3.1 x 62.4) cu. ft = 3.5 cu. ft

Sand:
From equation (1)
Specific gravity of sand = 1692/(Volume of sand x Density of water)
2.6 = 1692/(Vol. of sand x 62.4)
Vol. of sand = 1692/(2.6 x 62.4) cu. ft = 10.4 cu. ft

Aggregates:
From equation (1)
Specific gravity of aggregates = 2030/(Volume of aggregates x Density of water)
2.65 = 2030/(Vol. of aggregates x 62.4)
Vol. of aggregates = 2030/(2.65 x 62.4) cu. ft = 12.3 cu. ft
Total volume of cement, sand and aggregates = 3.5 + 10.4 + 12.3 = 26.2
One cu. yd contains 27 cu. ft.
Volume of water = 27 - 26.2 = 0.8 cu. ft

1 cu. ft = 7.48 gallons

Volume of water = 0.8 x 7.48 = 5.98 gallons
Water cement ratio = 5.98 gallons per cu. yd of concrete

In this example, 7.2 bags of cement were mixed per 1 cu. yd of concrete.
Water cement ratio 5.98/7.2 = 0.83 gallons per bag.

Note: See my **"Three Sample Exams for the Civil PE construction Module"** and **"Civil PE Construction Module Practice Problems, Second Edition"** for more problems and solutions.

6.0 Temporary Structures

6.1   Construction Loads:
Dead loads, live loads, wind loads, snow loads are some of the loads that need to be resisted. Formwork, scaffolding, shoring are some of the methods used to resist loads that occur during construction.

6.2   Formwork:
Concrete is the major construction material in the world today. Beams, columns and slabs need to be formed prior to concreting.

Timber Formwork:
Timber formwork is the cheapest formwork available. Timber formwork is built on site by carpenters. Timber formwork construction is time consuming compared to steel formwork.

Timber formwork for a footing

Steel Formwork:
Ready-made steel formwork is widely gaining popularity for larger projects. Material cost for steel formwork is higher than timber. Since the formwork is already made, only assembling will be done in the site. Due to this reason, labor cost may be smaller compared to timber formwork.

Steel formwork is assembled by screws and can be done quickly. Unlike timber formwork, steel formwork can be used many times repeatedly.

Steel formwork for a wall

6.3   Falsework and Scaffolding: Falsework is built to support formwork.

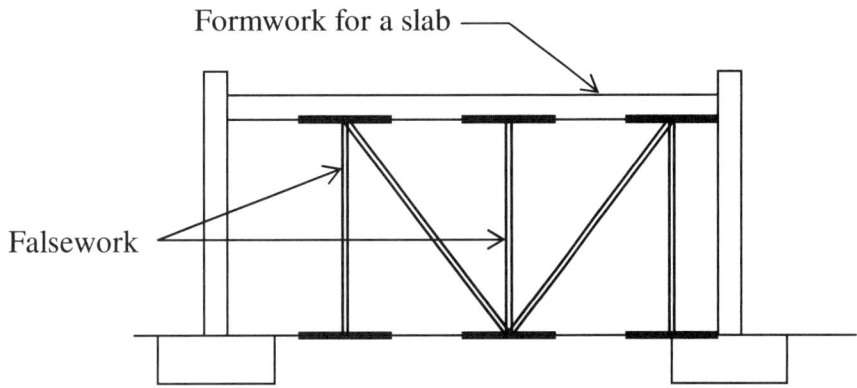

Formwork for a slab

Falsework

Falsework

Falsework supporting formwork

Falsework needs to be designed by professional engineers since failure of falsework may cost lives of workers who work underneath or above.

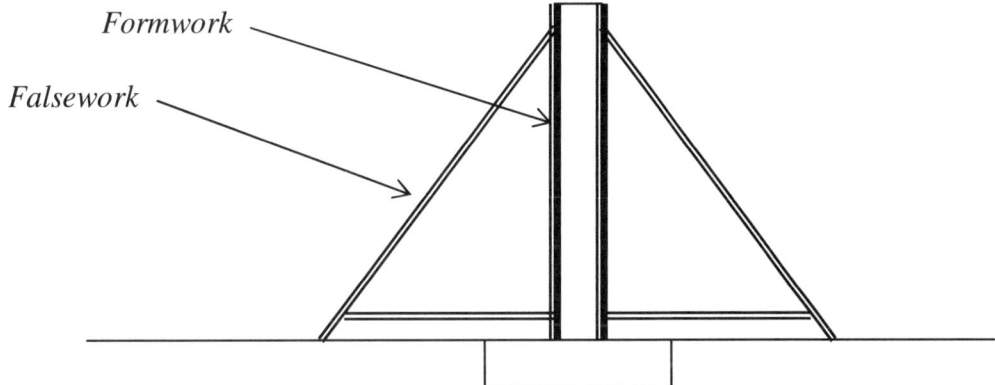

Formwork

Falsework

Formwork and falsework for a wall

Scaffolding: Scaffolding is constructed for men to work and store construction material such as windows, timber, concrete and steel.

Workers on metal scaffolding

Scaffolding for a painting project

As per Means guidelines, tubular scaffolding is cost effective up to 60' high or five stories. Above this, it is usually better to use hung scaffolding if construction permits. Swing scaffolding operations may interfere with tenants. In this case, the tubular is more practical at all heights.

In repairing or cleaning the front of an existing building, the cost of tubular scaffolding per SF of building front increases as the height increases above the first tier. The first tier cost is relatively high due to leveling and alignment.

Scaffolding Types: Tube and coupler scaffolds are the most popular scaffold type today. Wooden scaffolding was popular in the past. In Asia, still bamboo is the most widely used material to build scaffolding. Tube and coupler scaffolding may be expensive but could save time and probably will last during the life of the project.

- Tube and coupler scaffolds
- Carpenter's bracket scaffolds
- Outrigger scaffolds
- Bricklayer's square scaffolds
- Putlog scaffold
- Hanging scaffold or suspended scaffold

Figure: Tube and coupler scaffold

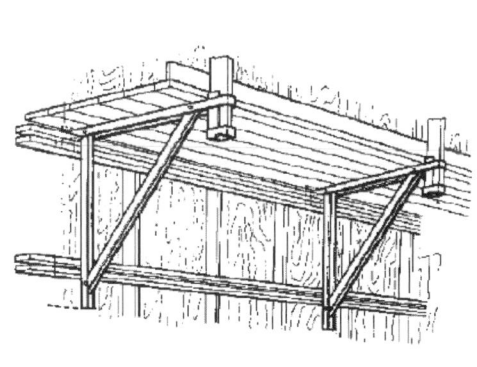

Figure: Carpenter's bracket scaffold

OUTRIGGER SCAFFOLD

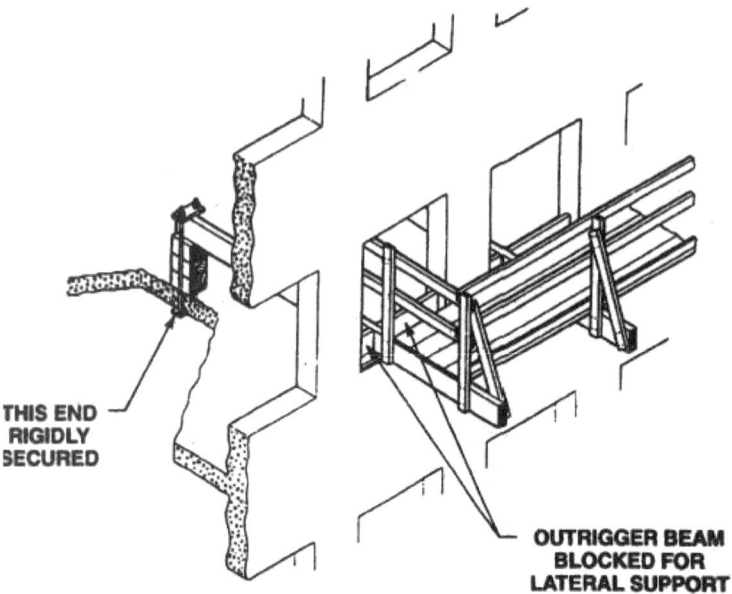

Figure: Outrigger scaffold

Outrigger scaffolds are built using outriggers that juts out from buildings. To build this type of scaffolds, one need openings in the building to place outriggers.

Hanging scaffold:

Figure: Hanging scaffold

Hanging scaffolds are hung from the roof. Roof assembly of a hanging scaffold is shown below.

Figure: Hanging scaffold roof assembly. The cantilevered beam supports the hanging scaffold below.

Putlog Scaffolds:

Putlog scaffolds are built by inserting beams into holes in the wall. These beams are known as putlogs.

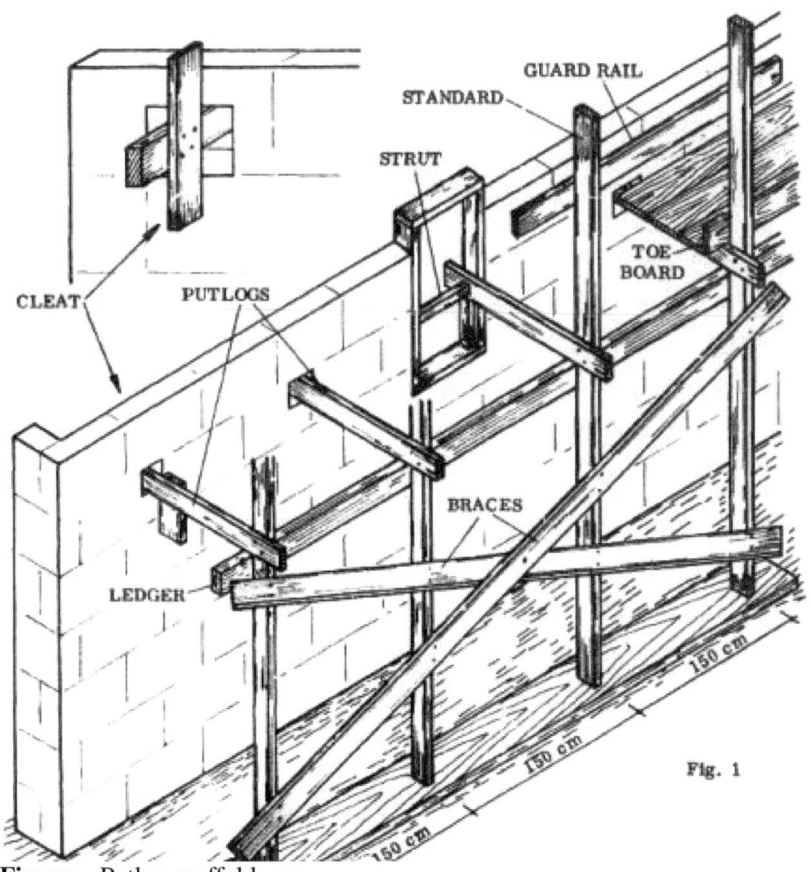

Figure: Putlog scaffold

(Metal Modular Scaffolding):

Pre-made modules are becoming common in many construction projects.

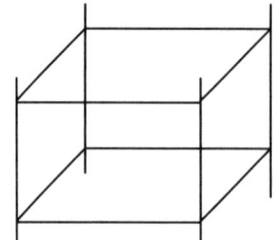

Scaffolding modules

Wood or metal Board

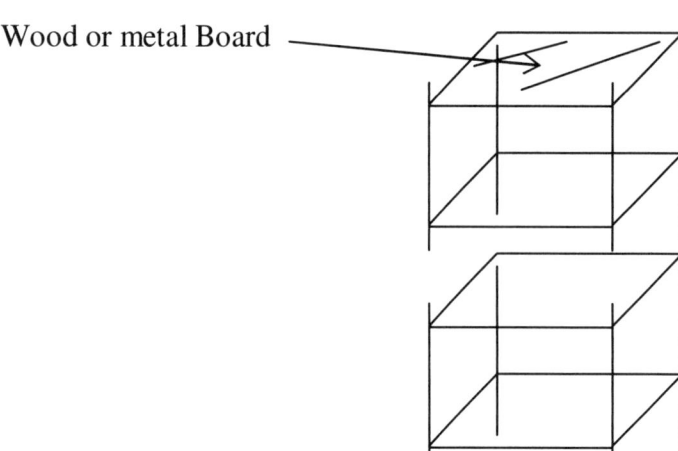

Scaffolding modules are fitted together to reach high elevations

Boards: Boards are made of metal or wooden planks attached to the scaffolding for people to stand and work.

Uprights also known as standards and poles are used to carry the load to base. False uprights are mainly used near entrances to the work platform. False uprights do not transfer any vertical loads to the ground. Though it may provide lateral support handrails it does not provide any lateral supports to the scaffold system.

Parts of a tube and coupler scaffolding:

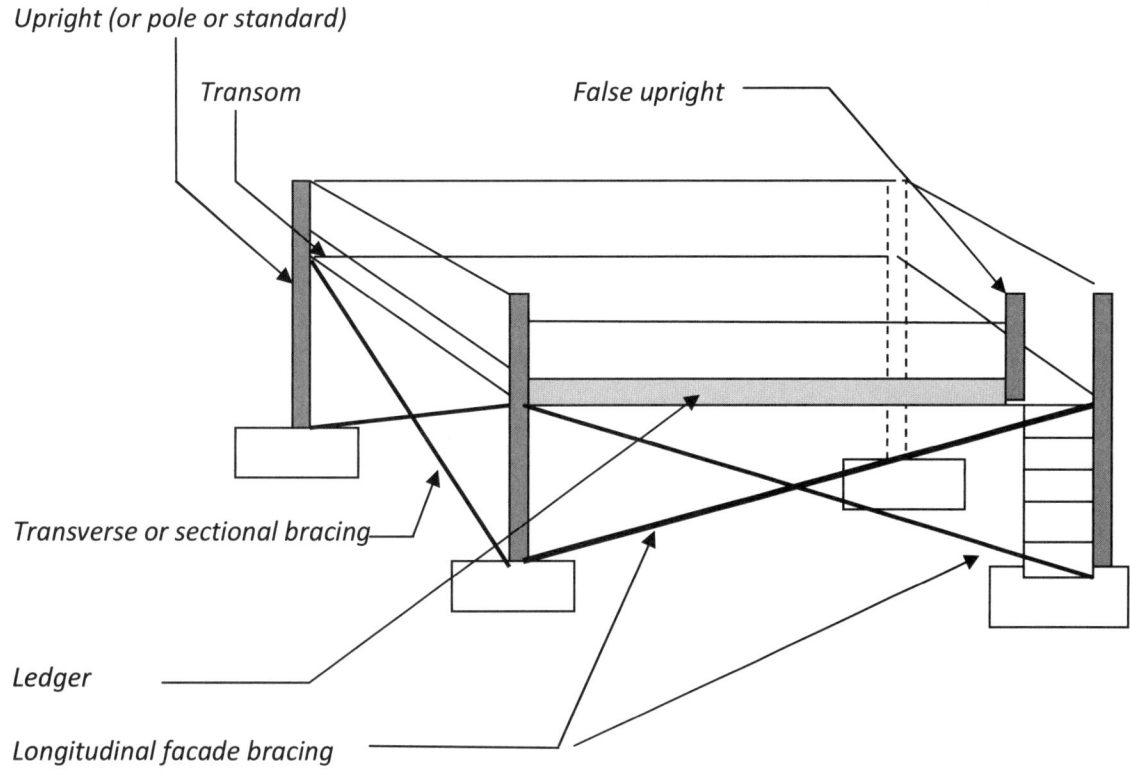

Upright (or pole or standard)

Transom   *False upright*

Transverse or sectional bracing

Ledger

Longitudinal facade bracing

Vertical poles: Vertical poles are transferring loads to the ground.   They are known as "standards". Some also call them uprights.

Horizontal poles: Horizontal poles along longer direction is known as ledgers. Horizontals along the shorter direction is known as transoms.

False Uprights: Uprights that do not go all the way to the ground are known as false uprights. They are needed near entrances.

Cross Bracings: Cross bracings along the longer direction is known as longitudinal bracing or facade bracing. Bracing in the shorter direction is known as transverse or sectional bracing.

Figure: Scaffold system

Exercise: Identify uprights, sectional bracings, facade bracing, ledgers, transoms, false uprights and toe boards in the above figure.

6.4   Shoring: Shoring is done to buttress existing building elements such as columns and structural walls.

Practice Problem 6.1:   Procedure to remove an existing column and building a new column is considered.

Deteriorated column

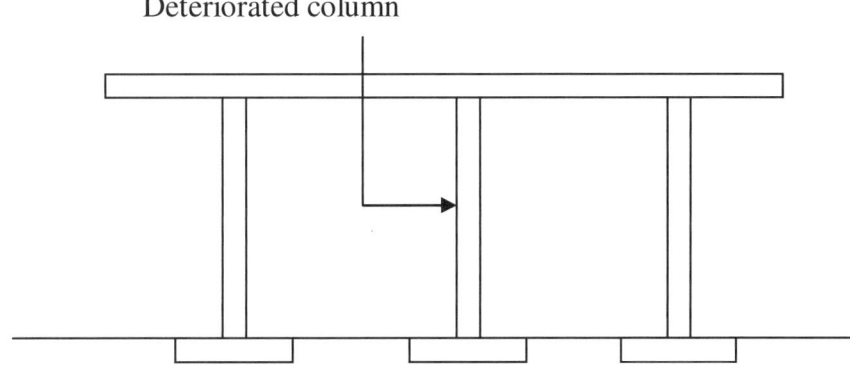

Removal of a deteriorated column

Shoring

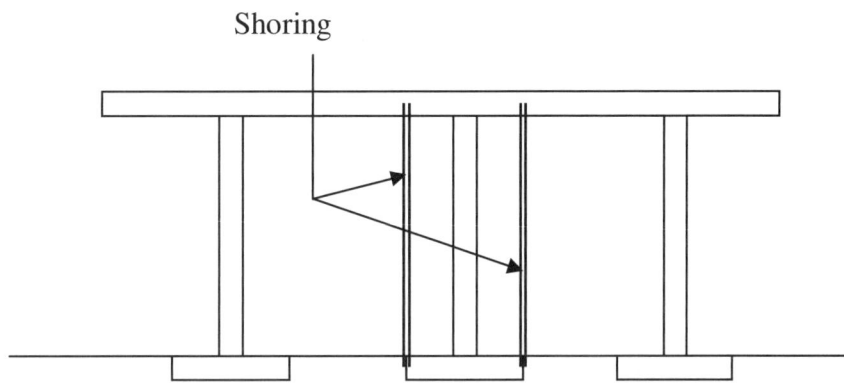

Provide shoring prior to removal of the column

Once proper shoring is provided and approved by relevant authorities, the contractor can remove the existing load bearing column and construct a new one.

6.4.1   Loads during Construction:

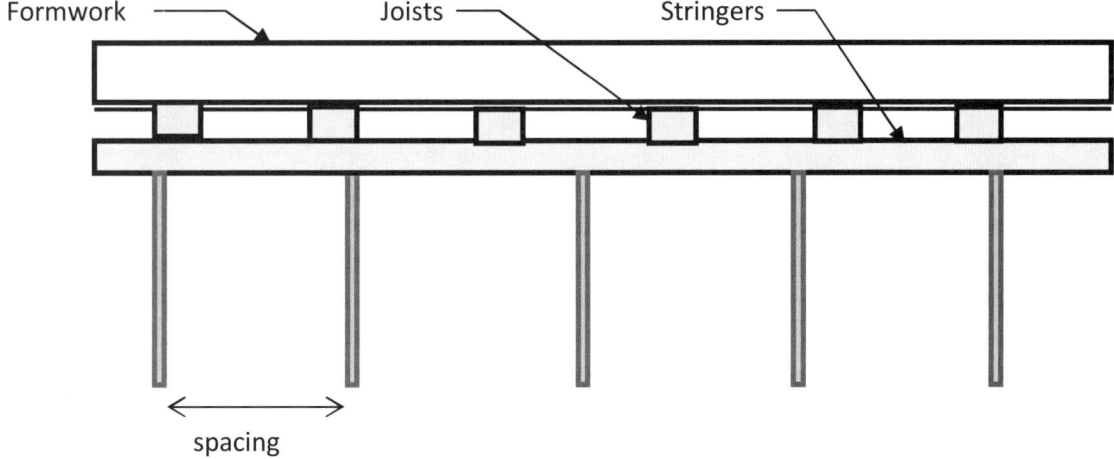

Formwork   Joists   Stringers

spacing

Loading during construction is different than permanent loading on a slab. During construction, workers will be working with their tools. Also concrete buggies, finishing equipment, hoses and vibrators also will be on the slab.

ASCE Standard, SEI/ASCE 37-02, 2002, defines following loads during construction. Note that load combinations and definitions are different during construction compared to permanent situation.

Dead load (D) – Dead load due to permanent structure constructed at a given time.   Shoring and other dead loads that are not part of the permanent structure are not considered for (D).

Construction dead load (C_D) - Dead load due to shoring, scaffolds and other construction related dead loads. These loads will be gone after the construction is completed.

Live load (L) – Live load due to occupants during construction. In many cases this would be zero. But occasionally occupants would like to use the structure during construction. Construction workers and their equipment are not part of this load.

Construction personal and equipment Load (C_P) – Construction workers working on the structure, concrete buggies, concrete pumping hoses, equipment for formwork and shoring, generators, gang boxes and compressors.

Horizontal Construction Load (C_H) – Construction activities can create horizontal loads. Moving vehicles, people, vibrating machines, compressors can generate horizontal loads.

Wind Load (W) –   Load due to wind acting on the structure. Wind load is mostly lateral and could uplift the structure as well. Lateral stability and resistance to uplift needs to be assessed. Wind load is a dynamic load. But for computation ease, wind load is considered to be a static horizontal load.

Snow load (S) and Ice Load (I):   Accumulation of snow on a structure during construction needs to be addressed. In some areas snow could turn into ice in a short period of time.

Earthquake Load (E):   Earthquake load is a dynamic load.   But for computation ease, earthquake load is considered to be a static load acting horizontally.

Material Loads: Load due to material during construction is divided into two. Fixed material loads (C_{FML}) and Variable material load (C_{VML}).

(C_{FML}) Fixed Material Loads :   During construction material have to be stockpiled in the structure that's been constructed. If the magnitude of the material load is fixed, then it is considered as C_{FML}. Load due to fuel and various other materials required during construction may be relatively fixed if they are replenished.

(C_{VML}) Variable Material Load: Load due to some material may be variable. Steel, nuts and bolts may be stored. Once they are constructed it becomes part of the permanent dead load (D).

Horizontal construction loads (C_H):   Moving wheelbarrows, moving personnel generates lateral loads on the structure. Wind load is not considered in this item since wind load is considered separately. It is assumed moving person would exert 50 lbs lateral load on the structure.

Load Combinations:

Load Combination 1: $1.4D + 1.4\,C_D + 1.2\,C_{FML} + 1.4\,C_{VML}$

Load Combination 2: $1.2D + 1.2\,C_D + 1.2\,C_{FML} + 1.4\,C_{VML} + 1.6\,C_P + 1.6\,C_H + 0.5L$

Load Combination 3: $1.2D + 1.2\,C_D + 1.2\,C_{FML} + 1.4\,C_{VML} + 1.3W + 0.5\,C_P + 0.5L$

Load Combination 4: $1.2D + 1.2\,C_D + 1.2\,C_{FML} + 1.4\,C_{VML} + 1.0E + 0.5\,C_P + 0.5L$

Load Combination 5: $0.9D + 0.9C_D + 1.3W$

Load Combination 6: $0.9D + 0.9C_D + 1.3E$

Apply all load combinations and find the highest load for design.

Practice Problem):   16 inch thick slab is under construction. The slab is supported by posts which are placed 4 ft x 4 ft grid. Construction related dead load on the slab is 20 psf. No occupants of the building is expected on the slab. Construction dead load is 8 psf. Construction personnel and construction equipment load is 120 psf. Fixed material load during construction is 10 psf and variable material load during construction is 15 psf. Wind, snow and earthquake loads are ignored. Density of concrete is 145 pcf. Assuming a factor of safety of 2.0, what is the capacity of posts.

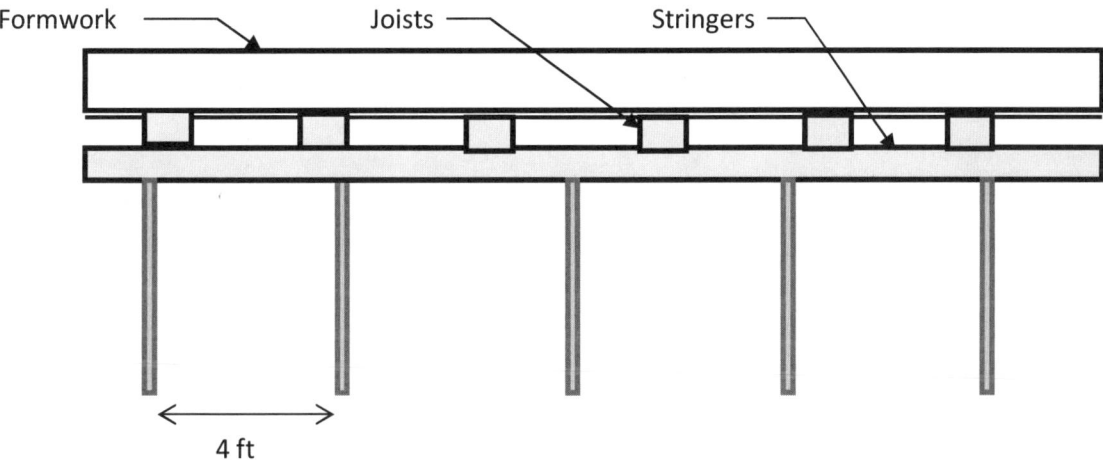

Formwork   Joists   Stringers

4 ft

Ans 14,929 lbs

Note: See my "**Three Sample Exams for Civil PE Construction Module**" for the worked solution.

6.5 Concrete Maturity and Early Strength Evaluation:

Concrete needs time to gain strength. Typically, concrete gain most of its strength after 28 days. Unfortunately, it is not possible to stop construction work until the concrete is fully hardened.

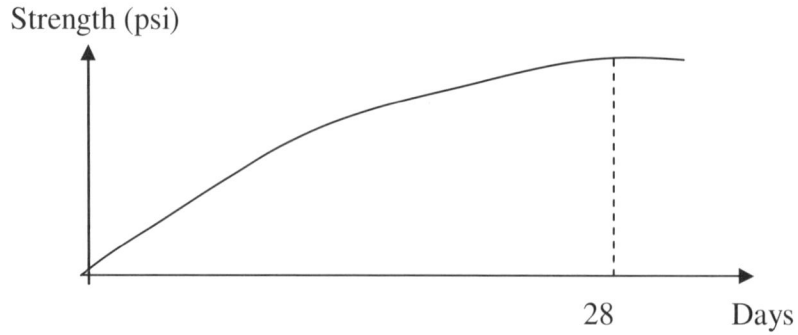

Normal Distribution:

In many cases, data can be considered to be distributed normally. Let us see what this means. Let us consider one thousand concrete break results. Following table was obtained from 1,000 concrete break results.

Break Range (psi)	No. of breaks
0 – 1,000	0
1,000 – 2,000	105
2,000 – 3,000	175
3,000 – 4,000	448
4,000 – 5,000	170
5,000 – 6,000	102
6,000 – 7,000	0
Total	**1,000**

As per above table none of the samples had a strength lower than 1,000 psi. There were 105 cylinders that had a strength between 1,000 and 2,000 psi. None of the cylinders had a strength greater than 6,000 psi.
Also we can say that probability of getting a break above 6,000 is zero.
Probability of getting a break result between 5,000 and 6,000 = 102/1,000 = 10.2%
Probability of getting a break result between 4,000 and 5,000 = 170/1,000 = 17.0%

Above results can be represented in a graph.

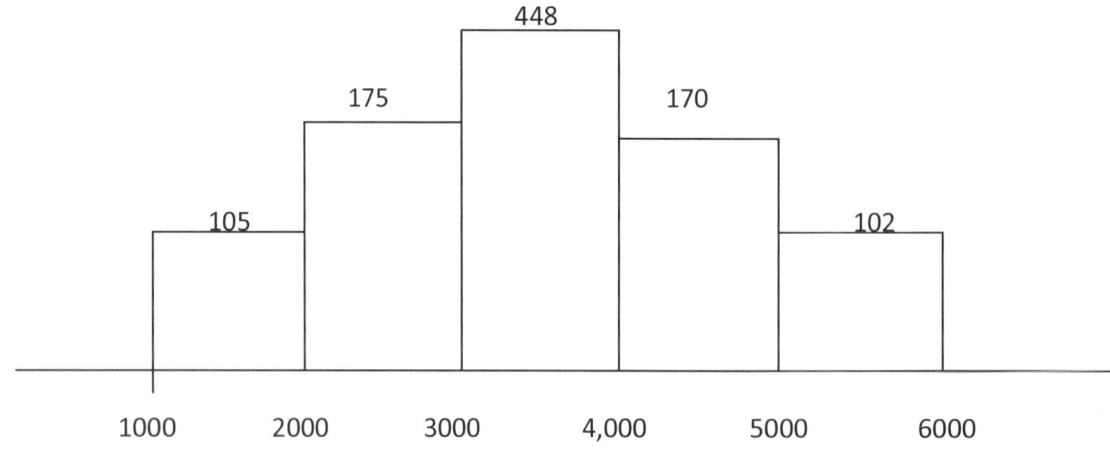

Above concrete break results follows the normal distribution curve. Area of the curve represents total number of breaks.

What is the probability that a break result is lower than 3,000 psi?
Probability of break results lower than 3,000 psi = No. of breaks below 3,000/Total breaks

Probability of break results lower than 3,000 psi = (175 + 105)/1,000 = 28%

What is the probability of breaks lower that 3,200 psi?
To find this probability, draw a line at 3,200 psi.

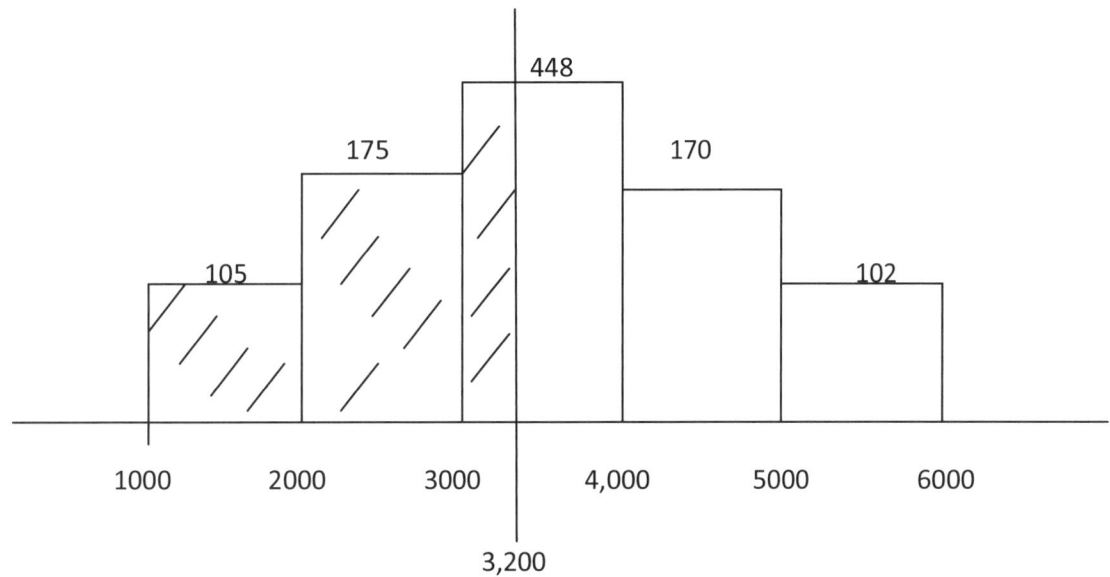

Probability of getting a break result less than 3,200 psi is given by the hatched area of the graph.

Hatched area of the graph = 105 + 175 + 448/5 = 369.6 psi
There are 448 breaks between 3,000 and 4,000. Hence there should be 448/5 break results between 3,000 and 3,200.
Probability of getting a break below 3,200 = 36.9%

What is the probability of getting a break result above 5,150 psi?

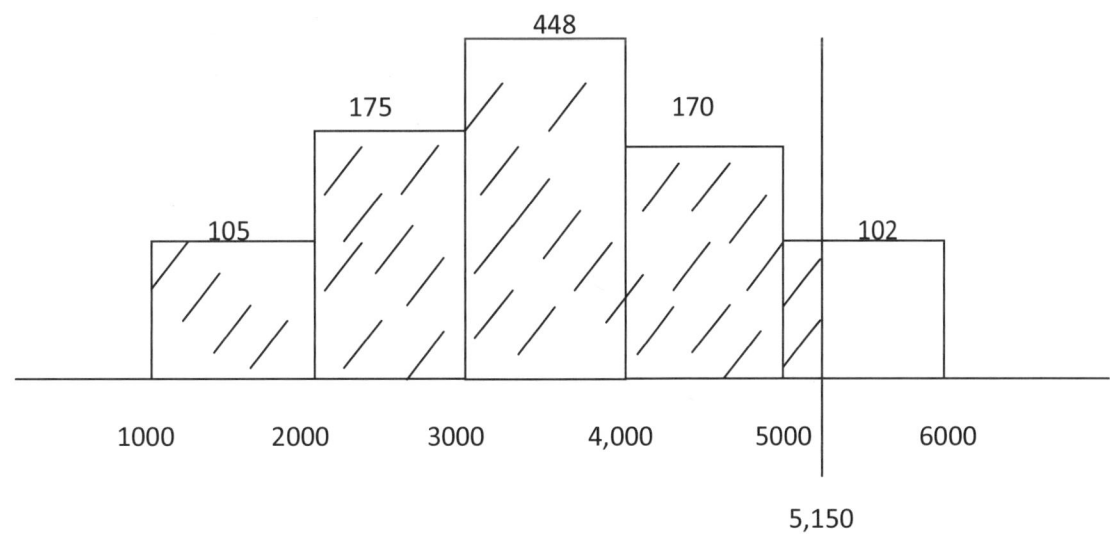

Probability of getting a result less than 5,150 psi = Hatched area
          = 105 + 175 + 448 + 170 + 102/1,000 x 150 = 913.3
          = 91.3%

Probability of getting a result larger than 5,150 psi = 100 − 91.3 = 8.7%
Now let us look at the normal distribution curve.

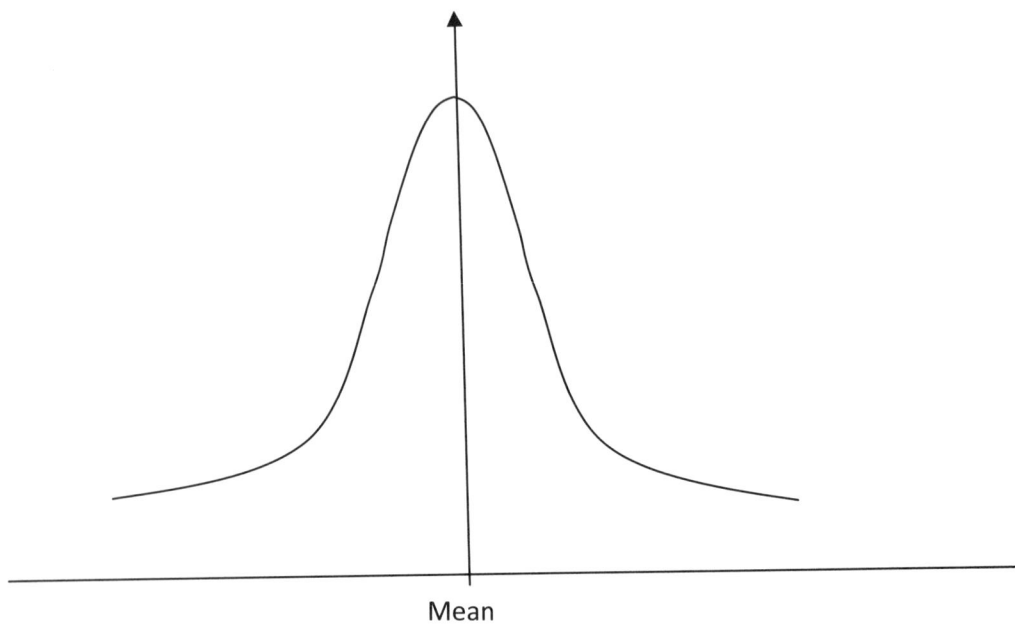

Mean

In a normal distribution curve, mean value is at the center. 50% of the results are larger than the mean and 50% are smaller than the mean.
What is the value of Y when 90% of the results less than Y?

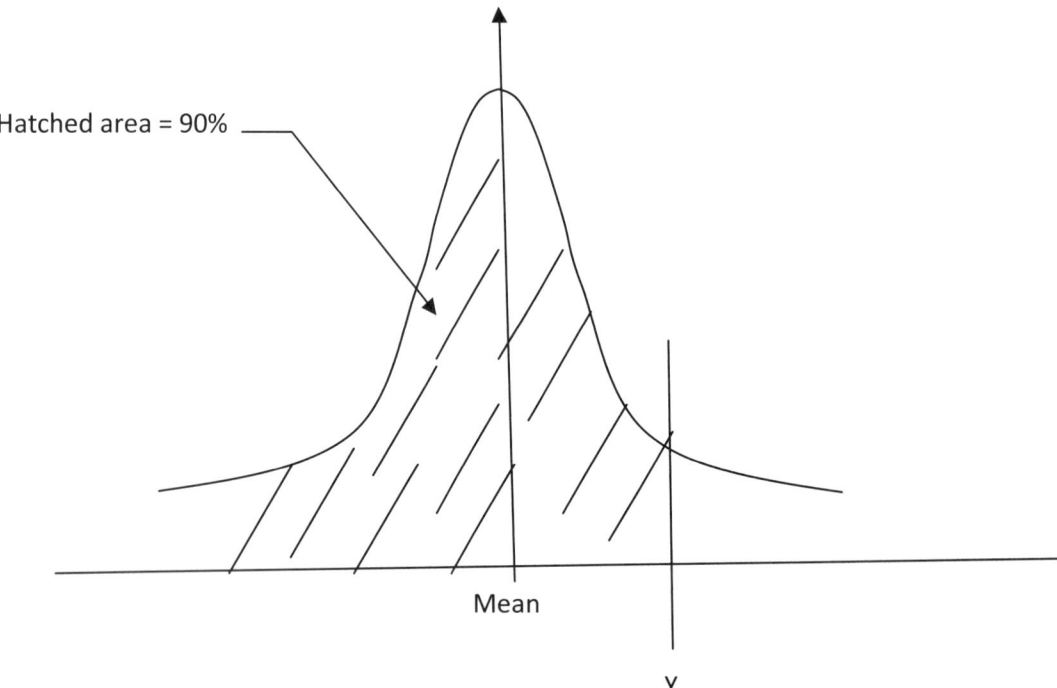

Hatched area = 90%

Mean

Y

This can be done easily using normal distribution tables. (Not provided in this book).

If you look a normal distribution table, 0.90 would yield 1.2816. What does this mean?
This means that 90% of the results are lower than 1.2816.Z. (Z is the standard deviation).

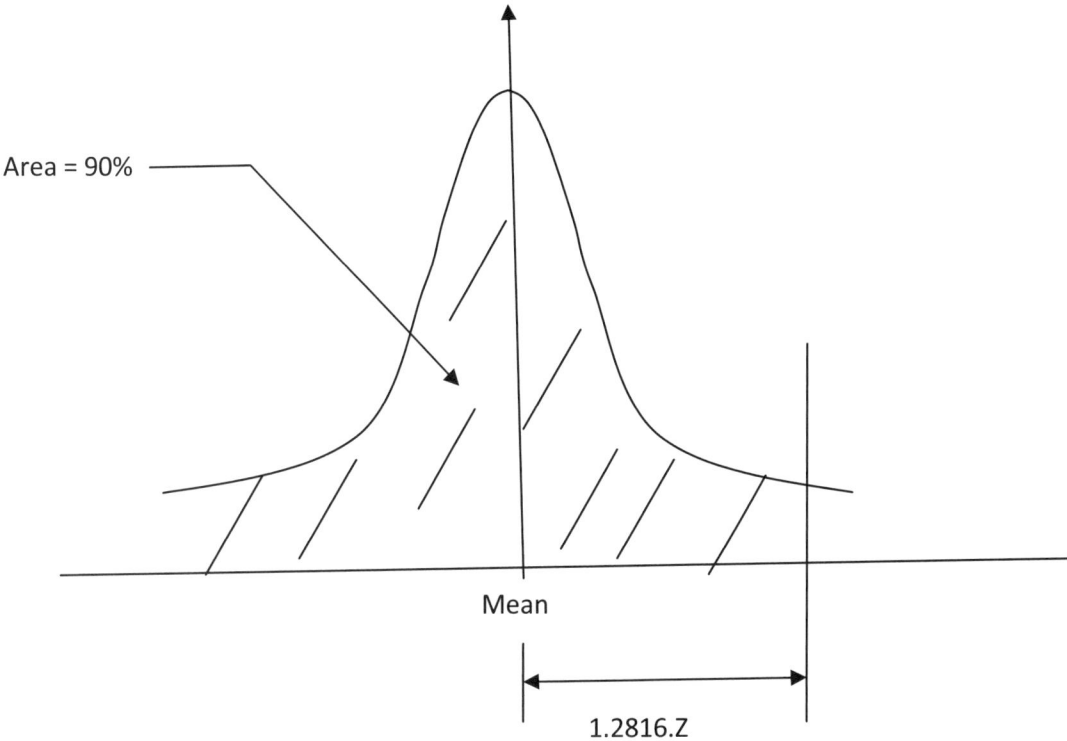

Similarly, normal distribution tables gives 0.6745.Z for 75%.

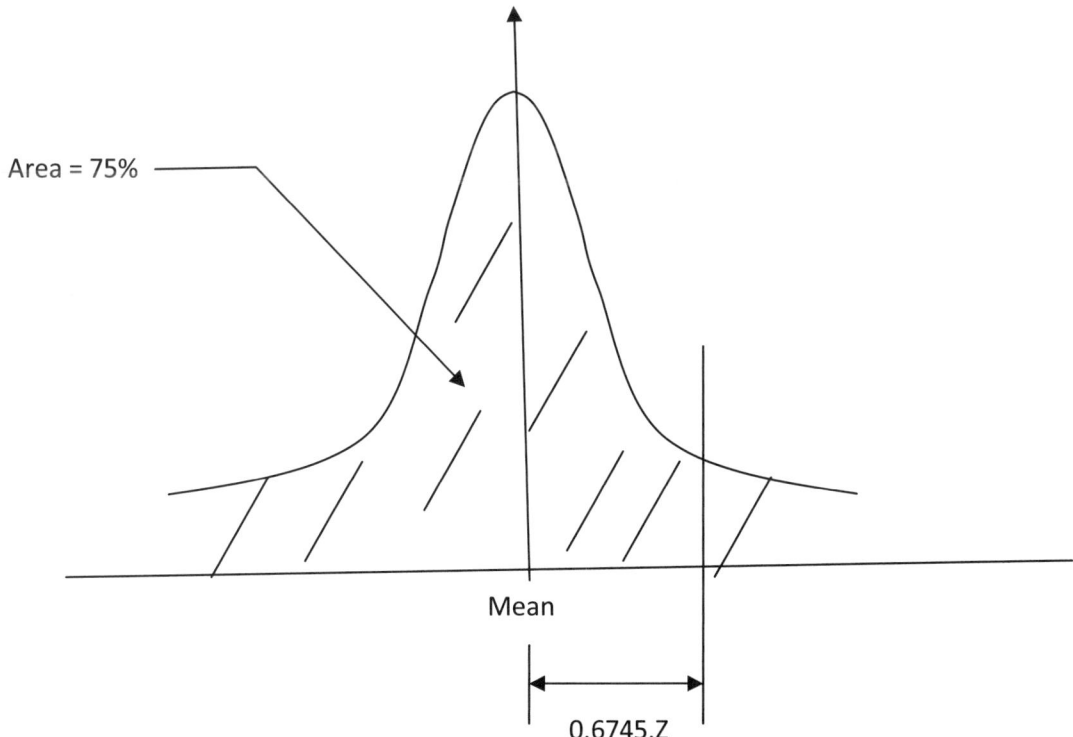

How to find mean of a sample:

Mean value of a sample is obtained by adding all the values and dividing by number of values.

$$\text{Mean} = \frac{\Sigma X_i}{n} = \frac{X1 + X2 + X3 + \ldots\ldots\ldots Xn}{n}$$

Example: What is the mean of following numbers;

4, 5, 1, 8, 9

$\Sigma X_i = 4 + 5 + 1 + 8 + 9 = 27$
n = Number of items = 5
mean = 27/5 = 5.4
Mean is represented by μ

Example: What is the standard deviation of the above numbers;

Standard deviation is given by;

$$Z = \frac{[\Sigma (X_i - \text{mean})^2]^{1/2}}{[(n - 1)]^{1/2}}$$

Mean = 5.4;   n = Number of items = 5

Top portion $= [\Sigma (X_i - \text{mean})^2]^{1/2} = [(4 - 5.4)^2 + (5 - 5.4)^2 + (1 - 5.4)^2 + (8 - 5.4)^2 + (9 - 5.4)^2]^{1/2} = 6.42$

Bottom portion $= [(n - 1)]^{1/2} = [5 - 1]^{1/2} = 2$
$Z = 6.42/2 = 3.21$
Standard deviation (Z) = 3.21

Example: Concrete break results have a mean of 3,000 psi and a standard deviation of 234 psi. The design requirement is to have 85% of the breaks above 3,000 psi. What is the new mean value of the concrete strength results assuming standard deviation and normal distribution curve was unchanged?

Let us draw a normal distribution curve.

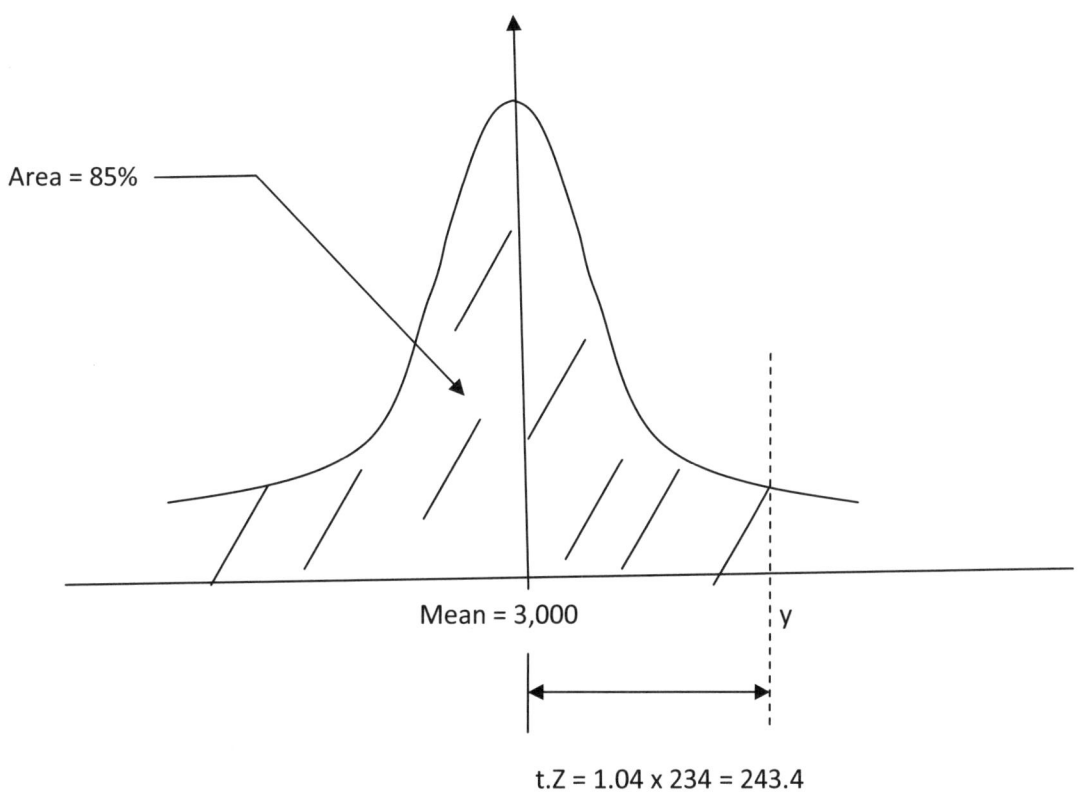

Area = 85%

Mean = 3,000   y

t.Z = 1.04 x 234 = 243.4

Mean (μ) is given to be 3,000 psi. This means 50% of the breaks are lower than 3,000 psi.

The goal is to increase the mean so that 85% of the breaks are above 3,000. In other words only 15% of the breaks would be lower than 3,000 psi.

Look up the normal distribution tables.
0.8508 (or 85.08%) gives a value of 1.04. This is the closest value to 85%,
Hence t = 1.04
Z = 234 psi (Given)
y = 3,000 + 1.04 x 234 = 3,243.4 psi

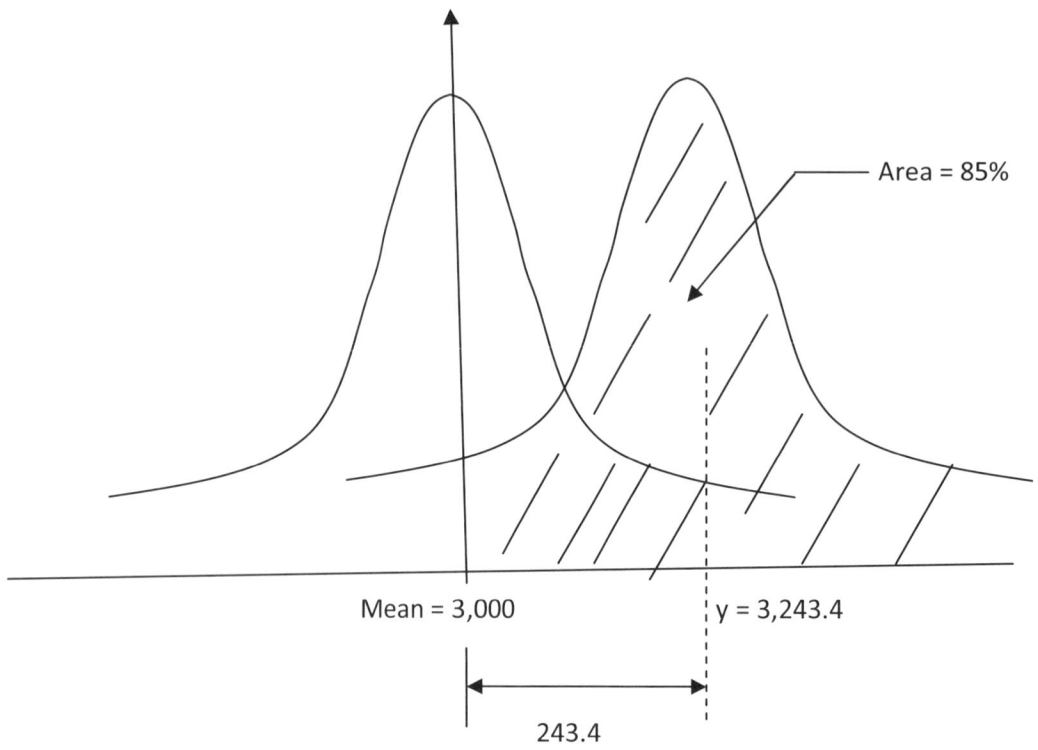

New mean is 3,243.4   Now you can see 85% of the breaks are above 3,000 psi.

See "**Three Sample Exams for the Civil PE Construction Module**" for more problems and ACI guidelines.

6.6 Bracing: Bracing is a support element provided to strengthen an existing structural element.

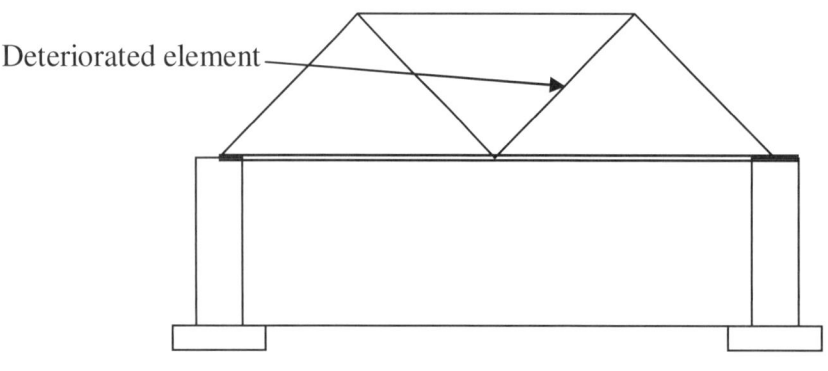

Deteriorated element in a structure

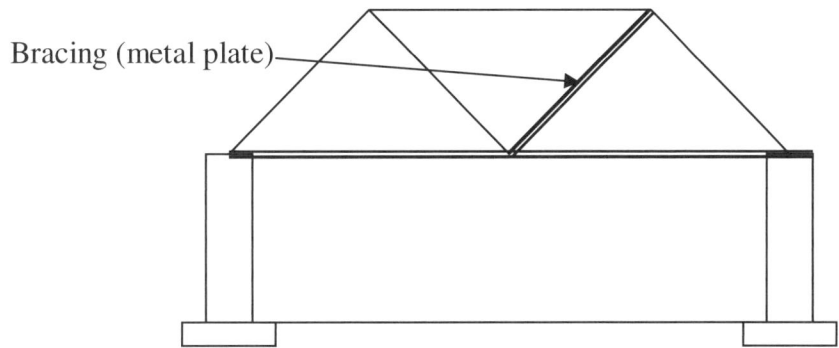

Bracing is provided for the deteriorated element

6.7 Anchorage: Anchoring of retaining walls, sheetpile walls, billboards, light poles, transmission towers, hangers are necessary to resist loads due to wind, soil and water. Anchoring is mainly done by anchor bolts, rock bolts, soil nails, sheetpile anchors and resin anchors.

Anchoring of a pipe hanger:

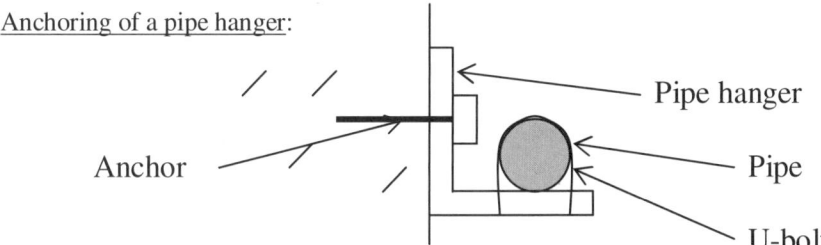

Above pipe is secured to the pipe hanger with a U-bolt. The pipe hanger is secured to the wall with a bolt, which acts as an anchor.

Anchoring of a retaining wall against soil pressure:

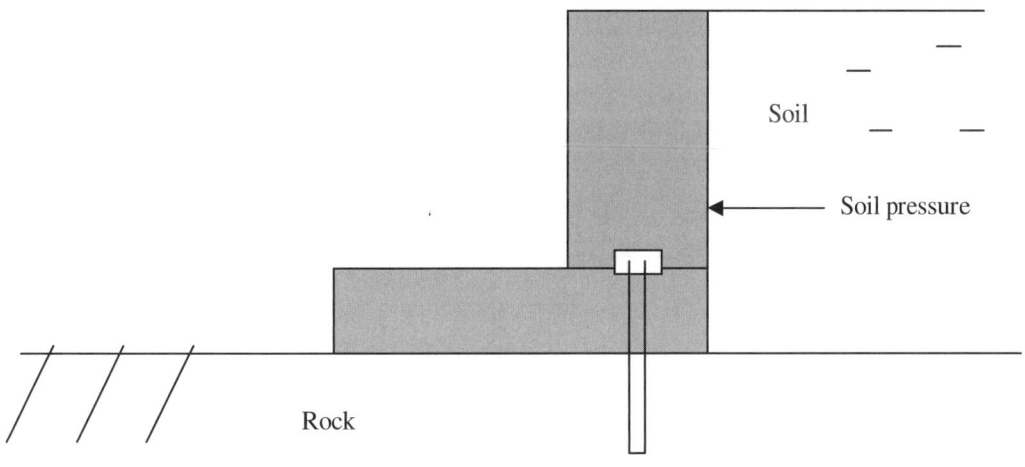

Retaining wall and a rock anchor

The above retaining wall is anchored to the rock using a rock bolt against soil pressure and moment. In such situations, rock bolts are used. There are many types of rock bolts.

Anchoring of a transmission tower against wind loads:

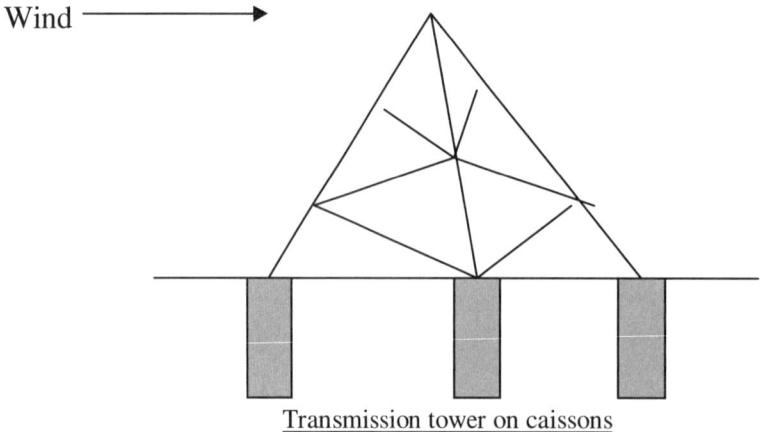

Transmission tower on caissons

Transmission towers are anchored to the ground using caissons or pile groups.

Sheetpile Walls: Sheetpile walls are anchored using sheetpile anchors.

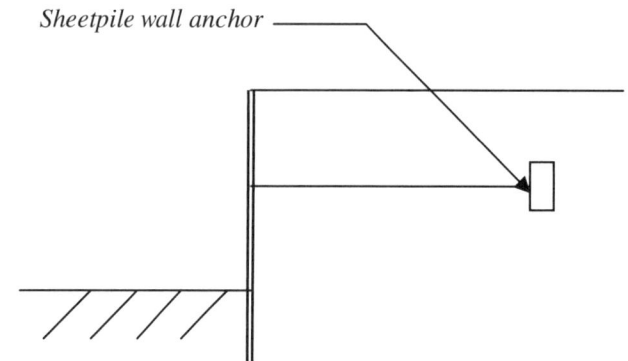

Sheetpile wall anchor

Sheetpile wall anchor system against soil pressure

Billboards:

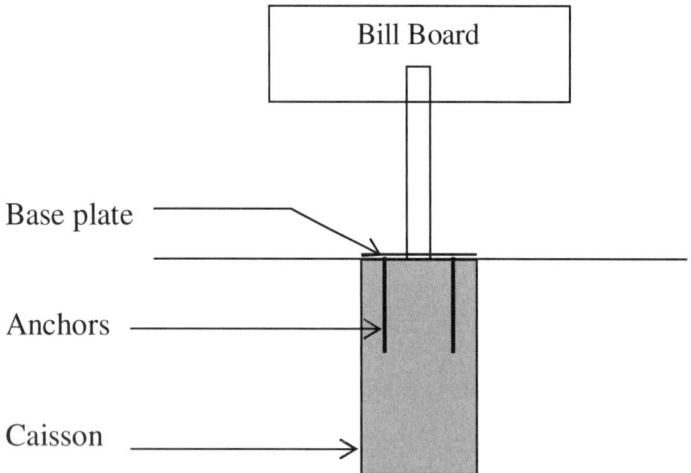

Billboards are typically welded to a base plate and the base plate is anchored to a caisson.

6.8 Cofferdams:

There are instances where construction has to take place near a river, lake or ocean. Bridge piers, harbor structures and flood control structures are some examples. In such situations water has to be kept away from the construction area. How can you concrete when water is pouring in? Some structure has to be built to keep the water away.

Figure: Bridge pier is shown in the above figure. How to build the foundation for this pier? Water has to be kept away from the foundation so that workers can place rebars and concrete.

In such situations, a temporary structure need to be constructed to keep the water away. These temporary structures are known as cofferdams.

Construction of a cofferdam   (Source: www.modot.com)

Cofferdams are temporary structures constructed to keep water out of the construction area. Majority of cofferdams are constructed in rivers mainly to build bridge piers. Thanks to improvement in caisson technology, most cases cofferdams may not be necessary anymore.

Cofferdams in Bridge Pier Construction:

Bridge piers are mostly constructed in rivers and water has to be kept out of the construction zone during construction. Typical bridge pier is shown below.

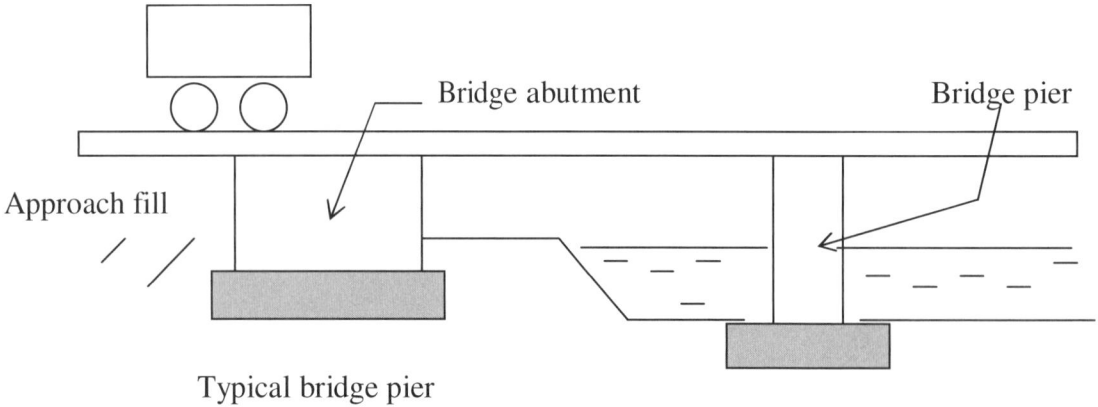

Typical bridge pier

Construction procedure of a typical cofferdam constructed using sheetpiles for a bridge pier is shown below.

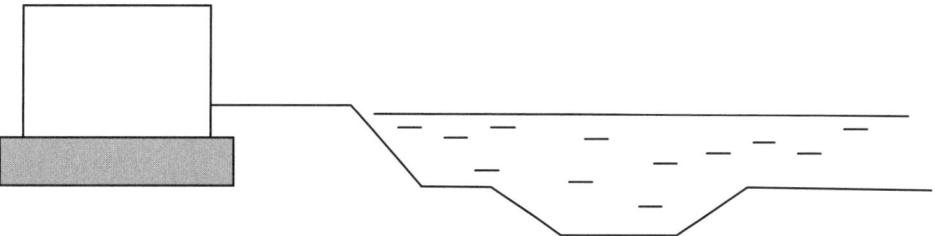

Dredge the bottom where the cofferdam to be constructed

STEP 1:   The bottom is dredged to remove lose sediments and to obtain hard bottom surface.

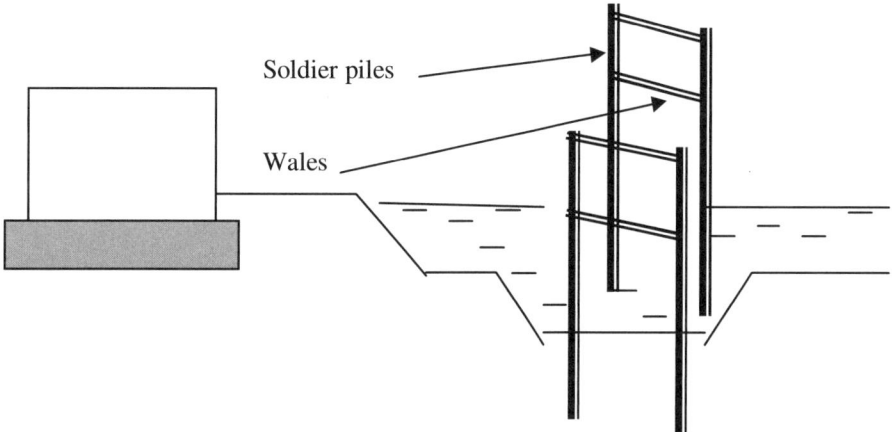

STEP 2: Drive soldier piles and construct wales (horizontal beams)
Soldier piles are driven first. These piles should extend deep into the riverbed. Soldier piles will take most of the load. Wales or the horizontal beams are constructed to provide stability to the structure.

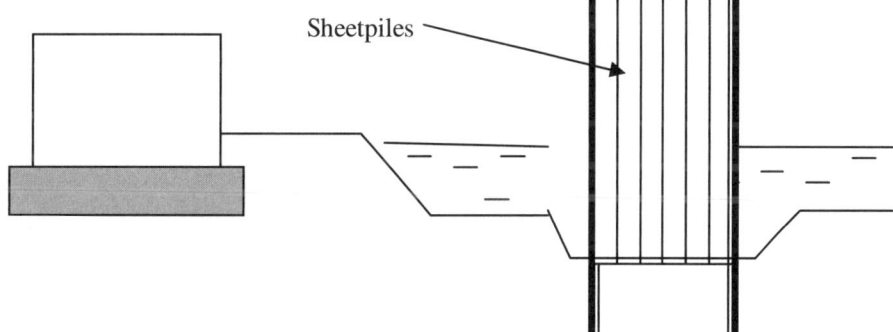

STEP 3: Drive watertight sheetpiles between soldier piles and attach them to the soldier piles
Watertight sheetpiles are driven and attached to the structure.   It is important to make sure that the cofferdam is stable during the construction process.

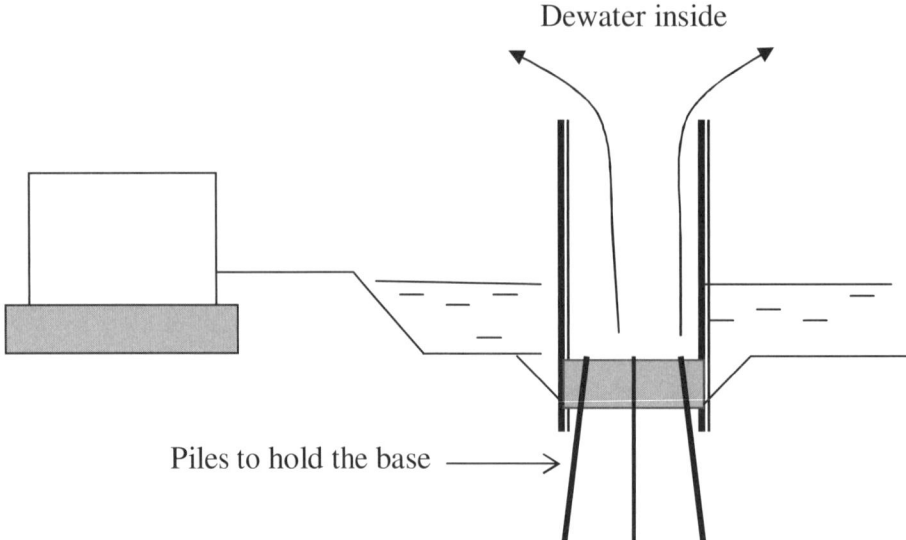

STEP 4: Concrete the bottom. Then dewater inside the cofferdam (sheetpiles are not shown). Piles are driven to hold the concrete base down.

Once the sheetpiles are driven and attached to soldier piles, the base is concreted. The concrete base has to be designed to make sure that it will not fail due to buoyant pressure of water. In some cases piles are driven prior to concreting the base to hold the base down. Piles can be driven after constructing the base as well by coring holes through concrete base. Driving of piles can be done from a barge from top and extra length can be cut off.

Some engineers place gravel on top of the concrete to hold the base down instead of driving piles.

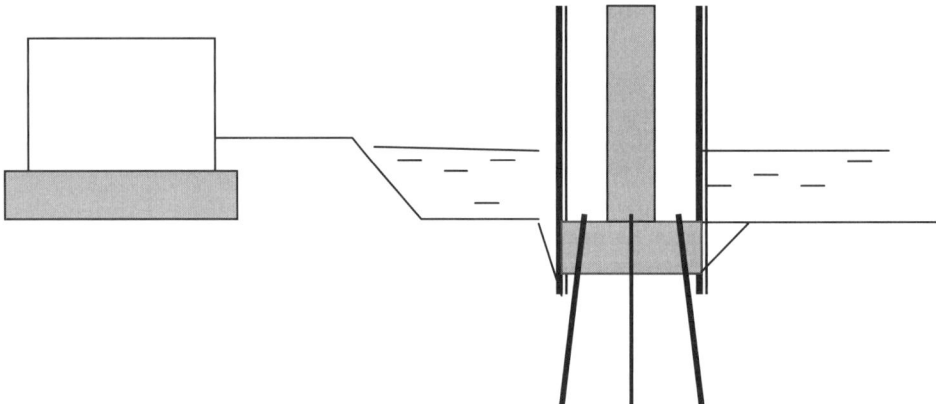

Construction workers can go inside the cofferdam and build the pier:

It is needless to say that the construction methodology depends upon the site conditions. If rock is encountered, concrete base can be placed on the rock. In that case, piles may not be necessary to hold the base. Again, one has to be careful of cracks and fissures in the rock. If water can migrate thru cracks and fissures in the rock, concrete base will be subjected to uplift forces.

Forces acting on cofferdams:

Force due to water flow: Main force on a cofferdam is the force due to flowing water. If the cofferdam is placed in the middle of a river, large forces could occur due to river flow. Force due to water flow is given by;

$$D = A. \, C_d. \, \gamma_w. \, V^2/2g$$

D = Force due to water flow
A = Projected area normal to the current
C_d. = Drag coefficient (depends on the roughness of sheetpile material and overall shape of the structure)
γ_w. = Density of water
V = Velocity of flow
g = 9.81 in SI units and 32 in fps units.

As can be seen from the above equation, higher the velocity of flow, higher the force on the cofferdam.

Static water pressure: Static water pressure occurs due to difference in hydrostatic heads.
Static water pressure is given by;

$p = \gamma_w. h$

p = Pressure due to water
γ_w. = Density of water   h = Hydrostatic head

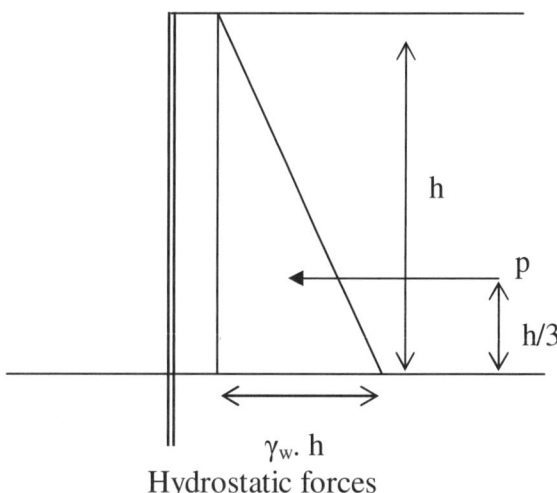

$\gamma_w. h$
Hydrostatic forces

Total force acting on the wall = Area of the triangle
$$= ½ \text{ x } (\gamma_w. h) \text{ x } h$$
$$= ½ \text{ x } \gamma_w.h^2$$
The hydrostatic force acts h/3 distance from the bottom.

Force due to waves: Wave action can develop additional forces on cofferdams.

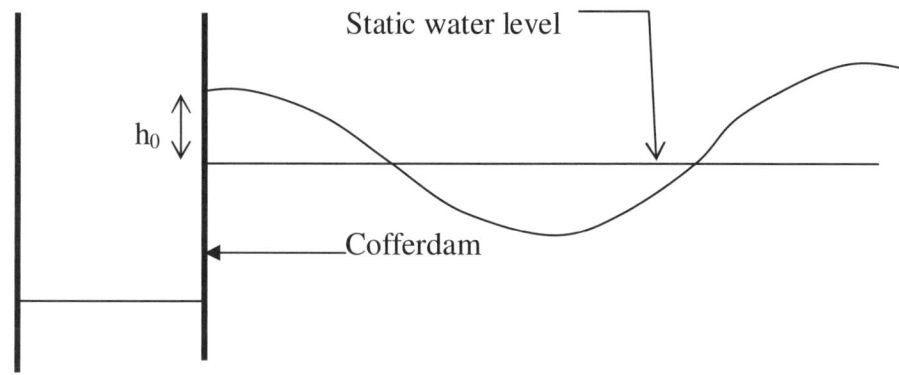

Additional hydrostatic head due to wave action also need to be computed.

<u>Forces due to ice action</u>:   When water becomes ice, volume increases. The increase in volume exerts additional pressure on sheetpile walls.

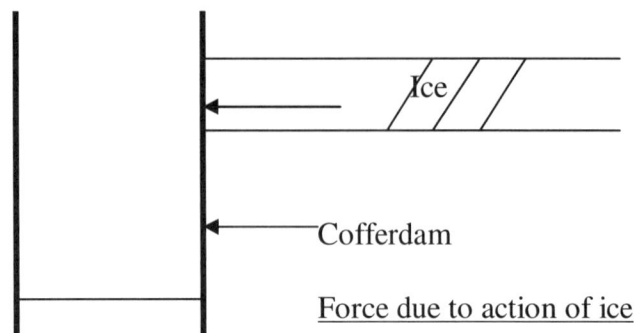

Cofferdam

<u>Force due to action of ice</u>

Cofferdam Types:

Most common cofferdam types are;

      1)   Single wall cofferdams
      2)   Double wall
      3)   Cellular wall
      4)   Diaphragm wall
      5)   Earth type
      6)   Timber crib
      7)   Rock fill

<u>Single Wall Cofferdams</u>:   As the name indicates single wall cofferdams have only one wall. Typically single wall cofferdams are built using sheetpiles.

<u>Figure:</u> Single wall cofferdam

Double Wall Cofferdam:

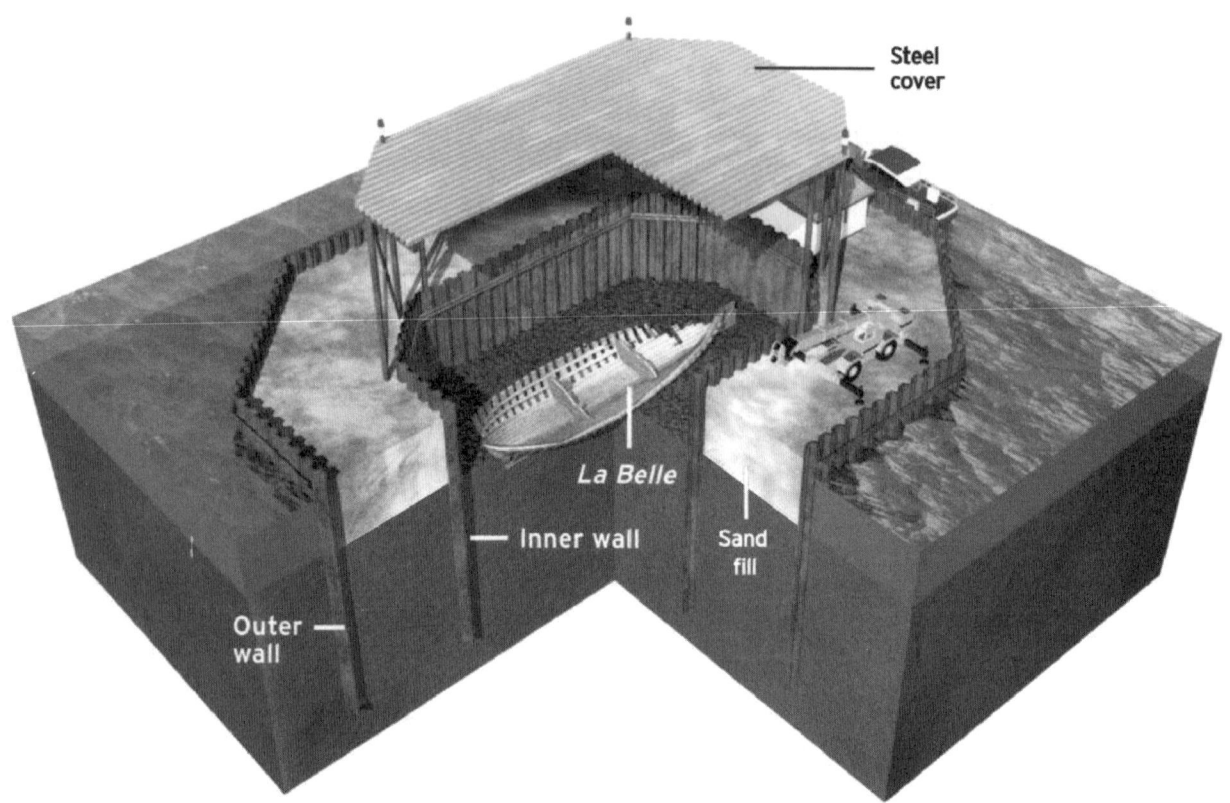

Figure: Double wall cofferdam (Inner wall and outer walls are shown).

Double wall cofferdams are somewhat permanent in nature and built to last for few years. When construction work can take many years, single wall cofferdams may not be suitable. Single wall cofferdams leaks and dewatering is required in a regular basis. This problem can be avoided with a double wall cofferdam.

- Single wall cofferdams can be built quickly with less cost.
- Dewatering and constant repairs needed for single wall cofferdams.
- Cost is less for single wall cofferdams.
- Double wall cofferdams are costly and need less maintenance. Also dewatering inside the work site is negligible.

Cellular Cofferdams:

Cellular cofferdams are built when large areas need to be kept dry. Cellular structures can stand alone and need not be braced.

Figure: Cellular Cofferdam

Note: Please see "**Three Sample Exams for the Civil PE Construction Module**" and "**Civil PE Construction Module Practice Problems**" for worked cofferdam examples.

7.0 Worker Health, Safety, and Environment:

7.1 OSHA Regulations (Introduction):
Laws of USA are made not by the president, but by the congress. Once the congress agree upon a piece of legislature (law) it has to be published. Federal government uses the code of federal register (CFR) to publish the laws of the country. Health and safety of construction workers are addressed in CFR 1926.

CFR 1926 is written in legal jargon and may be difficult to understand. Fortunately, simplified versions of CFR 1926 are published by various organizations.
This chapter will provide an overview of CFR1926.
CFR 1926 is divided into different subparts.

Safety Training: As per OSHA, It is the responsibility of the employer to provide safety training for workers. Special types of construction work such as confined space entry, working in high-rise buildings, working in hazardous environments require special training. For an instance OSHA 40 hr hazardous training certificate is required for workers who work in hazardous environments.

Exposure to Noise: 1926.52 deals with exposure to noise. OSHA provides a table where noise is considered to be a hazard.

Duration per day, hours	Sound level dBA slow response
8	90
6	92
4	95
3	97
2	100
1 1/2	102
1	105
1/2	110
1/4 or less	115

Permissible Noise Exposure (OSHA 1926.52)

For an example, as per above chart, if a worker is subjected to a noise of 102 decibels for more than 1.5 hours, the employer need to provide hearing protection.

7.2 CFR 1926 Subpart A (Right of Entry):
Subpart A deals with issues related to inspections and right of entry.

It says that the secretary of labor or representatives of the secretary of labor (OSHA) has the legal right to enter a workplace to investigate compliance of safety standards.

7.3 CFR 1926 Subpart B (Health Standards):
Subpart B deals with the rules of OSHA applying safety and health standards. This subpart covers various government regulations.

7.4 CFR 1926 Subpart C: (General safety and health provisions):

This section is of importance to both construction workers and employers. Hence, questions from this section can be expected in the exam. Following is a list of some of the laws and regulations included in this subpart.

It is the responsibility of the employer to provide a safe working condition to the workers.

The employer should monitor the work area and work procedures in a regular manner.

The employer should allow only qualified personnel to operate machinery.

Employer should inform the employees of any harmful substances in the workplace. The employee has the right to know of any hazardous material in the work place.

The employer should provide first aid facilities to the workers.

The employer should provide fire protecting and suppression equipment and maintain a fire-protecting program.

During construction, good housekeeping should be practiced. Nails, lumber, construction debris should be removed regularly.

Construction work site should be properly illuminated.

The employer should require that all employees wear proper personnel protective equipment.

Employee has the right to inspect exposure records. This piece of regulation provides employees the right to obtain data collected by the employer. In construction industry, certain chemicals such as organic vapor, metal vapor, CO, dust level and other chemicals are monitored. The employee has the right to request data obtained by the employer.

Employer has the right to delete information given to outside sources if the information is considered to be a trade secret. In such situations, the employer has to notify that some information has been deleted and alternative means should be provided to assess the health and safety issues.

7.5   CFR 1926 Subpart D: (Environmental Control):

Subpart D deals with first aid kits, noise exposure, exposure to radiation, gases and dust. Further, it deals with proper illumination and ventilation in the work site.

Employer should provide means to obtain prompt medical attention in case of injury. This may include providing first aid kits, telephones, radios, post maps and directions to nearby hospitals.

In the absence of a hospital nearby, the employer should provide a person who is trained in first aid from a reputed organization such as Red Cross or US Bureau of Mines.

Potable water and toilets should be provided by the employer.

Subpart D provides guidelines regarding noise exposure.

Subpart D provides threshold limit values for gases and vapors. If the site contains any chemical more than the threshold limit value, the employer should require the employees to wear proper personal protective equipment.

Subpart D provides minimum illumination acceptable in construction sites. General construction areas should have 5 foot candles of illumination.

Subpart D provides guidelines for ventilation in construction sites.

7.6   Personal Protective Equipment: 1926 Subpart E:

OSHA 1926 subpart E deals with personal protective equipment. Normally hard hats, boots, safety vests and eyeglasses are mandatory in construction sites.

Foot Protection (Boots):   Generally, all construction sites require boots. In some cases, steel toe boots are required. OSHA says the following;
OSHA 1926.97: Safety-toe footwear for employees shall meet the requirements and specifications in American National Standard for Men's Safety-Toe Footwear, Z41.1-1967.

Head Protection (Hard Hats):   In many construction sites, it is customary for safety professionals to require all workers wear hard hats.   However, OSHA does not require workers wear hard hats in construction sites if not needed.

OSHA says the following on hard hats;
OSHA 1926.100:   Employees working in areas where there is a possible danger of head injury from impact, or from falling or flying objects, or from electrical shock and burns, shall be protected by protective helmets.
As per OSHA, hard hats are required only when there is a possibility of head injury from impact or electrical shock.

Fall Protection (Safety belts, lifelines and lanyards): OSHA 1926.104

Lifelines should be able to withstand a load of 5,400 lbs. This includes the structural members that are used to attach the lifeline. Safety belts and lanyards should have a breaking point greater than 4,000 lbs.

7.7   Safety Nets 1926.105:

Safety nets shall be provided when workplaces are more than 25 feet above the ground or water surface. Nets shall extend 8 feet beyond the edge of the work surface where employees are exposed and shall be installed as close under the work surface as practical but in no case more than 25 feet below such work surface.

If the net is more than 25 feet lower than the workers, that would create a bigger drop and the workers may be subjected to high "g" forces.
OSHA also specifies net sizes. The mesh size of nets shall not exceed 6 inches by 6 inches. Safety nets shall be able to withstand an impact force of 17,500 foot-pounds.   Edge ropes that are used to tie the net shall provide a minimum breaking strength of 5,000 pounds.

Safety nets

Working near water: OSHA 1926.106:

Employees working over or near water, shall be provided with U.S. Coast Guard-approved life jacket or buoyant work vests.

Construction workers wearing life jackets

7.8   Fire Protection and Prevention: 1926 Subpart F:

Subpart F deals with fire protection and prevention. OSHA set the burden of fire protection on the employer. Employer is responsible of providing all fire protection equipment and training.

7.9   Signs Signals and Barricade: 1926 Subpart G:

Signs are a very effective way to communicate hazards to workers in a construction site.

Danger Signs: As per 1926.200 Danger signs should be used when there is an immediate hazard.
Caution Signs: Caution signs are used when there is a potential hazard due to unsafe practices such as smoking, not wearing PPE etc.

OSHA provides the color and designs for danger and caution signs.

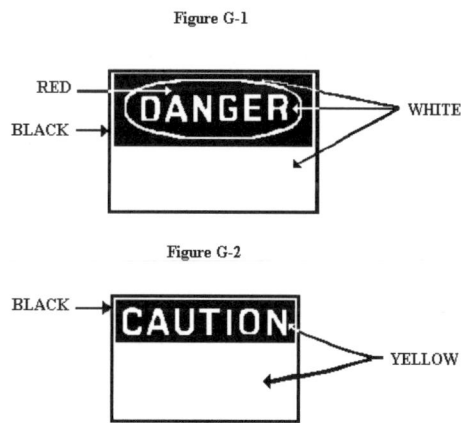

OSHA mandated danger and caution signs.

Danger signs should be red background with white letters. Black border is added to the red background. White space is left underneath the sign for the message. White space can be used to warn the workers of the danger. Something such as flammable area, lead contaminated area or radioactive area can be used in the white space.

Caution signs should be black background with yellow letters. Yellow space underneath can be used to inform of the site-specific condition.

7.10   Materials Handling, Storage, Use, and Disposal: 1926 Subpart H:

This section deals with storage of materials and equipment. If the material is stored indoors, safe load capacity of the floor should be posted. Aisles and passageways shall be kept clear to provide for the free and safe movement of material handling equipment or employees. Such areas shall be kept in good repair.

Material stored inside buildings under construction shall not be placed within 6 feet of any hoist way. or inside floor openings, nor within 10 feet of an exterior wall which does not extend above the top of the material stored. Materials shall not be stored on scaffolds or runways.   There is an important provision on storing bricks. OSHA indicates brick stacks to be not more than 7 feet in height. When a loose brick stack reaches a height of 4 feet, it shall be tapered back 2 inches in every foot of height above the 4-foot level.

This brick stack does not comply with OSHA guidelines

<u>Storage of Masonry Blocks</u>:   When masonry blocks are stacked higher than 6 feet, the stack shall be tapered back one-half block per tier above the 6-foot level.

<u>Storage of Lumber</u>:   Used lumber shall have all nails withdrawn before stacking. Lumber piles shall not exceed 20 feet in height. If the lumber to be handled manually then lumber stacks should not be more than 16 feet.

Left: Manual lumber stacking
Right: Automatic lumber stacking (Lumber is loaded to a conveyor belt and transported to the top of the stack)

Rigging Equipment for Material Handling: Rigging means lifting and moving. Rigging is required during construction. However, subpart H deals only with rigging of material for storage only.

General rigging safety includes making sure that the load does not exceed the rated value of hooks, shackles and all other equipment. In addition, employers must ensure that rigging equipment has permanently affixed and legible identification markings as prescribed by the manufacturer that indicate the recommended safe working load.

Slings should be inspected before each workday. The types of slings covered are those made from steel chain, wire rope, metal mesh, natural or synthetic fiber rope and synthetic web.

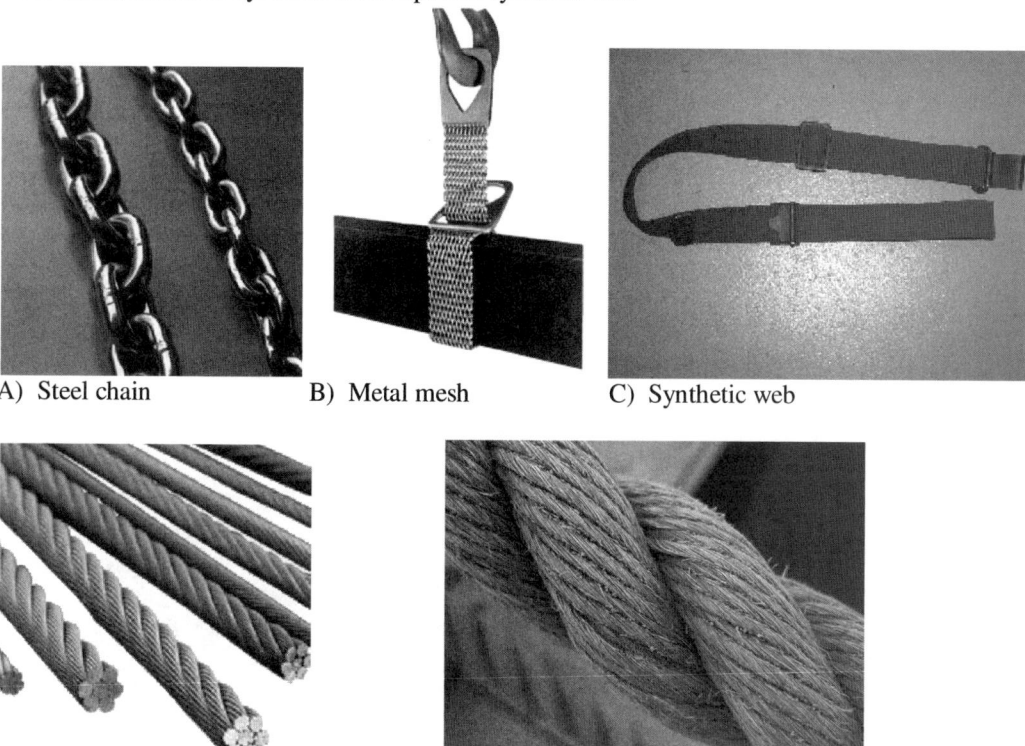

A) Steel chain   B) Metal mesh   C) Synthetic web

D) Wire rope   E) Ropes (Natural fiber or synthetic fiber)

Synthetic web can be made of Nylon, polyester or polypropylene. Wire ropes are typically made of steel.

Slings alone will not be enough for lifting. Hooks, rings, shackles and links are needed to attach slings and objects to be lifted.

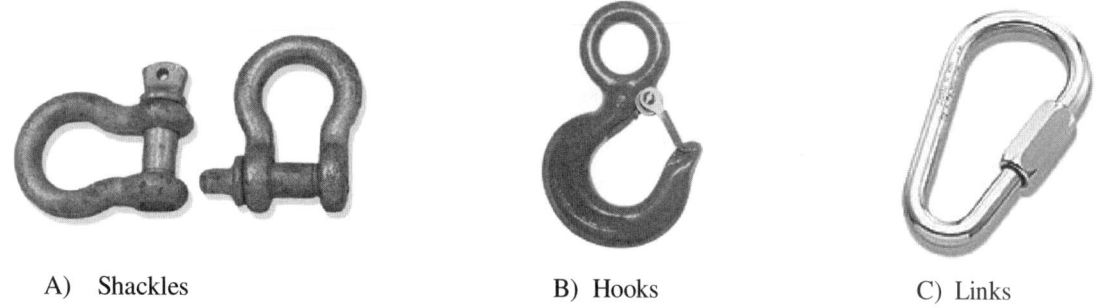

A)   Shackles   B) Hooks   C) Links

D) Rings used as links

7.11   Tools (Hand Tools and Power Tools) - Subpart I:

Subpart I deals with tools.   OSHA indicates the all hand and power tools and similar equipment, whether furnished by the employer or the employee, shall be maintained in a safe condition. Power tools need to have guards. All tools should be used in conjunction with proper personal protective equipment.

Left: *Power saw with a guard*
Right: *Power saw without a guard*

OSHA has named machines that need mandatory guards. They are Guillotine cutters, shears, alligator shears, powered presses, milling machines, power saws, jointers and portable power tools.

7.12   Welding and Cutting: OSHA 1926 Subpart J:

Gas cylinders are a common site in construction sites. Gas is used for cutting and welding.

Left: *Improper storage of gas cylinders. Gas cylinders should be stored upright position.*
Middle: *Proper storage of gas cylinders*
Right: *Proper moving of gas cylinders*

Valve protection caps shall be in place while transporting, moving, and storing compressed gas cylinders. Gas cylinders should not be hoisted with magnets or choker slings.

As per OSHA, correct way to move gas cylinders by tilting and rolling them on their bottom edges. They shall not be intentionally dropped, struck, or permitted to strike each other violently. When cylinders are transported by powered vehicles, they shall be secured in a vertical position.
Unless cylinders are firmly secured on a special carrier intended for this purpose, regulators shall be removed and valve protection caps put in place before cylinders are moved.

What is the best way to store compressed gas cylinders? OSHA says compressed gas cylinders shall be stored in an upright position at all times. It is important to separate Oxygen cylinders from fuel-gas cylinders or combustible materials (especially oil or grease), a minimum distance of 20 feet (6.1 m) or by a noncombustible barrier at least 5 feet (1.5 m) high having a fire-resistance rating of at least one-half hour.

When working in confined spaces, cylinders containing oxygen or acetylene or other fuel gas shall not be taken into confined space. Oil and grease are combustible material and creates a fire hazard. Oil and grease shall be kept away Oxygen or fuel gas cylinders.

Arc Welding Safety Issues: Electrical arcs are created during arc welding. All arc welding and cutting cables shall be completely insulated. These cables should be flexible type, capable of handling the maximum current requirements of the work in progress.
In some occasions, cables may need to be spliced. In that situations OSHA recommends substantial insulated connectors of a capacity at least equivalent to that of the cable shall be used.

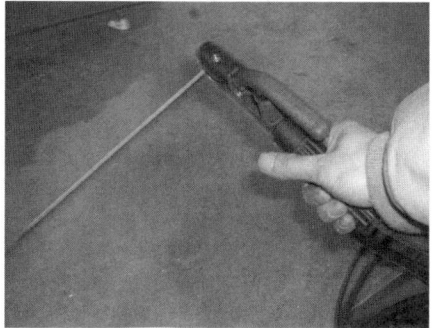 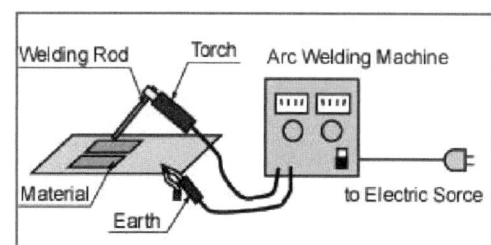

Left: *Arc welding electrode is shown*
Right: *Arc welding system (Welding machine, torch, electrode or welding rod, material to be welded and ground wire or earth.*

When electrode holders are to be left unattended, the electrodes shall be removed and the holders shall be so placed or protected that they cannot make electrical contact with employees or conducting objects.

Hot electrode holders shall not be dipped in water. This could short circuit the electricity and electrocutes the operator. When the arc welder has to stop work for any appreciable length of time, the power supply should be switched off.

Fire Prevention during Welding:

Fires due to welding and cutting activity are very common. Hence, OSHA has addressed this issue in great detail.

As per OSHA, No welding, cutting, or heating shall be done where in the presence of other flammable compounds
During welding, suitable fire, extinguishing equipment shall be immediately available in the work area and shall be maintained in a state of readiness for instant use.

Fire Watch: Fire watch is a worker dedicated to keep an eye on possible fires. Fire watch should be provided during cutting or welding operation. As per OSHA wording fire watch is not mandatory but recommended. Fire watch should stay after the work is done to make sure that there are no smokes or unnoticed fires in the area.

Drums and Containers: Before welding drums, completely remove all material from the drum. Also before heat is applied to a drum opening shall be provided for the release of any built-up pressure during the application of heat.

Ventilation during Welding or Cutting Operation: It is no secret that welding and cutting operations generate toxic fumes. Hence, proper ventilation should be provided. Mechanical fans or open windows as appropriate should be used to make sure that the area has proper ventilation. Contaminated air exhausted from welding operation should be discharged.

Air Respirators: In some confined spaces, sufficient air ventilation is not possible to provide for the workspace. In such situations air line respirators should be provided. When airline respirators are used, a worker should be placed outside to maintain communication with those working inside. The person outside should call for help during an emergency.

Eye Protection: Welders should use proper eye protection during welding or cutting. Eye injuries account for large percentage of all welding injuries.

Welding helmets are recommended to be used during welding. There are two types of welding helmets.

- Welding helmets with fixed shade filters
- Welding helmets with auto darkening filters

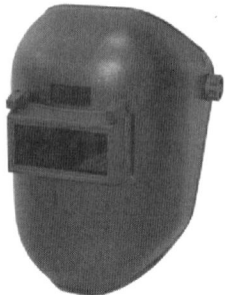

Welding helmet

Fixed shade welding helmets have one shade to protect against arcs. When there is no arc, welder cannot see the surroundings. Hence, the welder needs to move the helmet down to look at the finished weld. In addition, the welder needs to look at the weld prior to starting a new weld.

On the other hand, helmets with auto darkening filters, darkening of the lens happen only when the arc is generated. When there is no arc, darkening goes away. Hence, the welder does not have to move the helmet to look at the finished weld. The downside of this type of filter is they operate from a battery. The welder should check the battery prior to use them.

- Goggles or safety glasses are used during Oxy Fuel welding.

7.13 Electrical Safety: OSHA 1926 Subpart K:

<u>Electricity (Introduction)</u>: Electricity is a flow of electrons through a conductor. Copper wires are used as conductors.

<u>Electric Circuit</u>: Basic electric circuit has an electric source, useful service such as a light bulb and a switch to shut it on and off.

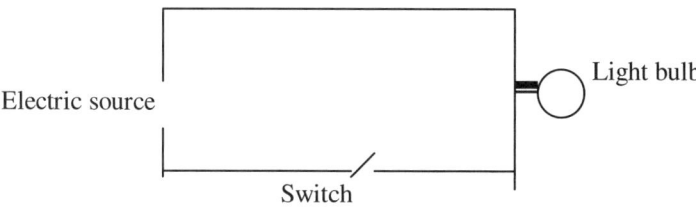

Electric Circuit

Electric source could be the supply from an outside source or generator.

<u>Switch Boards: (Electric Panels)</u>: In buildings, there could be large number of circuits. In such situations, there would be large number of switches. These switches are included in metal boxes. Such boxes are known as switchboards (or electric panels).

Typically, these boxes are waterproof. Only qualified electricians are allowed to make repairs or changes to switch boards.

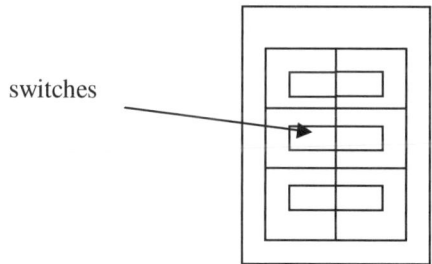

Electric Panel

Electric Panels:

Panel Directory: Panel directory would indicate the circuits allocated to a given switch. For an instance if repairs need to be done to the boiler, one can switch off the power to the boiler. If there is no directory indicating what switch is for what purpose then one may not be able to figure out how to switch off the electricity for the boiler. In such situations electrician has to conduct various tests to figure out the proper switches.

Ground wire	Green
Phase 1	Black
Phase 2	Red
Phase 3	Blue
Neutral	White

Color Code for Electric Wires

Circuit Protective Devices: (Circuit Breakers):   Circuit breakers shut off a circuit when the current is above the normal limit. Circuit breakers are essential for the safe operation of an electric circuit.

Ground Wires: Circuits are grounded in case there is a short circuit.

Hazards of electricity: Electricity is an invisible killer. Innocent looking cable could kill you in an instant. When electricity travels through the body, organs in the body would be damaged. The damage is dependent upon the current. One could be electrocuted by standing on water where there is contact with an electric circuit.

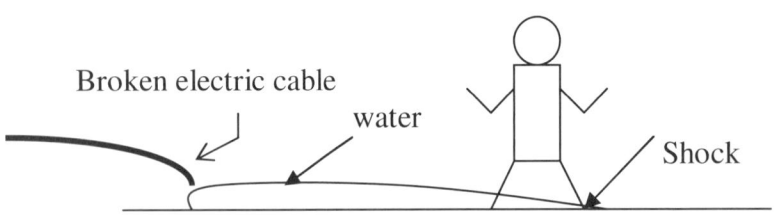

Broken electric cable

water

Shock

Electricity can travel through water

In areas where there is a possibility of a stray current, rubber mat should be placed. Electricity rarely travels through rubber mats.

Electricity and Burns: Another hazard of electricity is arcing. If you are closer to a high voltage circuit, it can arc.

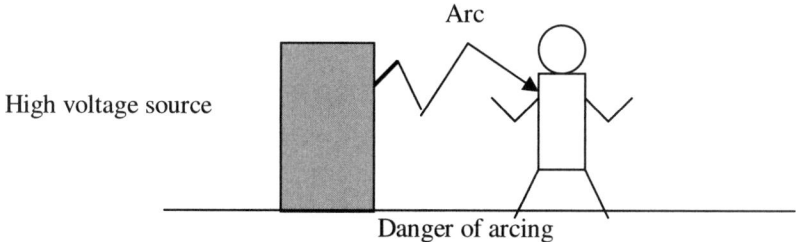

High voltage source

Arc

Danger of arcing

Severe burns can occur due to electric arcing.

Explosions: When the air is saturated with ignitable vapors electricity can provide the ignition needed for an explosion.

Electric Fires: Water infiltration into electric panels, switchgear can cause electric fires. Other main reason for electric fires is the wearing of insulation. When two or more wires start to rub with each other without insulation, fire could arise.

Summary of OSHA safety guidelines:

All electrical conductors and equipment shall be approved.
Electrical equipment shall not be used unless the manufacturer's name is not exhibited.
Arcing parts should be separated and enclosed from other parts.
Sufficient access and working space should be provided around all electrical equipment.
Electrical conductors should have a clearance of 3 ft from building openings.
Signs warning of electrical hazards should be posted when other employees may come to that area.
Switchboards that have any live parts should be placed in permanent dry locations.
Panels and switches installed in wet locations should be weatherproof.
Cords passing through holes should be protected by installing bushings.

OSHA refers to National Electrical Code ANSI/NFPA 70-1984, for guidance for electrical work.

All electrical conductors and equipment shall be approved prior to installation. As per OSHA it is the responsibility of the employer to ensure that electrical equipment is free from recognized hazards that are likely to cause death or serious physical harm to employees.
Following hazards are identified as regarding to electrical equipment.

- Mechanical strength and durability.
- Electrical insulation
- Heating effects under conditions of use
- Arcing effects.

No electrical equipment should be used unless the manufacturer's name or trademark on the equipment is present.

Working Space: Sufficient access and working space shall be provided and maintained about all electric equipment to permit ready and safe operation and maintenance of such equipment.

Lockout and Tagging of Circuits: If equipment is not in use that equipment should be properly locked out and tagged.

Maintenance of Equipment: When it comes to maintenance, electrical equipment needs special attention. Many accidents occur due to ill-maintained electrical equipment. The employer shall ensure that all wiring and equipment in hazardous locations are maintained in a dust-tight, dust-ignition-proof, or explosion-proof condition. There shall be no loose screws, gaskets, threaded connections, seals, or other impairments to a tight condition.

7.14   Scaffolds: OSHA 1926 Subpart L:

OSHA indicates that alls scaffolds should have a capacity of carrying its own weight plus four times the working weight. Ropes and connecting hardware should be able to withstand 6 times the working load. OSHA has a higher safety factor for ropes since ropes are prone to damage over time.

Scaffolds:

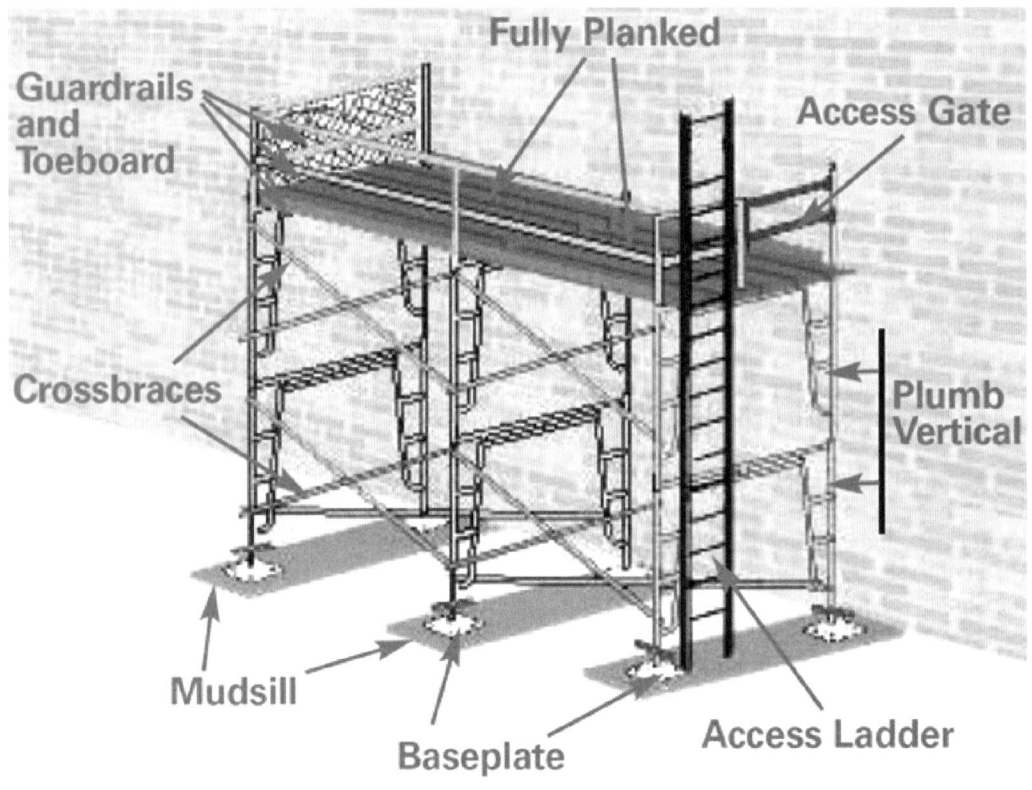

Different items of a scaffold

Base plates: Base plates are needed to distribute the load to the ground.
Vertical posts: Vertical posts carry the most load and should be properly installed.
Cross braces: Cross braces connect vertical posts for lateral stability.
Platform: Platform is provided for the workers to work.

Scaffold Platforms: As per OSHA, each platform on all working levels of scaffolds shall be fully planked or decked between the front uprights and the guardrail supports as follows:

7.15   Fall Protection: OSHA 1926 Subpart M:

When does fall protection is needed?

As per OSHA, when workers are working at a height greater than 6 ft, fall protection is needed. Fall protection methods commonly used are:

- Guardrails
- Safety net system
- Personal fall arrest system

Also, note that fall protection is needed when workers are working near an excavation greater than 6 ft.

<u>Fall Arrest Systems and Positioning Device Systems</u>**:**   It is important to understand the difference between the two systems. Fall arrest systems are designed to protect the workers in the case of a fall. Positioning device systems are designed to hold the worker in place while working.

<u>Left</u>:   *<u>Fall Arrest System</u>*
<u>Right:</u>   *<u>Fall Arrest System at Work</u>*

<u>Positioning Device System</u>:

Positioning device systems are different than fall arrest systems. Positioning device systems are designed to hold a person at place so that the worker can use both his hands.

Fall Arrest System

Positioning Device System

Positioning Device System

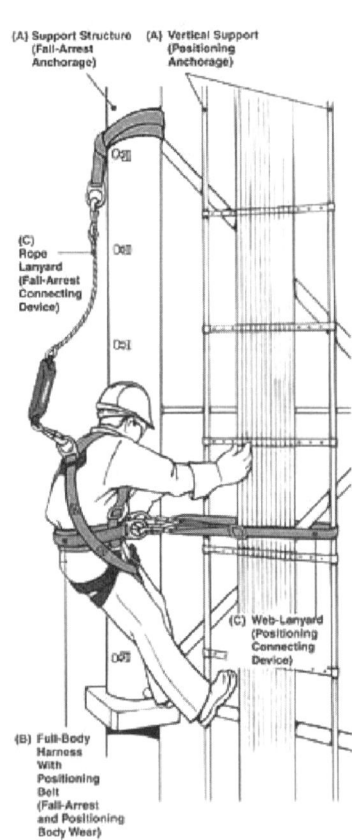

Both Positioning Device System and a Fall Arrest System

The worker shown on right is using both positioning device system and a fall arrest system.

Note that positioning device system cannot be considered as a fall arrest system.

Guard Rail Systems: Guardrail systems should be 42 inches plus or minus 3 inches above the walking/working level. Mid rail should be installed midway between top rail and working surface. Guardrail systems shall be capable of withstanding, without failure, a force of at least 200 pounds (890 N) applied at the top edge, in any outward or downward direction, at any point along the top edge.

<u>Safety Net Systems</u>:   Safety nets shall be installed as close as practicable under the walking/working surface on which employees are working, but in no case more than 30 feet below such level. In other words, OSHA do not want workers to fall more than 30 ft in the case of a fall.

Safety nets should extend beyond the vertical plane of the working surface. See the figure below for "x" and "y".

Depth to the safety net (y)	Min. required horizontal width of the net (x)
Up to 5 ft	8 ft
5 to 10 ft	10 ft
More than 10 ft	13 ft

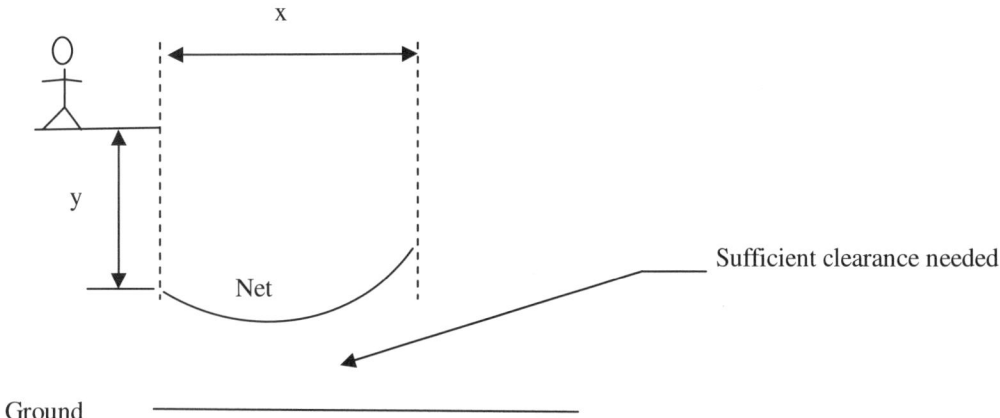

There should be sufficient clearance below the net so that net can move downward without hitting the ground.

<u>Drop Test for Safety Nets</u>:   The drop test shall consist of a 400-pound bag of sand 30 in diameter dropped into the net from the highest walking/working surface at which employees are working. If the working surface at a height less than 42 inches above the safety net, then drop test should be conducted for 42 inches.

<u>Safety Net Inspection</u>:   Safety nets shall be inspected once a week for damage. In addition, safety nets shall be kept clean. Any materials, told dropped onto the net shall be removed.

<u>Maximum Size of Mesh</u>: The maximum size of each safety net mesh opening shall not exceed 36 square inches nor be longer than 6 inches on any side.

<u>Personal fall arrest systems</u>:   All connectors shall be able to withstand 5,000 lbs and must have tested for 3,600 lbs. Body belts for personal fall arrest systems shall be at least one and five-eighths (1 5/8) inches wide. Personal fall arrest systems shall not be attached to guardrail systems, nor shall they be attached to hoists except as specified in other subparts of this Part.

<u>Lifelines</u>:   Lanyards and vertical lifelines shall have a minimum breaking strength of 5,000 pounds. It is important to protect lifelines from damages.

<u>Positioning device systems</u>:   Positioning devices shall be rigged such that an employee cannot free fall more than 2 feet. Positioning devices shall be secured to an anchorage that is capable of supporting at least twice the potential impact load of an employee's fall or 3,000 pounds, whichever is greater. Connecting assemblies of positional device systems shall have a minimum tensile strength of 5,000 pounds. Connectors shall be proof-tested to a minimum tensile load of 3,600 pounds.

<u>Safety monitoring systems</u>:   The employer shall designate a competent person to monitor the safety of other employees and the employer shall ensure that the safety monitor complies with the following requirements:

<u>Training for Workers</u>:   Employer should provide training for all workers who will be using the fall protection. The workers should be trained to wear and maintain personal fall arrests systems and positioning devices if they are planning to use them.

7.16   Helicopters, Hoists, Elevators, and Conveyors: OSHA 1926 Subpart N:

<u>Helicopter Cranes</u>:   Helicopters are increasingly used to hoist materials.

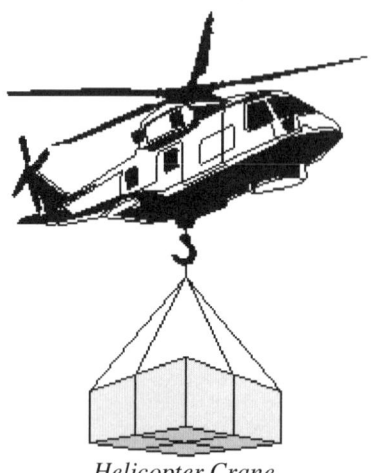

Helicopter Crane

<u>Daily Safety Briefing</u>:   Prior to start of work every day safety briefing shall be conducted with all the workers involved and the pilot.

<u>Signal System</u>:   Helicopter crane operation need to include a signal system between ground crew and pilot.

<u>Approach Distance</u>:   When the rotor blades are running only prior, authorized personnel are allowed to be within 50 ft of the helicopter.

<u>Material Hoist Safety</u>:   Material hoists are widely used for high-rise building construction work.

Material Hoists

Compliance with Manufacturer's Specifications: The contractor shall comply with the manufacturer's specifications and limitations. Rated load capacities, recommended operating speeds, and special hazard warnings or instructions shall be posted.

Inspection: All hoists shall be inspected and tested at not more than 3-month intervals. The employer shall prepare a inspection reports.

Most hoists use wire ropes. Wire rope shall be taken out of service, if six randomly distributed broken wires in one lay or three broken wires in one strand in one lay. Alternatively, wear of one-third the original diameter of outside individual wires. In addition, wire ropes shall be taken out of service if there is any evidence of heat damage.

Wire rope with broken wires

Overhead Hoists:

Overhead hoist

Manufacturer's specifications and safe loads shall be followed by the operator. Hoist shall be located in such a manner that the operator can stand clear of the load. Inspection of the hoist shall be conducted as per manufacturer's guidelines.

7.17   Motor Vehicles, Mechanized Equipment, and Marine Operations: OSHA 1926 Subpart O:

This section may not be too important for the exam. But I recommend you read it at least once.

7.18   Excavations: OSHA 1926 Subpart P:

Excavation safety problems are common in PE construction exams. Hence, it is important to pay attention to excavation safety.

Protecting Utilities: Prior to excavation work, the employer shall contact the utility companies and inform of the excavation work. In most cases, they would come to the site and mark out utility locations. If a certain utility company is unable to provide the utility mark up, the contractor shall use detecting devices to locate utilities.

Means of Egress: Exit locations need to be provided every 25 ft, in trenches deeper than 4 ft. Stairways, ladders, ramps or other safe means of egress shall be provided.

Oxygen Level: If the trench or excavation may possibly contain low level of Oxygen (less than 19.5 Oxygen) or high level of hazardous gases, such as in excavations shall be tested before employees enter excavations greater than 4 feet in depth.

Inspections for Cave-ins: Excavations need to be inspected daily prior to work for possible cave-ins.

When Excavation Protection is not Needed:
As per OSHA, excavations protection is not needed when following conditions are met;

- Excavation is conducted in stable rock
- Excavation is less than 5 ft and a competent person had determined that there is no risk of cave-in.

It should be mentioned here that in many cases contractors assume that all excavations less than 5 ft may not need excavation support. This is a false assumption. Competent person needs to certify that excavation does not require support, even if the excavation is less than 5 ft.

Sloping and Benching: Sloping and benching can be done instead of protection of slopes for some situations.

OSHA provides the following table for sloping and benching.

TABLE B-1
MAXIMUM ALLOWABLE SLOPES

SOIL OR ROCK TYPE	MAXIMUM ALLOWABLE SLOPES (H:V)(1) FOR EXCAVATIONS LESS THAN 20 FEET DEEP(3)
STABLE ROCK	VERTICAL (90°)
TYPE A	3/4H:1V (53°)
TYPE B	1:1 (45°)
TYPE C	1 ½H:1V (34°)

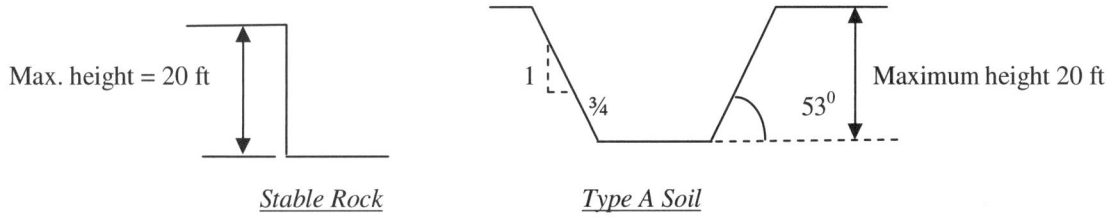

Stable Rock   *Type A Soil*

Stable Rock: Excavations in stable rock do not need any support and can have a vertical surface as shown above as long as the height is less than 20 ft.

Excavations in Type A Soil: Type A" soils are clayey soils with an unconfined, compressive strength of 1.5 tsf or greater. Unconfined compressive strength test is shown below.

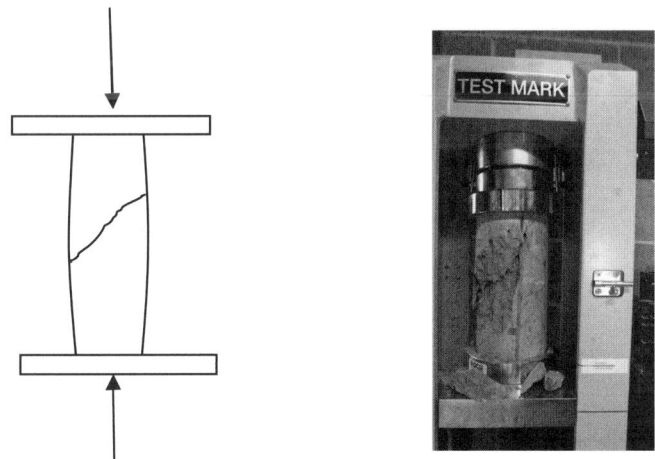

Unconfined compressive strength test

Unconfined compressive strength test is conducted by placing a soil sample between two plates and applying a force. This test can be done only for clay soils. Clay soils with high cohesion would fail at a higher load. Higher the unconfined compressive strength test value, higher the resistance to slope failure.

In type A soils, maximum slope angle allowed is 53 degrees up to a height of 20 ft. (53 degrees is same as 3/4H:1V)

In addition to simple slope as shown above, OSHA also provides benching methods.

Excavations in Type B Soil: Type B soils shall have a unconfined compressive strength less than 1.5 tsf and greater than 0.5 tsf.

In type B soils, maximum slope angle allowed is 45 degrees up to a height of 20 ft. (45 degrees is same as 1H:1V). Since type B soils have a lesser-unconfined compressive strength value, slope shall be less steep than type A soils.

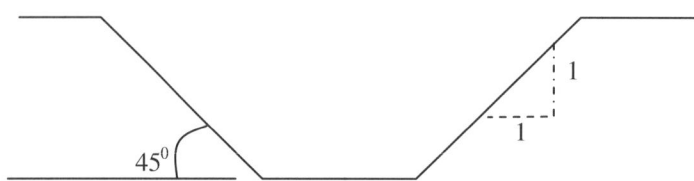

Excavations in Type C Soil: Type C soils shall have an unconfined compressive strength less than 0.5 tsf.

In type C soils, maximum slope angle allowed is 33.7 degrees up to a height of 20 ft. (33.7 degrees is same as 1.5H:1V).

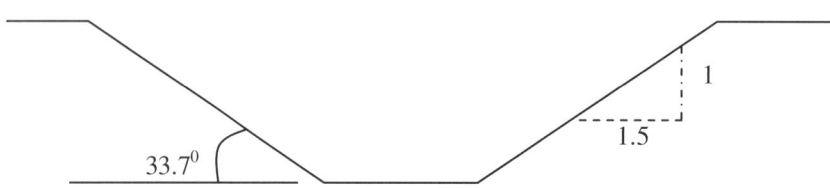

Timber Shoring: In some cases, sloping may not be feasible due to nearby buildings, roads and various other obstructions. In such situations, shoring is done. Timber shoring is still very popular and probably the cheapest.

Timber shoring picture is shown below.

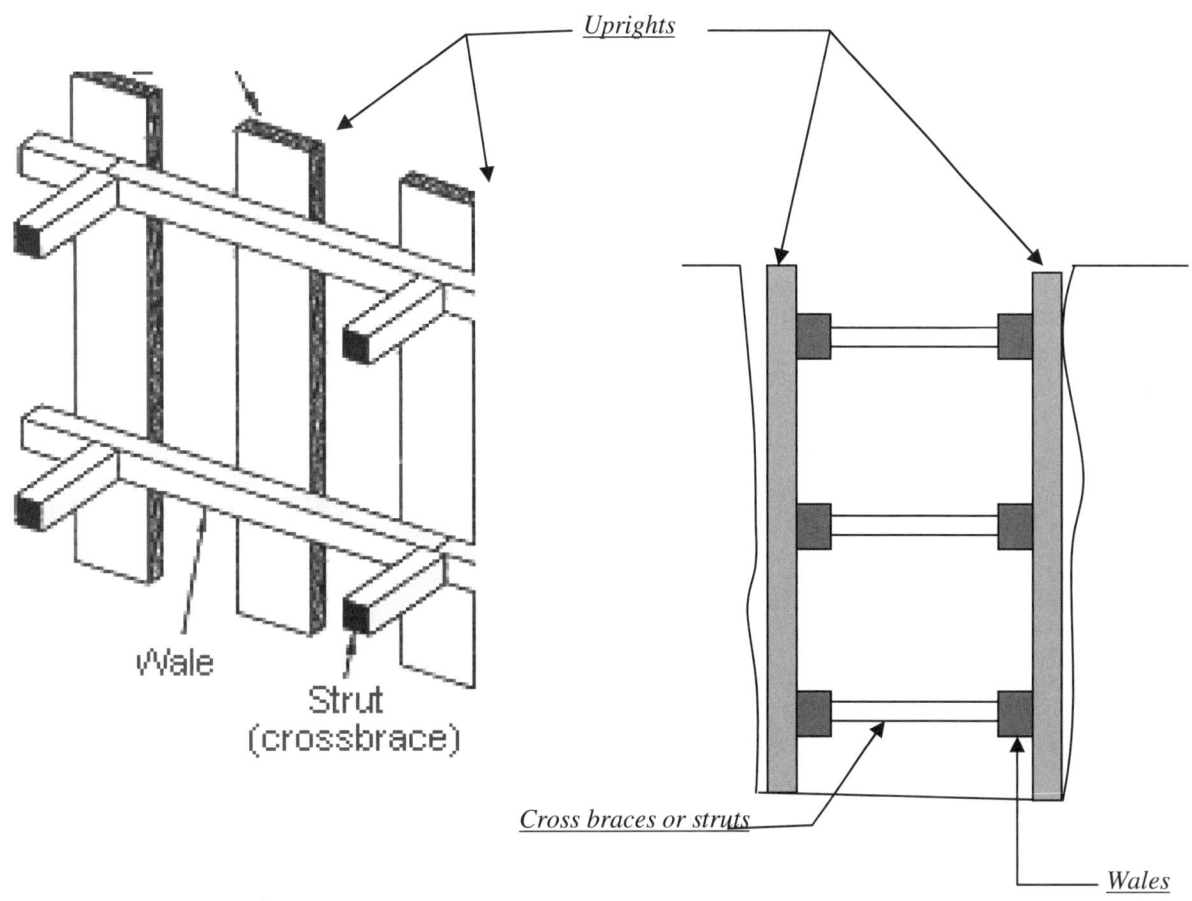

Elements of a timber shoring system:

- Cross braces (also known as struts)
- Uprights
- Wales (Sometime not needed)
- Sheathing (Sometimes not needed)

Cross braces, uprights and wales are timber elements. Sheathing is timber boards or plywood.

OSHA provides tables to design timber shoring.

<u>Design of Cross braces</u>:   Use Table C.1.1 in OSHA.
Portion of the table is shown below.

Table C.1.1 Design of Cross braces

Depth of trench	Hor. Spacing	Width of Trench					Vert. Spacing (ft)
		Up to 4 ft	*Up to 6 ft*	*Up to 9 ft*	*Up to 12 ft*	*Up to 15 ft*	
5 to 10 ft	Up to 6 ft	4 x 4	4 x 4	4 x 6	6 x 6	6 x 6	4
	Up to 8 ft	4 x 4	4 x 4	4 x 6	6 x 6	6 x 6	4
	Up to 10 ft	4 x 6	4 x 6	4 x 6	6 x 6	6 x 6	4
10 to 15 ft	Up to 6 ft	4 x 4	4 x 4	4 x 6	6 x 6	6 x 6	4
	Up to 8 ft	4 x 4	4 x 4	6 x 6	6 x 6	6 x 6	4
	Up to 10 ft	6 x 6	6 x 6	6 x 6	6 x 8	6 x 8	4
15 to 20 ft	Up to 6 ft	6 x 6	6 x 6	6 x 6	6 x 8	6 x 8	4
	Up to 8 ft	6 x 6	6 x 6	6 x 6	6 x 8	6 x 8	4
	Up to 10 ft	8 x 8	8 x 8	8 x 8	8 x 8	8 x 10	4

Example: A trench with a depth of 18 ft need to be constructed. The width of the trench is 10 ft. What is the size of the cross bracing required? The contractor would like to place cross bracing every 10 ft.

Solution: The depth is 18 ft. Hence, locate the row with depth 15 to 20 ft. The width is 10 ft. Hence, locate the column "up to 12 ft". Now the contractor has three choices. The contractor wishes to place cross bracing every 10 ft.
Hence the size of the cross bracing required = 8 x 8
Nominal size 8 x 8 (8 in x 8 in) is not the actual size. Actual size is 7.5 in x 7.5 in.

<u>8 x8 Timber (Actual size 7.5 in x 7.5 in)</u>

Design of Uprights:

Table C.1.1 Design of Uprights and Wales

Depth of trench	Wale Size	Wale vertical spacing (ft)	Maximum allowable horizontal spacing of Uprights and Size				
			Close	4 ft	5 ft	6 ft	8 ft
5 to 10 ft	Not required	---				2 x 6	
	Not required	---					2 x 8
	8 x 8	4			2 x 6		
	8 x 8	4				2 x 6	
10 to 15 ft	Not required	---					3 x 8
	8 x 8	4			2 x 6		
	8 x 10	4				2 x 6	
	10 x 10	4					3 x 8

OSHA provides tables to design wales, cross bracings and uprights for all types of soil.

Aluminum Hydraulic Shoring: Instead of timber, there is another alternative. That is Aluminum hydraulic shoring. These shoring can be reused many times. Though the initial cost is high, cost per given year may be less with this type of shoring.

Aluminum Hydraulic Shoring

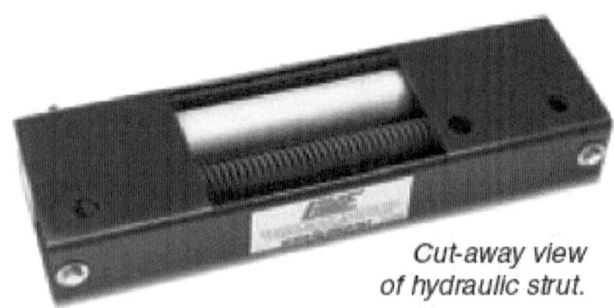

Cut-away view
of hydraulic strut.

Hydraulically operated struts

Length of hydraulically operated cross bracings can be adjusted to tighten the cross bracings. OSHA table D1.1 is used to design Aluminum struts and uprights.

Trench Shields: In urban environments, trench shields are much easier and faster.

Trench shields.
Left: *Excavation is done with the trench shield*
Right: *Excavation is completed prior to placing the trench shield*

7.19   Concrete and Masonry Construction: OSHA 1926 Subpart Q:

Many workers work in concrete and masonry construction work.   Concrete is considered to be the most popular construction material in the world.

General Safety Requirements:

Construction loads: Construction loads include tools, machines and construction workers. OSHA states that no construction loads shall be placed on a concrete structures unless the employer determines, based on information received from a person who is qualified in structural design, that the structure or portion of the structure is capable of supporting the loads.

Reinforcing steel: All protruding reinforcing steel need to be capped to avoid impalement.

Rebar caps

Post-tensioning operations: Post tensioning is the process of applying a compressing concrete beams and slabs using tendons. Note that post tensioning is different than pre stressing. Post tensioning tendons do not have a bond with concrete. On the other hand, pre stressed tendons are bonded to concrete.

Post tensioning method: A concrete beam is cast with tendons inside. Then after the concrete is hardened, tendons are pulled and attached to the beam.

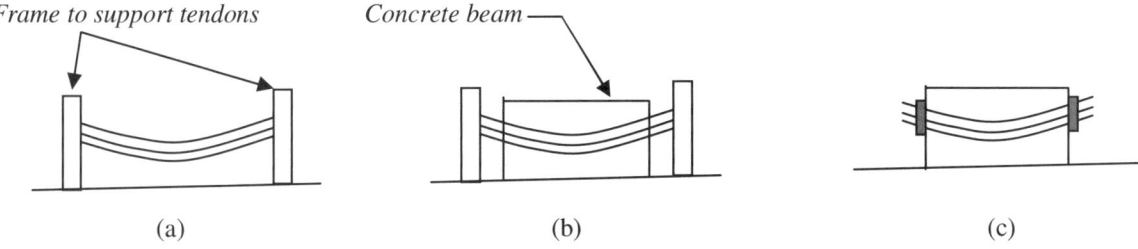

Frame to support tendons   *Concrete beam*

(a)   (b)   (c)

(a)   Place the frame and install the tendons. Tendons are inside a duct.
(b)   Cast the concrete beam and wait till the beam is hardened
(c)   After the beam is hardened, pull the tendons and tighten them at the end. Once the tendons are released, concrete beam will be compressed.

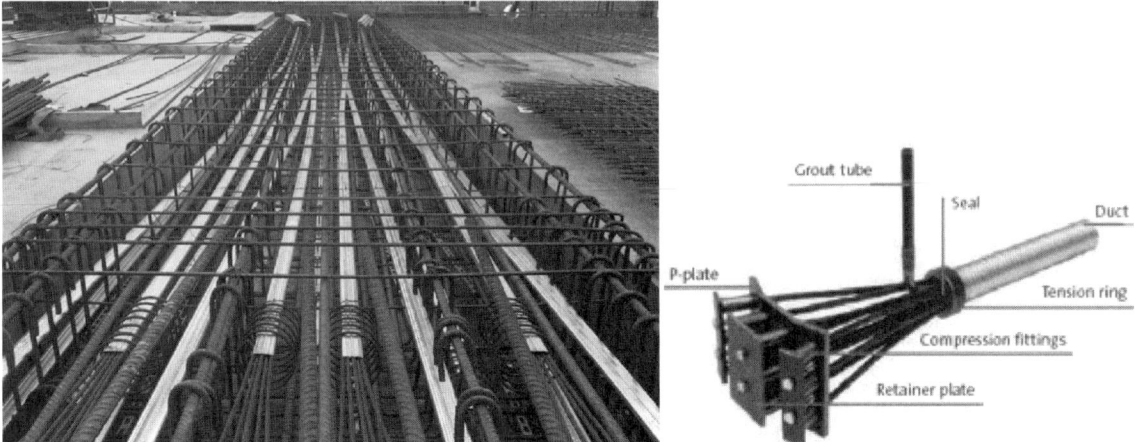

Left: Post tensioning tendons are inside ducts (Prior to casting the beam)
Right: Tendons and duct

Left photo shows post tensioning tendons and ducts prior to casting the beam. Right photo shows the tendons, duct and locking mechanism.

No employee (except those essential to the post-tensioning operations) shall be permitted to be behind the jack during tensioning operations. Signs and barriers shall be installed to maintain the post tensioning area free of visitors and other construction workers who are not involved in post tensioning activities.

<u>Concrete Buckets:</u>   Concrete buckets are widely used to pour concrete in high-rise buildings. As per OSHA, no employee shall be permitted to ride concrete buckets.

Concrete bucket

No employee shall be permitted to work under concrete buckets while buckets are being elevated or lowered into position.

<u>Power concrete trowels:</u>   Powered and rotating type concrete troweling machines shall be equipped with an automatic shutoff control switch that will automatically shut off the power whenever the hands of the operator are removed from the equipment handles.

<u>Formwork:</u>   Formwork drawings shall be available in the job site.

<u>Shoring and Reshoring:</u>   Shoring equipment shall be inspected immediately prior to, during, and immediately after concrete placement. Reshoring shall be erected, as the original forms and shores are removed, whenever the concrete is required to support loads in excess of its capacity.

<u>Removal of formwork:</u>   Many contractors would like to remove formwork early as possible to accelerate the project. However, as we all know wet concrete has less strength than hardened concrete. Seven-day-old concrete has approximately 65% of the 28-day strength. As per OSHA, removal of forms should be done as per plans and specifications. In case plans and specifications do not address this issue, the concrete should be tested as per ASTM method for strength. Forms shall be removed after required strength is achieved.

<u>Precast Concrete:</u>
Concrete structures can be built two ways.
- Cast in-situ
- Precast

Large majority of concrete structures built using cast in-situ method. This is the standard method where formwork and rebars are installed and concreted. In the case of precast concrete, concrete elements are manufactured in a plant and brought to the site and installed. It is fair to say that precast concrete is increasingly becoming popular.

Precast Concrete Elements

It is important to adequately support the precast units during construction. Precast units are held in place by fasteners and inserts. As per OSHA these fasteners that are used to stop precast elements from overturning shall be capable of supporting at least two times the maximum intended load.

On the other hand, lifting inserts shall be capable of supporting at least four times the maximum intended load.
No employee shall be permitted under precast concrete elements during construction except the workers who are involved with precast work.

<u>Masonry Construction</u>:   Masonry structures are very unstable before the mortar is hardened. Hence, OSHA recommends a limited access zone to be established. Only the workers who are actively engaged in masonry construction will be allowed in this zone. Limited access zone shall be equal to the height of the wall to be constructed plus four feet, and shall run the entire length of the wall. The limited access zone shall be established on the side of the wall which will be unscaffolded.

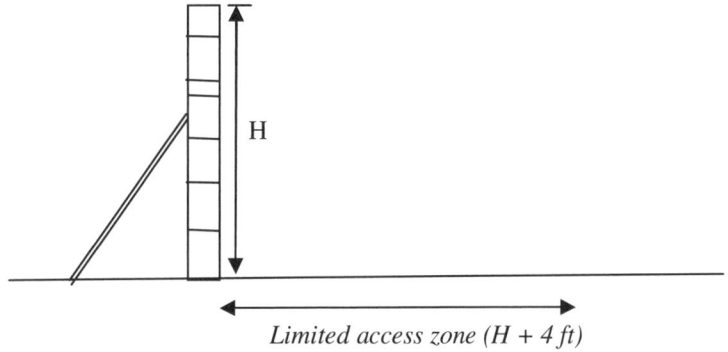

Limited access zone (H + 4 ft)

7.20   Steel Erection Safety: OSHA 1926 Subpart R:

<u>Iconic photographs from 1930s. Today such behavior would cost worker's job and a fine from OSHA</u>

Steel erection is considered to be one of the most dangerous activities.

<u>Start of Erection</u>: A steel erection contractor shall not erect steel unless he has received written notification that the concrete in the footings has attained at least 75 percent of the design strength or sufficient strength to support the loads imposed during steel erection.

Here it is important to note that one may not need to wait till 75% of the design strength. If the structural engineer decides that the footings have enough strength to hold the steel structure, then the erector can start work.

<u>Site Access</u>:   Steel erection requires bring in cranes, steel beams, columns, and various other deliveries. Adequate access roads, flagmen, fences and pedestrian control mechanisms should be in place prior to start of steel erection.

Site-specific Erection Plan: A site-specific erection plan shall be developed by a qualified person and be available at the work site.
Guidelines for establishing a site-specific erection plan are;

Preconstruction Meeting: Preconstruction meeting shall be held between the erector, fabricator and other parties involved before the start of steel erection.

Components of a site-specific erection plan:

Sequence: Sequence of erection activity shall be developed. What areas to be started first and what beams and columns to be erected. Typically the structure will be divided into portions and each portion and floors will be numbered. Then a sequence will be developed.

When developing the sequence of erection, one may need to consider following aspects;
- Material deliveries
- Material staging and storage
- Coordination with other trades
- Other construction activities such as excavation, concrete, fencing, retaining wall construction etc.

Crane Selection: Erection plan should address the process of crane selection. Site should be prepared for the crane. There need to be a path for overhead loads.

Fall Protection: Fall protection procedures should be established.

Certifications: All steel erecting workers shall be certified for their trade.

Emergency Action Plan: Procedure during an emergency shall be developed. Emergency action plan shall address issues such as access to first aid equipment, exit locations, address of the nearest hospital etc.

Rigging Safety: Rigging is the process of lifting and moving construction equipment and material. Cranes are widely used to lift and move in construction sites. As per OSHA, cranes should be visually inspected prior to every shift.

Items need to be observed in a crane prior to start of a shift;

- All control mechanisms for maladjustments;
- Safety devices, boom angle indicators, boom stops, boom kick out devices, anti-two block devices, and load moment indicators.
- Air, hydraulic, and other pressurized lines for deterioration or leakage.
- Hooks and latches for deformation, cracks, or wear
- Wire ropes for damage
- Electrical apparatus for malfunctioning
- Tires for proper inflation and condition
- Ground conditions around the hoisting equipment for proper support, including ground settling under and around outriggers, ground water accumulation, or similar conditions.
- The hoisting equipment for level position

OSHA states that the headache ball (also known as the overhaul ball) hook or load shall not be used to transport personnel. Headache ball is device that has a swivel inside. If the wire rope twists, swivel mechanism will make sure that the load will NOT twist. In the past headache ball and loads were used to transport people.

Left: Headache ball or the overhaul ball
Right: Riding the ball (This practice is against OSHA regulations).

As per OSHA, cranes may be used to hoist employees only if there is a personnel platform.

Working Under Loads: Sometimes it may be necessary to be under the load. As per OSHA, only the workers who are hooking, unhooking or connectors are allowed to be under the load.

Structural Stability:

During erection, erection crew will assemble steel beams and columns with few bolts. Bolting crew would then follow and complete all the bolts. Next comes the welding crew followed by the detailing crew. Hence, it is possible there are many floors that are not fully completed.

OSHA states the following;
 "*There shall be not more than eight stories between the erection floor and the upper-most permanent floor, except where the structural integrity is maintained as a result of the design*".

Let us see what this means. During erection temporary floor are erected for workers to work on. OSHA states that at any given time, when the erection is taking place at a certain floor, permanent floor shall be installed eight stories below.

As an example, let us say that erectors are erecting at floor 20 and they have installed temporary floors up to floor 16. On the other hand, they have only erected the permanent floors up to floor 10. In this case, the erector does not comply with the OSHA rule. To be in compliance, the erector should stop erecting and complete the permanent floors up to floor 12. OSHA also says;

"*At no time shall there be more than four floors or 48 feet (14.6 m), whichever is less, of unfinished bolting or welding above the foundation or uppermost permanently secured floor, except where the structural integrity is maintained as a result of the design*"

What does this OSHA rule means?
Let's say that the bolting crew is bolting an unfinished floor at floor 15. They have fully completed all the floors up to floor 10. In this case, the contractor is not in compliance. As per OSHA When a crew is working on the 15th floor, they should have finished the 11th floor completely.

Tripping hazards.   Shear connectors (such as headed steel studs, steel bars or steel lugs), reinforcing bars, deformed anchors or threaded studs shall not be attached to the top flanges of beams, joists or beam attachments so that they project vertically from or horizontally across the top flange of the member until after the metal decking, or other walking/working surface, has been installed.

<u>Shear Studs</u> (Shear studs should not be installed until the deck is installed)

<u>Covering roof and floor openings</u>*:*   Openings in decks are needed for ducts, elevator shafts and pipes. As per OSHA, openings shall have covers that are capable of supporting twice the weight of the employees, equipment and materials that may be imposed on the cover at any one time.

Also all covers shall be secured when installed to prevent accidental displacement by the wind.

All covers shall be painted with high-visibility paint or shall be marked with the word "HOLE" or "COVER" to provide warning of the hazard.

<u>Column Stability</u>:   As per OSHA, all columns shall be anchored by a minimum of 4 anchor bolts.

Each column anchor rod (anchor bolt) assembly, including the column-to-base plate weld and the column foundation, shall be designed to resist a minimum eccentric gravity load of 300 pounds located 18 inches from the extreme outer face of the column in each direction at the top of the column shaft.

Columns shall be set on level finished floors, pre-grouted leveling plates, leveling nuts, or shim packs which are adequate to transfer the construction loads.

All columns shall be evaluated by a competent person to determine whether guying or bracing is needed; if guying or bracing is needed, it shall be installed.

Anchor bolts shall not be repaired, replaced or field-modified without the approval of the project structural engineer of record.

Prior to the erection of a column, the controlling contractor shall provide written notification to the steel erector if there has been any repair, replacement or modification of the anchor rods (anchor bolts) of that column.

Anchor bolts in a column. As per OSHA at least 4 anchor bolts shall be installed at all times. Anchor bolts shall not be repaired or replaced without the approval of engineer on record. Additionally, general contractor shall notify the erector of any repairs to anchor bolts.

Other subparts of OSHA 1926 are;

Subpart S: Underground construction, caissons, cofferdams and compressed air
Subpart T: Demolition
Subpart U: Blasting
Subpart V: Power transmission
Subpart W: Overhead protection
Subpart X: Ladders

Guard Rails: Guardrails should be 39 to 45 inches in height.
Guardrails must be able to withstand a force of 200 lbs applied within 2 inches of the top of the guardrail.

CFR 1926 Subpart N: (Cranes, Derricks, Hoists, Elevators and Conveyors):

Cranes and derricks are needed to lift steel beams, equipment and material. Hoists are used to lift material and personnel. Conveyor belts are used for transporting material.

7.21 Safety Management: Safety management is an important aspect of any project. Some projects such as high-rise buildings, bridges may have more stringent safety management plans. Safety management plans should address following issues.

1) Safe operating procedures
2) Safety training of workers
3) Safety inspections and protocols

Some organizations such as oil refineries conduct exams for workers. OSHA approved courses are available for construction and hazardous waste management workers.

7.22   Safety Statistics:

Incidence rate means number of injuries or lost workdays per 100 full time workers per year. One worker works 40 hours a week. Assuming he works 50 weeks, one worker would work 2,000 hours per year. 100 workers would work 200,000 hours per year. (2,000 x 100).

$$\text{Incidence Rate} = N \times 200{,}000/EH$$

N = Number of injuries
EH = Number of work hours per year

Practice Problem: A company has 300 workers working 45 hours per week. The work crew works 50 weeks. There were 9 injuries. What is the incidence rate?

Solution: Total number of work hours (EH) = 300 x 45 x 50 = 675,000
Incidence Rate = N x 200,000/EH = 9 x 200,000/675,000 = 2.67

8.0 *Other Topics:*

8.1 Groundwater and well fields: Groundwater control is important during construction work.
Groundwater can be controlled by dewatering methods such as pumping, well fields and trenches discussed in chapter 3.3. Apart from dewatering, groundwater cutoff walls are also widely used.

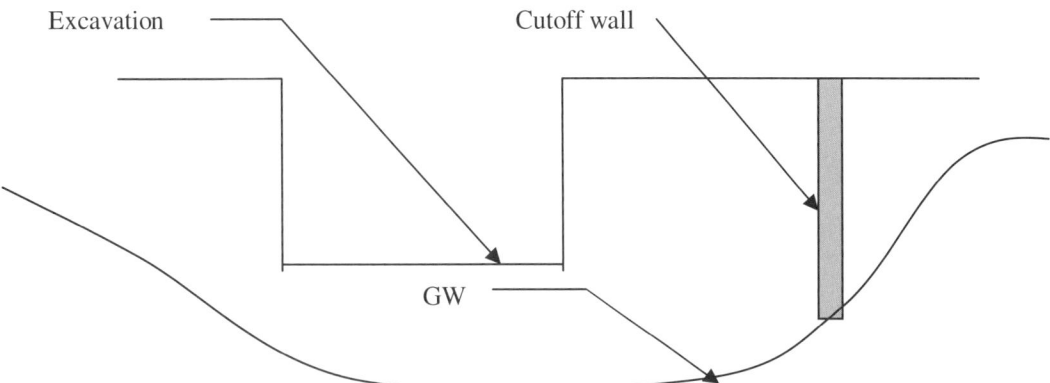

Groundwater cutoff walls can be constructed using slurry or jet grouting. In the case of slurry, a trench is excavated and filled with slurry. (Cement, sand and water mixture).

Confined Aquifers: Confined aquifers could be under pressure. In some cases, such aquifers would raise the water level to many feet.

Sigiri, An ancient rock fortress of Sri Lanka. Water for the pond on top of the rock comes from a confined aquifer.

8.2   Slurry Cutoff Wall Types:

Two types of slurry cutoff walls are popular.
Soil – Bentonite walls (SB walls)
Cement – Bentonite walls (CB walls)

<u>Soil Bentonite Walls (SB Walls)</u>:   A trench is excavated and filled with a mixture of soil, Bentonite powder and water. Normally soil coming out of the trench is used. Theoretically, any type of soil can be used. More fines (smaller than sieve #200) the soil have, the permeability would be lower. If clay is in a lumpy form, the permeability will not be low, even though clay particles are finer than sieve #200.

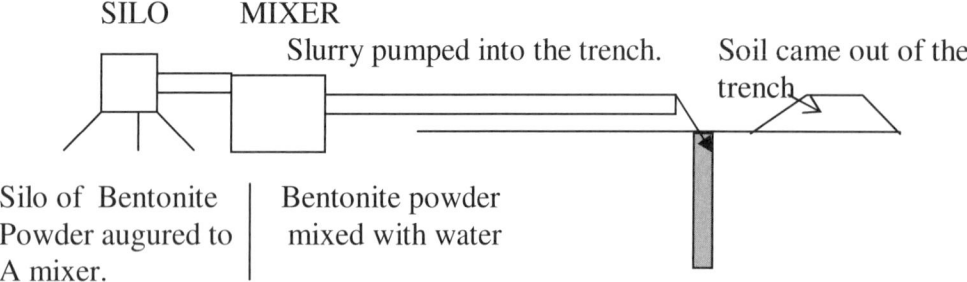

The slurry is pumped straight to the trench to keep the trench open. A backhoe would take the slurry out of the trench and mix with the soil that came out of the trench. The density of a soil Bentonite slurry is approximately 120 pcf. The cost of soil Bentonite walls is much less than sheetpile walls.

The permeability of soil Bentonite walls depends on the type of soil. If the soil contains more sandy material, then the permeability would be higher. Bulging of the trench due to high density of the soil Bentonite mixture is considered one of the problems of SB walls.

<u>Cement Bentonite Walls (CB Walls)</u>:   A slurry is produced using cement and Bentonite instead of soil and Bentonite. The slurry is pumped into the trench to harden. The density of a cement Bentonite slurry is approximately 70 pcf.   CB walls do not bulge as much as SB walls.

8.3   <u>Subsurface Exploration and Sampling</u>:
Prior to sub-surface exploration work, field visit is conducted.

<u>Field Visit</u>:   Field visits would provide information regarding surface topography, unsuitable areas, slopes, hillocks, nearby streams, soft grounds, fill areas, potential contaminated locations, existing utilities and possible obstructions for site investigation activities. Geotechnical engineer should bring a hand augur to the site so that he or she could observe the soil few feet below the surface.

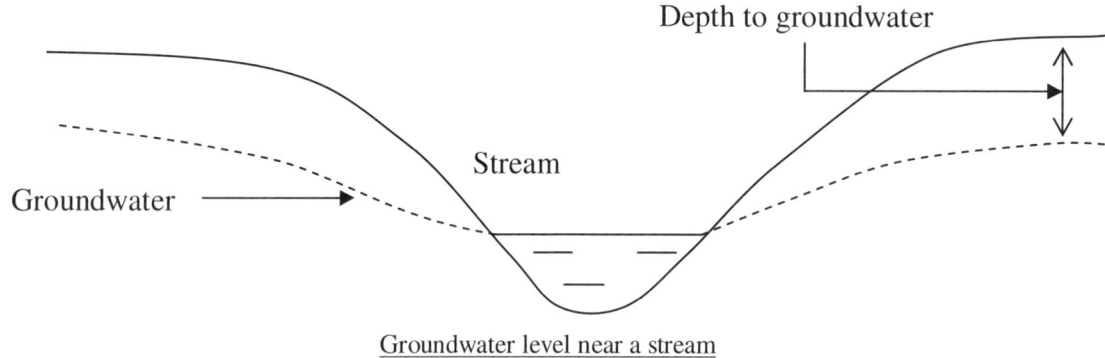

<u>Groundwater level near a stream</u>

Nearby streams could provide excellent information regarding depth to groundwater.

<u>Hand Auguring</u>: Hand augurs can be used to obtain soil samples to a depth of approximately 6 feet depending upon the soil conditions. Downward pressure (P) and a torque (T) are applied to the hand auger. Due to the torque and the downward pressure, the hand auger would penetrate into the ground. The process stops when the human strength is not capable of generating enough torque or pressure.

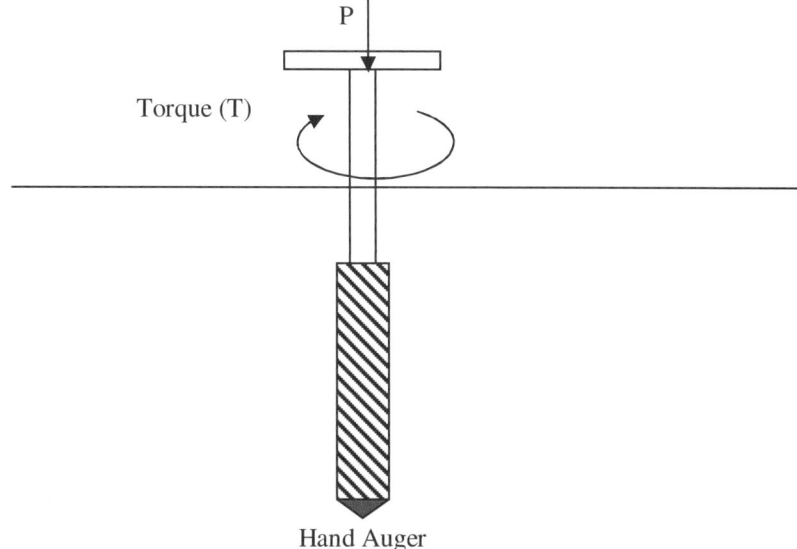

<u>Hand Auger</u>

Sloping Ground: Steep slopes in a site escalate the cost of construction because compacted fill is required. Such areas need to be noted for further investigation.

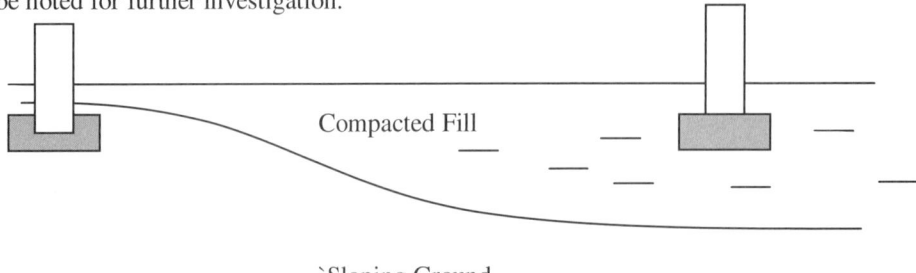

`Sloping Ground

Nearby Structures: Nearby structures could pose many problems for proposed projects. It is always good to identify these issues at the very beginning of a project. Distance to nearby buildings, schools, hospitals and apartment complexes should be noted. Pile driving may not be feasible if there is a hospital or school close to the proposed site.   In such situations, jacking of piles can be used to avoid noise.
 If the proposed building has a basement, underpinning of nearby buildings may be necessary.

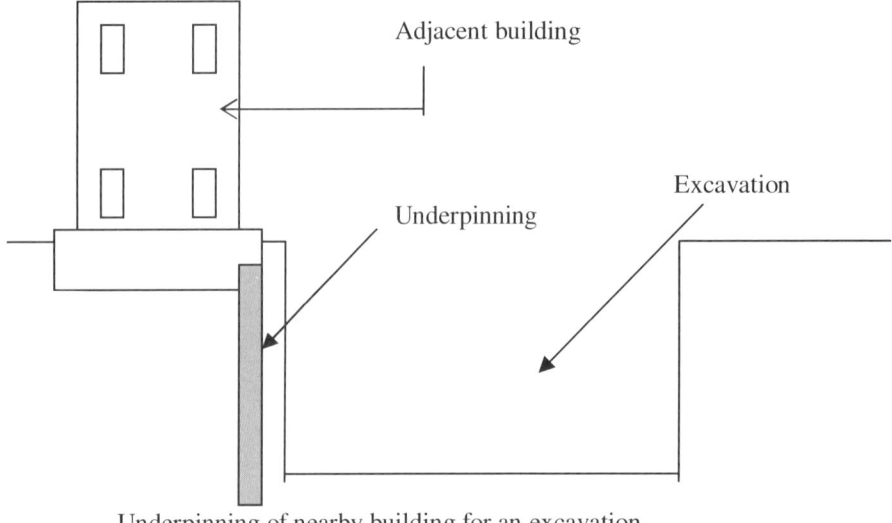

Underpinning of nearby building for an excavation

Contaminated Soils: Soil contamination is a very common problem in many urban sites. Contaminated soil will increase the cost of a project or in some cases could even kill a project entirely. Identifying contaminated soil areas at early stages of a project is desirable.

Underground Utilities: It is a common occurrence for drilling crews to accidentally puncture underground power cables or gas lines. Early identification of existing utilities is important. Electrical poles, electrical manhole locations, gas lines, water lines should be noted so that drilling can be done without breaking any utilities.
Existing utilities may have to be relocated or undisturbed during construction.
Existing manholes may indicate drainpipe locations.

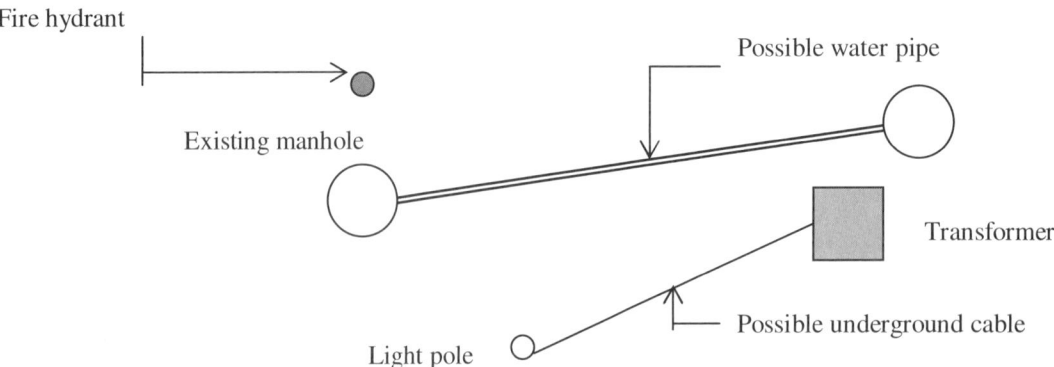

<u>Overhead Power Lines</u>:   Drill rigs need to keep a safe distance from overhead power lines during the site investigation phase. Overhead power line locations need to be noted during the field visit.

<u>Manmade Fill Areas</u>:   Most urban sites are affected by human activities. Man made fills may contain soils, bricks and various types of debris. It is possible to compact some manmade fills so that they could be used for foundations. This is not feasible when the fill material contain compressible soils, tires or rubber. Fill areas need to be further investigated during subsurface investigation phase of the project.

<u>Field Visit Checklist</u>:   Geotechnical engineer needs to pay attention to issues during field visit with regard to;
- Overall design of foundations
- Obstructions for the boring program - Overhead power lines, marsh areas, slopes, poor access may create obstacles for drill rigs
- Issues relating to construction of foundations   (High groundwater table, access, existing utilities)
- Identification of possible man made fill areas
- Nearby structures (Hospitals, schools, courthouses etc).

<u>Subsurface Investigation Phase</u>:   Soil strength characteristics of subsurface are obtained through a drilling program. In a nutshell, the geotechnical engineer needs following information for foundation design work.

<u>Soil strata identification   (Sand, clay, silt etc)</u>:
Depth and thickness of soil strata
Cohesion and friction angle (Two parameters responsible for soil strength)
Depth to groundwater

Subsurface soil strata information obtained using drilling.

Most common drilling techniques are;

- Auguring
- Mud rotary drilling

Auguring: In the case of auguring, the ground is penetrated using augers attached to a rig. The rig applies a torque and a downward pressure to augers. Same principal as in hand augers is used for the penetration into the ground.

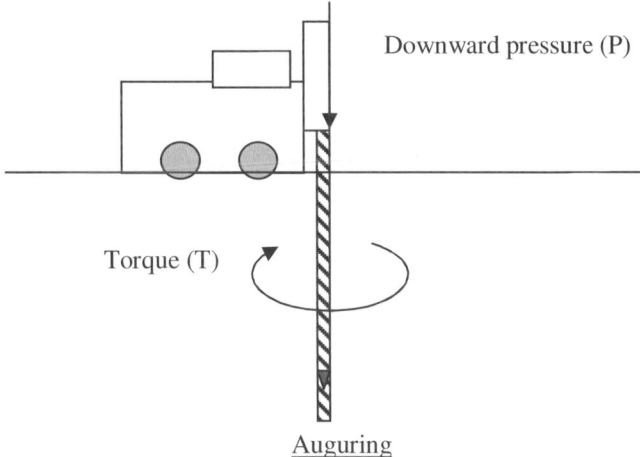

Auguring

Mud Rotary Drilling: In the case of mud rotary drilling, a drill bit known as roller bit is used for the penetration. Water is used to keep the roller bit cool so that it will not over heat and stop functioning. Usually drillers mix Bentonite slurry (also known as drilling mud) to the water to thicken the water. Main purpose of Bentonite slurry (also known as mud) is to keep the sidewalls from collapsing.

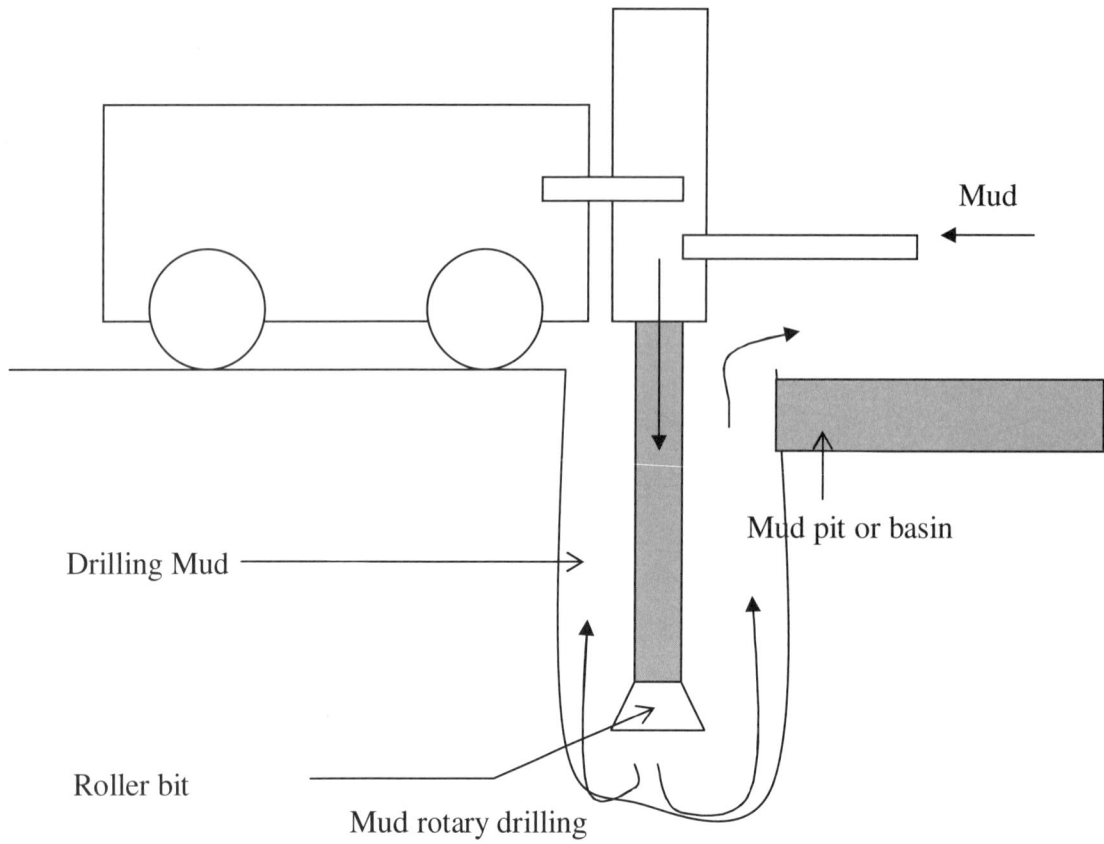

Mud

Drilling Mud

Mud pit or basin

Roller bit

Mud rotary drilling

Drilling mud goes through the rod and the roller bit and comes out from the bottom removing cuttings. The mud is captured in a basin and re-circulated.

Boring Program: Number of borings that need to be constructed may sometimes regulated by local codes. For an example, New York City building code requires one boring per each 2,500 square feet. It is important to conduct borings as close as possible to column locations and strip footing locations. In some cases, this may not be feasible.
Typically, borings are constructed 10 ft below the bottom level of the foundation.

Test Pits: In some situations, test pits would be more advantageous than borings. Test pits can provide information down to 15 ft below the surface. Unlike borings, soil can be visually observed from the sides of the test pit.
Soil Sampling:
Split spoon samples are obtained during boring construction. Split spoon samples are typically 2-inch diameter and have a length of 2 ft. Soil obtained from split spoon samples is adequate to conduct sieve analysis, soil identification and Atterberg limit tests. Consolidation tests, tri axial tests and unconfined compressive strength tests need large quantity of soil and in such situations, Shelby tubes are used. Shelby tubes have a larger diameter than split spoon samples.

Hand digging prior to drilling: Damage of utilities should be avoided during the boring program. Most utilities are rarely deeper than 6 feet. Hand digging the first 6 feet prior to drilling boreholes is found to be an effective way to avoid damaging utilities. During excavation activities, the backhoe operator is advised to be aware of utilities. The operator shall check for fill materials, since in many instances utilities are backfilled with select fill material. It is advisable to be cautious since there could be situations where utilities are buried with the same surrounding soil. In such cases, it is a good idea to have a second person present exclusively to watch the backhoe operation.

8.4   Shallow Foundations: Shallow foundations are the very first choice of foundation engineers.
They are primarily cheap and easy to construct compared to other alternatives such as pile foundations and mat foundations. Shallow foundations need to be designed for bearing capacity and excessive settlement. There are number of methods available to compute the bearing capacity of shallow foundations. Terzaghi bearing capacity equation, which was developed by Karl Terzaghi still widely used.

Buildings: Shallow foundations are widely used to support buildings. In some cases, doubt is cast upon the ability of shallow foundations to carry necessary loads due to loose soil underneath. In such situations, engineers use piles to support buildings. Shallow foundations are much more cost effective than piles. Building footings are subjected to wind, earthquake forces and bending moments. Hence, shallow foundations need to be designed to withstand all these forces.

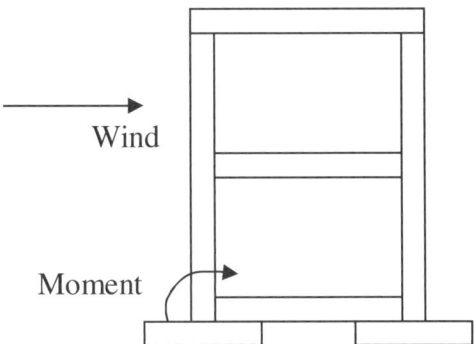

Building footings are subjected to both vertical and lateral forces

Buildings with Basements: Footings in buildings with basements need to be designed for lateral soil pressure as well. In most cases, the building frame has to support forces due to soil.

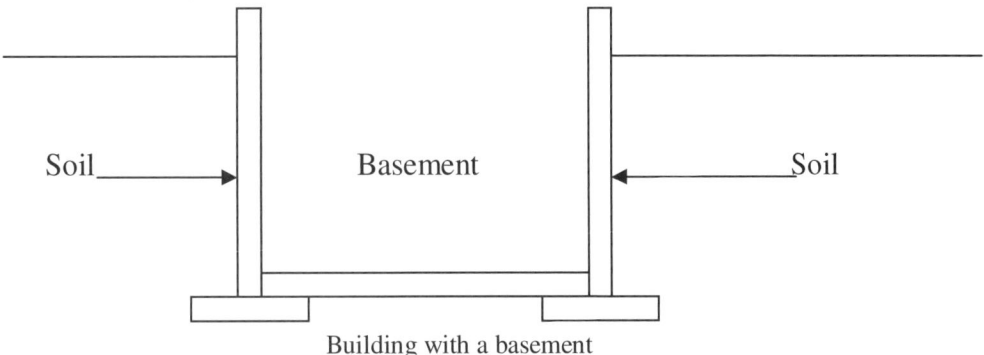

Building with a basement

Bridges: Bridges consist of abutments and piers. Due to large loads, many engineers prefer to use piles for bridge abutments and piers. Nevertheless, if the site conditions are suitable, shallow foundations can be used for bridges.

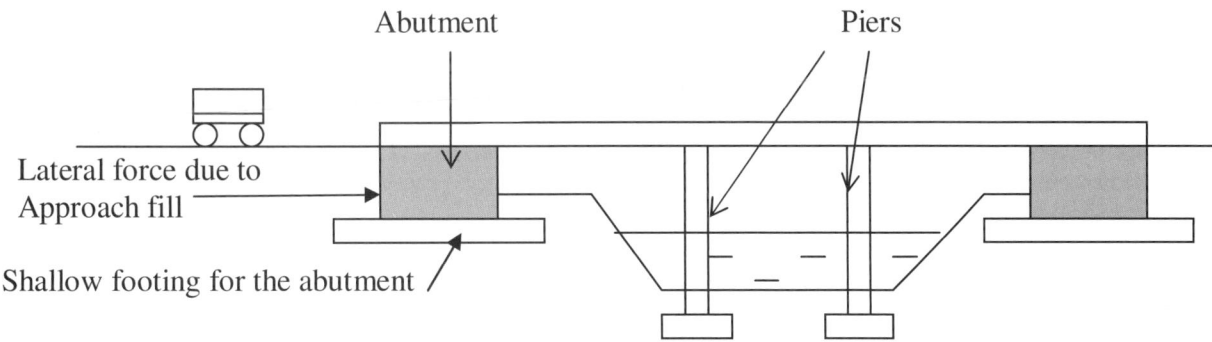

Lateral forces in a bridge abutment due to approach fill

Frost Depth: Shallow foundations need to be placed below frost level. During wintertime periods, soil at the surface will be frozen. During the summer, frozen soil will melt again. This freezing and thawing of soil generate a change in volume. If the footing is placed below the frost depth, freezing and melting of soil would generate upward forces and eventually cause cracking in concrete.

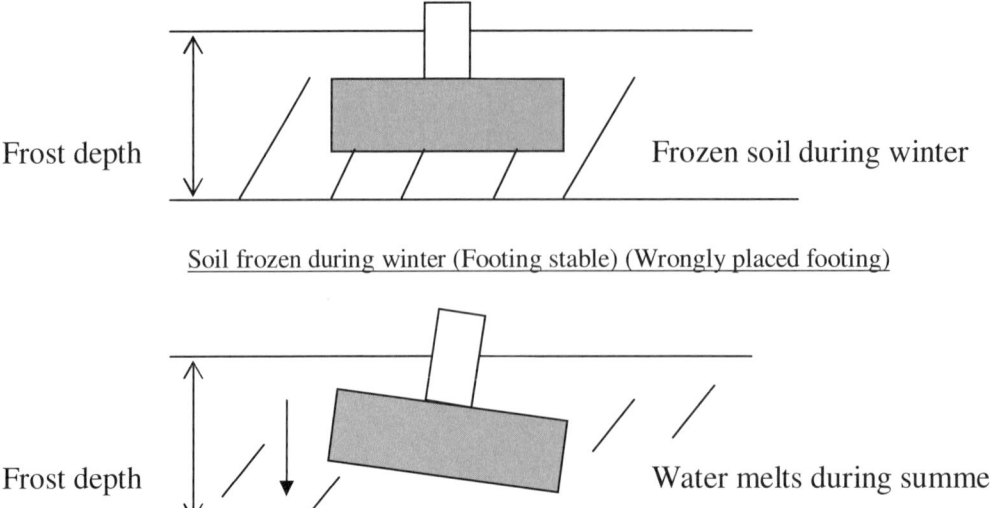

Soil frozen during winter (Footing stable) (Wrongly placed footing)

Soil during summer (water melts and footing unstable)

During summer, the water in soil will melt and the footing would settle. Due to this reason, all footings should be placed below the frost depth in that region.

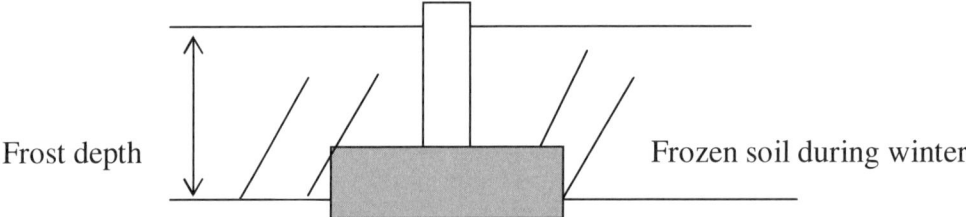

Footing placed below the frost depth (No effect due to soil freezing) (Correctly placed footing)

Frost depth is dependent upon the region. Frost depth in Siberia and some parts of Canada could be as high as 7 feet while in places like New York it is not more than 4 feet. Since there is no frost in tropical countries, frost depth is not an issue.

8.5   Raft (Mat) Foundations:
Rafts are known as mat foundations or floating foundations. Rafts are constructed in situations where shallow foundations are not feasible. The foundation engineer has the choice of picking either rafts or piles depending on the situation.

Slabs are needed for any building to function. Slab loads are carried to columns and taken to the ground. Column loads can be supported by column footings or piles. In the case of rafts, columns are placed on the raft. Hence, column load is absorbed by the raft and distributed evenly to the ground below.

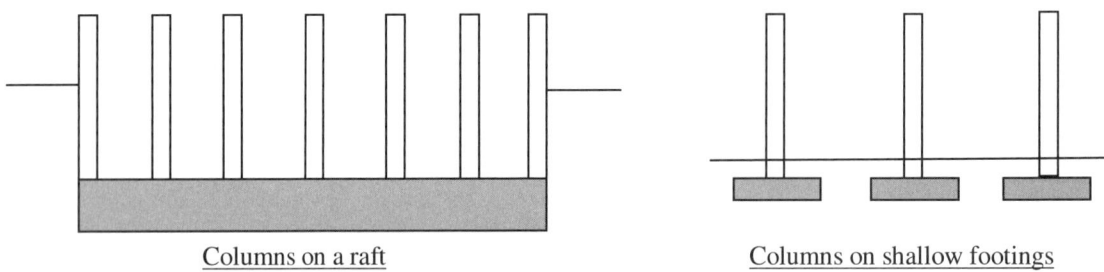

Columns on a raft   Columns on shallow footings

Rebars for a mat foundation

Raft should be thick enough and well reinforced to absorb column loads.

8.6   Earth Retaining Structures:

Introduction: `In many situations soil has to be retained. In roadwork, building basements, bridge abutments, and soil has to be retained. In such situations, earth retaining structures are built.

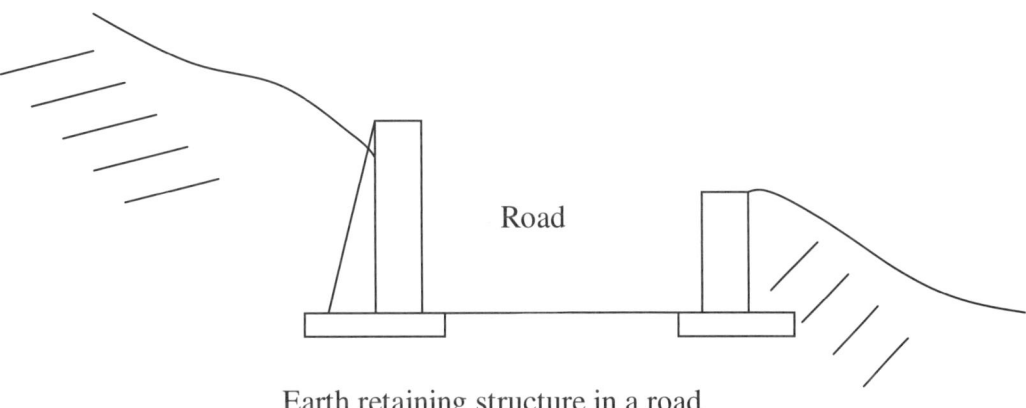

Earth retaining structure in a road

Gravity Walls: Earth retaining structures are important to hold back soil. Gravity retaining walls as the name indicates hold soil through its weight.

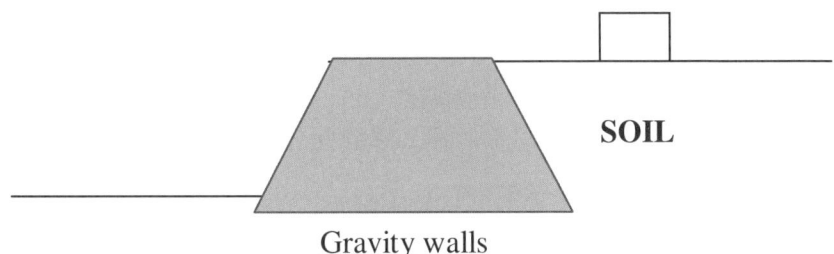

Gravity walls

In the case of gravity walls, pure weight of the retaining wall holds the soil. Gravity walls are made of rock, concrete and masonry. Presently concrete has been the most common material to construct gravity walls.

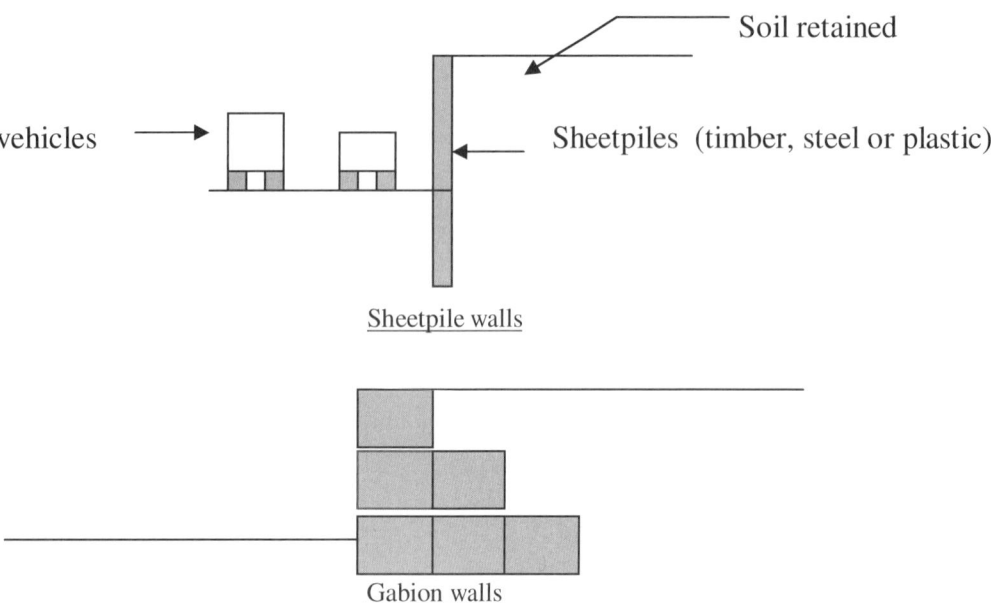

Sheetpile walls

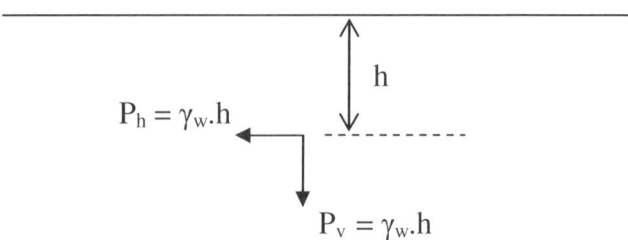

Gabion walls

Gabions are baskets filled with rocks. These rock baskets can be used to construct retaining walls. Gabion walls are designed as gravity walls. Easy drainage through gabions is a major advantage. Gabion walls are in most cases cheaper than concrete gravity walls.

Water Pressure Distribution: Before we discuss the horizontal force due to soil, let us look at the horizontal force due to water. Water pressure is same in all directions since it is a liquid.   Vertical stress at a point inside water is same as the horizontal stress at that location.

$P_h = \gamma_w.h$

$P_v = \gamma_w.h$

h

Pressure in water

$P_h = P_v = \gamma_w.h$

P_h = Horizontal pressure P_v = Vertical Pressure
γ_w = Density of water, (Usually taken as 62.4 pcf or 9.81 kN/m^3)
h = Depth to the point of interest

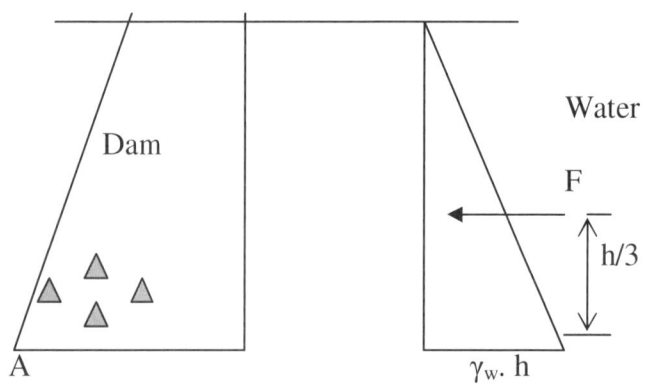

Dam

Water

F

h/3

A

$\gamma_w. h$

<u>Water pressure on a dam</u>

$F = \gamma_w . h . h/2 = \gamma_w . h^2/2$
The moment around point "A" can be computed.
Total Moment (M) = Force x Distance to the force
$M = \gamma_w . h^2/2 \; x \; h/3 = \gamma_w . h^3/6$
The resultant pressure of the triangle acts h/3 distance from the bottom.

Practice Problem: Find the horizontal force of the dam shown.

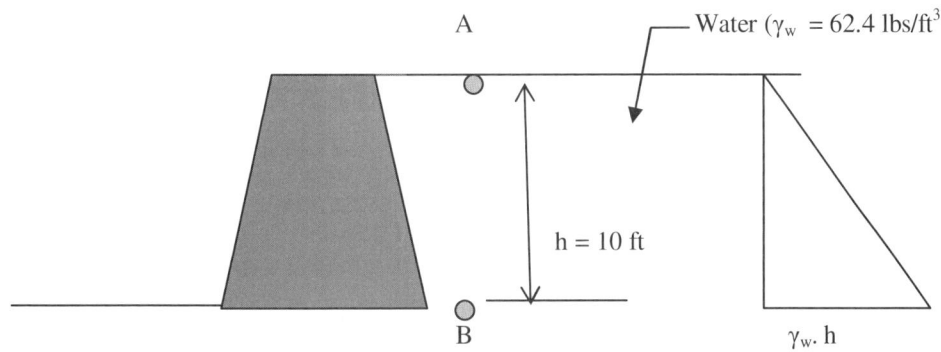

<u>Dam subjected to water pressure</u>

Solution: Find the pressure at point B.

$\gamma_w . h = 62.4 \; x \; 10 = 624 \; lbs/ft^2$.

Total pressure acting on the dam due to water is obtained by computing the area of the pressure triangle.

Total force acting on the dam = Area of the pressure triangle = ½ x 10 x 624 = 3,120 lbs

In the case of water, pressure in all directions is the same.

Computation of Horizontal Pressure in Soil:
Following equations are used to compute the horizontal pressure in soils.
Vertical pressure in soil = density of soil x depth = $\gamma \; x \; h$
(This is when there is no groundwater).
Horizontal pressure in soil = Lateral earth pressure coefficient (K) x density of soil x depth

$$= K \; x \; \gamma \; x \; h$$

K = Lateral earth pressure coefficient
There are three lateral earth pressure coefficients.
- Active earth pressure coefficient (K_a)
- Passive earth pressure coefficient (K_p)
- Lateral earth pressure coefficient at rest (K_0)

Active earth pressure coefficient (K_a):
Active earth pressure coefficient is used when the retaining wall has the freedom to move.

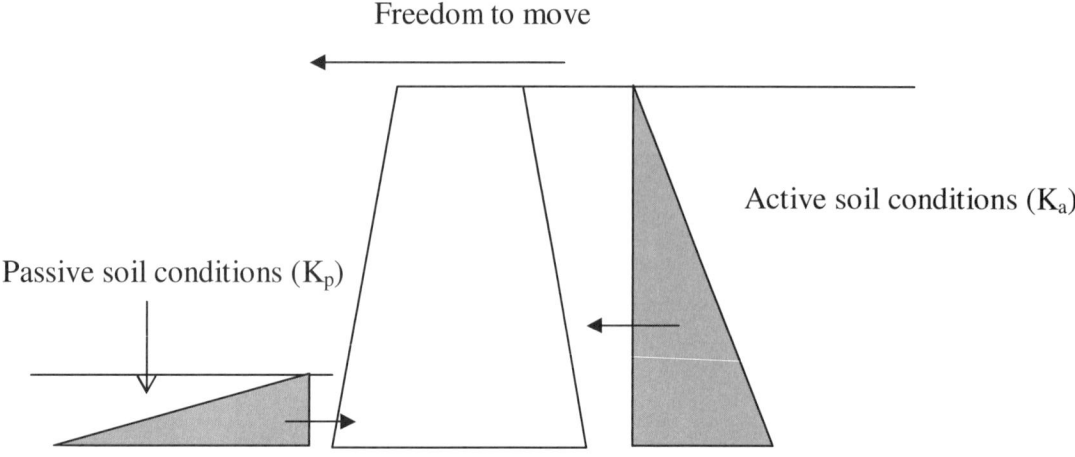

Freedom to move

Active soil conditions (K_a)

Passive soil conditions (K_p)

Freedom of movement of the retaining wall

The retaining wall is free to move to the left. When slight movement in the retaining wall occurs, pressure on the right hand side will be reduced. On the other hand, pressure on the left hand side will be increased.

Hence, we can see that K_a is smaller than K_p.
Following equation is used to compute K_a and K_p.

$$K_a = \tan^2(45 - \phi/2)$$
$$K_p = \tan^2(45 + \phi/2)$$

Many designers do not consider the passive soil conditions in front of the retaining walls. Some codes require that erosion protection to be provided when passive earth pressure in front of a retaining wall is considered for the design.

Earth pressure coefficient at rest (K_0):   Following equation is used to compute K_0.

$$K_0 = 1 - \sin \varphi$$

Earth pressure coefficient at rest is used for cantilever retaining walls.

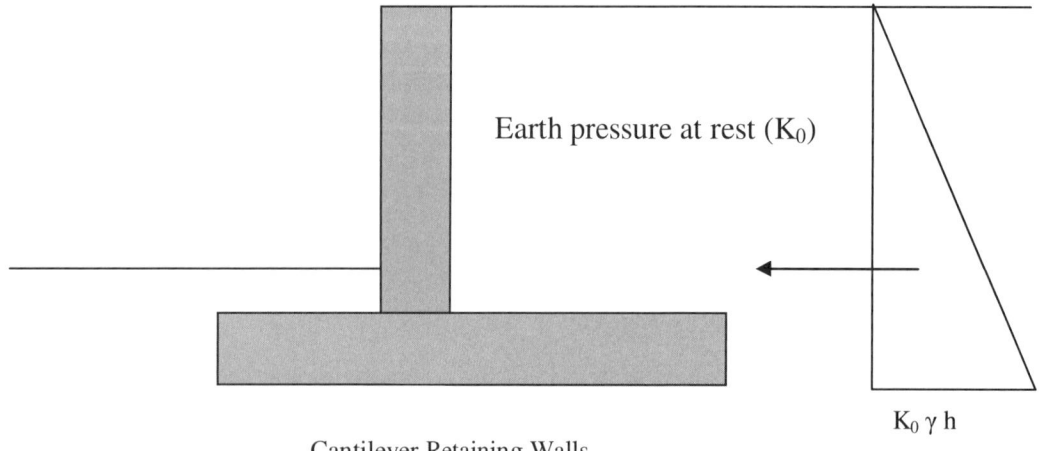

Earth pressure at rest (K_0)

$K_0 \, \gamma \, h$

Cantilever Retaining Walls

In a cantilever retaining wall, it is difficult to say whether the wall move enough to create active conditions behind the wall. Hence, earth pressure coefficient at rest (K_0) is used for cantilever retaining walls. K_0 is larger than K_a.
$$K_a \; < \; K_0 \; < \; K_p$$

Gravity Retaining Walls: (Sand Backfill):   In gravity walls, soil pressure is restrained by the weight of the retaining wall.

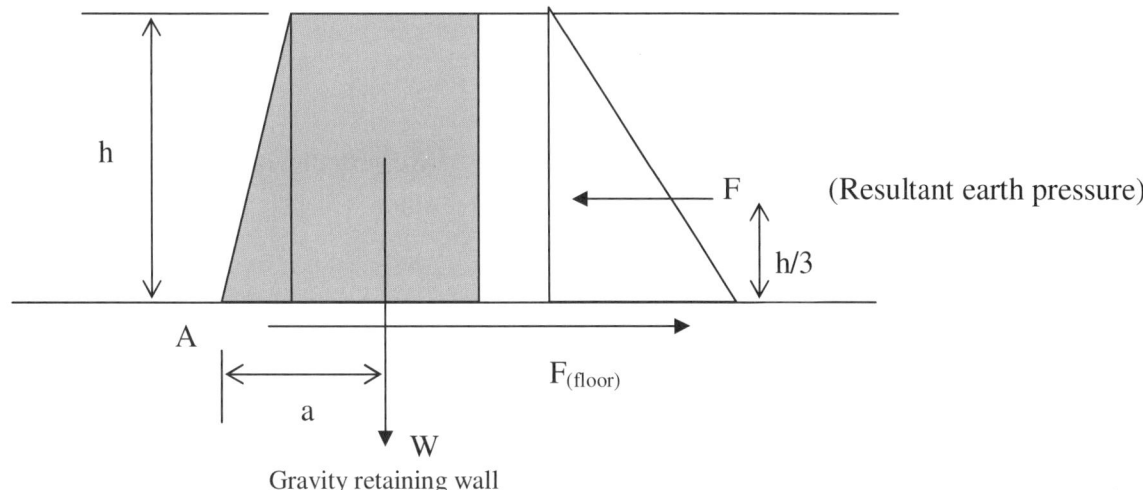

Gravity retaining wall

In the above figure, simple gravity retaining wall is shown. Modern gravity retaining walls are made of concrete. The retaining wall can fail in three different ways.

1) The retaining wall can slide - Sliding failure
2) The retaining wall can overturn around the toe (point A)
3) Bearing failure of the foundation

Resistance against Sliding Failure:

For stability; $F_{(floor)} > F$

F = Resultant earth pressure
$F_{(floor)}$ = Friction between concrete and soil at the bottom face
$F_{(floor)} = \tan \delta \times W$
W = Weight of the retaining wall
δ = Friction angle between concrete and soil.

Factor of safety against sliding failure = $F_{(floor)}/F$

Resistance against Overturning: The retaining wall can overturn around the toe. (point A).

Overturning moment = $F \times h/3$
Resisting moment = $W \times a$

Factor of safety against overturning = Resisting moment/Overturning moment = =3Wa/Fh

How to find the resultant earth pressure?
Earth pressure at any given point is given by $K_a \gamma h$

K_a = Active earth pressure coefficient = $\tan^2 (45 - \varphi/2)$
γ = Density of soil h = Height of the soil

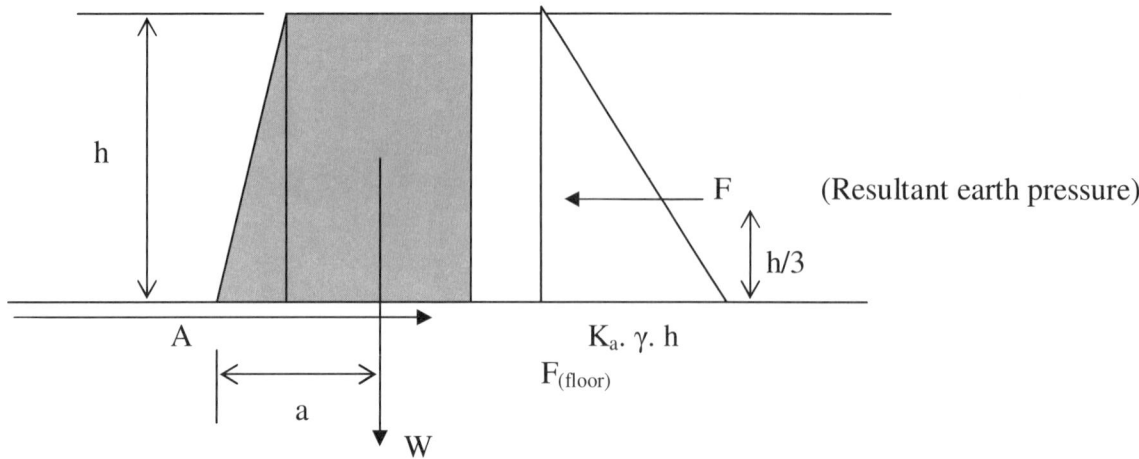

Gravity retaining wall with soil pressure

Resultant earth pressure (F) = Area of the pressure triangle
$$= K_a \gamma h \times (h/2)$$
$$= K_a \gamma h^2/2$$

The resultant earth pressure acts at the center of gravity of the pressure triangle, h/3 above the bottom.
Total Moment (M) around point A = Force (F) x distance to the force
$$M = (K_a \cdot \gamma \cdot h^2/2) \times h/3 = K_a \cdot \gamma \cdot h^3/6$$

Practice Problem: (Gravity retaining wall with sand backfill – No groundwater, fps units)
Find the factor of safety for the retaining wall shown. Height of the retaining wall (H = 10 ft), weight of the retaining wall 7 kip for 1 ft length of the wall. Vertical through center of gravity is at a distance of 5ft from the toe (point X). Friction angle of the soil backfill is 30^0. The soil backfill is mainly consists of sandy soils. Density of the soil is 110 pcf. Resultant earth pressure force acts H/3 distance from the bottom of the wall. Friction angle between soil and earth at the bottom of the retaining wall was found to be 20^0.

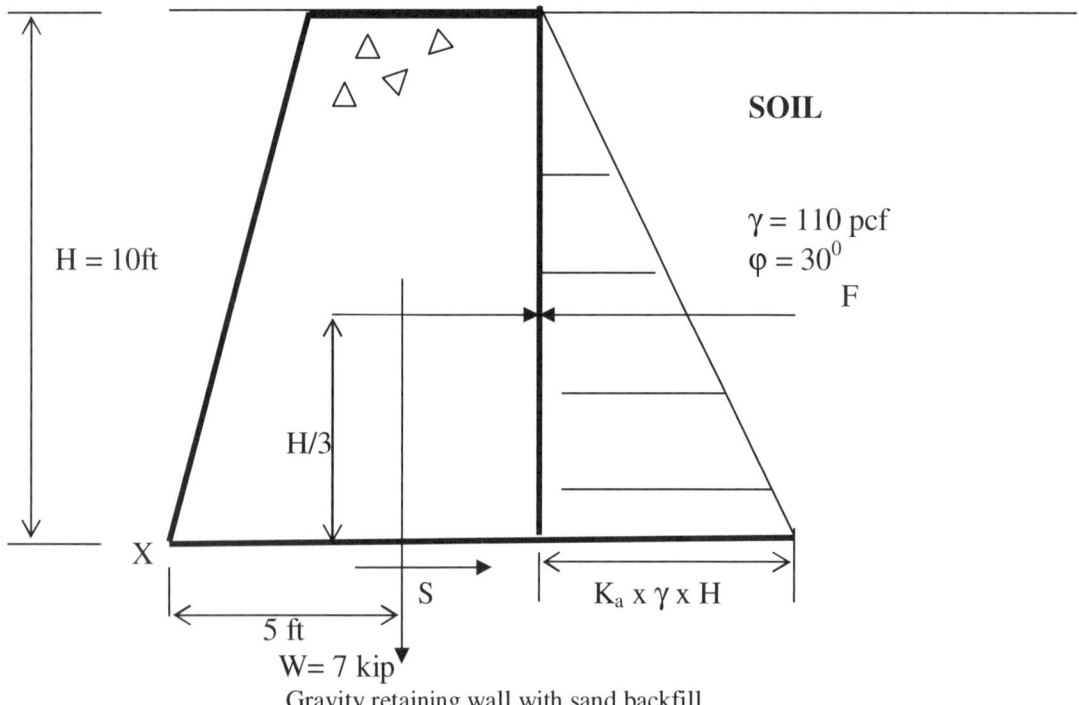

Gravity retaining wall with sand backfill

Solution:
STEP 1: Find the resultant earth pressure
Due to soil pressure gravity wall will slightly move. Hence, K_a is used to compute the lateral earth pressure.
$K_a = \tan^2(45 - \varphi/2) = \tan^2(45 - 30/2)$
$K_a = \tan^2 (30) = 0.33$
Earth pressure at the bottom of the base = $K_a \gamma H = 0.33 \times 110 \times 10 = 363$ psf.
Resultant earth pressure (F) = Area of the pressure triangle = $363 \times 10/2$
           = 1,815 lbs per 1 ft length of the wall = 1.815 kip per 1 ft length of the wall
STEP 2: Find the resistance against sliding at the base (S)
S = Weight of the wall x tan (δ)
δ = Friction angle between concrete and soil at the bottom of the retaining wall
S = W x tan (δ) = 7 x tan (20^0) = 7 x 0.36397 = 2.548 kip per 1 ft length of the wall
Weight of the retaining wall is given to be 7 kip per 1 ft length of the wall.
Factor of safety against sliding = S/F = 2.548/1.815 = 1.4
Factor of safety of 2.5 or more is desirable. Hence, it is necessary to increase the weight of the wall.

STEP 3: Find the resistance against overturning (O)

Overturning will occur around point "X" of the retaining wall.
Resistance to overturning is provided by the weight of the retaining wall.

Overturning moment = F x H/3 = 1.815 x 10/3 kip. ft
                        = 6.05 kip. ft (per 1 ft. length of the wall)
Resisting moment = W x a = 7 x 5 = 35 kip. ft (per 1 ft length of the wall)
Factor of safety against overturning = Resisting moment/Overturning moment
                        = 35/6.05 = 5.78
Similar problem in metric units is conducted below.

Lateral Earth Pressure Coefficient for Clayey Soils (Active Condition):

Earth pressure in clay soils is different than sandy soils. In the case of clay soils lateral earth pressure is given by the following equation.
Lateral earth pressure = $\gamma h - 2c$
"c" is cohesion and "γ" is the density of the clay. When clay backfill is used, portion of the clay layer will crack. The thickness of the cracked zone is given by $2.c/\gamma$.

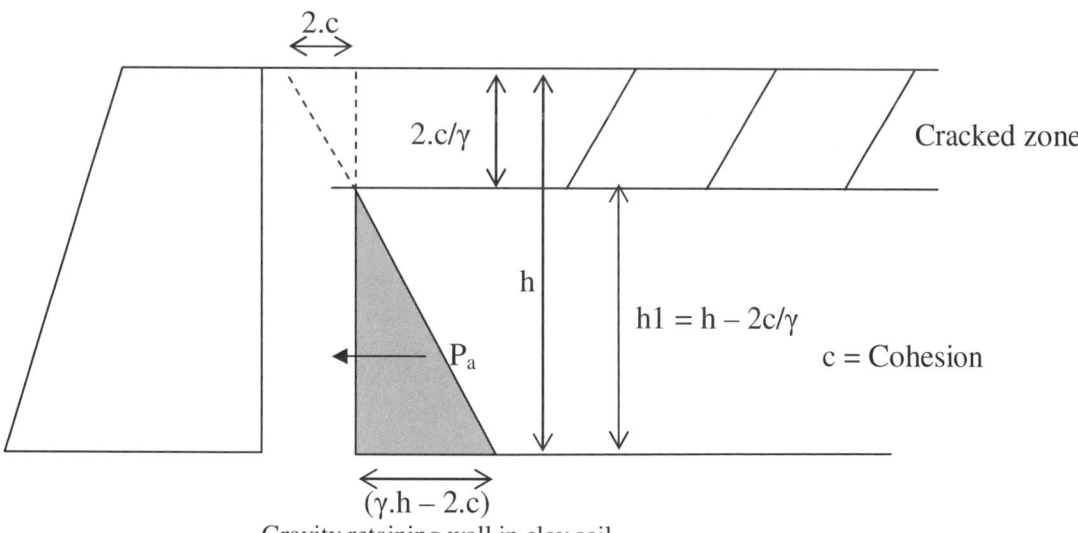

Gravity retaining wall in clay soil

No active pressure is generated within the cracked zone.
Force (P) = Area of the shaded portion of the triangle.

$P_a = (\gamma.h - 2.c) \times h1/2$

Since $h1 = h - 2.c/\gamma$

$P_a = (\gamma.h - 2.c) \times (h - 2.c/\gamma)/2$

Usually, cracked zone will get filled with water. Hence pressure due to water also needs to be accounted for.

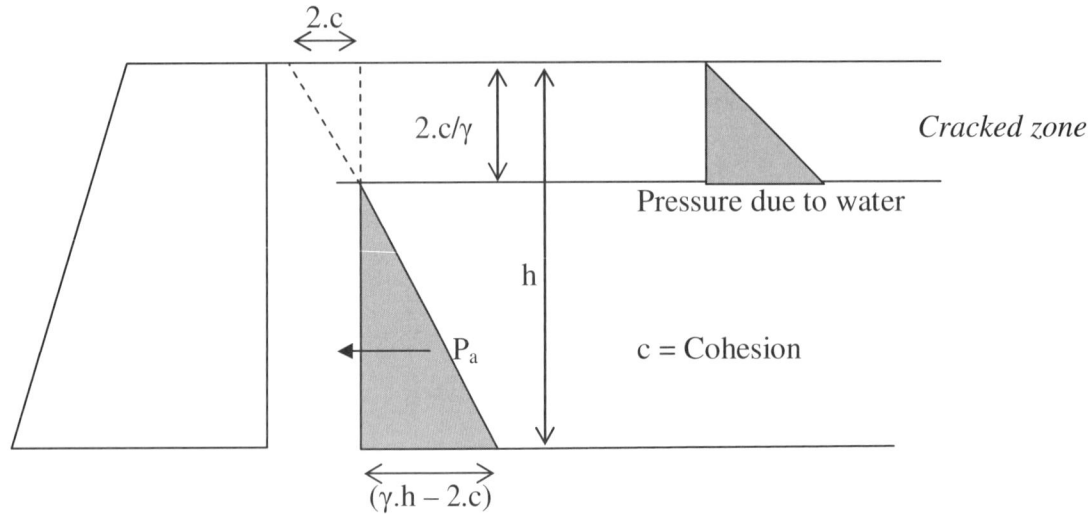

Forces due to clay soil

Practice Problem 7.5:   (Gravity retaining wall with clay backfill – fps units)

Find the factor of safety of the retaining wall shown against sliding failure and overturning. Cohesion of the clay backfill is 400 psf. Density of soil is $\gamma = 110$ pcf. Assume cracked zone is **not** filled with water. Weight of the retaining wall is 5,000 lbs per 1 foot run of the retaining wall. The weight is acting 1.1 ft from the toe of the retaining wall (X) as shown. Height of the retaining wall is 12 ft. Friction angle between base of the retaining wall and soil is 25^0. Assume tension cracks are not filled with water.

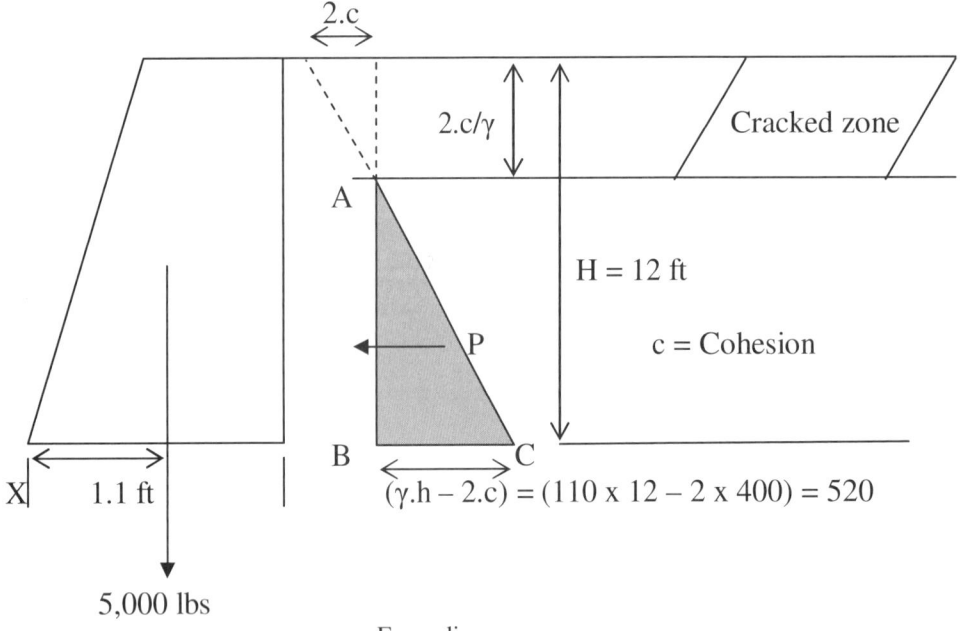

Force diagram

Solution:

STEP 1: Find the thickness of the cracked zone:

Thickness of the cracked zone = $2. c/\gamma = 2 \times 400/110 = 7.27$ ft

Length of AB = 12 – 7.27 = 4.73 ft

STEP 2: Find the pressure at the bottom:
Pressure at "B" = (γ.h – 2.c) = (110 x 12 – 2 x 400) = 520

STEP 3:   Find the lateral forces acting on the wall.
Lateral forces acting on the wall = Area of triangle ABC
Note: In this case it is assumed that the cracked zone is not filled with water.
Total horizontal force = Area of triangle ABC = ½ x 520 x AB = ½ x 520 x 4.73 = 1,230 lbs

STEP 4: Find the resistance to sliding:
Resistance to sliding = Friction angle x Weight of the retaining wall
Resistance to sliding = tan 25^0 x 5,000 lbs = 0.466 x 5,000 = 2,330lbs.
Factor of safety against sliding = Resistance to sliding/ Total horizontal force= 2,330/1,230 = 1.89
Usually, factor of safety of 2.5 is desired. Hence increase the weight of the retaining wall.

STEP 5:   Overturning Moment:
Resultant of the triangle ABC acts 1/3 distance from the base.
Distance to the resulting force = 4.73/3 = 1.58 ft
Overturning moment is obtained by taking moments around point "X"
Overturning moment = Force x moment arm = 1,230 x 1.58 = 1,943.4 lbs. ft
Resistance to overturning is provided by the weight of the retaining wall.
Resistance to overturning = 5,000 x 1.1 = 5,500 lbs. ft

Factor of safety against overturning = 5500/1943.4 = 2.83
Resistance against overturning is sufficient.

Gabion Walls: Gabion walls are also a type of gravity walls. Computations involved in Gabion walls are no different than regular gravity earth retaining walls. Earth pressure forces are computed as usual and stability of the wall with respect to rotation and sliding is computed. Gabion baskets are manufactured in different sizes. Typical basket is approximately 3 feet in size. Smaller baskets are easier to handle. At the same time smaller baskets would have more seems to be connected. Not all Gabion baskets are perfect cubes. Some baskets are made with elongated shapes.

Gabion basket

Gabion baskets are connected to build a wall.

Mechanically Stabilized Earth Walls: Mechanically stabilized earth walls are also known as reinforced earth walls are increasingly becoming popular due to ease of construction and low cost. Reinforced earth walls are becoming increasingly popular. Reinforced earth walls are constructed by holding the lateral earth pressure through metal strips.

Facing units

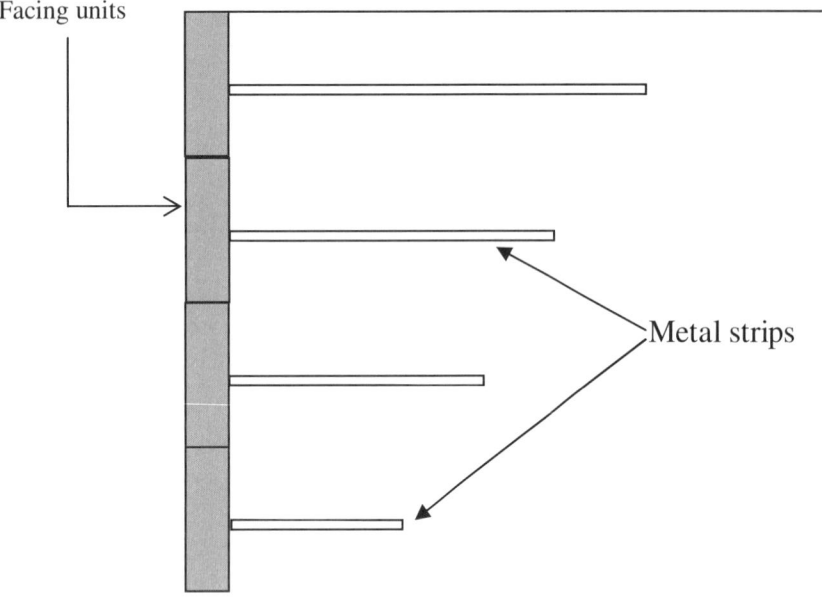

Metal strips

Reinforced Earth Wall

Soil pressure in reinforced earth walls are resisted by metal strips.

Lateral soil force (H)

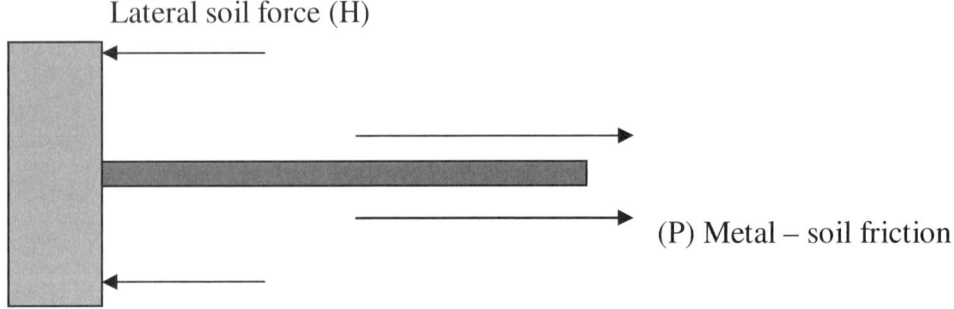

(P) Metal – soil friction

Forces acting on facing units and metal strips

Following equations can be developed to compute the lateral earth force acting on a facing unit.

Equations to Compute the Horizontal Force on the Facing Unit (H):

σ_v' = Vertical effective stress
σ_h' = K_a x σ_v' = Horizontal stress
K_a = Lateral earth pressure coefficient = $\tan^2(45 - \varphi/2)$

Lateral soil pressure (H) = $(K_a$ x $\sigma_v')$ x Area of the facing unit

Equations to Compute the Metal – Soil Friction (P):

The metal soil friction depends on the vertical effective stress acting on the strip, area of the metal strip and the friction angle between metal and soil.

Metal – Soil Friction (P) = 2 x $(\sigma_v'$ x $\tan \delta)$ x Area of the strip
δ = Friction angle between metal and soil
σ_v' = Vertical effective stress
The quantity is multiplied by 2, since there are two surfaces, top and bottom in the metal strip.
Factor of safety (FOS) = P/H

Construction of metal strips (Source: California DOT)

Practice Problem: Find the length of metal strips A, B and C in the figure below. The density (γ) of soil is found to be 17.5 kN/m3 and the friction angle (φ) of soil is 250. Facing units are 1m x 1m and the metal strips are 0.5 m wide. Find the length of the metal strips if required factor of safety is 2.5. Metal - soil friction angle (δ) is 200.

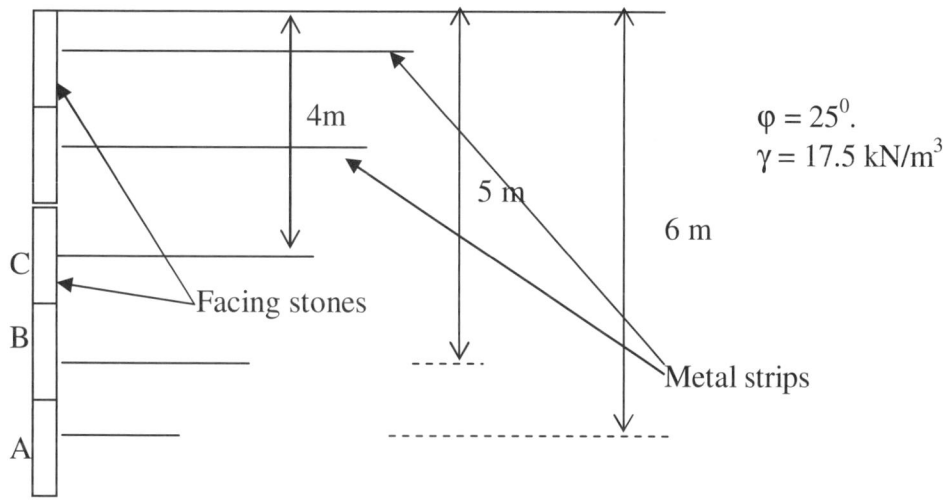

$\varphi = 25^0$.
$\gamma = 17.5$ kN/m^3

Reinforcing strips

Solution:

STEP 1: Find the vertical effective stress at the center of the facing unit

Facing unit "A"
Find the vertical effective stress at the center of the facing unit (σ_v');
$$\sigma_v' = \gamma \times h = 17.5 \times 6 \text{ kN/m}^2 = 105 \text{ kN/m}^2$$

Find the lateral earth pressure coefficient (K_a);
$$K_a = \tan^2 (45 - \varphi/2)$$
$$= \tan^2 (45 - 25/2) = 0.406$$

Find the horizontal stress at the center of the facing unit (σ_h')

$$\sigma_h' = K_a \times \sigma_v'$$
$$= 0.406 \times 105 \text{ kN/m}^2 = 42.6 \text{ kN/m}^2.$$

Area of the facing unit "A" = Width x length = 1 x 1 m2. = 1 m2.
Total horizontal force on the facing unit = Horizontal stress x Area of the facing unit
                = 42.6 kN
STEP 2: Find the metal – soil friction in facing unit "A;
Metal – Soil Friction (P) = 2 x (σv' x tan δ) x Area of the strip
                = 2 x 105 x tan 20 x 0.5 L   = 38.2 L

Required factor of safety (FOS) = 2.5
FOS = Metal soil friction/Horizontal force on the facing unit
2.5 = 38.2L/42.6
L = 2.79 m   (L = length of the facing unit)

The length of the metal strip within the active soil zone does not contribute to the strength. Hence the metal strip should extend 2.79 m beyond the active failure zone.

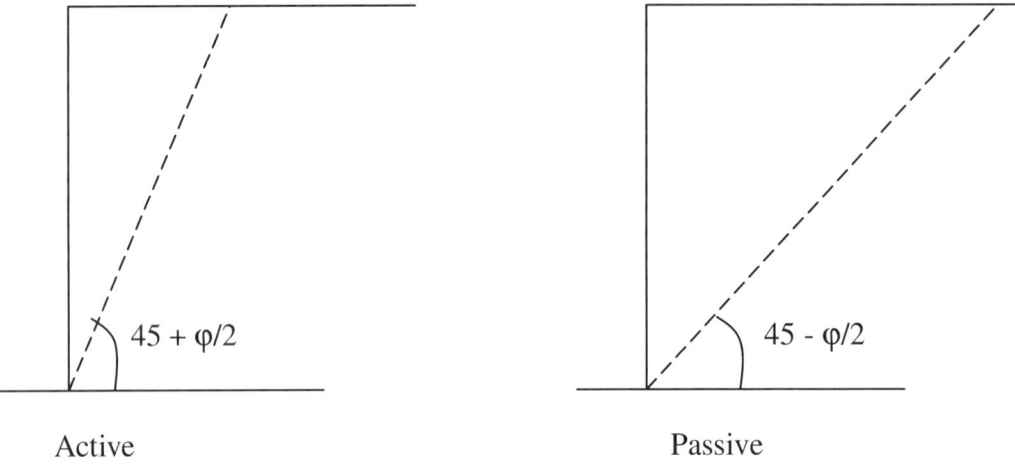

45 + ϕ/2

45 - ϕ/2

Active   Passive

Active and passive failure planes

Active failure plane

4m

5 m

6 m

$\phi = 25^0$.
$\gamma = 17.5$ kN/m^3

C

B

A   45 + ϕ/2

Metal strips and active failure plane

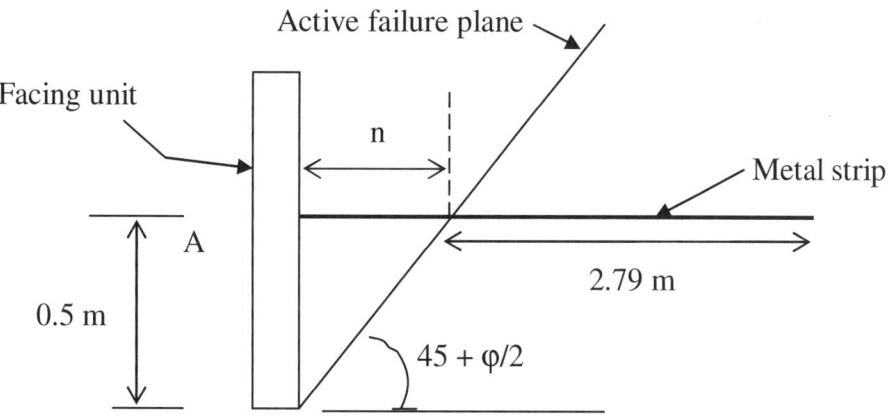

Facing unit "A" and the active failure plane

Above figure shows the facing unit "A" and the active failure plane.

Distance "n" can be computed since the distance to the center of the facing unit is 0.5 m.
n = 0.5 x tan (45 - φ/2)   (From trigonometry)
n = 0.5 x tan (45 – 25/2) = 0.32 m

Total required length of the strip = 0.32 + 2.79 = 3.11 m

The metal strip has to extend beyond 2.79 m beyond the failure plane to generate soil resistance.

Soil and Rock Anchors:

Soil Anchors: Soil anchors are mainly of two types.
Mechanical soil anchors
Grouted soil anchors

Mechanical soil anchors use mechanical methods to anchor to the surrounding media. Grouted soil anchors use the adhesive properties of grout to adhere to the surrounding media.

Mechanical Soil Anchors: Mechanical soil anchors are installed in retaining walls, shallow foundations and slabs that are subjected to uplift. End of soil anchor consist an anchor mechanism. The soil anchor is drilled into the soil. Then the anchor is pulled to activate the anchor mechanism.

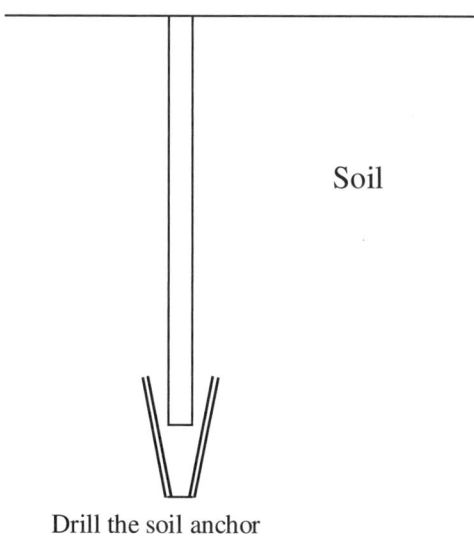

Drill the soil anchor

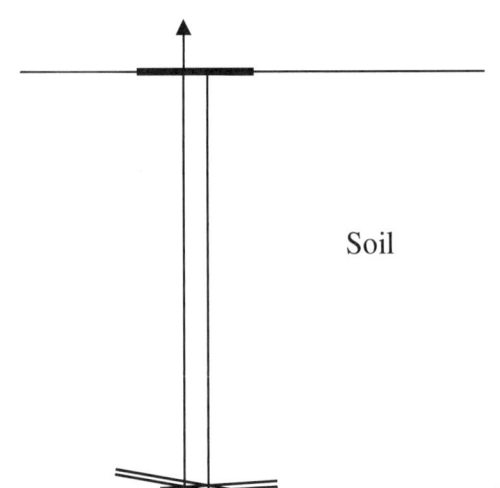

Soil

<u>Pull the anchor to activate the anchor mechanism</u>.

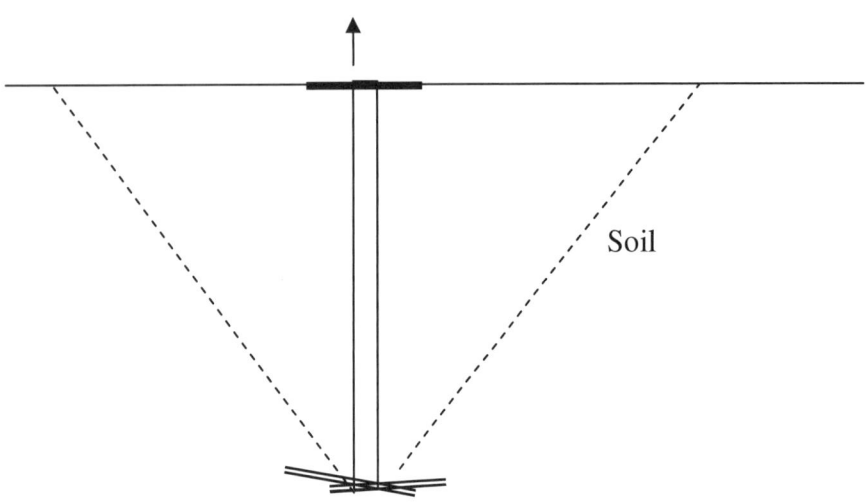

Soil

Failure cone for mechanical soil anchors

Grouted Soil Anchors:

Principal of grouted soil anchors is same as the grouted rock anchors. Grouted soil anchors could be non-stressed or pre-stressed.

Installation procedure for non-stressed grouted soil anchors is given below.

Step 1:	Drill a hole
Step 2:	Insert the soil anchor
Step 3:	Grout the hole

Installation procedure for pre-stressed grouted soil anchors is slightly different.

Step 1:	Drill a hole
Step 2:	Insert the soil anchor
Step 3:	Grout the desired length of the hole
Step 4:	Wait till the grout is set
Step 5:	Apply the desired pre-stress
Step 6:	Grout the rest of the hole

Auguring for horizontal soil anchors   *Source: California DOT*

8.7   Rock Anchors:

Rock bolts, dowels and cable bolts are some of the names used for rock anchors. Nomenclature changes from area to area. Generally, rock anchors (also known as rock bolts) can be non stressed or pre-stressed. Non stressed anchors are usually known as rock dowels. When there is a slight movement in the rock mass, rock dowels get tensioned and provide a resisting force.

Cable bolts are basically a group of wires used to create a cable. Cable bolts are used for high capacity applications. Rock anchors are used for shallow foundations, retaining walls, bridges and tunnels.

Basic types of rock anchors:
1)   Mechanical rock anchors or rock bolts (Non-stressed or pre-stressed)
2)   Grouted (non stressed or pre-stressed)
3)   Resin anchors
4)   Non stressed rock anchors are also known as rock dowels.

Applications:

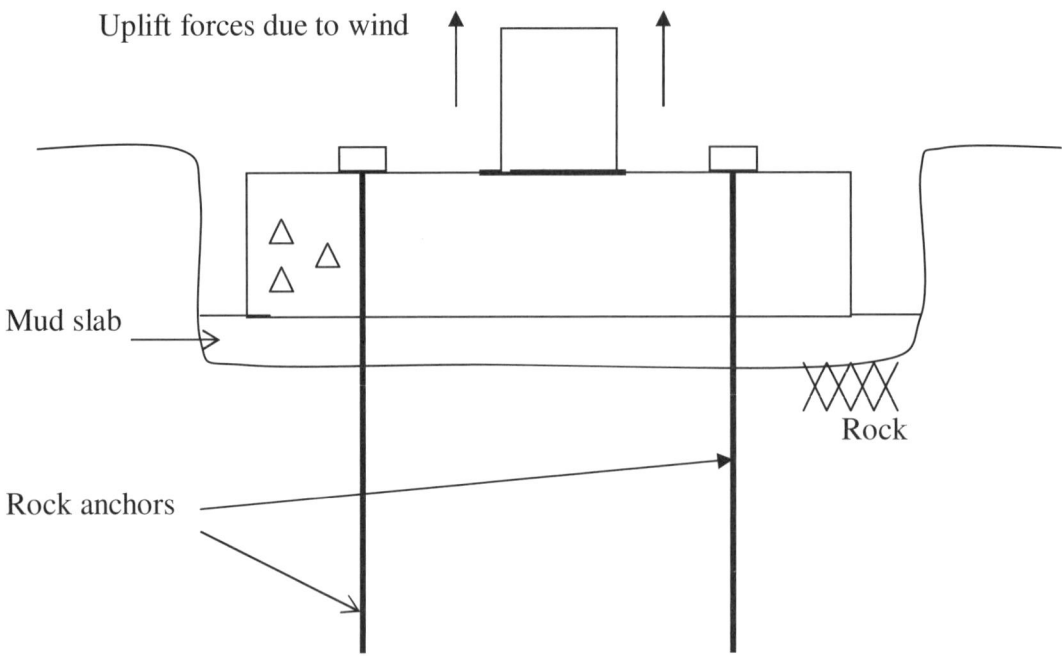

Uplift forces due to wind

Mud slab

Rock

Rock anchors

Rock anchors to resist uplift forces in a shallow foundation

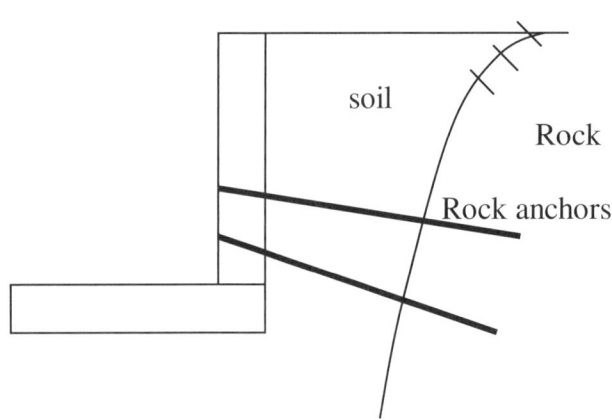

soil

Rock

Rock anchors

Rock anchors in a retaining wall

Rock anchors are widely used in retaining walls when rock is close enough for the anchors.

Rock anchors

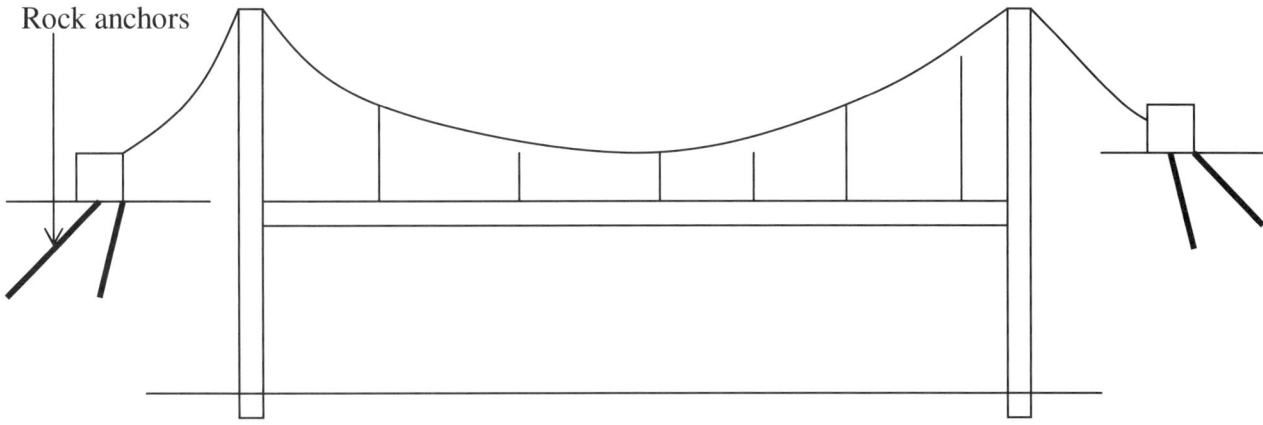

Rock anchors in a bridge

Mechanical rock anchors:

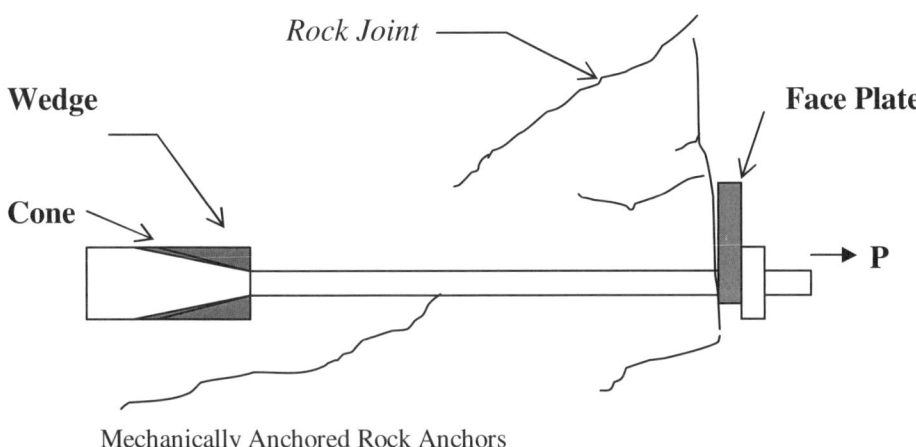

Mechanically Anchored Rock Anchors

Most popular mechanical anchor system is expansion shell anchors. A hole is drilled in the rock and the rock bolt assembly is inserted. Then tensile force (P) is applied. When the force is applied, the cone would try to move to the right. (See the figure above).

The movement of the cone would expand the two *wedges* and locks the bolt into the rock.

Typical installation procedure for mechanical anchors is provided below.

Step 1:   Drill a hole in the rock
Step 2:   Insert the mechanical anchor
Step 3:   Activate the mechanical wedge assembly at the end to attach the anchor to the rock. Rock anchors have a wedge assembly at the end which expands when rotated.
Step 4:   Grout the hole to avoid corrosion in the anchor

•   Initial tension applied = 70% of the total capacity of the rock bolt is recommended by E. Hoek. (*Ref. Underground Excavations in Hard Rock*)

Mechanical anchor failure:

Main reason for the failure is corrosion. Corrosion of mechanical anchors can be avoided by grouting the hole. Grouting of the hole is very important when there is water in the rock. Most permanent rock bolts are grouted.

Grouting may not be necessary for temporary rock bolts. It should be mentioned that groundwater in some regions could be acidic and can accelerate the corrosion process.

Design of Mechanical Anchors:

Failure surface of mechanical anchors is a cone.

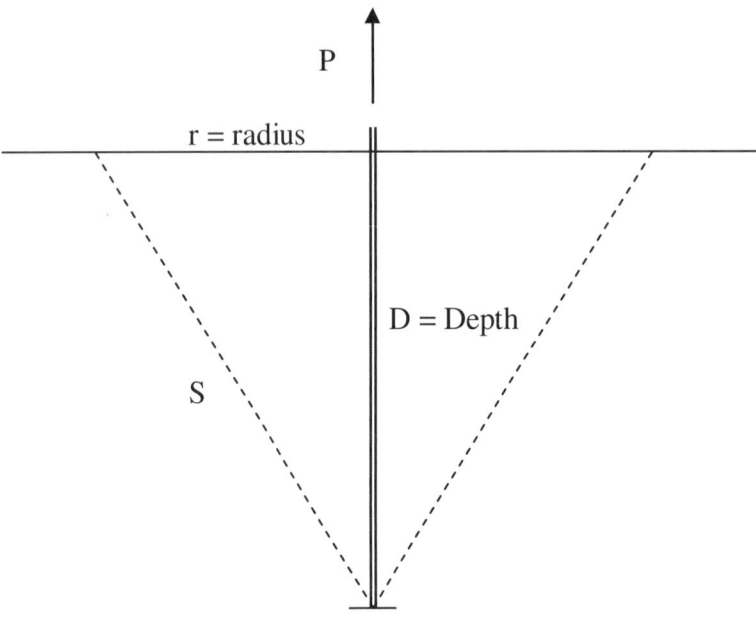

Failure cone of rock anchors

When a mechanical anchor is subjected to failure, failure cone is developed. Weight of the cone and rock cohesion along the cone surface acts against failure.

Resistance against failure = Weight of the cone + Cohesion along the surface of the cone.

Surface area and volume of cones are given by following equations.

Volume of a cone = $1/3 \times (\pi \times r^2) \times D$

Surface area of a cone = $(\pi \times r) \times S$

$S = (r^2 + D^2)^{1/2}$

Weight of the cone can be found if the density of rock is known.

Practice Problem: Find the failure force of the mechanical anchor shown in the figure below. Following information is obtained. Assume the angle of the stress triangle to be 30^0. Length of the rock anchor is 5 ft. Ignore the weight of rock. Rock cohesion = 100 psi,   Rock density = 150 pcf.

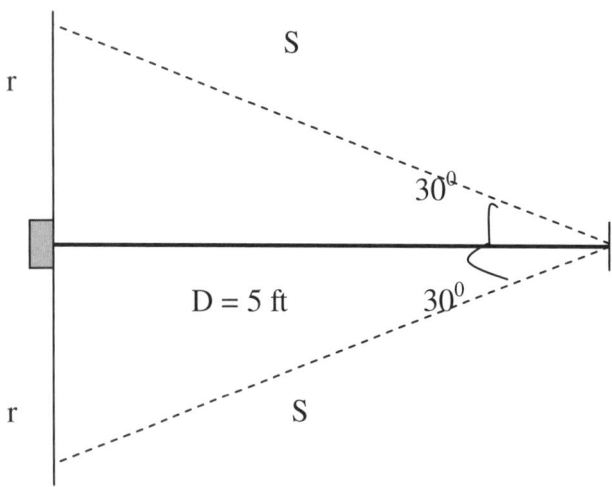

Failure mechanism of the rock anchor

Solution:
Radius = r = 5 x tan 30 = 5 x 0.577 = 2.89 ft
$\quad$ $S^2 = r^2 + D^2 = 2.89^2 + 5^2 = 8.35 + 25 = 33.35$
$\quad$ S = 5.78 ft
Surface area of the cone = (π x r) x S = (π x 2.89) x 5.78 = 52.5 ft^2.
Cohesive force = surface area of the cone x rock cohesion
$\qquad\qquad$ = 52.5 x (100 x 144)
$\qquad\qquad$ Rock cohesion is 100 psi which has to be converted to psf.
$\qquad\qquad$ = 378 tons (Ultimate capacity of the anchor)

Resin Anchored Rock Bolts: $\qquad$ One major disadvantage of mechanical anchors is that the mechanical anchor could loosen when there are vibrations in the rock due to blasting, train movement, traffic movement or construction activities. Further it is difficult to obtain a good mechanical anchor in weak and weathered rock. Shale, mudstone and highly weathered low RQD rocks are not good candidates for mechanical anchors. These difficulties could be avoided by using resin anchored rock bolts.

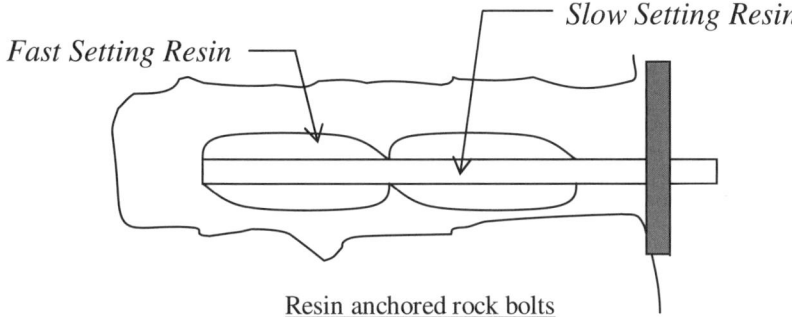

Resin anchored rock bolts

Two resin cartridges are inserted as shown. When the resin cartridges are broken (by spinning the rock bolt), fast setting resin would solidify first. The fast setting resin, would anchor the rock bolt into the rock. The tensile force is applied at this point. Slow setting resin still has not solidified yet. Slow setting portion is still in a liquid state. When the tension is applied, the rod is free to extend within the slow setting resin area. After the tension is applied and locked in, slow setting resin would solidify. For temporary applications slow setting resin may not be necessary. Its purpose is to provide corrosion protection.

Disadvantages:
- In fractured rock, the resin could seep into the rock and leaving little resin inside the hole.
- Some rocks contain clay seams. Resins may not be able to provide a good anchor in this type of rocks.
- Some researchers have expressed concern regarding the long term corrosion protection ability of resins. Further groundwater chemicals may react with resins and compromise its effectiveness.

Advantages:
- Resins work well in fractured rocks.
- Installation is very fast compared to other methods.

Rock Dowels: $\quad$ Rock dowels are not pre-stressed. Hence rock dowels do not apply a positive force to the rock. Rock dowels are called into action, when there is a movement in the rock. Simplest form of rock dowel is a grouted steel bar inserted into rock. This type is called grouted dowels. Other types include split set stabilizers and Swellex dowels.

Types of Rock Dowels:
1) Cement Grouted Dowels
2) Split Set Stabilizers
3) Swellex Dowels

Cement Grouted Dowels

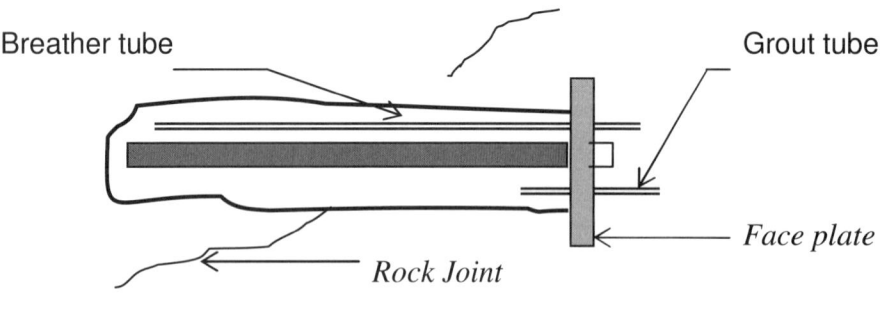

Cement grouted dowels

Note: If the rock, moves along the joint, the dowel would be tensioned.

Split Set Stabilizers: These rock dowels are different than grouted dowels. What happens when a steel rod is pushed into a small hole (smaller diameter than the steel bar) drilled in the rock? The steel bar would be compressed and will be tightly entrapped inside the hole. Split set stabilizers are designed based on this principal.

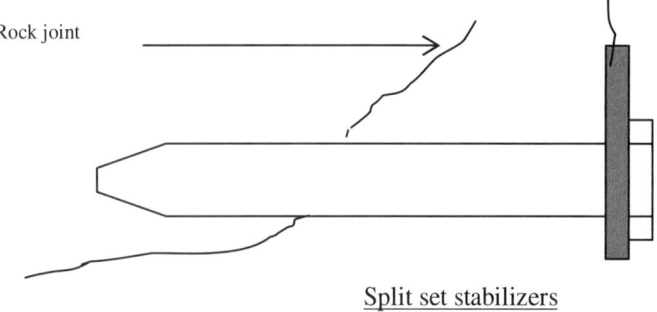

Split set stabilizers

Note: A hole smaller than the split set dowel is drilled.   Then the dowel is pushed into the rock.
Split set stabilizer can resist a force of 10.9 tons. (diameter = 33 mm). The recommended drill hole size = 31 mm. (Note that the hole diameter is smaller than the dowel).

Advantages and Disadvantages: These dowels are very quick and easy to install, since there is no grouting involved. The main disadvantage is corrosion. The cost factor also may play a part in their selection.

Grouted Rock Anchors: (Non Stressed):   In the case of grouted rock anchors, bonding between rock and anchor is achieved by grout.

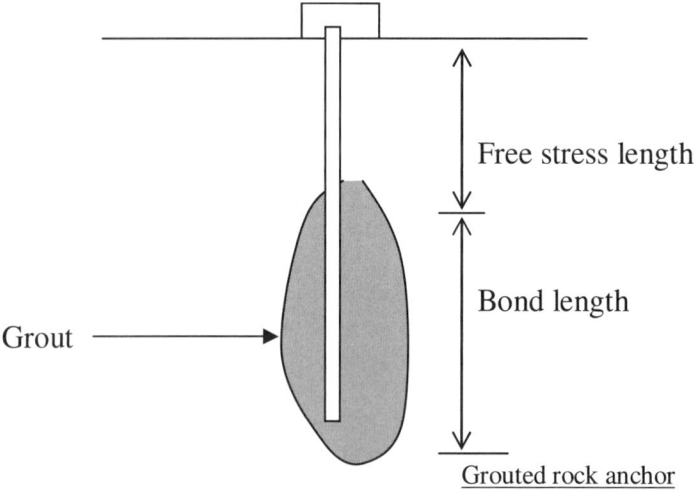

Grouted rock anchor

The anchor develops its strength through the bond strength between rock and grout.

Installation Procedure of grouted anchors:

STEP 1: Drill a hole to the desired length
STEP 2: Install the rock anchor
STEP 3: Grout the hole
STEP 4: Wait sufficient time for the grout to harden before applying the load

References:

Wiley, D.C., "Foundations on rock", Taylor and Francis, 1999.
Prior to discuss earth retaining structures it is important to discuss effective stresses in soils.

8.8   Pile Foundations:

Introduction: Piles are used to transfer the load to a deeper more stable layers of soil. Large structures were built in Egypt, Asia and Europe prior to advent of piles. Ancient engineers had no choice but to dig deep down to the bedrock.

Pile Types: All piles can be categorized as displacement piles and non-displacement piles. Timber piles, closed end steel pipe piles and precast concrete piles displace the soil when driven into the ground. These piles are categorized as displacement piles. Some piles displace soil during installation by a small degree. (H- piles, open end steel tubes, hollow concrete piles).

Displacement Piles: When a pile displaces soil during the driving process, such piles are known as displacement piles. Some piles such as closed end pipe piles and timber piles displaces large amount of soil compared to open end pipe piles or H-piles.

Large displacement piles

Timber piles
Precast concrete piles   (Reinforced and prestressed)
Closed end steel pipe piles
Jacked down solid concrete piles

Small displacement piles

Tubular concrete piles
H-piles
Open end pipe piles
Thin shell type
Jacked down hollow concrete cylinders

Non Displacement Piles: When a hole is augured and concreted, soil is not displaced.   During the auguring process soil is removed and surrounding soil is not displaced.

- Steel casing withdrawn after concreting (Alpha piles, Delta piles, Frankie piles, Vibrex piles)
- Continuous flight auger drilling and concrete placement. (with or without reinforcements)
- Auguring a hole and placing a thin shell and concreting
- Drill or augur a hole and placement of concrete blocks inside the hole.

Pile Types in Detail:

Timber Piles: Timber piles are the cheapest piles available. For small loads, timber piles are still used. One of the main problems of timber piles is that they could decay. Timber piles decay due to living microbes. Microbes need two ingredients to thrive. They are "*Oxygen*" and "*Moisture*". If one of these ingredients are missing, timber piles will not decay. Below groundwater level, there is ample moisture but very little Oxygen. Hence timber piles submerged in groundwater will not decay due to lack of Oxygen microbes are unable to live under the water table.

On the other hand, above groundwater level, there is ample "Oxygen". States like Nevada, Arizona and Texas, there is very little moisture above the groundwater level. Since microbes cannot survive without water, timber piles could last for a long period of time in dry states.

This is not the case for states in northern part of USA. Significant amount of moisture will be present above groundwater level due to snow and rain. Hence both Oxygen and moisture is available for the fungi to thrive. Timber piles would decay under such conditions. Creosoting and other techniques should be used to protect timber from decay above groundwater level.

When the church of St. Mark was demolished due to structural defects in 1902, wood piles driven in 900 AD were in good condition. These old piles were re-used to construct a new tower in place of the old church. Venice is a city with very high groundwater level and piles were under water for centuries.

Timber Pile Installation: Timber piles need to be installed with special care. Timber piles are susceptible for brooming and damage. Any sudden decrease in driving resistance should be investigated.

Splicing of Timber Piles: Splicing of timber piles should be avoided if possible. Unlike steel or concrete piles, timber piles cannot be spliced effectively. Usual practice is to provide a pipe section (known as a sleeve) and bolt it to two piles.

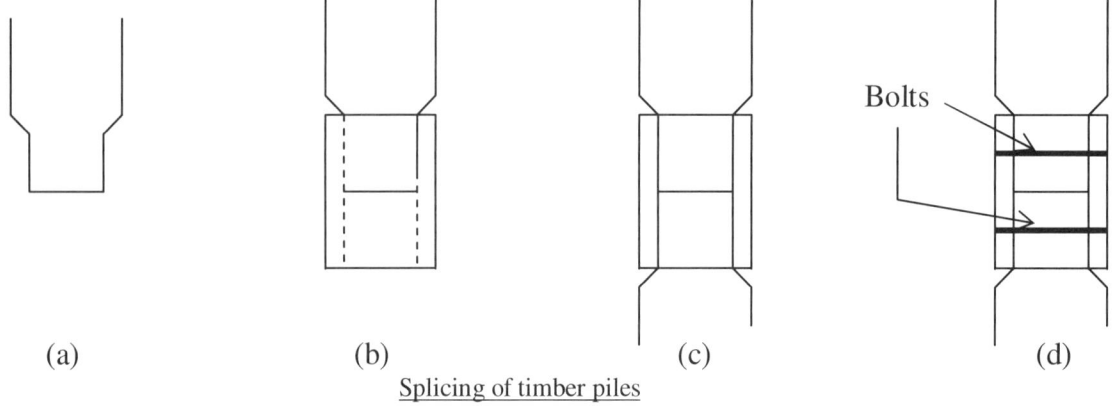

(a)   (b)   (c)   (d)

Splicing of timber piles

(a):   Usually, timber piles are tapered prior to splicing as shown in Fig. 1.
(b):   The sleeve (or the pipe section) is inserted.
(c):   Bottom pile is inserted
(d):   The pipe section is bolted to two piles.

Sleeve joints are approximately 3 to 4 ft in length. As one could see easily, the bending strength of the joint is much lower than the pile. Splice strength can be increased by increasing the length of the sleeve. Most building codes require, no splicing to be conducted on upper 10 feet of the pile since the pile is subjected to high bending stresses at upper levels. If splicing is absolutely required for timber piles in the upper 10 feet of the pile, it is recommended to construct a composite pile with upper section filled with concrete. This type of construction is much better than splicing.

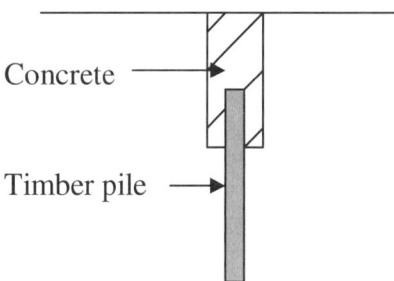

Concrete – Timber Composite Pile

Uplift Piles: Timber splices are extremely vulnerable for uplift (tensile) forces and should be avoided. Other than sleeves, steel bars and straps are also used for splicing.

Steel "H" Piles: Though timber piles are cheaper, they are not practical in some situations. Timber piles cannot be driven through hard ground. On the other hand steel H-piles can be driven through hard soils and fill material without much damage. Main disadvantage of H-piles is low skin friction due to limited perimeter. Hence steel "H" piles are essentially end bearing piles. Corrosion is a major problem for steel "H" piles. The corrosion is controlled by adding copper into steel. One of the main advantages of h-piles is that they can be easily spliced. H- piles are ideal for highly variable soil conditions. H- piles could bend under very hard ground conditions. This is known as "*dog legging*" and the pile installation supervisor needs to make sure that the piles are not out of plumb.

Steel H-Piles

Another problem with H-piles is that they can get plugged with soil during the driving process.

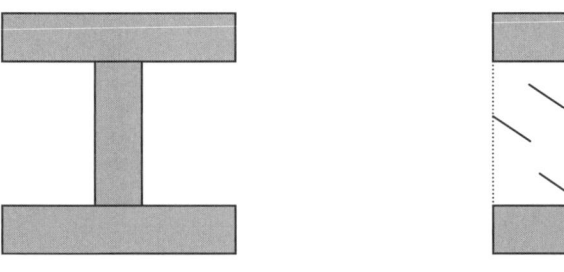

Unplugged   **Plugged**

H- piles (plugging of soil)

If a H-pile is plugged, end bearing would increase due to larger area. On the other hand, skin friction would become smaller due to lesser wall area. When H-piles are driven, both analysis should be done (unplugged and plugged) and use the lower value for design.

Unplugged: Low end bearing but high skin friction;
Plugged: Low skin friction but high end bearing;

Splicing of "H" Piles:

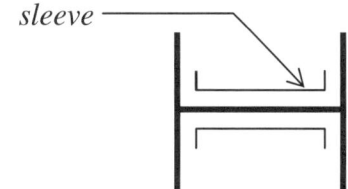

Plan view of a steel "H" pile   Plan view of a steel "H" pile, with the sleeve inserted

Splicing of H-piles

STEP 1: The sleeve is inserted into the bottom part of the "H" pile as shown and bolted to the web.
STEP 2: the top part of the pile is inserted into the sleeve and bolted.

Pipe Piles: Pipe piles may not be as strong as H-piles in hard driving conditions. Pipe piles are available in many sizes.   12-inch diameter pipe piles have a range of thicknesses. Pipe piles can be driven either open end or closed end. When driven open end, the pipe is cleaned with a jet of water.

Closed End Pipe Piles: Closed end pipe piles are constructed by covering the bottom of the pile with a steel plate. In most cases pipe piles are filled with concrete. In some cases, pipe piles are not filled with concrete to reduce the cost. If pipe piles were not filled with concrete, then corrosion protection layer should be applied.
If a concrete filled pipe pile is corroded, most of the load carrying capacity of the pile would remain intact due to concrete. On the other hand, empty pipe pile would lose significant amount of its load carrying capacity due to corrosion.
Pipe piles are a good candidate for batter piles. Structural capacity of pipe piles is calculated based on concrete strength and steel strength. The thickness of the steel should be reduced to account for corrosion. (Typically reduced by 1/16 in. to account for corrosion).

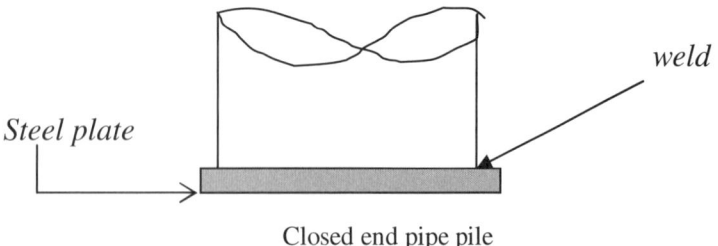

Closed end pipe pile

A pipe pile is covered with an end cap. The end cap is welded as shown. In the case of closed end driving, soil heave can occur. There are occasions where open end piles also generate soil heave. This is due to plugging of the open end of the pile with soil. Pipe piles are cheaper than steel H-piles or concrete piles.

Open End Pipe Piles: Open end pipe piles are driven and soil inside the pile is removed by a water jet.

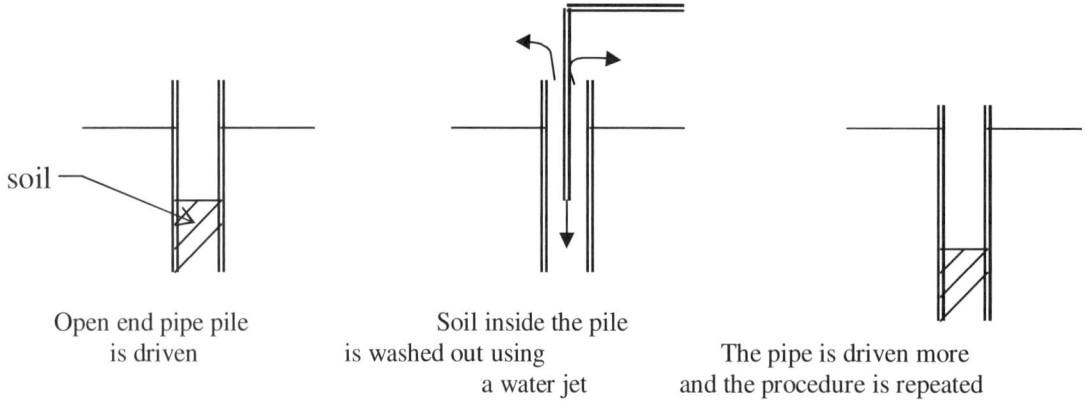

Open end pipe pile   Soil inside the pile
is driven   is washed out using   The pipe is driven more
                        a water jet   and the procedure is repeated

Driving of open end pipe piles

Open end pipe piles are easier to drive through hard soils than closed end pipe piles.

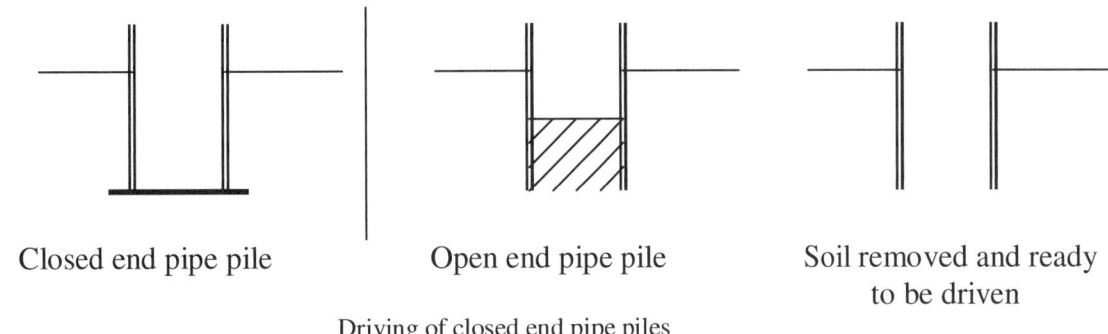

| Closed end pipe pile | Open end pipe pile | Soil removed and ready to be driven |

Driving of closed end pipe piles

Precast Concrete Piles: Precast concrete piles are gaining popularity among engineers. Precast concrete piles could be either reinforced concrete piles or prestressed concrete piles.

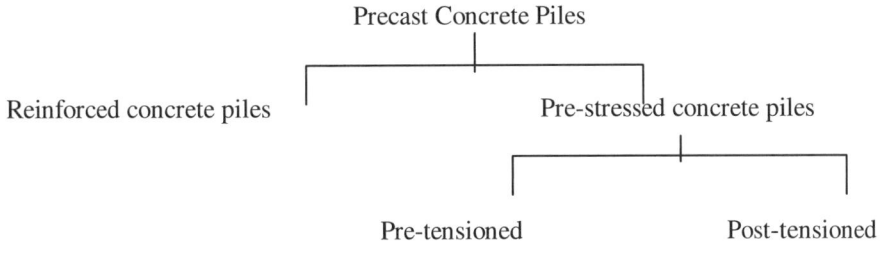

Precast concrete piles

Reinforced Concrete Piles:

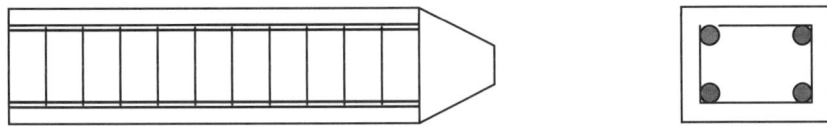

Reinforced concrete piles

Reinforced concrete piles are constructed by reinforcing the concrete as shown.

Prestressed Concrete Piles:

Pre - Tensioning Procedure

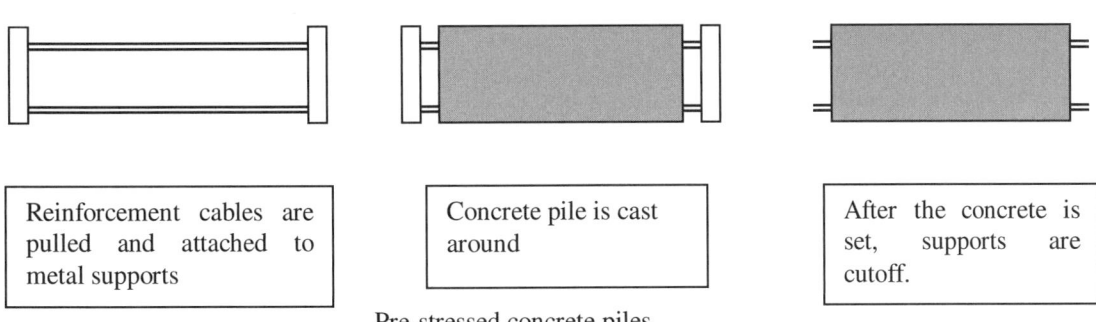

| Reinforcement cables are pulled and attached to metal supports | Concrete pile is cast around | After the concrete is set, supports are cutoff. |

Pre-stressed concrete piles

Post - Tensioning Procedure

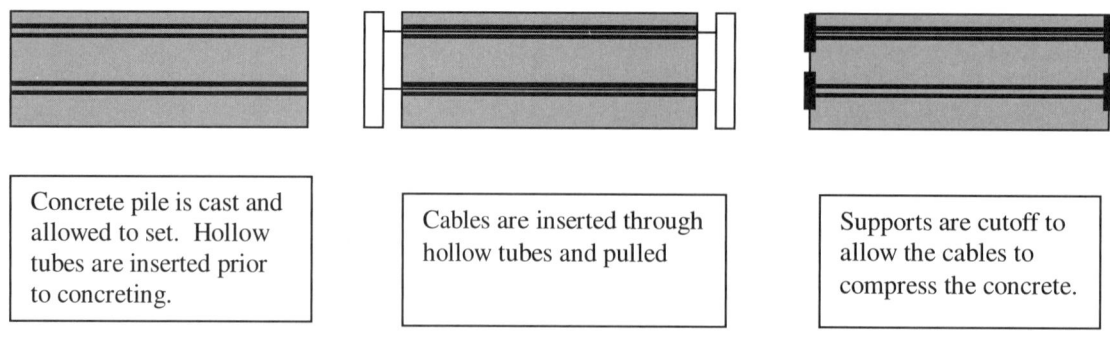

| Concrete pile is cast and allowed to set. Hollow tubes are inserted prior to concreting. | Cables are inserted through hollow tubes and pulled | Supports are cutoff to allow the cables to compress the concrete. |

Post tensioned concrete piles

Hollow Tubular Section Concrete Piles: Most hollow tubular piles are post tensioned to withstand tensile stresses. Hollow tubular concrete piles can be driven either closed end or open end. A cap is fitted at the end for closed end driving. It has been found that these piles are not suitable for dense soils. Splicing of these piles is expensive. It is a difficult and expensive process to cutoff these piles. It is very important to know the depth to the bearing stratum with reasonable accuracy prior to using these piles.

8.9 Loadings:

Dead Loads: Dead loads are the loads due to slabs, columns, beams, roofs and other permanent elements of a building.

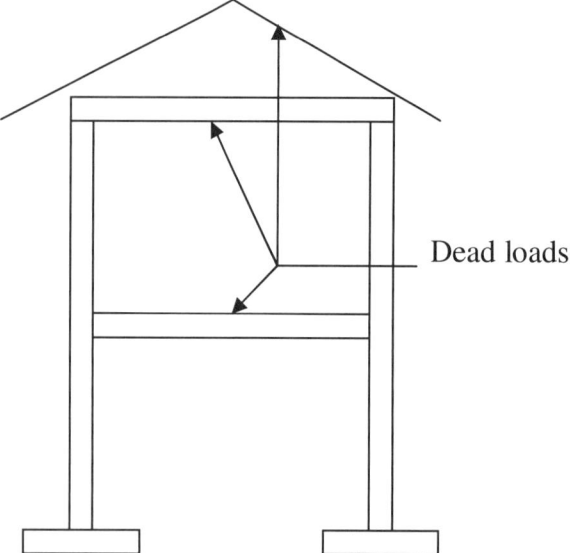

Dead loads

<u>Live Loads</u>:   Live loads are basically, people and non permanent furniture.

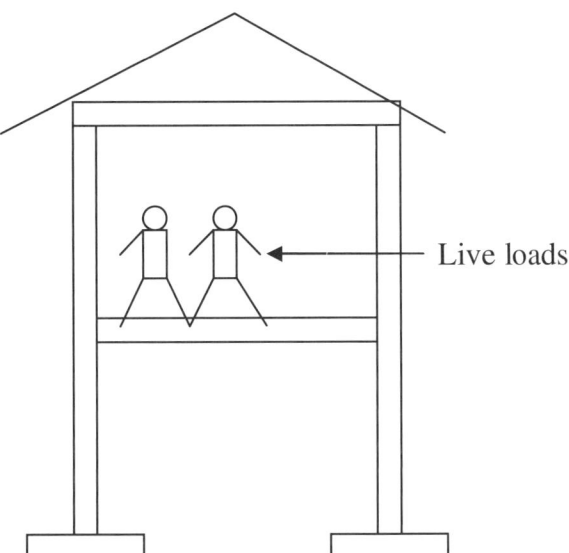

<u>Wind Loads</u>:   Wind loads as the name indicates are caused by wind.   Wind loads could act laterally or vertically upwards.

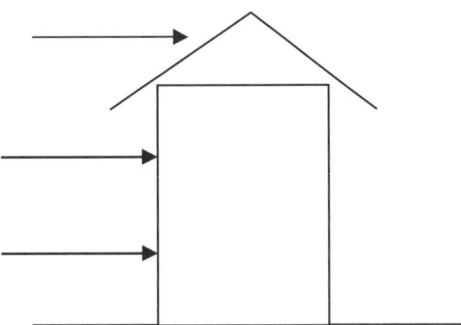

<u>Snow Loads</u>:   Snow loads can be the most critical load on roofs in northern US states.

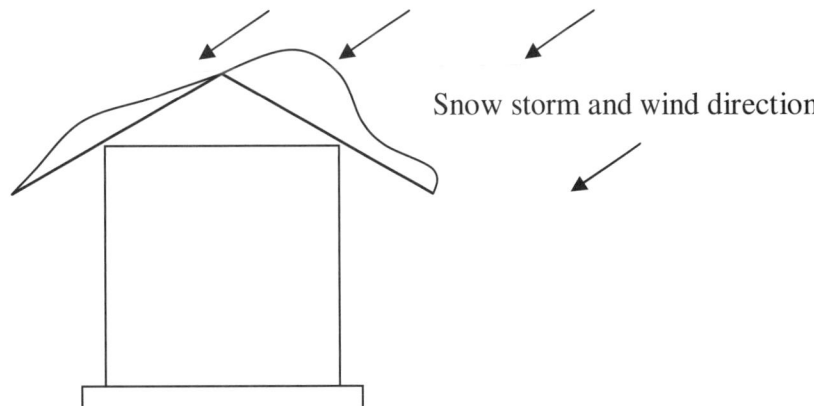

Accumulation of snow can be distributed in the roof in an uneven manner.

<u>Load Paths</u>:   Load path is the route load would take to reach the footings.   Bracings, connections and all other structural elements need to be analyzed and designed based on the load path.

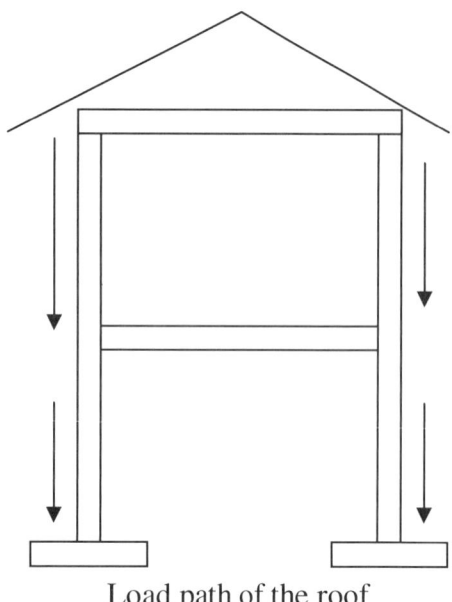

Load path of the roof

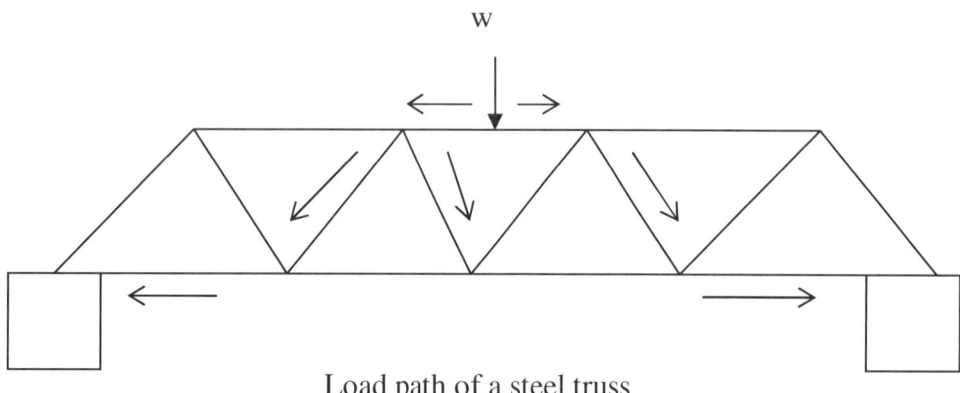

Load path of a steel truss

Load path in a truss can be complicated. Load path due to load "W" in a truss is shown above. Typically these computations are done using computer programs.

8.10 Mechanics of Materials: Mechanics can be divided into two parts.

- Statics – Deals with static objects and forces
- Dynamics – Deals with moving objects and forces

Statics: It may have been a while that you have performed any force computations. Hence it is important to look at some of the fundamentals in force computations.

Forces:

Consider the force shown below.

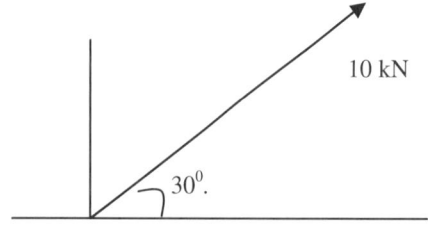

Find the components in horizontal and vertical directions.

Horizontal component = 10 x cos (30^0) = 10 x 0.866 = 8.66 kN
Vertical component = 10 x sin (30^0) = 10 x 0.5 = 5 kN

Resultant Forces: When two or more forces acting on a body, these forces can be resolved into one resultant force.

Parallelogram of Forces: When two forces are acting at an angle θ, they can be resolved into one force using parallelogram.

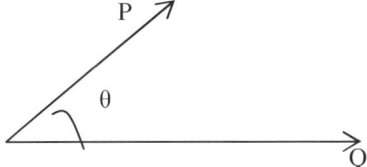

Draw a parallelogram as shown.

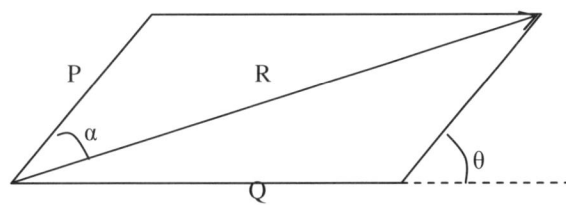

The angle θ is the angle between two forces P and Q.
Resultant R can be found by drawing the parallelogram as shown above. Resultant force R is given by the diagonal. From geometry it can be shown that

$$R^2 = P^2 + Q^2 + 2PQ \cos θ$$

Hence

$$R = (P^2 + Q^2 + 2PQ \cos θ)^{1/2}$$

The angle α is given by

$$\tan α = Q \sin θ/(P + Q \cos θ)$$

Practice Problem: Two forces P and Q are found to be 10 lbs and 22 lbs. The angle between them is 35^0. Find the resultant force and the angle of the resultant force.

Solution:

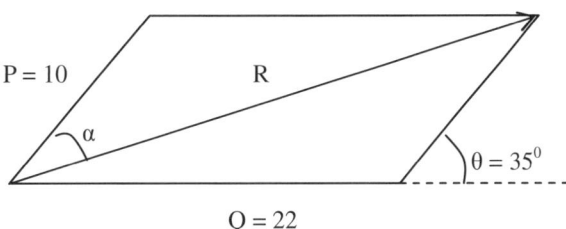

R = (P^2 + Q^2 + 2PQ Cos θ)$^{1/2}$ = (10^2 + 22^2 + 2 x 10 x 22 x cos 35)$^{1/2}$
R = 30.7 lbs

Tan α = Q Sin θ/(P + Q Cos θ) = 22 Sin 35/(10 + 22 Cos 35) = 0.45
Angle α = Tan^{-1}(0.45) = 24.5^0

<u>Equilibrium of Forces</u>:   When there are more than one force all forces can be resolved in two perpendicular directions. Typically forces are resolved in horizontal and vertical directions.
<u>For equilibrium</u>: $\Sigma H = 0$ and $\Sigma V = 0$

If the resolved forces are not zero, there would be a resultant force R.
R can be found using following equation.

$$R = (\Sigma H^2 + \Sigma V^2)^{1/2}$$

$$\text{Tan } \theta = \Sigma V / \Sigma H$$

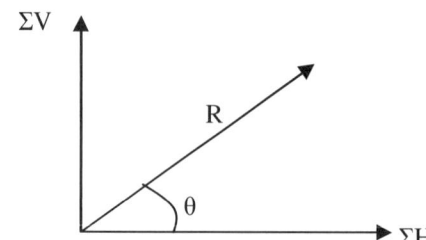

<u>**Practice Problem**</u>:   Find the resultant force of given forces and the resultant angle to the horizontal.

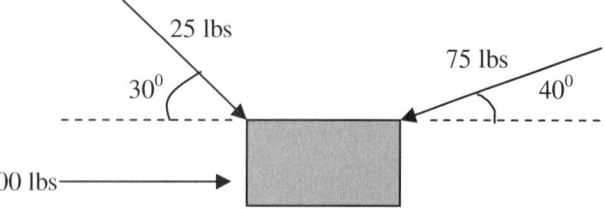

<u>Solution</u>:   STEP 1:   Resolve forces in the horizontal direction.

$\Sigma H = 100 + 25 \text{ Cos } 30 - 75 \text{ Cos } 40 = 100 + 25 \times 0.866 - 75 \times 0.766 = 64.2$ lbs
$\Sigma V = 25 \times \text{Sin } 30 + 75 \text{ Sin } 40 = 25 \times 0.5 + 75 \times 0.643 = 60.7$
$R = (\Sigma H^2 + \Sigma V^2)^{1/2}$
$R = (64.2^2 + 60.7^2)^{1/2} = 88.4$ lbs

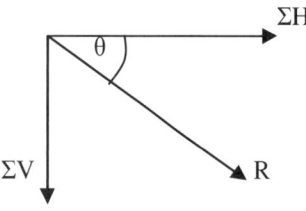

$\text{Tan } \theta = \Sigma V / \Sigma H = 60.7/64.2 = 0.95$
Angle $\theta = 43.5^0$

<u>**Center of Gravity:**</u>   Knowing the center of gravity is important for construction engineers. There is plenty of lifting, moving, loading and unloading work and construction engineers should know where the weight is concentrated.
Center of gravity of some objects shown below.

Triangle:

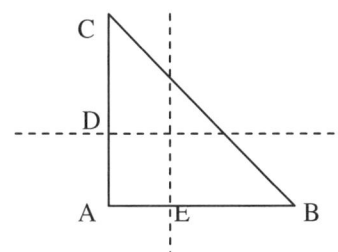

AD = AC/3 and AE = AB/3
CD = 2AC/3 and EB = 2AB/3

Semi Circle:

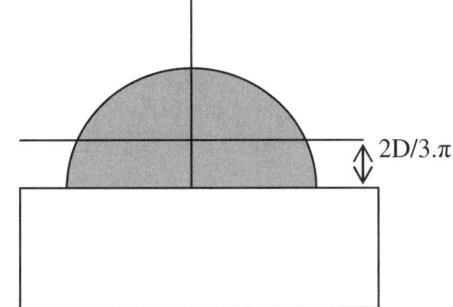

$2D/3.\pi$

Curve:

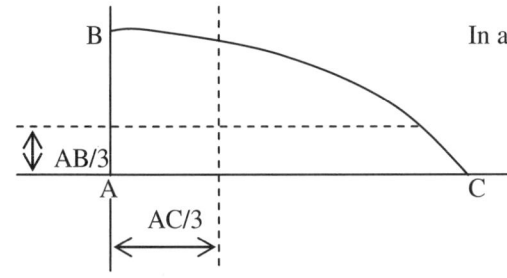

In a curve, center of gravity acts 1/3 of the leg.

Area of a curve = 2/3 x AB x AC

Cone:

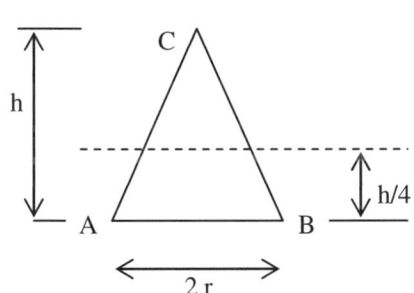

Area of a cone = $1/3. \pi r^2 h$

Trapezium:

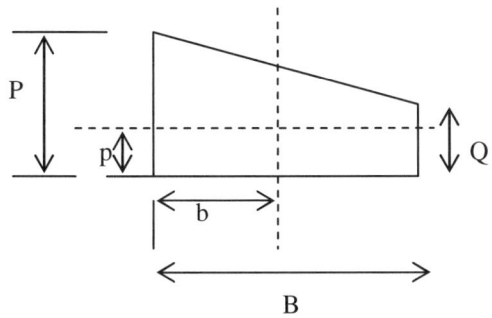

Area = ½ (P + Q).B

$p = (P^2 + PQ + Q^2)/3(P + Q)$

b = B/3 x (2Q + P)/(P + Q)

Q is the shorter side and P is the longer side.
b is measured from the longer side P.

Center of Gravity of Multiple Figures: Center of gravity of many objects can be found using the following equation.

$$X = (a1.x1 + a2.x2 + a3.x3…..)/(a1 + a2 + a3……)$$

Similarly

$$Y = (a.y1 + a2.y2 + a3.y3…….)/(a1 + a2 + a3……)$$

a1, a2, a3 are areas of figures. x1, x2, x3 are distances to center of gravity of each object.

Practice Problem: Find the distances X and Y to the center of gravity of the composite figure.

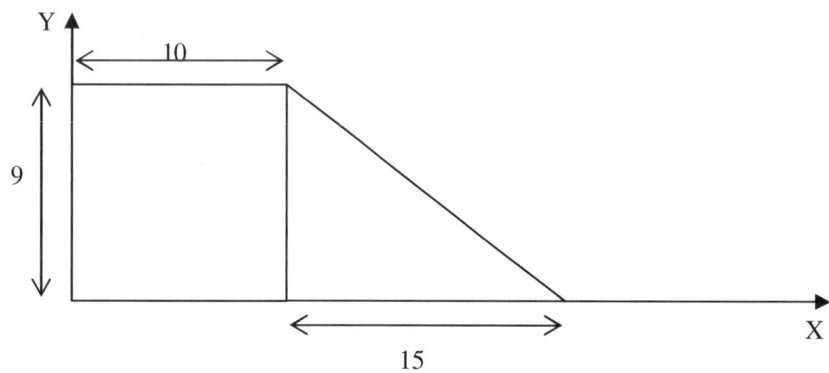

Area of the rectangle = a1 = 90
Area of the triangle = a2 = 15 x 9/2 = 67.5

Next we have to find x1 and x2 or distances to center of gravity of each object.

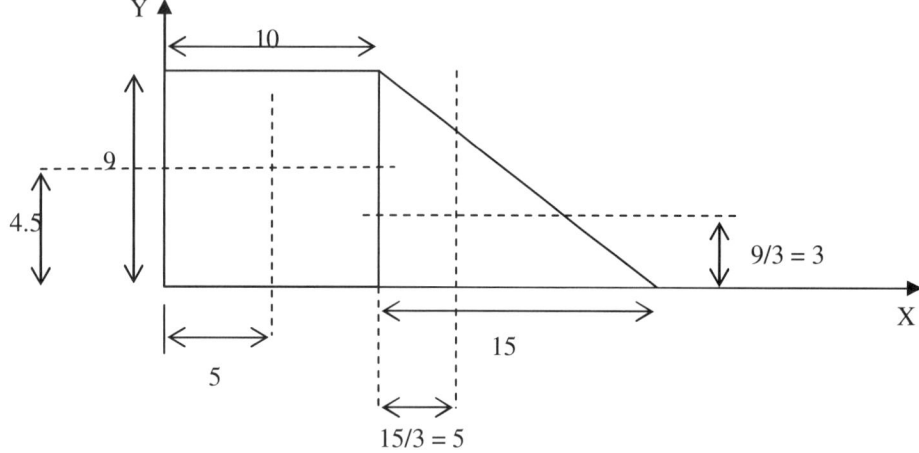

Distance to center of gravity from Y axis = X = (a1.x1 + a2.x2)/(a1 + a2) = [90 x 5 + 67.5 x (10 + 5)]/[90 + 67.5]
          X = 9.3

Distance to center of gravity from X axis = Y = (a1.y1 + a2.y2)/(a1 + a2) = [90 x 4.5 + 67.5 x 3]/[90 + 67.5]
          Y = 3.86

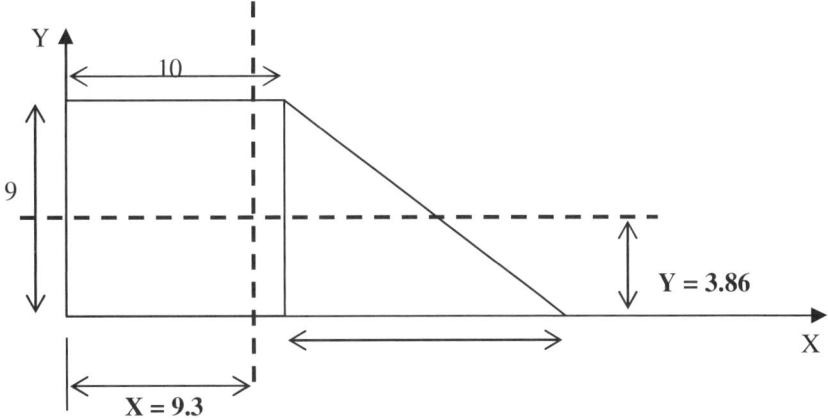

Note that X value is measured from the Y axis and Y value is measured from the X axis.

Moment: Moment of a force about a given point is obtained by multiplying the force with the perpendicular distance to that force.

Practice Problem: Find the moment of the force given from point A.

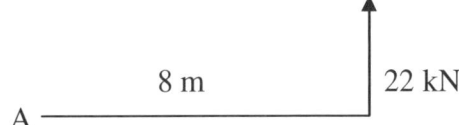

Moment around point A = 8 x 22 = 176 kN. m

Practice Problem: Similarly find the moment of forces around point A of the forces given below.

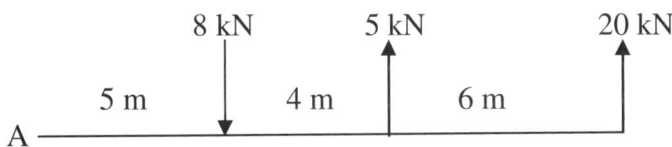

In the above figure, 8 kN acts downward while 5 kN and 20 kN act upwards. Assume downward moment to be positive and upward moment to be negative.
Moment around point A = (8 x 5) – 5 x (5 + 4) - 20 x (5 + 4 + 6) = -305 kN. m
Above negative sign indicates that the moment is acting upwards since we considered downward to be positive.

Uniform Loads: Weight of a beam is a good example for a uniform load.

Practice Problem: Assume the weight of the beam shown is 20 lbs per linear ft. Length of the beam is 15 ft. Find
a)   Total weight of the beam
b)   Two reactions (P and Q)
c)   Moment around point A.

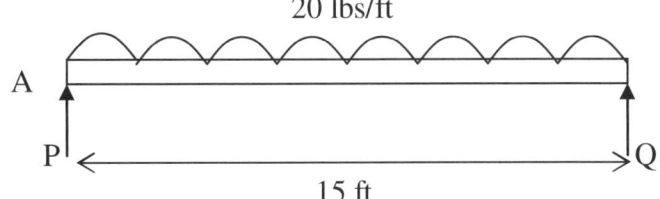

Solution:
a)   Total weight of the beam = 15 x 20 = 300 lbs.
b)   Two reactions:

Due to symmetry, two reactions P and Q has to be equal.
P + Q = 300 lbs.
Since P and Q are equal;   P = 150 and Q = 150

c)   Moment around point A;
The center of gravity of the uniform load act at the center of the beam.
Moment due to uniform load = 20 x 15 x (15/2) = 2,250 lbs. ft
Moment due to Q = -150 x 15 = -2,250
Moment due to Q is minus since it acts opposite to the uniform load.
Net moment around point A = 0

Practice Problem: Find the moment due to force T around point A. Force T is given to be 120 kN.

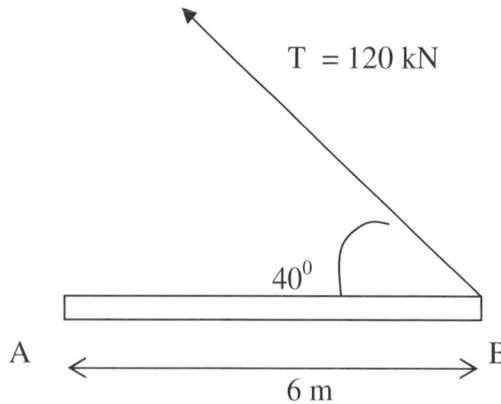

Solution: Draw a perpendicular to force T from point A.

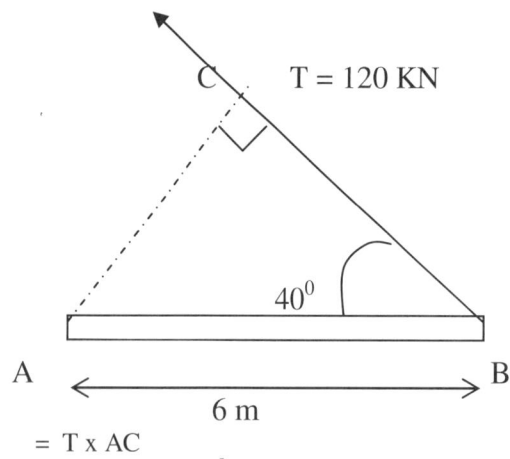

Moment around point A   = T x AC
                              = T x (AB sin 40^0)
                              = 120 x 6 x sin 40^0 = 462.8 kN. m

Friction: Friction acts opposite to movement. Friction is proportional to the normal force.

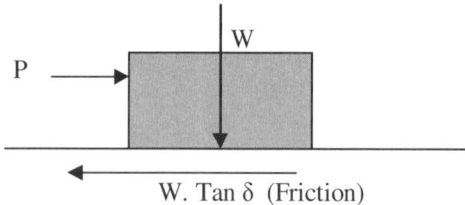

W is the weight of the object and δ is the friction angle. For the block to move P should be greater than W. Tan δ.

Practice Problem: Investigate whether the block placed on the inclined plane would move. Friction angle $\delta = 15^0$. Inclination angle (α) is 20^0.

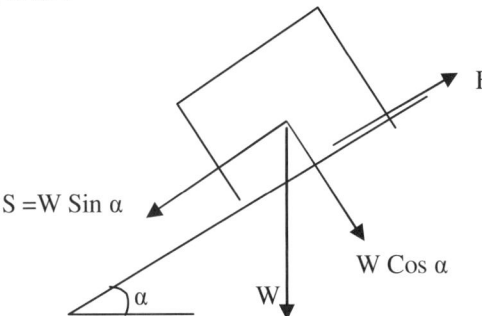

Solution:
STEP 1:   Find the force due to friction:
Frictional force $F = W. \cos \alpha \tan \delta. = W. \cos 20 \times \tan 15 \times = W \times 0.94 \times 0.268 = 0.252 W$

STEP 2:   Find the sliding force:
Sliding Force $S = W \sin \alpha = 0.34 W$
Sliding force S is greater than the frictional force. Hence the block would slide down.

Dynamics: Dynamics deals with moving objects.
Mass and Weight: Weight of an object would change from planet to planet. Person who weighs 100 kg would weigh only 33 kg in the moon and zero in space. In Jupiter, he would weigh more than thousand kg.

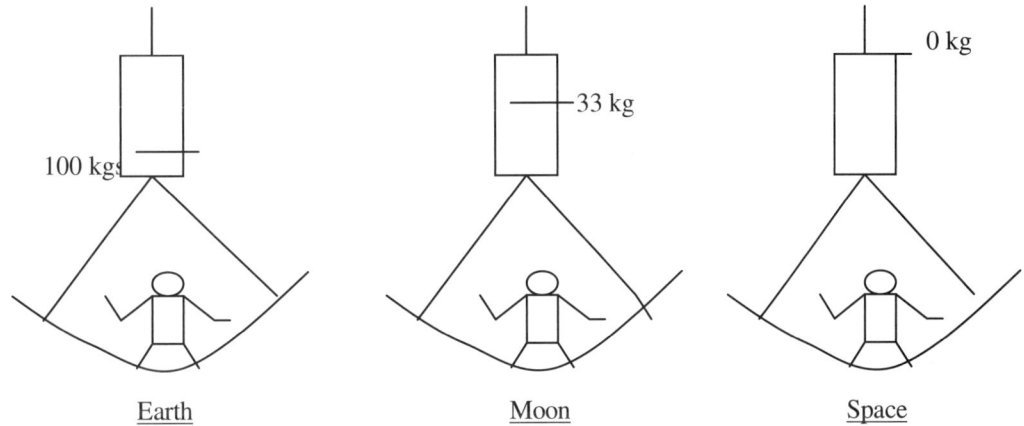

Now let's pay attention to Newton's second law, P = mf.
Let's take an object that has a mass of 1N and accelerate by 1 m/s^2. The mass (m) is 1N and acceleration (f) is 1 m/s^2.
$P = 1 \times 1 = 1$

Velocity and Distance and Acceleration Relationship: Following three relationships are widely used.

$$v = u + ft \qquad \text{-----------------------------------(1)}$$
$$s = u.t + \tfrac{1}{2}. f .t^2 \qquad \text{-----------------------------------(2)}$$
$$v^2 = u^2 + 2 f. s \qquad \text{-----------------------------------(3)}$$

u = Initial velocity   v = final velocity   t = time elapsed   f = acceleration   s = Distance

Practice Problem: A train is moving at a constant velocity of 30 mph. Then it starts to accelerate at 0.8 ft/s^2 for a time period of 2 minutes. What's the new velocity of the train?

Solution:

u (initial velocity), f (acceleration) and time (t) are given.
u = Initial velocity = 30 mph   f = 100 ft/s^2.   t = 5 minutes
Let's convert all to ft, and seconds.

u = 30 mph = 30 x 5280/3600 ft/s = 44 ft/s
t = 2 minutes = 2 x 60 = 120 sec
f = 0.8 ft/s^2

Use equation (1) above. $v = u + f.t$
                                 $v = 44 + 0.8 \times 120 = 140$ ft/sec = 140/5280 x 3600 mph = 95.5 mph

Practice Problem: A train is moving at a constant velocity of 30 mph. Then it starts to accelerate at an unknown acceleration for a time period of 2 minutes. During these two minutes, the train had traveled 3 miles. What's the acceleration of the train?

Solution:

u (initial velocity), s (distance) and time (t) are given.
u = Initial velocity = 30 mph = 44 ft/s   s = 3 miles = 3 x 5280 = 15,840 ft   t = 2 minutes = 120 sec

Use equation (2) $s = u.t + \frac{1}{2}.f.t^2$
                          $15,840 = 44 \times 120 + \frac{1}{2} f \times (120)^2$
                          $f = 1.47$ ft/s^2.

Practice Problem: A ship is moving at an unknown velocity. Then the ship accelerates at 0.4 ft/s^2 for an unknown time period. During this time period the ship has traveled 2 miles and has attained a velocity of 120 ft/sec. What is the initial velocity of the ship?

Solution:
f (acceleration), s (distance) and final velocity (v) are given.
v = final velocity = 120 ft/s   s = 2 miles = 2 x 5280 = 10,560 ft   f = 0.4 ft/s^2

Use equation (3) $v^2 = u^2 + 2 f. s$

                          $120^2 = u^2 + 2 \times 0.4 \times 10,560$
                          u = Initial velocity = 77.14 ft/sec.

Practice Problem: Ball is dropped from the third floor of a building which is 40 m above ground. Find the time it would take for the ball to hit the ground.

Solution:

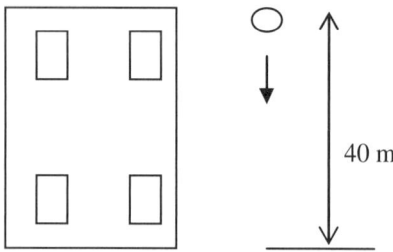

40 m

Known values: Initial velocity (u) = 0,   Acceleration = f = g = 9.81 m/s^2.

Use equation (2) $s = ut + \frac{1}{2} f. t^2$
                          $40 = 0 + \frac{1}{2} \times 9.81 \times t^2$
                          t = 2.86 sec.

Practice Problem: Contractor has to transport soil from site to the dump yard and come back. The dump yard is 10 miles away. Maximum velocity allowed for the truck is 60 mph. Truck can accelerate from 0 to 60 mph in 1 minute. It needs another minute to decelerate from 60 mph to zero. Find the time the truck would take to go to the dump yard.

Solution:

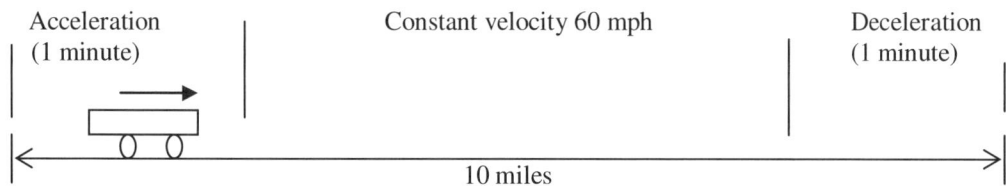

Acceleration Phase: The truck accelerates from 0 to 60 mph in one minute. We need to find the distance during the acceleration phase.

Given data: u = 0,   v = 60 mph = 60 x 5280/3600 = 88 ft/sec,   t = 60 sec.
From v = u + ft
          88 = 0 + f x 60
          f = 1.47 ft/s².
Distance (s) = u.t + ½ f .t²
          s = 0 + ½ x 1.47 x 60² = 2,646 ft

Deceleration Phase: Acceleration phase lasted for 2,646 ft. By symmetry one can see that deceleration phase also last for 2,646 ft.

Constant Velocity Phase: Total distance = 10 miles = 10 x 5280 ft = 52,800 ft
Constant velocity phase = 52,800 – 2,646 – 2,646 = 47,508 ft
Time taken to travel 47,508 ft at 60 mph = 47,508/88 = 539 seconds = 9 minutes
Note that 60 mph is equal to 88 ft/sec.
Total time to travel to dump site = 1 + 9 + 1 = 11 minutes.

Practice Problem: A post is stabilized by guy wires as shown. Following information is given.
P = 1,200 lbs,   α = 60⁰,   β = 100⁰,   Find horizontal components of Q and R.

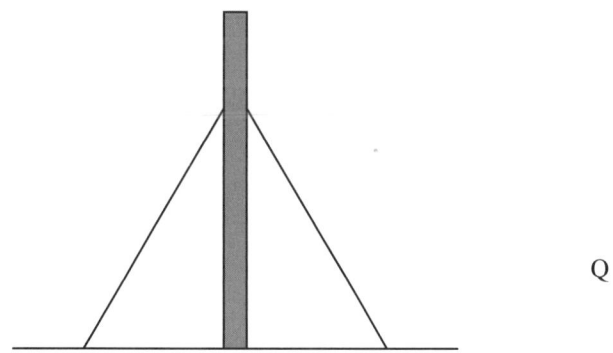

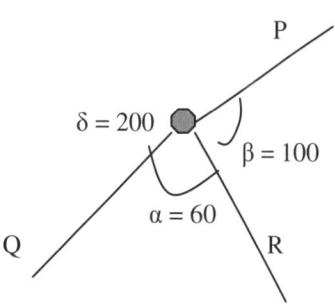

δ = 360⁰ – (60 + 100) = 200⁰

Following equation can be used. This equation is known as the "**Sine Rule**" and widely used.

$$\frac{P}{\sin \alpha} = \frac{Q}{\sin \beta} = \frac{R}{\sin \delta}$$

$$\frac{1,200}{\sin 60} = \frac{Q}{\sin 100} = \frac{R}{\sin 200}$$

$$\frac{1,200}{\text{Sin }60} = \frac{Q}{\text{Sin }100}$$

$Q = 1,200 \times \text{Sin }100/\text{Sin }60 = 1,365$ lbs

$$\frac{1,200}{\text{Sin }60} = \frac{R}{\text{Sin }200}$$

$R = 1,200 \times \text{Sin }200/\text{Sin }60 = -474$ lbs

Practice problem:

A ladder is placed as shown. The friction coefficient of the floor is 0.4. Weight of the ladder is 50 lbs. Will the ladder slip and fall? Assume the wall is smooth and has no friction.

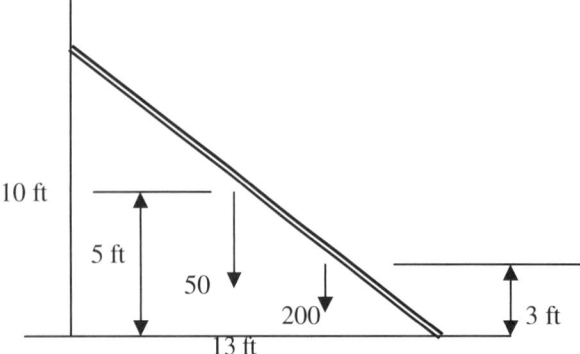

Vertical height of the ladder is 10 ft and the center of gravity of the ladder is 5 ft above the ground. Forces on the ladder are as shown below.

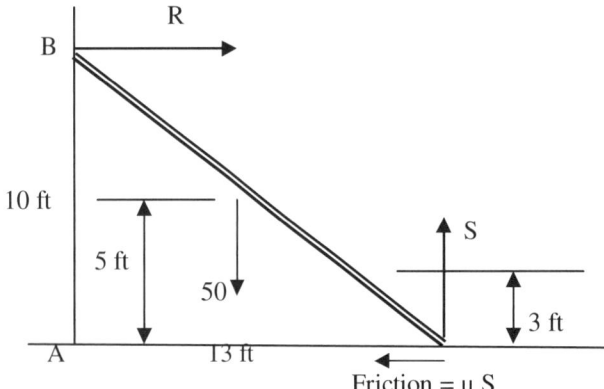

Solution:

Normal reaction due to wall on the ladder is taken to be R. Normal reaction on the ladder due to floor is S. Friction force on the ladder is 0.4 S. Friction is always acting against the direction of failure. The ladder will slide away from the wall. Hence the friction would act towards the wall.

Resolve all forces along vertical direction:

$50 = S$

Take moments about point B

S x 13 = 50 x 6.5 + μ S x 10

S (13 – 10 μ) = 325

50 (13 – 10 μ) = 325

13 – 10 μ = 6.5
μ = 0.65

μ = 0.65 is the friction coefficient required for stability. Friction coefficient available is only 0.4. Hence the ladder would slip and fall.

Projectiles: Projectiles move under the force of gravity. Projectiles have to be sent out with an initial velocity. The initial velocity would have two components, vertical and horizontal. Gravity acts downward on the projectile. Air resistance acts on the horizontal movement.

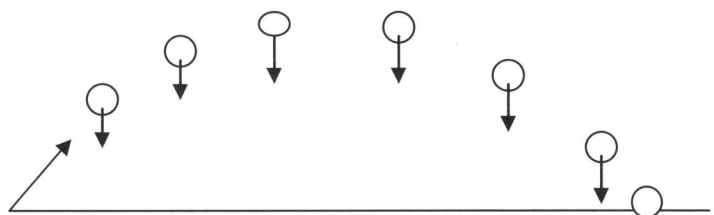

9.0 MUTCD: Manual of Uniform Traffic Control Devices

MUTCD is a document that deals with traffic signs published by FHWA. (Federal Highway Authority). There are questions in the PE exam on this subject. MUTCD manual can be downloaded free of charge from Federal Highway Authority website. (*mutcd.fhwa.dot.gov/*). If that link does not work, students can google to find the correct document. For the construction PE exam, all you need is Part 6 of MUTCD. That is very good news since complete MUTCD is about 1,000 pages.

PART 6 (MUTCD):   TRAFFIC CONTROLS FOR STREET AND HIGHWAY CONSTRUCTION, MAINTENANCE, UTILITY, AND INCIDENT MANAGEMENT OPERATIONS

9.1   Brief Overview of MUTCD Part 6:

Let us say a contractor is conducting repairs to a building near the street. Assume that the contractor needs a small crane to reach higher floors.

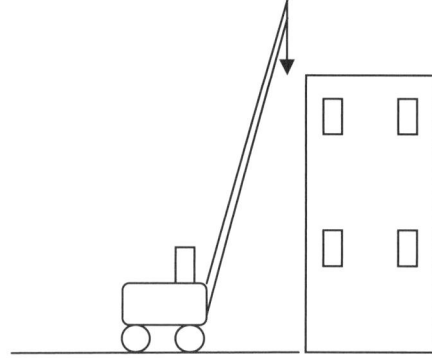

In this situation, one of the lanes of the road may need to be closed. In addition, pedestrian bridge may be required to protect the pedestrians.

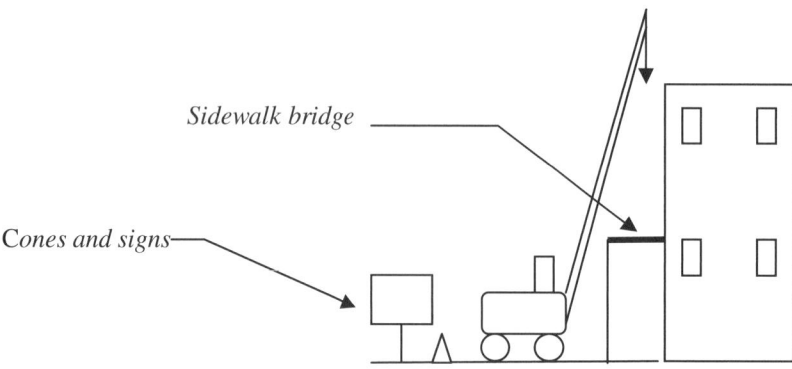

Sidewalk bridge

Cones and signs

9.2   TTC: Temporary Traffic Control:

Temporary traffic control or TTC is required during construction activities. Prior to establishing TTC devices, a TTC plan needs to be prepared. The plan should consider passenger traffic, commercial traffic and pedestrians. Commercial traffic may not be able to go over certain bridges due to weight restrictions. Hence TTC planners need to be aware of special considerations for commercial traffic when diverting traffic.

When developing a TTC plan, one has to assume that drivers would reduce the speed only if they clearly perceive a need to do so.

Seven fundamental principles to follow when developing a TTC:
1) General plans or guidelines should be developed to ensure safety of motorists, bicyclists and pedestrians.
2) Road user movement should be inhibited as little as practical.
3) Motorists, bicyclists and pedestrians should be guided in a clear and positive manner while approaching
and traversing TTC zones and incident sites.
Which means, signs should be visible and clear? Cones and other traffic guidance equipment should be properly used.
4) Routine day and night inspections of TTC elements should be performed:
Cones and signs could be misplaced due to wind, rain and kids playing around. Workers should routinely inspect cones and signs.
5) Attention should be given to maintenance of roadside safety during the life of the TTC zone
6) All personnel involved in developing and maintenance of a TTC program should be adequately trained.
7) Good public relations should be maintained. This can be done by providing advance notices of road closing and diversions etc. That way motorists can plan alternate routes.

Traffic Control Devices:

Traffic Signs: Traffic signs are a major part of any TTC plan. Traffic signs will let the motorists know what to expect.

Crash Attenuators:

When workers are working in the side of the road, crash attenuator will protect the workers.

Cone Placing Trucks:

In this cone placing truck, the worker who places the cones has a place to stand up and place the cones. It is important that the truck provide a place to stand on.

Components of Temporary Traffic Control Zones:

TTC (Temporary Traffic Control) zones are divided into four areas:
A) The advance warning area
B) The transition area
C) The activity area,
D) The termination area.

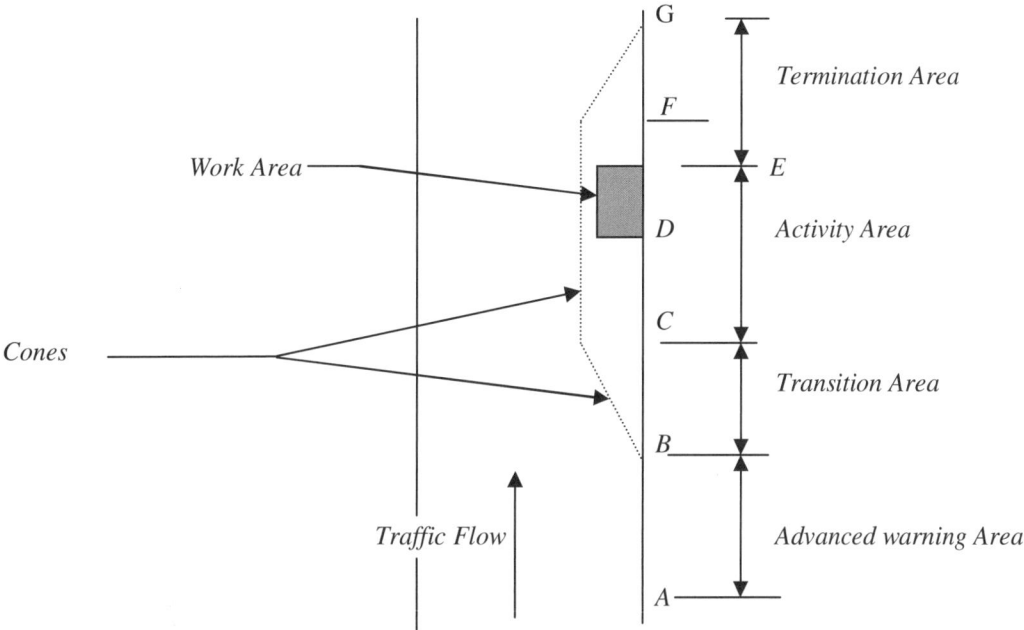

Above figure shows the four temporary traffic control zones. These four are further divided as shown below.

- A to B: Advance Warning Area: Advance warning area consists of signs such as "Construction Ahead", "Your Tax Dollar at Work", or various signs indicating that construction zone is ahead.

- B to C: Transition Area: In this zone, cones will be placed to guide the traffic.

- C to D: Buffer Zone: Buffer zone is created to provide a safety area for workers. In case a runaway driver to come thru the cones, the workers will be able to see the vehicle that is coming towards them. In some cases, speed attenuators are placed in this zone.

- D to E: Work Zone: Workers will be working in the work zone.

- E to F: Buffer space: Another safe space for workers to move around.

- F to G: Downstream Taper: Traffic is guided back.

Development of a TTC Plan:

TTC plan should be developed by qualified personnel. Depending upon the complexity of projects, TTC plans can be simple to very complicated. Generally, TTC plans are costly. Placing and maintaining cones, barriers, pillow trucks in a daily basis costs significant amount of money for contractors.

Flaggers:

One Lane Two-Way Traffic: (Conditions for No Flagmen)

As per MUTCD, if the workspace on a low-volume street or road is short and road users from both directions are able to see the traffic approaching from the opposite direction through and beyond the worksite, the movement of traffic through a one-lane, two-way constriction may be self-regulating. In other words, a flagman is not necessary.

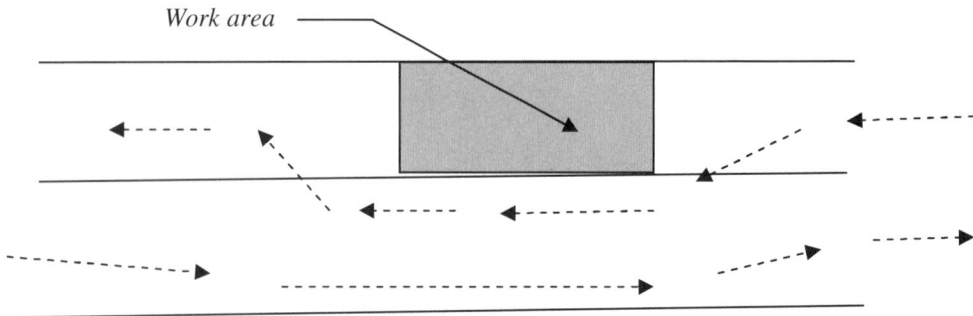

Work area

If the traffic is high or drivers cannot see each other due to a curve then flaggers are necessary.

One Lane Two-Way Traffic: (Conditions for One Flagman):

One flagman may be used only if the flagman can see one end to the other. When the road construction area is too long, the flagman may not be able to see the traffic coming from the other end.

One Lane Two-Way Traffic: (Conditions for Two Flagmen):

When one flagman cannot see the full length of the road, then two flagmen should be used.

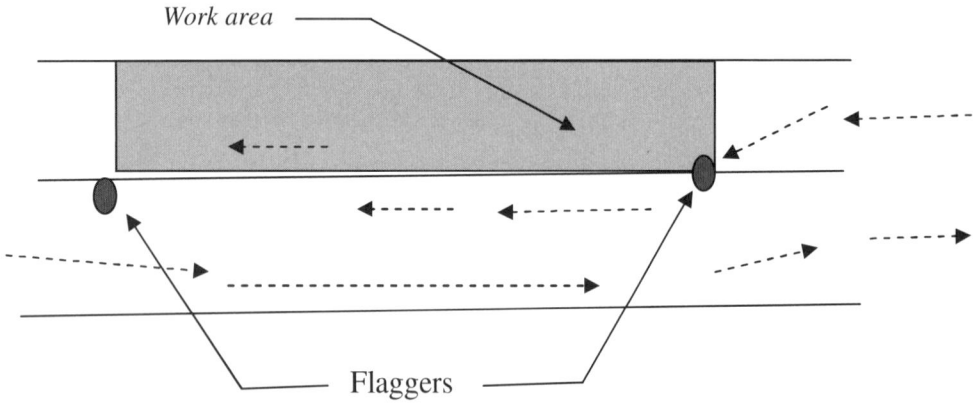

Work area

Flaggers

6D.01: Pedestrian safety around construction sites:

MUTCD 6D.01 deals with safety of pedestrians near construction work.

MUTCD provides following three Guidelines to follow when dealing with pedestrians.

Guideline A: Pedestrians should not be led into conflicts with vehicles, equipment, and operations.

Guideline B: Pedestrians should not be led into conflicts with vehicles moving through or around the worksite.

Guideline C: Pedestrians should be provided with a convenient and accessible path that replicates as nearly as practical the most desirable characteristics of the existing sidewalk(s) or footpath(s). Also, pedestrian route should not be severed and/or moved for non-construction activities such as parking.

Proper pedestrian movement near construction site

Let us look at the above photo. Let us see whether three Guidelines mentioned in MUTCD was followed by this contractor.

Guideline A: Pedestrians should not be led into conflicts with vehicles, equipment, and operations:

The traffic is delineated with jersey barriers in the above photo. A wooden barrier separates construction equipment and operations. Hence, the first guideline is followed.

Guideline B: Pedestrians should not be led into conflict with construction vehicles moving through or around the worksite:

When supply trucks or new equipment is brought to the site, it should be done in a manner that would not hinder the movement of pedestrians.

In addition, it seems in the photo above, pedestrians have a clean path without obstructions to walk. Hence, guideline C also followed.

Construction activity near a road

Does the worksite shown above follow three MUTCD guidelines regarding pedestrian access?

MUTCD Chapter 6D.03   Construction Worker Safety Near Traffic:

Many construction workers who work near roads are killed by vehicular traffic. Hence, MUTCD provides following guidelines to protect construction workers from traffic.

Guideline A: Worker Training:
All workers should be trained on how to work next to motor vehicle traffic in a way that minimizes their vulnerability. Workers having specific TTC responsibilities should be trained in TTC techniques, device usage, and placement.

Guideline B: Temporary Traffic Barriers:
Temporary traffic barriers should be placed along the workspace depending on factors such as lateral clearance of workers from adjacent traffic, speed of traffic, duration and type of operations, time of day, and volume of traffic.

Guideline C: Speed Reduction:
Reducing the speed of vehicular traffic, mainly through regulatory speed zoning, funneling, lane reduction, or the use of uniformed law enforcement officers or flaggers, should be considered.

Guideline D: Activity Area:
Planning the internal work activity area to minimize backing-up maneuvers of construction vehicles should be considered to minimize the exposure to risk.

Guideline E: Worker Safety Planning:

A trained person designated by the employer should conduct a basic hazard assessment for the worksite and job classifications required in the activity area. This safety professional should determine whether engineering, administrative, or personal protection measures should be implemented.

MUTCD Chapter 6E: Flagger Control:

Chapter 6E mainly deals with flagger control. This is a long chapter with subject matter ranging from flagger qualifications, flagging signs, flagger assistance devices and flagger stations.

Flagger Qualifications:
A). Ability to receive and communicate specific instructions clearly, firmly, and courteously;
B). Ability to move and maneuver quickly in order to avoid danger from errant vehicles;
C). Ability to control signaling devices (such as paddles and flags) in order to provide clear and positive guidance to drivers approaching a TTC zone in frequently changing situations;
D). Ability to understand and apply safe traffic control practices, sometimes in stressful or emergency situations; and
E). Ability to recognize dangerous traffic situations and warn workers in sufficient time to avoid injury.

9.3   Hand Signaling Devices: MUTCD recommends STOP/SLOW sign as the primary device of the flagger.

STOP/SLOW sign - One side has the STOP sign and the other side has the SLOW sign

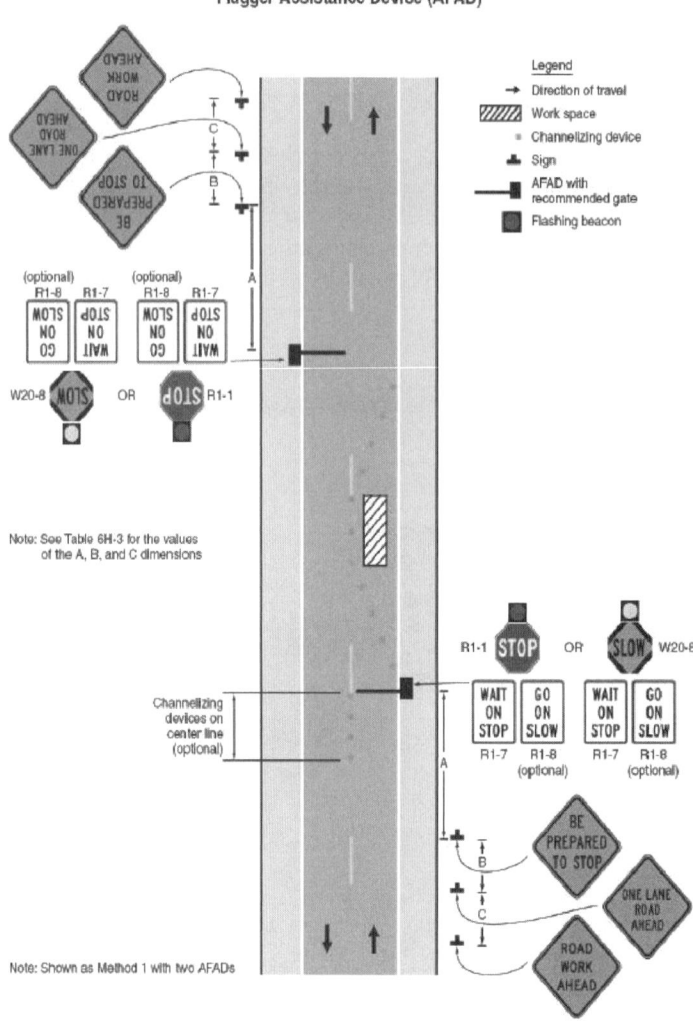

Figure 6E-1. Example of the Use of a STOP/SLOW Automated
Flagger Assistance Device (AFAD)

MUTCD flagger procedure for one lane closing

In the above figure, construction site is shown on the side of the road with a rectangular box. Three signs are placed for the oncoming traffic.

- Road Work Ahead
- One Lane Road Ahead
- Be Prepared to Stop

The drivers will see these signs and understand that construction area is ahead. A flagger will be placed before the construction site with a STOP/SLOW sign. There is another flagger on the other side of the work area as well. Two flaggers will communicate thru a radio or thru hand signals when to stop the traffic and when to let the traffic go.

Figure 6E-3. Use of Hand-Signaling Devices by Flaggers

| PREFERRED METHOD STOP/SLOW Paddle | EMERGENCY SITUATIONS ONLY Red Flag |

MUTCD flagger procedure

Let us look at the MUTCD flagger signs. Topmost signs are to stop traffic. Bottom two signs are to alert the oncoming traffic to slow down. The middle two signs are to instruct the stopped traffic to go ahead.

Top Two Figures: To STOP Traffic: If the flagger is using STOP/SLOW sign, then he/she should hold the STOP sign as shown in the figure. If the flagger is using a red flag, he/she should hold the arm horizontally and firmly as shown.

Middle Two Figures: To Instruct Stopped Traffic to Go: In this case, the flagger would hold the SLOW sign and gestures with the arm to move. If the flagger is using a red flag, he/she should drop the flag and signal the traffic to go.

Bottom Two Figures: To Slow Oncoming Traffic: If the flagger is using STOP/SLOW sign, he/she should hold the slow sign and gesture with the other hand to slow down by moving the hand up and down as shown. If the flagger is holding a red flag, he/she should move the flag up and down as shown at the bottom of the figure.

A

Accelerating Admixtures, 33
ACI, 7, 35, 37, 38, 39, 41, 42, 49, 50, 51, 52, 59, 60, 61, 85, 88
Activity Area, 439, 442
activity on arrow diagrams, 288
ACWP, 230, 231
admixtures, 60
Admixtures, 33
Advanced warning Area, 439
aggregates, 295, 296, 309, 323, 324
Aggregates, 295, 296, 324
Aluminum Forms, 58
American Concrete Institute, 7, 59
Angle of operation, 112, 113
Angle of Operation, 112
Aquifers, 254, 389
arrow side, 314, 315, 316
Artesian, 253, 254
ASCE, 336
Atmospheric head, 260, 261, 263
Azimuth, 134

B

Backfill, 180, 181, 196, 401
backhoe, 111, 112, 113, 115, 192, 263, 264, 265, 390, 394
Backhoes, 16, 112, 115
Bank Volume, 194, 195, 196
Base Pay, 189
BCWP, 230, 231
BCWS, 230, 231
Bearing Type Joints, 319
Bentonite, 390, 393
Blast furnace slag, 32, 87
Blast Furnace Slag, 32
block, 77, 80, 86, 234, 235, 236, 237, 240, 243, 245, 246, 247, 360, 384, 430, 431
Block and Tackle, 236
Bolt Tension, 320
Bolt tension indicator, 321
Bolting crew, 93, 94, 385
Bonding Admixture, 54
Borrow Pit, 124, 130, 132
Braces, 63, 207, 208
Bracing, 344, 345
Bracings, 80, 423
Breaking rock, 21
Bricks, 181, 182
Bucket efficiency, 111, 113
Bucket struck capacity, 113
Bull float, 45, 46, 88
Bull Float, 45, 89
Butt joints, 310
BVC, 148, 149, 150

C

Calibrate d Wrench Tightening, 320

C_c, 59, 60
Cement, 30, 31, 37, 60, 295, 298, 324, 389, 390, 415, 416
cement blocks, 298
center of gravity, 171, 402, 426, 427, 428, 430, 434
Chain hoists, 247, 248
Channels, 183, 184, 297
Chemical admixtures, 33
Clearing rakes, 21, 22
cleats, 203, 204, 205, 206
Closed end pipe piles, 420
Coarse Aggregates, 30
Coefficient of Permeability, 307
Coefficient of Traction, 122
cofferdam, 348, 349, 350, 351
Cofferdam, 351, 352
compact volume, 195
Compaction, 18, 117, 304, 305
concrete, 3, 7, 17, 18, 19, 30, 31, 32, 33, 34, 35, 36, 37, 38, 39, 40, 41, 42, 43, 44, 45, 46, 47, 48, 49, 50, 51, 52, 53, 54, 55, 56, 58, 59, 62, 63, 65, 86, 87, 88, 89, 90, 121, 178, 186, 188, 196, 197, 198, 199, 200, 201, 202, 206, 215, 216, 217, 218, 234, 251, 265, 278, 282, 291, 292, 293, 295, 296, 298, 299, 323, 324, 325, 327, 338, 350, 380, 381, 382, 383, 384, 395, 397, 398, 401, 403, 417, 418, 420, 421, 422
Concrete, 60
Concrete Admixtures, 33
Concrete Buckets, 39, 382
Concrete Buggies, 39
Concrete Chutes, 39
Concrete Cylinders, 34, 298
Concrete Finishing, 45
Concrete Formwork, 56
Concrete Grinding, 48
Concrete Pumping, 40
Concrete retarders, 33
Concrete Retarders, 33
Concrete Scarifiers, 48
confined aquifer, 254, 389
Connecting crew, 93, 94
Construction Joints, 86, 87
Contour lines, 174
Corner joints, 310, 313
Cost, 58, 123, 188, 189, 197, 198, 201, 202, 208, 209, 210, 211, 212, 213, 214, 215, 216, 217, 219, 225, 227, 228, 229, 230, 231, 232, 233, 263, 264, 265, 293
Cost - Benefit Analysis, 225
Cost variance, 231
CPI, 230, 231, 232, 233
crane, 19, 97, 102, 103, 104, 112, 114, 215
Crane Mechanism, 243
crawler type, 111, 120
Creasoting, 418
crew hour, 188, 189, 198, 200, 210, 213, 214, 216, 217, 219
critical path, 276, 286, 287, 289, 290, 291
Critical path method, 270
CSI format, 178
Cumulative cut, 161, 166, 168, 169, 170, 173
Cut and fill, 21, 158, 159, 174
Cut and Fill, 124, 173, 174, 177
Cut and fill diagram, 159

cutting trees, 17, 20, 21
C_w, 59, 60

D

dead load, 336
Decking crew, 93
Degree of saturation, 125, 129
Demolition, 21, 23, 387
Depreciation, 191, 192, 193, 194
Depth of Operation, 112
Detailing crew, 93
Dewatering, 251, 252, 253
Direct Tension Indicator, 321
Dowels, 415, 416
Dozer, 17, 106, 108, 120, 123
Drag coefficient, 351
Dragline, 114
Drainage, 24, 28, 177
Drawbar pull, 120
Drawbar Pull, 120, 122, 123
Dry Density, 125
dummy activities, 289
Dummy Activities, 289
dummy activity, 289

E

Early start time, 273, 274, 275
Earned value, 229, 230
Earned Value Management, 229
Earth pressure coefficient, 400
Earthquake Load, 336
Earthwork, 157, 188
Edge joints, 310
Edge Joints, 313
Elevating Scrapers, 107
Erection Drawings, 93
erosion, 17, 265, 266, 267, 400
Erosion, 25, 265, 266, 267
estimating, 5, 7, 17, 178, 188, 197, 198
Estimating, 178, 188
excavation, 112, 194, 212, 213, 251, 252, 253, 267, 392, 394
Excavation, 18, 28, 124, 180, 181, 188, 194, 196, 197, 212, 213, 252, 263, 267, 270, 374, 380, 389, 392
Excavations, 151, 251, 252, 267, 413
Excavators, 111
External Vibrators, 43

F

fabrication, 214, 215, 273
Fabrication, 214, 215, 273
Falsework, 327
fbm, 203, 205, 208, 209, 214, 218, 219
Fillet Weld, 313, 314
Fine aggregates, 41, 323
Fine grading, 21
Finished grade, 156
Flange, 183, 184, 185
Flow, 256

Fly Ash, 32, 87
footboard measure, 203
footing, 62, 136, 179, 180, 197, 198, 200, 207, 211, 252, 271, 278, 294, 326, 394, 395, 396
formwork, 59, 336
Formwork, 7, 18, 56, 57, 58, 179, 196, 197, 199, 200, 201, 202, 203, 204, 206, 207, 208, 215, 216, 217, 218, 270, 291, 326, 327, 382
forward pass, 116, 117, 272, 277, 278, 283, 284, 285
Forward pass, 116, 272, 273, 274, 275, 281, 285
Free Float, 286, 287
Free haul distance, 168, 169
Fringe Benefits, 189
frost depth, 395, 396
future worth, 220

G

Gabions, 398
Gantry cranes, 19, 102
General liability insurance, 189, 190, 191
General Liability Insurance, 189
Geographic North, 133
Grader, 116, 117
Graders, 115, 116
Grapples, 21, 22
Groove Weld, 316
Groundwater, 252, 253, 254, 389, 390
Gun Tackle, 237, 242
Gusset, 215

H

Hand augurs, 391
Hand Signaling Devices, 443
Hand trowel, 89
Head added by the pump, 255
headache ball, 247, 384
Heap volume, 111
Heap Volume, 111
hoist cable, 114
Hoist Cable, 114
honeycombing, 43
Horizontal Construction Load, 336
Horizontal curves, 139
Horizontal Curves, 139, 142
horsepower, 119, 120, 123
Horsepower, 110, 120, 122
Hot Weather Concreting, 50, 51, 52
HP - Piles, 185

I

impermeable, 254
Incidence Rate, 388
independent float, 287, 288
Independent float, 287, 288
Independent Float, 286, 287
Information stake, 152, 153, 154, 155
Information Stake, 152

J

Jumping Jacks, 118

K

Kelly Ball Test, 34

L

L - Angles, 185
labor hours, 189, 200, 210, 214, 216, 217
lag, 278, 282, 283
Landscaping, 21, 29
Lap joints, 310, 312
Lap Joints, 312
Late finish time, 272, 274, 276
late start, 289
late start time, 274, 275, 276, 282
Lateral earth pressure, 399, 403, 406
Lateral pressure, 58, 59
Lattice Boom Cranes, 98
lifting, 97, 98, 215, 234, 426
Light weight aggregates, 41, 42
limited access zone, 79
Liquid limit, 300, 306, 307
Live load, 336
Loader Cycle Time, 110
Loaders, 109, 110
Luff tackle, 240
Luffing jib, 99
lump sum, 222, 224, 229

M

M - Sections, 184
Machine power, 119
Magnetic North, 133
manhole, 26, 392
Manual of Uniform Traffic Control Devices, 436
masonry, 178, 181, 293, 397
Masonry, 77, 79, 83, 178, 181, 295, 298
Mass diagram, 159, 161, 162, 164, 167, 169
Mass Diagrams, 157, 159
Material Loads, 336
MC Sections, 185
MCAA, 77, 79, 80
mechanical advantage, 234, 237, 241, 245
Meridian, 134
Metal Ties, 62, 63, 207
Micro silica or silica fume, 32, 87
Mobile Cranes, 97
Modified proctor, 117
Modified Proctor test, 304
moisture content, 128, 130, 131, 132, 305, 306
Monitoring wells, 253
mortar, 81, 82, 83, 84, 178, 181, 182, 183, 298
Mortar, 181, 182, 183, 298
mud rotary drilling, 393
Mudrotary drilling, 393
MUTCD, 7, 436, 440, 441, 442, 443, 444, 445

N

negative lag, 282
net positive suction head, 260
NPSH, 260, 261, 262, 263

O

Open end pipe piles, 417, 420, 421
Original shoring, 65, 66, 67, 68, 69, 70, 71, 72
OSHA, 78, 79, 356, 367, 387
Overhang, 209, 210
Overhaul, 170
Overturning moment, 401, 403, 405

P

Parts of Line, 236, 237
performance curve, 257, 262
Performance Curve, 257
Permeability Test, 307
Piezometers, 253
Pipe piles, 420
planned value, 229, 230, 232
Plastic limit, 306, 307
Plates, 62, 63, 207, 208
Plywood, 58
Plywood Forms, 58
point of tangent, 142
Point of vertical curvature, 146, 147
Point of Vertical Curvature, 145
Point of Vertical Intersection, 145
point of vertical tangent, 146
point of Vertical Tangent, 145
Poorly Graded, 302
Porosity, 125, 128, 129, 316
Pozzalans, 32, 87
Predecessors, 273, 274
Present value, 220, 225, 226, 227, 228
Pulley, 238, 239
Pulleys, 234, 241
pump, 255, 256
Pump, 251, 252, 255, 256, 257, 258, 259, 260, 261, 262, 263
Pump horse power, 255, 256
PVC, 145, 146, 147, 148, 253, 254
PVI, 145, 147, 148, 149, 150
PVT, 145, 146, 147, 148

R

radians, 140, 141
Rafter, 209
Rebar chairs, 53
reference stake, 153, 154, 155
Reshoring, 65, 66
Resisting moment, 103, 104, 401, 403
restricted zone, 79
retaining wall, 177, 180, 181, 283, 345, 397, 400, 401, 402, 403, 404, 405, 412
Retaining walls, 21
Ride on trowel machine, 89

Ride on Trowel Machines, 47
rigging, 234
Rigging crew, 93
Rim pull, 119, 120, 122
Rip Rap, 266, 267
Riprap, 25
rock bolts, 345, 411, 413, 415
Rolling resistance, 119, 120, 121

S

Sag vertical curve, 149
Sand streaking, 44
Scaffolding, 327, 328, 332
Schedule, 229, 230, 231, 232, 233, 293
Schedule variance, 231
scrapers, 106, 107, 108, 171, 172, 173
Sediment Control, 25
Series Payments, 221, 222
sheathing, 63, 64, 202, 203, 204, 205, 218, 219
Sheathing, 57, 62, 63, 64, 207, 208
sheave, 234, 235, 236, 240
Sheaves, 100, 234
Sheepsfoot rollers, 117
Sheet piles, 27
sheetpiles, 27, 212, 213, 348, 349, 350
Sheetpiles, 212, 268, 349, 398
shoring, 336
Shoring, 65, 196, 251, 335, 336
Shrinkage factor, 163, 164, 165, 195
Sieve analysis, 300, 301
Silica Fume, 32
Silt fences, 265, 266
single whip, 236
Site clearing, 21, 188, 270, 271
Site Layout, 133
Site Work, 20, 28
slump, 33, 34, 38, 40, 51, 299
Slump Test, 33, 299, 300
Slurry, 390
Snow load, 336
Snow loads, 423
Social security tax, 189, 190, 191
Social Security Tax, 189
Soil stabilization, 21
soldier piles, 268, 269, 349, 350
SPI, 230, 231, 232, 233
Split spoon, 394
Splitting Tensile Strength Test, 35
ST Sections, 185
standard bricks, 182
Static water pressure, 351
Steel Construction, 7, 90, 91
Steel Erection, 18, 215
Steel Forms, 58
Struck volume, 111
Struck Volume, 111
Studs, 62, 63, 64, 207, 208
Stump pullers, 21
Stump splitters, 21
submersible pumps, 252, 253

Suction head, 256, 260
Sum of the Years Digits Method, 192
Superplasticizers, 33
Swell factor, 194, 195
System curve, 258, 259, 261

T

T – Joints, 311
Temporary Traffic Barriers, 442
Temporary Traffic Control, 7, 437, 439
Tension vs Torque Debate, 322
Termination Area, 439
test pits, 394
Timber piles, 417, 418, 419
Tolerances, 49
total float, 289
Total float, 289
Total Float, 286, 287
Total stations, 135
Towed Scrapers, 107
Tower Cranes, 101
Traffic Control Devices, 7, 437
Transition Area, 439
Traverse, 135
Tremie Pipes, 42
truss, 273, 424
TTC Plan, 440
Twofold purchase, 240
Type II cement, 30, 87

U

Unemployment Insurance, 189
uniform series, 223, 224, 227, 228
Uniform Series, 223, 224
Unit Weight Coefficient, 59, 60
Usable Force, 122

V

V groove, 310, 316
Variable Material Load, 336
Vertical Curve Equation, 149
Vertical curves, 139, 147
Vertical Curves, 139, 144
V-groove butt weld, 311
Vibratory Plates, 118

W

W Shapes, 183, 296
wales, 62, 63, 64, 207, 208, 212, 213, 349
Wales, 62, 64, 207, 208, 212, 349
Wall Forms, 59, 62
Washers, 318, 319, 321
Water Cement Ratio, 295
Water Reducing Admixtures, 33
Waterstops, 55
Web, 183, 184, 185
Weld Testing, 316

welding, 18, 215, 314, 316
Welding crew, 93, 95
Welding Symbols, 314
Well Graded, 302
well points, 251, 252, 253
Well points, 252, 253
Whalers, 57
Wide Flange, 183, 296
Winch, 243, 244, 245, 246
Wind Load, 336

Wind loads, 423
wood yokes, 204, 205, 206
Worker's compensation insurance, 190, 191
Workers Compensation Insurance, 189
WT Sections, 185

Z

zenith, 134